WORLD DEVELOPMENT

1997

THE
STATE
IN A
CHANGING
WORLD

PUBLISHED FOR THE WORLD BANK

OXFORD UNIVERSITY PRESS

Oxford University Press

OXFORD   NEW YORK   TORONTO   DELHI   BOMBAY   CALCUTTA
MADRAS   KARACHI   KUALA LUMPUR   SINGAPORE   HONG KONG
TOKYO   NAIROBI   DAR ES SALAAM   CAPE TOWN   MELBOURNE
AUCKLAND

and associated companies in

BERLIN   IBADAN

© 1997 The International Bank for Reconstruction and
Development / The World Bank
1818 H Street, N.W., Washington, D.C. 20433, U.S.A.

Published by Oxford University Press, Inc.
200 Madison Avenue, New York, N.Y. 10016

Interior design and typesetting by
Barton Matheson Willse & Worthington.

Manufactured in the United States of America
First printing June 1997

ISBN 0-19-521115-4 clothbound
ISBN 0-19-521114-6 paperback
ISSN 0163-5085

Text printed on recycled paper that conforms to the American Standard
for Permanence of Paper for Printed Library Material Z39.48-1984

FOREWORD

WORLD DEVELOPMENT REPORT 1997, THE TWENTIeth in this annual series, is devoted to the role and effectiveness of the state: what the state should do, how it should do it, and how it can do it better in a rapidly changing world.

These issues are high on the agenda in developing and industrial countries alike. For many, the lesson of recent years has been that the state could not deliver on its promises: transition economies have had to make a wrenching shift toward the market economy, and much of the developing world has had to face up to the failure of state-dominated development strategies. Even the mixed economies of the industrialized world, in response to the failures of government intervention, have opted for a decided shift in the mix in favor of market mechanisms. Many have felt that the logical end point of all these reforms was a minimalist state. Such a state would do no harm, but neither could it do much good.

The Report explains why this extreme view is at odds with the evidence of the world's development success stories, be it the development of today's industrial economies in the nineteenth century or the postwar growth "miracles" of East Asia. Far from supporting a minimalist approach to the state, these examples have shown that development requires an effective state, one that plays a catalytic, facilitating role, encouraging and complementing the activities of private businesses and individuals. Certainly, state-dominated development has failed. But so has stateless development—a message that comes through all too clearly in the agonies of people in collapsed states such as Liberia and Somalia. History has repeatedly shown that good government is not a luxury but a vital necessity. Without an effective state, sustainable development, both economic and social, is impossible.

History and recent experience have also taught us that development is not just about getting the right economic and technical inputs. It is also about the underlying, institutional environment: the rules and customs that determine how those inputs are used. As this Report shows, understanding the role the state plays in this environment—for example, its ability to enforce the rule of law to underpin market transactions—will be essential to making the state contribute more effectively to development.

The pathways to an effective state are many and varied. The Report makes no attempt to offer a single recipe for state reforms worldwide. It does, however, provide a framework for guiding these efforts, in the form of a two-part strategy:

- First, focus the state's activities to match its capability. Many states try to do too much with few resources and little capability. Getting governments better focused on the core public activities that are crucial to development will enhance their effectiveness.
- Second, over time, look for ways to improve the state's capability by reinvigorating public institutions. The Report puts particular emphasis on mechanisms that give public officials the incentive to do their jobs better and to be more flexible, but that also provide restraints to check arbitrary and corrupt behavior.

Drawing from examples of successful and unsuccessful states, and of state reform around the world, the Report elaborates this two-part strategy and shows how it can be implemented from a number of starting positions. Significantly, although there is an enormous diversity of settings and contexts, effective states clearly do have some common features. One is in the way government has set rules underpinning private transactions, and civil society more broadly. Another is in the way government has played by the rules itself, acting reliably and predictably and controlling corruption.

Building a more effective state to support sustainable development and the reduction of poverty will not be easy. In any situation many people will have a vested interest in keeping the state as it is, however costly the results for the well-being of the country as a whole. Overcoming their opposition will take time and political effort. But the Report shows how opportunities for reform can open, and widen, with the help of careful sequencing of reforms and mechanisms to compensate losers. Even in the worst of situations, very small steps toward a more effective state can have a large impact on economic and social welfare. As we approach the twenty-first century, the challenge for states is neither to shrink into insignificance, nor to dominate markets, but to start taking those small steps.

James D. Wolfensohn
President
The World Bank

May 30, 1997

This Report has been prepared by a team led by Ajay Chhibber and comprising Simon Commander, Alison Evans, Harald Fuhr, Cheikh Kane, Chad Leechor, Brian Levy, Sanjay Pradhan, and Beatrice Weder. Valuable contributions were made by Jean-Paul Azam, Ed Campos, Hamid Davoodi, Kathleen Newland, Kenichi Ohno, Dani Rodrik, Susan Rose-Ackerman, Astri Suhrke, and Douglas Webb. The team was assisted by Ritu Basu, Gregory Kisunko, Une Lee, Claudia Sepulveda, and Adam Michael Smith. Stephanie Flanders was the principal editor. The work was carried out under the general direction of the late Michael Bruno, Lyn Squire, and Joseph Stiglitz.

The team received useful advice from a distinguished panel of external experts comprising Masahiko Aoki, Ela Bhatt, Kwesi Botchwey, Peter Evans, Atul Kohli, Klaus König, Seymour Martin Lipset, Douglass North, Emma Rothschild, Graham Scott, and Vito Tanzi.

Many others inside and outside the World Bank provided helpful comments, wrote background papers and other contributions, and participated in consultation meetings. These contributors and participants are listed in the Bibliographical Note. The International Economics Department contributed to the data appendix and was responsible for the Selected World Development Indicators.

The production staff of the Report included Amy Brooks, Valerie Chisholm, Kathryn Kline Dahl, Joyce Gates, Stephanie Gerard, Jeffrey N. Lecksell, and Michael Treadway. Rebecca Sugui served as executive assistant to the team, and Daniel Atchison, Elizabete de Lima, Michael Geller, and Thomas Zorab as staff assistants. Maria Ameal served as administrative officer.

This Report is dedicated to the memory of Michael Bruno, Senior Vice President and Chief Economist of the World Bank from 1993 to 1996, whose life's work, including his contributions to this and past editions of *World Development Report,* immeasurably advanced our understanding of development.

CONTENTS

TEXT FIGURES

TEXT TABLES

Definitions and data notes

The countries included in regional and income groupings used in this Report (except those for the private sector survey) are listed in the Classification of Economies tables at the end of the Selected World Development Indicators. Income classifications are based on GNP per capita; thresholds for income classifications in this edition may be found in the Introduction to Selected World Development Indicators. Group averages reported in the figures and tables are unweighted averages of the countries in the group except where noted to the contrary.

The use of the term "countries" to refer to economies implies no judgment by the World Bank about the legal or other status of a territory. Statistics reported for "developing countries" include economies in transition from central planning except where noted to the contrary.

Dollar figures are current U.S. dollars except where otherwise specified.

Billion means 1,000 million; *trillion* means 1,000 billion.

The following abbreviations are used:

CEE	Central and Eastern Europe
CIS	Commonwealth of Independent States
GDP	Gross domestic product
GNP	Gross national product
IMF	International Monetary Fund
NGO	Nongovernmental organization
OECD	Organization for Economic Cooperation and Development
PPP	Purchasing power parity

AROUND THE GLOBE, THE STATE IS IN THE SPOTlight. Far-reaching developments in the global economy have us revisiting basic questions about government: what its role should be, what it can and cannot do, and how best to do it.

The last fifty years have shown clearly both the benefits and the limitations of state action, especially in the promotion of development. Governments have helped to deliver substantial improvements in education and health and reductions in social inequality. But government actions have also led to some very poor outcomes. And even where governments have done a good job in the past, many worry that they will not be able to adapt to the demands of a globalizing world economy.

The new worries and questions about the state's role are many and various, but four recent developments have given them particular impetus:

- The collapse of command-and-control economies in the former Soviet Union and Central and Eastern Europe
- The fiscal crisis of the welfare state in most of the established industrial countries
- The important role of the state in the "miracle" economies of East Asia
- The collapse of states and the explosion in humanitarian emergencies in several parts of the world.

This Report shows that the determining factor behind these contrasting developments is the effectiveness of the state. An effective state is vital for the provision of the goods and services—and the rules and institutions—that allow markets to flourish and people to lead healthier, happier lives. Without it, sustainable development, both economic and social, is impossible. Many said much the same thing fifty years ago, but then they tended to mean that development had to be state-provided. The message

of experience since then is rather different: that the state is central to economic and social development, not as a direct provider of growth but as a partner, catalyst, and facilitator.

What makes for an effective state differs enormously across countries at different stages of development. What works in the Netherlands or New Zealand, say, may not work in Nepal. Even among countries at the same level of income, differences in size, ethnic makeup, culture, and political systems make every state unique. But this very diversity enriches this Report's inquiry into *why* and *how* some states do better than others at sustaining development, eradicating poverty, and responding to change.

Rethinking the state—the world over

The world is changing, and with it our ideas about the state's role in economic and social development. Today's intense focus on the state's role is reminiscent of an earlier era, when the world was emerging from the ravages of World War II, and much of the developing world was just gaining its independence. Then development seemed a more easily surmountable—and largely technical—challenge. Good advisers and technical experts would formulate good policies, which good governments would then implement for the good of society. State-led intervention emphasized market failures and accorded the state a central role in correcting them. But the institutional assumptions implicit in this world view were, as we all realize today, too simplistic. Flexibility to implement the policies devised by technocrats was accorded pride of place. Accountability through checks and balances was regarded as an encumbrance.

In a few countries things have indeed worked out more or less as the technocrats expected. But in many countries outcomes were very different. Governments embarked on fanciful schemes. Private investors, lacking confidence in public policies or in the steadfastness of leaders, held back. Powerful rulers acted arbitrarily. Corruption became endemic. Development faltered, and poverty endured.

Over the last century the size and scope of government have expanded enormously, particularly in the industrial countries (Figure 1). The pre-World War II expansion was driven by, among other factors, the need to address the heavy toll on economic and social systems brought on by the Great Depression. The postwar confidence in government bred demands for it to do more. Industrial economies expanded the welfare state, and much of the de-

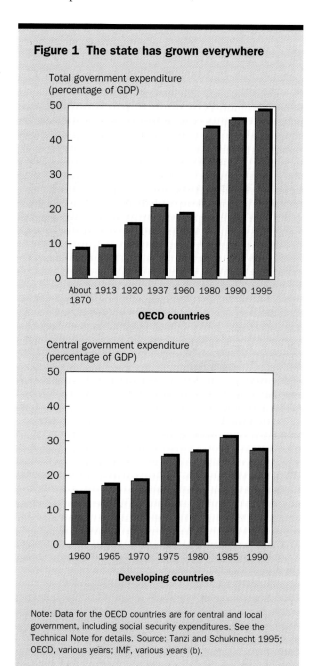

Figure 1 The state has grown everywhere

Total government expenditure
(percentage of GDP)

OECD countries

Central government expenditure
(percentage of GDP)

Developing countries

Note: Data for the OECD countries are for central and local government, including social security expenditures. See the Technical Note for details. Source: Tanzi and Schuknecht 1995; OECD, various years; IMF, various years (b).

veloping world embraced state-dominated development strategies. The result was a tremendous expansion in the size and reach of government worldwide. State spending now constitutes almost half of total income in the established industrial countries, and around a quarter in developing countries. But this very increase in the state's influence has also shifted the emphasis from the quantitative to the qualitative, from the sheer size of the state and the scope of its interventions to its effectiveness in meeting people's needs.

As in the 1940s, today's renewed focus on the state's role has been inspired by dramatic events in the global economy, which have fundamentally changed the environment in which states operate. The global integration of economies and the spread of democracy have narrowed the scope for arbitrary and capricious behavior. Taxes, investment rules, and economic policies must be ever more responsive to the parameters of a globalized world economy. Technological change has opened new opportunities for unbundling services and allowing a larger role for markets. These changes have meant new and different roles for government—no longer as sole provider but as facilitator and regulator. States have come under pressure even where governments have previously seemed to perform well. Many industrial countries find themselves grappling with a welfare state that has grown unwieldy, and having to make difficult choices about the services and benefits that people should expect government to provide. Markets—domestic and global—and citizens vexed by state weaknesses have come to insist, often through grassroots and other nongovernmental organizations, on transparency in the conduct of government, and on other changes to strengthen the ability of the state to meet its assigned objectives.

The clamor for greater government effectiveness has reached crisis proportions in many developing countries where the state has failed to deliver even such fundamental public goods as property rights, roads, and basic health and education. There a vicious circle has taken hold: people and businesses respond to deteriorating public services by avoiding taxation, which leads to further deterioration in services. In the former Soviet Union and Central and Eastern Europe it was the state's long-term failure to deliver on its promises that led, finally, to its overthrow. But the collapse of central planning has created problems of its own. In the resulting vacuum, citizens are sometimes deprived of basic public goods such as law and order. At the limit, as in Afghanistan, Liberia, and Somalia, the state has sometimes crumbled entirely, leaving individuals and international agencies trying desperately to pick up the pieces.

A two-part strategy

How can we cut through the maze of questions and pressures now facing the world's states? No one-size-fits-all recipe for an effective state is suggested here. The range of differences among states is too enormous, as are their starting points. Rather this Report provides a broad framework for addressing the issue of the state's effectiveness worldwide. It points to a number of ways to narrow the growing gap between the demands on states and their capability to meet those demands. Getting societies to accept a redefinition of the state's responsibilities will be one part of the solution. This will include strategic selection of the collective actions that states will try to promote, coupled with greater efforts to take the burden off the state, by involving citizens and communities in the delivery of core collective goods.

But reducing or diluting the state's role cannot be the end of the reform story. Even with more selectivity and greater reliance on the citizenry and on private firms, meeting a broad range of collective needs more effectively will still mean making the state's central institutions work better. For human welfare to be advanced, the state's capability—*defined as the ability to undertake and promote collective actions efficiently*—must be increased.

This basic message translates into a two-part strategy to make every state a more credible, effective partner in its country's development:

- *Matching the state's role to its capability* is the first element in this strategy. Where state capability is weak, how the state intervenes—and where—should be carefully assessed. Many states try to do too much with few resources and little capability, and often do more harm than good. A sharper focus on the fundamentals would improve effectiveness (Box 1). But here it is a matter not just of choosing what to do and what not to do—but of how to do it as well.
- But capability is not destiny. Therefore the second element of the strategy is to *raise state capability by reinvigorating public institutions.* This means designing effective rules and restraints, to check arbitrary state actions and combat entrenched corruption. It means subjecting state institutions to greater competition, to increase their efficiency. It means increasing the performance of state institutions, improving pay and incentives. And it means making the state more responsive to people's needs, bringing government closer to the people through broader participation and decentralization. Thus, the Report not only directs attention to refocusing the state's role, but also shows how countries might begin a process of rebuilding the state's capability.

Matching role to capability

Matching role to capability is not a simple message of dismantling the state. In some areas much greater focus is badly needed to improve effectiveness: choosing what to

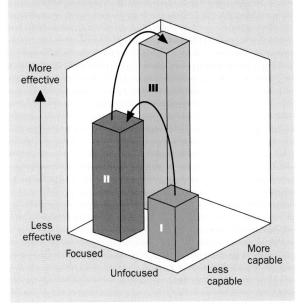

Box 1 The pathway to a more effective state

A more capable state can be a more effective state, but effectiveness and capability are not the same thing. *Capability*, as applied to states, is the ability to undertake and promote collective actions efficiently—such as law and order, public health, and basic infrastructure; *effectiveness* is a result of using that capability to meet society's demand for those goods. A state may be capable but not very effective if its capability is not used in society's interest.

The path to a more effective state, although not linear, is likely to be a two-stage process. First, the state must focus what capability it has on those tasks that it can and should undertake. As it does this, it can then focus on building additional capability. As the figure illustrates, countries in Zone I pursue a broad range of activities in an unfocused manner despite little state capability, and their efforts prove ineffective. But countries cannot move to Zone III overnight—building capability takes time. The pathway to greater effectiveness leads, first, to focusing on fundamental tasks and leveraging the state's limited capability through partnerships with the business community and civil society (Zone II). Countries then can move gradually to Zone III by strengthening their capability over time.

do and what not to do is critical. But this also involves choosing how to do things—how to deliver basic services, provide infrastructure, regulate the economy—and not just whether to do them at all. The choices here are many and must be tailored to the circumstances of each country.

The first job of states: Getting the fundamentals right

Five fundamental tasks lie at the core of every government's mission, without which sustainable, shared, poverty-reducing development is impossible:

- Establishing a foundation of law
- Maintaining a nondistortionary policy environment, including macroeconomic stability
- Investing in basic social services and infrastructure
- Protecting the vulnerable
- Protecting the environment.

Although the importance of these fundamentals has long been widely accepted, some new insights are emerging as to the appropriate mix of market and government activities in achieving them. Most important, we now see that markets and governments are complementary: the state is essential for putting in place the appropriate institutional foundations for markets. And government's credibility—the predictability of its rules and policies and the consistency with which they are applied—can be as important for attracting private investment as the content of those rules and policies.

A survey, specially commissioned for this Report, of domestic entrepreneurs (formal and informal) in sixty-nine countries confirms what was already known anecdotally: that many countries lack the basic institutional foundations for market development (Box 2). High levels of crime and personal violence and an unpredictable judiciary combine to produce what this Report defines as the "lawlessness syndrome." Weak and arbitrary state institutions often compound the problem with unpredictable, inconsistent behavior. Far from assisting the growth of markets, such actions squander the state's credibility and hurt market development.

To make development stable and sustainable, the state has to keep its eye on the social fundamentals. Lawlessness is often related to a sense of marginalization: indeed, breaking the law can seem the only way for the marginalized to get their voices heard. Public policies can ensure that growth is shared and that it contributes to reducing poverty and inequality, but only if governments put the social fundamentals high on their list of priorities.

Too often, policies and programs divert resources and services from the people who need them most. The political clout of the more affluent in society sometimes leads governments to spend many times more on rich and middle-class students in universities than on basic education for the majority and scholarships for the less well off. In many regions poverty and inequality are often biased against ethnic minorities or women, or disfavored geographic areas. Marginalized from public discussion and excluded from the broader economy and society, such groups are fertile ground for violence and instability, as many parts of the world are increasingly learning.

Public policies and programs must aim not merely to deliver growth but to ensure that the benefits of market-led growth are shared, particularly through investments in basic education and health. They must also ensure that people are protected against material and personal insecurity. Where poverty and economic marginalization stem from ethnic and social differences, policies must be carefully crafted to manage these differences, as Malaysia and Mauritius have done.

Government regulation is not the only answer to pollution. An expanding toolkit of innovative and flexible incentives is now available to get polluters to clean up their act. Although there is no substitute for meaningful regulatory frameworks and information about the environment, these new tools, which rely on persuasion, social pressure, and market forces to help push for improved environmental performance, can often succeed where regulation cannot. Countries are using some of these tools, with promising results, in four areas:

- Harnessing the power of public opinion
- Making regulation more flexible
- Applying self-regulatory mechanisms
- Choosing effective market-based instruments.

Going beyond the basics: The state need not be the sole provider

There is a growing recognition that in many countries monopoly public providers of infrastructure, social services, and other goods and services are unlikely to do a good job. At the same time, technological and organizational innovations have created new opportunities for competitive, private providers in activities hitherto confined to the public sector. To take advantage of these new opportunities—and better allocate scarce public capability—governments are beginning to separate the financing of infrastructure and services from its delivery, and to unbundle the competitive segments of utility markets from the monopoly segments. Reformers are also moving to separate programs of social insurance, designed to address the problems of health and employment insecurity for all, from programs of social assistance, intended to help only the poorest in society.

COPING WITH HOUSEHOLD INSECURITY. It is now well established that the state can help households cope with certain risks to their economic security: it can insure against destitution in old age through pensions, against devastating illness through health insurance, and against job loss through unemployment insurance. But the idea that the state alone must carry this burden is changing. Even in

Box 2   Credibility, investment, and growth

A survey of local entrepreneurs in sixty-nine countries shows that many states are performing their core functions poorly: they are failing to ensure law and order, protect property, and apply rules and policies predictably. Investors do not consider such states credible, and growth and investment suffer as a consequence.

Firms were asked to rank each of several indicators on a scale from one (extreme problem) to six (no problem). Averaging the answers, as the left panel does for each world region, yields an overall indicator of the

reliability of the institutional framework (normalized here to the high-income OECD countries) as perceived by private entrepreneurs—we call it credibility. The other two panels show that, once differences in income and education and policy distortions have been controlled for, there is a strong correlation between countries' credibility rating and their record of growth and investment. The credibility ratings are based on investors' perceptions. But it is these perceptions that determine investment behavior.

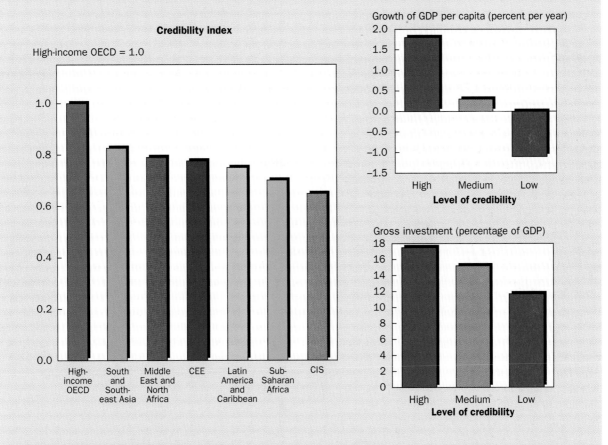

Note: The credibility index (left panel) is a summary indicator that combines the measures in Figure 2.3. Each bar in the two right panels is the average for a group of countries. The graphs are based on regressions for the period 1984–93 of GDP growth (thirty-two countries) and investment (thirty-three countries) on the index, controlling for income, education, and policy distortion. South and Southeast Asia and Middle East and North Africa are each represented by only three economies. Source: World Bank staff calculations using data from the private sector survey conducted for this Report and Brunetti, Kisunko, and Weder, background papers.

many industrial countries the welfare state is being reformed. Emerging economies from Brazil to China will be unable to afford even pared-down versions of the European system, especially with their rapidly aging populations.

Innovative solutions that involve businesses, labor, households, and community groups are needed to achieve greater security at lower cost. This is especially important for those developing countries not yet locked into costly solutions.

EFFECTIVE REGULATION. Well-designed regulatory systems can help societies influence market outcomes for public ends. Regulation can help protect consumers, workers, and the environment. It can foster competition and innovation while constraining the abuse of monopoly power. Thanks to regulatory reforms initiated in the early 1980s, Chile's telecommunications industry has enjoyed sustained private investment, increasing service quality and competition, and declining prices. By contrast, until some recent reform initiatives, dysfunctional regulation led the Philippine telecommunications industry—long privately owned—to underinvest. The result was poor and often high-priced service, imposing a high cost on citizens and other firms. Making the best use of the new options emerging for private provision of infrastructure and social services will also rely, often, on a good regulatory framework.

INDUSTRIAL POLICY. When markets are underdeveloped, the state can sometimes reduce coordination problems and gaps in information and encourage market development. Many of today's oldest industrial economies used various mechanisms to spur the growth of markets in their early stages of development. More recently, Japan, the Republic of Korea, and other countries in East Asia used a variety of mechanisms for market enhancement, in addition to securing the economic, social, and institutional fundamentals. Sometimes these interventions were quite elaborate: the highly strategic use of subsidies, for example. Other times they were less intrusive, taking the form of export promotion and special infrastructure incentives. But the ability to choose wisely among these interventions and use them effectively is critical; ill-considered trade, credit, and industrial policies can and have cost countries dearly. Many developing countries pursued ill-thought-out activist industrial policies, with poor results. Countries that have pursued an activist industrial policy successfully could not have done so without strong institutional capability.

MANAGING PRIVATIZATION. Carefully designed regulations and other active government initiatives can enhance the growth of markets. But in many countries this can take time, as private initiative is held hostage to a legacy of antagonistic state-market relations. And poorly performing state enterprises are often a big drain on the state's finances. Privatization provides an obvious solution. In general it is easier to sell off state assets once a supportive environment for private sector development is in place. Economies such as China, Korea, and Taiwan (China) have therefore opted not to give top priority to privatization, but to allow the private sector to develop around the state sector. This option, however, may not be available where the fiscal burden is very high, and where the presence of poorly performing state enterprises impedes much-needed overall restructuring of the economy.

Experience has shown that the way privatization is managed is terribly important to the end result. The key factors are transparency of process, winning the acquiescence of employees, generating broad-based ownership, and instituting the appropriate regulatory reform. Where privatization has been managed carefully, it is already showing positive results: in Chile, for example, and the Czech Republic. Its importance in the strategy to foster markets may vary, but for many developing countries seeking to scale back an overextended state, privatization must be kept on the front burner. A carefully managed privatization process brings very positive economic and fiscal benefits.

Knowing the state's limits

The key to predictable and consistent implementation of policy is a good fit between the state's institutional capabilities and its actions. In well-developed states, administrative capability is normally strong, and institutionalized checks and balances restrain arbitrary action, even as they provide government organizations the flexibility to pursue their mandates. By contrast, states with weaker institutions may need to err on the side of less flexibility and more restraint. This can be done in two ways:

- Through self-restricting rules, which precisely specify the content of policy and lock it into mechanisms that are costly to reverse. Regional common-currency arrangements, such as the CFA currency zone in francophone Africa or quasi currency boards as in Argentina, are examples of such mechanisms in the field of monetary policy. "Take-or-pay" contracts with independent power producers serve a similar function in utilities regulation.
- Through working in partnership with firms and citizens. In industrial policy, for example, states can foster private-to-private collaboration. In financial regulation they can give bankers an incentive to operate prudently. And in environmental regulation they can use the spread of information to encourage "bottom-up" citizen initiatives.

Countries in transition face a special challenge: not only are roles changing as a result of the adoption of market-based systems; so are capabilities. Some transition countries retain inherent capabilities in the form of qualified people and usable equipment, but they are not organized to perform in their new roles. Sometimes islands of excellence are found in countries where overall effectiveness has suffered. The task of improving effectiveness here is in some ways easier and in some ways more difficult: easier because capability does not start from a low base, more difficult because rebuilding capability means changing attitudes. Reform is not a matter of simply assigning people new responsibilities.

Reinvigorating state institutions

Acknowledging the state's existing, possibly meager capabilities does not mean accepting them for all time. The second key task of state reform is to reinvigorate the state's institutional capability, *by providing incentives for public officials to perform better while keeping arbitrary action in check.*

Countries struggle to build the institutions for an effective public sector. One reason the task is so difficult is political. Strong interests may develop, for example, to maintain an inequitable and inefficient status quo, whereas those who lose out from this arrangement may be unable to exert effective pressure for change.

But the problem of continued ineffectiveness, or of corruption, is not entirely political. Often politicians and other public officials have strong incentives and a sincere interest in improving public sector performance. But managing a public bureaucracy is a complex business that does not lend itself to clear, unambiguous solutions. In fact, building institutions for an effective public sector requires addressing a host of underlying behavioral factors

that distort incentives and ultimately lead to poor outcomes. Three basic incentive mechanisms can be used, in a variety of settings, to combat these deeper problems and improve capability (Figure 2):

- Effective rules and restraints
- Greater competitive pressure
- Increased citizen voice and partnership.

Effective rules and restraints
Over the long term, building accountability generally calls for formal mechanisms of restraint, anchored in core state institutions. Power can be divided, whether among the judicial, legislative, and executive branches of government or among central, provincial, and local authorities. The broader the separation of powers, the greater the number of veto points that can check arbitrary state action. But multiple veto points are a double-edged sword: they can make it as hard to change the harmful rules as the beneficial ones.

In many developing countries legislative and judicial oversight of the executive is weak. The setting of goals and the links to the policies needed to achieve them are sometimes diffuse, legislatures suffer from limited information

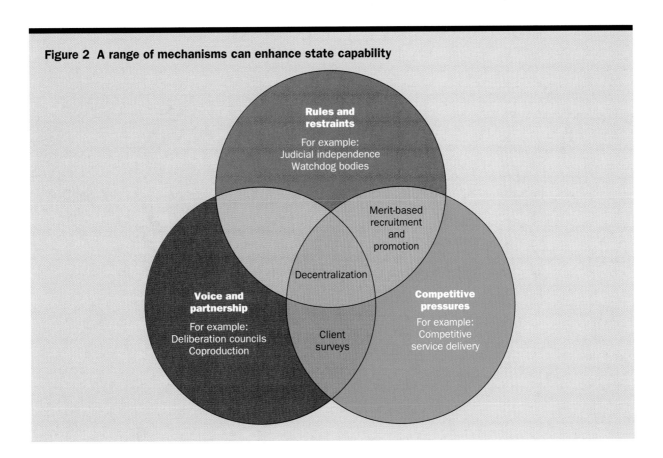

Figure 2 A range of mechanisms can enhance state capability

and capability, and judicial independence is compromised. An independent judiciary is vital to ensure that the legislative and executive authorities remain fully accountable under the law, and to interpret and enforce the terms of a constitution. Writing laws is the easy part; they need to be enforced if a country is to enjoy the benefits of a credible rule of law. These institutions of restraint take time to establish themselves, but international commitment mechanisms such as international adjudication, or guarantees from international agencies, can serve as a short-term substitute.

A major thrust of any effective strategy to reinvigorate the public sector will be to reduce the opportunities for corruption by cutting back on discretionary authority. Policies that lower controls on foreign trade, remove entry barriers for private industry, and privatize state firms in a way that ensures competition—all of these will fight corruption (Figure 3). Such reforms should not be half-

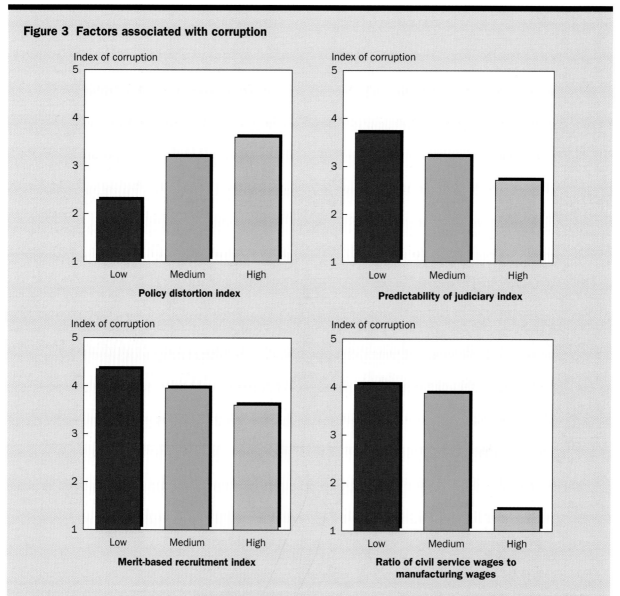

Figure 3 Factors associated with corruption

Note: Each index score is the average for a group of countries. See the Technical Note for details and definitions of the indexes. Higher values of the corruption index mean more corruption, and similarly for the other variables. The top left panel is based on a simple correlation for thirty-nine industrial and developing countries during 1984–93 (for the policy distortion index) and 1996 (for the corruption index). The top right panel is based on a regression using data from fifty-nine industrial and developing countries during 1996. The bottom left panel is based on a regression using data for thirty-five developing countries during 1970–90. The bottom right panel is based on a simple correlation for twenty industrial and developing countries in the late 1980s to the early 1990s; wage data are means. Source: World Bank staff calculations.

hearted: reforms that open opportunities for private entry into closed sectors of the economy, but leave that entry to the discretion of public officials rather than establish open and competitive processes, also create enormous scope for corruption. Formal checks and balances can also help reduce official corruption, but they are seldom enough. Reforming the civil service, restraining political patronage, and improving civil service pay have also been shown to reduce corruption by giving public officials more incentive to play by the rules.

Where corruption is deeply entrenched, more dramatic efforts will be needed to uproot it. These efforts should be focused on better monitoring of official action—both by formal institutions and by individual citizens—and punishment of wrongdoing in the courts. In Hong Kong (China, as of July 1, 1997), an independent commission against corruption is one successful example of such an approach. Likewise, recent reforms in Uganda have incorporated several elements of the anticorruption strategy outlined here, with some encouraging results. The same mechanisms could be applied around the globe: corruption, despite claims to the contrary, is not culture specific. Reducing it will require a multipronged approach, which must include the private sector and civil society more broadly. The briber has as much responsibility as the bribed; effective penalties on domestic and international business must be part of the solution.

Subjecting the state to more competition

Governments can improve their capability and effectiveness by introducing much greater competition in a variety of areas: in hiring and promotion, in policymaking, and in the way services are delivered.

BOOSTING COMPETITION WITHIN THE CIVIL SERVICE. Whether making policy, delivering services, or administering contracts, a capable, motivated staff is the lifeblood of an effective state. Civil servants can be motivated to perform effectively through a combination of mechanisms to encourage internal competition:

- A recruitment system based on merit, not favoritism
- A merit-based internal promotion system
- Adequate compensation.

Starting in the nineteenth century, all of today's established industrial countries used these principles to build modern professional bureaucracies. More recently these principles have been applied in many countries in East Asia, which have transformed weak, corrupt, patronage-based bureaucracies into reasonably well functioning systems. But many developing countries do not even need to look overseas or to history for role models: they exist at home. Central banks, for example, often continue to work

effectively and retain their competence even when all other institutions have declined. These agencies work well for all the reasons listed above. They are less subject to political interference. They have limited but clear objectives. They are given adequate resources and training. And their staff are usually better paid than their counterparts in other parts of government.

Cross-country evidence reveals that bureaucracies with more competitive, merit-based recruitment and promotion practices and better pay are more capable. In several countries (Kenya, the Philippines) political appointments run quite deep, whereas countries such as Korea have benefited from reliance on highly competitive recruitment and a promotion system that explicitly rewards merit. Ongoing reforms in the Philippines are examining these issues in an effort to improve bureaucratic capability. By and large, countries in which broader checks and balances are weak need to rely more heavily on more transparent and competitive systems. The experience of certain high-performing East Asian economies also shows that meritocracy and long-term career rewards help build an esprit de corps, or a shared commitment to collective goals. This reduces the transactions costs of enforcing internal constraints and builds internal partnerships and loyalty.

In many countries civil servants' wages have eroded as a result of expanding public employment at lower skill levels and fiscal constraints on the total wage bill (Figure 4). The result has been a significant compression of the salary structure and highly uncompetitive pay for senior officials, making it difficult to recruit and retain capable staff. Some countries, such as Uganda, are undertaking far-reaching reforms to reduce overstaffing dramatically, increase average pay, and decompress the salary structure. But in many countries these problems have yet to be addressed.

MORE COMPETITION IN THE PROVISION OF PUBLIC GOODS AND SERVICES. In many developing countries services are delivered badly or not at all. Politicians often intervene in the day-to-day operations of public agencies, and managers have limited flexibility. There is limited accountability for results. And in many countries the public sector has assumed a monopoly in delivery, eliminating pressures for better performance.

Building an effective public sector in these circumstances will mean opening up core government institutions, to improve incentives in areas that the public sector has long monopolized. Dozens of countries throughout the Americas, Europe, and Asia have capitalized on changes in technology and introduced competition in telecommunications and electric power generation. This has resulted in lower unit costs and a rapid expansion of service. Competition is also being enhanced by contracting out services through competitive bids and auctions.

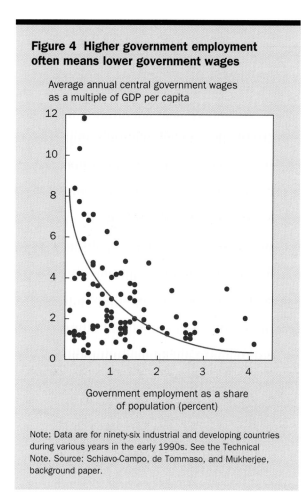

Figure 4 Higher government employment often means lower government wages

Average annual central government wages as a multiple of GDP per capita

Government employment as a share of population (percent)

Note: Data are for ninety-six industrial and developing countries during various years in the early 1990s. See the Technical Note. Source: Schiavo-Campo, de Tommaso, and Mukherjee, background paper.

This is a significant trend in industrial countries (the United Kingdom, Victoria State in Australia), but such mechanisms are also being used to improve efficiency in developing countries (for example, that of road maintenance in Brazil). Faced with weak administrative capacity, some countries (Bolivia, Uganda) are also contracting out the delivery of social services to nongovernmental organizations.

There is a growing trend to set up focused, performance-based public agencies with more clarity of purpose and greater managerial accountability for outputs or outcomes. New Zealand provides the most dramatic example among the high-income countries. It broke up its conglomerate ministries into focused business units, headed by chief executives on fixed-term, output-based contracts with the authority to hire and fire and to bargain collectively. Singapore has long followed a broadly similar approach with its performance-based statutory boards. Other developing countries are following suit, with Jamaica, for example, establishing executive agencies along the lines of the British model.

But countries with inadequate controls and weak capacity need to proceed with caution. For these countries, giv-

ing public managers more flexibility will merely increase arbitrariness and corruption with no commensurate improvement in performance. And writing and enforcing contracts, particularly for complex outputs, require specialized skills that are scarce in many developing countries. These countries need first to strengthen rule-based compliance and financial accountability (as Argentina and Bolivia have done) within the public sector, provide greater clarity of purpose and task, and introduce performance measurement (as in Colombia, Mexico, and Uganda). As output measurement and ex post controls on inputs are strengthened, agencies can be provided more flexibility in exchange for their greater accountability for results.

Bringing the state closer to people

Governments are more effective when they listen to businesses and citizens and work in partnership with them in deciding and implementing policy. Where governments lack mechanisms to listen, they are not responsive to people's interests, especially those of minorities and the poor, who usually strain to get their voices heard in the corridors of power. And even the best-intentioned government is unlikely to meet collective needs efficiently if it does not know what many of those needs are.

GIVING PEOPLE A VOICE. Partnership involves bringing the voice of the poor and of marginalized groups into the very center of the policymaking process. In many countries, voice is distributed as unequally as income. Greater information and transparency are vital for informed public debate and for increasing popular trust and confidence in the state—whether in discussing expenditure priorities, designing social assistance programs, or managing forests and other resources. Client surveys (in India, Nicaragua, and Tanzania) and citizen charters (in Malaysia) are providing new options for making voices heard.

The best-established mechanism for giving citizens voice is the ballot box. In 1974 only thirty-nine countries—one in every four worldwide—were independent democracies. Today, 117 countries—nearly two of every three—use open elections to choose their leaders. But periodic voting does not always mean the state is more responsive. Other mechanisms are needed to ensure that the concerns of minorities and the poor are reflected in public policies. Getting genuine intermediary organizations represented on policymaking councils is an important first step in articulating citizen interests in public policymaking. Even more effective in local and provincial government, these organizations have recently become very active in developing countries—especially where the state has performed poorly and where such organizations are not suppressed.

BROADENING PARTICIPATION. Evidence is mounting that government programs work better when they seek the participation of potential users, and when they tap the community's reservoir of social capital rather than work against it. The benefits show up in smoother implementation, greater sustainability, and better feedback to government agencies. Higher returns from water-borne sanitation systems in Recife, Brazil; housing schemes for the poor in Port Elizabeth, South Africa; forest management efforts in Gujarat State, India; and health care in Khartoum, Sudan, are all testament to the power of partnership—the participation of local people. This is in contrast with top-down approaches, which often fail.

In successful countries policymaking has been embedded in consultative processes, which provide civil society, labor unions, and private firms opportunities for input and oversight. In East Asia public-private deliberation councils—such as Korea's monthly export promotion meetings, Thailand's National Joint Public and Private Consultative Committee, and the Malaysian Business Council—have provided mechanisms for feedback, information sharing, and coordination.

DEVOLVING POWER, CAREFULLY. The typical developing country has a more centralized government than the typical industrial country. But with some significant exceptions, the past thirty years have seen a small shift in public spending power in developing countries from the national to lower levels. The industrial economies have seen an opposite trend, with spending power moving to the center. Neither of these observations, of course, takes into account the decentralization implicit in recent market reforms, which have clearly reduced the direct power and resources of central government in a broad range of countries.

Decentralization is bringing many benefits in China, India, much of Latin America, and many other parts of the world. It can improve the quality of government and the representation of local business and citizens' interests. And competition among provinces, cities, and localities can spur the development of more-effective policies and programs. But there are three big pitfalls to watch out for:

- *Rising inequality.* The gap between regions can widen— an issue of considerable concern in China, Russia, and Brazil. Labor mobility provides a partial solution, but it is seldom easy, especially in ethnically diverse countries where migrants are not always welcome.
- *Macroeconomic instability.* Governments can lose control of macroeconomic policy if local and regional fiscal indiscipline leads to frequent bailouts from the center, as occurred in Brazil.
- *Risk of local capture.* A serious danger is that of local governments falling under the sway of special interests, leading to misuse of resources and of the coercive power of the state.

These dangers show, once again, how central government will always play a vital role in sustaining development. The challenge is to find the right division of labor between the center and the other tiers of government.

Strategic options for reform

Building a more responsive state requires working on mechanisms that increase openness and transparency, increase incentives for participation in public affairs, and where appropriate, lessen the distance between government and the citizens and communities it is intended to serve. This yields four broad imperatives for policymakers:

- Where appropriate, ensure broad-based public discussion of key policy directions and priorities. At a minimum this includes making available information in the public interest and establishing consultative mechanisms—such as deliberation councils and citizen committees—to gather the views and make known the preferences of affected groups.
- Encourage, where feasible, the direct participation of users and other beneficiaries in the design, implementation, and monitoring of local public goods and services.
- Where decentralization is considered desirable, adopt a carefully staged and/or sectoral approach in priority areas. Introduce strong monitoring mechanisms and make sure sound intergovernmental rules are in place to restrain arbitrary action at the central and the local level.
- At the local level, focus on mechanisms—and horizontal incentives in government's relations with the rest of the community—that build accountability and competition.

Of course, a strategy of more openness and greater decentralization has its dangers. The more numerous the opportunities for participation, the greater the demands that will be made on the state. This can increase the risk of capture by vocal interest groups, or of gridlock. Bringing government closer to some people must not result in taking it even further away from others. Equally, without clear-cut rules to impose restraints on different tiers of government, and incentives to encourage local accountability, the crisis of governance that afflicts many centralized governments will simply be passed down to lower levels. But there are some safe ways to start the ball rolling, including the use of communication and consensus building to render reform intelligible to citizens and firms and enhance its chances of success.

Beyond national borders: Facilitating global collective action

Globalization is a threat to weak or capriciously governed states. But it also opens the way for effective, disciplined states to foster development and economic well-being, and it sharpens the need for effective international cooperation in pursuit of global collective action.

Embracing external competition

The state still defines the policies and rules for those within its jurisdiction, but global events and international agreements are increasingly affecting its choices. People are now more mobile, more educated, and better informed about conditions elsewhere. And involvement in the global economy tightens constraints on arbitrary state action, reduces the state's ability to tax capital, and brings much closer financial market scrutiny of monetary and fiscal policies.

"Globalization" is not yet truly global—it has yet to touch a large chunk of the world economy. Roughly half of the developing world's people have been left out of the much-discussed rise in the volume of international trade and capital flows since the early 1980s. Governments' hesitance to open up to the world economy is partly understandable. Joining the global economy, like devolving power from the center, carries risks as well as opportunities. For example, it can make countries more vulnerable to external price shocks or to large, destabilizing shifts in capital flows. This makes the state's role all the more critical, both in handling such shocks and in helping people and firms grasp the opportunities of the global marketplace. But the difficulties should not be exaggerated, particularly when laid against the risks of being left out of the globalization process altogether.

The cost of not opening up will be a widening gap in living standards between those countries that have integrated and those that remain outside. For lagging countries the route to higher incomes will lie in pursuing sound domestic policies and building the capability of the state. Integration gives powerful support to such policies—and increases the benefits from them—but it cannot substitute for them. In that sense, globalization begins at home. But multilateral institutions such as the World Trade Organization have an important role to play in providing countries with the incentive to make the leap.

Promoting global collective action

Global integration also gives rise to demands for states to cooperate to combat international threats such as global warming. Economic, cultural, and other differences between countries can make such cooperation difficult—even, at times, impossible. But stronger cooperation is clearly needed for at least five major concerns that transcend national borders:

- *Managing regional crises.* The threat of nuclear war between the superpowers has given way to a mushrooming of smaller conflicts, entailing costly problems of refugee relief and rehabilitation. No solid international framework exists for managing these conflicts or helping avoid them. A more integrated assessment of how state policies (and international assistance) help manage nascent conflict is needed in designing economic and social policy.

- *Promoting global economic stability.* Concern has been growing about the potentially destabilizing effects of large and rapid flows of portfolio capital, particularly when a crisis in one country can spill over into other markets. A variety of international mechanisms have been suggested to guard against such problems, and the International Monetary Fund has recently created a new facility to help members cope with sudden financial crises. But prudent and responsive economic policies at home will be countries' best protection. Growing international labor mobility is also raising a host of issues requiring international collective action.

- *Protecting the environment.* Urgent global environmental issues include climate change, loss of biodiversity, and protection of international waters. International collective action can help through better coordination, greater public awareness, more effective technological transfer, and better national and local practices. Progress has been slow, however, raising the worry that it will take a major environmental catastrophe to goad countries into concerted action.

- *Fostering basic research and the production of knowledge.* Now being revitalized to meet renewed challenges in food production, the Consultative Group on International Agricultural Research has shown how technology can be developed and disseminated through international collective action. Similar consultative mechanisms need to be developed to tackle other pressing research problems in the domains of environmental protection and health.

- *Making international development assistance more effective.* To become more effective, foreign aid needs to be tied more closely to the policies of the recipient countries. A high priority for aid agencies is to systematically channel resources to poor countries with good policies and a strong commitment to institutional reinvigoration.

Removing obstacles to state reform

The history of state reform in today's established industrial countries offers hope—and gives pause—to today's developing countries. Until the last century many of the problems that now appear to have reduced the effectiveness of the state in the developing world were in plain evidence in Europe, North America, and Japan. But the problems were addressed, and modern states with professional systems emerged. This gives us hope. But it also gives us pause, because institutional strengthening takes time. The reforms of the Meiji restoration, which launched Japan onto the path of development, took almost twenty-five years to take root. A more capable state can be built, but the process will be slow and will require immense political commitment. It is urgent to act now.

Over the past fifteen years many governments have responded to internal and external pressure by launching far-reaching reforms to improve their performance. Typically, changes in macroeconomic policy—dealing with exchange rates, fiscal policy, and trade policy—have come fastest. These reforms have political implications but do not require the overhaul of institutions. They can be undertaken quickly, often through decree, by a small group of competent technocrats. All it takes is the political decision to make the change.

But other state reforms, dealing with regulation, social services, finance, infrastructure, and public works, cannot be accomplished so rapidly because they involve changing institutional structures established for different purposes, to fit different rules of the game. This kind of institutional reform involves wrenching changes in the way government agencies think and act, and often a complete overhaul of long-established systems of patronage and corruption. But such change is absolutely essential if the capability of the state is ever to improve. The two together—good policies and more capable state institutions to implement them—produce much faster economic development (Figure 5).

Comprehensive reform along these lines will take a great deal of time and effort in many developing countries, and the agenda varies considerably from region to region (Box 3). Reform will also encounter considerable political opposition. But reformers can make a good start by strengthening central agencies for strategic policy formulation, introducing more transparency and competition, hiving off activities and agencies with easily specified outputs, seeking more feedback from users about the delivery of services, and working with labor unions on programs that will enable workers to seek security in change rather than seek security against change.

When do reforms occur?

Deep distributional conflicts and constraints embedded in state institutions are at the heart of the explanation for so many countries' failure to reform. But they are not immutable. Ultimately, change comes when the incentives to throw out the old policies and old institutional arrangements become stronger than the incentives to keep them. An economic crisis or an external threat, or the arrival of a new government with fewer vested interests in the old system, may provide the impetus for reform. But reform can be delayed if those in power stick with outdated policies because it is in their (or their allies') interest to do so. And the delay can sometimes be painfully long, as in Haiti under the Duvaliers, or Zaire today.

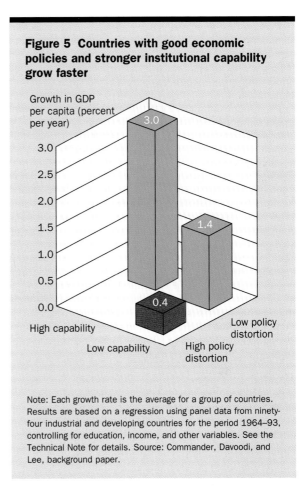

Figure 5 Countries with good economic policies and stronger institutional capability grow faster

Growth in GDP per capita (percent per year)

3.0

1.4

0.4

High capability
Low capability

Low policy distortion
High policy distortion

Note: Each growth rate is the average for a group of countries. Results are based on a regression using panel data from ninety-four industrial and developing countries for the period 1964–93, controlling for education, income, and other variables. See the Technical Note for details. Source: Commander, Davoodi, and Lee, background paper.

Neighbors, too, can be a powerful motivator for change. There is a clear domino effect at work in the wave of reform sweeping East Asia, Latin America, and much of Eastern Europe and the former Soviet Union. The threat of being left behind can goad countries to improve the functioning of their bureaucracies. But research has yet to explain why some countries respond to crises and others do not. Why, for example, does popular tolerance of inflation seem to be much lower in Asia than in parts of Latin America? And why can some countries endure a long period of economic decline before responding, while others take action much sooner?

Often the analysis of winners and losers yields a prediction of when—or at least whether—reforms will be undertaken. Reforms have little appeal if the winners cannot compensate the losers. Even when the potential gains are enough to allow for compensation, reform can be hard to achieve because the gains are spread over many people, whereas the losers, although smaller in number, are powerful and articulate. A further problem is that the benefits are often realized in the future, whereas the losses are immediate. Yet sometimes conditions have deteriorated so

---

Box 3 The regional agenda

The key features and challenges of improving the effectiveness of the state in the various developing regions are summarized below. These are of necessity broad generalizations, and each region includes several countries whose experiences are very different.

- Many countries in *Sub-Saharan Africa* are suffering from a crisis of statehood—a crisis of capability. An urgent priority is to rebuild state effectiveness through an overhaul of public institutions, reassertion of the rule of law, and credible checks on abuse of state power. Where the links between the state, the private sector, and civil society are fragile and underdeveloped, improving the delivery of public and collective services will require closer partnerships with the private sector and civil society.
- The capability of the state in most *East Asian* countries cannot be considered a problem. But states' ability to change in response to the new challenges facing the region will play a critical role in their continued economic success.
- The main issue in *South Asia* is overregulation, both a cause and an effect of bloated public employment and the surest route to corruption. Regulatory simplification and public enterprise reform, and the resulting contraction of the role of the state, will be complex and politically difficult.

- The job of reorienting the state toward the task of "steering, not rowing" is far from complete in *Central and Eastern Europe*. But most countries have made progress and are on the way to improving capability and accountability.
- Low state capability in many countries of the *Commonwealth of Independent States* is a serious and mounting obstacle to further progress in most areas of economic and social policy. Reorientation of the state is still at an early stage, and a host of severe problems have emerged from a general lack of accountability and transparency.
- In *Latin America,* decentralization of power and of spending, coupled with democratization, has dramatically transformed the local political landscape, in what some have called a "quiet revolution." A new model of government is emerging in the region. But greater emphasis is also needed on reform of the legal system, the civil service, and social policies.
- In the *Middle East and North Africa,* unemployment is by far the greatest economic and social problem and makes government downsizing especially difficult. Because the political and social difficulties of reform are considerable, although not insurmountable, a promising approach might be to begin decentralizing selected services, and focus on reforming state enterprises, while preparing the ground for wider-ranging reforms.

---

far that the winners far outnumber the losers. Then reform can produce immediate economic and political gains.

How can reforms be sustained?
Reform-oriented political leaders and elites can speed reform by making decisions that widen people's options, articulate the benefits clearly, and ensure that policies are more inclusive. In recent years farsighted political leaders have transformed the options for their people through decisive reform. They were successful because they made the benefits of change clear to all, and built coalitions that gave greater voice to often-silent beneficiaries. They also succeeded—and this is crucial—because they spelled out a longer-term vision for their society, allowing people to see beyond the immediate pain of adjustment. Effective leaders give their people a sense of owning the reforms—a sense that reform is not something imposed from without.

Reforming the state requires cooperation from all groups in society. Compensation of groups adversely af-

fected by reform (which may not always be the poorest in society) can help secure their support. Although compensation may be costly in the short run, it will pay off in the long run. Deep-seated differences and mutual suspicions among groups can also delay reform. There are no quick fixes for removing age-old enmities, but social pacts, such as Spain's Moncloa Pacts and Benin's National Economic Conference, can help.

International agencies can encourage and help sustain reform in four ways. First, they can provide important technical advice on what to do and what not to do. This assistance is often invaluable, especially for smaller states that lack the resources to handle all the technical issues internally. But it must be complemented by local expertise, to adapt reforms to local conditions and institutions. The World Trade Organization plays a major role in trade reform, the World Health Organization on health issues, and the International Labour Organisation on labor legislation and employment policy. Second, international agencies can provide a wealth of cross-country experience on a wide range of issues. Often staffed by people from all over the world, they can bring in experts from different backgrounds. Third, the financial assistance these agencies provide can help countries endure the early, painful period of reform until the benefits kick in. Fourth, they can provide a mechanism for countries to make external commitments, making it more difficult to backtrack on reforms. If the history of development assistance teaches anything, however, it is that external support can achieve little where the domestic will to reform is lacking.

Good government is not a luxury—it is a vital necessity for development

The approach of the twenty-first century brings great promise of change and reason for hope. In a world of dizzying changes in markets, civil societies, and global forces, the state is under pressure to become more effective, but it is not yet adapting rapidly enough to keep pace. Not surprisingly, there is no unique model for change, and reforms will often come slowly because they involve a fundamental rethinking of the roles of institutions and the interactions between citizens and government. But the issues raised in this Report are now an integral part of the rethinking of the state in many parts of the world and are on the agenda of the international organizations that assist them.

People living with ineffective states have long suffered the consequences in terms of postponed growth and social development. But an even bigger cost may now threaten states that postpone reforms: political and social unrest and, in some cases, disintegration, exacting a tremendous toll on stability, productive capacity, and human life. The enormous cost of state collapse has naturally turned attention to prevention as a preferable and potentially less costly course of action—but there are no shortcuts. Once the spiral into collapse has occurred, there are no quick fixes.

Instances of state collapse are both extreme and unique, but they are growing. As the Report elaborates, no simple generalizations about their causes or effects can be made, nor, for that matter, are there any easy solutions to their reconstruction; each case brings its own challenges for countries, their neighbors, and the international system. The consequences, however, are almost uniformly borne by ordinary people, illustrating once again how fundamental an effective, responsive state is to the long-term health and wealth of society.

The quest for a more effective state even in the established industrial countries suggests that the returns to incremental improvements are high. This is especially true in countries where the effectiveness of the state is low. Over time, even the smallest increases in the capability of the state have been shown to make a vast difference to the quality of people's lives, not least because reforms tend to produce their own virtuous circle. Small improvements in the state's effectiveness lead to higher standards of living, in turn paving the way for more reforms and further development.

A tour of the world's economies in 1997 would turn up countless examples of these virtuous circles in action. But it would provide equally plentiful evidence of the reverse: countries and regions caught in vicious cycles of poverty and underdevelopment set in train by the chronic ineffectiveness of the state. Such cycles can all too easily lead to social violence, crime, corruption, and instability, all of which undermine the state's capacity to support development—or even to function at all. The crucial challenge facing states is to take those steps, both small and large, toward better government that set economies on the upward path, using the two-part framework suggested in this Report. Reform of state institutions is long, difficult, and politically sensitive. But if we now have a better sense of the size of the reform challenge, we are also much more aware of the costs of leaving things as they are.

PART ONE

RETHINKING THE STATE— THE WORLD OVER

THROUGHOUT HISTORY, NOTIONS OF THE STATE'S ROLE HAVE SHIFTED DRAMAT-ically. For much of this century people looked to government to do more—in some cases a great deal more. But during the past fifteen years the pendulum has been swinging again, forcing the world to look at government from a range of conflicting perspectives. The end of the Cold War and the collapse of command-and-control economies, the fiscal crises of welfare states, the dra-matic success of some East Asian countries in accelerating economic growth and reducing poverty, and the crisis of failed states in parts of Africa and else-where—all of these have challenged existing conceptions of the state's place in the world and its potential contribution to human welfare.

Governments are also having to respond to the rapid diffusion of technol-ogy, growing demographic pressures, increased environmental concerns, greater global integration of markets, and a shift to more democratic forms of govern-ment. And amid all these pressures remain the formidable—and persistent—challenges of reducing poverty and fostering sustainable development.

It is not surprising, then, that countries are again putting the state under scrutiny, asking what government's role ought to be and, critically, how that role should be played. This Report explores why and how some states have been more effective than others at playing a catalytic and sustainable role in economic development and the eradication of poverty. This part of the Report provides a broad historical and conceptual introduction to the issues (in Chapter 1) and examines the empirical evidence of the impact of state policies and institutions on development (in Chapter 2). It conveys three principal messages:

- Development—economic, social, and sustainable—without an effective state is impossible. It is increasingly recognized that an effective state—not a minimal one—is central to economic and social development, but more as partner and facilitator than as director. States should work to complement markets, not replace them.

- A rich body of evidence shows the importance of good economic policies (including the promotion of macroeconomic stability), well-developed human capital, and openness to the world economy for broad-based, sustainable growth and the reduction of poverty. But as our understanding of the ingredients of development improves, a deeper set of questions emerges: why have some societies pursued these actions with greater success than others, and how, precisely, did the state contribute to these differing outcomes?

- The historical record suggests the importance of building on the relative strengths of the market, the state, and civil society to improve the state's effectiveness. This suggests a two-part strategy of matching the role of the state to its capability, and then improving that capability. These are the subject, respectively, of Parts Two and Three.

CHAPTER 1

THE EVOLVING ROLE OF THE STATE

A CENTURY AGO, A CANADIAN FARMER AND AN Ivorian probably felt little connection with their governments, and none at all to each other. Government affected their lives only to the extent that it provided a handful of classic public goods, such as law and order and basic infrastructure, and collected taxes from them.

Today the state has expanded dramatically—and the world has shrunk. The same farmers' descendants send their children to government-run schools, receive medical treatment from publicly supported clinics, rely on an array of publicly provided services, and may benefit from government price controls on the seed and fertilizer they buy, or the wheat or coffee they sell. These later generations of Canadians and Ivorians are therefore likely to be much more concerned than their ancestors were about the effectiveness of government and the checks and balances on its decisions. And they are likely to be much more aware of how their own government's performance compares with others'. Vastly expanded communications, trade and investment, radio and television, friends and relatives traveling to foreign lands as tourists or migrant laborers—all of these give Canadians and Ivorians today a much better idea of how the government services they receive measure up to those in other countries. The state's behavior, and the consequences of that behavior, are being scrutinized like never before.

This scrutiny might lead to better government. But if states are unable to respond constructively to the challenges they face, the result could simply be further erosion of the state's credibility, as the gap between what the state can do, and what people ask it to do, widens even further. The terminal phase of this process is visible in the recent agonies of Angola, Somalia, and Zaire. The state collapses from within, leaving citizens bereft of even the most basic conditions of a stable existence: law and security, trust in contracts, and a sound medium of exchange. These crises

recall Thomas Hobbes' insight, in his 1651 treatise *Leviathan*, that life without an effective state to preserve order is "solitary, poor, nasty, brutish and short."

This Report aims to show how every state, regardless of its point of departure, can improve its effectiveness and move ever further away from this doomsday scenario. Toward that end, this chapter begins with a reminder of how we got here. Surveying the history of the state from its early beginnings, it shows how notions of the state's role have evolved to produce, in both industrial and developing countries, a dramatic expansion of the state and, more recently, a change of emphasis from the quantity of government to the quality. The chapter then lays out a simple framework for rethinking the state, introducing a two-part strategy for greater state effectiveness that the rest of the Report explores. The message is that the state can rise to the challenges it faces, but only by, first, matching what it tries to do to what it can do, and second, working to increase the number of things it can do capably by reinvigorating public institutions.

Where the state began

From earliest times human beings have banded together into larger associations, starting with household and kinship groups and extending through to the modern state. For states to exist, individuals and groups have to cede authority in key areas, such as defense, to a public agency. That agency has to possess coercive power over all other organizational forms within a designated territory.

States have come in all shapes and sizes, depending on a mix of factors including culture, natural endowments, opportunities for trade, and distribution of power. The ancient Athenian state, for example, was underpinned by slavery and colonial spoils. Further east, elaborate state structures were built from early times on the basis of state ownership of land or, in Mughal India and

Box 1.1 State and government: Some concepts

State, in its wider sense, refers to a set of institutions that possess the means of legitimate coercion, exercised over a defined territory and its population, referred to as society. The state monopolizes rulemaking within its territory through the medium of an organized government.

The term *government* is often used differently in different contexts. It can refer to the process of governing, to the exercise of power. It can also refer to the existence of that process, to a condition of "ordered rule." "Government" often means the people who fill the positions of authority in a state. Finally, the term may refer to the manner, method, or system of governing in a society: to the structure and arrangement of offices and how they relate to the governed. While keeping these distinctions in mind, we also use the terms *state* and *government* colloquially and sometimes interchangeably—as they are often used in discussion and writing around the world.

Government is normally regarded as consisting of three distinct sets of powers, each with its assigned role. One is the *legislature,* whose role is to make the law. The second is the *executive* (sometimes referred to as "the government"), which is responsible for implementing the law. The third is the *judiciary,* which is responsible for interpreting and applying the law.

Classifications of government are many but have tended to concentrate on two criteria: the arrangement of offices, which is more narrow in conception, and the relationship between government and the governed. The first classification is based on the relationship between the executive and the legislature. In a *parliamentary* system the executive's continuance in office depends on its maintaining the support of the legislature. Members of the executive are commonly also members of the legislature. A prime minister may be the most powerful member of the executive, but important decisions within the executive are usually made collectively by a group of ministers. In a *presidential* system the executive's position is independent of the legislature. Members of the executive are not normally also members of the legislature, and ultimate decisionmaking authority within the executive lies with one person, the president.

The second classification concentrates on the distribution of power between levels of government. In a *unitary* state, all authority to make laws is vested in one supreme legislature whose jurisdiction covers the whole country. Local legislatures may exist, but only with the sufferance of the national legislature. In a *federal* state, local legislatures are guaranteed at least a measure of autonomous decisionmaking authority. In a *confederation,* a group of sovereign states combine for specified purposes, but each state retains its sovereignty.

---

imperial China, highly developed systems of administration and tax collection. The combination of public ownership of land and a complex bureaucracy long impeded the emergence of modern, market-based economies in these regions.

Yet despite this diversity of origins, states over time came to acquire several common and defining features worldwide. Modern states have a consolidated territory and population, and within these they play a centralizing and coordinating role. Sovereign authority commonly encompasses separate judicial, legislative, and executive functions (Box 1.1). Since the eighteenth century, through conquest and colonization, nation-states have incorporated most of the world into their own mutually exclusive territories. As empires disintegrated and minority groups established claims to statehood, the number of nations increased sharply. Membership in the United Nations jumped from 50 independent countries in 1945 to 185 in 1996 (Figure 1.1).

Modest beginnings

The configuration of states has varied widely across continents and centuries, but arguments over the proper roles of the public and private spheres have not. Whether in Niccolò Machiavelli's *The Prince,* Kautiliya's *Arthashastra,* Confucius' writings, or Ibn Khaldoun's *The Muqaddimah,* the discussion has revolved around the mutual rights and obligations of states and citizens. Almost all these traditions have included a role for the state in providing basic public goods (although the weight accorded to public, as opposed to private, goals has varied considerably). Using public resources to provide critical public goods and to raise private productivity is nothing new.

Beyond these minimal functions, however, there has been much less agreement on the appropriate role of the state in promoting development. Seventeenth-century mercantilists saw a major role for the state in guiding trade. Not until Adam Smith wrote *The Wealth of Nations* in the late eighteenth century was it generally recognized that the market was the best instrument for realizing growth and improving welfare. The state, on this view, was best held to certain core functions—providing public goods such as defense, ensuring the security of persons and property, educating the citizenry, and enforcing contracts—deemed essential for the market to flourish.

Figure 1.1 One world, many more states

Number of United Nations member countries

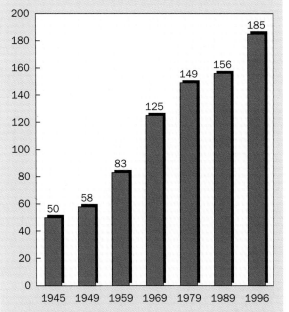

Note: Data are as of the end of the year. Source: United Nations data.

Box 1.2 U.S. government action to support market development: Some examples

The United States is the country that produced and believes in the dictum that "That government is best that governs least." Whereas in many parts of the world the role of the government has evolved gradually, the United States was founded on a revolution. The framers of the Constitution explicitly asked, What should be the role of the government?

Yet even in the United States, where laissez-faire and distrust of government are central to the framing of the state's role in society, government action has often proved critical to the growth and development of markets. For example:

- The global telecommunications industry has its roots in U.S. government support for the first telegraph line between Washington and Baltimore in the early 1840s.
- The enormous increase in agricultural productivity in the nineteenth and twentieth centuries can be traced to the federally supported program of research and extension services dating from the Morrill Act of 1863.
- The Northwest Ordinances of 1785 and 1787 committed the government to supporting education, and to devoting the revenues from the sale of certain lands to that purpose. And in 1863 the federal government helped establish the public university system.
- In 1863, in the midst of the Civil War, the Congress recognized the need for a national financial system and passed the National Banking Act, establishing the first nationwide bank supervisory agency. In later years the government created the Federal Reserve System (the U.S. central bank) as well as a series of public financial intermediaries.
- The interstate highway system and federal support for the establishment of railroads are cases of vital public involvement in transport infrastructure that helped the development of markets in the United States.

But even then, state intervention went on to play a vital, catalytic role in the development and growth of markets in Europe, Japan, and North America. In the United States, where state involvement in the economy has historically been more limited than in Europe or Japan, government was instrumental in constructing the first telegraph line, which spurred development of the telecommunications industry, and in agricultural research and extension, which stimulated productivity gains (Box 1.2).

In the nineteenth century the state's role in redistributing income was still quite limited. Redistribution in Europe came mainly through private charity and other voluntary action. Tax systems were usually restricted to customs, excise, monopoly, and commodity taxes. Income taxation, which had been introduced in France and Britain by the end of the eighteenth century, was not a major source of revenue. The first faint stirrings of the modern welfare state were seen in Germany, at the end of the nineteenth century, where Chancellor Otto von Bismarck introduced the first nationwide systems of social insurance.

The expanding state in industrial countries . . .
States remained small by modern standards until well into this century. A series of dramatic events in the aftermath of World War I marked the turning point. The first was the Russian Revolution of 1917, which led to the abolition there of most private property and put the state in control, through central planning, of all economic activity. The second was the Great Depression of the 1930s, which caused such economic devastation in the noncommunist world that states were spurred to experiment with

countercyclical policies to restore economic activity. The third event, unleashed by World War II, was the rapid breakup of European empires. That geopolitical change—as well as the clamor for social insurance in the industrial economies—ushered in fifty years of policy debate focused around a more activist role for government.

The postwar paradigm coalesced around three basic themes, all of which commanded broad, if not uniform, agreement. This three-pillared consensus remained largely undisturbed until the first oil price shock of 1973. First was the need to provide welfare benefits to those suffering from transitory loss of income or other deprivation. Second was the desirability of a mixed public-private economy, which would often mean nationalizing a range of strategic industries. Third was the need for a coordinated macroeconomic policy, on the grounds that the market alone could not deliver stable macroeconomic outcomes that were consistent with individuals' objectives. In time, the goals of macroeconomic policy were made explicit: full employment, price stability, and balance of payments equilibrium.

States thus took on new roles and expanded existing ones. By mid-century the range of tasks performed by public institutions included not only wider provision of infrastructure and utilities, but also much more extensive support for education and health care. In the three-and-a-

half decades between 1960 and 1995, governments in the industrial countries swelled to twice their starting size (Figure 1.2), with much of the expansion driven by increases in transfers and subsidies.

Indeed, by the early 1990s it was fair to say that most industrial-country governments spent more time moving money around the economy in the form of transfers and subsidies than they spent providing traditional public goods. Spending on defense and on law and order had shrunk to some 10 percent of general-government outlays, while over half of all tax revenues were transferred to individual beneficiaries (Figure 1.3). Demographics accounted for some of the shift, as aging populations forced an increase in outlays for pensions and health care. But national preferences also made a difference. Thus, from a point of rough equivalence in 1960, the Swedish state grew to nearly twice the size of that in the United States by 1995, in terms of both spending as a share of income and public employment as a share of the population.

. . . And in developing countries

Governments in developing countries were also reaching into new areas. They, too, grew dramatically in the second half of the twentieth century (Figure 1.2). Initially, much of the growth came from state and nation building after

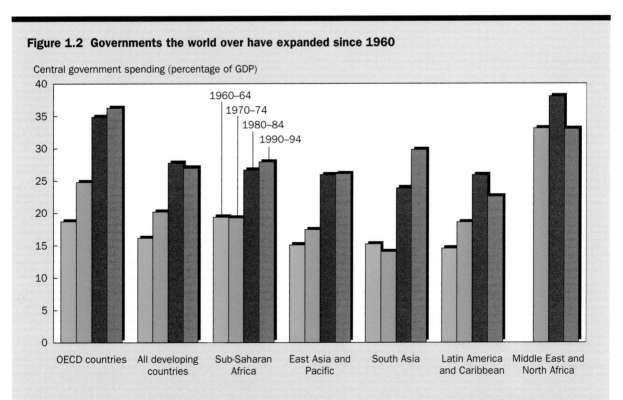

Figure 1.2 Governments the world over have expanded since 1960

Central government spending (percentage of GDP)

1960–64
1970–74
1980–84
1990–94

OECD countries All developing countries Sub-Saharan Africa East Asia and Pacific South Asia Latin America and Caribbean Middle East and North Africa

Note: Data are in current national prices. Data for Middle East and North Africa for 1960–64 are unavailable. Source: IMF, various years (a) and (b); World Bank data.

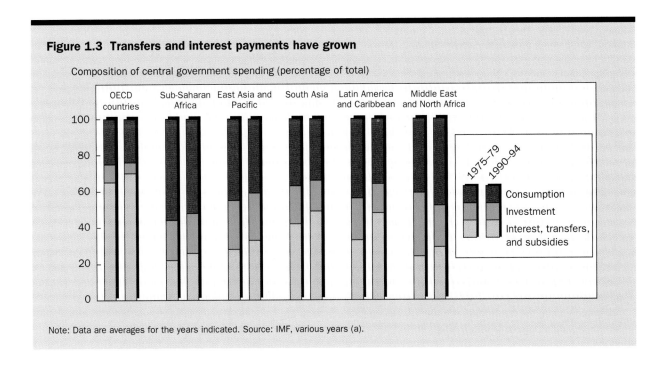

Figure 1.3 Transfers and interest payments have grown

Composition of central government spending (percentage of total)

Note: Data are averages for the years indicated. Source: IMF, various years (a).

the collapse of colonialism. The ups and downs in international commodity markets also had an impact. Resource-rich economies such as Mexico, Nigeria, and Venezuela tended to use the revenue bonanzas from the oil price rises of the 1970s and other commodity booms to expand their public sectors, sometimes with reckless abandon. Oil-importing countries, under the imperative of fiscal austerity, were less able to expand their spending.

Perhaps more significant than these forces has been the shift in thinking about the role of the state over the past fifty years. Most developing countries in Asia, the Middle East, and Africa came out of the colonial period with a strong belief in state-dominated economic development. The state would mobilize resources and people and direct them toward rapid growth and the eradication of social injustice. State control of the economy, following the example of the Soviet Union, was central to this strategy. (How it was followed in one country, India, is described in Box 1.3.) Many Latin American, Middle Eastern, and African countries also followed this postwar pattern of state-dominated, import-substituting industrialization.

This belief was reinforced by the popularity of state activism worldwide. The Great Depression was seen as a failure of capitalism and markets, while state interventions—the Marshall Plan, Keynesian demand management, and the welfare state—seemed to record one success after another. The new interventionist credo had its counterpart in the development strategy of the day, adopted by many developing countries at independence, which emphasized the prevalence of market failures and accorded

the state a central role in correcting them. Centralized planning, corrective interventions in resource allocation, and a heavy state hand in infant-industry development were part and parcel of this strategy. Economic nationalism was added to the mix, to be promoted through state enterprises and encouragement of the indigenous private sector. By the 1960s states had become involved in virtually every aspect of the economy, administering prices and increasingly regulating labor, foreign exchange, and financial markets.

By the 1970s the costs of this strategy were coming home to roost. The oil price shocks were a last gasp for state expansion. For the oil exporters they created a bonanza, which many threw into even greater expansion of state programs. As long as resources were flowing in, the institutional weaknesses stayed hidden. The oil-importing countries, for their part, got caught on a treadmill of heavy borrowing of recycled petrodollars to keep the state growing. The costs of this development strategy were suddenly exposed when the debt crisis hit in the 1980s and oil prices plunged.

The collapse of the Soviet Union—by then no longer an attractive model—sounded the death knell for a developmental era. Suddenly, government failure, including the failure of publicly owned firms, seemed everywhere glaringly evident. Governments began to adopt policies designed to reduce the scope of the state's intervention in the economy. States curbed their involvement in production, prices, and trade. Market-friendly strategies took hold in large parts of the developing world. The

Box 1.3   Evolution of the role of the state in India: The past fifty years

When India became independent in 1947, income per capita had been stagnating for half a century, and modern industry was minimal.

The Nehru years, 1947–64. India's first prime minister, Jawaharlal Nehru, saw industrialization as the key to alleviating poverty, and a powerful state with a planned economy as essential if the country was to industrialize rapidly, accelerate public saving and investment, and reduce the role of foreign trade and achieve self-sufficiency. Unlike many East Asian countries, which used state intervention to build strong private sector industries, India opted for state control over key industries. Believing the potential of agriculture and exports to be limited, Indian governments taxed agriculture by skewing the terms of trade against it and emphasizing import substitution. They saw technical education as vital for industrialization.

Garibi hatao, 1966–77. Under Prime Minister Indira Gandhi, two major shifts took place in the role of the state. First, the neglect of agriculture was reversed through state activism in subsidizing new seeds and fertilizers, agricultural credit, and rural electrification. The green revolution took off, and by the mid-1970s India was self-sufficient in grain. The second shift was the tightening of state control over every aspect of the economy. Under the slogan of *garibi hatao* ("abolish poverty"), banks were nationalized, trade was increasingly restricted, price controls were imposed on a wide range of products, and foreign investment was squeezed. The state achieved a stranglehold on the economy. Yet growth of gross domestic product (GDP) failed to accelerate, remaining during this period at 3.5 percent a year.

The spending boom and rising fiscal deficits, 1977–91. Between 1977 and 1991, most stringent controls on imports and industrial licensing were gradually relaxed, stimulating industrial growth. The government expanded antipoverty schemes, especially rural employ-

ment schemes, but only a small fraction of the rising subsidies actually reached the poor. Competition between political parties drove subsidies up at every election. The resulting large fiscal deficits (8.4 percent of GDP in 1985) contributed to a rising current account deficit. India's foreign exchange reserves were virtually exhausted by mid-1991, when a new government headed by Narasimha Rao came to power.

The reform phase, 1991 to the present. Rising interest payments on India's foreign debt meant that neither the central government nor the state governments could continue to finance both subsidies and heavy public investment. The former won out, and the government began to woo private and foreign investment. Thus, impending bankruptcy drove the reform process and changed the state's role from that of principal investor to that of facilitator of entrepreneurship. This shift was expected to free up government finances for more social spending, but in practice the fiscal crunch prevented a significant increase.

Rao's government abolished most industrial and import licensing, devalued the rupee, drastically reduced import tariffs, liberalized the financial sector and foreign investment, and allowed private investment in areas previously reserved for the government. The new coalition government that came to power in 1996 has by and large sustained these reforms. And the 1997 budget takes very positive steps in that direction.

Thus the old national consensus on socialism has given way over the course of a few years to a new consensus on liberalization. But formidable challenges remain. Most parties agree on the need for reform, yet no party is eager to retrench surplus labor, close unviable factories, or reduce subsidies. The reforms so far are a positive step but must be extended and accelerated if India is to catch up with the East Asian tigers.

---

pendulum had swung from the state-dominated development model of the 1960s and 1970s to the minimalist state of the 1980s.

As often happens with such radical shifts in perspective, countries sometimes tended to overshoot the mark. Efforts to rebalance government spending and borrowing were uncoordinated, and the good was as often cut as the bad. To meet their interest obligations, countries mired in debt squeezed critically important programs in education,

health, and infrastructure as often as—or more than—they cut low-priority programs, bloated civil service rolls, and money-losing enterprises. Cuts came primarily in capital budgets and, in Africa, in operating and maintenance outlays, further reducing the efficiency of investment. The result, seen most starkly in Africa, the former Soviet Union, and even parts of Latin America, was neglect of the state's vital functions, threatening social welfare and eroding the foundations for market development.

The consequences of an overzealous rejection of government have shifted attention from the sterile debate of state versus market to a more fundamental crisis in state effectiveness. In some countries the crisis has led to outright collapse of the state. In others the erosion of the state's capability has led nongovernmental and people's organizations—civil society more broadly—to try to take its place. In their embrace of markets and rejection of state activism, many have wondered whether the market and civil society could ultimately supplant the state. But the lesson of a half-century's thinking and rethinking of the state's role in development is more nuanced. State-dominated development has failed, but so will stateless development. Development without an effective state is impossible.

Rethinking the state: A framework

A central difficulty in redefining the state's role is that the ground beneath governments' feet is always changing. If we consider how global economic and social forces have changed prevailing notions of the state, it is clear that it retains a distinctive role in providing the public goods that promote economic and social development. And market failures continue to offer powerful economic arguments for state intervention (Box 1.4). But changes in technology are transforming the nature of market failure: in infrastructure, for example, technology has created new scope for competition in telecommunications and electric power generation. And many of the most successful examples of development, recent and historical, entail states working in partnership with markets to correct their failures, not replacing them.

Equity also remains a central concern of the state. New evidence, especially from East Asia, shows that the familiar tradeoff between growth and equity is not inevitable, as was once thought. Appropriately designed policies in basic education and health care can reduce poverty and increase equity while promoting economic growth. Neglecting these social fundamentals of development can be fatal. But the mere fact of market failure, and other problems of inequality and insecurity, does not mean that only the state can—or should—resolve these problems. The state's coercive authority within its boundaries gives it unique strengths in seeking to address these concerns, but also unique weaknesses. Governments must keep a firm eye on both in deciding whether, and how, to respond.

The state's unique strengths are its powers to tax, to prohibit, to punish, and to require participation. The state's power to tax enables it to finance the provision of public goods. Its power to prohibit and punish enables it to protect personal safety and property rights. And its power to require participation enables it to minimize free riding: those who would reap the benefits of public goods can be made to pay their share of the costs. The same

power can help resolve problems of collective action that would otherwise reduce the social benefits of insurance markets, or prevent mutually complementary private investments from being made, to take just two examples.

At the same time, however, the state confronts unique challenges both in clarifying its objectives and in ensuring that its employees pursue them. First, even though elections and other political mechanisms help mediate between citizens and the state, citizens' mandates can remain vague—and powerful special interests continually try to direct the focus of government in their favor. Second, monitoring performance is difficult in many government activities such as primary education, environmental protection, and preventive health care. This can make it hard to set standards or put other mechanisms in place to ensure accountability. Both problems can lead to state bureaucracies being granted enormous room for discretion. When that happens, state officials at all levels may pursue their own agendas rather than the society's. Haiti under the Duvaliers provides a vivid example of where the use of arbitrary public power for personal profit, rather than for the social good, can lead.

In many countries the voluntary sector has stepped in to address some of the gaps in collective goods and services left by market and by government failure. The voluntary sector brings its own strengths to the table, but also its own weaknesses. It does a lot of good in increasing public awareness, voicing citizens' concerns, and delivering services. Local self-help organizations are sometimes the preferred providers of local public goods and services, because of their closeness to local concerns. But their concern is often for certain religious or ethnic groups and not society as a whole, their accountability is limited, and their resources are often constrained. The challenge, then, for the state is to build on the relative strengths of private markets and the voluntary sector while taking into account and improving its own institutional capability.

All these considerations point to a two-part strategy to improve the state's ability to enhance economic and social welfare. The first task is to match the state's role to its existing capability—to establish the institutional rules and norms that will enable the state to provide collective goods and services efficiently. The second is to reinvigorate the state's capability through rules, partnerships, and competitive pressures outside and within the state.

Matching role to capability: What states do and how they do it

Part Two of this Report discusses the first part of the strategy: matching the state's role to its capability, to improve the effectiveness and efficiency of public resource use. It advocates ways in which states can provide the fundamentals for development, especially where capability is low

Box 1.4 The economic rationale for state intervention and some definitions

Market failure and the concern for equity provide the economic rationale for government intervention. But there is no guarantee that any such intervention will benefit society. Government failure may be as common as market failure. The challenge is to see that the political process and institutional structures get the incentives right, so that their interventions actually improve social welfare.

Market failure refers to the set of conditions under which a market economy fails to allocate resources efficiently. There are many sources of market failure and many degrees of failure. The implications for the role of the state and the form of public intervention can be quite different in each case.

Public goods are goods that are *nonrival* (consumption by one user does not reduce the supply available for others) and *nonexcludable* (users cannot be prevented from consuming the good). These characteristics make it infeasible to charge for the consumption of public goods, and therefore private suppliers will lack the incentive to supply them. National public goods, such as defense, benefit an entire country; local public goods, such as rural roads, benefit a smaller area. *Private goods* are those that are both rival and excludable, *common property goods* are nonexcludable but rival (an example is groundwater irrigation), and *club goods* are nonrival but excludable (examples are interurban highways and toll roads).

Externalities arise when the actions of one person or firm hurt or benefit others without that person or firm paying or receiving compensation. Pollution is an example of a *negative externality*, which imposes uncompensated costs on society; the broader benefit to society at large of a literate population is a *positive externality* of primary education. Governments can curb negative and promote positive externalities through regulation, taxation or subsidy, or outright provision.

A *natural monopoly* occurs when the unit cost of providing a good or service to an additional user declines over a wide range of output, reducing or eliminating the scope for competition. But left to operate freely, monopoly providers can restrict output to in-

crease prices and profits. Governments have addressed this problem by regulating private monopolists or providing the good or service themselves. Changes in technology have created new scope for competition in services once considered natural monopolies, such as telecommunications and power generation.

Incomplete markets and *imperfect* or *asymmetric information* are pervasive problems and can result in inefficient outcomes. Markets are incomplete whenever they fail to provide a good or service even though the cost would be less than what individuals are willing to pay. Imperfect information on the part of consumers can lead to systematic undervaluation of some services, such as primary education or preventive health care. Asymmetry of information—when suppliers know more than consumers, or vice versa—can lead to excessive or supplier-induced demand, for example in the provision of medical care. Problems of adverse selection and moral hazard can lead to the failure of insurance markets. *Adverse selection* occurs when buyers of a service tend to impose higher-than-average costs on the service provider, or when sellers are able to exclude such high-cost customers. Health insurance provides an example: those who are more likely to need care are more likely to buy insurance, and more likely to be turned down by insurers. *Moral hazard* is present when persons carrying insurance have an incentive to cause or allow the insured-against event to happen. An example is the tendency of health care consumers to seek, as well as providers to provide, more treatment than they need when a third party, the insurer, is paying most of the cost. Governments have sought to address these problems by ensuring widespread coverage and holding down costs. They have done this by either regulating private insurance, financing or mandating social insurance, or providing health care themselves.

Equity may prompt state intervention even in the absence of market failure. Competitive markets may distribute income in socially unacceptable ways. Persons with few assets may be left with insufficient resources to achieve acceptable living standards. Government action may be required to protect the vulnerable.

(Chapter 3). Chapter 4 looks at more demanding state functions, such as regulation and industrial policy, and shows how getting the right fit between roles and capabilities is vital for improving the state's effectiveness. Table 1.1 presents a framework for thinking about these issues. It classifies the functions of government along a continuum,

from activities that will not be undertaken at all without state intervention to activities in which the state plays an activist role in coordinating markets or redistributing assets:

■ Countries with low state capability need to focus first on basic functions: the provision of pure public goods such

Table 1.1 Functions of the state

	Addressing market failure			Improving equity
Minimal functions	*Providing pure public goods:* Defense Law and order Property rights Macroeconomic management Public health			*Protecting the poor:* Antipoverty programs Disaster relief
Intermediate functions	*Addressing externalities:* Basic education Environmental protection	*Regulating monopoly:* Utility regulation Antitrust policy	*Overcoming imperfect information:* Insurance (health, life, pensions) Financial regulation Consumer protection	*Providing social insurance:* Redistributive pensions Family allowances Unemployment insurance
Activist functions	*Coordinating private activity:* Fostering markets Cluster initiatives			*Redistribution:* Asset redistribution

as property rights, macroeconomic stability, control of infectious diseases, safe water, roads, and protection of the destitute. In many countries the state is not even providing these. Recent reforms have emphasized economic fundamentals. But social and institutional (including legal) fundamentals are equally important to avoid social disruption and ensure sustained development.

- Going beyond these basic services are the intermediate functions, such as management of externalities (pollution, for example), regulation of monopolies, and the provision of social insurance (pensions, unemployment benefits). Here, too, the government cannot choose whether, but only how best to intervene, and government can work in partnership with markets and civil society to ensure that these public goods are provided.

- States with strong capability can take on more-activist functions, dealing with the problem of missing markets by helping coordination. East Asia's experience has renewed interest in the state's role in promoting markets through active industrial and financial policy.

Matching role to capability involves not only *what* the state does but also *how* it does it. Rethinking the state also means exploring alternative instruments, existing or new, that can enhance state effectiveness. For example:

- In most modern economies the state's regulatory role is now broader and more complex than ever before, covering such areas as the environment and the financial sector, as well as more traditional areas such as monop-

olies. The design of regulation needs to fit the capability of state regulatory agencies and the sophistication of markets, and give greater emphasis to personal responsibility.

- Although the state still has a central role in ensuring the provision of basic services—education, health, infrastructure—it is not obvious that the state must be the only provider, or a provider at all. The state's choices about provision, financing, and regulation of these services must build on the relative strengths of markets, civil society, and state agencies.

- In protecting the vulnerable, countries need to distinguish more clearly between *insurance* and *assistance*. Insurance, against cyclical unemployment for example, aims to help smooth households' income and consumption through a market economy's inevitable ups and downs. Assistance, such as food-for-work programs or bread subsidies, seeks to provide some minimum level of support to the poorest in society.

Reinvigorating the state's capability

Reinvigorating the state's capability—the second, equally vital part of the reform strategy—is the subject of Part Three. Its theme is that such improvements are possible only if the incentives under which states and state institutions operate are changed. Improving capability is not easy. The modest successes, and many failures, of technical assistance efforts over the decades underscore that it is a matter of changing the incentives that determine behavior as much as it is one of training and resources. The key is to find rules and norms that create incentives for state agencies and officials to act in the collective interest, while restraining arbitrary action. This can be achieved through:

- *Rules and restraints.* Mechanisms for enforcing the rule of law, such as an independent judiciary, are critical foundations for sustainable development. Along with appropriate separation of powers and the presence of watchdog bodies, they also restrain arbitrary behavior.
- *Competitive pressure.* Competitive pressure can come from within the state bureaucracy, through recruitment of civil servants on the basis of merit. It can come from the domestic private sector, through contracting out for services and allowing private providers to compete directly with public agencies. Or it can come from the international marketplace, through trade and through the influence of global bond markets on fiscal decisions.
- *Voice and partnership.* The means to achieve transparency and openness in modern society are many and varied—business councils, interaction groups, and consumer groups, to name a few. Institutional working arrangements with community groups can contribute to greater state effectiveness by giving citizens a greater voice in the formulation of government's policies. And partnerships between levels of government and with international bodies can help in the provision of local and global public goods.

All three mechanisms are a recurrent theme of Part Three, which starts (in Chapter 5) by looking at the basic building blocks of a more effective public sector. The emphasis there is on rules and forms of competition to enhance the three basics: policymaking, service delivery, and the lifeblood of the public sector, the civil service. But history tells us that rebuilding public trust in government—and therefore its capability—will involve putting restraints on arbitrary action. These issues are taken up in Chapter 6, which analyzes the checks and balances in the constitutional structure of the state and the best ways to control arbitrary behavior and corruption.

A third layer, which supports the other two, is efforts to open up the government and make it more responsive.

A remote, imperious state, whose deliberations are not transparent, is much more likely to fall into the downward spiral of arbitrary rule and decreasing effectiveness. Chapter 7 looks at the benefits of making government reach out to people and grant them a greater role in deciding and implementing policy. And it shows how, carefully pursued, decentralization—the transfer of powers and resources to lower levels of government—can support this effort. Finally, Chapter 8 provides a reminder that collective action increasingly involves looking across national borders. The chapter examines the various ways in which national governments can and must cooperate to meet demands that, although felt at home, can only be addressed effectively at the international level.

Strategic options: Initiating and sustaining reforms

This two-part strategy for improving state effectiveness is far easier said than accomplished. The difficult job for reformers will be not only devising the right kind of reforms but combating the deep-seated opposition of those with a vested interest in the old ways. Matching role to capability means shedding some roles, including some that benefit powerful constituencies. Proponents of a more capable state will quickly discover that it is in many people's interest to keep it weak. Nevertheless, politicians have an incentive to undertake reforms if they result in net gains to important constituencies. Windows of opportunity occasionally open in response to crisis or external threat, and effective political leadership is skilled at devising strategies for building consensus or compensating losers.

Part Four explores the challenge of initiating and sustaining reforms of the state (Chapter 9). Its central argument is that constraints on reform are largely political and institutional. Hence fundamental institutional reform is likely to be long term, but reform opportunities arise, or can be created, and these must be seized. Finally, Chapter 10 lays out the prospects for change and the reform agenda for each developing region. The message is that reform will be difficult and must be tailored to its circumstances, but the special challenge of collapsed states provides a salutary reminder of the risks of failure.

CHAPTER 2

REFOCUSING ON THE EFFECTIVENESS OF THE STATE

Men are powerless to secure the future; institutions alone fix the destinies of nations.

—Napoleon I, *Imperial séance* (June 7, 1815)

FIFTY YEARS AGO, WORLD WAR II HAD ENDED AND reconstruction was under way in much of Europe, the Soviet Union, and Japan. Many developing countries were starting to emerge from colonialism, and the future seemed full of promise. The difficulties of economic development were not yet haunting us. Improving people's lives looked so achievable, a simple matter of applying the right ideas, technical expertise, and resources. And so it proved—in some cases. But in others progress was meager. Despite five decades of effort, enormous disparities remain in the quality of life of people around the world. Indeed, by some measures the gap between rich and poor has widened.

Explanations for these huge international differences in living standards have changed over the years. For centuries, access to natural resources—land and minerals—was considered the prerequisite for development. Much of Africa, Asia, and the Americas was colonized to acquire these resources, and countries went to war over them. Gradually, however, the thinking changed, and physical capital—machines and equipment—was held to be the key to development. "Industrialized" became synonymous with "developed." But around the middle of this century economic theorists realized that even this was too simplistic. Embodied in machines and equipment was technology—knowledge and ideas. But no one could explain in simple terms why technology developed better and faster in some parts of the world than others.

Other factors, such as human capital, have since attracted much attention as possible solutions to the puzzle. Investment in human capital both leads to new knowl-

edge and ideas and increases the speed with which they are absorbed, disseminated, and used. Since the 1980s the focus has shifted to the role of sound policies in explaining why countries accumulate human and physical capital at different rates. This, in turn, has led to yet another shift of focus, to the quality of a country's institutions. New, more complex questions have emerged. What institutional arrangements best allow markets to flourish? What is the role of the state both as a direct agent (mostly in the provision of services) and as a shaper of the institutional context in which markets function? How do policies and institutions interact in development?

The answers to these questions are central to our understanding of the deeper sources of differences in development outcomes—and of why the response to economic reform often varies so widely from one country to another. They help explain, for example, why investment and economic activity have revived more strongly following the embrace of the market in Poland than in Russia. They also help explain why many countries in Africa and Latin America have yet to see much of the improvement in the quality of life they were promised when they embarked on their economic reforms a decade ago.

The state has much to do with whether countries adopt the institutional arrangements under which markets can flourish. Not only is the state the arbiter of rules; through its own economic activity it shapes the environment for business and the rest of the economy. For good or ill, the state sets the tone.

This chapter makes the empirical case for shifting the focus of our thinking about development toward the quality of a country's institutions and the capability of the state—for bringing institutions into the mainstream of our dialogue about development. That case is supported by three new sets of findings:

- First, panel data analyzed for this Report, covering thirty years and ninety-four industrial and developing countries, show that policies and institutional capability matter for economic growth and for other indicators of the quality of life, such as infant mortality.
- Second, and taking the analysis a step further, are the results of a survey, specially commissioned for this Report, of over 3,600 domestic firms in sixty-nine countries (including local affiliates of international firms). These results, too, provide strong evidence that institutional capability—or the lack of it—has a major impact on growth and investment.
- The third set of findings explores how institutional capability affects not just the environment for business, but also the overall setting for a country's development. Using the results from the survey on institutional capability, we show that these cross-country differences help

explain much of the difference between countries in rates of return on development projects.

The state, institutions, and economic outcomes

What does the state do? For one thing, it sets the formal rules—laws and regulations—that are part and parcel of a country's institutional environment (Figure 2.1). These formal rules, along with the informal rules of the broader society, are the institutions that mediate human behavior. But the state is not merely a referee, making and enforcing the rules from the sidelines; it is also a player, indeed often a dominant player, in the economic game. Every day, state agencies invest resources, direct credit, procure goods and services, and negotiate contracts; these actions have profound effects on transactions costs and on economic activity and economic outcomes, especially in developing economies. Played well, the state's activities can accelerate development. Played badly, they will produce stagnation or, in the extreme, economic and social disintegration. The state, then, is in a unique position: not only must it establish, through a social and political process, the formal rules by which all other organizations

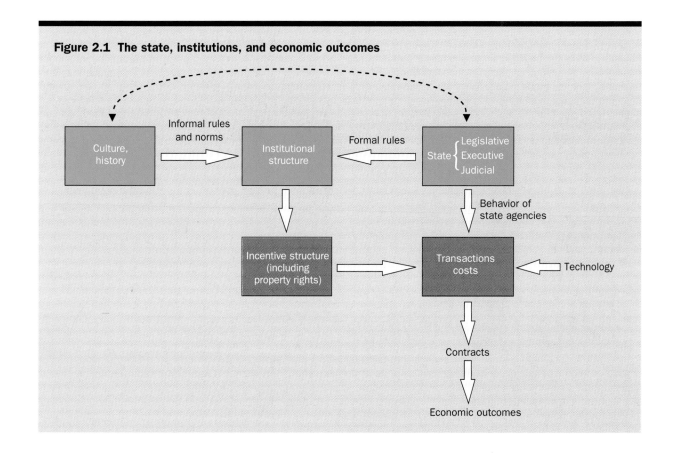

Figure 2.1 The state, institutions, and economic outcomes

must abide; as an organization itself, it, too, must abide by those rules.

Examples of the power of the state to improve the quality of people's lives are not hard to find. From the clean water and sanitation systems of ancient Rome to the elimination of smallpox in this century, public actions in the areas of health and sanitation have achieved repeated breakthroughs in public health. And states have long played a vital role in stimulating lasting development gains by providing infrastructure, security, and a stable macroeconomy. The Internet is only the latest in a long line of remarkable scientific and technical advances made possible by early and significant public support (Box 2.1).

Distilling the lessons of centuries, we see that the state can improve development outcomes in a number of ways:

- By providing a macroeconomic and a microeconomic environment that sets the right incentives for efficient economic activity

- By providing the institutional infrastructure—property rights, peace, law and order, and rules—that encourages efficient long-term investment, and

- By ensuring the provision of basic education, health care, and the physical infrastructure required for economic activity, and by protecting the natural environment.

Yet history also teaches that the state can do enormous harm:

- The wrong kind of rules can actively discourage the creation of wealth. For example, the state may penalize private wealth by distorting prices—through an overvalued currency, for example, or by creating agricultural marketing boards that tax farmers' output and give them little in return.

- Even if the rules themselves are benign, they may be applied by public organizations—and their employees— in harmful fashion. They may, for example, impose

---

Box 2.1 Building the Internet: A contemporary example of fruitful public-private interaction

The precursor of what we today call the Internet was launched in the United States in 1969. Then called ARPANET, the system comprised just four interconnected computers. By mid-1996, however, the Internet was accessible in 174 countries and on all seven continents, linking together nearly 13 million host computer systems. By 2000 that number could well be 100 million.

ARPANET owed its existence to the economics of defense research in the 1960s. Its original purpose was to link government computers in far-flung locations and so avoid duplication of what were then quite costly computing resources. In 1968 the U.S. Department of Defense invited proposals from 140 private companies to design and build the first four interface message processors, or routers. With these in place, public contracts with leading universities then led to development of the crucial set of protocols that could link diverse computer networks. It was these protocols that later made the Internet possible.

Complementary to this public financial support has been the partnership of academia, business, and government led by the U.S. National Science Foundation (NSF). Initially this partnership primed the connection of university computer science departments, but its influence soon expanded. NSFNET replaced ARPANET in 1990. Besides providing the critical

finance for a high-speed backbone infrastructure for the system, the NSF made grants available to universities to encourage them to form regional networks that would feed into the system. But the networks were also told that they would have to become self-sustaining.

The private sector's involvement has deepened over time. The NSF encouraged commercial carriers of electronic mail to link to the Internet. Companies also began to create their own backbone facilities, and the number of firms supplying access to the Internet multiplied. These trends were accelerated by the creation and rapid growth of the multimedia part of the Internet—the World Wide Web. Developed at the laboratories of the European Organization for Nuclear Research in Switzerland—another publicly supported agency—the Web drew in talent from universities and firms, leading to yet another explosion in use: from 130 sites in July 1993 to over 230,000 in June 1996.

In 1995 NSFNET was replaced by a fully commercial system. Major telephone companies now provide not only backbone facilities but also Internet access to their customers. Cable and direct broadcast satellite companies are also entering the market. The public sector is still involved in some advanced research, but its focus has shifted to such questions as how to ensure equitable access (for example, through pricing rules), freedom of expression, protection from fraud, and privacy.

huge transactions costs, in the form of red tape or bribery, on entrepreneurs setting up new businesses or restructuring old ones.

■ But potentially the largest source of state-inflicted damage is uncertainty. If the state changes the rules often, or does not clarify the rules by which the state itself will behave, businesses and individuals cannot be sure today what will be profitable or unprofitable, legal or illegal, tomorrow. They will then adopt costly strategies to insure against an uncertain future—by entering the informal economy, for example, or sending capital abroad—all of which impede development.

Economic growth and the state

Government's enormous impact on development is well illustrated by the contrasting economic performance of developing countries in Sub-Saharan Africa and East Asia. In 1960 incomes per capita in much of East Asia were only a little higher than in Africa. Governments in the two regions were also similar in size, although not in composition: African governments were already spending more on consumption, primarily on public employment. By the mid-1990s, however, incomes in East Asia were more than five times those in Africa. And government consumption in Africa, relative to GDP, had ballooned to one-and-a-half times that in East Asia. The sources of this divergence are complex, but it is widely believed that the superior performance of the state in East Asia—the limits it set on its own growth, the soundness of the policies it adopted, and the effectiveness with which it delivered services—made a powerful contribution to the growing gap in the quality of life experienced by the average citizen between these two parts of the world (Figure 2.2).

In considering the effect of government size on growth, it is useful to distinguish between public consumption and public investment (Box 2.2). Where government consumption spending is very high, it has generally been found to be a drag on growth: a net tax on society with few corresponding benefits. Conversely, certain types of public investment spending, particularly investment in infrastructure, have tended to exert a positive effect on growth, in part by raising the returns to private investment. Complicating the picture is the fact that some public consumption—teachers' salaries, for example, or purchases of medicine—can affect people's lives for the better, and even raise the efficiency of investment. Cutting consumption indiscriminately to boost equally indiscriminate investment is clearly not the answer.

But even sophisticated measures of the size of the government only tell part of the story. As noted above, governments also play a leading role in setting the broader

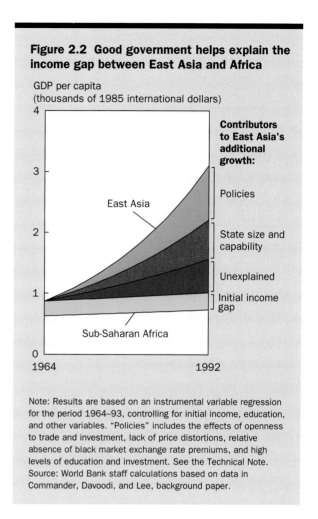

Figure 2.2 Good government helps explain the income gap between East Asia and Africa

GDP per capita
(thousands of 1985 international dollars)

Contributors to East Asia's additional growth:
Policies
State size and capability
Unexplained
Initial income gap

East Asia

Sub-Saharan Africa

Note: Results are based on an instrumental variable regression for the period 1964–93, controlling for initial income, education, and other variables. "Policies" includes the effects of openness to trade and investment, lack of price distortions, relative absence of black market exchange rate premiums, and high levels of education and investment. See the Technical Note.
Source: World Bank staff calculations based on data in Commander, Davoodi, and Lee, background paper.

institutional environment for behavior: the incentive structure to which economic agents respond. The private sector's ability to function will depend critically on the reliability and effectiveness of institutions such as the rule of law and the protection of property rights. None of these benefits—and costs—of the quality of government are ever likely to appear in the national accounts.

The analysis in this section tries to show this distinction between what the state does and how well it does it, by reporting on both policy content and institutional capability. Figure 5 in the Overview showed the effect of both factors on income growth over the last three decades across a large sample of industrial and developing countries. In countries with weak state capability and poor policies, income per capita grew only about half a percent per year. In contrast, in countries with strong capability and good policies, income per capita grew at an average rate of about 3 percent per year. Over a thirty-year period, these differences in income growth have made a huge difference to the quality of people's lives. A country with an

Box 2.2 Measuring the state—its size, its policies, and its institutional capability

A common measure of government size is the ratio of government expenditure to the economy's total expenditure or total output. But such data are generally not comprehensive, and coverage of public enterprises is especially sketchy in many developing countries. This measure of size also tends to ignore important off-budget items. Government expenditure itself can be broken down into consumption and investment. Government consumption—which mostly consists of the public wage bill—gives a narrow but more precise indicator of consumers' current benefits from government spending. Transfers, such as pensions or disability benefits, can be included in government expenditure, but transfers only redistribute resources. Further complicating matters, nominal and real ratios for expenditure will vary significantly over time. An alternative measure of government size that avoids these problems is government employment, but this, too, has its drawbacks. For example, it ignores changes in the productivity of government workers.

The results reported in this chapter use data on real government consumption, because the concern is mainly with how the division of output across public and private goods affects performance. Information on physical investment is also used, but this is normally available only as an aggregate of public and private investment. To facilitate cross-country comparisons over time, these ratios are translated into international or purchasing-power-parity (PPP) values—a not entirely innocuous transformation, particularly for low-income countries where much of government consumption is labor intensive. For these countries, using international prices markedly increases the government consumption ratio.

A more inclusive picture of the economic presence of government requires a measure that captures key government interventions through policy and institutions, in addition to fiscal interventions. We summarize a government's policy stance over time through an index that combines three key indicators: the openness of the economy (the share of trade in GDP), overvaluation of the currency (the black market exchange rate), and the gap between local and international prices. We also attempt to evaluate the quality of a key component of government, its bureaucracy. This evaluation is drawn from survey responses by foreign investors (in the next section we evaluate the responses of local investors) that focus on the amount of red tape involved in any transaction, the regulatory environment, and the degree of autonomy from political pressure.

average income per capita of $600 in 1965 (in international PPP dollars), with distorted policies and weak institutional capability, would after thirty years have reached an average income of only about $678 at 1965 prices. On the other hand, a country with strong institutional capability and good policies would have more than doubled its average income, to $1,456 at 1965 prices. Many countries in East Asia have done even better than that.

Good policies by themselves can improve results. But the benefits are magnified where institutional capability is also higher—where policies and programs are implemented more efficiently and where citizens and investors have greater certainty about government's future actions. Thus, good policies such as those being pursued more recently by many countries in Latin America and Africa would increase growth in income per capita by around 1.4 percent per year. Such a country starting with an average income of $600 in 1965 would see it rise to around $900 after thirty years. But it would rise even higher with good policies *and* strong institutions. The lesson is that reformers cannot afford to focus solely on improving policies; they must also look for ways to strengthen the institutional environment those policies have to work within.

Important though income growth is, it is only one of several measures of well-being. Our interest in the wide range of factors that make people better or worse off suggests that countries' performance should also be judged by other standards of well-being, such as infant mortality. High-quality government institutions lower infant mortality by improving outcomes for a given amount of social spending. Thus, the capability of the state has an important role in the quality of human life generally—not simply the pace of income growth. This explains why countries at the same income level can have widely disparate quality-of-life indicators—why Sri Lanka, for example, had an infant mortality rate of only 18 per 1,000 live births, whereas some countries with higher incomes per capita had substantially higher rates: 67 per 1,000 live births in Egypt, and 68 per 1,000 in Morocco, for example. The amount of social spending as well as the care with which services are delivered makes a huge difference.

Understanding institutional capability better: The private investor's view

As this chapter has already stressed, the mark of a capable state—besides its ability to facilitate collective actions—is its ability to set the rules that underpin markets and permit them to function. Although private arrangements can sometimes supplement formal property and contract rights, they can only take the development of markets so far. Governments, of course, have to do more than establish sound rules of the game; they also have to make sure those rules are enforced consistently and that private actors—business, labor, trade associations—can have confidence that the rules will not be changed overnight. States that change the rules frequently and unpredictably, announce changes but fail to implement them, or enforce rules arbitrarily will lack credibility, and markets will suffer accordingly.

How good are governments at providing credible rules that will nurture the development of markets? Hard evidence is difficult to come by. To begin with, credibility is tricky to measure: it depends as much on perceptions as on hard facts. At first glance, for example, one would think that the number of times a country has changed its government might be a good indicator of the degree of uncertainty about market rules, and therefore of the government's credibility. Yet businesses in Thailand generally considered their environment to be relatively stable, despite numerous coups and changes in government. By the same token, the environment for business can be highly volatile and unpredictable even if the government does not change. Peruvian entrepreneurs reported severe credibility problems in the 1980s because rules were being drawn up hastily, implemented by presidential decree, and often overturned soon thereafter.

Measures of corruption might seem another good signal of government credibility. But simple estimates of corruption, like measures of political instability, may not capture entrepreneurs' concerns. Some forms of corruption entail large uncertainties and risks, whereas others may be more predictable and act more like speed money. In the words of one entrepreneur, "There are two kinds of corruption. The first is one where you pay the regular price and you get what you want. The second is one where you pay what you have agreed to pay and you go home and lie awake every night worrying whether you will get it or if somebody is going to blackmail you instead." The best way to understand the problems holding back private sector development is to ask entrepreneurs directly.

To this end a large-scale survey of the private sector was conducted for this Report. The aim was to capture the full array of uncertainties that entrepreneurs face and to build an overall measure of the credibility of rules in a given country. The responses showed that in many countries private investors give the state very poor marks for credibility indeed.

Credibility: How private investors perceive the state
The private sector survey covered sixty-nine countries and over 3,600 firms. Entrepreneurs were asked for their subjective evaluation of different aspects of the institutional framework in their country, including security of property rights, predictability of rules and policies, reliability of the judiciary, problems with corruption and discretionary power in the bureaucracy, and disruptions due to changes in government.

Sometimes the source of uncertainty is the instability of the rules to which firms are subject. Two key indicators included in the survey were:

Predictability of rulemaking: the extent to which entrepreneurs have to cope with unexpected changes in rules and policies about which they have had no say.

■ The survey showed that entrepreneurs in some parts of the world live in constant fear of policy surprises. In the Commonwealth of Independent States (CIS) almost 80 percent of entrepreneurs reported that unpredictable changes in rules and policies seriously affected their business. In Central and Eastern Europe (CEE), Latin America, and Sub-Saharan Africa around 60 percent of entrepreneurs voiced the same complaint. By contrast, in the industrial countries and in South and Southeast Asia, only about 30 percent of respondents considered this a problem for their business (top left panel of Figure 2.3). A large part of the unpredictability of rule changes came from companies' having little or no role in the state's decisionmaking process; indeed, they may not even be informed of important rule changes before they take place. This problem appeared to be particularly severe in the CIS, CEE, and Sub-Saharan Africa, whereas Asian entrepreneurs (even small ones) considered themselves well informed—even better informed, in fact, than their industrial-country counterparts did. Unsurprisingly, perhaps, the survey also revealed that small companies tend to have less knowledge of, and involvement in, the drafting of new regulations and were therefore more subject to policy surprises.

Figure 2.3 Reliable institutions make for credible states

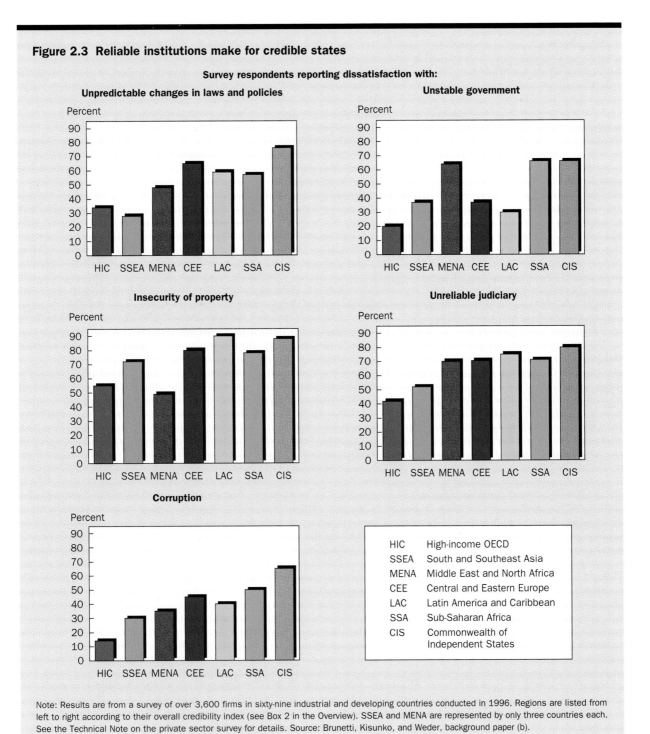

Survey respondents reporting dissatisfaction with:

Note: Results are from a survey of over 3,600 firms in sixty-nine industrial and developing countries conducted in 1996. Regions are listed from left to right according to their overall credibility index (see Box 2 in the Overview). SSEA and MENA are represented by only three countries each. See the Technical Note on the private sector survey for details. Source: Brunetti, Kisunko, and Weder, background paper (b).

Perceptions of political stability: whether changes in government (constitutional or unconstitutional) are usually accompanied by far-reaching policy surprises that could have serious effects on the private sector.

■ Entrepreneurs in many regions felt that the institutional framework was not well enough entrenched to withstand changes in government without serious disruption. In the CIS, Africa, and the Middle East over

60 percent of entrepreneurs said that they constantly feared government changes and the painful policy surprises that tended to go with them (top right panel of Figure 2.3).

Uncertainty may relate less to the rules themselves than to the way they are enforced. The relevant indicators here were:

Crime against persons and property: whether entrepreneurs felt confident that the authorities would protect them and their property from criminal actions, and whether theft and other forms of crime represented serious problems for business.

■ Private entrepreneurs in many countries complained of the lack of even the most basic institutional infrastructure for a market economy. Across the globe, crime and theft were listed as serious problems, which substantially increased the cost of doing business. A complete institutional vacuum seems to prevail in some countries, leading to crime, violence, and a generalized insecurity of property rights. In Latin America, Sub-Saharan Africa, the CIS, and CEE almost 80 percent of entrepreneurs reported a lack of confidence that the authorities would protect their person and property from criminals (middle left panel of Figure 2.3).

Reliability of judicial enforcement: whether the judiciary enforces rules arbitrarily, and whether such unpredictability presents a problem for doing business.

■ A well-functioning judiciary is a central pillar of the rule of law. Unfortunately, in many countries it seems to be the exception rather than the rule. In developing countries over 70 percent of entrepreneurs said that judicial unpredictability was a major problem in their business operations (middle right panel of Figure 2.3). Disturbingly, in most regions entrepreneurs felt that these problems had increased over the last ten years.

Freedom from corruption: whether it is common for private entrepreneurs to have to make irregular additional payments to get things done, and whether, after paying a bribe, they have to fear blackmail by another official.

■ The survey confirmed that corruption is an important—and widespread—problem for investors. Overall, more than 40 percent of entrepreneurs reported having to pay bribes to get things done as a matter of course. In industrial countries the figure was 15 per-

cent, in Asia about 30 percent, and in the CIS over 60 percent (bottom panel of Figure 2.3). Furthermore, over half the respondents worldwide did not regard a bribe as a guarantee that the promised service would be delivered, and many lived in fear that they would simply be asked for more by another official.

Lack of credibility reduces investment, growth, and the return on development projects

When the private sector does not believe that the state will enforce the rules of the game, it responds in a variety of ways, all of which worsen economic performance. An unreliable judiciary forces entrepreneurs to rely on informal agreements and enforcement mechanisms. A corrupt bureaucracy that is allowed too much discretion creates incentives to seek economic rents rather than in productive activity. A generalized environment of crime and insecurity of property rights prompts entrepreneurs to enlist the help of private security agents, or forces them to pay organized crime for "protection"—if it does not put them off going into business altogether.

Investment suffers because entrepreneurs choose not to commit resources in highly uncertain and volatile environments, especially if those resources will be difficult to recover should the business environment turn unfavorable. Where even the most basic types of property are not protected, investors move their resources to other countries, or invest them in projects that offer lower returns but require less capital commitment. Thus, trade and services may survive even in low-credibility environments, but manufacturing and, especially, high-technology projects are unlikely to flourish. A similar distortion occurs when highly talented people choose to become tax inspectors or customs officials rather than train to become engineers. Therefore, credibility affects not only the level of investment in physical and human capital but also its quality. As a consequence, in a low-credibility environment, growth suffers.

The top two panels of Figure 2.4 show how credibility relates to investment and growth in the countries surveyed for the period 1985–95. After controlling for other economic variables, countries with high credibility had investment rates significantly higher than countries with low credibility; a shift from a low- to a high-credibility environment makes a substantial difference in growth as well. Low credibility may also help explain why many countries do not see the expected private sector response after implementing stabilization and structural adjustment programs.

Finally, the credibility of rules affects not only the business environment, but also the environment for the implementation of development projects. The same fac-

Figure 2.4 Perceived credibility and economic performance go hand in hand

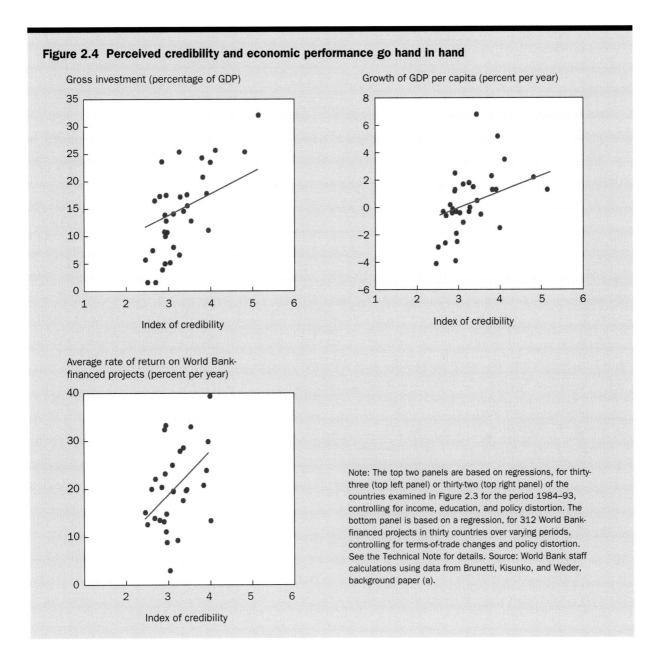

Note: The top two panels are based on regressions, for thirty-three (top left panel) or thirty-two (top right panel) of the countries examined in Figure 2.3 for the period 1984–93, controlling for income, education, and policy distortion. The bottom panel is based on a regression, for 312 World Bank-financed projects in thirty countries over varying periods, controlling for terms-of-trade changes and policy distortion. See the Technical Note for details. Source: World Bank staff calculations using data from Brunetti, Kisunko, and Weder, background paper (a).

tors—crime, corruption, uncertainty about policy, and judicial behavior—affect the outcome for all such projects. One reason is that these concerns are part and parcel of any contractual environment. If corruption affects the private sector, it is likely to affect the outcome of development projects as well. A second reason is that many public projects are implemented by private contractors who, in an environment of weak institutions, are subject to the same behavioral problems that affect private firms. The contractor is awarded a project, pays off corrupt officials, and gets more projects regardless of how the first turns out. Pilfering, theft, and enforcement problems are even more widespread in many public projects than in the private sector. As a result, many projects are delayed because of cost overruns.

The bottom panel of Figure 2.4 shows the correlation between government credibility and rates of return for 312 development projects in thirty countries. On average, in countries with a low-credibility environment rates of return are substantially higher than in countries with a high-credibility environment. These results take account of differences in economic policies and other project- and country-specific factors. The lesson, once again, is that institutions make an enormous difference to development outcomes. Napoleon's insight, cited at the beginning of this chapter, is as true today as it was in 1815.

Strategic options: Refocusing on the state's institutional capability

A clearer understanding of the institutions and norms embedded in markets shows the folly of thinking that development strategy is a matter of choosing between the state and the market. As this brief review of the evidence on the relationship between institutions and development has confirmed, the two are inextricably linked. Countries need markets to grow, but they need capable state institutions to grow markets.

Reformers the world over need to apply this lesson by refocusing attention on institutional capability. The task is particularly urgent in many developing countries, where weak and arbitrary governments are feeding the uncer-

tainties that have kept markets weak and underdeveloped. Countries suffering from such an institutional vacuum risk postponing economic and social development indefinitely. There is also a danger that dissatisfaction with the state—whether expressed through social protest, capital flight, or the ballot box—will undermine economic prospects even further.

The state's capability—its ability to deliver collective goods efficiently—is central to providing a viable institutional framework for development. As we have seen, many developing countries are starting out from a very low base indeed in this regard. But the state's ability to provide the institutional support that development requires can be improved over time, through matching the state's role to its capability, and then rebuilding that capability by focusing on the incentives that drive the behavior of the state. We turn to these issues in Parts Two and Three.

PART TWO

MATCHING ROLE TO CAPABILITY

AS PART ONE HIGHLIGHTED, AN EFFECTIVE STATE PROVIDES VITAL INGREDIENTS for development. This part of the Report argues that governments will achieve better results by being realistic in what they set out to accomplish. They must strive to match what they do—and how they do it—to their institutional capabilities, not to some idealized model.

Where government has a long record of failure, seeking a better match between the state's role and its capability can sound like a recipe for dismantling the state altogether. But market development without a functioning state is not an option. Rather, as Chapter 3 explains, the point is to prioritize. In many countries the state is still not securing the economic and social fundamentals: a foundation of lawfulness, a benign (and stable) policy environment, basic social services, and some protection of the vulnerable. At the same time, it is overproviding many goods and services that private markets and voluntary initiative could deliver instead. For development to proceed, such governments need to go back to the basics.

Chapter 4 explores how governments can find the right match between role and capability in a second area of policy where the state's behavior will inevitably make a large difference to development outcomes: regulation, liberalization, and industrial policies designed to foster markets. Markets and society need and benefit from effective regulation of certain activities. But many states are stifling private sector development by overregulating or, often, monopolizing large chunks of the economy by attempting complex strategic interventions in industry that are beyond their institutional capabilities. Deregulation, privatization, and less demanding approaches to regulation and industrial support in these circumstances will deliver large and immediate payoffs.

These chapters carry four basic messages for policymakers:

- States at all levels of institutional capability should respect, nurture, and take advantage of private and voluntary initiative and competitive markets.

- States with weak institutional capabilities should focus on providing the pure public goods and services that markets cannot provide (and that voluntary collective initiatives underprovide), as well as goods and services with large positive externalities, such as property rights, safe water, roads, and basic education.

- Credibility is vital for success. States with weak institutional capabilities should also focus on the tools for policymaking and implementation that give firms and citizens confidence that state officials and organizations will not act arbitrarily and will live within their fiscal means.

- Matching role to capability is a dynamic process. As institutional capability develops, states can take on more difficult collective initiatives (initiatives to foster markets, for example), and use efficient but difficult-to-manage tools for collective action, such as sophisticated regulatory instruments.

CHAPTER 3

SECURING THE ECONOMIC AND SOCIAL FUNDAMENTALS

W EAK STATES MUST TAILOR THEIR AMBITIONS TO their capability, yet some tasks are inescapable. The challenge, addressed in this chapter, is to find ways for states—even states with relatively weak capability—to get those basic government tasks right. Sustainable, shared, poverty-reducing development has five crucial ingredients:

- A foundation of law
- A benign policy environment, including macroeconomic stability
- Investment in people and infrastructure
- Protection of the vulnerable
- Protection of the natural environment.

The importance of these fundamentals for development has long been widely accepted. But as is shown below, new insights are emerging on the appropriate mix of market and government activities for achieving them. It is now much clearer that markets and governments are complementary, that government action can be vital in laying the institutional foundations for markets. Also much clearer is that faith in governments' ability to sustain good policies can be as important for attracting private investment as the policies themselves.

The track record of developing countries in managing the fundamentals has been mixed. Many countries in East Asia—plus others elsewhere such as Botswana, Chile, and Mauritius—have done a good job. But others have not. As Box 3.1 reveals, private firms in many developing regions are seriously constrained by the absence of such basic state functions as the protection of private property. Institutional impediments are largely to blame and will be hard to overcome. Yet windows of opportunity for reform can open and widen even in the most inhospitable of settings. And a major theme of this chapter is that even a modest shift in policy priorities in favor of the bare essentials can

do much to put long-stagnant economies back on track. We address the various approaches to government's role in effective environmental protection in Chapter 4.

Establishing a foundation of law and property rights

Markets rest on a foundation of institutions. Like the air we breathe, some of the public goods these institutions provide are so basic to daily economic life as to go unnoticed. Only when these goods are absent, as in many developing countries today, do we see their importance for development. Without the rudiments of social order, underpinned by institutions, markets cannot function.

The lawlessness syndrome

Markets cannot develop far without effective property rights. And property rights are only effective when three conditions are fulfilled. The first is protection from theft, violence, and other acts of predation. The second is protection from arbitrary government actions—ranging from unpredictable, ad hoc regulations and taxes to outright corruption—that disrupt business activity. These two are the most important. Unhappily, as Figure 3.1 makes evident, and as the regional patterns in Figure 3.2 highlight, in many countries neither is in place. The third condition is a reasonably fair and predictable judiciary. This is a tall order indeed for countries in the earliest stages of development, yet firms in more than half the countries surveyed considered it a major problem.

The absence of these critical supports for property rights gives rise to what this Report terms the lawlessness syndrome. Firms in twenty-seven of sixty-nine countries surveyed—including more than three-fourths of those in the CIS, and about half in Latin America and Africa (but none in the OECD)—are subject to this triple curse on markets: corruption, crime, and an unpredictable judiciary that offers little prospect of recourse.

Box 3.1 Weaknesses in fundamentals constrain firms the world over

In many countries the fundamentals needed to allow firms to go about creating wealth are not in place. The survey of businesspeople described in Chapter 2 asked firms to rank the relative importance of eight distinct obstacles to economic activity, to identify which aspects of government action most need improving. As the table below shows:

■ Obstacles associated with uncertain property rights and dealing with arbitrariness—corruption and crime—rank among the top three everywhere except among the high-income countries of the Organization for Economic Cooperation and Development. Regulation does not emerge directly as a major obstacle.

■ Policy-related problems—notably regarding taxation and the operation of financial markets—also tend to rank high (except in Latin America). But it is impossible to tell from the survey results alone whether these widespread perceptions reflect the universal desire of firms to pay lower taxes and to borrow more at lower interest rates, or whether they are symptomatic of fundamental policy shortcomings. More telling is the perception in countries of the CIS that policy instability is a major constraint.
■ Poor infrastructure emerges as the leading constraint in South Asia and the Middle East and North Africa, and as one of the top three constraints in Latin America and Sub-Saharan Africa.

Firms' rankings of obstacles to doing business
(Worst = 1)

Obstacle	Sub-Saharan Africa	Latin America and Caribbean	East and South Asia	Middle East and North Africa	CIS	CEE	High-income OECD
Property rights							
Corruption	1	1	3	2	3	3	5
Crime and theft	5	3	8	8	4	6	6
Regulation	8	8	7	7	8	8	4
Policy							
Taxes	2	5	2	3	1	1	1
Financing	6	4	5	4	5	2	2
Inflation	4	7	4	6	6	4	8
Policy instability	7	6	6	5	2	7	7
Public investment							
Poor infrastructure	3	2	1	1	7	5	3

Source: Private sector survey conducted for this Report.

Corruption emerged from the survey as a major problem. Its consequences often do not end with paying off officials and getting on with business. Arbitrary government entangles firms in a web of time-consuming and economically unproductive relations. More than half of senior managers in firms surveyed in the CIS—but only about 10 percent of those in the OECD countries—reported spending more than 15 percent of their time negotiating with government officials over laws and regulations (Figure 3.2). The burden of red tape is less in other developing countries, but still consistently worse than in the OECD countries. Chapter 6 examines in some detail how the scourge of corruption can be tamed.

The high ranking by CIS firms of the two other elements of the lawlessness syndrome—crime and judicial unpredictability—partly reflects the unique institutional vacuum created by the rejection of central planning in the transition economies. Yet indicators from other regions suggest that institutional decay is widespread. In Latin

America, for example, between 1980 and 1991 the murder rate rose from 12.8 per 100,000 people in 1980 to 21.4 per 100,000 in 1991, with increases evident in virtually all countries and subregions.

Much remains to be learned about how to reverse lawlessness among private citizens. But the solution is likely to embrace many of the reform priorities highlighted by this Report, including better protection of the vulnerable and stronger overall capability of state institutions. A community's descent into lawlessness can evoke a sense of helplessness among the law-abiding. But as Box 3.2 describes, a recent initiative in Cali, Colombia, has shown that, even under the most difficult of circumstances, civic action can start a reversal from despair to hope.

More complex institutional underpinnings
Containing lawlessness is necessary to secure property rights, but it may not be sufficient. Information and coordination problems can also impede development by under-

mining markets and property rights, a problem often found in low-income countries.

Information problems occur because people and firms inevitably have limited information and understanding, or because the rules of the game are unclear. The scope of property rights—including the right to use an asset, to permit or exclude its use by others, to collect the income generated by the asset, and to sell or otherwise dispose of it—may not be well defined. People and firms may lack knowledge of profit opportunities, or of the probity of potential business partners. The costs of seeking out such information decline as markets thicken and their supporting institutions develop, making economies more information intensive. In developing countries, however, the costs of learning can be high.

Coordination of economic activity is difficult because self-interested people and firms behave strategically—they generally are willing to share information only when they do not lose by doing so. The presence of moral hazard—the risk that other parties might opportunistically renege on agreements—hinders firms from taking advantage of opportunities for mutual gain. As markets develop, institutional arrangements evolve to facilitate cooperation among firms. Again, however, in developing countries where those institutions are underdeveloped, such cooperation can be difficult to achieve.

Spot markets can emerge even when information and enforcement mechanisms are weak, since the fact that the exchange is simultaneous makes it more difficult to cheat. But for other transactions the costs of providing adequate information and enforcement mechanisms to enable business to proceed can be formidable.

Well-functioning institutions can reduce these transactions costs. History provides abundant examples of the

symbiotic development of markets and institutions: new industries create demand for more-complex institutions, which in turn enable the industry to develop further. Consider the example of mining in the "Wild West" Nevada territory of the nineteenth-century United States.

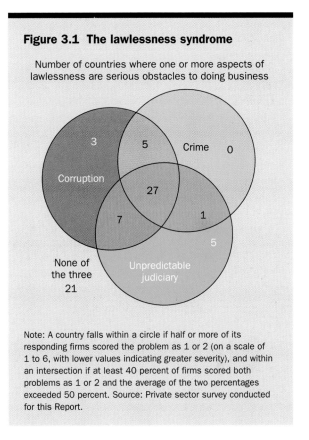

Figure 3.1 The lawlessness syndrome

Number of countries where one or more aspects of lawlessness are serious obstacles to doing business

Corruption 3
5
Crime 0
27
7
1
5
None of the three 21
Unpredictable judiciary

Note: A country falls within a circle if half or more of its responding firms scored the problem as 1 or 2 (on a scale of 1 to 6, with lower values indicating greater severity), and within an intersection if at least 40 percent of firms scored both problems as 1 or 2 and the average of the two percentages exceeded 50 percent. Source: Private sector survey conducted for this Report.

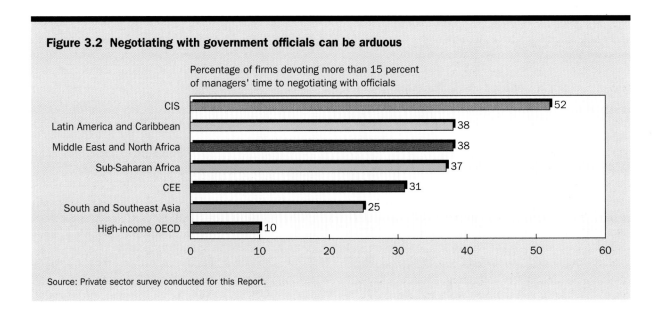

Figure 3.2 Negotiating with government officials can be arduous

Percentage of firms devoting more than 15 percent of managers' time to negotiating with officials

Region	Percentage
CIS	52
Latin America and Caribbean	38
Middle East and North Africa	38
Sub-Saharan Africa	37
CEE	31
South and Southeast Asia	25
High-income OECD	10

Source: Private sector survey conducted for this Report.

Box 3.2 Standing up to crime in Cali, Colombia

One of the centers of the illegal world trade in cocaine, Cali saw its homicide rate leap from 23 per 100,000 citizens in 1983 to over 100 per 100,000 in the early 1990s. Many murders could be directly attributed to drug trafficking, but many more seemed due to a spreading culture of violence. Fed up with the growing lawlessness, in 1992 the city elected as mayor a respected physician who put combating violent crime at the center of his political platform.

Within months the new mayor had mounted a major anticrime initiative, the Program for the Development of Safety and Peace. Starting from the principle that prevention should take precedence over repression—and after an exhaustive analysis of the patterns of crime—the program worked to combat crime across a variety of fronts:

■ Organizations of civic order were upgraded. Special education and housing programs were established for police officers, and improvements were made in the quality of services (including legal aid and conciliation services) available in the frontline inspectorate offices where citizens file complaints of criminal action.

■ Public education campaigns promoted tolerance and respect for the rights of others. Community leaders were trained in peaceful dispute settlement; children were encouraged to join a Friends of Peace program; humorous TV commercials aimed to re-educate citizens to follow the rules of everyday life, such as obeying traffic signals, or waiting in line to board a bus.

■ Public services were directed at reducing inequities. Primary and secondary schools were expanded in depressed areas of the city; water, light, and sewerage services were introduced into squatter areas; and youth centers and enterprise development programs worked to bring teenage gang members back into society's mainstream.

■ Catalysts of violent crime were directly confronted. The city banned the carrying of handguns on certain high-risk weekends, and sales of alcohol were restricted late at night and during holidays.

In 1995, after seven consecutive years of increase (to a peak of over 120 murders per 100,000 people), Cali's murder rate finally began to decline.

In the 1850s a few hundred miners worked a forty-square-mile area of seemingly marginal value. Only loosely tied to the U.S. polity, they operated under entirely unwritten and informal ownership agreements. The discovery of the gold- and silver-bearing Comstock Lode in the late 1850s precipitated a flood of prospectors. Within five months the new miners had established a formal mining camp government, which enacted written rules on private holdings and enforced them through a permanent claim recorder and an ad hoc miners' court.

By 1861 the surface ore was exhausted and miners resorted to subsurface mining—a substantially more expensive and capital-intensive undertaking. With more at stake financially and with disputes over underground mining rights increasing in complexity, the miners pressured for, and won, creation of a formal territorial government with a more extensive judiciary—subsidized in part by the U.S. Congress.

By 1864, with mining production still expanding, the territorial judicial system was overwhelmed by a massive case load, which could have taken up to four years to clear. At the end of that year Nevada was admitted to the union as a state, and within a year some important judicial rulings resolved disputes over subsurface rights. Property rights stabilized, and legal uncertainty ended.

The progress of land titling in Thailand is a more contemporary illustration of how the formal specification of property rights can unleash "locked-up" assets and accelerate private sector-led development. Thailand has issued more than 4 million title deeds since 1985, in two land titling projects. A third project to title another 3.4 million parcels is under way. Land is an ideal form of collateral, so possession of secure title has improved access to formal credit. Three years after the first titles were issued, Thai farmers who had received titles had increased their borrowing from the formal sector by 27 percent. By enhancing security of tenure, title to land can boost investment in land improvements (irrigation, fencing, destumping). Newly titled Thai farmers increased their use of inputs by 10 to 30 percent, their rate of capital formation by 30 to 67 percent, and their investment in land improvements by 37 to 100 percent. Even after adjusting for other factors, productivity on titled land was between 12 and 27 percent higher than on untitled land.

Not every country is in a position to achieve such results. In Thailand certain background conditions played an important role. First, formal credit markets were already well developed, and lack of formal title (and hence of collateral) was the only reason why many farmers could not get loans. By contrast, in a number of African countries with weak credit markets, no measurable impact of titling on borrowing and investment could be discerned. Second, the Thai titling projects took place against a backdrop of land disputes that threatened security of tenure but could no longer be adequately resolved through traditional mechanisms. This is not always the case. Indeed, where land is cultivated individually but owned communally, strengthening traditional, community-based systems of land administration could increase security at a fraction of the cost of establishing individual titles. This is a particularly attractive option where communities can switch to individual titles once the efficiency gains from allowing sales to outsiders, and from being able to collateralize land for borrowing, outweigh the benefits associated with communal tenure.

But some complex transactions can proceed even with simple judicial systems. A well-functioning judiciary is an important asset, which developing countries would do well to build up. As Chapter 6 details, creating a workable formal judicial system from scratch can be slow and difficult. But the best should not become an enemy of the better. Even less-than-perfect judicial systems that are cumbersome and costly can help sustain credibility. What matters is not so much that judicial decisionmaking be fast but that it be fair and predictable. And for that to happen, judges must be reasonably competent, the judicial system must keep judges from behaving arbitrarily, and legislatures and executives need to respect the independence and enforcement capability of judiciaries.

Without a well-developed judicial system, firms and citizens tend to find other ways of monitoring contracts and enforcing disputes. These can often make quite complex private transactions possible. In the early Middle Ages, for example, European merchants devised their own sophisticated legal code, the *lex mercatoria,* to govern commercial transactions; the code helped revive long-distance trade. A widespread alternative to legal mechanisms is social enforcement, based on long-term personal relationships. Cheating is deterred, not by the law, but by the "long shadow of the future": both parties pass up the one-time gains from cheating in expectation of the larger gains from a long-term business relationship. The extended family plays just this role in supporting business transactions in many Latin American countries. Although family size limits the number and variety of possible transactions, families find ways to, in effect, expand their membership, for example through marriage among business families or "adoption" of trading partners as godfathers, uncles, and aunts.

The extensive business networks created by Chinese clans, some of which have global reach, are another example of social enforcement at work. Against the backdrop of sound economic policies in large parts of East Asia, these networks have been very successful in generating wealth for their members. Indonesia's Chinese (non-*pribumi*) business community used its extended Southeast Asian network to kickstart exports of garments and furniture. A World Bank survey showed that over 90 percent of the initial export marketing contacts of non-*pribumi* firms were made through private business connections. Indonesia's non-Chinese exporters relied much more on initial support from public agencies.

Even when parties cannot rely on social enforcement, mechanisms of information sharing can allow quite complex transactions to take place. Box 3.3 shows how in Brazil, for example, sophisticated credit information systems have developed to enable firms to bypass some of the problems created by a predictable, but cumbersome, judicial system.

Focus on the foundations
Taken together, the evidence presented here offers reasons for hope—and a major challenge. The hope comes from the fact that simple institutions can do much to facilitate market-based economic development. The challenge comes from the recognition that so many countries presently lack even the most basic underpinnings of markets. The first priority in such economies must be to lay the initial building blocks of lawfulness: protection of life and property from criminal acts, restraints on arbitrary action by government officials, and a judicial system that is fair and predictable.

Once a foundation of lawfulness is in sight, the focus can turn to the ways in which specific parts of the legal system can buttress property rights. The legal terrain is vast, ranging from land titling and the collateralization of movable property to laws governing securities markets, the protection of intellectual property, and competition law. However, reforms in these areas—especially the more sophisticated ones—will yield fruit only where institutional capabilities are strong. In many countries, more basic challenges remain to be met first.

Sustaining a benign policy environment

Property rights are the foundation for market-led growth and poverty reduction. But much more is needed. Firms need an environment that induces them to allocate resources efficiently, to improve productivity, and to innovate. And unless firms are confident that policies will remain reasonably stable over time, they will fail to invest, and growth will lag.

This section reviews international experience with some key policies that support development. It highlights some institutional reasons why countries find it so difficult to put good policies in place—and the increasing risks, in a more integrated world, of pursuing bad policies. The emphasis throughout is on finding ways in which countries with different institutional capabilities can lock in good policies.

Box 3.3 Contracting and the judicial system in Brazil

The Brazilian judicial system is exceedingly cumbersome from a firm's perspective. A complex maze of laws may apply to an otherwise simple business transaction. In 1981, for example, getting an export license took 1,470 separate legal actions involving thirteen government ministries and fifty agencies. The legal process is also exceedingly slow, primarily because of a complex appeals procedure. Yet surprisingly, when asked to evaluate the relative importance of a diverse array of constraints on doing business, firms assigned a low ranking to problems associated with the legal system.

One reason is that, cumbersome though it is, Brazil's judicial system nonetheless seems to provide a secure backdrop of judicial recourse for business transactions. Most firms report that the judiciary is reasonably fair and predictable, and they do on occasion turn to it: two-thirds of a sample of Brazilian firms have disagreed with a government official and sought to have a ruling changed; 60 percent have taken the government to court, and over 80 percent would do so again. Similarly, one in every 1,000 transactions among produc-

ers and buyers of garments finds its way into court—only one in every 2,600 does so in Chile, and one in every 20,000 in Peru.

A second reason why firms shrug off the slowness of the judicial system is that (as in all private market economies) private institutional arrangements have evolved to restrain opportunism in business dealings, while bypassing court proceedings. We cite three examples. First, Brazilian firms readily provide short-term credit even to new customers with whom they have had no prior dealings; they base their confidence on a well-developed credit information system (backstopped by a juridically sanctioned mechanism for publicizing information on people who fail to pay their debts). Second, although it is difficult to claim pledged property when loans are not repaid, under Brazilian law leased property can be reclaimed much more readily—so Brazilians make liberal use of leasing arrangements. Third, for some simple financial transactions, special judicial mechanisms allow the usual proceedings to be bypassed.

Good policies promote growth

The past few decades have yielded a rich crop of lessons about the kinds of economic policies that support development. The East Asian miracle shows how government and the private sector can cooperate to achieve rapid growth and shared development. The recent recovery of some Latin American economies, breaking out of a long history of inflation and into renewed growth, has further confirmed the power of market liberalization, budget restraint, and credibility-enhancing institutions. Africa, especially south of the Sahara, has been slower in joining this movement, with the exception of a few countries such as Mauritius and Botswana. But several more—Côte d'Ivoire since the devaluation of the CFA franc, Uganda more recently—have embarked on promising new development paths.

Analyses of these and other experiences consistently find a core set of policies that appear to be essential for growth:

- Providing macroeconomic stability
- Avoiding price distortions
- Liberalizing trade and investment.

These policies help position an economy to benefit from competitive market forces. These forces provide the right

signals and incentives for economic agents to accumulate resources, use them efficiently, and innovate. Over time, as we saw in Chapter 2, getting these basics right can have a dramatic effect on living standards.

The relationship between growth and *macroeconomic stability* is well known. Empirical work has shown that high rates of inflation (above single digits) adversely affect growth. High inflation creates uncertainty about the returns on saving and investment, thus creating a disincentive for capital accumulation. Inflation also makes it difficult to maintain a stable but competitive exchange rate, impeding the country's ability to exploit the benefits of openness and creating wage volatility.

As Box 3.4 shows, governments around the world find it difficult to achieve the strong fiscal and monetary discipline required for economic stability. Maintaining such policies is harder still. But reforming governments will not inspire the confidence necessary to generate growth unless people believe the new discipline will be sustained. We discuss below a range of institutional arrangements that can help inspire such confidence.

Limiting price distortions is an essential element of good policies, because price distortions impede growth. They can discourage necessary investment, divert effort into unproductive activity, and encourage inefficient use of re-

Box 3.4 International track records on fiscal deficits and inflation

As the figure shows, fiscal deficits in the industrial countries as a whole rose progressively for two decades starting in the early 1960s, stabilized briefly in the late 1980s, and then began to grow again. Persistently high deficits have boosted public debt (even before unfunded pension liabilities are included) from about 40 percent of GDP in 1980 to 70 percent in 1995. Developing countries in the aggregate have shown considerable improvement in fiscal discipline, although with substantial variation. Fiscal deficits started falling in the early 1980s, mainly because of expenditure cuts.

However, this aggregate picture reflects mainly successes in Asia and Latin America, where sustained and dramatic deficit reductions have been achieved. By contrast, in the first half of the 1990s neither the African nor the Middle Eastern countries have been able to follow through on deficit reductions achieved in the second half of the 1980s.

Inflation rates have varied across regions even more than have fiscal deficits. The inflationary episode of the 1970s and early 1980s spread quickly around the world. The cooldown of inflation that started in the industrial countries in the early 1980s has begun to take hold, but with a lag. In the developing countries inflation began to moderate in the early 1990s, but not everywhere. In some developing regions, inflation rates are showing signs of convergence toward those of the industrial countries.

Fiscal deficits

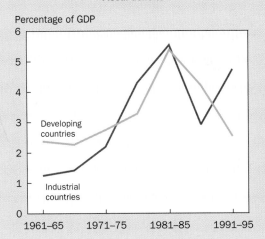

Inflation

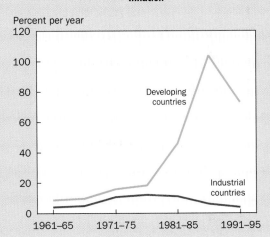

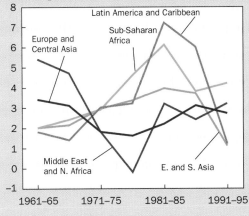

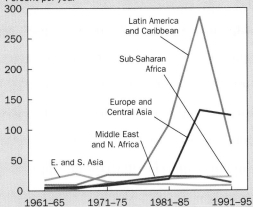

Source: IMF, various years (a).

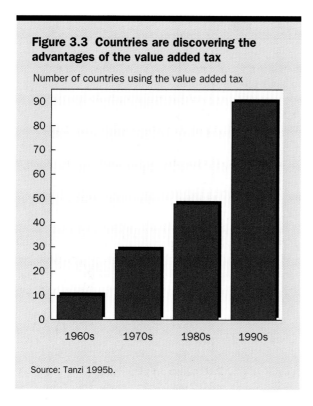

Figure 3.3 Countries are discovering the advantages of the value added tax

Number of countries using the value added tax

Source: Tanzi 1995b.

sources. Price distortions come in different forms, depending on their historical origins. The most common, however, involve discrimination against agriculture, overvaluation of currencies, unrealistic wages, and hidden taxes or subsidies on the use of capital.

African agriculture illustrates vividly how price distortions can undermine economic development. Agriculture accounts for about 35 percent of Africa's GDP, 40 percent of exports, and 70 percent of employment. Yet historically, African farmers have faced high rates of both explicit and implicit agricultural taxation. Explicit taxes (notably on agricultural exports) were high because administrative weaknesses precluded raising adequate revenue from other sources. Implicit taxes were high because pro-urban and pro-industry policies combined with high levels of import protection resulted in currencies being seriously overvalued in real effective terms. In addition, in some countries public sector monopolies raised border prices well above those at the farm gate, absorbing much of the difference in in-house expenditures. The combination of high explicit taxes and overvalued currencies contributed to alarming declines in Sub-Saharan Africa's agricultural growth rates: from an annual average of 2.2 percent in 1965–73 to 1.0 percent in 1974–80 and 0.6 percent in 1981–85.

Since the mid-1980s many African countries have made great strides in reversing the long-standing bias against agriculture. By the early 1990s two-thirds of a sample of twenty-seven countries had reduced the degree of

distortion by cutting explicit taxes and, often, correcting overvaluations. The 1994 devaluation of the CFA franc (see Box 3.5) significantly reduced the bias against agriculture among virtually all the franc zone countries that had not reformed earlier.

Harder to detect, but also widespread, are price distortions in labor and capital markets. Legal minimum wages, for instance, may be set too high, unintentionally making it more difficult for unskilled and low-wage workers to find jobs in the formal economy. Similarly, the price of capital—the interest rate—is sometimes kept falsely high through heavy taxation of financial transactions or high reserve requirements. When the authorities respond to borrowers' complaints by clamping a lid on lending rates, or by handing out subsidies to investors, yet another layer of distortion is added to the price system.

Maintaining *liberal trade, capital market, and investment regimes* is also essential for growth. As Chapter 8 details, many countries have recently moved toward greater openness. Open markets offer opportunities for citizens and businesses by increasing access to supplies, equipment, technology, and finance. Trade linkages with the world economy also help domestic prices adjust to global market conditions, so that prices reflect the scarcity values of goods and services. And improved incentives and opportunities allow entrepreneurs to use resources more efficiently.

Recent changes in the way developing countries raise tax revenues show how increased global integration can affect domestic policies. Internationalization of business and relentless competition for foreign investment—plus the presence of tax havens and low-tax jurisdictions— imply that countries cannot hope to tax corporate or personal income at rates much higher than global norms and still attract investment. And a growing worldwide consensus for lower national trade barriers has put pressure on the collection of border taxes, historically a major source of tax revenue for developing countries. (As a group, developing countries still derive about 30 percent of their revenue from trade taxes.) With increasing integration, the share of trade taxes in the total revenue of developing countries may be expected to fall further.

With these new constraints on traditional sources of revenue, many countries are turning toward consumption-based taxes such as the value added tax (VAT). Indeed, the combination of its revenue potential and pressures on other sources of revenue has led to dramatic growth in the number of countries using the VAT (Figure 3.3).

A liberal and open trade regime is also a powerful discipline on the other elements of economic policy. More-open economies are more exposed to external risks, making it more costly for governments to pursue inconsistent policies. Consequently, economies in which trade looms relatively large tend to have lower fiscal deficits than those where it does not. The need to comply with the rules and conventions of international treaties will be another spur to good behavior.

An economy without sound policies is unable to engage fully in international trade and investment. But being part of an integrating world economy also carries new risks. Where markets for goods and capital are open, the state has a hard time suppressing the consequences of monetary indiscipline. If it prints too much money, the foreign exchange market will quickly expect higher inflation, and the local currency will depreciate. This market feedback causes domestic interest rates to rise, and with them the government's financing costs. Good policies are needed to cope with the risks of capital flight, volatile arbitrage activity, and sharp movements in commodity prices. Box 3.4 summarized some differences in how countries have responded to the new global environment.

Foreign capital inflows also impose discipline on policymakers. Inflows tend to make the currency appreciate in real terms, and they can affect competitiveness and domestic saving. They can also be seriously destabilizing because they respond quickly to short-run financial turbulence. Recent experience suggests that this turbulence can be contagious, spilling over to other countries and even other regions in ways not necessarily commensurate with the change in risk. Countries experiencing sizable capital inflows may need to run positive fiscal balances, using these precautionary savings as a hedge against the possibility of sudden capital outflows. Capital inflows also have major implications for exchange rate policy; fixed exchange rates, for example, are unlikely to be a workable option if a country is vulnerable in financial markets. In short, the quality of a government's management of the economy is critical.

The risk of capital flight and financial turmoil is vividly illustrated by Mexico's experience in 1994–95. An important reason for the loss of confidence there was an overvalued peso, maintained despite very large current account deficits. As foreign exchange reserves fell below the domestic monetary base late in 1994, the authorities failed to bring about the necessary monetary contraction. More-consistent policies could have limited the loss of confidence.

An open economy is also exposed to price shocks arising from world markets. Energy and food prices are particularly volatile and can affect a country's external payments and fiscal positions. Exchange rates and interest rates are also volatile. Prudence calls for anticipating adverse shocks (a sharp price increase for importers, a price drop for exporters) by not borrowing excessively and maintaining scope for new borrowing and by holding adequate foreign exchange reserves, and in the medium term by establishing a more diversified economic base.

Favorable surprises can cause as much trouble as adverse ones. The prudent response to a positive economic shock is to set aside part of the windfall for future use. When the 1990–91 Gulf War pushed up oil prices, Nigeria used its windfall oil revenue to expand spending (Figure 3.4). So in spite of the large increases in revenue, Nigeria's fiscal deficit actually rose in 1990. When oil prices and revenue fell in 1991, spending remained at the new higher levels. By contrast, Indonesia responded to its oil windfall with fiscal discipline, explicitly budgeting a reserve fund to keep the increase in expenditure below the increase in revenue and maintain budget balance.

Good policies are hard to achieve

Although the recipe for good policies is well known, too many countries still fail to take it to heart, and poor performance persists. This often signals the presence of political and institutional incentives for maintaining "bad" policies.

Policies that are bad from a development perspective are often highly effective at channeling benefits to politically influential groups. Many macroeconomic problems—inflation, exchange rate misalignment—are in fact covert ways of levying unexpected taxes on the private sector or of redistributing economic benefits. Similarly, a broad array of microeconomic restrictions on the operation of markets—import restrictions, local monopoly

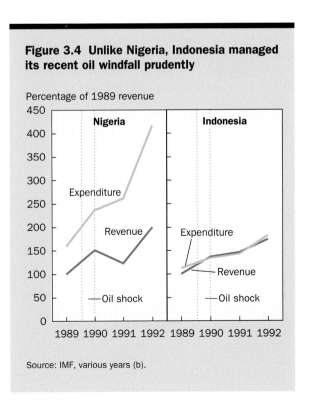

Figure 3.4 Unlike Nigeria, Indonesia managed its recent oil windfall prudently

Percentage of 1989 revenue

Source: IMF, various years (b).

privileges, regulatory red tape—serve to shelter powerful incumbent firms or other favored segments of society.

The political system in some countries has a built-in tendency toward chronic budget deficits. Legislators exchange favors, each promising to vote for benefits to the other's constituents, without specifying how these benefits will be paid for. So fiscal deficits rise.

When revenues fall short and politicians have little stomach for cutting spending, governments have to choose either to levy or raise taxes that are desirable from an efficiency standpoint, or impose hidden taxes such as the so-called inflation tax—the tax on real incomes that comes from financing government spending with debased currency. The latter course is often the easier. Increasing formal tax collection requires an efficient and honest tax administration. Achieving that may first require deep structural reform of fiscal administration. A change in the VAT rate might take a vote of parliament, implying delays and political compromise. But an increase in the inflation tax might involve no more than a ministerial order to the central bank.

Even when intentions are good, governments may sometimes be forced to use hidden taxes like the inflation tax—although they recognize that in the long run this brings huge costs and undermines credibility. How does a government with a history of inflationary financing convince potential bondholders that it will not inflate its way out of its obligations this time, or simply default? How can it convince trade union members that it will not cut their real income by raising the cost of living? If it cannot, investors will protect themselves by demanding a higher interest rate on government debt, and workers will protect themselves by demanding bigger raises. Their doubts may then become self-fulfilling: the government could be forced to bring about the inflation that these private agents expect, by loosening monetary policy and allowing real wages or interest rates to rise.

These perverse but powerful institutional incentives can make policy reform very difficult. And even if reforms are initiated, the skepticism of businesses, workers, and consumers may be borne out by events, unless the government can communicate the seriousness of its intent.

Locking in good policies

Once reforms are announced, their lasting success may depend on designing and implementing policies in ways that credibly signal that the government will not renege on its promises. A number of possible lock-in mechanisms are available, all with the same basic logic: to provide checks that restrain any impulse to depart from announced commitments. If institutional capabilities are strong enough to allow some flexibility to adapt rapidly to unexpected events, so much the better. If not, experience

suggests that long-run goals are better served by sticking to self-imposed restraints and living with the rigidities they inflict. The examples here concern fiscal and monetary policy; further examples in the field of regulation are discussed in Chapter 4.

FISCAL POLICY. Many macroeconomic disturbances start life as fiscal imbalances. Recent research suggests that changing the institutional features of the budgeting process can improve fiscal performance significantly.

Increasing the transparency of budgeting is particularly important. Although society as a whole will lose from budgetary ambiguity, it can be a boon for politicians, blurring the cost of favors to special interests, for example, or understating the long-run costs of short-term profligacy. When budgets are not transparent, "creative accounting" practices, such as off-budget spending and overoptimistic revenue and growth projections, become all too easy. Needless to say, all of these gimmicks make it harder to control spending.

How budgets are formulated and approved is also important. The evidence suggests, for example, that it matters whether a country takes a hierarchical approach to budgeting—giving considerable power over departmental spending totals to the finance ministry—or one that is more collegial. In principle, the hierarchical approach ought to foster greater fiscal discipline by enabling more "top-down" control of spending and limiting the scope for legislators to expand the budget piecemeal.

A recent study of twenty Latin American countries suggests that moves toward more transparent, hierarchical budgeting could deliver improved restraint (Figure 3.5). It found that budget deficits tended to be higher among countries that used collegial and nontransparent approaches to budget preparation. Countries with the least transparent and least hierarchical systems ran public deficits averaging 1.8 percent of GDP. The middle third ran an average budget surplus of 1.1 percent, while those with the highest combined hierarchy-transparency scores had budget surpluses, on average, of 1.7 percent. These results highlight that countries looking to improve their aggregate fiscal management need to scrutinize not just their balance sheets, but also the institutional environment that shapes the incentives to spend.

MONETARY POLICY. A well-functioning, independent central bank can effectively reduce the threat of politically motivated monetary expansion while maintaining some flexibility to accommodate unavoidable outside shocks. Many countries seeking credibility for their monetary policy have chosen the model of central bank independence.

In many cases this enthusiasm sprang from evidence that OECD countries with independent central banks generally had lower rates of inflation than others—with no slowdown in growth. But attempts to find a similar pattern in developing countries have yielded mixed results, depending on how central bank independence is defined. Russia's move to central bank independence in the early 1990s, for example, did not seem to restrain that country's inflation. This more complex story for developing countries suggests that monetary restraint through central bank independence cannot simply be manufactured by fiat. It may require a prior foundation of checks and balances on arbitrary action by public officials.

Choosing a conservative central bank governor, one who is more opposed to inflation than society in general, may be one way for developing countries to reap the benefits of central bank independence while containing the risks. Another way is to assign the bank only instrument independence—the day-to-day setting of policy to achieve a certain goal—while leaving the choice of the goal itself to the political authorities. A third option is to establish a contract for the central bank governor that provides for some penalty for deviating from an announced inflation target. This mimics the effect of employing a conservative central banker without relying on subjective judgments about the person holding the position.

The mixed success of independent central banks in restraining inflation raises the possibility that some developing countries may simply be unable to put in place mechanisms that credibly signal monetary restraint and at the same time maintain the capacity to respond flexibly to outside shocks. For these countries the choice may be between commitment through rigid mechanisms and no commitment whatsoever. A variety of inflexible approaches have been tried:

- Argentina, in breaking away from a long tradition of inflation, enacted a currency convertibility law in April 1991 that essentially turns the central bank into a quasi currency board. The money stock must be fully backed by foreign exchange.
- Many Latin American countries switched to a fixed nominal exchange rate to anchor prices and coordinate private sector expectations. A fixed rate precludes the use of devaluation to accommodate short-run external shocks. But as Mexico discovered to its dismay in 1994, a fixed nominal exchange rate can become dangerously destabilizing when capital inflows or domestic policies pull the real exchange rate out of line.
- Most of the francophone countries of Africa affiliated themselves with the CFA franc zone and its supranational central bank. Central bank advances to a member government are limited to 20 percent of tax revenues collected the previous year. This prevents countries from substituting the inflation tax for conventional taxes (Box 3.5). But the same mechanism can also provoke deflation if growth turns negative, as happened in the 1980s.

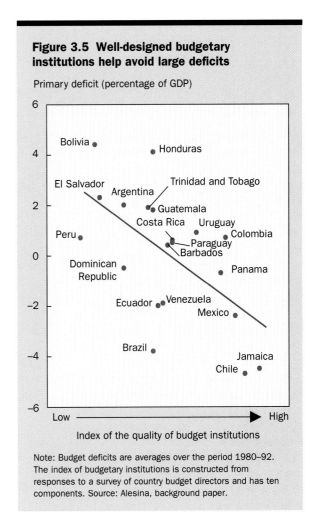

Figure 3.5 Well-designed budgetary institutions help avoid large deficits

Primary deficit (percentage of GDP)

Note: Budget deficits are averages over the period 1980–92. The index of budgetary institutions is constructed from responses to a survey of country budget directors and has ten components. Source: Alesina, background paper.

These hard-line approaches represent a high-stakes race against time. By raising the cost of policy reversal, such policies contribute to a belief that the government will hold fast. In time, however, some exogenous shock will be strong enough—or, perhaps, political opposition to some side effect of the policy will be strong enough—to demand a reconsideration. At that point, countries that have won the race against time will already have put in place more flexible approaches to monetary restraint, or will have won enough credibility that adapting the strategy will not be interpreted as a reversal.

Investing in people and infrastructure

Well-functioning markets are usually the most efficient means of providing the goods and services an economy needs—but not always. In particular, markets undersupply a range of collective goods—public goods, and private goods that have important spillover benefits for society at large. Generally these are goods that have a significant impact on the quality of life: clean air and safe water, basic literacy and public health, and low-cost transportation

Box 3.5 Commitment versus flexibility in the CFA zone

The CFA franc zone of West and Central Africa is both a currency union and a monetary standard: the CFA franc is convertible to French francs at a fixed nominal exchange rate. France established the zone after World War II to oversee monetary and financial policies in its African colonies, and France continues to play a central role in its operation.

In exchange for France's guarantee of convertibility, member countries surrender the right to print new currency. Policy changes require multilateral negotiations among the member states and France. Short of withdrawing completely from the zone, a single country cannot unilaterally renege on its commitment.

Compared with similarly endowed neighbors, zone members experienced lower average inflation and faster growth throughout the 1970s and early 1980s. By the second half of the 1980s, however, certain costs of zone membership had become apparent. The CFA zone was hit by a pair of external shocks: a real appreciation of the French franc against the dollar, which led directly to a real appreciation of the CFA franc; and a dramatic drop in the prices of some members' major exports. The fixed exchange rate ruled out adjustment through a nominal devaluation. Inflation remained low in this period, but at the cost of stagnant growth. The very factors that had contributed to the credibility and stability of the CFA zone now made it extremely difficult to devalue the CFA franc. By the early 1990s, however, a consensus was finally reached that a devaluation was necessary.

A 50 percent devaluation was announced in January 1994. Its dramatic size signaled that the devaluation was a once-and-for-all measure. Thus its benefits could be reaped without undermining the future credibility of the fixed exchange rate. Indications to date suggest that the devaluation has proved largely successful on both counts.

and communications. They are also goods whose provision can dramatically affect the welfare and life prospects of the poorest in society.

Public investments in health, education, and infrastructure yield high returns

Access to safe water and the control of infectious disease are public goods and services with large externalities that will be underprovided, or not provided at all, by the private sector. Infectious diseases still account for a large proportion of deaths in developing countries, and the poor suffer the most. Nearly 1 billion people in the developing world lack access to clean water, and 1.7 billion have no sanitation. Water-borne diseases such as cholera, typhoid, and paratyphoid remain a pervasive threat in many developing countries, especially for the poor. Evidence from Malaysia shows that traditional public health interventions, such as immunizations and provision of safe water, can make a significant difference in rates of illness and death, especially in infant mortality.

Returns to education are especially high at the primary level, because universal basic literacy yields large externalities to society. Educating girls, for example, is linked to better health for women and their children and to lower fertility rates. Many attribute a good part of the East Asian countries' economic success to their unwavering commitment to public funding for basic education as the cornerstone of economic development.

As *World Development Report 1994* highlighted, public investment in infrastructure boosts private activity in developing and industrial countries alike. A study of eighty-five districts in thirteen Indian states found that lower transport costs led to considerable agricultural expansion by making it easier for farmers to get their goods to market. More broadly, competing for new export markets requires high-quality infrastructure, to transport goods large distances at lowest cost.

Yet public resources often do not go to these high-return investments

The world over, too few resources are devoted to vital basic services. Governments spend roughly $1 per capita on public health, against a minimum requirement of $4 per capita. About 130 million primary-school-age children—60 percent of them girls—were not enrolled in schools in 1990. Half the children in Africa do not go to school. Girls, the rural poor, and children from linguistic and ethnic minorities are less likely to be in school than others.

Part of the problem is misallocation of resources *across* sectors—among defense, state enterprises, and social services, for example. In many developing countries, state enterprises produce goods that private markets could supply; the funds these enterprises absorb could be better spent on public goods. Turkey's state-owned coal-mining company lost $3.5 billion between 1990 and 1996. Tanzania's central government spent one-and-a-half times what it spent on public health to subsidize money-losing state enterprises. In low-income countries state enterprises' losses averaged 2.3 percent of GDP between 1978 and 1991.

Another part of the problem is the misallocation of resources *within* sectors. Spending on infrastructure and social services tends to be concentrated in areas where markets and private spending can meet most needs—urban hospitals, clinics, universities, and transport—rather than on essential public goods. These expenditures often benefit the rich disproportionately, while the poor receive only a small fraction.

For example, governments often try to finance the entire range of health care services. Yet public health interventions directed at improving the health status of large sections of the population, including the poor, warrant a higher priority. Most curative health care is a (nearly) pure private good—if government does not foot the bill, all but the poorest will find ways to pay for care themselves. This may explain why the public provision of clinical care services had no effect on health status in Malaysia, where people have the option of using private clinical services.

Although some governments are beginning to spend more on primary and secondary education, higher education is still heavily subsidized relative to other tiers. Whereas the Republic of Korea, for example, allocates 84 percent of its education budget to basic schooling, Venezuela allocates just 31 percent. Thirty-five percent of Bolivia's education budget—but only 11 percent of Indonesia's—is allocated to higher education. The tilt toward higher education is most acute in Africa, where public spending is about forty-four times greater per student in higher education than in primary schools. At the extreme—in Tanzania—the ratio was 238 to 1.

This emphasis on clinical health services and higher education entrenches social inequities. Evidence from Vietnam confirms that wealthier groups benefit disproportionately from hospital care: the richest fifth of the population are estimated to enjoy some 30 percent of the benefits of hospital spending, while the poorest fifth get only 11 percent (Figure 3.6).

Government decisions about what kind of services to supply are not the only reason why the benefits of public spending are unequally distributed. Differences in demand, especially those related to gender, are also important. In Côte d'Ivoire, for instance, almost two-thirds of public spending on education goes to boys. In Pakistan, boys benefit from about one-and-a-half times as much public spending on their education as do girls. Often the relative disadvantage of girls is even greater in poorer households, reflecting differences in demand in these households for education for girls and boys.

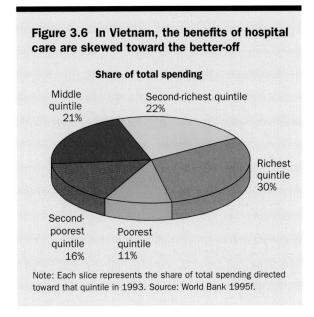

Figure 3.6 In Vietnam, the benefits of hospital care are skewed toward the better-off

Share of total spending

Middle quintile 21%

Second-richest quintile 22%

Richest quintile 30%

Second-poorest quintile 16%

Poorest quintile 11%

Note: Each slice represents the share of total spending directed toward that quintile in 1993. Source: World Bank 1995f.

Making better use of public resources

To focus public resources more efficiently on providing collective goods and services, countries will need to reallocate expenditures and learn to use their resources more efficiently. In many countries this will take both political and institutional change. The vital first step in institutional change is a readiness to embrace a pluralistic approach to delivery: to permit private participation while focusing direct public involvement on genuinely collective goods and services (although, as discussed below, governments might also choose to subsidize needy groups' consumption of goods even when the returns are wholly private). Viewed against the common postwar presumption that infrastructure and social services are the exclusive domain of public monopolies, pluralistic approaches might seem radical and untested. In fact, private and community participation in infrastructure and social services has a long historical pedigree (Box 3.6).

Only in the twentieth century did governments, first in Europe and later elsewhere, become important providers of services, in extreme cases excluding the private sector altogether. This transition to a more pervasive government role evolved differently for different services and in different countries, giving rise to wide variation in patterns of financing and delivery within and across income groups. Among low-income countries, for example, the private share of total education expenditure ranges from around 20 percent in Sri Lanka to around 60 percent in Uganda and Vietnam (Figure 3.7). The breakdown of health spending shows similar variation. In Latin America the private share ranges widely: from one-third of total health expenditures in Ecuador to 43 percent in Mexico

Box 3.6 Private provision of social services: A historical perspective

Only in the twentieth century did the state assume an important role in providing social services such as education and health care. The ability of the state to provide these services has varied, however, resulting in different public-private mixes.

Today's modern education systems were founded on private—often religious—initiatives. From the Islamic schools in Indonesia and West Africa to the Hindu gurus in India, the Christian churches in most of Europe, and the village teachers of China, private religious schools have been teaching children for centuries. In general, however, education was a privilege of the elites. Mass public education is a nineteenth-century invention, originating in Europe and North America and spreading to former colonies after independence. Significant public investment led to expanding public sector enrollments, accompanied in several countries by a shrinking role for private schools. In Malawi, for example, enrollment in private primary schools went from 77 percent of the total in 1965 to 10 percent in 1979. Elsewhere the inability of governments to keep up with demand or overcome dissatisfaction with public school quality led to an increase in private school enrollments.

Historically, most medical services were privately provided by midwives, traditional healers, and neigh-borhood doctors. Not until the first antibiotics were mass-produced after World War II did Western medicine begin to benefit large groups of people. In developing countries, increased urbanization and industrialization led to the formation of labor groups, which organized themselves to provide health insurance through "sickness funds" or pressed for publicly financed social insurance systems. By 1950 sixteen Latin American countries had enacted laws to provide health insurance to selected groups, but only two African and four Asian nations had done so.

The International Conference on Primary Health Care, held in Alma-Ata, Kazakstan, in 1979, proclaimed health a "basic human right" and urged governments to take "responsibility for the health of their people." Several governments in developing countries created national health systems that purport to provide free medical care to the entire population. These efforts met with mixed success, and the private sector expanded to fill the void. In Malaysia, for example, physicians in private practice rose from 43 percent of the total in 1975 to 90 percent of the total in 1990. But large parts of the population still lack access to basic services, while others rely chiefly on private providers paid out of pocket.

and 57 percent in Brazil. Eighty percent of health expenditures in Thailand are private.

In many settings unbundling the delivery of infrastructure and social services can help achieve a better match between roles and capabilities. In bundled systems of delivery a diverse array of activities—private and collective, subsidized and unsubsidized, competitive and monopolistic—are all undertaken by a single public provider. When services are unbundled, it becomes possible:

- To distinguish between activities that could be financed and delivered entirely through private markets, and those that have important collective elements—and to begin to shed the former
- To distinguish between those collective activities whose delivery should remain in public hands, and those whose financing should be public and their delivery private—with vouchers, contracting, and similar mechanisms providing the bridge between the public and the private sector (Chapter 5 explores these options in more detail)
- To take advantage of new opportunities for competition among the array of goods and services that can now be delivered privately (sometimes, as we see in Chapter 4 for utilities, taking advantage of these new opportunities may require new regulatory arrangements)
- To increase the transparency of the uses to which public money is being put (much harder when many diverse activities are bundled together within a monopoly public provider).

Yet organizational changes will not do it all. Perhaps the most important change in the incentive environment is to empower users themselves with "voice"—not only to work in partnership with providers where localized information is key to efficient delivery, but also to monitor providers' performance and to enforce, through the political process, a commitment to quality. How this can be achieved is the subject of Chapter 7.

Protecting the vulnerable

Over the long term, rapid growth and investment in people will cut poverty dramatically. Yet regardless of a country's income level—and regardless of the gains accruing to the economy as a whole—some citizens will be left behind, and others will suffer temporary hardship. This sec-

Figure 3.7 The balance of private and public education differs enormously worldwide

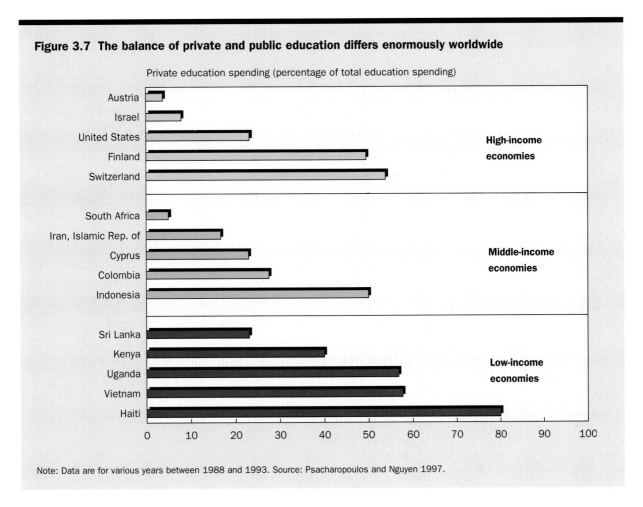

Private education spending (percentage of total education spending)

Note: Data are for various years between 1988 and 1993. Source: Psacharopoulos and Nguyen 1997.

tion examines how states have wrestled with the challenge of protecting the vulnerable.

A wide variety of protective measures
Table 3.1 offers a glimpse of the rich variety of initiatives governments have tried to protect the vulnerable in developing countries. All of these initiatives fall into one of two broad categories:

- Pension, unemployment, and other *social insurance* programs aim to support people who—for reasons of age, the business cycle, or other circumstances—are outside the wage economy for some part of their lives.
- Programs of *social assistance* aim to help the poorest in society, those who are barely able to support themselves.

In industrial countries the universal welfare state, which has influenced welfare programs around the world, has blurred this distinction. Most of the main transfer programs—pensions, unemployment insurance, family assistance—began during the 1930s and 1940s in response to the Great Depression and World War II, and following the realization that the elderly were especially

vulnerable in industrial societies. These three programs, pensions especially, absorb a rapidly increasing share of national income, and rich countries around the world are revisiting some aspects of their welfare programs (Figure 3.8). Even Sweden, where the commitment to the welfare state remains firm, and which has an unrivaled record in eradicating poverty, has embarked on wide-reaching reforms to find a better balance between the social benefits and the heavy—often invisible—economic costs.

In Central and Eastern Europe and the former Soviet Union the state has traditionally provided a wide range of social services. Before their transition to the market these states offered comprehensive benefits, but they differed from those in industrial market economies in four respects. First, because the system was premised on full employment guaranteed by the state, there was no unemployment insurance. Second, social protection focused on those (such as the old and the disabled) who could not work. Third, benefits were decentralized at the firm level. And fourth, in-kind subsidies (housing, energy) played an important role.

With an unprecedented economic contraction and tight budgets accompanying transition, some countries in Central and Eastern Europe and the former Soviet Union

Table 3.1 Social insurance, social assistance, and poverty-targeted programs in developing countries: Characteristics and lessons

Program type	Coverage and regional patterns	Design issues and lessons	Positive stories
Pensions	Nearly universal in transition countries, very low in Sub-Saharan Africa, medium to high in Latin America. Pay-as-you-go schemes dominate.	Actuarial imbalances, even in some countries with young populations, threaten macroeconomic stability, especially in transition countries, Brazil, and Uruguay. Transition countries need to increase pensionable age. Separate redistribution from insurance.	Innovative schemes in Argentina and Chile
Family assistance	Included in middle- to high-income countries as part of social insurance. It is universal at the enterprise level in transition economies.	Family size correlates highly with poverty in the Central Asian republics but not in Eastern Europe and the rest of the CIS. Poverty incidence determines the degree of progressivity. Where incidence is low, means testing is crucial to containing cost.	
Social assistance (cash)	Limited in transition countries, rare in Asia, nonexistent in Latin America and Africa.	More suitable to countries with relatively low poverty incidence.	Chile's family subsidy and old-age social assistance pension
Food subsidies	General price subsidies dominate in Africa and the Middle East. Quantity rationing is prevalent in South Asia. Food-for-work schemes are used in Latin America. Countries are shifting toward food stamp and targeted programs.	Open-ended price subsidies are fiscally unsustainable, distortionary, and regressive. Leakages can be prevented by innovative targeting. Nutrition programs are more cost-effective than quantity rations or general subsidies. Programs that set work requirements are more cost-effective than rations. Political economy often entails an urban bias.	Tunisia's price subsidy reform, which reduced costs by 2 percent of GDP and improved targeting; 1993 Food for Education Program in Bangladesh
Housing subsidies	Prevalent in transition economies, mostly on-budget; less prevalent in other regions, mostly off-budget.	Often regressive. Urban poor are best protected by increasing and encouraging low-cost housing production. Community organizations and cooperatives have been more successful at targeting. Subsidies in the former Soviet Union complicate functioning of housing and labor markets.	Chile's one-time subsidies for housing purchase on the private market
Energy subsidies	Prevalent in transition countries and oil-producing countries, such as Venezuela.	In Asia, Africa, and Latin America gasoline subsidies largely benefit the nonpoor. They are also somewhat regressive in transition countries because of their importance in the consumption basket of the nonpoor. Elimination of subsidies would affect the urban poor.	
Public works	The Maharashtra Employment Guarantee scheme in India and social funds in Africa and Latin America are funded domestically and by international donors.	Provide both insurance and assistance. They are appropriate in areas where poverty is transient and there is scope for unskilled labor-intensive projects. The program wage should not exceed the prevailing market wage. In-kind payments attract more women.	India's Maharashtra scheme; Korea's introduction and cancellation of work program
Credit-based programs	Prevalent everywhere, especially in Africa, South Asia, and Latin America.	Main problem is the inability to borrow in the absence of collateral. Programs should subsidize transactions costs but not interest rates, use local groups instead of direct targeting programs, organize beneficiaries, and incorporate incentives to both borrowers and lenders to enforce repayment. Incorporate saving as a necessary component.	Grameen Bank in Bangladesh

Source: Adapted from World Bank 1996e.

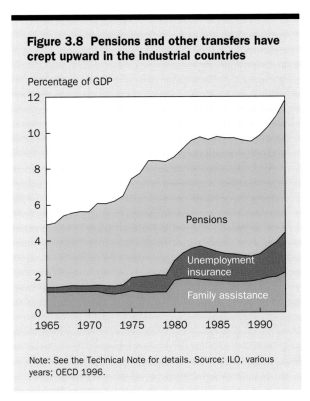

Figure 3.8 Pensions and other transfers have crept upward in the industrial countries

Percentage of GDP

Pensions

Unemployment insurance

Family assistance

Note: See the Technical Note for details. Source: ILO, various years; OECD 1996.

are beginning to realize that this system of universal coverage is no longer affordable and must be replaced by more-targeted programs. Cash transfers as a percentage of GDP are high. But adapting the welfare system to the new conditions is proving politically difficult. In Poland transfers doubled from 9 percent of GDP in 1988 to 18 percent in 1993.

In contrast to the OECD countries, the vast majority of developing countries have created "oasis" social insurance systems, which grant family benefits and pensions to formal sector workers and civil servants. The size of this oasis increases with income per capita. It covers 6 percent of the labor force in Sub-Saharan Africa, 23 percent in Asia, and 38 percent in Latin America. Formal unemployment insurance is rare, but the use of the public sector as employer of last resort is a form of disguised unemployment insurance.

Developing countries have also experimented with a variety of social assistance measures for meeting the basic needs of the poorest. These have ranged from programs that bundle cash assistance and insurance, to price subsidies (food, housing, energy) and labor-intensive public works (Table 3.1). The design of social assistance programs has often been heavily influenced by international aid. The prevalence of food aid from the United States in the 1950s and 1960s, for example, led to the adoption of many food-for-work programs, particularly in South Asia. The emergence of social funds in the 1980s, especially in

Latin America, reflects the shift to nonfood aid and greater cooperation with nongovernmental organizations (NGOs) and community-based groups in the delivery of targeted assistance. Labor-intensive public works programs have risen in popularity, particularly in South Asia and Africa.

In many countries, social insurance and assistance programs have failed to achieve their objective of protecting the vulnerable. Often they have resulted instead in transfers of resources to elite groups, sometimes with fiscally destabilizing consequences. New approaches are beginning to emerge for both insurance and assistance. We examine each in turn.

Social insurance—options and hazards

The generosity of social insurance programs has sometimes wrought havoc with long-term fiscal policy. As Table 3.2 suggests, in many countries the liabilities implicit in individuals' accrued pension rights far outweigh any reasonable measure of the government's tax-raising capacity.

Demographic changes partly explain these ballooning pension liabilities. Aging populations account for more than half of the expansion of pension and other welfare benefits in the OECD countries over a recent thirty-year period. Ukraine and Hungary, too, have older populations, which partly account for their high implicit pension debt. Demographic pressures on pension programs are likely to intensify especially rapidly in some developing countries. China's over-60 population will double from 9 to 18 percent of the total in thirty years—a transition that took a century in France and Britain.

Table 3.2 Implicit pension debt in selected countries
(percentage of GDP)

Country	Implicit pension debt of governments
Uruguay	296
Hungary	213
Brazil	187
Ukraine	141
Turkey	72
China	63
Cameroon	44
Peru	37
Congo	30
Venezuela	30
Senegal	27
Mali	13
Ghana	9
Burkina Faso	6

Note: Data are for various years between 1990 and 1996 and are net present values calculated at a discount rate of 4 percent.
Source: Kane and Palacios 1996.

Box 3.7 The new Chilean unemployment insurance scheme

Chile has a severance pay scheme but no system of unemployment insurance. The government has drafted a law to create one (called PROTAC). The design of this scheme departs from models prevailing in the OECD countries. The proposed scheme tries to circumvent the disincentives to work often associated with unemployment insurance. It would create individual accounts to which workers and employers would jointly contribute 4.4 percent of the worker's salary. These accounts would accumulate up to five months of salary and would be privately managed, possibly by the same institutions that now manage Chile's private pensions. A laid-off worker would receive severance pay of one month of salary per year of service, to a maximum of five years, and could make up to five monthly withdrawals from his or her individual account while unemployed. Workers who became unemployed following a resignation would only be entitled to the monthly withdrawals. The state would regulate these unemployment insurance accounts and guarantee a minimum unemployment benefit. As with pensions, this minimum guarantee would be provided only after funds in the account are exhausted. The individual account would thus act as a deductible.

But at their root the problems go beyond demographics. Civil servants in many countries view their pensions as an entitlement, rather than a form of savings: they make limited contributions to a retirement scheme but receive a full salary as pension after thirty to thirty-five years of service. More generally, influential constituencies successfully lobby for transfers from the budget, which they are unwilling to see scaled back even in the face of a severe fiscal crunch. Or, as in some African countries, public bureaucracies direct toward themselves resources intended for social insurance or for vulnerable groups.

Whatever the cause of these problems, unless social insurance can be put on a sounder financial footing, either the programs will collapse, or countries will be plunged into deep fiscal crisis, or both. An essential first step toward reform is for governments to distinguish between the goals of insurance and those of assistance—especially in developing countries where the gap is often vast between the poorest citizens (generally the targets of assistance programs) and those who participate in the formal economy (generally the targets of insurance programs). Experience suggests that failure to make this distinction is virtually certain to undermine both the fiscal viability of insurance programs (because the "insured" can lobby for unfunded benefits) and the impact of assistance programs (because nontargeted groups are likely to capture resources intended for the poor).

With insurance clearly distinguished from assistance, states can bring private participation and competition into insurance systems previously dominated by public monopolies. This can be done in several ways:

- The redistributive component of pensions can be unbundled from the saving component through a mandatory multipillar system, with the saving pillar fully funded, privately managed, and publicly regulated. Redistribution can be accomplished through a flat public pension (as in Argentina).
- States can introduce mandatory savings accounts for unemployment insurance, as well as pensions (Box 3.7 describes a Chilean initiative along these lines).
- Companies and individuals can be allowed to choose between public and private providers, as in Japan, Sri Lanka, and the United Kingdom.
- Management of the assets of public insurance programs can be contracted out to the private sector (as in Malaysia).
- States can enlist independent professionals, rather than political appointees, for the boards of trustees of public programs.

Of course, private provision of social insurance is only workable if financial markets are well enough developed so that private intermediaries can readily match these long-term liabilities with long-term assets. Yet even in poor regions such as Sub-Saharan Africa, thin capital markets need not be a bar to the development of private pension funds. Given an appropriate—and enforceable—legal framework for financial sector development, countries could set up regional equity markets. This is a particularly attractive option for countries of the CFA zone, which share a common currency. Already some equity markets in Sub-Saharan Africa compare favorably in terms of market capitalization with those in Latin American countries that have recently privatized their pension systems (such as Peru).

Sustainable approaches to social assistance

Unlike social insurance, which can be self-financing, social assistance requires direct expenditure of public funds. Balancing the objectives of poverty alleviation and fiscal prudence is thus vital to success. (Table 3.1 summarized the wide variety of approaches that have been tried.) In the past the debate was primarily over the relative merits of broad-based subsidies and means-tested programs. Today, the limitations of both have become more apparent.

Because means-tested programs (in which benefits are set according to the recipient's income) are administratively demanding, they are likely to achieve their goal at reasonable cost only in countries with strong institutional capability. But broad-based subsidies have also lost their appeal: they are expensive and relatively inefficient at reducing poverty. Housing and infrastructure subsidies, for example, turn out to benefit higher-income households disproportionately (Figure 3.9). Food subsidies can be more effective if they are targeted toward items consumed primarily by the poor. Tunisia has effectively moved from a nontargeted to a targeted program by eliminating all subsidies on goods consumed disproportionately by the nonpoor and, for those food products still subsidized, by differentiating product lines through differences in packaging and the use of generic ingredients. These reforms have reduced the cost of food subsidies from 4 percent of GDP in the mid-1980s to 2 percent by 1993, while still maintaining a food safety net for the poor.

With both means-tested and more broad-based assistance programs increasingly in question, attention has shifted to self-targeted approaches. One approach is to focus delivery on those localities, urban and rural, with disproportionate numbers of poor residents. Another is to set the level of benefits low and build in some kind of quid pro quo. Food-for-work programs incorporate these features. So, too, do lending programs for microenterprises in poor communities. Box 3.8 illustrates how Indonesia, which has made huge strides in reducing poverty through broad-based growth, is initiating a variety of self-targeted programs in an effort to eliminate poverty by 2005.

The challenge of sustaining programs of social assistance is political as well as fiscal: since the marginalized poor are politically weak almost everywhere, in times of fiscal belt tightening even prudently designed programs risk losing support. Self-targeted programs—especially those that impose reciprocal obligations on recipients—seem more politically resilient than those targeted more narrowly, but they too are vulnerable. At its root, then, the task—explored in Chapter 7—is to find ways of giving voice to the concerns of the poor, enabling them to become more effective advocates of their own interests.

Strategic options: Doing better on the fundamentals

Each of the four sets of economic and social fundamentals poses distinctive challenges, but all have some challenges in common.

First, prioritization is vital. As this chapter shows, in all too many countries the state still does not provide the full complement of core public goods and services: a foundation of lawfulness, a stable macroeconomy, the rudiments of public health, universal primary education, adequate transport infrastructure, and a minimal safety net. At the same time states are overproviding a wide variety of goods and services that private markets could supply in their stead. Especially in countries with weak institutional capabilities, the need is therefore urgent to focus the state's role on the fundamentals.

Second, skillful use of private, competitive markets and voluntary activity can support development while sharply reducing the burden on states with weak institutional capabilities. Market-led growth in a supportive incentive environment is fundamental. Additionally, markets can provide a variety of private goods and services that in many countries have somehow wandered into the domain of public provision, such as higher education, curative

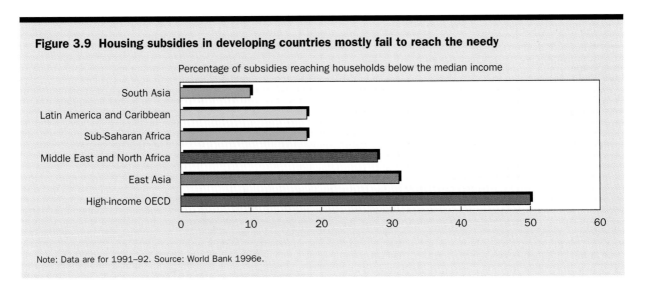

Figure 3.9 Housing subsidies in developing countries mostly fail to reach the needy

Percentage of subsidies reaching households below the median income

Note: Data are for 1991–92. Source: World Bank 1996e.

Box 3.8 Reducing poverty in Indonesia—how social assistance complements broad-based growth

Indonesia's rapid and broad-based growth has had a spectacular effect on poverty reduction. Between 1970 and 1990 the proportion of the population living below the official poverty line declined from 56 to 15 percent; other indicators of welfare, such as infant mortality, showed similar improvement. The government has now set itself the ambitious target of eradicating absolute poverty within the next decade. The challenge is that the remaining poor are concentrated in isolated pockets of poverty with poor natural resource endowments, low population densities, and other socioeconomic characteristics that make them difficult to reach. Several targeted interventions have been initiated in recent years, including the following:

■ The Inpres Desa Tertinggal (IDT) program, launched in 1994, is directed at villages that the country's development has left behind. The program distributes grants totaling $200 million per year among 20,000 villages—the poorest one-third of all Indonesian villages—to be used as seed capital for income-generating activities. The program is combined with public works programs.

■ The Prosperous Family program, launched in 1996, aims to improve the conditions of families living in non-IDT villages, and whose living standards are below a certain level, through small grants and subsidized credit.

■ Under the Transmigration Program about 750,000 families, or over 3.6 million people, have been resettled at government expense from overpopulated Java to less populated outer islands. The program aims to address landlessness as a cause of poverty and provide new settlers with agricultural land and other benefits.

■ The Kampung Improvement Program is targeted at improving the provision of social services and infrastructure to densely populated, low-income, urban neighborhoods.

health services, and pensions and other forms of insurance. In a range of other areas—using social funds for poverty alleviation, enhancing the quality of primary education, encouraging participation by NGOs and communities—reform can greatly improve service delivery. Countries with weak public institutions should assign high priority to finding ways to use markets and involve private firms and other nongovernmental providers in service delivery.

Finally, states should seek ways to enhance the credibility of their actions. In the short run, while weak domestic institutions are being reinforced, stronger ties with external actors—for example, through stabilization programs with the IMF—can help governments signal their commitment. In the long run, however, as Part Three explores in depth, the vital challenge is to build homegrown commitment mechanisms, rooted in domestic institutions.

CHAPTER 4

FOSTERING MARKETS: LIBERALIZATION, REGULATION, AND INDUSTRIAL POLICY

F EW DISPUTE THE CENTRAL ROLE OF THE STATE IN securing the economic and social fundamentals discussed in Chapter 3. There is much less agreement, however, about the state's precise role in regulation and industrial policy. A counterpart to the rise of state-dominated development strategies in the early postwar years was a dramatic expansion in government regulation in many countries. As countries have liberalized, those aspects of the regulatory framework that have proved counterproductive are being abandoned. But governments are learning that market reforms and fast-changing technology pose their own regulatory challenges. States cannot abandon regulation. The task, rather, is to adopt approaches to regulation that fit not merely the shifting demands of the economy and society but, critically, the country's existing institutional capability.

Attention to the proper match between the state's role and its institutional capability helps reconcile some seemingly clashing prescriptions for state action. Many, for example, would argue that, in complex industries such as telecommunications, regulators ought to have considerable flexibility in devising and implementing market rules. Yet where institutional capability remains weak, the scope for flexible initiatives is limited; the focus should instead be on winning credibility with firms and citizens, convincing them that the state will follow through on its commitments and will refrain from arbitrary and capricious action.

The same applies even more forcefully to more interventionist policies—those aimed at not merely laying the foundations of industrial development but actively accelerating it. In principle, there seems to be room for government to play such a role. But in practice its scope for doing so turns out to rely heavily on a range of stringent institutional conditions being fulfilled. Except where role and capability have been skillfully matched, activist industrial policy has often been a recipe for disaster.

Many countries with weak institutional capability are saddled by their history with governments whose reach is overextended; for them, privatization and market liberalization is a key part of the policy agenda. As capability develops, public organizations and officials will be able to take on more challenging collective initiatives, to foster markets and to make increasing use of efficient—but difficult to manage—regulatory tools.

Privatizing and liberalizing markets in overextended states

Interest has revived in finding ways for the government to work with the private sector in support of economic development, and to provide regulatory frameworks supportive of competitive markets. Yet in all too many countries, state and market remain fundamentally at odds. Private initiative is still held hostage to a legacy of antagonistic relations with the state. Rigid regulations inhibit private initiative. And state enterprises, often buttressed by monopoly privileges, dominate economic terrain that could more fruitfully be given over to competitive markets. At the extreme, a mass of inefficient state enterprises blocks private dynamism entirely, even as it imposes an unmanageable fiscal and administrative burden on the rest of the public sector. In such countries the first step toward increasing the state's effectiveness must be to reduce its reach.

The recent economic performance of such countries as China and Poland provides dramatic evidence of the benefits of shrinking the state in former centrally planned economies. But relaxing government's grip, whether that grip is maintained through public ownership or regulation, can also yield large dividends in more mixed economies. It can:

■ *Free up public resources for high-priority activities.* Diverting subsidies away from money-losing state enterprises and toward basic education would have

Table 4.1 Estimates of welfare gains from deregulation in the United States
(billions of dollars)

Industry	Gains to consumers	Gains to producers	Total gains	Further potential gains
Airlines	8.8–14.8	4.9	13.7–19.7	4.9
Railroads	7.2–9.7	3.2	10.4–12.9	0.4
Trucking	15.4	–4.8	10.6	0.0
Telecommunications	0.7–1.6	. .	0.7–1.6	11.8
Cable television	0.4–1.3	. .	0.4–1.3	0.4–0.8
Brokerage	0.1	–0.1	0.0	0.0
Natural gas	. .	. .	. .	4.1
Total	32.6–43	3.2	35.8–46.2	21.6–22.0

. . Not available.
Source: Winston 1993.

increased central government education expenditures by 50 percent in Mexico, 74 percent in Tanzania, and 160 percent in Tunisia.

■ *Pave the way to better, cheaper services.* Divestiture of state assets had positive effects in all but one of twelve carefully studied cases in Chile, Malaysia, Mexico, and the United Kingdom. The benefits came in the form of increased productivity and investment as well as more efficient pricing. Deregulation in five hitherto tightly regulated sectors in the United States had by 1990 yielded gains of $40 billion (Table 4.1). In Argentina, liberalizing harbor terminals in Buenos Aires led to an 80 percent reduction in fees.

■ *Unlock opportunities for private sector development.* Excessive regulation can inhibit market entry, fuel the growth of informal activity, and even create new industries solely devoted to helping firms navigate the regulatory maze. Eliminating these excesses enables markets to function more flexibly, at lower transactions costs.

The challenges of scaling back the overextended state are as much political and institutional as they are technical. Success relies on the ability to proceed with reform in the face of opposition from powerful groups who benefit from the status quo. Chapter 9 examines how reforms in general can most effectively be initiated and sustained. Here we focus more narrowly on programs of market liberalization and privatization.

Initiatives to foster market liberalization and privatization can be segmented into three overlapping phases: preparing for reform, establishing an enabling business environment, and privatizing (or liquidating) state enterprises. Transparency is the vital ingredient as governments begin to prepare for reform. Ideally, transparent preparation includes:

■ An explicit statement of the main objective—to unleash a competitive market economy—with fiscal

and other objectives preferably at most secondary in importance

■ Clarification of the criteria to be used in assessing which regulations are useful, which should be discarded, and which should be strengthened to complement privatization

■ Preparation of financial statements and public budgets (including information on borrowing from banks) to assess which state enterprises are moneylosers and uncover the reasons for their losses

■ Specification of open and competitive mechanisms (such as auctions) for divesting state enterprises.

Such efforts have an added rationale. Often they will show whether or not a country is truly ready for reform— whether key political actors want reform and find it politically feasible to translate that desire into action. If political will is lacking, further efforts will be wasted. Indeed, they may prove counterproductive if interpreted as another in a long line of arbitrary shifts in policy.

With the initial preparation done, the second phase of reform is to put in place a business environment that supports competitive private markets. Such an environment includes rules of the game that facilitate entry and competition, and a complementary institutional, legal, and regulatory framework that can undergird property rights and markets, including (notably) financial markets.

The economic advantages of early reform of the business environment—even before privatization—are substantial. One advantage is that fostering external and domestic competition ensures that many of the benefits of privatization will be passed on to consumers, rather than simply result in a transfer from public coffers to private monopolies. Otherwise the latter are likely to become powerful, entrenched interests, willing and able to stifle subsequent efforts to introduce more competition into the economy. A second advantage is that, if clear regulatory structures are in place, bidders will have a better idea of the economic potential of companies being privatized—the risk premium will be lower—and government will receive higher bids.

More broadly, liberalization of the business environment can be a powerful catalyst, setting off a virtuous spiral whereby each reform makes the next one easier. The stronger the business environment, the greater the range of opportunities and supports available to entrepreneurs, bureaucrats, and workers—and thus the weaker the political opposition to dismantling dysfunctional rules and agencies and liquidating or privatizing state enterprises. The challenge is finding a way to set this virtuous spiral in motion. For at the outset those who prosper under the dysfunctional system will have much to lose, while the eventual winners are unlikely to have reached the critical mass needed to lobby for their own interests. Box 4.1 describes how Mexico was able to overcome initial resistance to the rollback of regulatory controls.

Because it takes time for the business environment to become supportive—and because privatization becomes easier as the environment improves—reformers may be tempted to give privatization a backseat. This is precisely the approach adopted by China and, in earlier years, by the Republic of Korea and Taiwan (China). In the early 1960s, state enterprises accounted for about half of manufacturing production in Taiwan (China) and one-quarter in Korea. By the mid-1980s their share had fallen to about 10 percent in both economies—not as a result of privatization, but because of the rapid expansion of their private sectors.

A strategy of "growing out" of state dominance appears to have worked in some East Asian economies. But elsewhere economic and political considerations will favor keeping privatization on the front burner. Delay imposes three major economic costs. First, money-losing state enterprises may continue to drain money from the public coffers (or from banks in the form of never-to-be-repaid "loans"). Unless such losses can be contained, the resulting fiscal instability can undermine an entire reform program. Second, anticipating privatization down the road, managers and workers in state enterprises can be tempted to steal the company's most valuable assets while the going is good. Third, poorly performing state enterprises may obstruct liberalization and restructuring in other sectors. In Zambia market liberalization created opportunities for smallholder farms to expand production and exports of cotton. But before being exported, cotton must be processed, and for some years after liberalization virtually all the country's processors were under the control of a monopoly state enterprise. Once the sector was restructured, the pace at which farmers and businesses took advantage of new market opportunities picked up dramatically.

Given the importance of keeping privatization on the front burner, its sequencing in relation to liberalization thus poses some difficult dilemmas. On the one hand, privatization will yield greater economic benefits, and impose fewer hardships on society, if it is preceded by liberalization and regulatory reform. On the other hand, the longer privatization is delayed, the more entrenched management of state enterprises can become. Box 4.2

Box 4.1 Mexico's deregulation czar

In 1988 the president of Mexico appointed a "deregulation czar." Each month this official reported directly to the president and his economic council of ministers. Every business in Mexico, large or small, had equal access to the czar's office to complain about burdensome rules and regulations. When the office received a complaint, it was obliged to find out why the rule existed, how it interacted with other regulations, and whether it should continue in effect. The office operated under a strict timetable: if it did not act to maintain, revise, or abolish the disputed rule within forty-five days, the rule was annulled automatically.

The work of the deregulation czar over his first four years is widely credited with greatly accelerating Mexico's reforms. It provided struggling private businesspeople with an effective, responsive champion at the highest level of government. The factors behind this success include:

- Unequivocal presidential support, signaling to both bureaucrats and citizens the need to comply with the czar's decisions
- The fact that his decisions could be overruled only at the highest level of government
- The setting of tough penalties for officials who failed to implement the rulings
- The time limit, which ensured quick and visible results
- The czar's staff, who were skilled in the economic consequences of regulations, their interactions with other regulations, and their administrative requirements—no one person can effectively carry out a government-wide program of deregulation
- Finally, the fact that the czar won credibility with officials and with the public by giving a fair hearing to the powerless and the influential alike, and setting a consistent record of impartiality.

Box 4.2 Six objections to privatization—and how to address them

"We can't throw public sector workers into the street. It's wrong—and they won't stand for it."

Winning the acquiescence of employees is essential to successful privatization. Some countries have given shares to employees or privatized through employee and management buyouts. Others have offered generous severance pay. Privatization becomes easier as countries develop programs to protect the vulnerable, of the kind described in Chapter 3.

"Privatization is just another way for powerful politicians and businessmen to scratch each other's backs, and get rich at the expense of the people."

Process matters. Privatization must be based on competitive bidding, with the criteria for selecting buyers carefully specified in advance. And it all should be done in the open, in full view of the media and citizens.

"Our citizens won't accept our handing over precious national assets to foreign (or local) fat cats."

Broad-based ownership can help win popular support for privatization. One approach, adopted in the Czech Republic, Russia, and Mongolia, is to distribute privatization vouchers to citizens to be redeemed for shares. Another approach, adopted in Argentina, Chile, and the United Kingdom, is to make an initial public offering of shares to citizens at attractive prices. Both approaches can be designed to make room for a strong strategic partner with the incentive and expertise to effectively restructure the enterprise.

"Our local private sector is too weak. Without state enterprises, our economy will grind to a halt."

Certainly, privatization is easier if a well-functioning market economy, including financial markets, is already in place. Thus, a key complement (and, if appropriate, antecedent) to privatization is market liberalization, perhaps accompanied by the activist initiatives to foster markets described later in this chapter. Even so, in most settings it is precisely the heavy hand of the overextended state that is restraining private activity—the objection confuses cause with effect.

"All that privatization will do is replace a public monopoly with a private monopoly."

Regulatory reform is another important accompaniment to privatization: deregulation to remove artificial monopoly privileges, and development of a regulatory system that credibly restrains the abuse of economic power in noncompetitive markets.

"Why put ourselves through this trauma? Let's just manage our state enterprises better."

True, if governments are willing to put hard budget constraints in place, to allow competition from private firms, and to give managers appropriate incentives, the performance of state enterprises can improve. The sad reality is that, although some committed governments have reformed their state enterprises in the short term, making these reforms stick is much harder. *World Development Report 1983* spotlighted a number of well-performing state enterprises around the world; by 1993 a majority of these had sunk into decline.

---

describes how reformers opting to push ahead with privatization have tried to contain the risks.

Rolling back overextended states: Two central lessons
Experience worldwide with attempts to scale back overextended states suggests that success contains two vital ingredients. First is a commitment to competitive markets and an accompanying willingness to eliminate obstacles to their operation. Market liberalization enables new entrants to create jobs and wealth. It also eases the difficulties of privatization while increasing the potential economic gains. The second lesson is that, although the overextended

state needs to own less, and although there is no good economic reason for state ownership to persist in tradable-goods industries, there is no single "correct" stage in the reform program to start privatizing. The appropriate timing will depend on the dynamics of reform in each country.

Better regulation

Skillful regulation can help societies influence market outcomes to achieve public purposes. It can protect the environment. It can also protect consumers and workers from the effects of information asymmetries: the fact that banks, for example, know much more about the quality of their portfolios than do depositors, or the fact that business managers may know more about health and safety risks in production or consumption than do workers or consumers. Regulation can also make markets work more efficiently by fostering competition and innovation and preventing the abuse of monopoly power. And more broadly, it can help win public acceptance of the fairness and legitimacy of market outcomes.

With economic liberalization, many areas of regulation have been recognized as counterproductive, and wisely abandoned. Yet in some areas the traditional rationales for regulation remain, and market liberalization and privatization have themselves brought new regulatory issues to the fore. The challenge, illustrated here with reference to three important regulatory domains—banking, utilities, and the environment—is not to abandon regulation altogether. Instead it is to find regulatory approaches in each country that match both its needs and its capabilities.

Some new rationales for regulation

FINANCE: FROM CONTROLS TO PRUDENTIAL REGULATION. Our understanding of financial sector development has changed dramatically over the past decade. We now know that the depth of a country's financial sector is a powerful predictor and driver of development. Just as important, we know that the control-oriented regulation widely adopted in the early postwar years—directing subsidized credit to favored activities at very negative real interest rates, limiting the sectoral and geographic diversification of financial intermediaries—may often work against financial deepening. The near-universal response has been to move away from controls over the structure of financial markets and their allocation of finance, and embark on a process of liberalization.

Yet liberalization in the financial sector is not the same as deregulation. The case for regulating banking is as compelling as ever. Only the purpose has changed, from channeling credit in preferred directions to safeguarding the health of the financial system.

The banking system needs effective prudential controls because banks are different. Without appropriate regulation, outsiders will be less able to judge for themselves a bank's financial health than that of a nonfinancial company. Why? First, because outstanding loans are banks' primary assets. So long as banks receive interest on their loans, outside observers may well judge their portfolios to be healthy, even if (unknown to the observers) the borrowers lack the resources to repay the principal or, worse, are effectively bankrupt and are only keeping up the interest payments by taking out new loans. Second, because unlike many companies, banks can be hopelessly insolvent without running into a liquidity crisis. So long as insolvent bankers can disguise their condition to outsiders,

they can continue to attract deposits—and even aggressively pursue them by offering favorable interest rates. Failing banks often engage in ever-more-reckless gambles to salvage their position, throwing good deposits after bad, and driving up their losses before the inevitable crash. And third, because banks' balance sheets can be difficult to interpret, especially because a rising share of their portfolios may now be taken up with derivatives and other new financial instruments that are hard to monitor.

This information asymmetry can be destabilizing. Depositors, fearing for the safety of their funds, might rush to withdraw them when they begin to hear stories about troubled banks. Bank failures tend to be contagious. When one insolvent bank goes under, nervous depositors may start runs on others. As liquidity drains out of the system, even solvent banks may be forced to close. And a systemwide run can have severe macroeconomic consequences. For all these reasons—the difficulties in assessing a bank's financial health, the adverse spillover and distributional effects of bank failures—banks' behavior needs to be tempered by regulatory and other public actions, outlined later in this section.

UTILITIES: REGULATION WITH COMPETITION. For utilities, too, regulation has taken on renewed prominence. Here, however, the reason is revolutionary technological and organizational change, not just conscious shifts in policy. The argument for utility regulation used to be straightforward. Utilities were natural monopolies. Consequently, unless they were regulated, private utility operators would act as monopolists, restricting output and raising prices, with harmful consequences for economy-wide efficiency and income distribution. Today, changes in technology have created new scope for competition, but would-be competitors may need special reassurance from regulators before entering.

In telecommunications, dozens of countries throughout the Americas, Europe, and Asia—plus a few in Africa, including Ghana and South Africa—have introduced competition in long-distance, cellular, and value added (fax, data transmission, videoconferencing) services. A few countries—Chile and El Salvador, for example—are even exploring options for competition in local fixed-link networks. Electric power generation (but not transmission or distribution) is also now viewed as an arena for competition. In China, Indonesia, Malaysia, and the Philippines, private investors are adding generating capacity through independent power projects, alleviating acute shortages and enabling private finance to fill the gap left by shortfalls in public resources.

In this new environment the degree of natural monopoly has been drastically reduced (although perhaps not eliminated entirely). But regulation is still crucial, for two reasons. First, it can facilitate competition. Consider the problem of interconnection. By failing for more than a decade to establish workable rules to allow different networks to connect with one another, Chile's telecommunications regulators seriously obstructed competition, leaving dominant incumbent firms in control of how the system evolved. After numerous court disputes a multicarrier system was introduced in 1994: customers can now choose their long-distance provider. Within months, six new providers had entered the market, and the price of long-distance calling had dropped by half. Similar interconnection problems can arise in the electric power industry when generators supply customers through common-carrier transmission lines. This is an issue that Argentina, among others, has had to grapple with in the wake of privatization.

A second reason for improved regulation is that competition may not suffice to insure private investors against "regulatory risk": the danger that decisions by regulators or other public agencies will impose new and costly demands some time down the line. A utility's assets are unique to its business, and nonredeployable in other uses. This means that utilities will be willing to operate as long as they can recover their working costs. That, in turn, makes them peculiarly vulnerable to administrative expropriation—as when, for example, regulators set prices below long-run average cost. Consequently, countries without a track record of respecting property rights may fail to attract private investors into utilities, regardless of any commitment to competition in utility markets. As the next sections show, a well-designed mechanism that commits the regulator to a clearly defined course of action can offer the reassurance that potential investors need.

THE ENVIRONMENT: BALANCING SCIENCE, ECONOMICS, AND CITIZEN PRESSURE. Economists have long recognized pollution to be a negative externality. Without some form of regulatory protection, the environment can become an innocent victim of bad business practices. Buyers seek goods that are attractively priced, and producers seek ways of providing these goods at lower cost to themselves than their competitors can provide them. Unless there is some countervailing incentive, the temptation to cut corners by producing in a cheaper but environmentally "dirtier" way can be great.

Even countries with strong institutions find environmental regulation immensely challenging. Noxious fumes, poisoned water, earsplitting noise—and their consequences—are easy to spot. But the costs of many other forms of environmental damage are diffuse, and may be invisible even to those closest to the source of pollution, who may suffer serious long-term effects. Polluting emissions can also be tricky to measure. And the environmental consequences may depend heavily on the demographic and ecological features of the surrounding area.

A further complication is that the political incentives of community, business, and political stakeholders can foster ambiguity and negotiated outcomes rather than predictable and consistent implementation. Poor communities daily confront a dismal bargain, borrowing immediate survival against long-term environmental degradation. Private firms weigh the predictable costs and the benefits of complying with well-defined environmental regulations against the prospect of cutting costs by avoiding regulation altogether. Consequently, politicians may often conclude that environmental inaction (perhaps veiled behind the appearance of activism) is the politically expedient course.

In this climate of ambiguity, as later sections will show, purely technocratic approaches to environmental regulation have little hope of success. Especially in developing countries where the institutional foundations for regulation are weak, the potential for successfully containing the environmental hazards of unfettered private markets may be greater with approaches that rely at least as much on public information and citizen participation as on formal rules.

Where capability is strong, regulation can raise credibility and efficiency

So how should states respond to continually changing, and often conflicting, regulatory demands? Three principles are key. First, different ways of regulating have different costs and benefits, which countries should assess explicitly before proceeding. Second, this assessment should also incorporate the administrative dimension: some forms of regulation are intensive in their requirements for information, whereas others require much less (or much more easily monitorable) information; likewise, some regulatory approaches depend on command-and-control, others more on market-like mechanisms. In general, information-light and market-like approaches are easier to implement, and often at least as efficient. Third, states differ markedly both in their institutional capabilities and in the structure of their economies. Their approaches to regulation should reflect these differences.

We begin to show how these principles can be applied in practice by considering some "best-case" scenarios: the range of regulatory options for banking, utilities, and the environment that only work well with strong institutions. These institution-intensive approaches combine three central elements (Table 4.2):

- Relying on public administrators to manage complex technical problems
- Giving regulators considerable flexibility to respond to changing circumstances
- Using an array of checks and balances to restrain arbitrary behavior by regulatory agencies and build their credibility.

BANK SUPERVISION. Banking sector regulation around the world tends to be institution intensive. Later sections

Table 4.2 The variety of regulatory experience

	Utilities regulation	Environmental regulation	Financial regulation
Institution-intensive options	Price-cap regulation, with the regulator setting the price adjustment factor Regulation by independent commission, with public hearings	Precise rules (command-and-control or, preferably, incentive based) established by the regulatory agency or legislature	Detailed regulation monitored by competent, impartial supervisory authorities (possibly including some deposit insurance)
Institution-light options	Regulation based on simple rules, embodied in transaction-specific legal agreements and enforceable domestically or through an international mechanism	Bottom-up regulatory approaches: public information, local initiatives to strengthen citizens' voice, and initiatives by local authorities	Incentives structured so that bankers and depositors have a substantial stake in maintaining bank solvency

discuss some new ideas for maintaining the solvency of banks where supervisory agencies are weak. In many countries, however, formal supervision remains a vital bulwark. The idea behind it is that well-designed regulation, monitored and enforced by competent supervisory authorities, can overcome the information asymmetries inherent in banking, and detect—or at least contain—potentially ruinous banking crises (Box 4.3). Key elements of such systems include:

- *Capital adequacy and entry criteria.* Minimum capital requirements impose discipline on banks by ensuring

that their owners have something to lose in the event of failure. Authorities should also be required to consider the qualifications and track record of proposed owners and managers.
- *Restraints on insider lending.* Restrictions on lending to bank insiders can cut down on fraudulent loans. Similarly, many countries also limit a bank's lending to a single client (commonly to a maximum of 15 to 25 percent of the bank's capital); this prevents any one client from becoming "too big to fail," prompting the bank to make unsound loans solely to keep that client afloat.

Box 4.3 How government supervision averted financial disaster in Malaysia

In 1985 a sudden fall in world commodity prices reversed Malaysia's decade-long boom. The Malaysian stock index, which had surged from 100 in 1977 to 427 in early 1984, fell below 200 by early 1986; the value of prime commercial property in Kuala Lumpur fell by even more. Banks, which had moved heavily into real estate lending in the boom years, faced the specter of rising nonperforming loans and doubtful debts.

Because Malaysia had maintained a fairly high degree of banking supervision, provisioning for nonperforming loans rose rapidly: from 3.5 percent of total lending in 1984 to 14.5 percent by 1988. Even so, supervisory inspections in 1985 identified three commercial banks whose solvency was threatened by problem portfolios (but whose management was reluctant to acknowledge the full scope of the problem). Additionally, twenty-four nonbank deposit-taking cooperatives—with over 522,000 depositors and about $1.5

billion in assets, but subject to much less supervision than the commercial banks—were in severe distress.

Bank supervisors at Bank Negara, Malaysia's central bank, devised a series of complex rescue packages for the three ailing commercial banks and the twenty-four cooperatives. All told, losses as a result of the banking crisis amounted to 4.7 percent of Malaysia's 1986 gross national product (GNP).

Malaysia's experience underscores the value of good supervision. Losses in the tightly supervised banking sector amounted to only 2.4 percent of deposits—far less than the 40 percent of deposits lost in the lightly supervised nonbank cooperatives. And macroeconomic disaster was averted. The economy recovered in 1987, and stock and property prices and bank balance sheets recovered with it. Prompt action had made it possible to identify and address problems early, while disciplined rescue was still affordable.

- *Rules governing asset classification.* Requiring that banks classify the quality and risks of their loan portfolio according to specific criteria, and define and identify nonperforming loans, can provide early warning of problems.
- *Audit requirements.* Minimum auditing standards and disclosure requirements can make reliable and timely information available to bank depositors, investors, and creditors.

Building a robust system of prudential regulation and supervision is administratively demanding. It means having reasonably reliable accounting and auditing information on the financial health of a bank's borrowers. And it means having a sufficient number of supervisors, not only skilled enough to do their job but politically independent enough to do it impartially.

Many countries have relied exclusively on prudential regulation and supervision to undergird their banking sec-

tors, without having these prerequisites in place. The consequences have often been disastrous. A recent World Bank study identified over 100 major episodes of bank insolvency in ninety developing and transition economies from the late 1970s to 1994. In twenty-three of the thirty countries for which data were available, the direct losses sustained by governments in these episodes exceeded 3 percent of GDP (Figure 4.1). In absolute terms, losses were largest in the industrial countries: official estimates put nonperforming loans in Japan in 1995 at about $400 billion; the cost of cleaning up the 1980s U.S. savings and loan debacle came to $180 billion. But in relative terms the largest losses were in Latin America: Argentina's losses in the early 1980s amounted to more than half of its GDP, and Chile's exceeded 40 percent. Later sections examine some ways to guard against bank failure that are not so heavily dependent on formal supervision.

PRICE CAPS FOR REGULATING UTILITIES. The use of price caps in utility regulation illustrates both the scope of

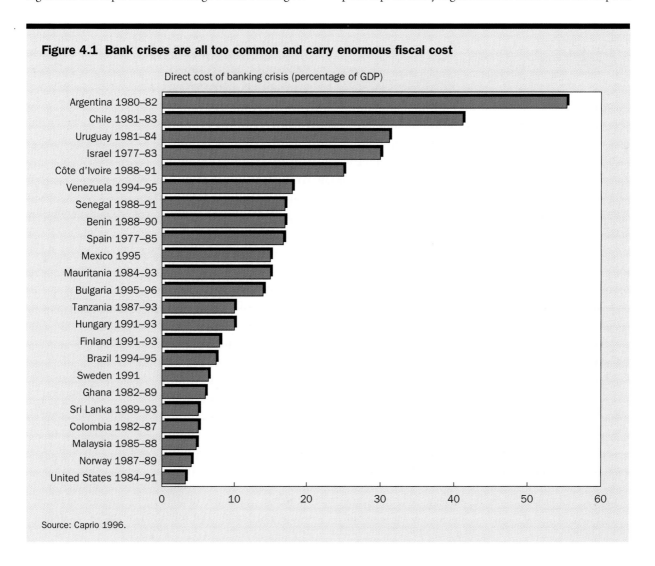

Figure 4.1 Bank crises are all too common and carry enormous fiscal cost

Direct cost of banking crisis (percentage of GDP)

Source: Caprio 1996.

authority of an independent regulator and the role of institutional checks on arbitrary action. Price-cap regulation gives the utility an incentive to be efficient and can encourage innovation, but it rests substantial discretionary power with the regulator. In the United Kingdom, which pioneered price-cap regulation, regulators impose an overall ceiling on utility prices, based on the annual rate of inflation minus an adjustment factor. The regulators decide the level of the adjustment factor, which they can change at defined (usually five-year) intervals.

The U.K. regulators are constrained by carefully designed checks and balances: any decisions that the utility opposes must be cleared by both the Monopolies and Mergers Commission and the Secretary of State for Trade and Industry. These checks have been strong enough to permit a highly flexible approach to regulation while still attracting substantial private investment. If countries with weaker checks and balances sought to adopt this type of regulation, private investors might reasonably expect the adjustment factor to increase dramatically at the first renewal of the price cap. Consequently, investors either would not invest or would demand very high rates of return to ensure a quick payback.

INSTITUTION-INTENSIVE APPROACHES TO ENVIRONMENTAL REGULATION. A central challenge for environmental regulation has always been finding ways to combine technical expertise with political legitimacy, to avoid the sense that scientists and technocrats are making decisions without regard for community or broader public concerns. In industrial countries, strong institutions have been the key to striking this balance. In France, Germany, and the United Kingdom, for example, elected legislators delegate the details of policy to environmental authorities, who consult with affected parties and respond to direct political pressure. Decisions by the U.S. Environmental Protection Agency are, like many other executive agency decisions, legally binding only if the public is given advance notice of rule changes and interested parties are able to make formal comments. The Dutch government provides more than half the funding for thirty to forty environmental NGOs and routinely consults them and other affected parties when preparing environmental legislation.

Viewed through the narrow lens of economic efficiency, even these mechanisms have produced imperfect outcomes. Both Germany and the United States, for example, have been strikingly successful in reducing emissions of some important pollutants. Yet partly because of the need to be seen as responsive to citizen concerns, both countries continue to rely overwhelmingly on command-and-control approaches to environmental regulation, even where market- and incentive-based regulation could achieve similar gains at much lower cost.

The shortcomings of top-down environmental regulation have been even more obvious in developing countries, many of which responded to the surge of interest in environmental issues by establishing new regulatory agencies modeled on this approach. Poland's regulatory agency, for example, although technically competent, found it had limited leverage in negotiations with plant managers in communities that were heavily dependent on one or a few large enterprises, which funded many community services. Chile's highly regarded environmental agency has spent four years trying, and failing, to implement a system of tradable permits for industrial emissions, because of difficulties in setting and later measuring baseline emissions.

The regulatory "fit" when institutions are weak
Countries with weaker institutions face a much greater risk that relying on administrators' skill and discretion will result in a mass of unpredictable and inconsistent regulation. The challenge for financial and environmental regulation in such countries is to prevent costly opportunism by private actors—be it banking fraud or pollution—when the regulatory agencies' authority cannot be relied upon. With regard to utilities, the trick will be to convince potential investors that regulators will not engage in arbitrary and expensive rule changes. Table 4.2 summarized some of the regulatory options available in such cases, each of which is discussed below.

FOSTERING INCENTIVES FOR PRUDENT BANKING. The incentives and interests of bank owners, managers, and depositors can themselves be a vital complement to supervision if they are aligned to be compatible with prudent banking. The history of banking offers examples of some unusually sophisticated self-enforcing arrangements for winning credibility. More recently, the World Bank and the European Bank for Reconstruction and Development collaborated on a project in Russia designed to influence banks' incentives: banks were chosen to on-lend funds provided they agreed to submit to annual audits by international accounting firms and to adhere to prudential norms.

Using regulation to raise the stakes for bankers is another institution-light way to protect the health of the banking system. It is less expensive to monitor the net worth of a bank than to monitor each of its transactions. A bank that has adequate net worth will have the right incentive to behave prudently. The following measures can all help raise net worth, and hence the cost of bank failure to bankers:

■ Very strict capital requirements on banks: not the modest 8 percent of deposits recommended by the Basel Committee for industrial countries, but 20 percent or more

- Tough restrictions on entry, in part to raise the franchise value of a banking license for incumbents and thereby strengthen the incentive to stay in business
- Ceilings on interest rates for deposits, not only to keep banks in business but also to create powerful incentives for banks to extend branch networks, so as to boost total deposits and accelerate financial deepening.

Another option that builds on prudential incentives is punitive contingent liability for bank owners, directors, and managers in the event of bank failure. Before the mid-1930s, U.S. authorities routinely imposed double liabilities on the shareholders of failed banks. Perhaps in part as a consequence, some 4,500 voluntary bank closures occurred between 1863 and 1928, but only 650 bank liquidations. New Zealand today imposes stringent requirements on banks for transparent reporting, coupled with tough sanctions on bank managers who violate them.

COMMITMENT MECHANISMS TO ATTRACT PRIVATE UTILITY INVESTORS. The Jamaican telecommunications industry vividly shows how private investment can affect the interplay between institutional capability and regulatory roles (Box 4.4). There the government was able to use regulatory commitment mechanisms capable of attracting

sustained private investment, but only at the cost of limiting flexibility. Since independence the industry has been on a regulatory roller coaster, thriving when the country was willing to forgo flexibility, but lagging behind when the mood shifted in favor of greater discretion.

Unlike Jamaica, the Philippines has until recently been unable to put in place a regulatory commitment mechanism capable of convincing private investors that the rules of the game would endure beyond the term of the current president. Consequently, from the late 1950s until the early 1990s the country's private telecommunications utility rode a political investment cycle. Investment was high immediately following the inauguration of a government aligned with the group controlling the utility, but tailed off in that government's later years, and stagnated in periods when relations with those in power were more distant. In the electric power industry, the government resolved the problem of commitment by agreeing on rigid legal "take-or-pay" agreements with private investors, sometimes enforceable offshore. Another option is to use third-party guarantees—such as those offered by the World Bank Group—to protect private investors and lenders against noncommercial risks, including the risk of administrative expropriation.

Box 4.4 Telecommunications regulation in Jamaica

During much of the colonial period and in the years immediately following independence, the terms under which Jamaica's largest telecommunications utility operated were laid out in a legally binding, precisely specified, forty-year license contract. Then as now, the ultimate court of appeal for Jamaica's independent judiciary was the Privy Council in the United Kingdom. This system was adequate to ensure steady growth of telecommunications services, and the number of subscribers tripled between 1950 and 1962. Yet a newly independent Jamaica chafed under the apparent restrictiveness of a concession arrangement that afforded virtually no opportunity for democratic participation. Consequently, in 1966 the country established the Jamaica Public Utility Commission. Modeled on the U.S. system, the commission held regular public hearings and was afforded broad scope to base its regulatory decisions on inputs from a wide variety of stakeholders.

However, Jamaica lacked the other institutions needed to make such a system workable. Whereas the U.S. system has a variety of constraints on regulatory discretion (including well-developed rules of administrative process and constitutional protections on property), Jamaica had virtually no checks and balances on

commission decisions. The result was that price controls became progressively more punitive—to the point that in 1975 Jamaica's largest private telecommunications operator was relieved to sell its assets to the government. In 1987, after a decade of underinvestment, Jamaica reprivatized its telecommunications utility, this time using a precisely specified, legally binding license contract similar to those used prior to 1965. In the next three years, average annual investment was more than three times what it had been over the previous fifteen.

Private investment came at a cost, however. To maintain long-standing (and politically difficult to eliminate) cross-subsidies between local and long-distance services, upon privatization Jamaica awarded a single telecommunications provider a twenty-five-year concession to operate the entire system. Revenues from the highly profitable long-distance network were used to extend the unprofitable local fixed-link network. Debate continues on whether, even within its political constraints, Jamaica could have retained room for competition in some value added services, thereby preserving at least a modicum of pressure for innovation and productivity improvements in an era of rapid global technological change.

COMMUNITY PRESSURE TO HELP PROTECT THE ENVIRONMENT. In settings where institutions are weak, public information and community pressure can be powerful spurs to ever more credible and efficient environmental regulation.

Experiments with transparent, information-intensive initiatives can help moderate industrial pollution even when enforceable formal rules are lacking. In Indonesia, for example, a largely voluntary Clean Rivers program, launched in 1989, had reduced total discharges of the 100 participating plants by more than a third by 1994. A program announced in mid-1995 to set, and publicize, environmental ratings for factories also seems to have induced many poorly rated factories to improve their performance. In both programs the secret to success was the reputation effect of making public to business peers, communities, and consumers the extent to which individual firms were good environmental citizens.

Environmental programs built entirely around public information have obvious limits. Nearly half the firms participating in the Clean Rivers program did not reduce the intensity of their polluting activities. Information-driven programs do help signal where the most severe problems are to be found, but often additional measures are necessary to get heavily polluting firms to clean up. And clearly, as countries develop they will need to move toward more institutionalized approaches that integrate community pressures with more formalized mechanisms for enforcing compliance.

In a pattern seen throughout the world, initiatives from the bottom up can set the stage for formal action at the national level. In the first two decades after World War II Japan rushed headlong into industrialization, with little concern for the environmental impact. At the national level this period of neglect ended in 1967, with the landmark Basic Law for Environmental Pollution Control. But well before then, grassroots initiatives in many localities had set in motion sustained environmental reform (Box 4.5).

Lessons: Clarifying regulatory options

The reality of imperfect markets brings regulation onto the development policy agenda. At the same time, however, the reality of imperfect government cautions against hasty enactment of institution-intensive regulatory systems in settings where institutions are weak. The key to success is to focus the regulatory agenda and adapt the available regulatory tools to fit the country's institutional capability. Two questions can help guide countries in the search for better regulation.

Are formal rules necessary to correct the market imperfections? Regulation's mixed record suggests that the use of formal rules to regulate markets is better viewed as a complement to other measures (or even as a last resort)

Box 4.5 Environmental activism in Yokohama, Japan

In 1960 local medical associations in Yokohama began to petition against oil refinery emissions and the health damages they caused. Shortly thereafter the municipal government, which had been dragging its feet on environmental issues, was ousted in elections by a reformist mayor who pledged to implement pollution prevention policies. A flurry of activity followed, punctuated by the establishment of a new pollution control unit within city government (which by the end of 1964 had a staff of ten), a residents' environmental organization, and a joint advisory group composed of community representatives, academics, and business experts.

Although the city had no legal authority to impose controls on pollution, by December 1964 it had entered into a formal, voluntary agreement with a new coal-fired power plant to drastically reduce emissions. This agreement offered a precedent for subsequent voluntary agreements with other new and existing large factories, which reduced emissions to just 20 percent of their earlier projected levels. Over the next two decades Yokohama progressively increased the stringency of these voluntary agreements—and consistently maintained higher environmental control standards than did Japan's national government (which itself was continually raising its standards).

---

than as an automatic response to problems. Moreover, countries' experiences with financial, utility, and environmental regulation show how competition, voice, and self-regulation can achieve social objectives once thought to require rule-based solutions.

Does the country have the institutional and political underpinnings necessary for formal rules to serve as a basis for credible regulatory commitments? On the political front, the relevant question is whether the country has the political will to follow through on what it enacts. On the institutional front, a critical issue is whether the country has an independent judiciary, with a reputation for impartiality, whose decisions are enforced. If not, other commitment mechanisms (sometimes extraterritorial) may be needed. In countries where political coalitions capable of amending rules are difficult to stitch together, legislation may suffice; in other countries it may be desirable to embed formal rules in binding legal agreements with individual firms.

If formal rules are called for, these must be workable not just in theory but in practice. In an ideal world flexible rules are preferable to rigid ones. But what constitutes a good regulatory "fit" in the real world may bear little relation to ideal conceptions of efficiency. In countries that lack appropriate checks and balances, flexibility may have to be sacrificed in the interests of certainty and predictability. What appears at first blush to be less than efficient may thus turn out to be the single best solution from the standpoint of matching the goals of regulation to the strengths and weaknesses of existing institutions.

Can state activism enhance market development?

Where externalities, lack of competition, or other market imperfections drive a wedge between private and social goals, most people accept that states may be able to enhance welfare through regulation. Much more controversial is whether states should also try to accelerate market development through more activist forms of industrial policy. The theoretical case for industrial policy rests on the proposition that the information and coordination problems identified above can be pervasive—more so in developing economies—and can go beyond those addressed by well-functioning institutions to protect property rights. In essence the argument centers on the fact that, in underdeveloped markets with few participants, learning can be extremely expensive. Information, more readily available in industrial countries, here becomes a zealously guarded secret, impeding coordination and market development more generally.

In theory, governments in such economies can act as brokers of information and facilitators of mutual learning and collaboration, and thereby play a market-enhancing role in support of industrial development. But whether governments can play this role in practice will depend, as ever, on their institutional capability. Even aggressive proponents recognize that activism can enhance markets only if three critical background conditions are in place.

First, and perhaps most important, companies and officials need to be working on a basis of mutual trust. Firms need to be confident, not only that additional coordination has merit, but that the government and the other firms involved will make good on their commitments. The participants also need confidence that a given set of arrangements will be flexible enough to adapt to changing circumstances. Ordinarily this will mean a credible government commitment to involve the private sector in implementation.

Second, initiatives to promote industrial development must be kept honest through competitive market pressures. Competition can come from other domestic firms or from imports, or take place in export markets. Unless firms are systematically challenged by one or more of these

forms of competition, they will have little incentive to use resources efficiently or to innovate, productivity will not improve, and industrial expansion will not be sustained.

Third, a country's strategy for industrial development has to be guided by its evolving comparative advantage— by its relative abundance of natural resources, skilled and unskilled labor, and capital for investment. Some proponents of activist measures have favored efforts to nurture a nascent comparative advantage by encouraging firms to risk more on a new market than they might otherwise have been willing to invest. Very few, however, would support wholesale leapfrogging: low-income countries, say, seeking to subsidize investments in highly technology-intensive activities. And there is broad agreement that high levels of protection to promote infant industries, without compensating pressures to encourage efficiency, can be fatal to a country's chances of achieving sustainable industrial development.

Industrial policy in practice

The many and varied approaches to activist industrial policy can be grouped under three broad headings: investment coordination, network thickening, and picking winners. In both the first two approaches the government attempts to enhance market signals and private activity— although the institutional demands of investment coordination are much greater than those of network thickening. The third approach involves government seeking to supersede the market altogether.

INVESTMENT COORDINATION INITIATIVES. The classic, "big push" rationale for government activism was that investment in an underdeveloped country posed a huge collective action problem. With markets undeveloped, firms could not perceive the demand for more and better products that the very act of producing them would create. Thus, it was argued, countries could benefit from coordinating such investments, which are mutually beneficial to firms but which they are unlikely to undertake by themselves. Postwar Japan's development of its steel, coal, machinery, and shipbuilding industries illustrates this rationale for intervention, as well as the stringent institutional prerequisites for success (Box 4.6):

- A domestic private sector capable of efficiently managing complex, large-scale projects
- A private sector willing to cooperate with government in pursuit of the shared goal of competitive industrial development
- Strong technical capabilities in public agencies for evaluating private analyses of investment options and, on occasion, generating independent industrial analyses
- Sufficient mutual credibility to enable each party to base its investment decisions on the other's commit-

---

Box 4.6 Japan's postwar big push in metals industries

A coordinated restructuring of the machinery, steel, shipbuilding, and coal industries contributed greatly to Japan's economic recovery after World War II. Machinery companies identified the high cost of steel as a major impediment to penetrating export markets. Steel companies, in turn, identified the high cost of coal as a principal reason for high steel prices. High coal prices were a consequence of continued mining from expensive Japanese mines and the high cost of shipping imported coal to Japan.

Building on institutional arrangements nurtured during wartime, in 1949 Japan's Ministry of International Trade and Industry (MITI) put in place a joint public-private deliberative structure, the Council for Industrial Rationalization. Composed of representatives of industrial associations, leading enterprises from each industry, and public officials, the council included twenty-nine sectoral branches and two central branches. Three of the council's branches—iron and steel, coal, and coordination—worked closely together and agreed on the following commitments:

- The steel and coordination branches identified the price of coal that would make it possible to produce export steel competitively.

- The coal industry committed itself to invest 40 billion yen to rationalize production from domestic mines, provided the steel firms agreed to purchase coal from them afterward at the new prices, which would be 18 percent below prevailing levels.
- The steel and coal industries agreed on an overall target price that steel firms would pay for coal, to be achieved by mixing domestic purchases and imports.
- The steel industry committed itself to invest 42 billion yen to upgrade its facilities. With this investment, and lower coal prices, it would be able to export steel at competitive prices.
- In return for lower steel prices, the machinery and shipbuilding industries were in a position to embark on large, export-oriented investment programs. These commitments provided the domestic market that the steel industry needed to embark on its investment program, and confidence that the shipping cost of imported coal would decline.

Once the Japan Development Bank (after careful technical analysis, and in consultation with both MITI and the Bank of Japan) agreed to participate in these projects, providing financing at only moderately subsidized interest rates, Japan's largest banks took the lead in mobilizing the investment funds.

---

ments, and to adapt its actions in response to changing circumstances without undermining the overall commitment to collaborate.

Pursuing this style of investment coordination presupposes levels of public and private institutional capability that are beyond the reach of most developing countries. The Philippine experience of the late 1970s and 1980s shows what can happen when the ambitions of policy do not match up to institutional reality, and efforts to coordinate investment are pursued where government is swayed by powerful private interests.

Driven in part by the desire to create new business opportunities for domestic allies, in 1979 the Philippine government announced a new $5 billion program of "major industrial projects," all in heavy, capital-intensive industries. Within a year of the announcement the government, responding to pressure from critics, agreed to subject the projects to another round of economic and financial scrutiny. Soon thereafter the political and finan-

cial turmoil surrounding the fall of President Ferdinand Marcos' regime intervened. By late 1987 five of the eleven initial projects, accounting for almost $4 billion of the $5 billion, had been shelved as infeasible. A sixth project had been abandoned because its lack of economic potential became apparent. A fertilizer plant, completed at a cost of $550 million, was suffering losses that were being shouldered by government. Only four projects, accounting for just $800 million, were operating profitably.

NETWORK-THICKENING INITIATIVES. Activist initiatives need not be large in scale—imposing commensurably large demands on public and private institutional capabilities—or solely devoted to increasing investment. They can also aim to strengthen the private-to-private networks that flourish in mature market systems. Domestic, regional, and international networks create numerous sources of learning and opportunity for firms: specialized buyers open up new market niches and offer information on product standards, equipment providers transfer technological know-how, input suppliers help with product and process innovations, and competitors are a rich source of new ideas. Often, clusters of firms, buyers, equipment suppliers, input and service providers, industry associations, design centers, and other specialized cooperative organizations come together in the same geographic region.

Countries whose markets are underdeveloped may need some catalyst, public or private, to set this cumulative process of market thickening and network development in motion. There are three leading examples.

The first is special support for exports. Participating in export markets brings firms into contact with international best practice and fosters learning and productivity growth. It can also be a useful measure of the effectiveness of government efforts at industrial promotion. Many countries have directed credit in favor of exporters and set up export promotion organizations. With few exceptions, most of them in East Asia, these bodies became expensive white elephants. Other export support measures have also been tried, with mixed results. World Trade Organization rules may well rule out future experiments along these lines.

A second type of effort focuses on strengthening local infrastructure: physical, human, and institutional. The history of Korea's once-lagging Cholla region illustrates the impact local infrastructure can have. In 1983 this southern region opened its first large-scale industrial estate. Its success set in motion a cumulative process of learning by local authorities about how to plan, finance, build, and operate such estates—three more followed. It also helped catalyze a transformation of the business environment, from one bogged down by red tape and other bureaucratic obstacles to one of close cooperation and coordination between the local government and the private sector. By 1991 Cholla accounted for 15 percent of industrial land in Korea, up from 9 percent in 1978, and the rate of growth of regional manufacturing output was above the national average.

Third, and increasingly popular, are public-private partnerships, with the public partners drawn from either local or regional governments. These can take a variety of forms, including:

- *Initiatives directed at individual firms or groups of firms.* Sometimes these are focused events, such as joint participation in a trade fair. Others are aimed at achieving a broader shift in the business culture to favor increased cooperation. A promising approach involves giving matching grants to firms, typically on a 50-50 cost-sharing basis, to help penetrate new markets and upgrade technologies. Easy to implement, with management delegated to private contractors, and demand-driven, with participating firms paying for half of any initiative, such programs are now under way in coun-

tries as diverse as Argentina, India, Jamaica, Mauritius, Uganda, and Zimbabwe.
- *Using public procurement to foster competitive private sector development.* In Brazil's state of Ceará an innovative cost- and quality-driven procurement program worked through associations of small producers to transform the economy of the town of São João do Arauru. Before the program the town had four sawmills with twelve employees. Five years later forty-two sawmills employed about 350 workers; nearly 1,000 of the town's 9,000 inhabitants were directly or indirectly employed in the woodworking industry; and 70 percent of output was going to the private sector.

SUPERSEDING MARKETS. Sometimes information and coordination problems are so severe—markets so underdeveloped, and private agents so lacking in resources and experience—that market-enhancing initiatives are unlikely to yield any response. As a way of kickstarting industrial growth, states have been tempted to supplant market judgments with information and judgments generated in the public sector. These efforts rarely work, although the success of some ventures by Korea's *chaebol* (interlinked business groups), made at the initiative of government, suggests that the quest to pick winners is not inevitably a fool's errand.

What distinguished Korea's success from others' failures was that these initiatives were channeled through the private sector, whereas most such efforts (including some in Korea) have been implemented by state enterprises. When state firms are used as implementing agencies, the opportunities for venality—or fanciful romanticism—are virtually limitless. A number of countries have subsidized money-losing state enterprises, to the severe detriment of fiscal performance. The generally sorry experience with investment in state enterprises has convincingly demonstrated that the production of tradable products is best left exclusively to private firms.

Walking the industrial policy tightrope
These experiences highlight why the debate over industrial policy has been unusually heated: industrial policy is combustible. Economic theory and evidence suggest that the possibility of successful, market-enhancing activism cannot be dismissed out of hand. But institutional theory and evidence suggest that, implemented badly, activist industrial policy can be a recipe for disaster. How, then, might countries proceed?

Taken together, the economic and institutional perspectives suggest drawing a sharp distinction between initiatives that require only a light touch from government (for example, some network-thickening initiatives) and initiatives that require high-intensity government support (such as coordinating investment or picking winners). High-intensity initiatives should be approached cautiously, or not at all, unless countries have unusually strong institutional capability: strong administrative capability, commitment mechanisms that credibly restrain arbitrary government action, the ability to respond flexibly to surprises, a competitive business environment, and a track record of public-private partnership.

By contrast, light-touch initiatives (those that are inexpensive, and supportive rather than restrictive or command-oriented) offer more flexibility. The essential institutional attribute for success is an unambiguous commitment by government to public-private partnership. When this commitment exists, when countries do not overreach their institutional capabilities, and when the business environment is reasonably supportive of private sector development, the benefits of experimentation with light-touch initiatives can be large, and the cost of failure low.

Strategic options: Focusing on the workable

In the realm of liberalization and privatization, regulation, and industrial policy—indeed, in the full range of state actions probed in this Report—there is no one-size-fits-all formula. Privatization and liberalization are the appropriate priorities for countries whose governments have been overextended. Every country must also look to build and adapt its institutions, not dismantle them. This chapter has distinguished between institution-intensive and institution-light approaches to regulation and industrial policy, stressing how the choice of approaches might appropriately vary with a country's institutional capability.

Successful institution-intensive approaches generally share two characteristics. They require strong administrative capability. And they delegate substantial discretion for policy and implementation to a public agency, embedded in a broader system of checks and balances that prevents that discretion from degenerating into arbitrariness. If institutions are strong, these state actions can contribute to economic well-being. If they are not, the evidence and analysis of this chapter suggest that such actions are likely to prove ineffective at best, and at worst a recipe for capture by powerful private interests or predation by powerful and self-interested politicians and bureaucrats.

How, then, should countries proceed if they lack the administrative and institutional wherewithal to make such approaches work? The long-run strategy, explored in Part Three, is to strengthen and build the requisite institutions. In the meantime this chapter has indicated two possible pathways toward reform. One is to focus on the essentials and take on a lighter agenda for state action. The second, which need not conflict with the first, is to experiment with tools for state action that are better aligned with the country's capability. Much remains to be learned, but this chapter has highlighted two strategies that appear to have great potential even where institutional capability is weak:

- Specify the content of policy in precise rules, and then lock in those rules using mechanisms that make it costly to reverse course: in utility regulation, for example, these might include take-or-pay contracts with independent power producers.
- Work in partnership with firms and citizens, and, where appropriate, shift the burden of implementation entirely outside government. In industrial policy this may mean fostering private-to-private collaboration rather than building a large industrial bureaucracy. In financial regulation it means giving bankers an incentive to operate prudently, rather than just building up supervisory capability. And in environmental regulation it means using information to encourage citizen initiatives, rather than promulgating unenforceable rules from the top down.

The policies that rely on these approaches may not be first-best policies in a textbook sense. But as state capability grows, countries can switch to more flexible tools, capable of squeezing out further efficiency gains. Throughout, states must maintain the confidence of firms and citizens that flexibility will not be accompanied by arbitrary behavior—else the foundation for development crumbles.

PART THREE

PARTS ONE AND TWO HAVE UNDERSCORED THAT THE STATE MAKES A VITAL CON-tribution to economic development when its role matches its institutional capa-bility. But capability is not destiny. It can and must be improved if governments are to promote further improvements in economic and social welfare. This part of the Report discusses how this can be achieved.

State capability refers to the ability of the state to undertake collective actions at least cost to society. This notion of capability encompasses the administrative or technical capacity of state officials, but it is much broader than that. It also includes the deeper, institutional mechanisms that give politicians and civil ser-vants the flexibility, rules, and restraints to enable them to act in the collective interest.

Three interrelated sets of institutional mechanisms can help create incentives that will strengthen the state's capability. These mechanisms aim to:

- Enforce rules and restraints in society as well as within the state
- Promote competitive pressures from outside and from within the state, and
- Facilitate voice and partnerships both outside and within the state.

Over the long term, sustainable institutions have been built on formal checks and balances, anchored around core state institutions such as an independent judiciary and the separation of powers. These are essential for ensuring that neither state officials nor anyone else in society is above the law.

But rule-based government is not enough. State capability will also be improved by institutional arrangements that foster partnerships with, and provide competitive pressures from, actors both outside and within the state. Partnerships with and participation in state activities by external stakeholders—businesses and civil society—can build credibility and consensus and supplement low state capability. Partnerships within the state can build commitment and loyalty on the part of government workers and reduce the costs of achieving shared goals.

The flip side of partnership is competitive pressure—from markets and civil society and within the state itself. Such pressure can improve incentives for performance and check the abuse of the state's monopoly in policymaking and service delivery. Similarly, competitive or merit-based recruitment and promotion are crucial for building a capable bureaucracy.

This part of the Report starts with a look at ways to reinvigorate state institutions, by building the foundations of an effective public sector (Chapter 5) and, more broadly, by instituting formal checks and balances and controlling corruption (Chapter 6). Chapter 7 then examines how to sharpen competitive pressure, strengthen voice, and promote partnership by bringing the state closer to the people—an important means of which is decentralization, or the shifting of power and resources to lower levels of government. Finally, Chapter 8 discusses partnerships and competitive pressures that cross the boundaries of nation-states, and how countries can cooperate in providing collective goods.

CHAPTER 5

BUILDING INSTITUTIONS FOR A CAPABLE PUBLIC SECTOR

Sire, a vast majority of civil servants are ill paid. . . . The result is that skilled and talented men shun public service. The Government of Your Majesty is then forced to recruit mediocre personnel whose sole aim is to improve their weak pecuniary situation . . . intelligent, hardworking, competent, and motivated individuals should direct Your Empire's civil service. . . . It is Your Majesty's prerogative to introduce the indispensable principle of accountability, without which all progress is retarded and work inevitably destroyed.

—From *The Political Testaments of Ali Pasha,* Grand Vizier to Ottoman Sultan Abdulaziz, about 1871 (quoted in Andic and Andic 1996)

THE SAME PROBLEMS THAT PLAGUED SULTAN ABDUL-aziz haunt today's public bureaucracies. The history of development in Europe and North America in the nineteenth century, and that of East Asia in this one, have shown the economic rewards of building an effective public sector. But examples of this kind of institution building are all too rare.

Building the institutions for a capable public sector is essential to enhancing state effectiveness, but also immensely difficult. Once poor systems are in place, they can be very difficult to dislodge. Strong interests develop in maintaining the status quo, however inefficient or unfair. And those who lose out from present arrangements may be unable to bring effective pressure to bear for change. Even when the incentives are there to improve public sector performance, formidable information and capacity constraints often thwart the attempt.

How can governments with ineffective public institutions begin to put things right? The complex problems involved in building and managing a public bureaucracy do not lend themselves to clear, unambiguous solutions. But this chapter outlines some institutional building blocks of an effective public sector and discusses promising options for putting these in place. This focus on institutions is very different from the traditional approach of technical assistance, which emphasizes equipment and skills and administrative or technical capacity. The emphasis here is on the incentive framework guiding *behavior*—what government agencies and officials do and how they perform. Few countries consciously set out to encourage bureaucratic corruption and inefficiency. But the mere existence of formal rules forbidding bribes, say, or the abuse of patronage will rarely be enough to root these things out. What matters is whether the actual rules and incentive mechanisms embedded in the system can translate the fine words into reality.

The foundations of an effective public sector

Evidence across a range of countries has shown that well-functioning bureaucracies can promote growth and reduce poverty (Chapter 2). They can provide sound policy inputs and deliver critical public goods and services at least cost. During the nineteenth century most industrializing states modernized their public administrations. Early leaders included France, Prussia, and the United Kingdom. The success of the British civil service reforms in the last century provides an early example of the importance of nurturing effective, rule-based bureaucracies. As Box 5.1 describes, these reforms heralded the careful cultivation of a professional meritocracy, which helped pave the way for a half-century of English dominance over international commerce.

More recently, some East Asian economies have established and nurtured the foundations of capable bureaucracies. Many low-income countries, however, have been

Box 5.1 Laying bureaucratic foundations: The Northcote-Trevelyan reforms in the United Kingdom

Until the early nineteenth century the affairs of the state in the United Kingdom were administered by public officials who owed their positions to political patronage and influence. There was no common system of pay, bribes augmented official salaries, and officeholders, who viewed their positions as property that could be sold, often engaged and paid their own staff. Although the system did not rule out advance by individual ability, it was not a basis for sound administration.

As the Victorian era progressed, however, the United Kingdom underwent a period of intense reform driven by social and economic change and the demands of an expanding, educated middle class. Universities, the armed forces, the judiciary, and central and local bureaucracies were all reformed.

The blueprint for civil service reform was the Northcote-Trevelyan Report of 1854, which advocated the creation of a modern bureaucracy based on a career civil service. Drawing on ideas advanced for the Indian civil service by Thomas Macaulay, Sir Stafford Northcote and Sir Charles Trevelyan proposed divid-

ing the government's work into two classes—intellectual (policy and administration) and mechanical (clerical)—and creating a career civil service to carry it out. Staff capable of performing the intellectual work would be recruited from the newly reformed universities; the best talent would be selected through tough competitive examinations supervised by a board of civil service commissioners.

Opposition was strong. Although a civil service commission was established in 1855, many government departments continued recruiting in their accustomed way until 1870, when patronage was abolished and the two grades were made compulsory for all departments. The Northcote-Trevelyan reforms were followed by reforms in the armed forces, the judiciary, and, later, municipal government. There were also extensive changes in the rules and restraints governing policy formation and implementation. By the end of the nineteenth century the United Kingdom had laid the foundations of a modern government and formally institutionalized the values of honesty, economy, and political neutrality.

unable to create even the most rudimentary underpinnings of a rule-based civil service. Their formal systems often resemble those of industrial countries on paper. But in practice informality remains the norm. Merit-based personnel rules are circumvented, and staff are recruited or promoted on the basis of patronage and clientelism; budgets are unrealistic and often set aside in any case by ad hoc decisions during implementation. At bottom, all these problems can be traced back to weaknesses in the underlying institutions: poor enforceability of the rule of law both within and beyond the public sector; a lack of built-in mechanisms for listening to, and forming partnerships with, firms and civil society; and a complete absence of competitive pressure in policymaking, the delivery of services, and personnel practices.

To tackle these problems at their root and lay the foundations of an effective public sector, countries need to focus on three essential building blocks:

- *Strong central capacity for formulating and coordinating policy.* This is the brains of the system. Politicians formulate visions and set goals, but for these to materialize they must be translated into strategic priorities. This requires mechanisms that lead to well-informed, disciplined, and accountable decisions. A constant challenge for all countries is to set rules that give politicians and

their expert counselors the flexibility they need to formulate policies, but embed their decisionmaking in processes that allow for inputs and oversight from stakeholders.
- *Efficient and effective delivery systems.* Here, too, reform involves setting the right balance between flexibility and accountability. For activities that are contestable (that is, where there is scope for actual or potential competition from various suppliers) and easily specified, market mechanisms and contracting out of services can often improve delivery dramatically. But for many other services there is often no substitute for delivery by the core public sector. Here giving citizens greater voice and allowing client feedback can exert pressure for better performance, but ultimately performance will depend on the loyalty of civil servants and their compliance with established rules.
- *Motivated and capable staff.* These are the lifeblood of the executive. Able and dedicated staff inject energy into the public sector. Uncommitted staff stifle it. Civil servants can be motivated to perform well through a range of mechanisms, including merit-based recruitment and promotion, adequate pay, and a strong esprit de corps.

Effective bureaucracies take decades to develop. And in seeking to build—or rebuild—the foundations of such a bureaucracy, reformers must, as always, be conscious of what they are building *on*. For example, where countries have been unable to establish credible controls over managers' use of resources, giving them greater flexibility will only encourage arbitrariness and corruption. But certain reforms can generate early payoffs even in the worst systems. These are discussed further below.

Strengthening institutions for policymaking

Politicians set goals and broad strategic directions. But sound institutional arrangements can determine whether the visions of political leaders get translated into effective policy priorities. They can make transparent the costs and benefits of competing policy proposals. And given that adequate information is inevitably in short supply, they can make sure that leaders are as well informed as possible, through processes that provide input and oversight from internal and external stakeholders. All these mechanisms will help produce better-informed decisions and raise the credibility of policymaking in general.

The rules and norms embedded in the policymaking process should be designed to curb the kind of uncoordinated political pressures that can lead to poor decisionmaking and bad outcomes. If politicians or bureaucrats pursue only their own or their constituents' immediate interests as they are voiced, the result may be collectively undesirable, even destabilizing—there is no invisible hand in statecraft, automatically shaping individual initiatives toward a common good. The aim must be to build mechanisms to discipline and coordinate the policy debate and call competing policy proposals into question. In some countries politicians have delegated macroeconomic and strategic policy coordination to capable, relatively autonomous central agencies, whose activities are guided by consultative processes that are transparent to outsiders. In others, politicians themselves collectively restrain and challenge each other in established forums where decisions are made in common. But many countries have none of these mechanisms, and their absence reveals itself in incoherent strategic policies and macroeconomic instability.

Although the precise institutional arrangements vary, effective public sectors the world over have generally been characterized by strong central capacity for macroeconomic and strategic policy formulation; by mechanisms to delegate, discipline, and debate policies among government agencies; and by institutionalized links to stakeholders outside the government, providing transparency and accountability and encouraging feedback. As discussed below, systems in many industrial countries and in much of East Asia exhibit many of these characteristics. Their absence in many developing economies is a major obstacle to building a more effective state. Policymaking

capacity in these countries tends to be weak and fragmented, with few institutionalized mechanisms for input or oversight.

Policymaking mechanisms in industrial countries
Many OECD countries have built up well-functioning policymaking mechanisms over time. At the heart of these systems are mechanisms for properly preparing policy proposals, estimating the costs of alternative proposals within a disciplined overall budget framework, ensuring their critical evaluation through consultation and debate, and reaching and recording decisions and monitoring their implementation. A vital complement to these mechanisms is effective capacity at the center of government—the Cabinet Secretariat in France, the Ministry of Finance in Japan, the Office of Management and Budget in the United States—to facilitate consultation and coordinate proposals among ministries before they are submitted.

There is always room for improvement. Australia is a good example of an industrial country that has introduced reforms explicitly aimed at making the policymaking process more transparent, competitive, and results-oriented. Several features of these reforms are of particular relevance to other countries: the emphasis on publicizing the medium-term costs of competing policies; the effort to facilitate debate and consultation on policy priorities, within hard budgets, both in the cabinet and among agencies; and the attention to results (Box 5.2).

The United States and some continental European countries have instituted other mechanisms for consultation and oversight in policymaking. Corresponding to the cabinet in a parliamentary system, congressional committees in the U.S. presidential system are the principal arena for policy debate and consultation. U.S. executive agencies, for their part, are governed by the Administrative Procedures Act of 1946, which imposes certain procedural requirements, enforceable in the courts, such as public announcement of new policies, while preserving flexibility in the substance of policymaking. This procedures-oriented approach to policy formulation allows legislators to shift the substance of policymaking to specialist agencies and other interested parties closer to the problem. This kind of decentralized mechanism uses citizen voice and the judiciary to ensure accountability, but with the inevitable side effect of slowing decisionmaking.

Many continental European countries rely on administrative law and specialized courts for judicial review of administrative actions. Citizens can challenge administrative decisions on legal grounds or for factual errors. The European Union has adopted this system for the European Court of Justice, allowing it to oversee decisions made by EU institutions.

Box 5.2   Australia's mechanisms for transparent, competitive, and results-oriented policymaking

One of the main objectives of Australia's public sector reforms has been to institute a process for disciplining and coordinating policies and exposing them to vigorous debate. Some of the challenges the Labor government faced when it came to power in the early 1980s were similar to those confronting many developing countries today: the new government had to manage both an immediate fiscal crisis and the unsustainable long-term fiscal commitments of previous policies.

To discipline policy formulation and win political support for a resetting of national strategic priorities, the new administration decided to publish estimates of future spending under existing policies. These projections painted a bleak picture of unsustainable real growth in spending requirements, underscoring the need to scale back. Once the government had published these estimates, however, it became incumbent upon the government to continue to do so, to show the continuing declines in future commitments that it had promised. Indeed, succeeding projections fell markedly, in what became called the "falling man" pattern (see figure at left). Open financial markets imposed additional discipline.

The reforms also required the government to publish a reconciliation table, showing how the projections for existing policies differed from those for the new policies. These measures helped make apparent the changes in the government's strategic priorities, as well as in the medium-term costs of new commitments. In addition, the projections made resource flows to the line ministries more predictable, since the projected figures were automatically rolled over into the actual budget if no changes in policy intervened. This helped improve decisionmaking and the operational efficiency of line agencies.

The reforms also required that line ministries proposing any new policy, or any changes in existing policy that would increase spending, also propose offsetting savings (see figure at right). This ensured that spending stayed within the resource envelope agreed to in the cabinet. The cabinet focused on changes in strategic priorities—which new policies to adopt and which existing ones to cut—to stay within macroeconomic constraints. Policy proposals were debated vigorously within the cabinet, and all affected ministries and agencies were required to submit written comments on the soundness of other agencies' proposals. This helped legitimize and build consensus on policy priorities. Finally, the reforms focused attention on results, through mandated periodic evaluation of new and existing policies and through reporting on performance and outcomes.

The results? Australia's deficit of 4 percent of GDP in 1983 became a surplus by the end of the decade. Accompanying this achievement were significant changes in the composition of public expenditures, reflecting both broad strategic shifts identified by the cabinet and changes in priorities within ministries, often identified by the line agencies themselves.

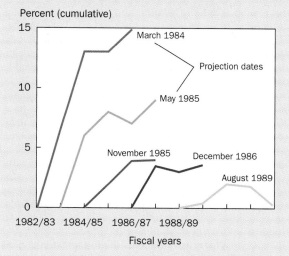

Projected growth in total spending

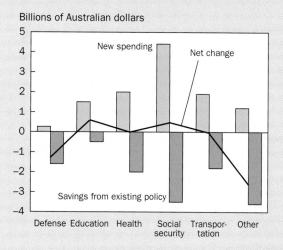

Changes by category, 1983/84 to 1992/93

Source: Adapted from Campos and Pradhan 1996; Dixon 1993.

Elite central agencies in East Asia

The successful East Asian economies have adopted a procedural approach to policymaking that shares some key aspects of systems in industrial countries. Several East Asian leaders have formulated long-term visions for their countries; examples include, in postwar Japan, the Liberal Democratic Party's declared aim to catch up with the West, and more recently, in Malaysia, Prime Minister Mahathir Mohamad's Vision 2020. They have then worked to create the institutional arrangements needed to translate their vision into a highly focused set of strategic priorities. Powerful elite central agencies have been delegated the authority to develop policies that will achieve the leaders' long-term objectives. Although relatively autonomous, these agencies' deliberations have always been embedded in processes—such as public-private councils—that provide input and oversight from private firms.

These elite agencies often play an immensely important role in setting their countries' economic course. The Ministry of International Trade and Industry (MITI) in Japan and the Economic Planning Board in the Republic of Korea are considered the prime movers behind their countries' industrial policies and use of administrative guidance. In Thailand the Ministry of Finance, the budget bureau, the central bank, and the National Economic and Social Development Board—the so-called gang of four—act in unison to cap spending and control inflation. In Indonesia the Ministry of Finance and the planning agency Bapennas have been the guardians of the purse and the brains of the civil service. These central agencies are staffed by professional and capable employees recruited on the basis of merit, often through highly competitive examinations.

The delegation of macroeconomic policy to competent and reputable technocrats has recently been a common feature in several Latin American countries as well, including Argentina, Colombia, Mexico, and Peru. The effects on performance have been noticeable. This delegated policymaking, combined with the kind of hierarchical and transparent budget procedures described in Chapter 3, was important in reducing inflation in these countries during the late 1980s and early 1990s. Chile, in particular, appears to have developed the kind of esprit de corps among senior officials that has long fostered partnerships in the Indonesian technocracy and Japan's MITI, among others. Most striking are the parallels between Chile's group of high-level advisers—the Chicago boys—and Indonesia's Berkeley mafia and Thailand's gang of four.

As already noted, although the central agencies in East Asia had considerable flexibility in policymaking, they were embedded in a larger network of deliberation councils and external think tanks. In Japan, Korea, Malaysia, Singapore, and Thailand, information about the costs of industrial policies was distributed through a range of public-private deliberation councils, which would expose costly programs to rigorous review. Such transparent and institutionalized consultation mechanisms gave those outside of government power to restrain or even veto its actions, while preserving flexibility for policymakers to adapt to changing circumstances.

Deliberation councils require substantial technical capability if they are to use the information supplied by private participants to make coherent policy. There is also the problem that such councils exclude broader segments of society from their deliberations. If a country's private sector is small, deliberation councils can all too easily degenerate into well-oiled mechanisms for unproductive rent extraction. This probably explains why African versions of deliberative councils—such as the francophone countries' experiments with economic and social councils—have generally been ineffective (with the notable exception of Botswana's). If such councils are to support sustainable development, they will need to be complemented, as they were in East Asia, by attempts to win legitimacy from society more broadly.

Weak capacity and fragmented policymaking in developing countries

Many developing countries, especially in Africa, Central America, and the Caribbean, lack the critical mass of effective capacity and internal coherence to formulate and coordinate macroeconomic and strategic policies. Central capacity is weak, stretched thinly among a handful of senior officials who must attend to numerous tasks. These strains are compounded by problems in the bureaucracy: low pay at senior levels, rampant political patronage, and an absence of meritocratic recruitment and promotion.

One especially costly consequence of weak central capacity is an inability to make budget forecasts based on sound and realistic assumptions. This undermines transparency and predictability in decisionmaking. For example, in recent years the difference between budgeted and actual recurrent expenditures has averaged more than 50 percent in Tanzania and more than 30 percent in Uganda. Transparency and coherence are also compromised by the use of extrabudgetary funds (equivalent to more than half of total federal expenditures in Nigeria, for example) and by long lags in the production of financial accounts and audits. Often decisionmakers will have little sense of the costs or outcomes of policies. Partly as a result, budgeting focuses almost exclusively on the allocation of inputs rather than the results they are intended to achieve.

In aid-dependent countries donors sometimes alleviate, but too often worsen, the problem of weak central capacity. To the extent that their policy advice supplements weak capacity at the center, they help solve the short-term problem at hand. But such advice does nothing to build long-term capacity if politicians fail to recognize the need ultimately to rely on local experts. Donors may also fragment central capacity for policy formulation, entering with ministries into bilateral deals on multiple projects without determining whether their cumulative effects are collectively sustainable or mutually consistent. In many countries public investment programs have become passive repositories of donor-driven projects, whose recurrent costs after completion continue to accumulate, contributing to an expansionary fiscal bias. Lack of coordination between the ministry of planning and the ministry of finance sometimes further impedes the integration of capital and current expenditures.

All these problems seriously erode the capacity to coordinate, challenge, and discipline decisionmaking. Guinea provides a case in point. Although the government has designated primary education, public health, and road maintenance as spending priorities, funds often end up being allocated to other areas instead. And no system exists for costing out policy proposals or subjecting them to rigorous scrutiny. An exercise to cost out Guinea's policies to meet the government's stated priorities revealed that the share of priority programs in total spending

would need to triple over the succeeding four years, implying drastic cuts in other expenditures (left panel of Figure 5.1). Moreover, the recurrent costs of donor-led investment projects were shown to be unsustainable (right panel of Figure 5.1). The same inadequacies play out across the developing world, as newly built roads fall into disrepair, and schools find themselves without textbooks and health centers without drugs.

Several initiatives have been launched to address these problems, but all are still in their early stages. The Africa Capacity Building Initiative seeks to strengthen the capacity of African governments in policy analysis through a more professional civil service, improved information systems, and enhanced external inputs from African universities and civil society more broadly. Governments and donors have also launched sectoral investment programs to coordinate donor assistance. The Agricultural Sector Investment Program in Zambia replaces 180 individual donor projects. But although they consolidate fragmented policies in a shared arena, such efforts can create coordination problems of their own as long as capacity remains weak. Malawi and Uganda are among those countries moving to the next, crucial level of reform: developing a

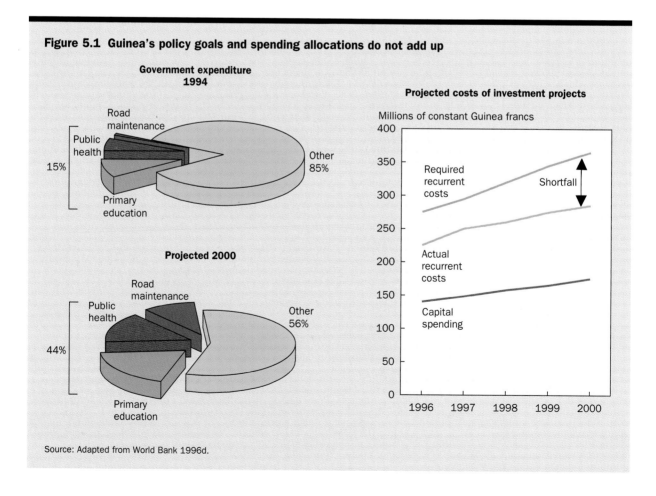

Figure 5.1 Guinea's policy goals and spending allocations do not add up

Source: Adapted from World Bank 1996d.

systematic process to set strategic priorities across sectors and within aggregate spending constraints. Colombia is instituting ex post evaluation systems to assess whether policies and programs already in place are achieving their intended outcomes.

Policy coordination in transition economies

Although the shortage of administrative expertise is not as much of a problem in the transition economies of Central and Eastern Europe and the former Soviet Union, their experience shows the equal importance of mechanisms that can channel that expertise into coherent policy. When the communist regimes in these countries collapsed, so did the centralized decisionmaking apparatus for coordinating the activities of ministries and departments. As a result, confused and overlapping responsibilities and multiple rather than collective accountability emerged—a sure-fire formula for policy disaster.

Ukraine exemplifies such problems in the extreme. Following independence in 1991, a central machinery of government was established which reflects many of the features of a former Soviet system. Decisionmaking

remains highly centralized. The Apparat of the Cabinet of Ministers has retained responsibility for policy formulation and coordination and directs the activities of central government departments. The number of central government bodies remains large (over 110), their responsibilities often overlap, and lines of accountability are unclear (Figure 5.2). The cumbersome structure makes coordination difficult, delays decisionmaking, and reduces transparency. However, efforts to reform this system are now under way following the adoption of a new constitution in July 1996.

Some Central and Eastern European countries with similar although perhaps less severe problems have initiated promising reforms of their central decisionmaking mechanisms. Poland and Hungary have both introduced reforms to streamline multiple and conflicting responsibilities and speed decisionmaking. In Georgia, streamlining has removed overlapping and conflicting positions, and the fate of draft laws is now decided in the presence of all members of the president's economic council before submission to the parliament. Such reforms have aided consultation and coordination in central government

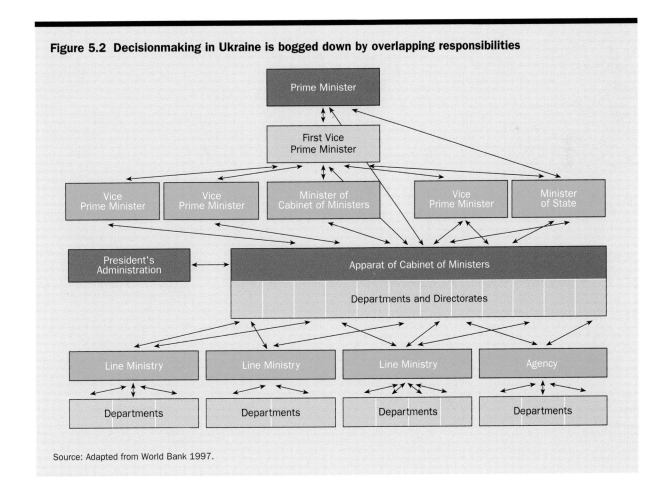

Figure 5.2 Decisionmaking in Ukraine is bogged down by overlapping responsibilities

Source: Adapted from World Bank 1997.

decisionmaking. But most countries have a long way to go to build the institutional capability needed to respond effectively to the many demands of transition.

Reforming institutions for delivery

The best-designed policy will achieve little if it is badly implemented. Poor quality, high cost, waste, fraud, and corruption have marred the delivery of services in many developing countries. More often than not, the problems can be traced back to a belief that government ought to be the dominant—if not the sole—provider.

The expansion of the state under the state-dominated development strategies outlined in Chapter 1 has provided countless opportunities for politicians to exploit their positions for political gain (Box 5.3). More broadly, governments have simply overextended themselves, with disastrous results. Examples abound of services not being delivered or being delivered badly. Power system losses in low-income countries are more than twice those in other

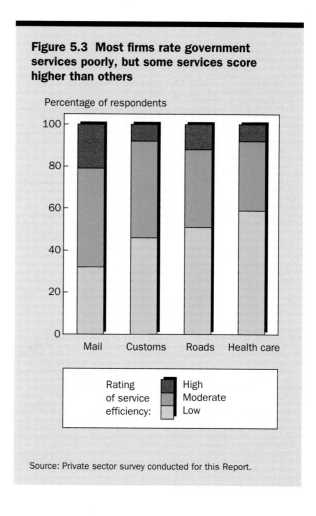

Figure 5.3 Most firms rate government services poorly, but some services score higher than others

Percentage of respondents

Rating of service efficiency: High / Moderate / Low

Source: Private sector survey conducted for this Report.

> #### Box 5.3 The mushrooming of Bangladesh's government
>
> Since independence in 1971 the government of Bangladesh has effectively doubled in size. The number of ministries increased from twenty-one to thirty-five over twenty years, and between 1990 and 1994 the number of departments and directorates went from 109 to 221. Public sector employment increased from 450,000 in 1971 to almost 1 million in 1992—a compound rate of increase of 3.6 percent a year, compared with population growth of 2.5 percent during the same period. Civil service pay has fallen considerably, especially for those at the top. The base pay of a permanent secretary (the most senior civil service position) has declined by 87 percent in real terms since 1971.
>
> New ministries, divisions, and departments were created in part to meet emerging needs such as environmental protection and women's issues. But the state has also spread its wings into commercial activities. Growth has often been stimulated by political considerations. The increase in ministries allowed new ministerial positions to be handed out to more intraparty groups—and, of course, created more lower-level jobs to be dispensed. Aside from its budgetary effects, this expansion has stretched implementation capacity, compounded coordination problems, and made regulation more intrusive. It has also created vested interests that have blocked efforts at rationalization and reform.

countries. In China nearly 1 million hectares of irrigated land has been taken out of production since 1980 because of insufficient maintenance. Only 6 percent of domestic businesspeople surveyed for this Report in fifty-eight developing economies rated government service delivery as efficient, while 36 percent rated them very inefficient. Mail delivery fared reasonably well, followed by customs and roads; health services scored the worst (Figure 5.3). These results indicate a broader pattern: the lower-rated services are delivered by government departments (as opposed to state enterprises) and produce outputs that are harder to measure and monitor.

What is needed is better management of the principal-agent relationships inherent in service delivery. In many countries delivery suffers because neither the principals (the politicians) nor the agents (the bureaucrats) live up to their side of the bargain. Politicians interfere in the day-to-day operations of public agencies; services are delivered through government departments whose managers have little operational flexibility and whose resource flows are unpredictable. Even where managers have been able to get around these rules, they have had few incentives to achieve better results. In the many countries where the public sector has assumed a monopoly role in the delivery of many services, external pressures for better performance are eliminated. And few countries have set credible restraints to hold managers accountable for their use of inputs or for the achievement of measurable outcomes.

Institutional mechanisms to improve delivery

Governments are experimenting with a range of institutional mechanisms to improve service delivery. Greater use of markets is creating competitive pressures and more exit options—alternatives to public provision for users seeking better quality or lower cost. Also expanding these options is the practice of contracting out service delivery to private firms or NGOs. Some governments are setting up performance-based agencies in the public sector and entering into formal contracts with these agencies, providing them greater managerial flexibility while holding them accountable for specified outputs or outcomes. Others are relying on more traditional bureaucratic forms in the core public sector, emphasizing accountability in the use of inputs, meritocratic recruitment and promotion, and the cultivation of an esprit de corps to build loyalty and improve performance. Finally, user participation, client surveys, published benchmarks, and other mechanisms for increasing citizen voice are providing external pressures for better delivery.

These initiatives can be classified into three broad categories: expanding exit options, strengthening voice, and improving compliance and loyalty. Which of these apply depends on the incentive environment through which the service can be delivered (Figure 5.4). Markets and contracts with the private sector offer primarily exit options for better performance. In the broader public sector—including corporatized state enterprises and performance-based agencies—exit options are fewer, but voice begins to become influential. For activities whose outputs are difficult to specify and that are not contestable, the core civil service remains the agency of choice, but it provides no realistic exit options and has considerably less flexibility in financial and personnel management. Here the more relevant instruments switch to citizen voice, the loyalty of the civil service, and well-specified rules for them to follow.

Recently, the so-called new public management reforms in industrial countries have sought to move delivery away from the core public sector (the center of the circle in Figure 5.4), primarily by using market mechanisms and formal contracting. New Zealand provides the most dramatic example. Beginning in the early 1980s, commercial and other contestable activities were hived off, corporatized, and often privatized. The remaining large, multipurpose ministries were split up into focused business units headed by managers on fixed-term, output-based contracts with considerable autonomy (including the right to hire and fire). These reforms helped turn a

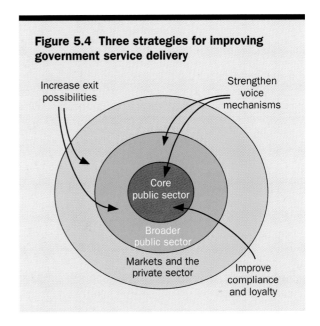

Figure 5.4 Three strategies for improving government service delivery

Increase exit possibilities

Strengthen voice mechanisms

Core public sector

Broader public sector

Markets and the private sector

Improve compliance and loyalty

budget deficit equivalent to 9 percent of GDP into a surplus during the 1980s and cut the unit cost of delivery by more than 20 percent in some agencies.

Several developing countries are now emulating these reforms. But what is feasible in New Zealand may be unworkable in many developing countries. It takes considerable capability and commitment to write and enforce contracts, especially for difficult-to-specify outputs in the social services. Which mechanism will prove most effective in improving performance depends on both the characteristics of the service and the capability of the state to enforce internal and external contracts (Table 5.1).

For instance, for services that are contestable—such as most commercial products and, more recently, telecommunications and electric power generation—market mechanisms can generate powerful competitive pressures for improved delivery. For services whose outputs the state can specify and enforce at low transactions cost, contracting out to private firms and NGOs is an attractive option. Countries with strong capability and commitment are setting up performance-based agencies and formal contracts even for complex activities within the core public sector, such as defense, education, and health care. But countries with little capability to enforce complex contracts, and weak bureaucratic controls to restrain arbitrary behavior under more flexible management regimes, need to proceed with caution.

Using competitive markets to improve delivery

Overstretched and with budgets increasingly tight, governments are relying more on market mechanisms to improve the delivery of contestable services. At the same time, a flood of innovation at both the technological and the policy level has been pushing back the boundaries of

Table 5.1 Mechanisms to improve service delivery

Environment	Service characteristics and state capability		
	Contestable	**Easy to specify outputs and enforce performance**	**Difficult to specify outputs and enforce performance**
Private sector	Strengthen markets through credible regulation Create markets, e.g., by issuing vouchers	Contract out to for-profit or nonprofit agencies	
Broader public sector	Enhance internal competition Set hard budgets and divest state enterprises	Set up performance-based agencies Corporatize state enterprises and establish enforceable performance contracts Strengthen voice mechanisms	
Core public sector			Ensure clarity of purpose and task Improve compliance with rules Strengthen voice mechanisms

what can be considered contestable. Chapter 4 showed how deregulation and the unbundling of activities in state-dominated industries such as electric power generation have led to significantly lower unit costs and a rapid expansion in services.

Other recent innovations such as vouchers and capitation grants have even increased the scope for competition in the provision of some social services. Experience remains limited, however, and confined largely to education. Chile's capitation grant system allows students to enroll in any school, public or private; schools receive a payment from the state based on enrollment (Box 5.4). Private enrollments have increased, but the program's effects on school performance are not yet clear. Vouchers are promising but carry a risk of increasing social polarization if not properly regulated.

Indeed, greater use of market mechanisms must be accompanied by effective regulatory capacity. As discussed in Chapter 4, this is not always easy to achieve. The difficulties of regulation are even more daunting in social services than in, say, infrastructure. For instance, the private delivery of health care services is unregulated in many developing countries (Brazil is a notable exception) because regulating the vast number of small-scale providers is beyond the government's capacity.

Contracting out to the private sector and NGOs
In those areas where competition *in* the market is not feasible, it may still be possible to foster competition *for* the

market: governments can contract with private firms, selected through competitive bids, to provide services. Contracting out is now a widespread practice in many industrial countries. Victoria State in Australia provides a particularly dramatic example: each local council contracts out at least half its annual budget through competitive tender, including complex community care services.

In developing countries, where both markets and state capacities are weak, options for contracting out are fewer. Still, where outputs are easily specified and direct competition is impossible, competition managed through such arrangements as service contracts, management contracts, leases, and long-term concessions can yield efficiency gains. In Brazil, for instance, contracting out road maintenance to private contractors led to savings of 25 percent over the use of government employees. Leases have increased the technical efficiency of water supply in Guinea and of the operation of Port Kelang in Malaysia.

Governments are also contracting out the delivery of social services, especially to NGOs. Even though outputs here are difficult to specify, governments have taken this route where NGOs are perceived to be committed to high quality or where, because of their religious or ideological orientation, they can better serve certain groups (for example, the Netherlands has long contracted with NGOs for education services). In Bolivia an arrangement with a local church organization to manage public schools is producing promising results (Box 5.5). And in Uganda the government is entering into partnerships with NGOs to

Box 5.4 Vouchers and school choice

Vouchers can increase the scope for competition in providing education. Students are given vouchers funded by public tax dollars but redeemable at any school, private or public. Letting parents choose the school their children will attend should induce schools to compete for students.

Opponents of vouchers claim that they would lead public school students—especially the better ones—to leave in droves, gutting the public system. Such an outcome would be wasteful and might lead to even poorer education for those who choose to remain. Yet in a 1993 pilot program in Puerto Rico, the 18 percent of students who did transfer to private schools were largely offset by the 15 percent who transferred from private to public schools—hardly a mass exodus. Puerto Rico's experiment was so successful that in its second year the number of applicants jumped from 1,600 to 15,500.

Public funding for private schools is nothing new. In the Netherlands two-thirds of students attend publicly funded private schools. When Chile reformed its education system in 1980, the Ministry of Education began providing capitation grants—fixed payments per student enrolled—to both public and private schools. Because the per-student payment was based on the average cost of education in the public sector, and expenditures per student were 70 percent less in the private sector, private schools eagerly vied for students. By 1986 primary enrollment in private schools had more than doubled, from 14 to 29 percent of total enrollment, and enrollment in private secondary schools had increased almost fourfold. The effects on school performance are not yet clear.

Vouchers also present potential risks. The ones most commonly cited are increased stratification among services and polarization among users. Some analysts have criticized the unfettered rush toward school choice in the former Soviet republics, arguing that it will exacerbate social tensions in rapidly polarizing societies. The underlying concern is that, in the absence of national controls, school curriculums will become divisive and parochial, and an essential role of the state—that of ensuring social cohesion—will be undermined.

deliver both preventive and curative health services previously in the public domain.

Like regulatory contracts and vouchers, however, contracting out is not a panacea. In general, contracting works best where outputs are easy to specify and markets are strong, so that the effectiveness of alternative suppliers can be readily judged. For activities that are complex or nonroutine, contracting out will inevitably incur higher transactions costs. Contracting is also prone to corruption and mismanagement, much as are contracts within the public sector. The Inspector General of Uganda, to take but one example, reported several instances of fraud in contracts with the private sector, including payments for roads that were never built or maintained.

Finally, competition in contracting does not necessarily mean that the private sector will outperform the public sector. In one of the most extensive U.S. experiments in public-private competition, the Public Works Department of Phoenix, Arizona, developed innovative strategies and outperformed private competitors on several contracts between 1984 and 1988. Competition provided the stimulus for reform in that case, but equally important was the strong partnership forged between management and labor through quality circles and labor-management productivity committees to build on workers' expertise and jointly identify competitive solutions.

Improving delivery through the broader public sector

Notwithstanding the growing opportunities for private participation, the public sector will inevitably continue to deliver a large number of services. Here the challenge is to create an enabling environment that provides incentives for better performance.

INTERNAL COMPETITION. Some industrial countries are experimenting with ways to increase competition within the public sector, to improve delivery of services for which neither market competition nor contracting out is feasible. In the United Kingdom, for example, an internal market has been created within the national health service by transforming local health authorities and groups of general practitioners into purchasers of hospital services on behalf of their patients. This arrangement has created competition among hospitals, acting as a decentralized mechanism for reallocating resources. Although internal competition can enhance efficiency, it is important to ensure that equity concerns are safeguarded in the process.

Decentralization of delivery—moving resources and responsibilities to lower levels of government—is another potentially powerful means of introducing internal competitive pressure, particularly for the provision of local public goods with few interjurisdictional spillovers or economies of scale. Local governments get the flexibility to match supply to local preferences or demands, while

Box 5.5 Contracting with NGOs for better schooling in Bolivia

In an experimental program in Bolivia, the government contracted with the church-based Fe y Alegría to manage a certain number of mostly secondary public schools. Before agreeing to do so, Fe y Alegría demanded (and received) the right to appoint principals and teachers and to allow teachers to work both the morning and afternoon shifts rather than the three-and-a-half hours allotted for instruction in the public schools.

In all other ways Fe y Alegría schools are identical to other Bolivian public schools. Although handpicked, teachers receive little special training and are paid the same salary as other public school teachers. Fe y Alegría schools receive no additional money for books or supplies, and their curriculums and teaching methods are the same as those used in other public schools.

The only comparative advantage Fe y Alegría schools have is an exceptional esprit de corps among students, parents, and staff. Teachers and students flock to Fe y Alegría schools, with many families paying extra fees for their children to attend. On the rare occasions when innovative teaching methods have been tried (such as a mathematics course transmitted over a public radio station), they have also proved popular, both in the schools and throughout the community. This public-private partnership between government and a religious NGO appears to be so successful that the government is studying it as a possible model for national education reform.

local accountability and interjurisdictional competition in supply provide potential restraints. But as discussed in Chapter 7, appropriate institutional preconditions need to be in place if decentralization is to improve efficiency and equity.

PERFORMANCE-BASED AGENCIES. The so-called new public management reforms in industrial countries have sought to break up the core public sector into a series of distinct business groups or special-purpose agencies. In general these agencies have greater managerial flexibility in the allocation of financial and human resources and greater accountability for results. Sweden and some other Nordic countries have long separated cabinet ministries from agencies with specific purposes. In the United Kingdom nearly two-thirds of the civil service has now been moved into executive agencies charged with specific delivery functions. These changes have been accompanied by substantial devolution of managerial authority and accountability for results. In Australia, Denmark, Ireland, and Sweden, for example, detailed and itemized administrative costs have been consolidated into a single budget line item, making it possible for managers to reallocate resources in accordance with changing priorities and needs.

Among developing countries, Singapore has perhaps the longest head start in creating focused business units. As early as the 1970s the Singaporean civil service was organized around the concept of statutory boards. Elsewhere, Jamaica has selected eleven pilot agencies for conversion into executive agencies.

But countries with inadequate controls over inputs and weak capacity need to proceed with caution. The industrial countries that have now relaxed detailed control over inputs did so from a position of strength, having developed over many years a series of credible restraints on arbitrary behavior. For the many countries that have not yet succeeded in instituting credible controls over the use of inputs, greater managerial flexibility will only increase arbitrary and corrupt behavior. Furthermore, writing and enforcing contracts, particularly for complex outputs, require specialized skills that are often in scarce supply.

Some of these concerns are borne out by a recent study of state enterprises, which found the overall record of performance contracts in developing countries extremely disappointing. Yet while performance contracts have not succeeded in most developing countries, many have sought to create performance-based agencies for easily specified and high-priority tasks such as road maintenance or tax collection. These agencies are typically set up as enclaves within the civil service, with greater managerial flexibility, better pay, and greater accountability for results. In Sub-Saharan Africa, for instance, performance-based agencies have been created to achieve tax collection targets in Ghana, Uganda, and Zambia. Other countries appear ready to follow suit.

In these instances, enclaving tax collection has been considered a prerequisite for boosting a government's capacity to raise revenues and improving incentives for the rest of the civil service. The results have been impressive. Ghana was the first country in Sub-Saharan Africa to introduce a performance-based approach to tax and customs revenue collection. Total revenues nearly doubled in the first five years, from 6.6 percent of GDP in 1984 to 12.3 percent in 1988, largely thanks to better collection. But the scheme was not without its problems. The rest of the civil service chafed at the special treatment afforded tax collectors, and the Ministry of Finance objected to its loss of authority. The program could not have gone forward without strong support from the top.

More troublesome has been the establishment of development project enclaves in several aid-dependent countries, each with its own system of remuneration and accountability. Often, donors have created these enclaves with little if any systematic consideration of the nature of the services provided or of the optimal sequencing of institutional reforms. And they have often created disparities.

As discussed in Chapter 9, enclaves are usually designed as quick fixes. Although they have sometimes accomplished short-term goals, they can create obstacles to deeper institutional reform. Where output is easily specified—tax revenues collected, for example—enclaves may be useful as an experimental stage of reform that can then be progressively extended, and as a demonstration that reforms can be effective. But it is important to employ systematic criteria in selecting which agencies to hive off. And although they are a useful first step, enclaves cannot substitute for the longer-term institutional reforms needed to create a motivated, capable civil service.

Improving delivery through the core public sector

Contracting out, setting up performance-based agencies, and ensuring formal accountability for results are not viable options for many services in countries with weak capacities. The challenge is particularly acute for street-level bureaucracies whose operators (police, irrigation patrollers, health workers, teachers, extension workers) interact daily with the people they serve, are geographically dispersed, are granted substantial discretion, and produce outputs that are difficult to monitor and are not subject to competitive pressure.

Experience across a range of countries suggests that a combination of mechanisms can boost incentives to perform in such areas. A study comparing irrigation agencies in India and Korea revealed that the Indian organization provided few incentives for conscientious work, whereas the Korean agency was full of such incentives. Korean irrigation patrollers had greater clarity of purpose and were subject to random monitoring from three separate agencies. Supervision techniques in India sought to discover grounds for punishment; in Korea they sought to solve problems. With staff from all parts of the organization traveling frequently up and down the canals in Korea, there was more external pressure from farmers, and stronger partnerships could be built for better performance.

PERFORMANCE ORIENTATION AND PREDICTABILITY IN RESOURCE FLOWS. An important starting point in raising the emphasis on performance within public sector organizations is greater clarity of purpose and task. Colombia, Mexico, and Uganda are introducing performance measurement to orient managers to achieving desired results. Whereas some countries (New Zealand is one) have stressed outputs as performance measures, others (Aus-

tralia, Colombia, Uganda) are emphasizing outcomes—the impact of outputs on beneficiaries—combined with ex post evaluation.

But even with greater clarity of purpose and task, public sector managers will not perform well if the flow of budgeted resources is highly uncertain. This brings home the downstream importance of building effective policy-making mechanisms at the center, as discussed earlier in this chapter. A credible medium-term expenditure framework, such as that in Australia (see Box 5.2), provides greater consistency between policies and resources and therefore more predictability in the flow of resources to units downstream. Malawi and Uganda are beginning to institute such frameworks.

FINANCIAL AND MANAGEMENT CONTROLS. Because public sector outputs are often difficult to measure and monitor, financial control and accountability are needed to keep managers honest, prevent the poor use—or abuse—of public resources, and improve service delivery. An expenditure tracking exercise in Uganda revealed that a significant portion of funds allocated for basic social services never reach the intended health clinics or schools, particularly in rural areas. In many countries public financial accounts and audits are outdated and inadequate and therefore do not provide credible restraint.

To improve the transparency and quality of their financial accounting and auditing systems and reduce lags, countries are modernizing their financial information systems. Countries as diverse as Bolivia, China, Indonesia, and Moldova are writing sound accounting principles into law, backed by strong professional associations both within government and in the private sector.

Although systematic evidence about the effects of these reforms is not available, some useful policy lessons can nevertheless be gleaned. Modern, computer-based information systems can both improve transparency and strengthen aggregate control while reducing the need for controls on specific transactions. Controls on inputs can be broadened sequentially as systems are expanded and trust is built up: countries can gradually move away from detailed, ex ante line-item controls to broader budget categories, salary scales with broader bands, and greater latitude in procurement and recruitment. The shift from ex ante to ex post transaction-specific input controls should proceed carefully and only as controls over budgetary aggregates are improved, as agencies demonstrate that they can be trusted with greater autonomy, and as ex post controls build strength through improved accounting and auditing capacities.

But experience also suggests that moving from a highly centralized, transaction-specific control regime to a more decentralized one can encounter resistance. For instance, in Ecuador a plan to devolve payment controls, although

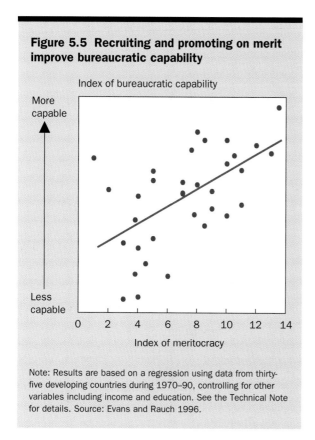

Figure 5.5 Recruiting and promoting on merit improve bureaucratic capability

Index of bureaucratic capability

Note: Results are based on a regression using data from thirty-five developing countries during 1970–90, controlling for other variables including income and education. See the Technical Note for details. Source: Evans and Rauch 1996.

proposed in 1995, has yet to be implemented, largely because of central agencies' fears of fiscal indiscipline. Trust needs to be built up first by strengthening systems of performance measurement and ex post input controls. As these systems become more credible, resistance to the changeover will fade, and managers can be provided greater flexibility, with stronger accountability for results.

LOYALTY, MOTIVATION, AND COMPETENCE. Better systems of monitoring, accounting, and auditing alone will not suffice to improve the delivery of many services. Mechanisms for enhancing the loyalty, motivation, and competence of the civil service are also needed. Loyalty promotes staff identification with an organization's goals and a willingness to take a longer-term view of responsibilities. Loyalty is essential in the core public sector, where activities are not easily specifiable or monitorable, and exit has no meaning.

The civil services of France, Germany, Japan, and Singapore all seek to ensure that the loyalties of a small group of professionals are fundamentally aligned with the interests of the state. Job security in the civil service was meant to foster this alignment of interests. It has worked in some contexts but not in many others. As discussed in the next section, the experience of successful countries suggests that building this commitment, and motivating

and attracting capable staff, require long-term career rewards, adequate pay, and mechanisms to instill an esprit de corps through, for instance, strong partnerships between management and labor.

STRENGTHENING MECHANISMS OF CITIZEN VOICE. Instituting credible bureaucratic controls takes time. Meanwhile, where internal monitoring and enforcement capacity are weak, clients and beneficiaries can exert powerful pressures to improve performance, and so help reduce monitoring costs until these capacities are built up. Coproduction and other forms of government partnership with the community in providing services, even if indirect, create incentives to press for better service. Feedback mechanisms such as the client surveys used in India, Nicaragua, and Uganda increase transparency and improve accountability by making more people aware of the agency's performance. Citizen charters, in which agencies publicly commit themselves to minimum standards of service provision—as applied in Belgium, Malaysia, Portugal, and the United Kingdom—can be a fulcrum for increased external and internal pressures to meet performance targets, and help focus the attention of clients and staff on service quality. Chapter 7 puts the use of voice and participation in the broader context of raising state capability.

Fostering motivated, capable staff

Whether making policy, delivering services, or administering contracts, capable and motivated staff are the lifeblood of an effective state. Efforts to build a competent and dedicated civil service usually focus almost exclusively on pay. Pay is certainly important, but so are other things, such as merit-based recruitment and promotion and esprit de corps. Meritocratic recruitment and promotion restrain political patronage and attract and retain more capable staff. A healthy esprit de corps encourages closer identification with an organization's goals, reduces the costs of making people play by the rules, and nurtures internal partnerships and loyalty.

A recent cross-country study shows why these things matter. The authors found that an index representing meritocratic recruitment and promotion and adequacy of pay was correlated with economic growth as well as with investors' perceptions of bureaucratic capability, even after allowing for income and educational differences (Figure 5.5). Clearly, then, finding the right institutional recipe for recruiting and motivating capable staff can reap sizable rewards.

Merit-based recruitment and promotion

Making a meritocracy of the civil service helps bring in high-quality staff, confers prestige on civil service positions, and can do a great deal to motivate good performance. In many countries (Japan and Korea, for example) a national civil service entrance examination uses tough standards to winnow the more skilled from the less skilled applicants. In others, academic (often college) performance is the primary filter. Pressure to perform is sustained after recruitment by specifying clear objectives and criteria for upward mobility and offering rewards for meritorious long-term service. In Korea, for instance, promotion is based on a formula that combines seniority with merit-based elements. Where instead promotions are personalized or politicized, civil servants worry more about pleasing their superiors or influential politicians, and efforts to build prestige through tough recruitment standards are undercut.

Meritocracy has not yet become established in many countries. Instead the state has often become a massive source of jobs, with recruitment based on connections rather than merit. Figure 5.6 shows that political appointments run much deeper in the Philippines than in other East Asian countries. This, combined with poor pay, has resulted in lower bureaucratic capability, which has also worsened over time. The Philippine government is undertaking reforms to introduce greater meritocracy in its civil service. Of course, political appointments can be quite extensive in industrial countries, such as the United States, as well. But countries with weak institutions and inadequate checks and balances are better off relying on more transparent and competitive mechanisms.

Even countries that have managed to install merit-based recruitment and limit political appointments can suffer from rampant political interference in employee transfers. In India, for example, senior civil servants are transferred frequently: the average tenure of field officers in some states

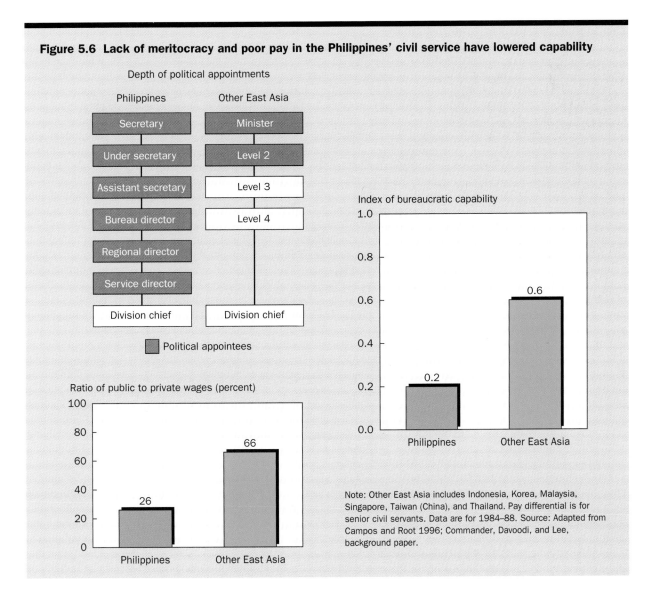

Figure 5.6 Lack of meritocracy and poor pay in the Philippines' civil service have lowered capability

Depth of political appointments

Note: Other East Asia includes Indonesia, Korea, Malaysia, Singapore, Taiwan (China), and Thailand. Pay differential is for senior civil servants. Data are for 1984–88. Source: Adapted from Campos and Root 1996; Commander, Davoodi, and Lee, background paper.

can be as low as eight months. Partly as a result, the once-legendary Indian civil service is no longer perceived as a model of efficiency and effectiveness.

Merit-based recruitment and promotion systems are of two broad but not mutually exclusive types: mandarin systems and open recruitment systems. Mandarin systems, such as those found in France, Germany, and Japan, are closed-entry, hierarchical systems with highly competitive entrance requirements (Box 5.6). Where well-qualified human resources are in short supply, mandarin systems may well be the preferred basis for a more selective approach to personnel development. Open recruitment systems, such as those in New Zealand and the United States, provide a more flexible, decentralized, and increasingly market-driven system of civil service recruitment. Open systems give more flexibility to managers to match job requirements with available skills, including hard-to-find technical expertise, although at the cost of making it

more difficult to maintain professional standards and esprit de corps.

Adequate compensation

As countries build prestige for their civil service through merit-based recruitment and promotion, government employment becomes more attractive. But if civil service compensation trails far behind that in the private sector, prestige alone will not make up the difference.

A rough benchmark for evaluating the adequacy of public sector compensation is the gap between public and private sector compensation, discounted somewhat to adjust for the fact that civil service employment is generally more secure. Precise comparisons are tricky, given differences in benefits and perquisites, job requirements, and the like. As a rule, however, civil servants nearly everywhere are paid less than their private sector counterparts. In the Philippines, for example, public pay averages 25

Box 5.6   Cultivating the best and the brightest: Mandarin versus open systems

Most countries have adopted one of two broad approaches to meritocratic recruitment. The first, called the mandarin system, is a hierarchical system with entry limited to promising candidates at the outset of their careers. "Mandarin system" traditionally referred to an elite group of civil servants in certain East Asian bureaucracies; in its more modern sense it refers to a "corps-career" system that also includes lower and middle levels of the civil service. Recruitment is centralized and highly selective, generally on the basis of a rigorous entrance examination. The successful candidates are placed on a fast track into the best jobs in government. For the most part these recruits, who are mostly generalists by educational background, are hired into a career stream or corps rather than for specific jobs.

France and Japan best exemplify the mandarin system. At France's National School of Administration, future high-level cadres are put through a one-year professional internship followed by fifteen months of coursework. Japan's Tokyo University produces that country's administrative elite, most of whom have a legal or generalist education, possibly supplemented with in-service technical training. Variants on the system are found in Singapore, where two-year cadetships rotate promising recruits, and Germany, where a "practicum" system offers practical, on-the-job internships for outstanding candidates.

The second system, known as open recruitment, is a more flexible, decentralized, and increasingly market-

driven approach to civil service recruitment. The U.S. system, for example, in stark contrast to the mandarin model, permits entry at any point in the hierarchy, without age restrictions. Centralized competitive entrance examinations have been replaced with profession-specific exams, and managers have been granted more autonomy in hiring. The United States, like Australia, complements its horizontal recruitment system with a Senior Executive Service aimed at building an elite group from within the civil service.

The boldest approach to open recruitment and career development is found in countries pursuing the "new public management" reforms. These countries have significantly devolved recruitment responsibilities. In New Zealand, for example, agency managers can hire staff at market salaries.

Countries with critical shortages of well-qualified human resources may find mandarin systems useful for establishing a selective rather than a comprehensive approach to personnel development. Moreover, a prestigious corps can have spillover effects, motivating other parts of the civil service to perform well. Open recruitment, on the other hand, gives managers greater flexibility in finding candidates with needed skills, including hard-to-find specialist expertise. And open systems discourage insularity in the civil service by bringing in, at all levels, staff with fresh perspectives and new ideas. The downside is that professional standards are less easy to maintain across the service, as is esprit de corps.

Figure 5.7 In Africa, as public employment has risen, wages have fallen

Average real central government wages relative to GDP per capita

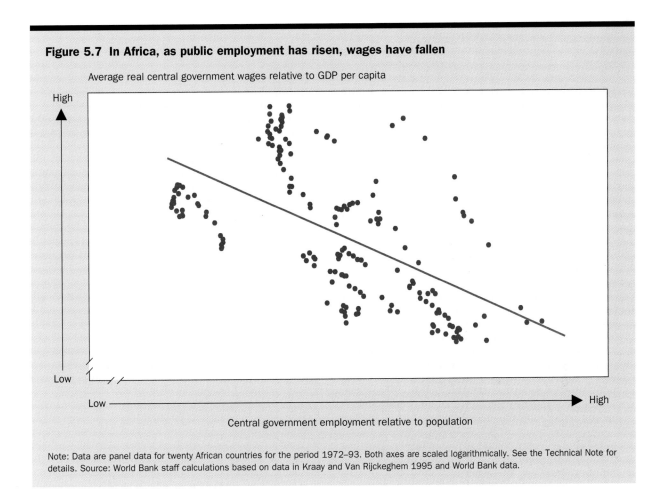

Central government employment relative to population

Note: Data are panel data for twenty African countries for the period 1972–93. Both axes are scaled logarithmically. See the Technical Note for details. Source: World Bank staff calculations based on data in Kraay and Van Rijckeghem 1995 and World Bank data.

percent of private wages; in Somalia the figure is 11 percent. (At the other extreme, public sector salaries in Singapore average 114 percent of those in the private sector, and in fact senior Singaporean civil servants are better paid than their U.S. counterparts.) The gap is widening in some countries. In Kenya, for instance, the disparity between public and private wages grew by 3 percent a year during 1982–92. Contributing in many countries to the relative erosion of public sector wages were fiscal austerity measures during the 1980s that tended to lower real wages rather than employment.

In many African countries, public employment has not merely been maintained in the face of rising fiscal pressures—it has actually risen, especially at lower skill levels (Figure 5.7). Governments have become employers of last resort and dispensers of political patronage, offering jobs to family, friends, and supporters. As a result, individual wages have often been low even though the overall wage bill has been high. Moreover, growth in the wage bill has often outpaced expenditures on operations and maintenance, leading to the familiar stories of teachers without textbooks and extension workers without bicycles.

The contrast between the size of the wage bill and the relative level of wages shows through in another major problem, which will not be solved by across-the-board increases. This is the relatively low level of remuneration for senior officials. In many countries the wages of higher-level civil servants are allowed, often for political reasons, to erode by more than those of the lower echelons; this wage compression makes it even harder to attract and retain high-quality staff at the vital senior levels. A study of ten African countries found that, on average, the ratio of the salaries of the highest- to those of the lowest-grade civil servants had declined from thirteen to one to nine to one during the 1980s.

Prompted by a desire to raise public sector salaries, and by the need to correct aggregate fiscal imbalances, some countries have embarked on initiatives to reduce employment, decompress the wage structure, and raise average pay in the civil service. These efforts have met with mixed success. A study of civil service reform in fifteen countries in various regions between 1981 and 1991 found that wage bill reduction and salary decompression had been achieved in fewer than half the cases. Employment had been reduced in more than half, but reversals were sometimes reported later, and the cuts were rarely adequate to finance substantial salary increases for higher-level staff. In Peru, for instance, some 250,000 workers were cut from the civil service over three years, but 163,000 of them were subsequently rehired; in addition, poor targeting of the cuts resulted in the departure of the most qualified staff.

This mixed and often disappointing experience with civil service reform nevertheless provides some lessons for future efforts. First, strategies have focused exclusively on pay and employment and, within those issues, on reducing numbers (the wage bill and employment). These are important, but so are other, complementary elements: merit-based recruitment and promotion, performance measurement and orientation, mechanisms to improve accountability, and esprit de corps.

A more careful sequencing of reforms is called for, starting with wage decompression. Even within constrained overall wage bills, wages at the top of the scale can be raised relative to lower levels, to attract more qualified people and concentrate scarce skills in strategic areas. In governments that are considerably overstaffed, reforms have been too modest to downsize them to sustainable levels. And they have tended to be one-shot reductions rather than a steady program to redimension government over the longer term.

Inevitably, pay and employment reforms will face political obstacles, although fears of political backlash have often been exaggerated. Some countries have viewed civil servants as partners in reform and have consulted extensively with them to find politically acceptable solutions. For instance, in the province of Santa Fe, Argentina, a close dialogue between the governor and the local civil service union helped the parties agree on measures for modernizing provincial public administration, including expenditure cuts of some 10 percent. In addition, the experience with civil service reform has helped develop a good set of technical tools—civil service censuses, functional reviews, better-designed severance packages—for managing and implementing reforms more effectively. But civil service reforms will generate losers, who can be important constituencies of the political leadership and therefore a force to be reckoned with. The political economy of reforms is discussed further in Chapter 9.

Building esprit de corps

Effective and capable bureaucracies share a commitment to their organization's objectives. This esprit de corps includes a common understanding about what is desirable and undesirable behavior, manifested in formal and informal norms and grounded in a set of objectives, and a devotion to upholding the honor of the group, based on this common understanding. An esprit de corps gives

members a sense of purpose and belonging and imposes self-discipline that guides members toward achieving the group's objectives. King Arthur's Knights of the Round Table, the samurai in Japan, and even the mafiosi of past generations all embodied some form of esprit de corps. A few of today's civil services are also said to do so, including those in Chile, France, Germany, Japan, Korea, and the United Kingdom. Most, however, do not.

It is not impossible to build an esprit de corps within the bureaucracy from scratch. Singapore's civil service is now well known for its coherence and sense of purpose, even though these characteristics barely existed in the early 1960s. Getting there was difficult, but the steps were straightforward enough. Each year prospective recruits are taken from the top 200 (less than 5 percent) of the graduating class at the National University of Singapore (and more recently the Nanyang Technological University) and put through a one-year training program. Their education and training give the recruits a common understanding of what is expected of them as civil servants and help build trust among them. The country's meritocratic promotion system gives officials a stake in achieving their agency's goals. The single-mindedness of Singapore's leadership and its continuous efforts to imbue the civil service with its desired values help strengthen the bond among civil servants. Some of Singapore's lessons are now being learned in Botswana, in twinning arrangements that emphasize the two key ingredients of teamwork and group performance.

Worker dedication and commitment are not confined to the industrial countries and East Asia. In Brazil's poor northeastern state of Ceará, steps to increase worker commitment dramatically improved the quality of public services delivered (Box 5.7). The state government promoted a sense of calling among workers and conferred new prestige on their jobs. These feelings were reinforced by innovative practices such as worker participation and self-managed worker teams, multitasking, and flexibly organized or specialized production. These practices involved greater worker discretion and flexibility, greater cooperation between labor and management, and greater trust between workers and customers. Such experiences also underscore the importance of nonmonetary rewards—recognition, appreciation, prestige, and awards—in motivating staff, over and above the adequacy of pay and meritocratic recruitment and promotion.

Strategic options: Steps toward an effective public sector

Some developing countries lack the most basic underpinnings of a professional, rule-based bureaucracy. Even reform-minded leaders cannot translate their goals into reality because the machinery linking policy statements to

---

Box 5.7 Building worker dedication: Good government in Brazil's Ceará State

In 1987 the state government of Ceará in northeastern Brazil confronted a crippling fiscal crisis, superimposed on a legacy of mediocre administrative performance. Yet within four years the fiscal crisis had been overcome, and the quality of services had improved dramatically. Vaccination coverage for measles and polio more than tripled, from 25 percent to 90 percent of the child population. The state's public works program employed more than 1 million unemployed farmers during droughts. And its business extension and public procurement program for small firms was saving more than 30 percent over its previous overall expenditure.

Much of the credit for this success is owed to the civil service itself. The state government contributed in an unusual and sometimes inadvertent way to public workers' newfound dedication. Using rewards for good performance, public screening methods for new recruits, orientation programs, and sheer boasting through the media about its successes, the state created a strong sense of mission around key programs and their workers. Highly motivated workers carried out a

larger variety of tasks than usual, often voluntarily. Granted greater autonomy and discretion, workers were able to provide more customized service. This greater discretion did not result, as it often does elsewhere, in greater opportunities for rent seeking because of pressures to be accountable. Workers wanted to perform better in order to live up to the new trust placed in them by their clients. This in turn was the result of the more customized arrangements of their work and the public messages of respect from the state. At the same time, the communities where these public servants worked monitored them more closely. The state's publicity campaigns and similar messages had armed citizens with new information about their rights to better government and about how public services were supposed to work. Thus government played a powerful role in monitoring, but it did so indirectly.

These mechanisms created a virtuous cycle in which workers reported feeling more appreciated and recognized, not necessarily by superiors, but by their clients and the communities where they worked. This, in turn, reinforced their dedication to the job.

---

action has ceased to function. As a result, a vast gap has opened up between what the state says it will do and what it does—between the formal rules of public institutions and the real ones. The first step toward building a more effective public sector in such countries must be to close these gaps: to reestablish the credibility of the government's policies and the rules it claims to live by, making sure they operate in practice. This includes setting hard budget limits, implementing budgets and other policies as approved, making the flow of resources predictable, instituting accountability for the use of financial resources, and curbing rampant political patronage in personnel decisions.

Where these preconditions are absent, the new public management must be introduced cautiously. If informal norms have long deviated significantly from formal ones (with regard to personnel practices, for example), simply introducing new formal rules will not change much. Where countries have been unable to establish credible controls over inputs, giving managers greater flexibility will only encourage arbitrary actions and corruption. And where specialized skills are in short supply, performance contracts and other output-based contracts for complex services may absorb a large share of scarce bureaucratic capacity to specify and enforce them. Nevertheless, countries can begin by providing greater clarity of purpose and

task and by introducing performance measurement on a selective, sequential basis. When output measurement is strengthened and credible controls over inputs are instituted, managers can be granted more operational flexibility in exchange for greater accountability for results.

Instituting a professional, rule-based bureaucracy will take time. In the meantime some other measures can be implemented more quickly, some of which can generate early payoffs. Well-functioning policymaking mechanisms make transparent the costs of competing policies and encourage debate and consultation among all stakeholders. Using the market to deliver contestable services—too many of which are now the sole domain of government—can lower costs and improve service quality. Likewise, contracting out easily specified activities through competitive bids can reduce the burden on overstretched capacity and build partnerships with markets and NGOs to improve efficiency. And reformers need not rely only on internal controls: creating more points of access for feedback from firms and the people who use public services can do a lot to generate external pressures for better performance while internal capacity and enforcement mechanisms are still developing.

As previous chapters have stressed, getting the state out of the business of providing many of the goods and services it now provides will still leave it plenty to do. Where it is no longer a direct provider, the state must become a partner and facilitator, regulating markets, enforcing contracts, and pursuing all the essential roles outlined in Chapters 3 and 4. That means attracting and keeping capable staff. Rule-based restraint on political patronage in recruitment and promotion, and more competition through meritocracy, will be necessary to build this capability. In countries where rapid employment expansion has taken place in the lower echelons, reforms to reduce employment are inevitable. But the relative attrac-

tiveness of salaries at the upper end can be raised, to attract capable staff, even within constrained wage bills, in part by reducing excess employment among the rank and file.

There is bound to be opposition to these and other reforms from those who stand to lose. But as discussed in Chapter 9, windows of opportunity for reform can open and widen. Reform-minded governments should seize these opportunities to build consensus, address the obstacles to change, and initiate and sustain reforms to build an effective public sector. The resulting reinvigoration of public institutions will generate large payoffs.

CHAPTER 6

RESTRAINING ARBITRARY STATE ACTION AND CORRUPTION

Aᴺ ᴇꜰꜰᴇᴄᴛɪᴠᴇ ꜱᴛᴀᴛᴇ ᴄᴀɴ ᴄᴏɴᴛʀɪʙᴜᴛᴇ ᴘᴏᴡᴇʀꜰᴜʟʟʏ to sustainable development and the reduction of poverty. But there is no guarantee that state intervention will benefit society. The state's monopoly on coercion, which gives it the power to intervene effectively in economic activity, also gives it the power to intervene arbitrarily. This power, coupled with access to information not available to the general public, creates opportunities for public officials to promote their own interests, or those of friends or allies, at the expense of the general interest. The possibilities for rent seeking and corruption are considerable. Countries must therefore work to establish and nurture mechanisms that give state agencies the flexibility and the incentive to act for the common good, while at the same time restraining arbitrary and corrupt behavior in dealings with businesses and citizens.

Chapter 5 focused on building the capability of the public sector. Many of the reforms discussed there will contribute to reducing arbitrariness and corruption. Particularly useful toward that end are instilling a rule-based culture in public institutions, and curbing patronage in the civil service. This chapter broadens that discussion to look at mechanisms to restrain arbitrary state action and corruption more generally.

The chapter examines first the formal checks and balances that need to be built into the structure of government, including judicial independence and the separation of powers. These promote credibility and accountability. But formal instruments of restraint are seldom enough, particularly in countries where corruption has become well entrenched. Therefore this chapter also analyzes the options for these states and others seeking to make a dent in corruption, by examining its root causes. One important lesson is that anticorruption efforts must proceed along many fronts, to reduce the opportunities for, and the payoffs from, corruption while raising the price and the probability of being caught.

Formal checks and balances

In framing a government to be administered by men over men, the great difficulty lies in this: you must first enable the government to control the governed; and in the next place oblige it to control itself.
— James Madison, *Federalist* No. 51 (1788)

Restraining the potential use and abuse of state power is a challenge for any country. Harder still is doing it without depriving state agencies of the flexibility they need to do their job. The misuse of state power creates serious problems of credibility, whose effects linger long after the event. The expropriation of property and the harassment of entrepreneurial Asian minorities in Uganda under Idi Amin left a legacy of distrust, which initially posed enormous problems when the current administration tried to attract private investment. But arbitrary and capricious state action undermines more than credibility. It undermines the rule of law itself, by weakening the force of whatever rules the state has set in place. And it fosters conditions that encourage state officials to place themselves above the law and tempt the rest of society to do the same. Development, in these circumstances, hits a brick wall.

Instruments of restraint

Sustainable development generally calls for formal mechanisms of restraint that hold the state and its officials accountable for their actions. To be enduring and credible, these mechanisms must be anchored in core state institutions; if these are too weak, external mechanisms such as international adjudication may substitute temporarily. The two principal formal mechanisms of restraint are a strong, independent judiciary and the separation of powers.

JUDICIAL INDEPENDENCE AND EFFECTIVENESS. To prosper, economies need institutional arrangements to resolve disputes among firms, citizens, and governments; to clarify ambiguities in laws and regulations; and to enforce compliance. Societies have devised a broad array of formal and informal mechanisms to do this, but none more important than the formal judiciary. It alone has access to the coercive authority of the state to enforce judgments. And it alone has the formal authority to rule on the legality of actions by the legislative and the executive branches. This special relation to the rest of the state puts the judiciary in a unique position to support sustainable development, by holding the other two branches accountable for their decisions and underpinning the credibility of the overall business and political environment. Yet judiciaries can play this role only when three core conditions are met: independence, the power to enforce rulings, and efficient organization.

Independence from the rest of government is the most important of these. Whatever the precise character of judicial relations with the legislature and the executive, all industrial countries—and many developing countries—rely on the judiciary to hold the executive accountable under the law and to interpret and enforce the terms of the constitution.

Judicial independence has been repeatedly compromised in some countries, and in no country has the judiciary been immune from political efforts to override its decisions. Legislatures and executives have used a variety of gambits to rein in their judiciaries:

- Judges of the superior court in Malta were suspended one hour before a case challenging executive actions was to be heard.
- A succession of Pakistani governments in the past appointed temporary judges, whose lack of tenure made them more vulnerable to political influence.
- Although Ukraine's constitution declares that the courts are independent of the executive, judges remain largely dependent on local authorities for their housing. Judges who have ruled against city officials appear to be particularly susceptible to long delays in getting housing.

The effectiveness of the judiciary also depends on its decisions being enforced. In practice that means that other branches of the government must consent to provide the resources needed for enforcement, including personnel authorized by law to serve court documents, to seize and dispose of property, and to turn the proceeds over to the winning party. In many countries this enforcement capability is constrained. In Poland, for instance,

bailiffs are not under the control of judges but are employed by the Ministry of Justice. Thus, although judges are competent and reasonably efficient, enforcement is slow and often ineffective because the number of bailiffs has not kept pace with the rising caseload.

Developing relationships among the judiciary, legislature, and executive that ensure judicial independence and reliable enforcement is a gradual process. Studies show that private sector confidence in the rule of law increases with each year a stable regime remains in place. More broadly, as Box 6.1 illustrates for Peru, the success of third-party mechanisms for enforcement depends in large part on citizens viewing those mechanisms as legitimate. In countries where judicial institutions are weak, it may be at least as important to demonstrate to citizens and firms the potential benefits of a well-functioning judiciary, and to win support for good laws and impartial enforcement, as it is to proceed with wholly technocratic programs of judicial reform.

The third component of judicial effectiveness is organizational efficiency, which is needed to avoid long delays in clearing cases. The average case takes 1,500 days to clear in Brazil and Ecuador, but only 100 days in France. Long delays raise the transactions costs for dispute resolution and may block access for some potential users; however, the internal efficiency of the judiciary is less critical than its independence and its enforcement authority. As discussed in Chapter 3, even when saddled with cumbersome and costly procedures, judicial systems can strengthen credibility in countries as long as their decisions are perceived to be fair. Any state beginning from a weak institutional base should consider building this aspect of judicial performance its first priority.

SEPARATION OF POWERS. Judiciaries may be capable of enforcing rules, but if the public has little faith in those rules remaining stable, the state's credibility can still be compromised. The classic constitutional mechanism for restraining constant legislative changes is the horizontal and vertical separation of powers.

Power can be divided horizontally among the judiciary, the legislature, and the executive, and vertically between central and local authorities. The patterns of a country's political party organization—which can range from a small number of highly disciplined parties to a large number of parties whose members only loosely abide by a party line, and that can govern only by forming multiparty coalitions—also influence the extent to which political power is concentrated or diffused.

The broader the separation of powers, the greater will be the number of veto points to be navigated to change any rule-based commitments. Thus the separation of powers increases confidence in the stability of rules. Multiple veto points can be a double-edged sword, however:

Box 6.1 How popular participation improved property rights and dispute resolution in Peru

Until 1989 most Peruvians living in marginal urban settlements and rural areas did not enjoy the security provided by formal ownership of their real property (70 percent of the population in urban areas and 80 percent in rural areas). The traditional system of property registration was run by the Ministry of Justice, and conflicts were resolved by the judiciary. The system was perceived by poor urban and rural property owners as a system for the rich, who could better afford the high transactions costs.

In the early 1980s the Institute of Liberty and Democracy (ILD), an NGO, began a campaign to improve the property rights of poor Peruvians. The ILD began by holding extensive public hearings to gather complaints, identify reasons why citizens did not formally register their property, and publicize the potential benefits and costs of registration and secure property. The group coupled this participatory process with a study of the laws and regulations governing property registration and enforcement. Based on the resulting diagnosis, the ILD then developed concrete proposals for reform. These were publicly debated and fine-tuned starting in 1986. Although the professional

monopolies that held a stake in the old system, such as lawyers' associations and notaries, strongly opposed the proposed reforms, community-level support carried the day.

In 1989 a new property registration system was enacted into law. The new system dramatically reduced transactions costs and uncertainty by reducing the power of the professional monopolies. Instead the system uses community norms, such as neighbors vouching for a party's ownership claim, to establish property rights and resolve conflicts. Subject to administrative requirements specified by the law, any lawyer may serve as a third-party verifier, sign the property titles, and resolve conflicts in the field. Contested or complicated cases are resolved by the new system's chief registrar, who is appointed by the Ministry of Housing, not the judiciary. Only after these mechanisms have failed can the conflict be taken to a judge.

By 1994 the new system had registered nearly 120,000 entities, and between 1994 and 1996 it registered an additional 170,000. Spurred by its demand-driven design, the system continues to evolve, and initiatives are under way to expand it nationwide.

---

they make it just as hard to change harmful rules as to change the beneficial ones.

Many developing countries, including some with formal separation of powers, have few effective checks and balances on the actions of political leaders. In some countries legislative oversight is weak because of poor capacity and inadequate information. In others the executive dominates a compliant legislature. But like the development of a well-functioning judicial system, the formal elaboration of constitutional checks and balances, or their more effective institutionalization, is a gradual process.

EXTERNAL MECHANISMS. To some extent, extraterritorial and international restraints can substitute for limitations on the ability of national institutions to enforce rules or to signal credibly that the rules will remain reasonably stable over time. One option is to use extraterritorial adjudication to underpin the domestic judicial system. Confidence in the Jamaican judicial system is buttressed by the fact that the United Kingdom's Privy Council serves as its appellate court of last resort. Because of the weaknesses of the Philippine judicial system, many firms, domestic as well as foreign, prefer to adjudicate their contracts offshore.

As Chapter 3 noted, international agreements are a second mechanism for strengthening commitments not

anchored by any domestic institution. On the trade front, both the European Union and the North American Free Trade Agreement have been able to play this role, and many countries will find it an important reason to join the World Trade Organization. Clearly, sovereign countries can still reverse course on, for example, trade policy by withdrawing from such agreements. But they then have to calculate not just the benefits and costs of the policy reversal, but also the broader costs of reneging on an international commitment for which their partners will hold them accountable. The threat of international censure makes countries less likely to reverse course.

Agreements with multilateral organizations, such as the IMF or the World Bank, often include some degree of policy conditionality: in order to borrow funds, for example, countries undertake certain reforms. This can have a similar benefit for some countries. These conditionalities can be viewed as a sign of national commitment to the policies that are included as conditions. Countries with weak domestic commitment mechanisms can strengthen their credibility by binding themselves to pay a penalty should they violate the agreement. One of the intentions behind World Bank guarantees is to accelerate the flow of private finance to developing countries by underpinning such commitments.

Building in flexibility

Instruments of restraint are a vital foundation for sustainable development. But excessive restraint can lead to paralysis. Instruments for restraining government need to be complemented by institutional arrangements that build in flexibility for the executive branch in formulating and implementing policies and adapting to new information and changing circumstances.

As discussed in Chapter 5, countries have tried a variety of institutional arrangements that combine flexibility with restraint. Some arrangements—such as deliberation councils in East Asia and the Administrative Procedures Act in the United States—delegate substantial autonomy to executive agencies to define the substance and undertake the implementation of policy. But they also require these agencies to follow procedures that open their decisions to input and oversight by other arms of the state and by civil society and businesses. Other arrangements rely on mechanisms within the executive branch to promote flexibility within restraints, such as the devolution of managerial authority to executive agencies within set budgets and performance targets.

But even if bureaucracies are embedded in processes that provide ample opportunity for outside input and oversight, the risk remains that officials will pursue personal rather than organizational goals. Self-seeking behavior can degenerate into corruption when private interests wield their influence in illegal and secret ways, circumventing the legal and bureaucratic rules designed to keep them out. Whether public institutions succumb to these and other sources of corruption will depend on the strength of their institutional defenses. How these are built and maintained is the subject of the next section.

Controlling corruption

A Congressional appropriation costs money. . . . A majority of the House Committee, say $10,000 apiece—$40,000; a majority of the Senate Committee, the same each—say $40,000; a little extra to one or two chairmen of one or two such committees, say $10,000 each. Then seven male lobbyists at $3,000 each; one female lobbyist, $10,000; a high moral Congressman or Senator here and there—the high moral ones cost more.

—A U.S. railroad company owner in Mark Twain and Charles Warner, *The Gilded Age: A Tale of Today* (1877)

Mark Twain's damning tale was a thinly veiled caricature of corruption in the U.S. Congress in the 1870s. Twain's novel followed closely on the heels of the infamous Crédit Mobilier scandal, in which two prominent businessmen brazenly bought their way into the Congress. In India in 1996 a blockbuster movie, *Hindustani,* expressed an extreme form of popular outrage over corruption. The movie depicts horrific tales of callous politicians and bureaucrats willing to let hospital patients die and poor pensioners starve unless they receive their cut.

Fiction thrives on exaggeration. But it is also a mirror that society holds up to itself to reflect entrenched problems. These tales—a century and a hemisphere apart—remind us that corruption is nothing new, nor is it confined to any particular corner of the world. It is a problem that has deeply affected the lives and stirred the resentment of citizens and businesspeople the world over.

Today, citizens everywhere demand greater probity of government officials, and the new transparency in domestic and global markets brings corruption more quickly to the public eye. In the past few years allegations of corruption have contributed to the fall of governments throughout the world. Two former presidents of the Republic of Korea have been prosecuted and indicted. A president of Brazil was impeached on charges of corruption. In October 1996 more than 250,000 people protested the Belgian government's handling of a pedophile ring and alleged corruption in judicial appointments and enforcement. And a fierce debate has erupted over the financing of political campaigns and its influence on public policy in the aftermath of the 1996 U.S. presidential election.

Corruption has been defined in many ways. This Report defines it as the abuse of public power for private gain. Although corruption tends to get the most attention, it is a symptom of a more general problem of perverse underlying incentives in public service. Corruption flourishes where distortions in the policy and regulatory regime provide scope for it and where institutions of restraint are weak. The problem of corruption lies at the intersection of the public and the private sectors. It is a two-way street. Private interests, domestic and external, wield their influence through illegal means to take advantage of opportunities for corruption and rent seeking, and public institutions succumb to these and other sources of corruption in the absence of credible restraints.

Corruption violates the public trust and corrodes social capital. A small side payment for a government service may seem a minor offense, but it is not the only cost—corruption can have far-reaching externalities. Unchecked, the creeping accumulation of seemingly minor infractions can slowly erode political legitimacy to the point where even noncorrupt officials and members of the public see little point in playing by the rules.

Studies have shown a clear negative correlation between the level of corruption (as perceived by businesspeople) and both investment and economic growth. This is confirmed for investment levels by the results of the private sector survey conducted for this Report (Figure 6.1). As we saw in Chapter 3, the survey identified corruption as one of the major obstacles to doing business in many countries. Yet it is not just a cost of doing business. Other surveys and anecdotal evidence suggest that the greatest victims of petty corruption are usually the poor.

Despite such evidence, many parts of the developing world retain a certain ambivalence toward corruption. A commonly heard view is that corruption merely greases the wheels of commerce, and that without it there would be no transactions and no growth. Apparent support for this argument comes from the fact that some countries that rank high in surveys of the level of corruption have also excelled in economic growth. The predictability of corruption—both that of the amount one has to pay and that of receiving the outcome one has paid for—provides some insights into this apparent paradox. For a given level of corruption, countries with more predictable corruption have higher investment rates (Figure 6.1). But even in these countries corruption has an adverse impact on economic performance. Figure 6.1 also shows that, no matter how high the degree of predictability of corruption in a country, its rate of investment would be significantly higher were there less corruption.

Countries that have so far achieved high rates of economic growth despite serious corruption may find themselves paying a higher price in the future. Tolerating corruption that siphons off payments of, say, 10 percent on average may generate pressures to increase the take to 15 or 20 percent. Corruption feeds on itself, creating a widening spiral of illegal payoffs until ultimately development is undermined and years of progress are reversed. And the very growth that permitted corruption in the past can produce a shift from productive activities to an unproductive struggle for the spoils. Over time corruption becomes entrenched, so that when governments finally do move to contain it, they meet powerful resistance.

Causes of corruption

Incentives for corrupt behavior arise whenever public officials have wide discretion and little accountability. Politicians, bureaucrats, and judges control access to valuable benefits and can impose costs on private citizens and businesses. Public officials may be tempted to use their positions for private gain by accepting bribes; for their part, private individuals may be willing to make illegal payments to get what they want from government. Thus, a necessary condition for corruption is that public officials have rewards and penalties at their disposal.

Some corruption stems from opportunities generated by the policy environment, at the bottom or the top of the hierarchy. Payoffs are frequent to lower-level officials charged with collecting tariffs, providing police protection, issuing permits, and the like. When corruption is

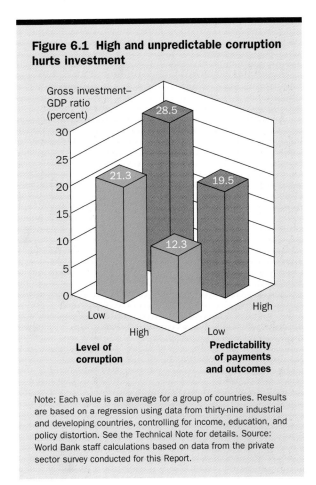

Figure 6.1 High and unpredictable corruption hurts investment

Gross investment–GDP ratio (percent)

Level of corruption

Predictability of payments and outcomes

Note: Each value is an average for a group of countries. Results are based on a regression using data from thirty-nine industrial and developing countries, controlling for income, education, and policy distortion. See the Technical Note for details. Source: World Bank staff calculations based on data from the private sector survey conducted for this Report.

endemic, these officials may create additional red tape and delays to induce even higher payments. Of course, corruption also occurs at the highest levels of government, in the awarding of major contracts, privatization, the allocation of import quotas, and the regulation of natural monopolies. This helps explain why corruption is more prevalent in countries with highly distorted policies, as measured by variables such as the black market exchange rate premium (top left panel in Figure 6.2). Any policy that creates an artificial gap between demand and supply creates a profitable opportunity for opportunistic middlemen.

The probability of being caught and punished (for the person paying the bribe and for the official receiving it) also affects the level of corruption. Economic analysis of the law suggests that individuals weigh the expected benefits of breaking the law against the expected costs (the probability of being caught and punished multiplied by the level of punishment). Corruption may be high in a country where the government system does little to deter bribes. Lawbreakers may believe that there is little chance of being caught or, if caught, of having to pay the penalty, since they believe that the system of justice itself can be

Figure 6.2 Some factors associated with corruption

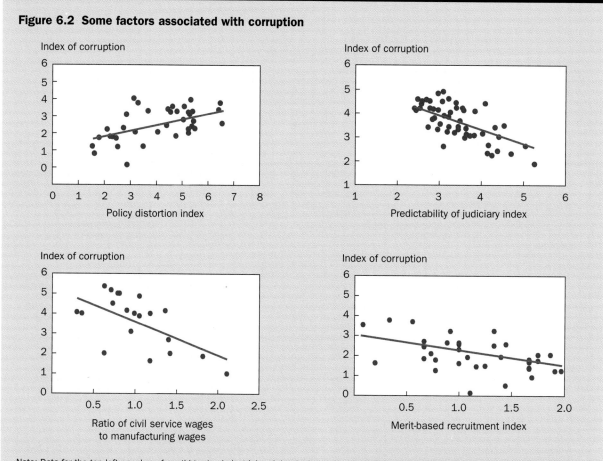

Note: Data for the top left panel are from thirty-nine industrial and developing countries during 1984–93 (for the policy distortion index) and 1996 (for the corruption index). The top right panel is based on a regression using data from fifty-nine industrial and developing countries during 1996. Data for the bottom left panel are from twenty industrial and developing countries in the late 1980s to early 1990s. The bottom right panel is based on a regression using data from thirty-five developing countries during 1970–90, controlling for income. See the Technical Note to Figure 3. Source: World Bank staff calculations (top two panels); Van Rijckeghem and Weder, background paper (bottom left panel); Evans and Rauch 1996 (bottom right panel).

corrupted. Corruption can even persist in countries with substantial press freedom and public resentment against it, if there is little hope of independent judicial resolution of important cases. This Report's private sector survey found a negative correlation between reported levels of corruption and judicial predictability (top right panel in Figure 6.2).

Finally, corruption may thrive if the consequences of being caught and disciplined are low relative to the benefits. Officials frequently control the allocation of benefits and costs whose value far exceeds their own salaries. Corruption becomes especially likely if the wages of public service do not reflect the comparable private wage. Where civil service wages are very low, officials may try to eke out a middle-class standard of living by supplementing their pay with illegal payoffs. The risk of being fired from a low-paying civil service job because of corruption is not

a serious threat if more remunerative positions are available legally in the private sector. Hence corruption is often positively associated with the difference between public and private salaries, or what may be termed the "rate of temptation" (bottom left panel in Figure 6.2). But simply raising civil service salaries may not reduce corrupt behavior. Pay reform must be combined with credible monitoring and law enforcement. Merit-based recruitment and promotion mechanisms that restrain political patronage and create a more impartial public service are also associated with lower corruption (bottom right panel in Figure 6.2).

Reducing corruption

Several countries have managed to reduce endemic corruption over time. The struggle of the Progressive movement against the power of U.S. urban political machines of the nineteenth century is a case in point (Box 6.2). Containing corruption requires an understanding of the benefits and costs under public officials' control. Many officials remain honest despite considerable temptation, and many ordinary people and businesses refuse to pay bribes despite the promise of short-term gain. But others succumb. It is unwise to deal with the possibility of corruption by assuming that government officials are of higher moral standing than the rest of the population.

The actual extent of bribery and other corruption depends not just on the potential gains and risks, but also on the relative bargaining power of the buyer and the seller of public favors. Reformers must also consider the fact that anticorruption efforts have marginal costs as well as marginal benefits; the efficient level of bribery will seldom be zero.

Corruption cannot be effectively attacked in isolation from other problems. It is a symptom of problems at the intersection of the public and the private sectors and needs to be combated through a multipronged strategy. Recent reforms in Uganda illustrate such an approach (Box 6.3). One part of the strategy focuses on a major

theme of Chapter 5: creating a rule-based bureaucracy with a pay structure that rewards civil servants for honest efforts, a merit-based recruitment and promotion system to shield the civil service from political patronage, and credible financial controls to prevent the arbitrary use of public resources. Here we focus on the remaining two parts of the strategy. The first is to reduce the opportunities for officials to act corruptly, by cutting back on their discretionary authority. The second aims at enhancing accountability by strengthening mechanisms of monitoring and punishment—using not only criminal law but also oversight by formal institutions and ordinary citizens.

REDUCING OPPORTUNITIES FOR CORRUPT PRACTICE. In general, any reform that increases the competitiveness of the economy will reduce incentives for corrupt behavior. Thus policies that lower controls on foreign trade, remove entry barriers to private industry, and privatize state firms in a way that ensures competition will all support the fight. If the state has no authority to restrict exports or to license businesses, there will be no opportunities to pay bribes in those areas. If a subsidy program is eliminated, any bribes that accompanied it will disappear

---

Box 6.2 Urban political machines in the United States and their reform

In the late nineteenth and early twentieth centuries many U.S. cities were dominated by political machines, defined by one scholar "as a political party in which a boss oversees a hierarchy of party regulars who provide private favors to citizens in exchange for votes and who expect government jobs in return." Machine-controlled cities also typically made corrupt, collusive deals with private businesses seeking contracts, franchises, or protected markets. The politicians driving these machines operated—and flourished—in nominally democratic environments.

Machines were costly to the communities they dominated. Spending per capita for general administration and for police and fire services—both areas with lots of patronage jobs—was 34 percent and 17 percent higher, respectively, in machine-controlled than in nonmachine cities. To take one extreme case, in Boston the number of city clerks increased by 75 percent between 1895 and 1907, while the population increased by less than a quarter; meanwhile growth in productivity fell by half.

The Progressive movement in the United States had as one of its main goals the reform of machine-dominated cities. Reform frequently meant property tax reform. Seth Low, New York's reform mayor in the early 1900s, was distressed by the favoritism shown to

wealthy property owners and introduced a plan to assess property at market value. The plan increased the assessed value of real estate, lowered the tax rate, and increased revenues. The city's budget was cut by $1.5 million as patronage appointees were removed from office. Reform mayors in many other U.S. cities followed similar policies.

Reform also involved municipal franchises. In Philadelphia, for example, the machine-controlled city council regularly awarded a gas franchise in return for contributions to the Republican Party. In 1905 reform mayor John Weaver vetoed the franchise bill, appointed a supporter to a key position on the city council to ensure that the veto would be upheld, and had machine adherents arrested on charges of corruption.

Cities dominated by machines paid a high cost in the form of inflated budgets and inequitable tax and spending systems. Although many people benefited from the jobs and patronage dispensed by the machines, the losers were more numerous still. It was they who eventually organized to elect reform candidates in many cities. The wave of reform mayors effected real change, which persisted even when the machines were returned to power, mainly because the reforms were popular and hard to reverse.

Box 6.3 Fighting corruption in Uganda

Uganda, long plagued by systemic corruption, has launched a multipronged battle against it. The effort enjoys support from the country's leaders, who seem committed to the goal of sound governance.

In the immediate postcolonial period Uganda was a kleptocratic state. By 1967 the regime ruled without holding elections. These beginnings set the stage for Idi Amin's rise to power in 1971. Under Amin, government became little more than a system of organized crime used to extract rents from the public. Their depredations took many forms, including support for economically irrational projects, exorbitant military expenditures, kickbacks on state contracts, extortionate import controls, and expropriation of the properties of Asians. Upon emerging from civil war in 1986, the new Ugandan government under President Yoweri Museveni inherited a weak, underpaid, and overstaffed

civil service (including thousands of "ghost workers") and a thin and porous tax base.

Cleaning up the civil service will take years, but Uganda is making some progress. The effort includes policy reform and deregulation to remove opportunities for rent seeking; civil service reform to streamline the public work force, improve remuneration, provide training, and instill a code of ethics; revival of the Public Accounts Committee of Parliament; a strengthened auditor general's office; and a public relations campaign against and prosecution of corruption, under the authority of an inspector general with powers to investigate and prosecute. Much remains to be done before corruption can be said to be under control. The inspector general, however, has announced prosecutions against common examples of rent seeking (such as customs and procurement fraud), which should have a deterrent effect.

as well. If price controls are lifted, market prices will reflect scarcity values, not the payment of bribes.

Needless to say, reducing official discretion does not mean eliminating regulatory and spending programs with strong justifications. Such programs must be reformed, not eliminated. Abolishing taxes is not a sensible way to root out corruption among tax collectors; a corrupt police force cannot simply be closed down. Several measures have proved effective in reducing official discretion in ongoing programs:

- *Clarify and streamline laws in ways that reduce official discretion.* Mexico's customs reforms cut the number of steps in the process from twelve to four; the remaining steps were streamlined to reduce delays.
- *Contract for services with a private company, possibly a foreign firm with no close ties to the country.* When Indonesia contracted with a Swiss firm for customs preinspection and valuation and for help in collecting import duties, corruption declined. Contracting out monitoring functions is pointless, however, unless the government makes use of the reports it receives—and that does not always happen.
- *Make rules more transparent.* Simpler, nondiscretionary tax, spending, and regulatory laws can limit opportunities for corruption. Sometimes a certain risk of corruption is tolerated because the benefits of a discretionary approach to program administration exceed the costs of corruption. But even then transparency and publicity

can help blunt the incentive to be corrupt. Police officers, for example, must have discretionary authority to make law enforcement decisions on the spot, but public complaints will often restrain any abuses.

- *Introduce market-based schemes that limit the discretion of regulators.* This approach also has the virtue of producing an economically efficient allocation of resources. The sale of water and grazing rights, pollution rights, and import and export licenses can improve the efficiency of government operations while limiting corruption.
- *Adopt administrative reforms that introduce competitive pressures into government.* Open, competitive bidding for public procurement contracts can reduce opportunities for corrupt deals. Creating overlapping, competitive bureaucratic jurisdictions can greatly diminish the bargaining power of individual officials. If clients can turn to a second official when the first demands a bribe, no single official has the power to extract a large payoff so long as applicants are eligible for the service. And if it is the applicants who are seeking something illegal, overlapping enforcement areas can help to check payoffs as well. For instance, when the state wants to control illegal businesses, police officers can be given overlapping enforcement areas to reduce opportunities for corruption.

STRENGTHENING MECHANISMS FOR MONITORING AND PUNISHMENT. Independent watchdog institutions that are part of the government structure can also curb corruption. Countries have experimented with various approaches:

- Some countries have independent anticorruption commissions or inspectors general that can investigate allegations and bring cases to trial. The most famous is the Independent Commission against Corruption in Hong Kong (China), which reports exclusively to the highest authority and has extensive powers (Box 6.4). Singapore and Botswana have similar institutions.
- Ombudsmen hear citizen complaints and can help increase the accountability of government agencies. Under the Ombudsman Act of 1991, South Africa has established a public protector to investigate alleged improprieties (malfeasance, corruption, human rights abuses) by public officials and to prepare reports, which are usually made public. The office cannot initiate legal actions but will refer cases to offices that can.
- Some public agencies, such as the School Construction Authority in New York City, have established internal units to root out corrupt contractors and propose ways to reorganize the agency to reduce corruption.
- Whistleblower statutes protect and reward public employees who report the malfeasance of co-workers or government contractors. The United States, for example, has a statute that calls for rewarding workers who report irregularities in government contracts. Such an incentive for reporting is often necessary, since people who report co-workers' misdeeds are frequently ostracized. Such measures are hollow, however, unless prosecutors follow up, courts are incorruptible and efficiently run, and penalties are severe enough to deter potential offenders.

Watchdog organizations should focus not only on those who receive bribes, but also on those who pay them. It takes two to tango, and penalties should be equally severe on both sides—usually a multiple of the bribes received or paid. Penalties for bribe payers should also include the prospect of being barred from contracting

Box 6.4 Hong Kong's independent commission against corruption

Corruption was endemic in Hong Kong (China) during the 1960s. Its entrenched character is suggested by expressions popular at the time: people had the choice of "getting on the bus" (actively participating in corruption) or "running alongside the bus" (being a bystander who did not interfere with the system). "Standing in front of the bus" (reporting or resisting corruption) was not a viable option.

Spurred to action by a scandal involving a high-ranking police officer, the then-governor general established the Independent Commission Against Corruption (ICAC) in 1974. The commission reports only to the governor and is independent of the police force. ICAC officials are paid more than other government workers and cannot be transferred to other departments. No one may leave the ICAC to work for senior officers who have been the subject of an investigation. The ICAC has the power to investigate and prosecute corruption cases as well as to sponsor public education campaigns. The government's commitment to reform was further indicated by the appointment of a person of unquestioned integrity as the first head of the commission and by a policy of investigating and prosecuting "big tigers" from the outset.

Early efforts to clean up corrupt syndicates within the police force, however, met with protests. The ICAC at first backed down and granted an amnesty for offenses committed before January 1, 1977. This setback was harmful to the commission's prestige, but it was able to recover with a vigorous public education campaign. Public surveys carried out between 1977 and 1994 indicate that public perceptions of corruption have fallen significantly. Indirect evidence suggests that active corruption has declined as well.

Still, the ICAC is not without its problems. The main one is that it reports only to the governor. An anticorruption commission reporting to an autocratic ruler could be used as an instrument of repression against political opponents, and the ICAC has not been immune to such charges. The ICAC's broad powers could be abused in systems less committed to the rule of law. A series of oversight committees and an independent judiciary act as a check on the ICAC, but even so the occasional scandal surfaces. As a further control on its power, such an agency might report not to the chief executive but to the legislature, as do Uganda's Inspector General and the U.S. General Accounting Office. A tough, independent anticorruption agency is a potent tool and represents a credible long-term commitment, but there should also be checks on its ability to be misused for political ends.

with the government for a period of years. Industrial countries with strong monitoring capacity can enforce such measures on their multinational companies conducting business overseas. But except for the United States, which adopted the Foreign Corrupt Practices Act in 1977, countries have been reluctant to act unilaterally for fear of subjecting their businesses to more stringent standards than their foreign competitors.

In this context, international organizations provide a forum for agreeing on common standards and coordinating action. Regional organizations such as the Organization of American States have sponsored international conventions making bribery, including international bribery, a crime. A recent initiative by the OECD encourages ending the tax deductibility of bribes and criminalizing the bribing of foreign officials. It makes recommendations to its member countries on how to deal with bribery in international business transactions. International organizations are also working to coordinate the fight against money laundering and, in particular, to expand the list of offenses, including corruption. The forty recommendations of the Financial Action Task Force on Money Laundering include nondrug criminal activities. This opens the way for countries to make illegal the use, deposit, or transfer of money acquired through corruption.

Citizens' groups can also be an important check on the arbitrary abuse of government power—if people can organize, and if they can find out what is happening. Governments should publish budgets, revenue collection data, statutes and rules, and the proceedings of legislative bodies. Financial data should be audited by an independent authority like the U.S. General Accounting Office. Unaudited secret funds or extrabudgetary funds available to chief executives are an invitation to corruption.

Freedom-of-information acts in the United States and a number of European countries are an important tool for public oversight. A recent directive of the European Union requires member states to pass freedom-of-information laws covering environmental information. Such laws enable citizens to obtain government information without having to show how their lives are affected by it. The availability of information helps citizens discipline public officials at the ballot box and through other avenues of protest, such as legal challenges and direct petitions to decisionmakers.

Information is of little value, however, without mechanisms for using the knowledge gained to influence government behavior:

- In democracies, citizens can vote officials out of office if they believe them to be corrupt. This gives politicians an incentive to stay honest and work for the interests of their constituents. (However, if corrupt payoffs are used to buy benefits for individual voters, knowledge of corruption may do little to stop it.)
- If courts are independent and citizens can sue to force the government to comply with the law, this opens another route to control government malfeasance.
- Public exposure of corruption through the media is another option. Even undemocratic rulers are likely to be sensitive to public opinion, if only because they wish to avoid being overthrown. A free press can be a vital check on abuses of power, especially in countries that lack other means of constraining politicians and bureaucrats.

Yet even if both the necessary information and the means of punishing corrupt practices are available, individual citizens are unlikely to act alone. Laws that make it easy to establish associations and nonprofits can help resolve this collective action problem. Such groups might not only seek information from government, but also supply information to government about citizens' opinions of the quality of public services. As discussed in Chapter 7, the nonprofit Public Affairs Centre in Bangalore is engaged in a promising experiment to publicize the performance of Indian public agencies. An international nonprofit organization, Transparency International, is working to mobilize citizens around the world to fight corruption and to publicize countries' track records. Yet precisely because open information can be so potent in promoting government reform, many countries limit such groups or make it costly for them to organize.

Strategic options: Balancing flexibility with restraints

Pressures for reform are on the rise everywhere. Private entrepreneurs and firms want the credibility of state actions anchored by a well-functioning system of property rights. Citizens are demanding more responsive and effective delivery of public services and greater probity in the use of public resources. At the same time, globalization is increasing demands for a more agile state, one that can respond quickly to changing circumstances. These pressures have magnified the state's dilemma: how to check arbitrary decisionmaking without building rigidities that inhibit innovation and change. The fundamental challenge is to devise institutional arrangements that sustain a workable balance between flexibility and restraint. Countries with strong institutions or track records of following through on commitments may have room to respond flexibly (even at the cost of some corruption), but countries with dysfunctional and arbitrary governments may not.

States in many developing countries have demonstrated a clear imbalance between flexibility and restraint. They have generally not been credible, accountable, responsive, or agile. In several countries the capricious exercise of state power coupled with rampant and unpredictable corruption has undermined development. States with too much flexibility and not enough restraint will find that their actions are not viewed as credible, and investment and growth will suffer. These countries need to strengthen the formal instruments of restraint—judicial independence, effective separation of powers—to enhance the credibility and accountability of the state. International commitment mechanisms can serve as a short-term substitute while these institutions are built up.

Yet these actions will not be enough to stop the rot in countries where endemic and entrenched corruption has undermined key functions of the state. Strengthening formal instruments of restraint is only one element of a multipronged strategy to control corruption. Reforming the civil service (for instance, by raising pay and restraining political patronage in recruitment and promotion), reducing opportunities for officials to act corruptly (for instance, by increasing competition and reducing officials' discretionary authority), and enhancing accountability are other essential steps. Strengthening mechanisms for monitoring and punishment—of the people who pay bribes as well as those who accept them—will require vigorous enforcement of criminal law. But it will also require oversight by formal institutions such as statutory boards and by ordinary citizens (through voice and participation). These efforts can help not only in controlling corruption but also in improving many other functions of the state, such as policymaking and service delivery. The use of voice and participation to reinvigorate public institutions is the subject of Chapter 7.

CHAPTER 7

BRINGING THE STATE CLOSER TO PEOPLE

And, tell me, what use is the ship-of-state if all are not on board?

—From Tijan M. Sallah, *The State* (1996)

PEOPLE ARE THE MEANS AND THE END OF DEVELOP-
ment. But they have different amounts of power
and resources, and different interests, all of which the state
must try to represent and respond to if it is to act effectively. In nearly all societies the needs and preferences of
the wealthy and powerful are well reflected in official policy goals and priorities. But this is rarely true of the poor
and the marginalized, who struggle to get their voices
heard in the corridors of power. As a result, these and other
less vocal groups tend to be ill served by public policies and
services, even those that should benefit them most.

A state that ignores the needs of large sections of the
population in setting and implementing policy is not a
capable state. And even with the best will in the world,
government is unlikely to meet collective needs efficiently
if it does not know what many of those needs are. Reinvigorating public institutions must, then, begin by bringing government closer to the people. That means bringing
popular voice into policymaking: opening up ways for
individual users, private sector organizations, and other
groups in civil society to have their say. In the right setting, it can also mean greater decentralization of government power and resources.

This chapter discusses a wide range of mechanisms to
ensure that policies and programs better reflect the full
panoply of society's interests. Informing and responding
to citizens will raise the state's effectiveness by improving monitoring of public goods and services and forcing
greater transparency in decisionmaking. Encouraging
wider participation in the design and delivery of these
goods and services, through partnerships among govern-

ment, business, and civic organizations, can also enhance
their supply. But effective citizen involvement does not
come easily. One lesson of many such experiments is that
effective participation requires enlightened government
intervention, including improving the institutional environment in which social and human capital is created.

There is another important lesson: bringing government closer to some people can risk taking it even further away from others. Not all organizations of civil society
are adequately accountable, either to their own members or
to the public at large. And although some groups may be
quite vocal, the interests they represent may not be widely
shared. In reaching out to groups in civil society, government must be conscious of the interests those groups represent, but also of those they do not. Otherwise its intervention risks creating new disparities between the newly
enfranchised and those whose voices remain unheard:
women and ethnic groups, for example, or people whose
interests have not been adopted by an active NGO.

Some of the same concerns arise with regard to decentralization. Carefully managed, decentralization can do
much to improve state capability, creating pressures for
better matching of government services to local preferences, strengthening local accountability, and supporting
local economic development. But there are pitfalls: policymakers in central government may lose control over the
macroeconomy as a result of uncoordinated local decisions, and regional disparities can widen, exacerbating
economic and social tensions. Local governments can fall
under the sway of particular interests, leading to abuse
of state power and even less responsive and accountable

government. The message, here as elsewhere, is that bringing government closer to the people will only be effective if it is part of a larger strategy for improving the institutional capability of the state.

Greater accountability and responsiveness through participation

Throughout history nearly all societies have grappled with how to make the state reflect the needs and interests of the population. But it is an especially relevant question today, with the spread of education and information and the growing pluralism of nations creating new pressures on states to listen and respond to the voices of their citizens. A sample of public opinion around the world suggests that belief in government remains solid, but that the performance of some state institutions is falling short of expectations (Box 7.1).

Electoral participation

In a democratic society elections are the primary manifestation of citizen voice. The number of democratically elected governments has increased sharply in recent decades, giving many citizens new opportunities to voice their opinions through the ballot. In 1974 only 39 countries—one in every four worldwide—were democratic. Today 117 countries—nearly two in three—use open elections to choose their national leadership, and two-thirds of the adult population in developing countries are eligible to participate in national elections (Figure 7.1). The trend is especially striking in Central and Eastern

---

Box 7.1 Public opinion and the state

Views on the state vary widely, reflecting perceptions of wide-ranging political and economic variables. To assess these perceptions and concerns, public opinion surveys have been carried out in various countries and regions. For example, a 1991–92 survey found that 49 percent of respondents in the United Kingdom, and 44 percent in the United States, felt excluded from public decision-making that directly affected their lives. Even so, satisfaction with the way their democracies are developing is relatively high in Western Europe and North America, ranging from 54 to 64 percent of respondents. By contrast, in Latin America and the transition economies of Eastern Europe only 30 to 40 percent of respondents report being satisfied with the way their democracies are working. In Latin America this negative perception may be related to the fact that 52 percent of respondents in a twelve-nation survey felt that the administration of elections in their country was fraudulent.

In Europe public support for the state and its services has been consistently strong since the 1970s. In 1990 large majorities—more than 70 percent—in seven Western European nations still believed that the government should provide health care, services to the elderly, aid to the unemployed, and assistance to industry, as well as reduce income differences. A 1996 poll across the fifteen countries of the European Union found that 51 percent of citizens believe their governments should maintain current social benefits and protection levels, compared with 12 percent who think they should be cut considerably to enhance EU competitiveness in world markets.

In Latin America 69 percent of citizens believe that the state should intervene to reduce income differences between rich and poor. Latin American respondents also regard as critical the government's role in maintaining law and order, but 65 percent have little or no confidence in the judiciary or the police force. Only 24 percent have some confidence in these institutions. These results closely mirror the concerns voiced by the region's entrepreneurs in the survey reported in Chapter 3.

In India a 1996 survey found that, despite strong support for the democratic system, voter trust in their representatives has fallen since 1971. Trust in some public institutions was also low, particularly the police (28 percent) and the bureaucracy (37 percent). Still, the poll found strong popular participation and involvement in politics: the number of respondents who said they participated in a social organization or political party doubled between 1971 and 1996.

In contrast to Europe, Latin America, and to some extent Asia, where statist traditions remain strong, in the United States 80 percent of respondents in a recent poll said they mistrusted the government because of its perceived inefficiency and waste. In addition, public support for welfare programs, particularly targeted welfare spending, has declined. A 1993 poll found that only one-sixth of Americans thought that the welfare system was working very well or fairly well, and in 1995 two-thirds thought that too much was being spent on welfare programs.

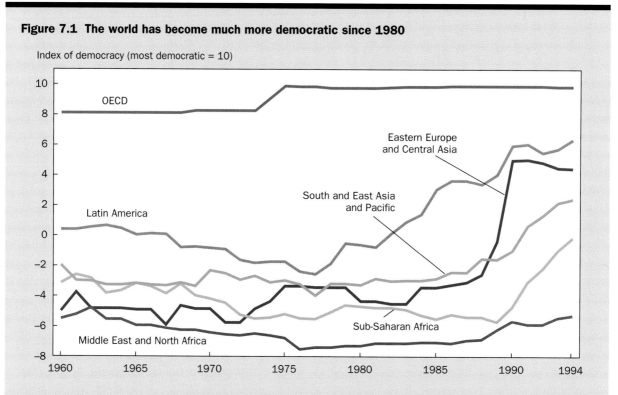

Figure 7.1 The world has become much more democratic since 1980

Index of democracy (most democratic = 10)

Note: This particular index of democracy is calculated for 177 countries from scores on five component indicators: competitiveness of political participation, regulation of political participation, competitiveness of executive recruitment, openness of executive recruitment, and constraints on the chief executive. The World Bank does not endorse any particular democracy index. See the Technical Note for details. Source: Jaggers and Gurr 1996.

Europe and Central Asia, where the fall of communist regimes in 1989 and 1991 sparked a series of major political changes across the region. These events had repercussions in other regions as well, particularly in Sub-Saharan Africa. In Latin America the gradual movement toward democracy started somewhat earlier. Now all but two countries in the region have democratically elected governments, and close to 13,000 units of local government are electing local leaders (such as mayors), compared with fewer than 3,000 in the late 1970s.

The principle of one person, one vote is fundamental to the representative purpose of elections. Without the necessary safeguards, however, political interference and electoral fraud can seriously affect representativeness and, thus, the legitimacy of electoral outcomes. As Box 7.1 noted, for instance, a majority of poll respondents in twelve Latin American countries felt that the administration of elections was fraudulent in their country; only 30 to 40 percent felt satisfied with the way democracy was working. Constitutional and institutional arrangements, compounded by inadequate information, also affect the ability of minority interests to gain effective representation. For example, a study of a number of European democracies in the 1980s shows that women's parliamentary representation and voter turnout are higher in systems based on proportional representation than in winner-take-all systems. Where women are better represented in parliament, their interests are better protected, through policies relating to maternity leave, child care, and flexibility in retirement systems. This suggests caution in making simple generalizations about the representativeness of formal electoral arrangements: it is important to analyze how they play out in practice.

Diversity and representation

Concern about the effects of majoritarian rule has sometimes led to changes in electoral arrangements to ensure adequate representation of minority groups. As the number of ethnic conflicts around the world attests, the belief of certain groups that they are being left behind—in terms of income, assets, or employment—can be a powerful source of frustration. This can spill over into direct conflict if the lagging groups lack adequate means of representing their concerns. Political elites who mirror ethnic differences in competing for power and distributing patronage will add fuel to the fire. In the contemporary world, states play a significant part in shaping ethnic relations through two related channels:

- The expansion of political authority enables states to create a competitive arena for the distribution of state resources and access to education, employment, land, and credit.
- The extension of political patronage, whether for administrative convenience or for enhanced control, lets governments favor certain ethnic groups over others.

Ethnic differences and conflicts are a part of most societies, yet some societies have managed them better than others. Techniques for alleviating such pressures have included dispersing the "points of power" (decentralization or devolution), supporting electoral arrangements that encourage cooperation among ethnic groups (electoral incentives and coalitions), and giving preferences to less privileged ethnic groups in public sector employment and other areas. Box 7.2 describes how constitutional change and preferential policies were used in Malaysia and Mauritius. By looking at some of the basic rules of the game, including elements of the political or institutional structure, both countries seem to have found a way to manage ethnic differences effectively.

Alternative strategies for voice and participation
Voting rules and electoral incentives can be reformed to make them more representative, but the simple fact that elections and referendums are held relatively infrequently (Switzerland is an exception, with an average of five local referendums each year since 1945) limits their scope for communicating timely information about societal preferences. In most societies, democratic or not, citizens seek representation of their interests beyond the ballot: as taxpayers, as users of public services, and increasingly as clients or members of NGOs and voluntary associations. Against a backdrop of competing social demands, rising expectations, and variable government performance, these expressions of voice and participation are on the rise.

The rapid growth of NGOs illustrates the trend most vividly. Since the late 1980s the number of NGOs operating in parts of Africa and Asia has almost doubled. In Central and Eastern Europe and the CIS the number of NGOs may have increased three- or fourfold from its very low base of 1989. In some countries of the OECD, operating expenditures in the voluntary or NGO sector now account for almost 4 percent of GDP.

NGOs have myriad organizational forms and functions, from labor unions to professional associations to neighborhood groups to philanthropic trusts. Among the most active NGOs today are those providing services directly to individuals and communities, from health and

---

Box 7.2   Managing multiethnic societies in Malaysia and Mauritius

Ethnic divisions in Malaysia have their roots in the colonial period, when large numbers of ethnic Chinese and Indians immigrated to take jobs and commercial opportunities that were not being filled by the largely agrarian native Malays (*bumiputra*). The 1957 constitution enshrined consociational principles, achieved through extensive negotiation among the major groups. In 1971, however, the new parliament passed a constitutional amendment that firmly established Malay primacy. The amendment made it illegal to "question publicly or even in Parliament the status of Malay language, the sovereignty of the Malay rulers, the special position of Malays or the citizenship rights of the immigrant communities." This ruling changed the character of electoral campaigns, since parties could no longer gain votes by arousing ethnic antagonisms.

A second initiative, the New Economic Program (1970–90), boosted the economic position of Malays. The program had two main elements. The first was the promotion of full, productive employment of Malays and an expansion of the supply of skilled Malay labor. Preferential university admissions standards for Malays almost tripled their enrollment, to three-quarters of the total. The second was the gradual redistribution of asset ownership. The government made it clear that it would not confiscate Chinese economic wealth, but that it would promote Malay participation in a growing economy. Strong growth allowed non-Malays to continue to gain, while the New Economic Program ensured that the growth would be shared by all citizens.

Mauritius has at least three major ethnic groups: Indo-Mauritians, Creoles, and Chinese. The designers of the electoral system, anxious to avoid creating institutions that might exacerbate the country's ethnic divisions, structured the system to force the main parties to seek support from all communities. Moreover, Mauritian governments have generally chosen broad-based growth and distribution policies over ethnic preferences. Formal preferences in employment and in education have never been used. And all governments since independence have had to form multiethnic coalitions in order to assume and maintain power. Growth with redistribution has tended to blunt the appeal of communal politics.

education to microcredit, vocational training, and professional services. In the OECD countries many NGOs operate alongside public providers. In Japan and the United Kingdom, for example, a large percentage of nonprofit organizations are active in education. In the United States they figure prominently in health care. But unlike public providers, most NGOs are not obliged to cater to the general needs of the population; this makes it simpler for them to provide services of a particular type and quality to specific groups.

In most developing countries NGOs engaged in service delivery are small in scale, working in communities and settings where the reach of government or private providers is weak or nonexistent. In the West Bank and Gaza, for example, an estimated 1,200 NGOs provide 60 percent of primary health care services, up to half of secondary and tertiary health care, and most agricultural services, low-cost housing schemes, and microcredit. In Cambodia some thirty to forty NGOs provide microcredit to rural and urban entrepreneurs in the absence of alternative government programs for poverty alleviation. The numerical importance of these NGOs reflects their ability to substitute for weak public sector capacity and to mobilize funds from a range of different sources, including national and international organizations.

Yet not all NGOs are involved in the delivery of services. Many others are research and civic education groups, advocacy organizations, and professional and business associations that represent particular interests or seek to educate the public about issues in their collective interest. The Socio-Ecological Union in Belarus, for example, is actively engaged in public education about industrial pollution and its consequences. The West Africa Enterprise Network is a business-oriented network, with some 300 members from twelve nations, representing the interests of domestic entrepreneurs in dealings with government. In many countries trade unions play an important role in generating and disseminating information on labor and policy-related issues. The growth of these intermediary organizations reflects the larger movement toward democracy in many regions and, in some countries, the need to bridge the "missing middle" between citizens and the state. Unlike the electoral process, however, where all votes are counted equally, not all these organizations are equally representative, either of their clients' interests or of the public interest more broadly.

Most intermediary NGOs tend to be one step removed from ordinary citizens; by contrast, grassroots organizations, community-based groups, and people's organizations engage them directly. In Umu-Itodo, a village in Enugu State, Nigeria, for instance, the Community Development Committee formed in 1986 has been responsible for numerous development and infrastructure projects that have had a direct impact on this isolated community. The committee has an elected executive board consisting of members from each part of the village; villagers rank it as the most relevant and effective organization in the village. Similar locally based organizations include rotating credit associations, farmers' associations, worker cooperatives, parent-teacher associations, and even religious congregations. These associations are valuable not only for their ability to meet basic needs, but also for the role they play in building trust and a sense of public connectedness among those excluded or alienated from the formal political process. But organizations such as these also face limitations, including narrowness of membership and representation, limited management capacity, and the risk of co-option by traditional power holders or political factions.

The institutional basis of participation

The depth and intensity of popular collective activity obviously differ by social and institutional setting. One explanation for these differences lies in differing endowments of *social capital,* the informal rules, norms, and long-term relationships that facilitate coordinated action and enable people to undertake cooperative ventures for mutual advantage. The presence of rules conducive to social organization can improve the collective efficiency of a community, but the absence of such rules is not necessarily a permanent condition. They can be generated by participation itself, and here governments and other formal organizations such as labor unions can play a positive role. Government efforts to improve the management of irrigation systems in Taiwan (China) and the Philippines, for example, have yielded numerous collective responses from farmers in managing operations and maintenance and in collecting water user fees. By accepting co-management of water resources by farmers, public officials achieved a substantial improvement in irrigation management. In the state of Ceará in northeastern Brazil (see Box 5.7 in Chapter 5), community monitoring of an innovative government health program provided the basis not only for a highly successful program but also for more effective cooperation among community members on other mutually beneficial courses of action.

The debate about the contribution of social capital to economic and social development is just beginning, and the early evidence is by no means unambiguous. But some studies are already demonstrating its potential impact on local economic development, on the provision of local public goods, and on the performance of public agencies (Box 7.3).

The social mechanisms that constitute social capital and the myriad forms of more formal nongovernmental activity directly reflect the heterogeneity of needs and preferences in society. At the same time there are no guarantees that these

Box 7.3 Does social capital matter?

A study of regional government in Italy during the 1970s and 1980s found that although political and economic failures were widespread, some regional governments, particularly those in the north, had performed well. Northern regional governments were notable for developing innovative day care programs and job training centers, promoting investment and economic development, managing the public's business efficiently, and satisfying their constituents. Regional governments in the south, by contrast, showed much weaker responsiveness and performance. The study attributed the better performance of northern governments to the external pressures created by dense networks of civic associations and citizen involvement in local public affairs.

A recent study of villages in rural Tanzania found that households in villages with high levels of social capital (defined in terms of the degree of participation in village-level social organizations) have higher ad-

justed incomes per capita than do households in villages with low levels of social capital. When other nonsocial capital determinants are controlled for, there also appears to be a strong correlation between a village's well-being and its level of social capital. This result points to important spillover effects at the village level arising from individual participation in local associations and groups. Although no general conclusions could be drawn about the impact of social capital on government performance, the study points to a number of important linkages, including a positive association between social capital and the quality of local schooling (see figure). The implication is that where parents can organize to monitor and pressure local government into maintaining local schools, school quality is enhanced. Even though the direct benefits of schooling accrue mainly to individuals, the benefits of monitoring local government performance accrue to all as a public good.

Social capital, household expenditure, and school quality in Tanzania

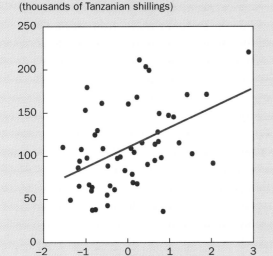

Household expenditure per capita
(thousands of Tanzanian shillings)

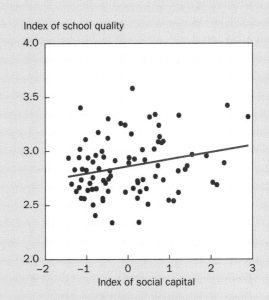

Index of school quality

Note: Data for the social capital index are from a 1995 survey of 1,376 Tanzanian households. The social capital index measures the prevalence of residents' participation in groups and voluntary associations. The school quality index measures households' perceptions of school quality. See the Technical Note for details. Source: Narayan and Pritchett 1997.

organizations are adequately addressing citizens' needs or that they are genuinely concerned with promoting the public interest. Most NGOs provide services of high quality, but some suffer from serious problems, including poor quality of service, inadequate community participation, and weak accountability. Some NGOs are created opportunistically, to advance the interests of narrow and privileged constituencies, often at the expense of the less vocal and less powerful. And the same social rules and norms that facilitate collective action among citizens can preserve inequalities and power differences within communities.

Yet given the many obstacles facing ordinary citizens, especially the poor, in articulating and pressing their needs, these associations play a vital role in channeling their voice and in building capacity for participation in public affairs. And those organizations that genuinely seek to work in the public interest can be valuable partners in economic and social development. Working from this premise, many governments are searching for new institutional arrangements for providing public goods, which involve both the private sector and groups in civil society (Figure 7.2). The next section sets these efforts in a broader context, exploring the range of mechanisms for increasing popular participation in the design and implementation of public policy.

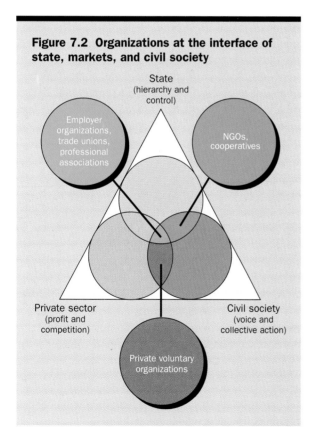

Figure 7.2 Organizations at the interface of state, markets, and civil society

State
(hierarchy and control)

Employer organizations, trade unions, professional associations

NGOs, cooperatives

Private sector
(profit and competition)

Civil society
(voice and collective action)

Private voluntary organizations

Improving institutional capability

Increasing opportunities for voice and participation can improve state capability in three ways. First, when citizens can express their opinions, formally or informally, and press their demands publicly within the framework of the law, states acquire some of the credibility they need to govern well. Broad-based discussion of policy goals can also reduce the risk that a powerful minority will monopolize the direction of government. States that achieve credibility are then allowed more flexibility in policy implementation and have an easier time engaging citizens in the pursuit of collective goals. This does not mean that Western-style democracy is the only solution. Experience from parts of East Asia suggests that where there is widespread trust in public institutions, effective ground-level deliberation, and respect for the rule of law, the conditions for responsive state intervention can be met.

Second, where markets are absent, as is the case for most public goods, popular voice can reduce information problems and lower transactions costs. Where incentive problems and weak state capability lead to inefficient public services, user groups and citizen associations can inform public officials of the problem and pressure them for improvements. A recent user assessment of the water supply system in Baku, Azerbaijan, for example, revealed not only significant problems of water leakage and water-related health problems, but the high costs that the city's unreliable water supply imposed on low-income consumers. Perhaps most interesting, users also revealed themselves willing to pay between two and five times more than they were actually paying for a reliable and safe water supply.

Third, no matter how dedicated, hardworking, or public spirited state officials are, they cannot anticipate all the public goods and services that citizens desire. The emergence of private and NGO alternatives to public provision can help meet gaps in the supply of public goods, as well as provide those goods and services that individuals are willing to pay for out of their own pocket. NGOs can be both partners and competitors in the delivery of public services. And when backed by citizen voice, they can exert useful pressure on government to improve the delivery and quality of public services.

There is no blueprint for finding the appropriate balance of voice, participation, and bureaucratic control in the provision of public goods. The solution depends on the capabilities of the public agencies in question and other providers and on the characteristics of the public good or service being provided. As discussed below, efficiency and equity dictate some degree of centralized government control and coordination when it comes to goods and services that have jurisdictional spillovers, are subject to economies of scale, or raise distributional concerns. In the technical and often sensitive area of economic management, for example, some insulation of decisionmaking from the pressure of political lobbies is desirable. In setting standards, such as in the provision of basic education, there is also an important role for centralized decisionmaking. But the process by which broad policy directions and standards are set should not be insulated from public discussion. And in the management of common-property resources, the production of basic infrastructure, and the delivery of essential services, there is considerable scope for involving people directly, both in the formulation of policy and in its implementation.

Participatory mechanisms

MECHANISMS FOR INFORMING AND CONSULTING. It is generally accepted that some areas of public decisionmaking require insulation from political pressure. In others, however, public and private interests coincide to such an extent—efforts to raise agricultural production, for example, or reforming the health system—that some level of public-private deliberation is not just desirable but in fact critical to success. In East Asia, by institutionalizing public-private deliberation councils comprising representatives of labor unions, industry, and government, policymakers were able to get broad agreement on economic policy issues and the necessary commitment to intervene quickly and flexibly. Other nations with very different institutional settings, such as Botswana, Chile, Mexico, Senegal, Uganda, and the United States, have also sought to implement deliberative mechanisms on issues ranging from economic policy to institutional reform.

By embedding the voice of powerful interest groups in mutually acceptable rules, public-private deliberation councils can reduce transactions costs by reducing the scope for opportunistic behavior. But these councils do not always succeed. Systematic evaluations of performance are not available, but a number of conditions and characteristics appear to affect success. These include broad enough representation and public education for the process to have widespread support, technical support and assistance to the councils, and an emphasis on building trust and mutual monitoring among both public and private sector participants.

Deliberative mechanisms are unlikely to enable governments to be effective in the long run if their policies appear illegitimate or unresponsive to crucial societal demands. Efforts to reach out to citizens must reach all the way down. At the very least, reforms and programs must be made intelligible to the public, for example by encouraging widespread media coverage of budget debates. In Singapore the Division of Public Feedback systematically gathers citizens' comments on a variety of national policies and invites interest groups to public hearings with ministers and senior officials. As discussed in Chapter 5,

legislation can also strengthen public accountability and responsiveness by requiring agencies to announce and enforce service norms and standards, provide public information, and respond to consumer complaints.

Specific techniques and mechanisms for consulting users and intended beneficiaries can also help improve the quality of specific public services. As the cases in Box 7.4 illustrate, feedback mechanisms such as client or user surveys can provide valuable information about an agency's performance and the type and quality of services reaching consumers. Simplified surveys such as the report card used in Bangalore, India, can be particularly useful when institutional capability is limited.

Besides increasing the flow of information to public officials, techniques for citizen and client consultation can introduce more openness and transparency into the system. As more people become aware of the performance of specific agencies or officials, they are more likely to exert collective pressure on the agency to perform better. At the same time public agencies will have less opportunity for arbitrary action.

But no mechanism for consultation automatically reaches all the appropriate individuals and groups. There are costs to acquiring and providing information, and the low income or subordinate position of some groups in society makes them nearly invisible to public officials. In consulting with users or clients, every effort must be made to identify all relevant social groups and ensure that they are represented.

MECHANISMS FOR DESIGN AND IMPLEMENTATION. Improving government performance does not end with improved consultation. There is also compelling evidence that arrangements that promote participation by stakeholders in the design and implementation of public services or programs can improve both the rate of return and the sustainability of these activities.

The education sector has proved particularly fertile ground for this kind of experimentation. Weak monitoring and supervision of local schools is a perennial problem for governments. But several are finding that these problems can be addressed by increasing the involvement of parents and communities in school management. In New Zealand, elected boards of trustees that manage schools are composed of parents of children at the school. Legislation enacted in Sri Lanka in 1993 established school development boards to promote community participation in school management. Many countries have also found that communities that participate in school management are more willing to assist in school financing.

Yet effective citizen involvement in school management does not come easy, nor is it a panacea. New Zealand realized after it had embarked on its reform that newly elected trustees required intensive training.

Box 7.4 Client surveys to motivate service improvements in India, Uganda, and Nicaragua

In several countries client surveys have helped motivate better public sector performance. By tapping the experience of citizens and having them monitor and evaluate services, surveys have helped identify problems and design and implement innovative solutions.

In Bangalore, India, "report cards" ask citizens and businesses to rate the public agencies they use to solve problems or get services. The report cards, administered by the Public Affairs Centre Bangalore, an NGO, assess the quality and cost of citizens' interactions with public agencies. In the first round of report cards the Bangalore Development Authority, responsible for housing and other services, scored the lowest in several categories, including staff behavior, quality of service, and information provided. Only 1 percent of respondents rated the authority's services as satisfactory. Rather than viewing the results as a threat, however, the authority's director took them as an opportunity, launching a citizen-government initiative to address delivery problems. Other agencies in Bangalore have also taken action inspired by the report cards. And groups in five other Indian cities,

including Mumbai (Bombay), have started using the report card approach.

Working with NGOs and communities, Uganda's government is also surveying views on service delivery. The first survey found that just 11 percent of rural households had ever been visited by an agricultural extension worker. Several districts have incorporated the survey findings into their district plans. One district has instituted further training for extension workers and is lobbying the central government for permission to spend more of its budget on extension workers.

Nicaragua's surveys, like Uganda's, were initiated by the government. The first survey, in 1995, found that 14 percent of bus riders had at some time been assaulted on a bus. It also found that 90 percent of bus drivers did not respect the official fare of 85 cordobas: they did not return the 15 cordobas in change from a 100-cordoba note to riders. Moreover, the survey revealed that people were willing to pay higher bus fares. Based on these findings, the fare was raised to one U.S. dollar. In a follow-up survey in 1996, 90 percent of users said that the official rate is respected.

Botswana found it difficult to attract qualified people to lower secondary school boards of governors, especially in rural areas. In Uganda, community training for parent-teacher associations and school management committees is being provided in two districts by an international NGO, to ensure that the quality of schooling and of school administration is enhanced.

Citizen participation may also be crucial in programs for the management of natural and common-property resources such as grazing lands, wildlife, forests, and water sources. Exclusive bureaucratic control of such resources has proved inadequate in many different institutional settings, in some cases leading to confrontation between the users of these resources and the public officials seeking to manage them. Recognizing the importance of participatory natural resource management, forestry officials, NGOs, and local communities in India are now undertaking a variety of initiatives. The National Forestry Policy embraces increased participation of local people in managing forests. In India's joint forest management programs, forest departments and local user groups share decisionmaking authority and control over forest lands and products and revenue. The result has been reduced conflict and increased productivity of the land.

Practices are also changing elsewhere. In Zimbabwe the CAMPFIRE program seeks to return the benefits of

protecting and conserving wildlife to local communities. And across Africa, Asia, and Latin America high levels of beneficiary participation in the design and management of rural water supply projects have been shown to be highly correlated with project success (Box 7.5).

However, the same study of rural water supply also revealed that, among the highly participatory projects, only half adequately involved women. The explanation was found in factors specific to women's participation, including time constraints and cultural barriers. Consequently, innovative participatory mechanisms are required that explicitly seek women's involvement in the design and implementation of projects that directly affect them. One such effort can be found in the Philippines, where a series of measures over more than two decades has gradually led to the integration of gender issues in the government's agenda, partly through greater participation of women in planning and implementing policies, and partly through specific programs for women. The expected payoff to such measures lies not just in improvements in the process of public policymaking but in the economic returns to better-designed and better-targeted public investments.

Making participation succeed will take hard work . . .
These illustrations suggest that in the provision of certain local public goods or shared services—where the people

who pay are also the direct and principal beneficiaries—using the institutional capacity closest to the client can improve the quality and effectiveness of public action. Capable states are therefore likely to be those that strengthen and increase the efficiency of local organizations and associations rather than replace them. But reaching out to citizens as co-managers or co-producers does not necessarily reduce the role of the state, nor is it costless or quick to implement. To get users or clients to become partners, public agencies often must invest considerable time and energy in building ties with communities, in building commitment among their own staff, and in ensuring that minimum standards of quality and equity are maintained.

In a pioneering case in Recife, Brazil, where the introduction of low-cost condominial sewers in low-income neighborhoods changed the relationship between the state agency and the sewer users, it took two years for public officials, working intensively and in multidisciplinary teams with residents, to figure out how to make the condominial system work. Even after the process was better understood, successful implementation took another four to six months in each neighborhood. An evaluation of the project showed that, by fostering an active and vocal constituency, the scheme not only generated considerable savings but also put in motion mechanisms for accountability that were critical for good agency performance.

Greater responsiveness means changing not only the way state agencies work with clients, but also the way those agencies are organized and reward their workers. Effective participation is more likely when opportunities for internal participation exist within the public agency. In addition, the overall incentive environment must reward higher-level staff for responsiveness to clients and must provide adequate support to street- or field-level workers in their efforts to work with clients. Without such measures, resistance to working with clients can be high, creating an atmosphere that is incompatible with a more participatory approach.

Working closely with people also often requires redefining tasks and responsibilities, reallocating staff resources, and developing new mechanisms for learning and experimentation. In Benin the Ministry of Health gave local health management committees decisionmaking control over resources. Committee members are elected democratically; anyone may serve, provided that at least one member is a woman. The committee is directly involved in preparing the health center's annual budget for submission to the ministry. It is responsible for collecting and accounting for funds paid to the health center for services and drugs. Representatives of local committees sit on the board of the government's new drug procurement agency, which is one way of keeping the agency accountable, and on the Health Sector Coordinat-

---

Box 7.5 Does participation improve project performance?

Using data from 121 diverse rural water supply projects in forty-nine countries in Africa, Asia, and Latin America, a recent study tested the relationship between participation and project performance. Participation was measured on a continuum ranging from simple information sharing through in-depth consultation with beneficiaries to shared decisionmaking to full control over decisionmaking. The authors found a strong correlation between high levels of beneficiary participation, especially in decisionmaking, and project success. Of the forty-nine projects with low levels of participation, only 8 percent were successful. But of the forty-two projects with high levels of beneficiary participation, 64 percent were successes.

Case studies support these conclusions. The first phase of the Aguthi Rural Water Supply Project in Kenya was conducted without community participation. The project, which involved piped water systems, was so plagued with problems that it came to a standstill and had to be redesigned. Working with project staff, local leaders, organized as the Aguthi Water Committee, mobilized community support for the project. Following public conferences with stakeholders, community members began to contribute labor and funds. Phase II of the project was completed on schedule and within budget. The communities continue to pay monthly tariffs for the new water service, and operation and maintenance are handled successfully in cooperation with the relevant government agency.

---

ing Committee, which gives local representatives a voice in national policy.

. . . And a supportive environment

Government can also support participation indirectly through its influence on the enabling environment. States have great power over individuals and organizations through the information they make public and through the laws they enact and administer. The rule of law that protects both persons and personal property is important to a healthy, vibrant civil society. Governments can facilitate participation by safeguarding the right of people to organize, to gain access to information, to engage in contracts, and to own and manage assets. The constitutions of Bolivia, Brazil, Colombia, and the Philippines explicitly encourage the development and participation of NGOs at all levels of decisionmaking. In Singapore the government helps NGOs recruit staff, allocates unused government buildings to them at nominal rents, and funds up to half the capital and operating costs of facilities run by NGOs for social welfare purposes. Without a credible legal environment that requires NGOs and public agencies to act openly and transparently, legitimate organizations are deprived of an opportunity to develop, or, perhaps worse, the door is left open for unhealthy or corrupt activities that taint the reputation of all NGOs. The aim must be to strike the right balance between regulations and reporting requirements that fosters growth of NGOs, while guarding against corruption and malpractice.

The benefits of greater consultation and partnership with civil society show up in improvements in the process of public policymaking, in the quality of service delivery, and, in some instances, in improved rates of return. They also manifest themselves in the greater flexibility afforded to public agencies and officials in the way they intervene. But without effective monitoring this flexibility can give rise to capricious or arbitrary action. Again, finding the right balance between participatory mechanisms and enlightened government control is crucial. The next section examines some of these concerns in the context of the debate over decentralization and the fostering of greater public accountability from below.

Decentralization: Matching services with local preferences

Decentralizing state power and resources seems a logical continuation of the many recent efforts to bring government closer to the people. Like the broad range of participatory mechanisms described earlier, decentralization offers the chance to match public services more closely with local demands and preferences and to build more responsive and accountable government from below. But decentralization also has its pitfalls, including the possibility of increased disparity across regions, loss of macroeconomic stability, and institutional capture by local factions, especially in highly unequal societies. This section focuses on some of the factors explaining recent trends in decentralization, and on some areas where it has been shown to have a positive impact, including bringing citizens into public affairs and stimulating local economic development. The section concludes by exploring the risks of decentralization and the implications for governments of differing capabilities starting out on the decentralization path.

The age of decentralization?

The rising demand for decentralization has come as part of the broader process of liberalization, privatization, and other market reforms in many countries. These reforms are distinct from one another, but their underlying rationale is similar to that for decentralization: that power over the production and delivery of goods and services should be rendered to the lowest unit capable of capturing the associated costs and benefits. In many countries this will involve scaling back the power of central government, but reformers must be discriminating. Depending on the institutional environment, decentralization can improve state capability by freeing it to focus on its core functions; it can also, however, undermine that capability.

The demand for formal, political decentralization has been driven by at least three major recent developments:

- *The minimum size of self-sufficient government has declined.* New technological options and new demands from citizens, producers, and consumers mean that some of the advantages (security, for example) that kept countries, regions, and provinces working together under a central government have become less important. In Europe and North America the pressure from global markets is creating strong demand for local and regional governments that can better provide the infrastructure and skilled labor force that multinational businesses need.
- *Political changes have given voice to local demands.* Centralized authority in Czechoslovakia, the Soviet Union, and Yugoslavia collapsed once the unifying force of the Communist Party disappeared. Elsewhere, regions and subnational governments benefited from the political vacuum created before and during regime changes, as in Argentina and Brazil in the late 1980s, and South Africa in the 1990s.
- *Countries often turn to local and regional governments when the central government has persistently failed to provide essential services.* In the second half of the 1980s, Colombia embarked on a path of decentralization and political reform that reversed a long tradition of centralism. A new government changed direction, transferring social services delivery to the local level and opening up the rigid political appointment system to local electoral choice. Similarly, in Venezuela and other countries in South America, active local governments have made local administration more responsive and improved the quality of services provided, often dramatically.

Before assessing how governments can act to meet such demands, it is worth asking what decentralization really means. In fact, the term encompasses a wide range of distinct processes. The main ones are administrative deconcentration, or the transfer of state functions from higher to lower levels of government while retaining central control of budgets and policymaking; fiscal decentralization, or the ceding of influence over budgets and financial decisions from higher to lower levels; and devolution, or the transfer of resources and political authority to lower-level authorities that are largely independent of higher levels of government. Rarely does decentralization embrace all three. This wide diversity of experience makes it difficult to compare trends across countries or draw many hard and fast conclusions.

Richer and larger countries tend to be more decentralized, in terms of the share of subnational governments in total public expenditure and revenue. In the aggregate, however, industrial countries have become slightly more centralized since 1974 (Table 7.1). This is especially true of the United Kingdom, whereas Australia, France, Spain, and the United States are continuing to decentralize central government functions. Developing countries, most of which went through a nation-building phase of development in the aftermath of colonialism in the 1950s and 1960s, have become more decentralized since the 1970s. Striking examples include Argentina, Brazil, and Colombia. In both groups of countries decentralization of expenditure has gone significantly further than that of corresponding revenue.

How to think about decentralization
As the above discussion has made clear, what constitutes the best structure of intergovernmental arrangements will be highly country-specific. The one-size-fits-all approach

is as fruitless here as in other aspects of state reform. But a number of important analytical principles are available to guide reformers. The clearest and most important principle (often referred to as subsidiarity) is that public goods and services should be provided by the lowest level of government that can fully capture the costs and benefits.

Applying this principle is no simple matter, however. Table 7.2 illustrates some of the demand and supply characteristics of goods and services that will be relevant to the decision. As already discussed, for some local goods, such as those with common-property characteristics, organizations outside of government such as forest or water user associations or NGOs may be the most appropriate institutional mechanism for delivery. More generally, where preferences or demands differ from one community to the next, local governments can better match supply to suit local tastes. Decentralized service provision can also enhance efficiency and interjurisdictional competition in supply, providing consumers (at least in theory) with the option to exit to other jurisdictions. On the other hand, where economies of scale or interjurisdictional spillovers are present on the supply side—as in the construction and maintenance of interurban highways—or where minimum standards (such as for primary schooling) and other consumption externalities apply on the demand side,

Table 7.1 Changes in subnational finance in selected countries
(percentage of expenditures or revenues for all levels of government)

Country	Subnational expenditures			Subnational revenues		
	1974	1994	Trend	1974	1994	Trend
Argentina	25	45	↗	25	37	↗
Australia	47	49		20	27	↗
Brazil	30	38	↗	23	25	
Canada	61	60		39	44	↗
Chile	2	9	↗	2	5	
Colombia	25	33	↗	16	18	
France	18	19		6	13	↗
Germany	44	40		34	30	
India	45	49		27	25	
Indonesia	11	15		3	3	
Iran, Islamic Rep. of	1	5		1	6	↗
Malaysia	18	14		13	8	↘
Romania	16	10	↘	12	6	↘
South Africa	24	41	↗	4	12	↗
Spain	10	34	↗	5	12	↗
Sweden	44	34	↘	28	32	
Thailand	17	8	↘	5	5	
United Kingdom	33	28		15	8	↘
United States	45	44		33	36	
Zimbabwe	26	25		24	15	↘

Note: Data are for all levels of government other than central government. Data include transfers from central government to subnational governments. Arrows indicate changes of 5 percentage points or more. Where data for 1974 or 1994 were unavailable (indicated by italics), data for the closest available year were used. Data for Germany for 1974 refer to the preunification territory.
Source: IMF, various years (a).

Table 7.2 Demand and supply characteristics of local and national public goods

Level of public provision	Demand-side factors	Supply-side factors
Local	Variation in local taste (street lighting, zoning) Common property (urban roads, waste disposal)	Potential for competition between jurisdictions (police protection, road maintenance)
National	Spatial consumption externalities (control of epidemics) Equity concerns (minimum standards for primary education)	Economies of scale (defense) Cross-jurisdictional externalities (inter-urban highways)

centralized control (whether at the national or the provincial level) is likely to be preferable.

Matching services to local preferences can lead to lower transactions costs (particularly information costs), efficiency gains, and incentives to local economic development. But even where a service might, in principle, seem a candidate for local provision, the benefits and costs of decentralization will vary by setting. And experience suggests that decentralization is unlikely to work without effective institutional arrangements to foster accountability at the local level, and fiscal restraint on the part of both local and national governments. This is best explained in terms of two separate but interrelated sets of relationships facing local governments, both of which need to be considered in gauging the scope for decentralization.

The first are horizontal relationships between local government and citizens, NGOs, and private businesses. Institutional arrangements, for example local elections or referendums, can create or influence such relationships, providing incentives for cooperation, accountability, and improved local government performance. The second set of relationships is vertical, between levels of government. Most countries have formal institutional arrangements that define the role and functions of each tier of government, particularly as they affect intergovernmental fiscal relations. Both vertical rules and horizontal incentives are essential if local governments are to perform their functions well (Figure 7.3). The next section discusses some of the ways in which horizontal relationships can encourage local governments to enhance their responsiveness, mobi-

lize resources, improve service delivery, and stimulate private sector development.

The benefits of improved local accountability and incentives
CITIZEN PARTICIPATION. In theory, decentralization can strengthen and complement the measures to broaden popular participation described earlier in this chapter. Like them, it can help guard against majoritarian tyranny by moving government closer to people and by facilitating local definition of issues and problems, especially those of minority groups. The contrasting situations of Oaxaca and Chiapas, two of the poorest states in Mexico, provide a telling example of these effects at work. The two states have similar resource endowments and development potential, and both have a high percentage of poor and indigenous populations. Yet the outcomes of antipoverty programs are generally regarded as good in Oaxaca, whereas neighboring Chiapas has a bad record. The difference seems to stem from the degree of popular participation in policy decisions and implementation. Oaxaca has a long tradition of participatory mechanisms for indigenous populations and the poor. In Chiapas, on the other hand, the denial of such options, coupled with widespread official corruption, has led to poor services and rising tensions, including armed conflict since early 1994.

Where public office is contested and people can participate in elections and decide on representatives at different levels of government, the number of political choices also increases, thus stimulating competition between levels of government. Local participation can also mean greater confidence in and acceptance of policy decisions by constituents. Decentralization can therefore increase local options for policymaking while holding local officials accountable for what they do and how they do it. Recent evidence from Latin America, particularly Colombia, suggests that once local policymakers are held accountable for their actions and made aware that their jobs depend to a large extent on citizens' assessments of their performance, they tend to be much more concerned with the quality of their staff and of the tools they have to run their offices effectively. In Pôrto Alegre, Brazil, an innovative process of public investment planning and management was launched in 1989, to mobilize citizen groups to take part in formulating the municipal budget. In 1995 some 14,000 people were engaged in the process through assemblies and meetings. Indirectly, an estimated 100,000 people were linked to "participatory budgeting" through local associations and popular organizations.

LOCAL SERVICE PROVISION. Many governments have responded to fiscal crises, the availability of new technologies, and citizen concerns by transferring resources and responsibility for service provision, especially in education and health, to local authorities. In many cases this has given rise to new and often creative arrangements among local governments, NGOs, and local businesses. Although relatively little comparative evidence is available with which to evaluate the relationship between decentralized government and service quality, some recent examples from Latin America are illustrative. In the 1980s the primary education system in the state of Minas Gerais, in southeastern Brazil, faced many of the problems common among education systems in developing countries: high repetition rates, low graduation rates, and low achievement scores. Contributing to these problems were overregulated and centralized management, inadequate funding, and poorly trained teachers. In the 1990s a series of measures, including the introduction of autonomy to elected boards in each local school (composed of teachers, parents, and students over 16), together with grants from central government based on enrollment and special needs, have produced some encouraging early results: achievement scores have risen by 7 percent in science, 20 percent in Portuguese language skills, and 41 percent in mathematics.

In Teocelo, a town in Mexico's state of Veracruz, decentralization has created opportunities to organize resources for health more efficiently by identifying the population's needs and designing strategies to foster participation through community organization and health education. Coverage increased for both preventive and curative care, the quality of services improved enormously, and infant mortality rates fell. In addition, users of health facilities reported that the attitudes of health personnel and the quality of services had improved greatly.

LOCAL ECONOMIC DEVELOPMENT. The participation of local businesses can also play a crucial role in decentralization, shaping incentives at the local level. Entrepreneurs have for centuries strongly influenced both the pace of development and intergovernmental relationships in industrial countries. Property-owning classes with command over local resources exerted considerable pressure on public entities. To spur expansion, private actors and public officials were encouraged to cooperate. Much of this began in local environments. Members of the business community often participated in local legislatures. Provided that rent seeking is minimized by effective competition policies—a function for higher levels of government—a strong local private sector may promote better administrative performance. And local governments that provide and maintain credible frameworks for local economic development end up promoting private investment, which over time increases local government revenues.

The world is replete with examples of local governments that have stimulated economic development in their communities, and of decentralized institutional arrangements that have contributed to growth. The cities of Greenville and Spartanburg, South Carolina, are small, inland, and far from major U.S. population centers. Yet they have the highest foreign investment per capita of any metropolitan areas in the United States. They are host to 215 companies from eighteen countries, seventy-four of which are headquartered there. Visionary decisionmakers with a strong private sector approach to local development have established a solid base of innovative small and

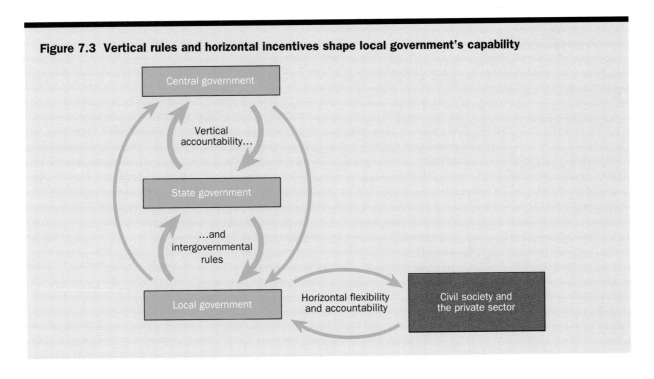

Figure 7.3 Vertical rules and horizontal incentives shape local government's capability

Central government

Vertical accountability...

State government

...and intergovernmental rules

Local government

Horizontal flexibility and accountability

Civil society and the private sector

medium-size enterprises, employing a work force whose skills are regularly upgraded.

On the other side of the world, the city government of Wuhan, in central China, decided in the early 1990s to transform the old city and build a new one on a large scale. To this end it relaxed controls on foreign investment in two development zones, opened a third, passed local regulations to supply foreign investors with a legal foundation for business operation, strengthened the management of real estate and land rentals, and undertook several projects to improve the infrastructure for foreign investment. As a result, in 1992 alone the number of foreign investment projects approved for the city was more than two-and-a-half times the total for the previous eight years, producing a threefold increase in total capital invested. Not satisfied, the city government organized a huge investment promotion mission in 1993, which garnered agreements worth $5 billion from Singapore and Hong Kong (China).

Despite such encouraging cases, experience suggests that successful decentralization may be short-lived, or difficult to replicate, without effective rules for intergovernmental collaboration. Horizontal incentives for improved performance tell only part of the story. In education, for example, involvement of higher levels of government may be needed to prevent fragmentation and to minimize differences in the quality of education in different communities. And in the health sector the appropriate allocation of responsibilities across levels of government is rarely clear-cut. Immunizations, tuberculosis surveillance, and vaccine storage all need strong, effective management from higher levels of government. In addition, localities may not provide the right framework for policy formulation and implementation. Consequently, decentralization should not become a rigid, doctrinaire exercise, pushing functions onto communities and municipalities or artificially separating levels of government. Instead it should be a practical endeavor to find the right balance between the roles of different levels of government, to ensure that high-quality services are provided in a timely manner. As the following sections describe, the quest for that balance must take place within a framework of credible rules.

The pitfalls of decentralization

In many cases decentralization is not the result of any carefully designed sequence of reforms, but has occurred in a politically volatile environment in which the level of trust is low and policymakers respond unsystematically to emerging demands from below. Such weak policy frameworks can lead to serious economic problems, including loss of macroeconomic control, regional disparities in service provision, and misallocation of resources as a result of local capture. The lesson, for all governments, is that there

must at any given time be clear rules specifying the range of responsibilities for each level of government.

MACROECONOMIC DIMENSIONS OF INTERGOVERNMENTAL FINANCE. Macroeconomic control is universally regarded as a function of central government. Centralization, or at least strong central guidance, in budget and financial matters has proved critical in ensuring sound public finances and a reliable framework for economic development in most industrial economies. Because decentralization increases the number of actors and of budgetary accounts, countries facing serious budgetary and inflationary pressures will be confronted with additional challenges and risks should they embark on decentralization.

Intergovernmental fiscal relations mainly affect the macroeconomy through three channels: the assignment and sharing of tax bases and expenditures, the match of tax and expenditure decisions, and levels of subnational borrowing.

Serious macroeconomic imbalances can occur if major tax bases are inappropriately assigned. In India, for example, important tax bases have been assigned to subnational governments. This has left the central government, despite a growing public debt and pension liabilities, with a tax base, consisting mainly of income, foreign trade, and excise taxes, that is too small to cope comfortably with its expenditure responsibility. The sharing of major tax bases also has the potential to dilute the impact of deficit reduction at the central government level. This happened in Argentina in the early 1990s, when increased tax revenues following a tax reform had to be shared with provincial governments. Provincial governments essentially took a free ride on the central government's efforts and used the extra revenue to expand their work forces.

Expenditures with national benefits and costs—national public goods—should be the responsibility of central government. These include the costs of economic stabilization and redistribution. But many local expenditures also affect income distribution, such as the provision of health and housing subsidies in transition economies and many developing countries. In addition, where the benefits of local public expenditure are concentrated within the jurisdiction doing the spending, but the costs (in the form of general taxes or negative spillovers) are spread more widely, subnational governments have an incentive to spend beyond their means. The effect on national fiscal policy can be severe.

SUBNATIONAL BORROWING. Borrowing by local governments can contribute to macroeconomic instability when the central government fails to impose hard budget constraints and there is no effective mechanism for monitoring debt obligations, particularly when there are multiple lenders. Another problem is asymmetric information on the part of borrowers (subnational governments) and lenders (central government and international capital markets). In China, for example, provincial governments are not allowed to finance budget deficits through borrowing. But in the early 1990s all-but-uncontrolled borrowing by state enterprises at the subnational level contributed to economic overheating and imperiled macroeconomic stability (Box 7.6). The combined indebtedness of the Brazilian states exceeds $100 billion, close to the levels of total federal and central bank debt. Unless the growth of this debt is curtailed, the federal government will have to reduce its own spending, raise taxes, or resort to inflationary financing to cover the states' debts.

Box 7.6 Pitfalls in intergovernmental relations: The experiences of Brazil and China

Democratization and constitutional revisions in the 1980s increased the amount of resources under subnational control in Brazil and the degree of local autonomy in their use. Local governments now account for half of total public spending.

Although decentralization shifted resources downward, there was no corresponding clarification or expansion of local responsibilities. Subnational governments were not prepared to assume new tasks, and were neither required to perform specific functions nor prohibited from performing functions already performed by other levels of government. As a result, local governments used much of their windfall to increase staffing and launch questionable new projects. There is scant evidence that the overall efficiency of public sector spending improved. Decentralization also increased the fiscal deficit, as large states used their improved political autonomy to extract federal resources: by the mid-1990s nearly a third of the growing federal deficit was due to subnational debt.

Brazil's experience shows that political and fiscal decentralization does not guarantee improved public sector efficiency, and may threaten macroeconomic stability. To achieve its objectives, fiscal decentralization must be accompanied by a corresponding decentralization of expenditure responsibilities; state and municipal governments' institutional capacities should be improved; and the federal government should impose hard budgets in its fiscal and financial relationships with subnational governments.

China's experience in the early 1990s demonstrates the pitfalls of decentralization that is not accompanied by parallel reforms and macroeconomic safeguards. Beginning in 1978, central authority over investment and allocation decisions was gradually decentralized to provincial governments, enterprises, financial institutions, and even households. This was a crucial element of China's economic liberalization and a key factor in the economy's impressive growth over the past two decades. At the same time, however, three consequences of decentralization undermined the central government's control over macroeconomic aggregates:

■ Government revenues as a share of GDP declined precipitously. By contributing to increased industrial competition, decentralization helped lower the profits of industrial state enterprises, previously the main source of tax revenues. Increasingly autonomous local governments reduced revenues even further by granting tax exemptions to improve the after-tax earnings of the state enterprises under their control.

■ The growing autonomy of local governments also made it difficult for the central government's investment planning system to control the investments of provincial governments and state enterprises under their control. Since tax revenues at the provincial level had declined and were inadequate to cover these investments, local branches of the state banks were usually prevailed on to lend for these projects.

■ Local branches of the central bank were given discretionary authority over 30 percent of the central bank's annual lending to the financial system. When local branches of the state bank needed additional resources to support investments by local governments and state enterprises, they turned to the local branch of the central bank for an infusion of liquidity.

The resulting overheating of the Chinese economy in 1992–93 posed considerable risks to stability. Inflation climbed to its highest level in several decades. Real GDP growth reached an amazing 14.2 percent in 1992 and 13.5 percent in 1993. Eighty percent of this growth came from growth in investment, most of it by state enterprises under the supervision of provincial governments.

The authorities responded quickly with a combination of measures. The most important of these were administrative restrictions on investment by provincial governments and state enterprises and a reassertion of authority by the central bank over lending to state banks. These measures and others helped bring the economy to a soft landing. By 1995 inflation had fallen below 7 percent, while GDP growth had been maintained at around 9 percent.

All three channels can lead to undesirable macroeconomic outcomes. But some of the channels are quantitatively more important in some countries than in others. Whether they generate macroeconomic instability will depend on the relative importance of each channel, the relative capacity of central and local government policymaking and implementation, and the central government's commitment to overall macroeconomic objectives, such as growth and price stability.

REGIONAL DISPARITIES AND INEQUALITIES IN SERVICE PROVISION. Rough national equality in living standards and in access to public services is an overarching goal—even a constitutional mandate—in many countries. Centralization allows the national government more discretion to counter regional income disparities by managing regional differences in levels of public service provision and taxation. With decentralization, an equitable outcome can no longer be guaranteed or, at least, may be more difficult to achieve. And wealthier local governments and regions may benefit disproportionately from being given greater taxing power.

In China, for example, disparities in real income per capita between provinces have been growing in recent years. Income per capita in the richest province, Guangdong, is now four times greater than that in the poorest, Guizhou. Some provinces on the southern coast, such as Fujian, Guangdong, and Hainan, have done better than the western, interior provinces largely because of their central location for transport and communications and their proximity to Hong Kong (China). These natural advantages have been reinforced by official policies that favor coastal provinces, including tax breaks to foreign investors locating in special economic zones near the coast, large allocations of credit (relative to population) through China's government-directed banking system, and registration requirements that discourage the poor from migrating to the booming coast.

In Russia income inequality across oblasts is high. The ratio of expenditure per capita between the lowest- and the highest-spending oblast is estimated to have risen to one to seven by 1992, with better-off regions receiving disproportionately high budgetary expenditure allocations and rural areas relatively ill served. Subnational taxation or sharing of federal revenues from natural resources on the basis of their origin could create even greater fiscal disparities. Both Russia's and China's experiences highlight the need to design appropriate equalization schemes to deal with rising inequality during periods of accelerated growth or macroeconomic stabilization.

RESOURCE MISALLOCATION AS A RESULT OF LOCAL CAPTURE. Economic and financial distortions may also arise from subnational governments' ability to exploit weaknesses at the center. In the absence of agreed intergovernmental rules, local governments may benefit from sources of income that have not been formally allocated to them under an appropriate fiscal decentralization scheme. In Poland, for example, the introduction of local self-government has seen many local authorities begin to act like pressure groups, eager to extract more benefits from Warsaw for local clienteles. As a consequence, inequalities have risen among jurisdictions, leading to new forms of social conflict.

In Pakistan decentralization has been accompanied by a subtle recentralization of functions at the provincial level and difficult intergovernmental relationships. Provincial governments, which have expanded their role in the provision of education and other local public services since the 1960s, have increasingly adopted an intrusive, centralist attitude toward municipal governments. Instead of being encouraged to assume new tasks and responsibilities, municipal governments are being denied opportunities to succeed. Increased provincial control has not led to any noticeable improvement in service delivery, however.

Industrial countries that have decentralized began the process with a strong legal framework, which ties subnational governments to credible rules. Many of these countries also have mechanisms in place, such as fiscal transfer policies and equalization schemes (Box 7.7), hard budget constraints, and limitations on local borrowing, to counterbalance negative outcomes. Some countries have experimented with participatory mechanisms (blue-ribbon commissions, for example), which bring stakeholders together and provide options for feasible and manageable policies within a mutually agreed time frame.

Lessons for successful decentralization

Ideally, policymakers would embark on decentralization by gradually phasing in the reassignment of revenue authority and of expenditure authority and responsibilities in ways that are compatible and consistent with previously defined needs and responsibilities. At the same time, they would develop a system of intergovernmental grants to cover gaps between expenditures and revenues at the local level and to correct imbalances in efficiency and effectiveness, preferably with built-in incentives for local resource mobilization. So much for the ideal. The real-life business of designing a successful decentralization program tends to be more complex.

ASSIGNING EXPENDITURE AND REVENUE AUTHORITY. This brings a host of problems. Information on the true distribution of benefits and taxes both within and between jurisdictions is imperfect. And economies of scale in revenue collection and in the production of services may partly negate the efficiency advantages of a decentralized system. In addition, the costs of alternative options

Box 7.7 Calculating fiscal equalization grants

Fiscal equalization programs compensate provinces whose fiscal capacities are below the average. In addition to safeguarding national objectives of providing minimum levels of public services nationwide, an equalization program can foster the participation of member provinces in a federation. Thus fiscal equalization is often viewed as the glue that holds a federation together. Economists have long recognized that equalization is justified on grounds of horizontal equity, and in recent years it has become clear that under certain conditions it can promote economic efficiency as well.

In Pakistan, for example, a representative tax system has been proposed to equalize fiscal capacity across regions. Designing such a system involves, first, calculating the revenue that could be raised if a provincial government used all the standard sources of revenues at the nationwide average intensity of use. Then, using

the arithmetic mean of all provinces as a standard, the province's equalization entitlement for a given revenue source is determined by the difference (if positive) between the average potential yield at the national average rate of taxation in all provinces in the aggregate, and the potential yield obtained in the province when the national average tax rate is applied to its revenue base. In this way the fiscal capacity of below-average provinces is brought up to the median, the arithmetic mean, or some other norm. Because the data on tax bases and tax collections required to implement a representative tax system are published regularly by various levels of government in many countries, implementing such a system does not impose new data requirements and could be implemented as a federal fiscal equalization program in lieu of revenue sharing by the population.

---

for service production are often unknown. Some possible tax and expenditure assignments are shown in Table 7.3.

DESIGNING INTERGOVERNMENTAL GRANTS. Intergovernmental grants are important sources of revenue for many subnational governments. In Brazil between 1970 and 1992, grants from the federal government financed 64 percent of local government expenditure. In South Africa grants from the central government to newly elected provincial governments account for about 90 percent of total revenues for the latter. By their nature, intergovernmental grants tend to divorce local spending from local resources, and the benefits of providing local public services from the costs. The separation of benefits and costs and the limited ability of local governments to mobilize revenues for themselves can reduce the transparency of local budgetmaking and the accountability of local governments to local citizens, leading to inefficient and inequitable delivery of public services. Clearly, then, any system of intergovernmental grants in developing countries will need to be designed extremely carefully.

No blueprint exists for an optimal system of intergovernmental grants, but a good system should have certain characteristics. Above all, it should be predictable and transparent and embody the relevant principles set forth in Table 7.4.

AGREEING ON THE RIGHT APPROACH. Clear-cut rules are essential for imposing restraints on actors at each level of government. Equally important seems to be the process by which the rules are agreed on. Although, in principle, rules could be imposed from the top down to restrain the

arbitrary action of all participants, experience suggests that it is difficult to force agreement and that the result may not be sustainable. This is especially true of developing economies. Lessons from a variety of countries indicate that key policy decisions are more likely to be sustained when they are based on a broad consensus among stakeholders. Thus, the prospects of successful decentralization are greater with institutional settings and processes that allow for articulation of interests and consensual policymaking, as spelled out, for example, in the European Charter of Local Government of 1985.

In the absence of agreed-on guiding principles, what can governments committed to decentralization do to get the process started? Some models already exist. In the early 1990s the government of Uganda established a consultative process with different stakeholders—community groups, agricultural producers, and government representatives—to decide on the best way to proceed with decentralization. The decision was made for a staged and gradualist approach. Other countries have opted for commissions made up of informed leaders from different levels of government, academia, and sometimes unions and business associations, drawing on foreign advice where necessary. South Africa's recent experience is interesting in this respect. The new constitution calls for a fiscal commission to deal with the intergovernmental structure of the country. The president, in charge of setting up the commission, provided different representatives with a constitutionally guaranteed forum for articulating their interests. Although it is too early to judge its success, the

Table 7.3 Possible tax and expenditure assignments by level of government

Central government	State government	Local or provincial government
Revenues		
Value added tax	Individual income tax	Property taxes
Individual income tax	Surcharges on national taxes	Vehicle taxes
Corporate income tax	Retail sales taxes	User charges
Excise taxes	Excise taxes	Licenses and fees
Natural resource taxes	Property taxes	
Customs duties	Vehicle taxes	
Export taxes		
Expenditures		
Tertiary health care (control of infectious diseases, research)	Secondary health care (hospitals, curative care)	Primary health care
University education	University and secondary education	Primary and secondary education
Roads and highways (intercity)	Roads and highways (intercity)	Roads and highways (intracity)
Public transportation (intercity)	Public transportation (intercity)	Public transportation (intracity)
Natural resource management	Air and water pollution	Air and water pollution
Defense	Natural resource management	Solid waste disposal, water, sewerage, fire protection
	Police protection	Land use regulation and zoning
		Housing
		Cultural policy
		Promotion of tourism
		Police protection

process created a widespread sense of expectation and generated demands to design appropriate decentralization measures.

Commissions may serve short-term interests well. Over the longer term, however, more-durable solutions may be needed to allow for formal representation of subnational governments' interests in national policymaking and legislation. Second-chamber institutions, such as the German Bundesrat, have often been used in this context. Such arrangements offer an institutionalized mechanism for articulating interests from below, while providing the means to develop widely accepted and credible rules for intergovernmental collaboration, which are essential for sustainable decentralization. They also help different tiers of government adjust to emerging needs over time.

ENSURING THAT THE INSTITUTIONAL GROUND IS READY. In principle, bringing policymaking and implementation closer to the communities they serve, and involving citizens in shaping policies, lead to greater accountability and improved local checks and balances. But as the above discussion of the potential for macroeconomic instability shows, government actions at the center can be undermined at the local level if there is no strong pattern of fiscal restraint and if there are no enforceable rules governing intergovernmental relations. In most federalized systems effective checks and balances between levels of government have evolved over long periods. What

history tells us, paradoxically, is that unless states have achieved a certain level of centralization and effective rules for overall macroeconomic control and sound policymaking, decentralization may be difficult to implement and may create imbalances. Decentralization, whether it occurs through gradual evolution or design (or both), can create additional momentum for development, but only if these conditions are met.

Any strategy of decentralization must begin with an assessment of institutional capability at the various levels of government (Table 7.5). Where there is weak central government capability to manage national fiscal and monetary policy, to enact and enforce credible rules for intergovernmental affairs, or to provide a framework for bringing stakeholders together, decentralization will be hard to pull off. Strongly polarized relationships between or within tiers of government and extremely weak organizational capacity at the subnational level will also be cause for concern. In these circumstances policymakers would do well to postpone decentralization, or eschew ambitious strategies in favor of a more carefully staged or sectoral approach. Decentralization might begin, for example, with certain priority areas such as education, health, or infrastructure. Strong monitoring mechanisms could provide opportunities for learning and for gradually phasing in new policies. Countries with greater capability at the central and the local levels have more options to choose from—but their preferences will vary. What may be important in one country (say, decentralized service delivery) may not be desired (or desirable) in others.

Strategic options: Bridging the gap between state and citizen

The evidence presented in this chapter has shown that improving the capability and effectiveness of the state rests with mechanisms to increase openness and transparency, to strengthen incentives for participation in public affairs, and, where appropriate, to bring government closer to the people and communities it is meant to serve. Building capability in this way will take time and careful attention to the dangers: efforts to open up government to a broader array of needs and interests will not improve effectiveness or accountability if they shut other groups further out. But the experience of governments the world over suggests some clear starting points:

- Where appropriate, states should work to ensure broad-based public discussion and evaluation of key policy directions and priorities. At a minimum this means making available information in the public interest and establishing consultative mechanisms such as deliberation councils and citizen committees to gather the views and preferences of affected groups.
- They should encourage, where feasible, the direct participation of users and beneficiary groups in the design, implementation, and monitoring of local public goods and services. And they should enhance the capacity and efficiency of accountable local organizations and institutions rather than replace them.
- Where decentralized service delivery is considered desirable, states should adopt a carefully staged or sectoral approach, beginning in priority areas such as health, education, or infrastructure. They should introduce strong monitoring mechanisms and make sure that

Table 7.4 Principles and best practices in grant design

Grant objective	Principles of grant design	Best practices	Practices to avoid
Bridging fiscal gap	Reassignment of responsibilities between levels of government Tax abatement Tax base sharing	Tax abatement in Canada Tax base sharing in Brazil, Canada, Pakistan, and South Africa	Deficit grants Tax-by-tax sharing as in India and Pakistan
Reducing regional fiscal disparities	General nonmatching grants Fiscal capacity equalization transfers	Fiscal equalization programs in Australia, Canada, and Germany	General revenue sharing using multiple-factor formulas
Compensating for benefit spillovers	Open-ended matching transfers with matching rate consistent with estimated spillover	Transfers for teaching hospitals in South Africa	
Setting national minimum standards	Conditional nonmatching block transfers with conditions on standards of service and access	Roads and primary education grants in Indonesia Education transfers in Colombia and Chile	Conditional transfers with conditions on spending alone Ad hoc grants
Influencing local priorities in areas of high national but low local priority	Open-ended matching transfers with matching rate varying inversely with local fiscal capacity	Matching transfers for social assistance in Canada	Ad hoc grants
Stabilization	Capital grants, provided maintenance is possible	Limited use of capital grants with encouragement of private sector participation through guarantees against political and policy risk	Stabilization grants with no future upkeep requirements

Table 7.5 Matching decentralization strategy to government capacity

Local government capacity	Central government capacity	
	Low	**High**
Low	Cautious decentralization strategy with pilot testing	Deconcentration of some priority services
	Delegation of some functions to NGOs and communities	Delegation of some functions to NGOs and communities
	Massive institutional strengthening at both levels, particularly in public finances (most Sub-Saharan African countries)	Targeted strengthening of local entities during transfer of responsibilities (e.g., Hungary, Mexico, Thailand)
High	Separatist or secessionist tendencies	Delegation or devolution of functions according to government priorities and preferences as well as articulated needs (most industrial countries)
	Delegation or devolution according to priorities of governments (e.g., Santa Cruz Province, Bolivia; parts of former Soviet Union)	

sound intergovernmental rules are in place to restrain arbitrary action at the central and the local levels.

■ At the local level, states should focus on the processes and incentives for building accountability and competition. Where local governments are weakly accountable and unresponsive, improving both horizontal accountability (to the public) and vertical accountability (to the center) will be a vital first step toward achieving greater state capability.

Certain dangers are inherent in any strategy aimed at opening and decentralizing government. Expanded opportunities for voice and participation increase the demands made on the state, which can increase the risk of gridlock or of capture by vocal interest groups. And if no clear-cut rules impose restraints on the different tiers of government, and no incentives encourage local accountability, the crisis of governance that now afflicts many centralized governments will simply be passed down to lower levels. However, as Part Four of this Report argues, the obstacles on the path to reform of the state are not insurmountable. The first step toward bringing government closer to people will be to make the objectives of reform clearly intelligible to citizens and the business community. Efforts at communication and consensus building will have a double benefit, increasing the support for reform as well as arming the government with a better sense of how to do it right.

CHAPTER 8

FACILITATING INTERNATIONAL COLLECTIVE ACTION

CHAPTER 7 EXPLAINED HOW NEW PARTNERSHIPS AND competitive pressures can enhance the state's effectiveness at home. But the challenge of reforming the state does not stop at the state's borders. In an increasingly interdependent world, one country's actions will often have implications for its neighbors and for the rest of the world. And there is a growing recognition that some needed public goods and services can only be secured through international cooperation. Thus, building state capability will mean building more-effective partnerships and institutions internationally as well as at home.

The need for international cooperation stems from global and regional manifestations of the problems described in earlier chapters, such as missing markets and the presence of externalities. World peace, a sustainable global environment, a single world marketplace for goods and services, and basic knowledge are all examples of international public goods. They will be underprovided without conscious, concerted, and collective efforts to provide them. Development aid, although not a public good in the strict sense, also justifies international cooperation because of global equity considerations.

This chapter discusses the ways in which governments might help ensure more effective global provision of international public goods. It begins by examining the voluntary mechanisms already established to coordinate international collective action. Although the evidence is clear that cooperation to achieve global collective goals brings global benefits, not every such action will bring benefits for all. Hence it will not always be in every country's interest to participate. Some international public goods may simply not be valued as highly by some countries as by others, and sometimes the domestic costs of complying with an agreement may outweigh the benefits. A major lesson of experience with voluntary agreements is that

they achieve little when countries have signed on without fully understanding, or accepting, the likely costs.

Funding and provision of international public goods

Not so long ago the standard policy advice with regard to the provision of public goods relied almost exclusively on state intervention. Depending on the circumstances, the prescription might be to introduce a subsidy, a tax, a new liability rule, a new regulation, or a new program for direct public provision of the good in question. But this approach usually fell flat when it came to the provision of international public goods. In a world of sovereign nations, voluntary cooperation becomes the only answer. But why would countries undertake cooperatively actions that they have little or no incentive to carry out individually?

Experience and a better understanding of how economies work have since led us to recognize a richer set of motives for collective action and to devise better institutional arrangements for carrying them out, be they national or global. As previous chapters have shown, states are setting aside monopolistic, command-and-control approaches to governing in favor of a more participatory approach involving civil society, markets, and local authorities. At the global level, the participatory approach goes a step further, since it relies on international cooperation without the use of coercive power. Today, the key mechanisms for the provision of international public goods are based entirely on voluntary action.

In international markets for trade and investment, countries have collaborated to develop common rules and norms of conduct and to institutionalize them through various formal arrangements. These have included regional arrangements such as the Asia-Pacific Economic Cooperation (APEC) forum and Mercosur in South America, as well as multilateral ones such as the

World Trade Organization (WTO) and its precursor the General Agreement on Tariffs and Trade (GATT). Although all these arrangements are based entirely on voluntary participation, they have attracted growing memberships, contributing hugely to growth in world trade and improvements in the participants' welfare. Organizing and operating these arrangements are costly, but members have deemed the benefits sufficient to justify the costs.

When is cooperation desirable?

For any country, the decision to cooperate in important international endeavors will be a complex one, conditioned by the country's social values and by its assessment of the long-term national interest. The balance of the costs and benefits of cooperating depends on the type of activity, the mechanisms proposed, and the social and economic conditions the country faces.

There is greater recognition today not only of the existence and benefits of international public goods, but also of the implications of failing to provide them adequately. History has shown what can happen when the community of nations is more fragmented, by war or by trade and investment barriers, than it is today. Without a forum for nation-states to discuss and negotiate orderly changes in national policies and standards, small economies may end up having to adopt the practices of the dominant economic powers, in a process of "imperial harmonization." And failure to provide effective foreign aid or support for basic research to meet the needs of poor countries diminishes the prospects of those countries ever developing into vibrant economies and profitable trading partners. International cooperation is critical to making events turn out significantly better.

But again, not all countries will in all cases wish to participate in the provision of international public goods. At the very least, cooperation can restrict a country's freedom to act. Often the benefits will exceed the costs of ceding some national autonomy, but not always. In many areas—macroeconomic policy coordination is one—there is inevitably some uncertainty about what kind of joint action to take. In others, such as environmental protection and climate change, there is uncertainty about the extent to which the key players will participate. Uncertainties such as these blunt the likely effectiveness and dilute the expected benefits of cooperation.

Even when the relevant facts are more certain, differing perceptions and priorities can still preclude cooperation. Many developing countries, for example, are reluctant to adopt the labor laws and pollution standards of the richer countries for fear of losing their competitive advantage and jeopardizing growth. And some countries may choose not to cooperate in certain activities out of a belief that private research and experimentation will ultimately produce cheaper solutions.

Collective provision of public goods generally requires balancing three principles: openness, diversity, and cohesion. Each has considerable merit, but pursuing any one to the extreme risks compromising the others. Openness to the global economy involves a commitment to transparency and clear rules, for example prohibiting discriminatory trade practices. Yet openness without diversity could lead to backsliding by countries that desire more freedom to differ, and thus to greater fragmentation of the world economy. Likewise, acceptance of diversity—for example in the mutual recognition of different national standards—fosters innovation but may be detrimental to cohesion among countries or among communities within a country. Cohesion, of course, is also generally desirable, but not when it involves sacrificing too much openness and diversity.

These considerations suggest that although there is much need for collective provision of international public goods, it is not the answer to all problems for all countries. Each country has to decide, on a case-by-case basis, whether to participate. An appropriate global framework for organizing collective action must therefore allow for multiple arrangements and institutions, all based on voluntary participation. One possible approach to organizational design is to think in terms of a series of groups, each with a different objective:

- Functional groups to deal with specific issues such as macroeconomic policy, environmental protection, labor standards, and international conflicts (for example, the International Labour Organisation and the Bank for International Settlements)
- Regional groups to deal with multiple issues of interest to neighboring countries (but preferably open to all that wish to join), including trade and investment (for example, the North American Free Trade Area, or NAFTA, and APEC)
- Coordinating groups to link the functional and regional groups and create a broader network for all members (for example, the OECD).

This framework provides for a reasonable balance among openness, diversity, and cohesion and may well be adequate to prevent fragmentation and imperial harmonization. Individual countries' interest and participation in the various arrangements at any given time will vary, and groups may be relatively inactive for long periods. But when the timing is right, with ideas and circumstances converging, groups may witness a surge of interest in their activities, as occurred, for example, in the concluding stages of the Uruguay Round negotiations of the GATT.

Ensuring more effective cooperation

There is no guarantee that participating states will always fully comply with external commitments. In the absence of some global authority with universal jurisdiction and coercive power, enforcing international agreements and treaties is up to the states themselves. Hence mechanisms are clearly needed to ensure compliance when commitments are not being honored voluntarily. Recent experience in international law suggests a few such mechanisms.

Countries fail to comply with international commitments for different reasons. The incentives to comply may be weak, because of changes in political priorities or in underlying economic conditions. Or the necessary capability, including the technical expertise and organizational skills needed to ensure timely action, may be lacking. Perhaps most common among developing countries, the requisite financial resources may not be available.

Where its incentives have become incompatible with fulfilling its international obligations, a country may need to reconsider its participation. The effectiveness of the agreement (or international organization) will be undermined if many members simultaneously face strong incentives not to abide by its provisions. In practice, however, states have perceived their self-interest broadly, recognizing the impact of their actions on the community of nations, on their own reputation, and on the possibility of entering into future reciprocal arrangements.

Lack of capacity and financial resources is often more manageable. Many international agreements take the capacity and financial constraints of some members into account. Provisions can be included to ensure that necessary personnel and financial resources are available to all members. Where such needs are not fully anticipated, mechanisms for communication and supervision can be devised to address emerging issues. Allocating responsibilities realistically and providing for necessary resource transfers in advance can improve implementation and reduce violations.

Traditional legal mechanisms often fail to address the root cause of compliance problems, instead relying on breach of the agreement to trigger action. This approach highlights the violation of commitment and is confrontational. Necessary remedial actions may come too late—the damage may have been done. Relations among members may sour, making future cooperation more difficult.

An alternative, more process-oriented approach promotes the observance of commitments on a continuous basis. The goal is not to condemn wrongdoing but to keep states in compliance with their obligations and prevent violations. This approach relies to a much greater extent on communication, consultation, monitoring, the sharing of information, and technical and financial assistance.

Recent conventions, particularly in the environmental domain, incorporate mechanisms for monitoring and facilitating compliance. These include conferences among the parties, separate secretariats, and financial assistance arrangements that ensure the submission and review of implementation reports by member countries. These bodies, however, lack enforcement power. They also have limited capacity to verify implementation unless countries cooperate in providing information. More sophisticated legal agreements, including some recent environmental conventions, add the element of supervision. A supervisory body can help by following up on reporting requirements and by disseminating information on the impact of the convention at the domestic level.

The procedure for noncompliance established under the Montreal Protocol on Substances that Deplete the Ozone Layer is a good example of this new approach. Any party to the agreement that has doubts about the correct application of the protocol by another party can initiate the procedure, as can the secretariat itself or any party having trouble meeting its commitments. NGOs and individuals also have access to this procedure: they can transmit information about possible noncompliance to the secretariat. The Committee on Implementation may try to bring about an amicable settlement, or recommend technical or financial assistance if the failure to apply the protocol is due to lack of capacity. It can also suspend the rights and privileges of parties in violation.

Continuous cooperation among national agencies is the foundation of this process-oriented approach. The building blocks include such facilities as permanent communication networks, periodic reporting or implementation, periodic review of legal provisions, and regular meetings of decisionmakers and staff. All these help maintain awareness among responsible officials of the goals being sought by the agreements and the means for achieving them, and keep the public informed of emerging issues. The Geneva-based International Register of Potentially Toxic Chemicals, which is founded on national regulatory decisions rather than international regulatory action, is a good example of such a facility.

Current provision of international public goods

This section reviews some of challenges and opportunities facing states as they seek in five selected areas to balance self-interest and the common interest in an increasingly interdependent world.

Expanding world markets

The liberalization of trade and investment laws around the world has contributed to an enormous increase in the volume of world trade and foreign direct and portfolio investment, whose impact on the welfare of participants has been considerable and for the better. Multilateral and regional agreements have supported market expansion, as greater economic interdependence has made it necessary to maintain and extend an international system of liberal trade and investment. Invigorated by buoyant trade, the global economy has grown rapidly, and that growth shows little sign

Box 8.1 The World Trade Organization—an international mechanism for bringing credibility to national policy

The WTO was established in January 1995 to administer multilateral trade agreements negotiated by its member countries. The WTO can be regarded both as an institution embodying a set of rules and principles on the use of policies that affect trade flows, and as a "market" in which members exchange market access concessions and agree on rules of the game. The WTO requires its members to ensure that their trade policies are largely nondiscriminatory and their rules and enforcement procedures transparent. The WTO also provides legal mechanisms for countries to signal the seriousness of their commitments, and improved dispute settlement procedures for resolving conflicts between member states.

In the first two years of its existence, the WTO dispute settlement system received a total of sixty-two cases involving more than forty-three distinct matters.

Of these matters, two have completed the entire process, and two further panel reports have been issued. Countries can no longer block the establishment of arbitration panels or ignore their findings, as they could under the GATT. And although they may appeal, the decision of the appeals body is final. Every stage of the process is subject to strict time limits, and countries that fail to comply face authorized trade sanctions.

The largest trading nations and customs territories continue to dominate the dispute settlement process, and the credibility of the system depends on their willingness to comply with judgments against them. But encouraged by the nature of the WTO system, including the right to redress, developing countries are turning to the dispute settlement process far more often than they did under the GATT.

of abating. International migration of people in search of work is the laggard in this story. As *World Development 1995* showed, annual migratory flows from developing countries are no greater now, relative to total population, than in the 1970s. Most workers in poorer countries are only beginning to experience the benefits—and the costs—of global migration. But the expansion of markets and the increase in competitive pressure will leave some unprepared countries highly vulnerable to unforeseen shocks and policy mistakes. As Chapter 3 explained, countries will need to adopt prudent, consistent, and credible policies at home to prepare for the new global environment. International collective action can help support these efforts by offering ways for countries to make external commitments that will give these policies more credibility.

The growing global consensus on the benefits of more liberal trade and international market expansion is reflected in the large and growing membership of the WTO (Box 8.1). The most recent series of multilateral negotiations toward trade liberalization, the Uruguay Round, led to significant reductions in both tariff and nontariff barriers to trade in goods and services, particularly among developing countries.

Yet reducing border barriers is only one of the preconditions for participating more actively in the global trading system. Countries also need a competitive exchange rate, good availability of foreign exchange, and a transport infrastructure that can support expanded trade. Thus, despite spreading trade liberalization, the share of trade in GDP fell in forty-four of ninety-three developing countries between the mid-1980s and the mid-1990s. Such disparity in the speed and extent of integration reflects how well different regions have succeeded in raising their volume of trade with the rest of the world. While East Asia, for instance, has consistently expanded its trade over several decades, that of Sub-Saharan Africa has actually fallen.

In addition to liberalizing trade, more countries are also gradually removing restrictions on cross-border movements of capital, either unilaterally or as part of regional initiatives. The number of countries with liberal or mostly liberal capital regimes has grown from nine to thirty in the past two decades, while the number of countries with relatively restrictive rules has dropped sharply, from seventy-three to fifty-three (Figure 8.1).

Just as countries differ markedly with respect to growth in trade, so there is considerable disparity in countries' ability to attract foreign capital. Although worldwide private and official capital flows have expanded by about a factor of ten in the past two decades, developing regions have fared unequally in attracting these flows. Much of the expansion has been in private flows, and among developing regions most of these go to East Asia and Latin America. One estimate suggests that more than half the population of the developing world has been little touched by this aspect of globalization.

Of particular concern to developing countries is the composition of these growing private capital flows. Whereas many developing countries actively seek foreign direct investment, they regard portfolio investment with ambivalence. Foreign portfolio investors can help develop

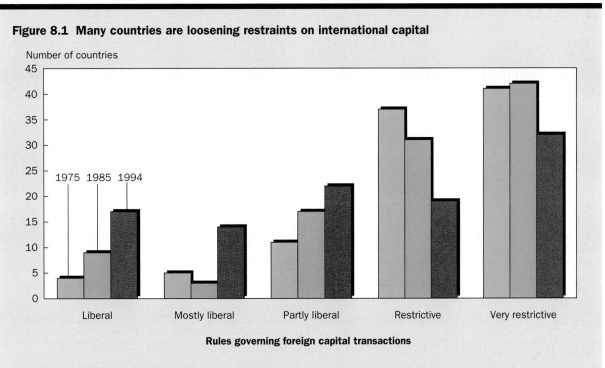

Figure 8.1 Many countries are loosening restraints on international capital

Number of countries

[Bar chart with categories: Liberal, Mostly liberal, Partly liberal, Restrictive, Very restrictive; bars for 1975, 1985, 1994]

Rules governing foreign capital transactions

Note: Data are for 102 industrial and developing countries. *Liberal* means no restrictions; *mostly liberal* means a few restrictions by industry; *partly liberal* means many restrictions on the size and timing of transactions; *restrictive* means that domestic investment by foreigners or foreign investment by domestic residents requires official approval; *very restrictive* means that all cross-border transactions require official approval. Source: Adapted from Gwartney, Lawson, and Block 1996.

local financial markets by providing liquidity and by influencing the regulatory framework and corporate governance. But they also bring the risk of sudden capital flight, whose destabilizing effects were dramatically illustrated by Mexico's crisis of 1994–95.

Managing the risk of capital flight, and of large capital flows generally, has been a challenge for most developing countries. Increasingly the risk is regarded as a welcome source of government discipline, which discourages capricious and irresponsible policies, and many countries have relaxed capital controls (see Chapter 3). Still, large flows in either direction can accentuate a country's vulnerabilities through large external imbalances, rising inflation or interest rates, or exuberant credit expansion that could compromise the soundness of banks.

The means at governments' disposal to keep themselves out of trouble are almost all a matter of domestic policy: in particular, prudent fiscal policies, credible monetary and exchange rate regimes, a sound and prudent banking system, and, possibly, measures that reduce the public's expectation that the government will bail them out if investments turn sour.

But the international community has important interests at stake in addressing the risks associated with capital

flows. A better understanding of these risks and greater confidence in managing them would encourage countries to participate more actively in world markets. More-open and better-functioning capital markets in developing countries would improve the use of global resources and increase portfolio diversification.

What kind of collective actions could help achieve these benefits? Closer consultation among central banks and financial regulators could help upgrade national regulatory frameworks and financial practices. And greater cooperation among national authorities could help establish procedures for mutual assistance in crises, such as the IMF's new facility to help member countries absorb external shocks.

Another concern is growing regionalism. The past two decades have witnessed a sharp increase in the number of regional market-opening agreements, including NAFTA, Mercosur, and APEC. Regionalism is not simply about trade. In the case of the European Union, for example, it also reflects the desires of neighboring nations for greater political integration in response to common security concerns, for cost sharing for infrastructure and institutions, and for increased bargaining power in international negotiations.

Opinion is divided on the merits of regional arrangements, and the evidence remains inconclusive. Some argue that regionalism will divert attention and resources away from the more important multilateral processes and undermine progress toward global nondiscriminatory trade rules. Others contend that regionalism enables states to undertake innovative market-opening measures that will eventually serve as building blocks for multilateral initiatives. Regional partners have indeed pioneered arrangements later adopted in multilateral agreements; an example is the European Union's treatment of trade in services.

Some of the concerns about regionalism may be legitimate. But regional arrangements can be made more consistent with more-open and integrated world markets. One way is to open membership in such arrangements to any trading partners that wish to join, rather than restrict it to countries within the region. Another option is to establish, through a multilateral mechanism, a time-bound convergence process for cutting differences between internal and external trade barriers to a stipulated minimum.

Supporting basic research and the creation of knowledge
Knowledge is an international public good whose benefits accrue to all. International collective action can direct research toward the needs of developing countries, where most research activities that exist are fragmented, poorly funded, and inadequately directed. International assistance can help in assessing needs, developing a cost-effective agenda, encouraging international exchange and collaboration, and providing additional funding where it is needed. Successes such as those of the Consultative Group on International Agricultural Research (CGIAR) and the World Health Organization suggest that the return on investment in research in developing countries can be substantial.

Basic research is a classic—and global—public good. The benefits, although uncertain beforehand, and hard to measure after, often prove exceptionally high. The transformation of the global economy and of entire societies has as its basis the knowledge gained from new discoveries. Yet the incentives to conduct and fund basic research are extremely weak: the benefits of greater knowledge are nonexcludable, and few constituencies lobby for more research. Governments in rich countries often regard research as a luxury. Governments in poor countries seldom pay it much attention.

Perhaps the greatest mismatch between potential returns and actual investment in research is to be found in developing countries. The scope for building human capital there is enormous, but the process is complicated by childhood malnutrition, debilitating diseases, and degradation of the natural resources that support agricultural

production. New knowledge can make a dramatic difference in people's lives, as it did with the eradication of smallpox, the containment of malaria and river blindness, and the significant increases in agricultural productivity made possible by the green revolution. But these successes are few and far between. And new breakthroughs are unlikely in the absence of assured continued support for well-directed efforts.

In developing countries research suffers from several disadvantages. First, research activity in these countries is usually given low priority. In Sub-Saharan Africa, for example, less than 2 percent of health budgets is spent on health research; the result is shortages of research institutions, facilities, and scientists. Second, the limited funding that is devoted to research is usually misallocated. Pneumonia and diarrheal diseases account for 15 percent of the disease burden in developing countries, yet only 0.2 percent of medical research funding in developing countries is directed toward studying these diseases. This misallocation often reflects a lack of basic information and of the skilled personnel needed to develop an appropriate research agenda. Third, there is little coordination and exchange by researchers across developing-country borders; the results are a considerable overlap in research activities and missed opportunities for cost saving.

The international community can do more to assist developing countries in generating the new knowledge that will address their needs. Through foreign aid, donors can help governments develop a research agenda based on careful assessment of needs, and help finance a higher but sustainable level of research spending. The industrial countries can also help alleviate brain drain—the exodus of skilled developing-country researchers—by providing competent researchers and scientists to work with institutions in developing countries to develop training capacity and research programs that encourage the retention of local personnel. Donors can help establish and fund regional research institutes to encourage cross-fertilization of ideas and limit redundant research activities. And international institutions can help disseminate the new knowledge gained to promote productivity, more effective treatment of diseases, and healthier lifestyles.

The scope for such efforts has been well illustrated by successful cooperation in many areas of research and dissemination. The CGIAR, for example, was instrumental in developing more productive crop varieties and promoting more efficient and environmentally friendly agricultural methods. A network of sixteen agricultural research centers around the world, the CGIAR is supported by fifty nations in its primary goal of alleviating hunger in developing countries. But the benefits of its activity have not been limited to those countries (Box 8.2).

International cooperation in health research has also led to important advances. The World Health Organization, for example, played a major role in the eradication of smallpox. But much scope remains for collective action. Of total worldwide spending on health research in the early 1990s, an estimated 95 percent was devoted to health problems of concern mainly to industrial countries, and only 5 percent to the health needs of developing countries.

Several research activities especially warrant more international support:

- Improving the understanding of tropical diseases, particularly those affecting children and rural dwellers of Sub-Saharan Africa
- Controlling the spread of the human immunodeficiency virus (HIV), which causes AIDS
- Improving treatment and prevention of noncommunicable diseases, which affect an increasing number of people in developing countries
- Finding or developing disease- and pest-resistant varieties of such crops as cotton, cocoa, rice, and yams, which play a key role in many economies
- Developing mining and farming technology to minimize soil erosion and deforestation.

Protecting the global environment

A severe threat to development comes from environmental degradation, at both the global and the local level. Particularly worrisome global environmental issues include climate change (Box 8.3), loss of biodiversity, and protection of international waters. At the local level the most pressing problems are urban air and water pollution, deforestation, and soil and rangeland degradation. International collective action can help mitigate these problems through better coordination, increased public awareness, technology transfers, cost sharing, and consultation to help shape national and local policies and practices.

International cooperation is now recognized as the cornerstone of a sustainable environmental regime. In the past two decades the number of international environmental agreements has grown significantly. The wide array of interests at stake means that activities must be coordinated at the international level to ensure stable and predictable patterns of behavior and to establish cooperative management systems. Although willingness to participate in international collective action implies recognition of a common objective, different countries have different interests at stake, and these, too, must be recognized. Article 4 of the 1992 Climate Change Convention, for example, requires that parties to the convention give full consideration to the interests of (among others) small island countries; countries with low-lying coastal areas,

Box 8.2 How international agricultural research benefits donors as well

In 1993 the United States produced about 12 percent of the world's wheat crop. The United States is also a major rice exporter, accounting for nearly 18 percent of international trade in the commodity. Most wheat and rice varieties grown in the United States were developed through crop improvement research. Many were developed through the work of two research centers in the CGIAR network: the International Center for Maize and Wheat Improvement (known by its Spanish abbreviation CIMMYT) and the International Rice Research Institute (IRRI). Both are supported in part by contributions from the U.S. government.

A recent study sought to measure the benefits to the U.S. economy from CGIAR research. It was estimated that, during 1970–93, gains from the use of improved wheat varieties developed by CIMMYT amounted to $3.4 billion to $13.7 billion. The benefit-cost ratio for U.S. government support of CIMMYT was as high as 190 to 1. IRRI research was linked to $20 million to $1 billion in gains in rice revenues, yielding a benefit-cost ratio of as much as 17 to 1. Thus even though U.S. investments in international agricultural research on wheat and rice were made primarily on humanitarian grounds, they have yielded direct benefits to the U.S. economy that far outweigh the costs of supporting the CGIAR. And as the study concludes, "international agricultural research is an investment in international stability and economic growth overseas, which reaps further rewards for the United States and other donor nations."

arid and semiarid areas, forested areas, or areas vulnerable to forest decay; and countries with areas prone to natural disaster.

Institutional and financial support is often needed to enable certain countries to meet their obligations. One of the outcomes of the 1992 U.N. Conference on Environment and Development in Rio de Janeiro, for example, was a commitment by the industrial countries to provide financial resources to meet the costs incurred by developing countries in implementing obligations set out in the conference's Agenda 21. The Global Environment Facility, conceived to finance the incremental costs of

Box 8.3 The challenges of global climate change for international cooperation

Although some doubts remain about the magnitude of global climate change and the urgency of dealing with it, a consensus is emerging that the problem is real and potentially dangerous, and that reasonable and appropriate measures should not be postponed. The Intergovernmental Panel on Climate Change has predicted that over the next 100 years the earth's surface will warm by an average of 1.5 to 6.3 degrees Fahrenheit, and sea levels will rise 6 to 38 inches. These changes would bring more frequent and intense droughts, the spread of disease, the retreat of mountain glaciers, and storms of greater malevolence.

What challenges does climate change pose for international cooperation? Under the auspices of the United Nations Framework on Climate Change, signed in 1992 and ratified by 159 countries, an international agreement to limit the greenhouse gas emissions that contribute to climate change is being negotiated and may be adopted by the end of 1997. But climate change, if it brings the dire effects that are predicted, will take far bolder cooperation—political, economic, and financial—to meet needs projected to reach $50 billion a year by 2040.

Recent analysis of climate change provides a strong economic rationale for adopting market-based instruments, such as tradable carbon emissions entitlements, to reduce greenhouse gas emissions. In a tradable permits system, permits corresponding to a targeted ceiling of greenhouse gas emissions would be issued, and emissions without a permit would be prohibited. Countries for which the costs of reducing carbon emissions are low would have an incentive to undertake those reductions and sell their unneeded permits to countries for which the costs of emissions reduction are high. A recent World Bank study estimates that cutting emissions in the countries of the OECD by 20 percent at least cost could require global trading of entitlements worth $30 billion to $40 billion annually. Allowing trading would generate savings equivalent to 65 percent of global abatement costs.

The barriers to implementing this global market are largely political. The market's very existence depends on governments' willingness to create and regulate it. (The financial resources for purchasing entitlements are expected to come from the private sector.) A crucial step in establishing the market will be the initial allocation of entitlements—this will have to be determined by a global climate change protocol. Although many formulas have been suggested, this contentious issue has not yet been resolved.

---

projects that have global environmental impact, plays a crucial role in implementing these obligations (Box 8.4).

Many of the most immediately pressing environmental problems facing developing countries, such as urban water and air pollution and soil degradation, are mainly local rather than global. But they have major implications for productivity, health, and the quality of life within these countries' borders. Progress in alleviating these problems has been slow, with lack of capacity and political will, at both the national and the local level, a major stumbling block.

The lesson of recent experience is that bringing about both local and global environmental integrity and sustainability will require a coordinated international effort, one that blends careful attention to financial incentives, market forces, laws, and national interests. Equally important, the international community must help raise public awareness of the dangers of environmental degradation, so as to change the political incentives facing leaders, which often work against the goal of environmental integrity.

Preventing and controlling conflict

For most of the twentieth century the world has lived under the specter of major war. The first half of the century witnessed two global conflicts, catastrophic destruction of lives and resources, and decades of rehabilitation and reconstruction. During the second half the Cold War loomed large, with the threat of even greater destruction from nuclear weapons. Global tensions led many countries to devote a substantial share of national output to the military. Only in the past ten years have these tensions begun to subside, providing an opportunity for nations to reduce military spending and reap the dividends of peace (Box 8.5).

The threat of nuclear war has been replaced by a proliferation of smaller conflicts, bringing costly problems of refugee relief and rehabilitation. Existing cooperative mechanisms have had limited success in managing these conflicts, or in helping to avoid them. The problems often spill over and engulf neighboring countries, as they did in Southeast Asia and much of southern Africa in past decades and are doing now in Central and West Africa.

These conflicts are not confined to the poorest countries, but can also break out in middle-income countries such as the former Yugoslavia and Lebanon. The challenge facing the international community is to find new ways to prevent such conflicts or to manage them at an early stage before they turn into tragedies.

The end of the Cold War brought rising optimism that many of the issues that had contributed to instability and conflict throughout the world would be resolved. Instead at least thirty major armed conflicts (defined as those causing more than 1,000 deaths in a year) have taken place worldwide in recent years. The fragile peace settlements in Cambodia and Mozambique now seem the exception rather than the norm. We have seen:

- A rising number of refugees and internally displaced persons, and a disproportionate number of women and children who lack access to the basic resources needed for repatriation or rehabilitation (Figure 8.2)
- A rise in the number of humanitarian emergencies, from an average of five a year in 1985–89 to twenty in 1990, twenty-six in 1994, and twenty-four in 1995
- The erosion or total collapse of legitimacy and authority in many states, including Afghanistan, Liberia, Rwanda, Somalia, and the former Yugoslavia, as a result of extended civil war or genocide.

The relationship between refugees and the state is inextricable. States are major actors in responding to and defining refugee crises. Indeed, international law defines "refugee" in relation to the state. Although NGOs and receiving countries and communities play essential roles in providing for displaced persons, the scale of displacement in recent years has required that states—unilaterally or within the framework of multilateral organizations—mobilize and deliver protection, relief, and assistance. In addition, states acting together, or as members of international organizations, have initiated the negotiations that have brought to an end several refugee-generating armed conflicts, including those in Cambodia, Mozambique, and the former Yugoslavia.

Nevertheless, the disincentives to cooperate on refugee issues are powerful. One is the difficulty in securing commitments in situations where a state may perceive no direct interest of its own. Another is the prospect of burden-sharing arrangements that require a state to accept refugees into its territory, often at high political and financial cost. The case of Rwanda illustrates the high cost of providing relief in large-scale humanitarian emergencies. Between April and December 1994 the international community allocated about $1.4 billion for relief in Rwanda and neighboring countries. Rehabilitation efforts were gradually introduced,

---

Box 8.4 Sharing the burden of environmental protection

The Global Environment Facility (GEF) was set up in 1991 to help developing countries finance the incremental costs of new environmental investments with global benefits in four areas: climate change, preservation of biodiversity, protection of the ozone layer, and protection of international waters. A joint undertaking of the United Nations Environment Programme, the United Nations Development Programme, and the World Bank, the GEF has led to new institutional arrangements for the provision of collective goods.

The GEF has more than 165 member states and is governed by a board of representatives from thirty-two countries, each representing a constituency. There are sixteen constituencies for developing countries, fourteen for industrial countries, and two for Eastern Europe. The countries in each constituency choose a board member and an alternate, and each constituency determines its own process of consultation and decisionmaking. New members join an existing constituency. This innovative arrangement thus combines representativeness with efficiency.

---

but by late 1996 an external refugee population of about 1.5 million remained dependent on international assistance.

States also differ in their ability to avoid or limit refugee flows. Stronger states are more effective at denying entry to refugees and asylum seekers. It is often the weaker states, with the most limited resources, that shoulder the greatest burden in protecting refugees and repatriating them when conflicts end.

Today's international collective response to refugee problems relies heavily on multilateral organizations. The Office of the United Nations High Commissioner on Refugees has seen its budget doubled and its mandate stretched in the 1990s. It has provided in-country humanitarian relief in Bosnia, cross-border operations in Somalia, assistance to internally displaced persons in Sri Lanka, and repatriation of refugees in Central America and Mozambique. These activities have required highly complex coordination: in Mozambique, for example, relief operations in 1991 involved twenty-six United Nations agencies, forty-four bilateral donors, six other multilateral institutions, and 180 NGOs. It is estimated that more

Box 8.5 How large the global peace dividend?

Global military spending has fallen significantly, from about 4 percent of GDP in 1990 to 2.7 percent in 1994 to 2.4 percent in 1995 (see figure). This drop, in sharp contrast to the rising trend of the previous two decades, resulted from the breakup of the Soviet Union, a changing global political climate, increased democratization, and a fall in military aid.

But has the reduction in military spending improved growth and welfare? The relationship between military spending and economic development depends on a variety of factors and circumstances. Empirical results vary, depending on the assumptions and methodologies used. Some studies show that global reductions in military spending have indeed generated a peace dividend in the form of faster output growth. Others suggest that the relationship between military spending and growth is not linear but quadratic: at low levels of military spending, increased spending contributes to faster growth; at higher levels further military spending slows growth. Once the highest-spending nations are excluded from the sample, the relationship between military spending and growth is not significant for most developing countries (in peacetime). In such cases the biggest dividend ultimately may come from a country's perceived security and increased investor confidence, rather than from reductions in military spending per se.

Military expenditure by industrial, developing, and former Soviet bloc countries

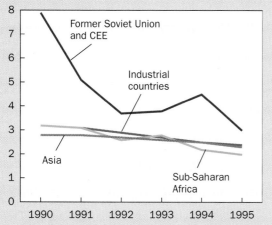

Percentage of GDP

Note: Data are averages of the countries in each group, weighted by GDP. Source: Gupta, Schiff, and Clements 1996.

than 16,000 NGOs are working to provide relief and humanitarian assistance worldwide.

Improving the effectiveness of foreign aid

Foreign aid is not strictly a public good, but it can be justified by considerations of international equity, particularly concerning the future productivity and well-being of people in poor countries. A vital part of improving the climate for development assistance must be to make foreign aid more effective from the standpoint of both the borrower and the donor. Recent research suggests that this can be achieved by linking aid more closely to recipients' policies.

The success or failure of aid-financed development projects, even in the social sectors, is particularly dependent on the quality of a country's macroeconomic policies. A project to expand primary education, for example, is more likely to succeed where macroeconomic policies are sound. If projects are the vehicle for development, macroeconomic policies can be seen as the fuel and lubricants that keep the vehicle going.

Moreover, only in a good policy environment will foreign aid have an impact on growth. In countries that have pursued the key economic policies for growth—which empirical research has identified as ensuring fiscal discipline, preventing high inflation, and maintaining a reasonably open economy—foreign aid has significantly increased economic growth (Figure 8.3). Countries that have achieved a good policy environment and received significant amounts of aid in recent years—Bolivia, El Salvador, Mali, and Uganda, for example—have grown faster than would have been predicted by their policies alone.

The clear implication is that foreign aid would be more effective if it were either more systematically targeted to poor countries with good economic reform programs or used to promote good policies. At the same time, donors share much of the responsibility for ensuring that foreign aid is dispensed responsibly and effectively.

The past decade has seen a trend toward economic liberalization in the developing world, indicating an improving climate for effective assistance. For example, India and Vietnam—populous countries that undertook good reform programs in the early 1990s—have built environments where foreign aid is likely to have a greater impact on growth and poverty reduction. But the track record of targeting aid to poor countries with good policies was generally weak between 1970 and 1993. Bilateral aid showed no tendency to favor good policies, whereas multilateral aid reflected only modest favoritism toward countries with good policies (as shown in a study that controlled for income and population). Clearly, a high priority for aid agencies is to channel resources more systematically toward poor countries with good policies.

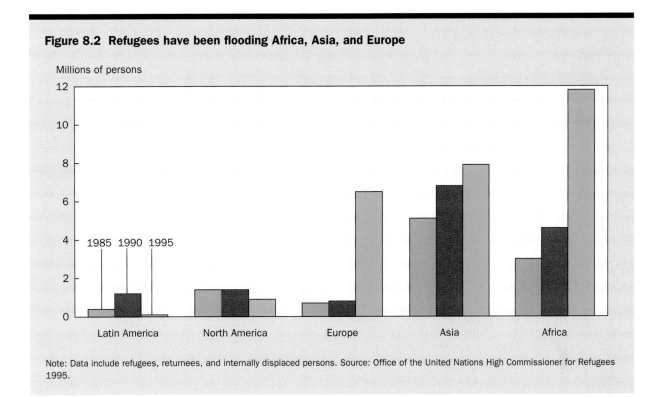

Figure 8.2 Refugees have been flooding Africa, Asia, and Europe

Millions of persons

Note: Data include refugees, returnees, and internally displaced persons. Source: Office of the United Nations High Commissioner for Refugees 1995.

Can aid help poor countries improve their policies and institutions? This is a difficult but critical question for the allocation of aid. There has been little systematic research into this question, but the available results are suggestive.

Structural adjustment lending to support policy reform has been more successful where local "ownership" of the reform program has been strong. Although adjustment lending can provide a useful support to an existing reform program, it is not likely to generate reform on its own: experience strongly suggests that donors cannot "bribe" governments to introduce policies for which there is no domestic support.

Where domestic social and political forces have initiated programs to reform policies and institutions, foreign aid can provide effective support by bringing technical expertise and lessons from other countries into a receptive environment. Good examples of such positive interaction are Indonesia, Mauritius, and Uganda. But where there is little domestic movement toward reform, assistance aimed at institution building and policy reform has had little impact.

Thus, in some environments it may be difficult for foreign assistance to accomplish anything beyond peace-keeping and emergency relief. But once domestic social and political forces have generated momentum for reform, foreign aid can provide important support for both policy reform and institutional development. And

once good policies and good institutional structures are in place, financial assistance can accelerate the transition to a more rapid growth path. The experience of successful economies shows that the need is temporary: as a track record of good policies and performance develops, private capital flows increase and gradually eliminate the need for foreign aid.

Strategic options: Furthering the provision of international collective goods

More effective international cooperation can expand opportunities and help nations cope with the new global challenges. Each country has to evaluate the merits of each proposed cooperative endeavor and decide on a case-by-case basis whether or not to participate. But this chapter has pointed to several areas where cooperation could be of great value:

- *Expansion and preservation of open world markets, including mitigation of the risk associated with volatile capital movements.* Many developing countries are concerned about more-open capital markets because of the possibility of sudden outflows that can destabilize economic management.
- *Basic research directed at the needs of developing countries.* The green revolution, made possible by the support of the CGIAR, shows that investing in research and

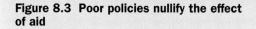

Figure 8.3 Poor policies nullify the effect of aid

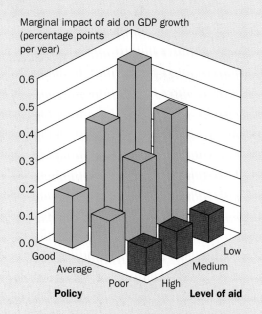

Note: Each value is an average for a group of countries. Results are based on a regression using data from fifty-six countries for the period 1970–73 to 1990–93. The level of aid is measured as a percentage of the recipient country's GDP. Source: Adapted from Burnside and Dollar 1996.

mental problems by improving coordination, increasing public awareness, transferring technology, and providing incentives for appropriate national environmental policies and enforcement.

■ *Peacekeeping and the prevention of armed conflicts.* The high human and financial cost of wars—and of associated relief and rehabilitation efforts—is well known, but existing mechanisms have had little success in preventing conflicts or in resolving them before they become large-scale human tragedies.

■ *Improving the effectiveness of foreign aid.* Linking aid more closely to recipients' policies can make aid more effective: for any level of foreign aid available to a country, economic performance rises with the quality of policy and governance. Recipients' policies appear to have influenced the allocation of multilateral but not of bilateral aid.

The appropriate catalyst for greater cooperation will vary, both according to the goal and according to the range of countries likely to participate. In several areas, new functional or regional groups may be useful in helping coordinate and enforce more effective voluntary collaboration. These groups can seek to develop common rules and mechanisms for pursuing designated objectives. But the credibility and effectiveness of any such effort will rely critically on striking the right balance among the competing values of openness, diversity, and cohesion. They will rely, too, on the political incentives—and the commitment—of participants. Attempts to improve the effectiveness of international collective actions, like similar domestic efforts, will bear fruit only if leaders are willing not merely to promise change, but to take the steps required to deliver it.

development can bring rich returns—for both the donors and the intended beneficiaries.

■ *Protection of the environment.* International collective action can help mitigate both global and local environ-

PART FOUR

REMOVING OBSTACLES TO CHANGE

CHAPTER 9

THE CHALLENGE OF INITIATING AND SUSTAINING REFORMS

The innovator makes enemies of all those who prospered under the old order,
and only lukewarm support is forthcoming from those who would prosper under the new.

—Niccolò Machiavelli, *The Prince* (1513)

PRECEDING CHAPTERS HAVE SHOWN HOW THE STATE can improve its effectiveness by matching its role more closely to its capability, and working to enhance that capability over time. Integral to this approach is a better understanding of why some countries do not meet even the most basic requirements for sound economic management, and why so few developing countries have managed to create effective state institutions. But understanding the problem and fixing it are two very different things. The basic questions remain: why and how is it that some countries have been able to throw off this legacy of failure and move forward with reform, while others have not?

This chapter looks for some answers to these questions by examining the main obstacles to reform and how they can be overcome. Three factors turn out to be critical: the distributional characteristics of reform (the likely winners and losers), the political strength of key groups (particularly those that will lose out), and the design of existing state institutions. Sometimes a reform will be politically undesirable because the likely losers are part of the political leadership's support base. Even when the political will to change is present, reformers can find their efforts derailed by constraints embedded in state institutions, which make it easier for opponents to maintain the status quo.

But the fact that opposition to reform can be rooted deeply in a country's institutions need not be a counsel of despair. To the contrary, close examination of the impediments to reform yields three pieces of practical advice for reformers. The first is that windows of reform opportunity do open; they tend to be those times when the normal rules of the game are in flux for some reason, however temporary. Thus, radical reforms have often been undertaken in response to an external threat or economic crisis, or during the "honeymoon" period of a new administration or regime, when incumbents with a strong vested interest in the old system have been displaced.

The second lesson is that, given such an opportunity, reformers can make the best use of the time available by adopting a strategy that understands the likely obstacles and seeks to mitigate them. Tactically designing and sequencing the reforms can help, as can measures to make institutions less susceptible to capture by special interests and gridlock, and, perhaps most important, building a consensus in favor of reform.

Finally, the message of the many reform successes—and failures—analyzed in this chapter is that breakthroughs will rarely happen by accident. At any given time, the forces favoring the status quo are likely to prevail. Reforms only succeed if they are directed by leaders with a clear vision of the way things could be, and a contagious determination to turn that vision into reality.

Obstacles to reform

The obstacles to reform in any country will be many and varied. The recipe for reform failure is no more susceptible to easy generalizations than the recipe for success. But chief among the barriers to change will always be the powerful interest groups who stand to lose by it. Resistance will be even stronger when the prospective losers are among the political leadership's core constituents. In short, the redistributive effects of a reform and the political strength of groups affected by it may simply render some policy changes politically undesirable. Yet even politically desirable reforms may fail because of constraints embedded in state institutions, which tilt the playing field firmly in the opponents' favor. Thus, policy outcomes can usually be seen as the combined effect of the characteristics of the reforms themselves, the political strength of different actors, and the design of existing state institutions.

Distributional conflicts, uncertainty, and reform
Some common types of reform and the groups that stand to gain or lose from them are listed in Table 9.1. These alignments do not apply in all circumstances. But the truth remains that resistance to reform is often triggered by the potential redistribution of resources among differ-

ent groups, whose precise composition will depend on the reform in question. For example, public sector reform, which is central to reinvigorating state institutions, can sometimes be thwarted by civil servants who run the risk of unemployment or finding themselves worse off in private sector employment. Politicians who use public employment as a source of patronage may also see an interest in blocking certain kinds of reform. Decentralization, for instance, raises the prospect of reallocating resources outside the political leadership's constituency. In Peru, a decentralization program that would have transferred resources for financing primary and secondary education to provincial municipalities was halted in 1993, following widespread victories by independents and opposition parties in the municipal elections.

Table 9.1 Alignment of interest groups, political costs, and tactical sequencing of reform by reform type

| Type of reform | Interest groups | | Determinants of political cost | Tactical sequencing | Other issues |
	Against	For			
Trade liberalization	Holders of import quotas Protected industrialists	Consumers, exporters, the treasury (if revenues will increase)	Redistribution (+) Efficiency gains (−)	Reduce quantitative restrictions before tariffs.	
Pension privatization	Trade unions Pensioners' associations Bureaucracies (labor ministry, social security agency)	Employers Financial institutions Young workers	Wealth reduction (+) Reduced coverage (+) Older median voter (+) Efficiency gains (−)	Allow participants to opt out of public scheme, then phase it out.	Young workers may be willing to forgo some of their acquired rights.
Decentralization Functional	Top officials and staff in central administration	Top officials and staff in local administrations, consumers, citizen beneficiaries, local businesses	Redistribution (+) Political contestability (+) Efficiency gains (−)	Build consensus, phase in pilot program, design grant schemes.	Need to mitigate fiscal imbalances and design new schemes for allocation of grants across jurisdictions
Political	Top decisionmakers in political parties	Local decisionmakers in political parties, associations, and labor unions; NGOs; taxpayers			
Fiscal	Top officials in ministry of finance and strategic planning (or public investment) commission	Department of finance in local administration, local planning and investment units			
Public sector reform	Employees and managers of public enterprises, politicians prone to patronage	Private business, rural elite, central agencies, taxpayers	Redundancy (+) Unemployment (+) Relative wages (+) Efficiency gains (−)	Eliminate ghost workers, encourage voluntary and early retirement, ensure retrenchment without revolving door.	Incentives: severance, buyouts, capitalization scheme, training, private sector placement, credit schemes

Note: A plus sign indicates a factor that increases, and a minus sign one that lowers, the political cost of reform.

Ranking policy changes according to their political costs and benefits can help policymakers design the tactical sequencing of a comprehensive reform program. Although such an exercise is highly country specific, a good starting point is to compare the expected redistributional effects of planned reforms with their expected efficiency gains. Some reforms, for example, are difficult to implement because in the short run they seem to be merely reshuffling opportunities and incomes. Although such reforms, if they increase efficiency, ultimately increase the size of the pie, their short-run redistributive effects may exceed even the immediate benefits. In that case, other things equal, reform will not occur, because the political difficulties of reforming outweigh the rewards. This political cost-benefit approach can be applied to a broad range of reforms, such as trade liberalization (Box 9.1).

Applying the redistributional calculus to the case of pension reform shows how conflicts of interest across gen-

---

Box 9.1 Weighing the political costs and benefits of reform

Efficiency-enhancing reforms are often difficult to implement because they create both winners and losers, and there may be no way to compensate the losers. Defusing opposition is even more difficult when the efficiency gains are low relative to the redistributive effects. Applying a rough political cost-benefit ratio to reform measures can show how much redistribution takes place for a given amount of efficiency gain. A policy that increases the income of one group without taking income away from another, for example, would have a ratio of zero.

For trade liberalization the political cost-benefit ratio is inversely related to the tariff rate, the share of imports in total consumption, and the elasticity of import demand. In Sub-Saharan Africa the average import tariff exceeds 30 percent, and the share of imports in total consumption is about 40 percent. Assuming an import demand elasticity of two (demand for imports rises by 2 percent for every 1 percent decline in price), the cost-benefit ratio of trade liberalization is more than four. Thus, for any given amount of efficiency gain, the redistributive effects would be four times that amount. When a reform program combines trade liberalization with a stabilization program that increases output, the ratio declines significantly. A stabilization program that increases GDP growth by 1 percentage point would be sufficient to lower the ratio from four to less than one.

---

erations can also affect policy outcomes. Most public pension schemes are unfunded, financed by current payroll taxes rather than past contributions. The resulting high marginal tax on labor and the weak link between contributions and benefits create distortions in the labor market. In mature systems these distortions are compounded by the low implicit return on pensions relative to the market return on capital. The distortions could be reduced by, among other things, strengthening the link between contributions and benefits and privatizing and funding pension schemes. But such reforms would affect different generations of workers differently. For example, privatizing and fully funding the U.S. Social Security system could generate net gains, including gains in efficiency, but younger workers would realize most of those gains, and older workers would lose (Figure 9.1). This dilemma helps explain why reform is so politically sensitive. Similarly, redistribution away from the elderly helps explain why countries in CEE and the CIS are resisting increasing the pension age. In Ukraine, for example, a uniform pension age of 65 would ease the system's actuarial imbalance but would also reduce the pension wealth of workers (in present value terms) by about 25 percent of GDP.

The difficulty of reforming universal pension programs thus stems from the anticipated reform's redistributive effects and the power of elderly voters. Meanwhile unborn generations, who would benefit the most from reform, have no voice in the decision. The political costs of reform in the United States have risen over time, as the gap in voter turnout between the young (those between 25 and 40 years of age) and those over 65 has widened in favor of the latter, to some 12 percentage points. Clearly, reforming public pension and health care financing programs for the elderly, however fiscally unsustainable, is a difficult feat to pull off, but should be a high priority. Even when one-time, comprehensive reform is not feasible, more-gradual changes and grandfathering of existing beneficiaries, in the recognition that changes are likely to be generational, with long lead times, may reduce opposition to reform.

In many countries utilities are inefficiently run public monopolies. Consumers would realize significant gains if these utilities were privatized and effective regulatory agencies established to watch over them. Witness the case of Argentina, which began privatizing its state-run infrastructure services in 1989. All income groups have benefited from the efficiency gains induced by privatization, and these gains (relative to spending on utilities) have been similar across income groups (Table 9.2). In Uruguay, for example, a 1989 plebiscite rejected privatization legislation. Yet a recent study shows that inefficiencies in public utilities add 30 percent to the average Uruguayan's electricity, water, and telephone bills. And as

Figure 9.1 Older workers will lose from reforming pensions, but the young will gain

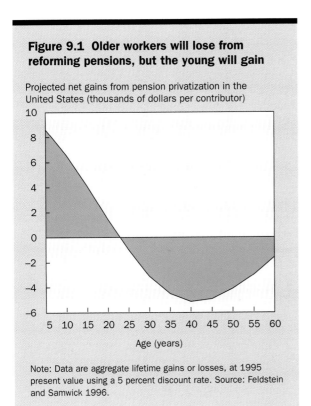

Projected net gains from pension privatization in the United States (thousands of dollars per contributor)

Age (years)

Note: Data are aggregate lifetime gains or losses, at 1995 present value using a 5 percent discount rate. Source: Feldstein and Samwick 1996.

we saw in Box 4.2, many of the arguments commonly offered against privatization are not valid.

So why is privatization still resisted in some countries? This reluctance to implement welfare-improving reforms is linked to at least three factors:

- The perceived uncertainty of the outcome of reform, which impedes the creation of a strong constituency for reform and raises concerns that the immediate response may be social unrest, while the benefits are only realized later
- The fact that private operators typically have to make changes that are detrimental to certain groups in order for the efficiency gains to materialize
- The fact that different groups may hold conflicting views about the role of the state—for instance, in many countries that have previously relied entirely on state utilities, many groups continue to resist privatization on ideological grounds.

Institutional design

The preceding discussion has identified the losers from reform as potentially powerful obstacles. But whether or not these groups prevail in a given instance will often be determined by the design of state institutions. Rather than attempt an exhaustive account of how state institutions

can be used to block reform, we focus here on two principal ones: the electoral and party system and the system of checks and balances. The point is not that institutions should be redesigned and changed frequently to facilitate reform, or that a single design is desirable for all countries and situations. The aim, rather, is to show how elements of the underlying institutional framework can condition both the attempt to reform and the response.

ELECTORAL AND PARTY SYSTEMS. As has been emphasized throughout this Report, institutional choices are seldom clear-cut: they will involve a careful tradeoff between allowing state officials flexibility and imposing appropriate restraints on them. Experience with proportional electoral systems is a case in point. Such systems are associated with coalition governments, which can be desirable to the extent that they bring more voices to the cabinet table and put a high value on consensus. Yet the same characteristics can also be a barrier to reform, leading to long delays in policymaking and higher fiscal deficits because of the need to buy off sectoral or regional interests. Research has shown that countries with large and fragmented coalitions tend to have more difficulty adjusting to external shocks, such as the 1973–74 oil price hikes. Both Belgium's and Italy's very high levels of public debt have been partly attributed to two decades of being governed by large and unstable coalitions.

Brazil provides another illustration of how electoral and party systems can interact with economic policy. The social security bill proposed by the administration of President Fernando Henrique Cardoso in June 1996 was defeated in the lower house of the legislature, despite a formal majority in favor of the government alliance, because certain interest groups (civil servants and teachers, among others) exploited constitutionally protected privileges and a political system that discourages stable voting majorities in the congress. The fact that deputies belonging to the alliance voted against the bill reflects the

Table 9.2 Estimated efficiency gains from privatizing utilities in Argentina

Income quintile	Efficiency gains (millions of 1993 dollars)	Gains per dollar of expenditure on utilities (percent)
Poorest	205	30
Second	222	27
Middle	342	34
Fourth	335	27
Richest	549	31
Total	1,653	30

Source: Chisari, Estache, and Romero 1996.

unusual autonomy of elected officials from political parties that characterizes Brazil's system of proportional representation. A 1991 study of Brazil's electoral and party system found that representatives had belonged to an average of three political parties, and that in 1987–90 one-third of the 559 representatives had switched parties since being elected in 1986. A bill to reform some aspects of party legislation may be voted in the congress in 1997.

In Uruguay a number of institutions have speeded some reforms—and held back others. One of the peculiarities of the country's electoral system, prior to the recent reform, was that party primaries and general elections were held simultaneously. As a result, the winning presidential candidate received only a minority of the total vote and had to build alliances with opponents in the parliament. In the November 1994 election the winning candidate received only 24 percent of the vote, and the three main parties each received more than 30 percent. Such an electoral system tends to be candidate centered and conducive to faction. Hence, groups that are able to mobilize politically reap the most benefits. Another distinctive feature of Uruguay's political system is its heavy reliance on direct democracy (through plebiscites) to decide on features of the public pension system. In 1992 voters reversed major privatization legislation. And a 1989 plebiscite, initiated by the association of pensioners, guarantees full wage indexation every three months. These institutional designs help explain why pension expenditures relative to GDP are about 35 percent higher in Uruguay than in the United States, even though the two countries have roughly the same proportion of elderly in the population (16 percent).

Uruguay has since recognized that its electoral system is an impediment to a well-functioning state. A new system was approved by the parliament in October 1996. It would end simultaneous voting for primaries and general elections, and it would require a second-round ballot between the two presidential front-runners when neither has managed to secure 50 percent of the vote. These changes are expected to strengthen party discipline and deter factionalism.

CHECKS AND BALANCES. Chapter 6 showed how and why inadequate checks and balances can lead to arbitrary government decisions and behavior. The veto points arise at three levels: the separation between the legislative and the executive branches, the division of the legislature into separate chambers, and the division of power between national and subnational governments. A bias toward the status quo develops when the state supports many institutional veto points, and groups that oppose change can exert power at one or more levels. In a presidential system, for example, gridlock can emerge when different parties or coalitions control the executive and the legislature. Simi-

larly, as Chapter 7 showed, an ill-designed decentralization that leads to capture of local authority by special interests can prevent the adoption of sound reforms.

Although the presence of many veto points can sometimes contribute to delays, some evidence suggests that it has helped contain the expansion of the welfare state. As Figure 9.2 shows, the constitutional division of power ranks second only to aging in explaining changes in welfare spending. As incomes per capita increase, demand for government transfers also rises. Countries with fewer veto points in their state structure (such as Sweden and Denmark) are more receptive to these demands. By contrast, the greater number of veto points in Switzerland—a federal state with a bicameral legislature—has blocked many initiatives to expand welfare programs. Reforming the welfare state will therefore require going beyond streamlining the functioning of transfer programs. Indeed, this was recognized by the 1992 Swedish commission on state reform, which recommended strengthening the executive by introducing a constructive vote of no confidence, allowing the government to ask parliament to vote on measures as a package rather than line by line, extending the time between elections from four to five years, and reducing the size of the parliament by half.

POLITICAL REGIME. The choice of political regime has justifications that go far beyond economic conditions. Yet the strong links between state institutions and policy out-

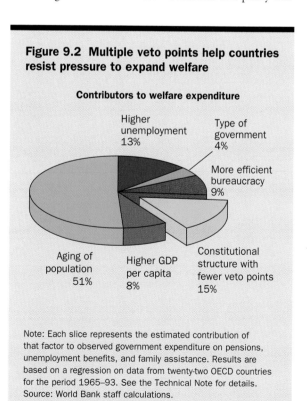

Figure 9.2 Multiple veto points help countries resist pressure to expand welfare

Contributors to welfare expenditure

Higher unemployment 13%

Type of government 4%

More efficient bureaucracy 9%

Aging of population 51%

Higher GDP per capita 8%

Constitutional structure with fewer veto points 15%

Note: Each slice represents the estimated contribution of that factor to observed government expenditure on pensions, unemployment benefits, and family assistance. Results are based on a regression on data from twenty-two OECD countries for the period 1965–93. See the Technical Note for details.
Source: World Bank staff calculations.

Box 9.2 The predatory state under the Duvalier dynasty in Haiti

Haiti became independent in 1804. A predatory state arose there between 1843 and 1915, a period characterized by short-lived rulers, often removed by coups, driven by the creation of personal wealth. Of twenty-two administrations during that period, eleven held office for less than a year, and only one managed to complete its term.

The United States occupied the country from 1915 to 1934, but the logic of a predatory state remained unchanged. In 1957 the democratically elected government of François (Papa Doc) Duvalier took that logic to a new level, starting with an unprecedented purge of civil society, the inherited army, political opposition, and other branches of government. Within two months of coming to power, Duvalier had jailed 100 political opponents. The Catholic Church was perceived as a threat, and spiritual leaders were expelled. The mass media were silenced through the expulsion of foreign journalists, and a 1958 code allowed the government to shoot reporters charged with spreading "false news." Imprisonment of the parents of striking students was made mandatory. After lifting parliamentary immunity in 1959, Duvalier dissolved both the Senate and the Chamber of Deputies. Modern military equipment was stored in the basement of the presidential palace, and more than 200 officers were removed in Duvalier's first eleven years of power. In 1964 Duvalier declared himself president for life.

The economic pillars of Haiti's predatory state were expropriation, extortion, the inflation tax, and corruption. Following a business strike in 1957, the police were authorized to open the shops of striking merchants and distribute their merchandise. Significant resources were devoted to protecting Duvalier himself: 30 percent of total expenditures during the first half of the 1960s. Agriculture, particularly coffee, was heavily taxed. Some sources estimate that Duvalier transferred more than $7 million a year out of Haiti for personal purposes. Large-scale bribes also took place, through deals with foreign investors on projects that often never materialized. Extortion under the veil of "voluntary" donations was institutionalized under the Mouvement de Rénovation Nationale. A pseudo-old-age pension with a 3 percent deduction was created, and government employees were forced to buy a $15 book containing Duvalier's speeches. An autonomous government fund collected taxes and levies, which were excluded from the budget, and no accounting was made of their use.

After nearly thirty years of rule, the Duvalier dynasty fell in 1986, when Jean-Claude (Baby Doc) Duvalier, who had inherited the presidency from his father, went into exile in France with an estimated $1.6 billion at his disposal. Haiti's history as a predatory state goes a long way toward explaining its dismal economic performance. During 1965–90 growth in GNP per capita averaged –0.02 percent, and social indicators remain the worst in the Western Hemisphere. Given the legacies of the predatory state, Haiti's history remains perhaps the biggest obstacle to change.

---

comes raise the question of whether obstacles to reform may be embedded in the political regime. Some observers have argued that nondemocratic regimes, by having fewer veto points, are more conducive to economic development. The reality is more complicated: no single type of regime can guarantee economic and social progress. We do know, however, that one kind of regime—the so-called predatory state—can be almost guaranteed to produce economic stagnation. The focus of such a state is on the extraction of economic rents from the citizenry by those in power. It does so by specifying property rights in a way that maximizes the revenue of the group in power, regardless of the impact on the wealth of the society as a whole. Haiti under the Duvalier regime (Box 9.2) and Romania under Nicolae Ceausescu are prime examples. A predatory state is inconsistent with economic development because it discourages productivity and leads to misallocation of resources, culminating sometimes in the collapse of the state itself.

The end of the Cold War, combined with pressure from citizens, should lessen the risks of extreme state capture embodied in a predatory state, with many countries now having adopted elements of democratic regimes (such as free and open elections). But researchers have yet to reach a consensus on the precise relationship between growth and democracy: about one-fifth of the studies find a positive relationship, one-fifth a negative relationship, and the rest are inconclusive. The analysis of the determinants of growth summarized in Chapter 2 found no statistically significant correlation between the two. And certainly, economic performance among developing countries classified as sustained democracies has varied considerably.

The experience of countries that have combined political transformation with the transition from a planned to a market economy suggests equally mixed conclusions with regard to the relationship between democracy and reform. As noted in Chapter 7, using the ballot box to punish or reward politicians for past performance (retrospective voting) could be a powerful way to ensure accountability and good policy outcomes. But the road can be rocky at first. Indeed, governments' initial reaction to greater political contestability may add to the difficulty of improving institutions, and transitions to democracy are sometimes associated with increased budget deficits and inflation.

Sub-Saharan Africa has witnessed about twenty-seven elections since 1990, twenty-one of which were in countries holding elections for the first time. Young democracies are not immune to the electoral cycle. Before Ghana's 1992 elections, the government increased outlays and the wage bill at the cost of macroeconomic stability and subsequent inflation. In Sub-Saharan Africa the numbers of ministerial positions and legislative seats have increased by 22 percent during the political transition that began in 1989. The governments of Cameroon, Malawi, and Senegal all have more than thirty ministers each. A careful prioritization of policy issues is difficult to achieve in such an atmosphere. Bolivia, for instance, has responded by putting legal restrictions on the size of the cabinet: only two additional ministries may be created, and those on a temporary basis. These experiences suggest that states need skill to manage the political transition in such a way that it does not impede the development agenda.

When and why do countries reform?

Insights about the circumstances under which reforms are likely to succeed are as useful as insights about the obstacles to reform. Indeed, the two are related. If circumstances are conducive to reform, the first step is to alter the dynamics that created the status quo. The following sections describe how an external threat or an economic crisis—real or perceived—may override resistance to change. They may. But they have not always done so. It remains a puzzle why some countries reform in such extreme circumstances and others do not.

External threat

A growing external military threat has often triggered reform. Until recently, a country's lagging technological and economic performance became evident only during wartime. In the 1700s and 1800s the leadership of the Ottoman Empire reorganized the military and made broad reforms in education and governance, in response to battlefield losses to European powers. Similarly, the Meiji restoration in Japan in 1868 was motivated by a desire to strengthen the state against the encroachments of Western powers (Box 9.3).

Today, military confrontation plays a smaller role in driving reform. But the perception that a country is lagging behind its neighbors economically often leads to

---

Box 9.3 Reform under external threat: The Meiji restoration in Japan

The intrusion of Western powers into national commerce was the impetus for reform in Japan. Starting in the 1840s, Japan was under increasing pressure from the West to grant commercial and trade privileges. The Tokugawa leadership was aware that Japan's technological and military prowess lagged, and in 1854 Japan had little choice but to accede to Commodore Perry's demand that some ports be opened to American ships. Similar arrangements with other foreign governments followed. By 1865 Western powers had restricted Japan's ability to levy import tariffs: the highest rate was set at 5 percent. In 1868 a coalition of feudal lords overthrew the Tokugawa family, which had ruled Japan for more than two centuries, and replaced it with a leadership that would modernize Japan and transform it into a country better able to face up to foreign threat. This so-called Meiji restoration marked the beginning of modern Japan's economic growth.

Reforms following the restoration transformed the Japanese state and society. The class system was abolished, a new system of local and national government was set up, and conscription into the army and the navy was instituted. To establish the basis for a sound fiscal system, the government undertook a land survey, established titles, and implemented a land tax payable in cash. Education was gradually made compulsory, so that by the mid-1880s almost half of school-age children were attending school. The Bank of Japan (the central bank) was created, and bureaucratic reforms were undertaken, laying the ground for the recruitment of state officials based on merit, not patronage. Moreover, the new regime undertook initiatives that today would be called industrial policies: it established and operated factories (silk, brick, glass, cement, textiles, shipyards), subsidized industries, imported technicians, and sent students abroad.

---

important demonstration effects. Chile's economic success clearly inspired other Latin American countries to undertake reform in the late 1980s, as did the success of Japan and, later, that of the Republic of Korea and Taiwan (China) in East and Southeast Asia. Economic reform in China can be explained by many factors. But among them was the demonstration effect of its neighbors' economic success and an unwillingness to be left behind.

Economic crisis

Since the early 1980s, economic crisis has been by far the most important factor driving the introduction of ambitious reforms. As the failure of prevailing policies becomes widely recognized, popular demands for reform become more vocal, and politicians more willing to risk radical change. Economic crisis—particularly hyperinflation and deep recession—preceded economic reform in, for example, Indonesia in 1961–64 and Peru in 1990. Yet other countries in dire economic straits have failed to take corrective measures, while several countries have not needed a deep crisis to spur reform. Economic crisis cannot be credited with stimulating reform in Australia (1983), Colombia (1989), or Portugal (1985).

Economic crisis and civil conflict often feed on one another, leading to near disintegration of the state (for example, in Liberia and Somalia). Such crises have immense social costs and offer little hope for quick resolution, for state capability matters when it comes to turning a crisis into an opportunity. Yet political leadership and political entrepreneurship are also important. And often political leaders who can convert opportunities for economic gain into reality can capitalize on the benefits of successful reform.

Even in time of crisis, incumbents are often more reluctant to embrace reform than are newcomers. Thus, a change in government in the middle of an economic crisis (as in Peru and Poland in 1990) may provide the added impetus needed to get reform started. Terrorism, hyperinflation, and the poor performance of traditional parties in Peru all gave the new president, Alberto Fujimori, room to maneuver. On the other hand, Colombia's reforms took place in 1989, toward the end of the administration of Virgilio Barco, when the economy was not in crisis. So honeymoon periods and economic crisis provide an opportunity, but not the only opportunity, for embarking on reform. More important, even in countries where economic crisis has triggered reform, the depth of reform has tended to be modest. Lasting improvements in economic performance have often remained elusive. Economic crisis may provide an opportunity to go beyond stabilization, but whether or not countries seize the opportunity depends on the redistributive effects, the state's initial capability, and political leadership. Deep institutional reforms are unlikely to result from a reform agenda triggered and driven by crisis alone.

Implementing and sustaining reform

Reform of the state means not only reform of policies but also an institutionalization of good rules of behavior for government agencies. Institutions must be created that help avoid heavy discounting of the benefits from reforms, paralysis due to unfamiliar new circumstances,

and problems of social mistrust. A balance must be struck between clear rules that circumscribe the freedom of state officials to act opportunistically, and the need for them to act flexibly and responsively. An effective state operates with clear and transparent rules, yet is quick to exploit opportunities and to reverse course when circumstances demand it.

The obstacles to building an effective state are not insurmountable. Change has a better chance of success when policymakers do three things: tactically design and sequence reforms, compensate losers, and build consensus. We take up each of these in the following discussion. But in some cases institutions must be modified to make the state function better: it is no longer a question of tactics but of fundamental reform. One lesson is clear: all these changes are a good deal more difficult—impossible, even—in the absence of leaders with a clear vision of the future.

Tactical design and sequencing

Tactical design and sequencing of reform can improve the chances of success by recognizing the constraints of existing state capabilities, diluting resistance to change, and building a constituency in favor of reform.

MATCHING ROLE TO CAPABILITY. As emphasized throughout this Report, a good match between the state's role and its capability is the key to effective policies. A mismatch between capability and action can compromise the sustainability and effectiveness of reforms even in the absence of political obstacles. Regulatory reform—whether of antitrust, environmental, or financial regulation—should reflect institutional capabilities (see Table 4.2). For instance, price-cap regulation, in which the regulator sets the adjustment factor used in determining a monopoly utility's prices, is more suited to countries with relatively strong institutions. Similarly, mechanisms to improve the delivery of services have to take into account not only the characteristics of the service but also the capability of the state (see Table 5.1). Within the core public sector (in education and health care, for example), using performance-based agencies and formal contracts requires an institutional capability that many developing countries lack. In these cases such institution-heavy approaches are unworkable. Capability constraints should also loom large in the choice of a decentralization strategy (see Table 7.5). Where capability is low in both central and local government, a cautious decentralization strategy with pilot testing is probably the best course. But, as Part Three of this Report showed, capability is not destiny. And the return to improving capability is significant indeed.

STRATEGIC SEQUENCING AS A FIRST STEP TO IMPROVING CAPABILITY. Where administrative capability is weak, rather than attempt comprehensive reforms of all institutions, countries might do better to reform key functions and agencies selectively. Besides being consistent with fiscal and human resource constraints, this approach has two advantages. First, it allows reformers to learn from the unavoidable mistakes associated with institution building. Second, by beginning with the most promising agencies, reformers can count on demonstration effects for the rest of the public sector. These two advantages increase the likelihood of achieving a series of success stories that will maintain political support of an overall reform program.

Many countries have used this strategic approach, beginning reform with a few critical enclaves. Candidates for early treatment typically include the ministry of finance, the central bank, and the tax collection agency. In both Peru and Ghana, for example, very low tax revenues forced the government to make swift changes in tax collection. Yet any country following such a strategy must ensure that the assignment of policy responsibilities among agencies and ministries takes into account where the relevant professional expertise is concentrated, and that mandates are broadly consonant with the public interest at large. For instance, a tariff regime that is managed out of the finance ministry is likely to emphasize revenue goals over industry protection—the priorities would probably be reversed if the ministry of commerce were in charge. Transforming quantitative restrictions into tariffs would typically receive more support from the treasury (see Table 9.1). The appropriate assignment of policy responsibilities can help sustain reform by influencing what gets approved and in what order.

The strategic enclave approach allows countries to adopt the first generation of reforms (Table 9.3). These reforms—which can mostly be enacted through executive order—typically involve stabilization and selected structural reforms. But an excessively narrow approach to enclaving can impede the deeper institutional changes required by the second generation of reforms. And progress in the social sectors has generally been modest. For example, in Ghana, one of the pioneer reformers in Sub-Saharan Africa, health expenditures have become even more regressive since reforms began. Deep institutional reforms take time and are complex, and opposition by interest groups (for example, the teachers union in Colombia) is often strong. For countries trapped in the first generation of reforms, sustainable long-term development will be elusive.

Countries can implement a strategy that enables them to escape the enclave trap. Such a strategy involves, above all, agreeing on clear rules for the conditions under which agencies outside the original enclave will be brought within the reform program. These rules provide a bridge between the first- and second-generation reforms, while mitigating animosities from agencies outside the enclave. The Bolivian civil service reform has rightly moved in that direction. Embedded in the 1990 Financial Administration Act and associated agency-specific regulations are a series of rules governing which entities are eligible to recruit highly paid civil servants, what conditions these entities have to meet in order to qualify, and what is expected from them once they have implemented the

Table 9.3 First- and second-generation reforms

	First generation	Second generation
Main objectives	Crisis management: reducing inflation and restoring growth	Improving social conditions and competitiveness, maintaining macroeconomic stability
Instruments	Drastic budget cuts, tax reform, price liberalization, trade and foreign investment liberalization, deregulation, social funds, autonomous contracting agencies, some privatization	Civil service reform, labor reform, restructuring of social ministries, judicial reform, modernizing of the legislature, upgrading of regulatory capacity, improved tax collection, large-scale privatization, restructuring of central-local government relationships
Actors	Presidency, economic cabinet, central bank, multilateral financial institutions, private financial groups, foreign portfolio investors	Presidency and cabinet, legislature, civil service, judiciary, unions, political parties, media, state and local governments, private sector, multilateral financial institutions
Main challenge	Macroeconomic management by an insulated technocratic elite	Institutional development highly dependent on middle management in the public sector

Source: Adapted from Naím 1995.

reform. Yet Ecuador's experience with a similar reform strategy illustrates that it requires a firm commitment to the program to ensure that these rules are implemented in practice. Two months after finalizing the rules governing administrative reform, the secretary in charge declared all central administration entities "restructured" and granted salary enhancement, although none had met the eligibility conditions. Rules can underpin a commitment to reform—but they cannot substitute for it.

GRADUAL PHASING OUT. Matching the state's role to its capability and going beyond enclaving sometimes require replacing a public agency with a private one. This, in turn, may call for a two-stage strategy to circumvent resistance. During the first phase, an opting-out mechanism might be put in place, to allow people to switch to private providers if they want to. Wider recognition of the benefits of better services can then make it easier to carry out the second phase: getting rid of the public providers.

Sri Lanka's 1991 Telecommunications Act shows the benefits of such a strategy. This act created the regulatory agency and allowed private operators to compete with the state monopoly Sri Lanka Telecom (SLT) in value added telecommunication services. The legal and regulatory framework has contributed to making Sri Lanka one of the most liberalized telecommunications markets in Asia. By 1995 there were four mobile cellular operators, five paging companies, three data transmission service providers, and one Internet provider. At the end of 1995, 20 percent of all telephone subscribers were connected to cellular services. Competition between the cellular operators has led to some of the lowest tariffs in the region, and these services are increasingly seen as a credible alternative to SLT's wired services. To reduce unsatisfied demand quickly, in early 1996 the telecommunications regulatory agency licensed two fixed wireless private operators for basic telecommunications services. These impressive results have created pressure for better performance by the public telecommunications company. Consistent with a two-stage phasing-out strategy, the government has announced the sale of 34 percent of SLT's equity to a strategic investor.

Peru's pension reform illustrates how gradual phasing out can be applied to the social sectors as well. When the reform was launched in 1993, workers were allowed to choose between public and private pension providers. In 1996 disincentives for joining a private provider were removed, leading to a de facto phasing out of the public scheme. During the second stage a strong constituency in favor of the reform was formed, comprising workers who had already shifted to a private provider and pension fund managers. By contrast, the sequencing of Pakistan's direct tax reform seems to have greatly reduced the chances of success. The government began the reform with a

reduction in rates, which was supposed to be accompanied by a removal of tax holidays. But the powerful agricultural lobby blocked the lifting of exemptions, and an attempt in 1993 to introduce a tax on rich farmers was circumvented by raising the exemption ceiling tenfold. By contrast, even a revenue-neutral tax rate reduction combined with a broadening of the tax base would have cut distortions without creating losers. A back-of-the-envelope estimate of the benefit of reduced distortions suggests it would be upward of 1.4 percent of GDP (see the Technical Note).

EFFICIENCY VERSUS TACTICAL SEQUENCING. The optimal sequencing from an efficiency standpoint may not be politically feasible. For example, efficiency considerations dictate setting up a credible and stable regulatory agency before privatizing telecommunications. This sequencing reduces the risk involved in the purchase, hence increasing the selling price of the company. Argentina, however, did not follow this sequence. Instead the country's telephone monopoly was sold a year before a new regulatory agency was set up. This strategy was adopted to speed privatization and prevent opposition to the reform. Regulatory uncertainty may have reduced the selling price, but the political feasibility of the reform was greatly enhanced. And as noted above, the efficiency gains induced by the overall privatization program were significant (Table 9.2). Moreover, countries choosing for political reasons to reverse the most efficient sequencing might mitigate the disadvantages of the lower initial selling price by selling shares in stages, as the reform's credibility improves.

COMBINING AND PACKAGING REFORMS. Introducing the right mix of reforms could allow key constituencies to balance their gains and losses, hence reducing the political cost of the reform (see Box 9.1). This strategy was pursued by New Zealand's Labour government in the 1980s. Minister of Finance Roger Douglas persuaded agricultural groups that losing their subsidies was essential to the total reform package, which benefited farmers by cutting tariffs, lowering inflation, and addressing the bias against exports. Similarly, in Bolivia the broad reform package introduced in 1985 by the government of Victor Paz Estenssoro, in a context of hyperinflation, managed to circumvent labor opposition, which had vetoed previous reform plans. Although support from the two main political parties helped, the speed and comprehensiveness of the reform prevented pressure groups from organizing to derail it.

When deep macroeconomic imbalances have to be corrected, packaging some reforms could increase their political feasibility. For example, trade liberalization is often easier to implement in conjunction with an adjustment program, because the gains from improved macroeconomic policy (in lower inflation and positive growth) can offset the distributive effects of liberalization (see Box

9.1). Broad reforms may also enhance credibility. In 1990 the Polish government freed 90 percent of prices, eliminated most trade barriers, abolished state trading monopolies, and made its currency convertible for current account transactions. After an initial decline in output in 1990–91, the Polish economy has recorded vigorous growth.

Compensation

SEVERANCE PACKAGES. Both matching the state's role to its capability and enhancing its capability require not only tactical design and sequencing but also the compensation of groups adversely affected by reform, to secure their support. These groups are not always the poorest in society. They may, for example, include bureaucrats whose jobs are being eliminated, managers of privatized state enterprises, and businesspeople used to operating behind high levels of trade protection. Although compensation might be economically costly in the short run, it will pay off in the long run to the extent that it eases opposition to reform. A recent study of retrenchment programs found that, on average, the associated benefits in terms of productivity gains and wage bill savings offset the compensation cost after only 1.7 years. Three factors show why severance payments can be so important to the success of reform. First, political feasibility may require that retrenchment be done on a voluntary basis. Second, even where political constraints are not a factor, the law may preclude involuntary separation, as in the case of the Central Bank of Ecuador. Third, most developing countries do not have an unemployment insurance scheme, and severance pay then becomes a close substitute.

Designing severance schemes that take into account broader characteristics of workers can help make politically feasible retrenchment less costly and better targeted. One such mechanism is to set ceilings on the number of departures by skill level. In Argentina, for instance, trained professionals from the National Institute of Agricultural Technology were made ineligible for voluntary retirement packages. It is also important when designing retrenchment programs to establish built-in mechanisms that prevent rehiring, which would defeat the purpose.

EQUITY INCENTIVES. In some cases compensation goes beyond generous severance payments: labor, management, or the public at large may be given a share of privatized enterprises. Bolivia's capitalization program is a very innovative approach. At least three features of the program increased its political acceptance without compromising on efficiency gains:

- By distributing shares to employees and pensioners, the program circumvented the resistance to privatization that often occurs when assets are sold entirely to foreign companies.

- Tangible benefits accrue to citizens early in the process. Beginning in May 1997 each person over 65 will get an annuity from the capitalization program with an estimated value of $200 to $225. Bolivia's income per capita, for comparison, was $770 in 1994.
- A concern often raised by opponents of privatization, namely, that it provides an opportunity for corruption, is somewhat mitigated (whether warranted or not) because the state does not receive funds.

The Bolivian and Czech experiences show how a carefully designed privatization program can enhance political feasibility and achieve sustainable efficiency gains, but poorly designed versions of these strategies can backfire.

Building consensus

Reforming the state requires cooperation from all major groups in society. Deep-seated differences and mutual suspicions among groups can delay or kill reform. There are no quick fixes for reversing age-old enmities, but social pacts can help. In a social pact, business, labor, and agricultural interests negotiate the terms of a contract with government leaders, setting clearly defined responsibilities for each group. This approach has proved successful in countries as diverse as Spain and Benin. In Spain a minority government was able to impose wage restraint by bringing all political parties to the negotiating table and developing a common program, later known as the Moncloa Pacts (Box 9.4). Benin's second democratically elected government organized a consultation with political parties and civil society on taking office in May 1996. This National Economic Conference created a number of sectoral working groups and made specific recommendations about the role of the state. Whether this initiative will translate into a consensus around an economic program remains to be seen.

Leadership and vision

There is no universal blueprint for reform. But almost all successful reform episodes in developing economies have had one common feature: they have been crafted by dynamic leaders who shepherded changes through complicated political terrain. Such leaders seize opportunities as they appear, but they also create them, by identifying and reaching out to potential beneficiaries, reshaping institutions, and articulating a compelling and achievable vision for the future. Political leadership is particularly important in countries that lack trust and cohesion among different social groups. When businesspeople mistrust bureaucrats, workers are wary of managers, and farmers are suspicious of everyone, sensible reforms can stall. Leaders must instill a sense of common purpose that minimizes polarization.

Box 9.4 The Moncloa Pacts in Spain

Adolfo Suárez was named chief of government by Spain's King Juan Carlos I in July 1976, early in the transition to democracy following Generalissimo Francisco Franco's death in November 1975. Suárez started by instituting political reforms: he recognized free trade unions and the right to strike, legalized all political parties (including the Communist Party), proclaimed a political amnesty, and passed a new electoral law. The first free elections since the Spanish civil war were held on June 15, 1977. Suárez won the elections, but his newly created party, the Center Democratic Union, held only 47 percent of the seats in parliament.

The elections took place as the economy was falling into a crisis. Inflation and unemployment were both on the rise, and the external balance was deteriorating rapidly. As part of its anti-inflationary drive and its policy of external liberalization, the Suárez government sought to reduce wage growth. But rather than confront the labor movement and the trade unions, Suárez took a consensual approach to incomes policy. Peak business and labor associations were brought together in late summer 1977 to forge a common position. These attempts failed, however, because of deep divisions within business and labor. Labor, for example, was represented by officials from at least four distinct political leanings. No one wanted to appear to be making concessions.

Suárez then changed strategy and sought agreement among party rather than class leaders. The resulting agreements, reached in October 1977, have come to be called the Moncloa Pacts. Agreement among the political parties proved easier to achieve because the party leaders were more moderate than the interest groups they represented, and because the far left (which had no parliamentary representation) could be excluded.

The pacts went far beyond wage restraint and encompassed provisions on monetary and fiscal policies and structural reforms as well. They promised a "new framework for labor relations" with increased labor market flexibility, a more progressive tax system, and the rationalization and decentralization of public enterprises. Importantly, the pacts contained measures to compensate workers for some of the costs that adjustment was expected to impose on them. Increased state spending on job creation and unemployment insurance, the progressive extension of unemployment insurance to all the unemployed, and some price controls were among the compensatory measures. Given that Spain already had the highest level of worker conflict in all of Europe, getting labor to go along with fundamental reforms without these concessions was a major achievement.

Although not all the promises made in the Moncloa Pacts (especially those in the areas of labor market reform and public enterprises) were fulfilled, the pacts were successful in achieving their primary targets. Price and wage inflation was sharply reduced after 1977, and the current account gap was closed.

The purpose of reform is to enhance economic well-being. The consequences of reform are often measured using quantifiable yardsticks, such as national income, exports, or inflation. But an equally important aspect of reform is whether it succeeds in reshaping the values and norms of the state and the state's relationship to the economy. It is this transformation that ultimately legitimates reforms in the public eye. Thus political leaders must offer a compelling vision, beyond the dry realities of economic efficiency, about where their societies are headed. Such a vision can motivate and rally support for reforms.

For example, in some transition economies—such as the Czech Republic, Hungary, and Poland—reform was aided by the prospect of joining the European Union. The same desire motivated reform in Spain and Portugal in the early 1980s. In other instances a clear vision does not present itself so easily. Venezuela's reforms under Carlos Andrés Pérez were a political failure because there was no coherent vision to help sell the reforms (Box 9.5). In Malaysia, by contrast, Prime Minister Mahathir Mohamad's policy initiatives in the 1990s were packaged in his Vision 2020, which set the eye-catching target of raising Malaysian living standards to industrial-country levels by 2020.

Strategic options: Finding the route to reform

Machiavelli rightly recognized that distributional conflicts lie at the heart of the difficulties of reforming the state. Yet such conflicts, and the constraints embedded in state institutions which can exacerbate them, are not immutable. Change will come when the incentives to throw out the old policies and institutional arrangements become stronger than the incentives to keep them. An economic crisis or an external threat may provide the impetus for initiating reforms. But its precise timing can be prolonged if those who control state power stick with outdated policies because it is in their (or their allies') interest that it be so. Sometimes the delays can be painfully long, as in Haiti under the Duvaliers or Zaire today.

Box 9.5 Venezuela's 1989 reform program and its reversal

In the late 1980s the Venezuelan economy was experiencing a deep crisis, with internal and external imbalances generated by an overextended state and a mismanaged economy. In 1989 Carlos Andrés Pérez, who had served as president in the 1970s, was reelected. His 1989 stabilization plan included a sharp devaluation of the bolívar and a lifting of price and interest rate controls. The plan restored internal and external balance and was accompanied by structural reforms such as trade liberalization, privatization, and increased central bank autonomy.

These reforms were made possible by the broad executive powers of the Venezuelan presidency. But the consensus on them did not last long. After a period of political instability, in February 1994 Rafael Caldera was elected as leader of a coalition government. The new government started by repudiating some of the reforms, eliminating the value added tax and returning to price and interest rate controls. The autonomy of the central bank was also compromised, prompting its president to resign. Constrained by international agreements, the administration did not reverse trade liberalization, but instead relied on nontariff protection. The program's lack of coherence caused an erosion of confidence in the international investment community. Venezuela's bond rating dropped 20 percentage points below its 1991 level. In 1994 real GDP dropped by 3 percent, and inflation soared to 71 percent. In the second quarter of 1996 the administration began adopting more orthodox economic policies, supported by an arrangement with the IMF. These have been implemented with some success thus far. How far-reaching and sustainable this program will be remains to be seen.

Venezuela's experience highlights some important points about the sustainability of reform. Economic reform is more susceptible to reversal when it is supported by only a few technocrats, without backing from political parties or other groups. Reforms linked to stabilization are easier to implement than are structural reforms requiring congressional approval. Moreover, economic reforms are harder to implement in an environment prone to political risk. Introducing new taxes is contentious in an environment where state control over natural resources (in this case petroleum) gives the appearance of cost-free public services. A crisis may be sufficient to create the conditions for initiating reforms, but sustaining them requires much more. Long-term performance requires vision and unity of purpose.

This chapter has shown how windows of opportunity can open, and how important it is to seize these opportunities to bring about change—through compensation of potential losers, the skillful choice of tactics, and building consensus. As emphasized throughout this Report, it is important to reckon on state capability when designing reforms. But reformers cannot afford to stop there: they must also have a strategy for improving capability. A more capable state can broaden the scope of policy options and significantly improve economic performance. Strategic sequencing, and even well-thought-out enclaving, are a good first step and are consistent with the budgetary and other constraints facing many developing countries. Early on, however, countries should design a strategy for going beyond reforming a few agencies, and thus escaping the enclave trap. This involves defining clear rules under which agencies outside the original enclave will be brought into the reform program. Rules and tactics, however, are no substitute for commitment and political leadership.

Leadership is not everything: even committed and visionary leaders are not always able to throw off the heavy legacy of years, perhaps decades, of poor performance. Choosing reform in these circumstances usually involves a leap of faith, a leap that can be as frightening to those who will ultimately gain as it is to the losers. In these circumstances the presence of someone who can convince the public that the leap is worth making is a potent reform weapon indeed.

CHAPTER 10

THE AGENDA FOR CHANGE

THIS REPORT HAS SHOWN THAT THE STATE HAS ENORmous sway over a country's economic and social development and whether that development is sustainable. The state's potential to leverage, promote, and mediate change in pursuit of collective ends is unmatched. Where this capacity has been used well, economies have flourished. But where it has not, development has hit a brick wall.

The process is not irrevocable: examples through history, and throughout the world, have shown that countries can change track, reforming policies and institutions to improve the state's effectiveness and forward development. But why do so many of these efforts fail to achieve their goals? Even more important, why is it that so many states, in desperate circumstances, do not even attempt them? Politics provides much of the answer. But it is not simply a matter of democracy versus authoritarianism. We need to go beyond those broad concepts of political organization to understand the incentives that inspire state organizations to work better. We need to understand better how and when the economic and political interests that favor development can be harnessed to bring about the institutional changes needed to make development happen.

Efforts to restart development in countries with ineffective states must start with institutional arrangements that foster responsiveness, accountability, and the rule of law.

Enabling the state to do more good for the economy and society means building confidence; people must have trust in the basic rules governing society and in the public authority that underpins them. The task is difficult for two reasons.

First, it requires patience. It takes time for judiciaries to convince firms and citizens that they are impartial in their decisions. It takes time for national and provincial legislatures, political appointees, judges, civil servants, public-private deliberation councils, independent watchdogs, and nongovernmental organizations—arrayed in unique relations to one another in different societies—to learn to respect the limits of one another's authority and to work together. It takes time to lay the foundations of a professional, rule-based bureaucracy. Still, it is possible to sequence reforms in a manner that yields some early payoffs. Such early measures can include strengthening the capacity of central government, raising upperend salary scales to attract capable staff, inviting more inputs into policymaking and making deliberations more open, hiving off contestable and easily specified activities for private sector involvement, and seeking more feedback from clients. In general, however, there are few quick fixes.

Second, the task is difficult because the same institutions that can foster credibility and accountability can also be constraining. The same rules that prevent abuse of state authority can also lessen the ability to use that authority well. The challenge is to devise institutional arrangements that provide flexibility within appropriate restraints.

In the end each country must strike its own balance. Countries with strong track records of following through on commitments, and whose state institutions have deep roots in society, are likely to have room to experiment and to respond flexibly to unanticipated events, with little cost to credibility. But countries emerging from long periods of arbitrary and dysfunctional government might be better off forswearing the short-term benefits of flexibility in favor of the long-term goal of building credible and sustainable institutions.

Where prospects for reform are strong, this Report has suggested a two-part approach to improving the effectiveness of the state:

- Matching role with capability, and
- Reinvigorating state capability by subjecting the state to more rules and restraint and greater competitive pressure, and making it more transparent and open.

Focusing limited state capability on the basics is a badly needed first step in a wide range of countries—especially in Africa, the CIS countries, and parts of Latin America, the Middle East, and South Asia.

Matching role with capability must come first. In many parts of the world the state is not even performing its basic functions: safeguarding law and order, protecting property rights, managing the macroeconomy, providing basic social services, and protecting the destitute.

In some cases the state has been overregulating the economy, even though it lacks the capability to enforce regulations systematically. One consequence has been the spread of corruption, which corrodes capability even further—sometimes rendering the state incapable of delivering even basic services. Reasonably well functioning bureaucracies have been weakened over the years and will now need considerable overhaul. Deregulating these economies is vital.

Reforms supported by the World Bank and other international organizations have tried to help countries design reforms to match the state's role to its capability. Many reforms over the last decade or so have tried to trim back the state's role in some areas of the economy and refocus the released resources on core functions. These are a start, but more is needed.

However, as this Report has shown, matching role to capability is not simply a matter of reducing the state's role. It is not just a question of what to do, but also a question of how to do it: how to manage the financial sector, how to regulate economic activity, how to protect the environment—all these choices depend critically on the state's institutional capability.

Efforts to focus the state's existing capability more effectively must be complemented by reforms to improve capability by reinvigorating public institutions. In many areas the state will only be able to improve its effectiveness by forging new partnerships with other organizations of civil society. In other instances it will become more effective only if its decisions and actions can be contested—if people and business have choices and if the state's monopoly is broken.

Improving state capability is not simply a matter of more technical assistance. It takes the right incentives.

The precise recipe for improved state capability will vary from country to country, since so much of the reform involved is institutional, and institutional change is path-dependent. We examine below some of the key opportunities and challenges facing states in each developing region. But the advice is premised on the assumption that there is, at least, a state there to reform. Increasingly, even this basic precondition for improving development outcomes does not apply. We turn first to these most extreme cases of institutional failure, when, for a period, the state itself as a legitimate and functioning order is gone.

When states collapse

In recent years a growing number of countries have seen virtually all of the functions and institutions of government collapse, often in the context of civil war. When the state ceases to perform even its most basic functions, the associated crisis can be prolonged and severe. Structures that might normally mitigate the impact of the crisis and provide a vehicle for eventual recovery are frequently destroyed, making the more generic prescriptions for enhancing state capability somewhat inapplicable.

The causes of state collapse

State collapse is not a new phenomenon. It does, however, seem to have become more common in the 1980s and 1990s than in the earlier postwar years, and it is a matter of grave concern for other states, individually and collectively. Collapsed states such as Afghanistan, Cambodia, Liberia, Rwanda, and Somalia have been the settings for some of the worst humanitarian disasters of recent years. These often spill over into neighboring countries in the form of violence, banditry, and refugee flows. They also send countries into arrears, destroy economic assets and infrastructure, claim huge amounts of international assistance—and, of course, waste countless lives. Three broad and overlapping pathologies of state collapse can be identified:

- States that have lost (or failed to establish) legitimacy in the eyes of most of the population notionally under their authority, and are therefore unable to exercise that authority
- States that have been run into the ground by leaders and officials who are corrupt, negligent, incompetent, or all three
- States that have fragmented in civil war, and in which no party is capable of reestablishing central authority.

What all these states have in common is a fundamental loss of institutional capability. As outlined in Chapter 1 (see Table 1.1), at a minimum the state must perform the most basic functions of maintaining law and order, providing national defense, and establishing a framework for managing economic transactions. A collapsed state, then, is not one that fails to do the right things, but one that fails to do much of anything effectively—even maintain repressive order. A collapsed state is not the same as a state defeated in war, or a state split apart into two or more states, where, despite some incapacity, systems continue to function more or less effectively. Nor is a collapsed state the same thing as a "predatory" or repressive state. Successful repression of a whole population can require considerable organizational capacity. Such acts may provoke the replacement of one state structure or regime with another, as in Cambodia or Rwanda, but do not necessarily—or even probably—bring about its collapse.

Factors perpetuating the conflict

In most countries where the state has collapsed, there are forces that have an interest in perpetuating a state of anarchy, and whose unbridled pursuit of riches or power would be constrained by a state with the capability to make rules, collect revenue, and enforce the law. The most troubling and intractable of collapsed states are those in which these forces predominate. In Angola, Liberia, and Somalia, for example, a self-sustaining economy of armed violence has emerged, based on looting, protection rackets, drug trafficking, money laundering, and the extraction of crude resources such as gems, minerals, and tropical timber (Box 10.1). Civil warfare in these countries has its roots in political or ethnic rivalries, but it has gradually shifted character and is now centered around the control of economic assets, which provide the source of financing for the war and for private enrichment.

In such countries factional warfare is the main system of resource allocation, and violence the source of power. These economies operate independently of any state institutions, and indeed would likely be hindered by them. Thus, strong economic forces are at work perpetuating the fighting. The role of economic factors as a driving cause of the war has been especially pronounced in the case of Liberia (Box 10.2), but it can also explain the prolongation of wars in Angola and Sierra Leone. Ordinary people pay a high price for their helpless proximity to these systems. Normal international economic transactions are disrupted and, often, corrupted by them.

Box 10.1 State collapse and beyond in Somalia

Somalia is one of the most ethnically homogeneous countries in Africa; one of the most common factors in state collapse—interethnic conflict—played no part in its collapse. Rather, the dynamic of Somalia's collapse was set in motion during a long period (1969–91) of dictatorial rule and egregious economic mismanagement by Mohamed Siad Barre, followed by a fierce contest for power after he was violently deposed. Siad Barre played off the Cold War superpowers against each other. His external support, first from the Soviet Union and then from the United States, unbalanced the fragile social ecology of Somalia's clan politics and introduced high levels of lethal weaponry. A north-south conflict inherited from the preindependence era, an irredentist war to seize Ethiopia's Somali-populated Ogaden region, and the suspension of economic and military aid in 1989 all further contributed to the erosion of state capability.

Since 1991, continuous civil war between rival clans and factions has completed the destruction of the formal economy and left Somalia with no state institutional or public administration. Physical infrastructure and economic assets have been destroyed, private businesses looted, and agricultural and pastoral production drastically reduced. Professionals, technocrats, and civil servants have fled. International intervention to halt a major war-induced famine brought a respite and some reconstruction from late 1992 to early 1995, but these gains were reversed after U.N. forces withdrew, and anarchy returned.

Some elements of the private, informal market have shown an extraordinary, if somewhat perverse, resilience to the chaos and violence that surrounds them. Merchants and entrepreneurs can operate only with clan protection; those who benefit from this protection, and from their clan's control of economic assets such as ports, mineral deposits, and agricultural lands, finance clan militias. With no government regulations or controls, the prices of goods and foreign currencies float freely. Transactions costs are high, but markets operate efficiently. The Somali shilling has value despite the absence of a central bank, but banknotes are physically wearing out. Remittances from abroad are handled quickly and reliably through clan networks.

Today, Somalia exemplifies a post-state economy. Productive capacity, private investment, and employment are extremely low; risks are high, and violence is the normal means of competition and resolution of economic disputes. If a functioning state with legitimate institutions were able to restore law and order without reverting to the heavy-handed economic mismanagement of the Siad Barre regime, the private sector has shown that it could weather the high risk and respond to the challenges of the market.

Box 10.2 The economic underpinnings of conflict: The case of Liberia

Initially, the war in Liberia was fought largely for social and political motives, with control over the central government as the central objective. Foreign support helped finance the launching of the war. Gradually control over Liberia's rich natural resources and other assets, in addition to being a means of ensuring funding for the war, has become an end in itself for the fighting factions.

The factions depend on a steady supply of income from the export of rubber, timber, iron ore, gold, and diamonds. During periods of intense conflict, much of the income is used to purchase arms and ammunition. When no fighting is taking place, a revenue "surplus" is created, which provides for the personal enrichment of the leaders and for the payoffs that keep faction members loyal. This, together with the uncertainty that faction members face regarding their economic prospects after the war, creates strong pressures down the ranks to share in the surplus. However, lower-rank fighters rarely receive direct payments, instead relying on looting and pillaging for their livelihood.

Because fighting actually runs down the "surplus," as long as the prospects for private enrichment remain high the incentives are strong for factions to maintain a "no war, no peace" equilibrium. This helps explain the difficulties in reaching a lasting peace agreement in Liberia.

Thus, to restore peace, any intervention will have to include actions that make the "surplus" accruing to the fighting organizations zero or negative, while simultaneously eliminating individual fighters' income from looting, or raising the associated risk. Such actions range from economic sanctions on the export of timber and rubber exports to international agreements that increase the cost of arms. In addition, combatants' incentives to continue the war must be removed through a combination of carefully planned demobilization and enforcement of criminal laws.

Although the diminishing returns of conflict and resource extraction imply that wars will eventually fade away without international intervention, this point is reached only after nearly all the assets of a country have been destroyed. This leaves other states, and intergovernmental organizations, facing two urgent questions: How can state collapse be prevented? And how can a functioning state be rescued from the ashes of a collapsed one?

Preventing state collapse

The enormous toll of collapsed states has naturally turned attention to prevention as a preferable and potentially less costly course of action. But there are no easy shortcuts. Preventing state collapse ultimately involves the whole gamut of institutions and policies that affect social, political, and economic relations within a society. Nevertheless, two interrelated approaches have emerged as ways of reducing the likelihood that political conflict will spiral down into a comprehensive collapse of the state.

The first strategy emphasizes the reinforcement of civil society as a way of increasing the resilience of social institutions that may be able to fend off anarchy even if the state is very weak. A rich associational life may enable communities to maintain local law and order, support a safety net, and resist official corruption or exploitation. The second approach, drawn from the East Asian experience, points to the need to build bureaucratic structures that are insulated from political interference, and to embed bureaucratic decisionmaking within appropriate restraints. The integrity and professionalism of the civil service are an important element in this.

> *An active civil society and a competent and professional bureaucracy are twin pillars of a constructive relationship between state and society. When comprehensive collapse of the state is a danger, these twin pillars may reduce the risk.*

The challenge of reconstruction

Rapid retrieval of a lost state is even more difficult—if not impossible. Most collapsed states are immersed in, or just emerging from, bitter internecine conflict. Politics is often highly charged with suspicion of complicity; mistrust is widespread. Cooperation among former rivals is difficult to achieve, and the desire for justice on the part of some may look like vengeance seeking to others. There may be little confidence that peace will be sustained, or policies maintained, and social and human capital has often been severely damaged.

External actors face unusual difficulties when they decide to become engaged in a country without a functioning state. A basic question arises: how and with whom should one work? One strategy involves choosing among local factions or leaders and attempting to reinforce the position of the chosen partner. This is risky. The chosen partner may be unreliable or may abuse the position of leadership. There is also the risk that another external force will pick an alternative winner, prolonging the conflict, as occurred in Mozambique and Angola. Alternatively, outsiders can choose to work with those local authorities and institutions that often retain legitimacy and capability long after central institutions collapse. Such a strategy can help rebuild local confidence and strengthen local decisionmaking capacity. But it can also prolong the period of state fragmentation if it is not combined with a strategy for rebuilding the authority of a central government. Somalia is a case in point.

In many instances external actors focus on mitigating the human cost of state collapse through relief and rehabilitation programs, rather than intervening directly in civil or political reconstruction. Recent experience suggests, however, that after some time these programs can lead to dependency among the population, and even undermine the rebuilding of state capability by drawing attention away from minimal state functions. By contrast, more-comprehensive peace approaches, such as adopted in Angola, Cambodia, and Mozambique, place far-reaching formal authority in the hands of international organizations to oversee peace agreements, deliver public services, and facilitate the repatriation of refugees. All this is with a view to handing over power to an indigenous authority after elections have been held. The international operations in Cambodia and Mozambique are generally considered to have been successful in this regard. But both were enormously costly, and external actors cannot and should not be expected to replace absent state capability indefinitely.

The choice of strategy for external actors will differ according to the particular pathology of state collapse involved. As the discussion in Chapter 8 suggests, there is an increasing awareness of the role that external donors and agencies may need to play in the future to allow for the long process of reconstruction and rehabilitation. Some of the challenges facing external actors are mentioned below.

REESTABLISHING SECURITY. The end of civil war does not lead automatically to the end of insecurity. Fear of personal violence or theft may actually increase after the war, and without measures to increase the opportunity cost of warfare for individual combatants, the end of the war may signal increased opportunities for criminal activity. Well-designed demobilization programs, like that in Uganda, that assure combatants of their reintegration into civil society after the war, and so give them a legitimate exit strategy, are therefore a priority. Also essential will be efforts to strengthen local police forces and tighten enforcement of criminal laws and other measures, to reduce the risks of banditry and criminal enterprise. The long-term response, however, must be to address the socioeconomic root causes of the conflict.

ECONOMIC RECOVERY. Although the elements of a postconflict stabilization and recovery program may differ little from programs applied elsewhere, there are grounds for caution and for examining the components of the standard policy package in light of the conditions and distortions peculiar to the postconflict environment. Civil conflict erodes the social capital that inspires trust and facilitates investment. Consequently, fear may be a bigger obstacle to the revival of investment than damaged infrastructure. Policies to spur the private sector's recovery should therefore avoid overly aggressive increases in taxation and should stress the early sequencing of investment-sensitive reforms, including the preservation of low inflation, the sale or restitution of expropriated housing stock, and restraint in revenue collection. Avoiding aggressive revenue collection does not, however, mean offering overly generous tax incentives for private foreign investment. As Cambodia's experience now shows, these may be counterproductive, depriving the government of substantial revenue for many years and taking government further from the all-important task of reviving domestic investment.

PROMOTING FUNDAMENTAL SOCIOPOLITICAL RECONCILIATION. Economic policy and sectoral projects need to be tailored to take account of the special problems of traumatized populations and societies with heavily damaged social capital. The sequencing of standard economic policy reform and of governance measures also needs to be tailored to avoid threatening the sustainability of peace agreements and to take account of the typically severe distortions in economic conditions.

BUILDING CAPABILITY. The problem at the heart of attempts to sustain recovery and reconstruction in postconflict situations is lack of capability. Yet even where effective macroeconomic and political reforms have been undertaken, improvements in bureaucratic capability have often lagged well behind (as in Uganda, for example). Various options have been tried to jump-start the capacity-building process, including drawing on a diaspora of professionals to occupy positions within the new government (as in Cambodia, Lebanon, and Haiti) and providing foreign experts to work as advisers to their local counterparts. As the strategy for enhancing state capability implies, conventional technical assistance is rarely effective in settings where even minimal rules and restraints on arbitrary action are lacking. The absence of such rules is a defining feature of a failed state. Thus, it is vital that imported technical assistance come with efforts to implement and enforce the most basic rules of accountability and restraint within government and so begin to rebuild its lost credibility.

The collapse of a state is an extreme phenomenon, and each case is unique. Hence there are no simple generalizations about their causes or effects. Each produces its own challenges for the afflicted nation and for the international system. The consequences are, however, almost uniformly borne by ordinary people, illustrating once again the critical importance of an effective, responsive state to the long-term health and wealth of society.

Some regional steps—and missteps

Inevitably, the elements of any strategy for improving the state's effectiveness will differ hugely from country to country, according to the institutional and political setting. The key features and challenges facing states in various regions are summarized below. These are necessarily broad generalizations: each region includes several countries whose experiences are entirely different.

It is in *Sub-Saharan Africa* that the deterioration in the state's effectiveness has been most severe—the result of eroding civil service wages, heavy dependence on aid, and patronage politics. There are a few exceptions, such as Botswana. But a recent report commissioned by a group of African finance ministers, echoing themes raised in the preceding chapters of this Report, concluded that the majority of countries in Sub-Saharan Africa now have lower capability (including state capability) than they did at independence. As a consequence, many are trapped in a vicious circle of declining state capability and, thus, declining credibility in the eyes of their citizens.

There is a crisis of statehood in much of Africa—a crisis of capability and of legitimacy.

The first part of the two-part strategy recommended by this Report is perhaps the more urgently needed in Sub-Saharan Africa. A sharp refocus of the state's priorities is badly needed. In a few cases this refocus has taken place, although only after protracted crisis. Typically, the reach and effectiveness of the state have withered away, and perforce the state has in effect withdrawn. Unfortunately, since the refocus has not been carefully managed, the state has also weakened or withdrawn from areas that are its legitimate function. An institutional vacuum of significant proportions has emerged in many parts of Sub-Saharan Africa, leading to increased crime and an absence of security, affecting investment and growth.

Achieving a turnaround in the effectiveness of the state will not be easy, since the roots of state failure are many and complex. Chief among them has been a continuing struggle between traditional forms of governance and social organization (often based on tribes, lineages, and language and kinship groups) and modern forms of government. High military expenditure and dysfunctional behavior of military personnel (in the absence of other checks and balances) have been other important impediments. These have often reduced the transparency and accountability of public institutions to the extent that

governments have felt a decreasing need to explain and justify their actions to the domestic population.

The urgent priority in Africa is to rebuild state capability through an overhaul of public institutions and credible checks on the abuse of state power.

The clear need in most African countries is for a thorough reform of the machinery of the state, so that it can deliver quality public services and facilitate private activity rather than impede both. As this Report has emphasized, the second part of the strategy—rebuilding capability—must also start on an urgent footing. In this it is essential to start in some areas of priority. Strengthening the rule of law must be a vital first step. Another is to strengthen the capability for legislative oversight of the executive. But strengthening the executive—particularly the central government's capacity to formulate macroeconomic and strategic policy, and its incentives to deliver core public goods efficiently—is also a key priority. Disappointingly, with some promising exceptions (Botswana and more recently Uganda), improving the effectiveness of the state in Africa has generally been limited to tinkering around the edges and to promulgating reforms on paper. But there are signs that these issues are now being taken seriously. Recent reform programs pay much greater attention to institutional strengthening, and macroeconomic management is improving across a broad swath of African economies.

An important constraint on systemic institutional reform of the state in Africa is its cost, but resources can be found if the priorities are clear. Most countries will need to redirect existing, misallocated resources to raise real public wages (more than proportionately to any savings from further retrenchment), increase spending on social services, and undertake vast investments in personnel management, retraining, and accountability. This major rebuilding of state capability cannot happen without international assistance. But an exceptional degree of cooperation between governments and external agencies has culminated in a pattern of external dependency. The types of assistance and the incentives it generates also need to be reexamined, to ensure that assistance supports coherent and well-contested policies and strengthens the overall framework of incentives within and outside the state. Prioritizing and even strategic enclaving are necessary, to start the reform process, but must be part of a well-thought-out plan to broaden and deepen the reforms.

Improving the delivery of public and collective services will require closer partnerships with the private sector and civil society. Such partnerships should be encouraged, especially when the links between the state and civil society are underdeveloped.

A hopeful recent development is a growing array of self-help community initiatives, particularly in elementary education, basic health care, and local services such as waste disposal. These initiatives have often sprung from the state's own failure to provide such services effectively. Although they can seldom fully substitute for a well-functioning government administration, they offer a partial escape from the current morass. That said, it is difficult to imagine how reform of the role of the state and improvement in its capability can be realized in most African countries without the stronger incentives that this Report also recommends: more competitive pressure, greater voice and transparency, and rules and restraints including the rule of law.

The situation in Asia is different. In the newly industrializing countries of *East Asia,* the state is generally viewed as effective, engaged in a productive partnership with the private sector. With few exceptions, it has matched its role to its capability very well and thereby enhanced its effectiveness. Whereas ineffective authoritarian states have been directly responsible for economic decline in Africa, many East Asian countries have experienced remarkable growth (with some improvement in equity) under authoritarian regimes. As the previous chapter implied, the link between authoritarianism and economic decline, so evident in Africa, has been inoperative in Asian countries, largely because of their powerful commitment to rapid economic development, strong administrative capability, and institutionalized links with stakeholders such as private firms, as well as their ability to deliver on the economic and social fundamentals: sound economic management, basic education and health care, and infrastructure.

In East Asia the state's ability to change in response to important new challenges will be critical to the region's continued economic success. At the same time, steps to modernize public administration and achieve effective decentralization will be critical.

Yet throughout East Asia there are major new challenges to the role and functioning of the state. China and Vietnam, the region's transition economies, are struggling with the need to redefine the state's role in the enterprise and financial sectors. Both countries have combined rapid growth with the maintenance of large public enterprise sectors, but these sectors appear increasingly fragile financially. There is also a continuing debate in these economies about the potential role for an activist industrial policy in guiding investment. However, the conditions facing these two economies appear to be very different from those prevailing in Japan and the Republic of Korea in their early stages of industrialization (Chapter 4).

Throughout the region substantial economic rents (flowing from legal monopolies or restrictions, or from influence and corruption) continue to coexist with great private sector dynamism and international engagement. Tolerance of these rents is probably declining—witness the recent anticorruption offensives in China, Korea, and Vietnam. And heightened international competition may mean that inefficient, protected sectors can no longer be carried on the shoulders of dynamic and efficient ones, either in Japan and Korea or in the newly emerging economies.

This suggests that deeper, modernizing reforms will be needed in much of East Asia to develop robust regulatory structures to support competition and, in areas of continued government action, mechanisms to ensure greater transparency and accountability. Particularly vital for these countries' long-term development prospects will be more efficient financing and delivery of infrastructure in partnership with the private sector. Although many high-profile projects are under way, East Asia needs to move faster in developing regulatory frameworks for creating competition, managing the contracting process, and regulating monopolies.

At the same time, many East Asian societies are likely to face new areas where enhanced state action is called for. These are likely to include formal mechanisms such as social and health insurance schemes, to help manage the new risks facing individuals and households in increasingly urbanized and aging societies, and more vigorous efforts to protect the environment. Public action will also be needed to reach those left behind by rapid development, for example the rural populations in some inland provinces of China, the relatively poorer populations of eastern Indonesia, and, in some countries, ethnic minorities. New mechanisms to respond to rising inequality may also be needed, for example in China, Malaysia, and Thailand.

Finally, many countries in the region face a need to build more-effective core government institutions (following the agenda laid out in Chapter 5) and address the problem of corruption (Chapter 6). Institution building is a high priority for those countries where the civil service is relatively weak (Indonesia, for example) and where traditional state capabilities have eroded somewhat (such as the Philippines and Thailand). Efforts to build bureaucratic capability at lower levels of government are also urgently needed in countries such as China, Indonesia, the Philippines, and Vietnam, where the decentralization of some government functions puts power in the hands of lower-quality staff and raises risks of local government capture (see Chapter 7).

The situation is different in South Asia, where in many countries state inefficiency and corruption have coexisted with a relatively competent and efficient civil service, albeit one whose quality has suffered a noticeable decline.

South Asia, too, suffers from a mismatch between the state's role and its capability. Here it is not that the state's capability was historically weak, as in Africa. In fact it was not, but the state pursued an overly activist agenda that went well beyond its capability. As a result, development suffered, and over time the state's capability declined as well. The agenda now is to refocus the state's role to match its current capability, stem its further decline, and improve that capability.

The main issue in South Asia is overregulation and an overextended state—both cause and effect of bloated public employment, and the surest route to corruption. As stressed in Chapter 4, regulatory simplification and public enterprise reform, and the resulting contraction of the role of the state, will be complex and politically difficult. But such measures stand to boost economic efficiency, increase competitive pressure, reduce corruption, and produce substantial fiscal savings. Another imperative is to build stronger partnerships with, and listen more effectively to, business and civil society, to improve feedback and supplement the state's capability.

Pervasive political interference is a second major barrier to state effectiveness in many countries of the region. As discussed in Chapter 5, India's bureaucratic capability suffers not merely from legendary amounts of administrative red tape, but from the fact that the autonomy of its highly qualified civil servants is severely circumscribed in practice (despite statutory protection from interference in their individual actions) by frequent, often politically motivated transfers of personnel and other arrangements.

In Pakistan the machinery of the state has come increasingly under pressure from powerful business and feudal interest groups. More recently the resulting erosion of state authority and effectiveness has spurred an attempt to reform the very machinery of the state. Here, too, a competent civil service, allied with an activist judiciary, offers grounds for optimism that reform is not only possible, but will occur. In Bangladesh, recent political developments have also created conditions for beginning to address the decline of the state's authority and effectiveness, using the pillars of strong top-level political commitment, popular participation, and decentralization, buttressed by competent and professional elements of the civil service. Similar possibilities for improving government and streamlining public administration are emerging elsewhere in the region.

As noted earlier, substantial differences exist among countries in all regions, and regional generalizations are useful only as a first approximation. This is particularly true of the countries of *Central and Eastern Europe* (CEE) and the *Commonwealth of Independent States* (CIS), now undergoing the transition from central planning. There are also broad differences between the CEE countries as a group and the CIS countries. Although both face a common challenge of economic and political transformation—and hence of a fundamental refocusing of state activities—the CIS countries (except Russia) face the gigantic, and historically unique, double challenge of economic transformation *and* state building: they have had no central government within living memory, nor have they constituted for centuries (most never) independent political entities within their present boundaries.

The challenge of bringing more effective government to these transition economies is in some ways easier and in other ways more difficult than—but certainly quite different from—that faced in most developing economies. The first part of the two-part strategy, that of matching role to capability, is critical, but especially difficult in a situation where both role and capability are changing rapidly. The extent of deterioration in capability varies enormously, with islands of excellence in a sea of declining effectiveness and huge problems of basic governance. In this context matching role to capability is not a simple matter of focusing on the fundamentals. It is not that the fundamentals are not critical—without them progress toward a market-based economic system will be rocky. But the challenge in these countries is providing these fundamentals while at the same time maintaining existing centers of excellence that have been developed over time, and providing the population with the mechanisms of social protection to which they are accustomed. Given the inherent capabilities of a highly educated, socially conscious population, the task of rebuilding state capability—the second part of the strategy—is here more than elsewhere one of changing incentives and the culture of bureaucracy. How quickly this reorientation is managed will determine how quickly the transition is completed.

The job of reorienting the state toward the task of "steering, not rowing" is far from complete in Central and Eastern Europe. But most countries have made progress in refocusing the state's role and are on the way to improving capability and accountability.

It is no surprise, then, that improvements in the effectiveness of the state have been more noticeable in CEE, especially in countries such as the Czech Republic, Hungary, and Poland. Much of this has come from a very swift refocusing of the state's role—part one of the two-part strategy. However, progress in southeastern Europe has generally been much less significant, both in terms of policy reform and on the public administration front.

In particular, several CEE countries have made advances toward setting up competitive systems for service delivery and toward relying much more on the private sector (including, in part, for education and health care). Autonomous professional associations are also beginning to take root in these countries, with healthy potential implications for institutional capability outside the government (capability that is needed to help implement the reforms) and for the rebuilding of social capital. And substantial regulatory reform and simplification have occurred, aided by support from the European Union. Again, in southeastern Europe progress in all these areas tends to have been much slower. The difficulty is not so much a lack of consensus on the desirability of these reforms, but a severe lack of capability at the core of government to formulate and guide them—compounded, in some countries, by a fluid political situation.

Low state capability in the former Soviet republics is a serious and mounting obstacle to further progress in most areas of economic and social policy.

In the CIS the process of reorienting the state is still at an early stage, and a host of severe problems have emerged. Unlike in CEE, in the CIS there is often no clear definition of the state's new role. And even where it is clear in principle, in practice weak central capacity has made it extremely difficult to translate those principles into reality. In most cases the basic institutional structures for an effective state are weak. The first and fundamental problem is the weak accountability of the executive to the legislature in most CIS countries. In the very early 1990s, parliaments in most of the new countries were the only repository of whatever political legitimacy existed after the collapse of the Soviet Union. There were even instances of excessive interference by the legislature in routine executive functions (which remains a problem in Ukraine). But the situation in most countries today is one of a dominant executive and weak legislative oversight.

Beyond the issue of increasing executive accountability, three further sets of problems face most CIS countries. Between them these problems not only produce enormous economic costs, but also give rise to pervasive corruption. This last is rightly decried almost everywhere in the region, and confirmed in the results of the survey of private business commissioned for this Report. First, weak and slow judicial systems severely handicap both reform and economic activity. As is well known, weak enforcement of the law and weak judicial procedures have permitted the unprecedented rise of organized crime. Second, fuzzy boundaries between private and public property rights have generated massive rent seeking, with officials often exploiting public assets, including those of state enterprises, for private profit. Third, opaque and still hugely complex regulatory frameworks have fueled corruption across the spectrum of interactions between the public and the private sectors.

Outside assistance and encouragement—to tighten the accountability of executives to legislatures, to strengthen legislative oversight capacity, to streamline and reinforce judicial systems, to clarify property rights and provide for accountable management and oversight of public assets, to radically simplify the regulatory framework and move rapidly toward rules and away from discretion, and, not least, to bring criminal activities under control and sever their links to the public sector—are clearly essential to improve the functioning of the state and promote economic recovery throughout the region.

Genuine administrative reform to improve bureaucratic capability has been conspicuous by its absence in most CIS countries. Staffing of central government tends to be low, and although government workers are often highly educated and technically knowledgeable, they lack the skills needed for administration in a noncommand economy. They are, moreover, deprived of basic supplies and resources and very badly paid. Unsurprisingly, during the first stage of the economic transformation, attention and financial resources were devoted to the urgent tasks of privatization, to reforming the price and foreign exchange system, and to establishing some measure of fiscal and monetary control. But it is equally unsurprising that the next stage of the transformation, that dealing with reforms that require decisive and clear administrative action, is now severely hampered by the absence of the mechanisms and of the government personnel and resources necessary to implement those reforms.

The role of the state in *Latin America and the Caribbean* has been undergoing profound change over the past decade, fueled by fiscal crisis and rising expectations born of the return of democracy and the emergence of civil society. Competitive pressures from globalization have made it increasingly urgent for government to privatize or to contract out activities in which it lacks comparative advantage, and to improve its efficiency and effectiveness in producing public goods.

But while the first-stage reforms have been implemented successfully in a number of countries in the region, progress has lagged in the second-generation reforms, where institutional change is vital. For example, civil service reform and reforms in the social services are being held back by political constraints and vested interests. Such reforms (recently begun in Argentina and a few other countries) cannot be undertaken in isolation, but must be part of a broader decentralization of political administration and financial management, already under way in many countries.

Governments in Latin America are rethinking their approach to the alleviation of poverty, particularly important in a region with highly skewed income distributions.

A number of Latin American countries, having launched major economic and structural reforms, have now created social investment funds for the poorer segments of society. At a broader level, governments in the region have been faced with the bankruptcy of highly inequitable, state-run, pay-as-you-go pension systems. Chile privatized its system in 1981, reducing the role of government to that of regulator; other countries (Argentina and Colombia, for example) have pursued dual systems. A third group of countries are just now starting to contemplate how pension reform should proceed. But more aggressive action will be needed on the social fundamentals, to complement reform on the economic fundamentals, if Latin America is to compete with East Asia.

The priority in Latin America is to reinvigorate the institutional capability of the state, and here some major initiatives are under way. Both unitary and federal states have turned to decentralization, particularly to improve service delivery. Authority and responsibility for both revenue and spending have been transferred, although often these have been mismatched at first. Strengthening institutional capability at the provincial and the local level is a major challenge in countries with federal systems, such as Argentina and Brazil, which have a legacy of overly indebted local governments and weak state or provincial banks. Nevertheless, examples abound of successful local government reforms (for example, through public-private partnerships) emerging in time of crisis, where dynamic local leaders have been able to foster reforms on a manageable scale.

Decentralization of power and of spending, coupled with democratization, has dramatically transformed the local political landscape in Latin America, in what some have called a "quiet revolution." A new model of governing is emerging in the region.

The first stages of local reform in Latin America, covering roughly the period 1983–90, created an institutional environment that nurtured a fresh generation of office seekers, more professional and more reformist than their predecessors. Leaders in scores of cities were drawn by the ineluctable logic of popular participation as a natural means of sounding out the wishes of voters. This same logic led to a strengthening of the fiscal link between government and the governed, making more obvious the connection between the public works and service improvements that neighborhood residents say they want, and the payment burdens that authorities say residents must bear to achieve cost recovery. For instance, many local governments tie improvements to user fees or betterment levies, or rely on referendums. Traditional models of government take this exchange—payment for goods and

services rendered—as axiomatic. But four decades of centralized systems in Latin America and the Caribbean have broken this unspoken bargain of trust, and poor cost recovery and low tax revenues are just two of the consequences. The outstanding feature of the new style of governing, and one bright prospect for the future, is the restoration of this critical fiscal link at the local level.

Governments are also moving to create more open administrations, reflecting the emergence of a more forceful civil society (media, private think tanks, nongovernmental organizations) demanding greater access to decisionmaking, particularly in the Commonwealth Caribbean through citizens' charters (in Jamaica, for example). Efforts are under way in countries such as Colombia to develop performance indicators (of economy, efficiency, effectiveness, service quality, and financial performance) that will provide accountability for public sector managers and politicians.

Court systems in most Latin American countries have suffered from major inefficiencies, widespread corruption, and political interference. For the new legislative and institutional structures to work effectively, the judicial system must work well and fairly. Needed reforms, already under way in a number of countries (including Bolivia, Ecuador, Trinidad and Tobago, and Venezuela) include legal education, better court administration and case flow management, and procedural reform, including the development of alternative dispute resolution systems outside the courts. Efforts are also needed to strengthen the criminal justice system, to address the growing problem of crime and violence, which is partly related to drug trafficking in the region.

In the Middle East and North Africa, unemployment is by far the single greatest economic and social problem and makes government downsizing especially difficult.

Countries in the *Middle East and North Africa* assigned vast economic responsibilities to the state in the 1960s and 1970s. More recently, governments have trimmed back their roles to some extent, but much remains to be done, within government and in the state enterprise sector. There has also been no proportionate slimming of the large civil services built up in those earlier years. With a few exceptions (Tunisia is one), regulation is excessive, as is state involvement in economic activity, and delivery of public services is inefficient.

Skilled civil servants are often in short supply, and the delivery of public services is often inadequate. Overregulation has produced a bloated work force, pervasive interference in private economic activity, and widespread corruption. Little effort has been devoted to streamlining agencies and improving state efficiency. And the system's capacity to change has slowly atrophied over time. Regional conflict has also distracted attention from state reform, but the end of the Cold War, the conclusion of the Gulf War, and the change in attitudes brought about by the peace process have led governments in the region to begin to give the issue more attention.

The first steps in most countries in this region must be to prevent any further growth in central government employment, and to liberalize the economy. These steps have begun in a few cases. Because the political and social difficulties of reform are considerable, although not insurmountable, one approach might be to decentralize selected services to improve responsiveness and accountability, and focus on selective state enterprise reforms while preparing the ground for more comprehensive state reform.

In the countries of the *Organization for Economic Cooperation and Development (OECD),* where the overall capability of the state is high, efforts are ongoing to improve its effectiveness. Driven in part by globalization and technology, changes are under way that will open greater opportunities in many OECD countries for government to enter into partnerships with the private sector and civil society, especially in the area of social insurance and assistance.

Some of the most comprehensive reforms of the state worldwide have occurred in OECD countries, driven primarily by the rising cost of government and citizens' demands for more value for money. It is too soon to render a definitive judgment on most of these efforts. But the depth of dissatisfaction with the effectiveness of the state in these countries suggests that the search for more effective government, for better public services at lower overall cost to society, will and must continue.

Even small steps can make a big difference to the state's effectiveness, leading to better standards of living and opening opportunities for more reforms. The challenge is to take those small steps that can open the way to virtuous cycles.

The two-part strategy laid out in this Report is only a broad guide for the many different agendas of reform being pursued throughout the world. Likewise, international assistance for state reform must go beyond a one-size-fits-all approach, or one based on donors' preferences rather than recipients' needs. It must be based on a clearer diagnosis of the case at hand and of how reforms would fit into broader political and social changes going on in each country.

An important component of the reforms discussed in this Report is institutional, and so will take time. Quick-fix capacity-building solutions have been attempted over the past twenty years, with limited impact. These efforts have focused largely on training, on building skills, and on importing technical systems. They have not focused on incentives, which come from competitive pressures, partnership, and transparency, and from rule-based systems. Reforms pushed forward too rapidly can produce new risks as well: they may be blocked by those likely to lose from change, and the danger is always present that the reforms will lead to fragmentation and the creation of an institutional vacuum.

International cooperation and decentralization are a potentially positive trend, since they create the opportunity to improve international collective action and the delivery of local public goods. The two trends, in fact, reinforce each other. But the gains will be realized only if the pitfalls are avoided. International cooperation will yield gains only if countries believe that they will benefit from international integration. This can happen only if the risks and uncertainties of globalization—for households, workers, the poor, and the vulnerable—are skillfully handled. Decentralization will also need careful management to ensure that the costs, such as loss of macroeconomic control and rising regional inequalities, do not overwhelm the benefits.

In the past, it seemed clear that reform delayed was growth merely deferred, that the cost of missing an opportunity to reform would be, at worst, continued stagnation. But a deeper understanding of the way in which declines in state effectiveness and credibility—and resistance to reform—can magnify over time, coupled with examples of collapsed states at the end of these downward spirals, suggests the costs are far greater. If governments cannot grasp the nettle of improving their effectiveness and reinvigorating public institutions, the prospects for significant improvement in economic and social welfare, in some countries, may be bleak indeed.

The approach of the twenty-first century brings enormous promise of change and reason for hope. In a world of dizzying changes in markets, civil societies, and global forces, the state is under pressure to become more effective. But it is not yet changing rapidly enough to keep pace. There is no unique model for change, and reforms will often come slowly, because they involve fundamental alterations in the roles of institutions and in interactions between citizens and government. This Report has shown that reform of state institutions is a long, difficult, and politically sensitive task. But if we now have a better sense of the dimensions of the challenge, we are also now much more aware of the costs of leaving things as they are.

TECHNICAL
NOTE

Overview

Data in *Figure 1* are at current national prices. Data for the OECD countries come from Tanzi and Schuknecht 1995, with updates from OECD, various years. The countries included are Austria, Belgium, France, Germany, Italy, Japan, the Netherlands, Norway, Spain, Sweden, Switzerland, the United Kingdom, and the United States. Data for the developing countries come from IMF, various years (b). Developing countries include low- and middle-income countries as defined by the World Bank; the countries included vary across the period.

The regional indexes in the left panel in *Box 2* are derived from averages of credibility indexes for the countries in the region. On construction of the credibility index see "The private sector survey" below and the Brunetti, Kisunko, and Weder background papers.

The other two panels in Box 2 are based on regressions reported in Table TN1. The GDP growth regression follows the instrumental variable (IV) methodology, using the Freedom House Index of Political Rights (Freedom House, various issues) as an instrument for the level of credibility. The regression for the share of investment in GDP reports ordinary least-squares (OLS) results. The credibility index is taken from the Brunetti, Kisunko, and Weder background paper (a). The index is normalized such that the level for the high-income OECD countries equals one. The source for the remaining variables is the Commander, Davoodi, and Lee background paper.

The methodology used to generate the two right-hand panels in Box 2 is routinely used in multiple regression analysis and is used throughout the Report unless stated otherwise. The height of the vertical bar associated with the medium category is the value of the dependent variable obtained by evaluating the estimated regression at the sample mean of all the right-hand-side terms (for example, the constant term, credibility, initial income, initial education, and policy distortion in Table TN1). The heights of the other two bars are the values of the dependent variable obtained by evaluating the estimated regression at the sample mean of all the right-hand-side variables except the variable of interest (credibility in Table TN1), which is evaluated at one standard deviation above the sample mean for the high category and one standard deviation below the sample mean for the low category.

In figures where a bar diagram is based on a simple correlation (for example, the top left panel of Figure 3 in the Overview), the following methodology is used unless otherwise stated. Countries in the sample are ranked according to their values for the variable on the horizontal axis. The low, medium, and high categories are then defined as follows. The medium category includes countries within one standard deviation of the sample mean, and the height of the bar is the average for those countries. The remaining countries, in the upper and lower tails of the distribution, then make up the high and low categories, respectively, and again the bar height is the average for the countries in the category.

The top left panel in *Figure 3* is based on a simple correlation between a policy distortion index (averages for 1984–93) and a corruption index (1996 data). The correlation coefficient is 0.53 with a *t*-statistic of 3.79. The policy distortion index is taken from the Commander, Davoodi, and Lee background paper. Higher values of the index mean more distorted policies. The corruption index is taken from the private sector survey conducted for this Report (see below). See the technical note for Figure 5 for the construction of the policy distortion index.

The top right panel in Figure 3 is based on a regression, reported in Table TN2, of an index of corruption on an index of predictability of the judiciary (higher values mean greater predictability), controlling for initial GDP per capita and education (data from the World Bank data

Table TN1 Regressions of growth and investment on level of credibility and other variables

Independent variable	Regression coefficient	
	Growth in GDP per capita (IV method)	Investment-GDP ratio (OLS method)
Constant	−9.550**	−36.841***
	(4.14)	(9.03)
Level of credibility	13.44**	17.54**
(0 worst, 1 best)	(6.34)	(7.53)
Log of initial GDP	−0.048	5.025**
per capita	(0.77)	(1.43)
Log of initial	−0.255	−1.109
mean years	(0.85)	(1.85)
of schooling		
Policy distortion	−0.256	0.628
	(0.64)	(1.51)
Adjusted R^2	0.264	0.674
No. of observations	33	33

***Significant at the 1 percent level.
**Significant at the 5 percent level.
Note: Numbers in parentheses are standard errors.

Table TN2 Regression of level of corruption on predictability of the judiciary and crime and theft

Independent variable	Regression coefficient
Constant	−7.63***
	(0.703)
Predictability of judiciary	−0.59***
	(0.10)
Log of initial GDP per capita in 1990	−0.51***
	(0.162)
Log of 1990 secondary school enrollment	0.39
	(0.185)**
Adjusted R^2	0.603
No. of observations	59

*** Significant at the 1 percent level.
Note: Numbers in parentheses are standard errors. Estimation is by the OLS method.

base). Data on level of corruption and predictability of the judiciary were taken from the private sector survey (see below). The statistical methodology for generating the bars is described in the technical note to Box 2.

The bottom left panel in Figure 3 is derived from a regression reported by Evans and Rauch 1996. The dependent variable is corruption, data for which are taken from various issues of the *International Country Risk Guide,* a publication of Political Risk Services, as compiled by the IRIS Center, University of Maryland (see also Keefer and Knack 1995), and rescaled so that higher values indicate more corruption. The regression includes a constant term and, as independent variables, real GDP per capita and a merit-based recruitment index. Higher values of this index indicate that a greater proportion of higher-level officials in the core economic agencies entered the civil service through a formal examination system, and that a higher proportion of those who did not enter through examinations have university or postgraduate degrees. The statistical methodology for generating the bars is described in the technical note to Box 2.

The bottom right panel in Figure 3 shows the relation between, on the one hand, civil service wages relative to manufacturing wages and, on the other, the index of corruption from the *International Country Risk Guide.* The overall correlation coefficient was 0.65 with a *t*-statistic of 3.61. Data are taken from the Van Rijckeghem and Weder background paper.

The correlation coefficient for the data in *Figure 4* is −0.35, with a *t*-statistic of −3.65.

Figure 5 is from the Commander, Davoodi, and Lee background paper and is based on the IV regression, with the interaction term, reported in TN3. The data are from both World Bank sources and the Summers-Heston world tables (National Bureau of Economic Research 1997). The state variables are the logarithm of initial GDP per capita at 1985 international prices, educational attainment (as measured by the logarithm of mean years of schooling among the working-age population), the population growth rate, and the logarithm of the share of investment in GDP at 1985 international prices. The control variables include the logarithm of the share of government consumption in GDP (government size) at 1985 international prices, a policy distortion index, a measure of the quality of bureaucracy or institutional capability, the average percentage change in the terms of trade, and decade and regional dummies. The regression with the interaction term estimates the combined effect of government size and bureaucracy on growth of GDP per capita.

The institutional capability variable is a composite index of measures of the quality of government and draws on Knack and Keefer 1995 and Mauro 1995, among others. This evaluation is put together from a set of responses by foreign investors that focus on the extent of red tape involved in any transaction, the regulatory environment, and the degree of autonomy from political pressure. Although responses by foreign investors are likely to be biased, these series are the only currently available large-scale, cross-country evaluations of the way in which government bureaucracies function. All responses have been rescaled to range from zero to one, with higher scores

Table TN3 Ordinary least-squares and instrumental variable regressions with growth of GDP per capita as the dependent variable

Independent variable	OLS method		IV method	
	Without interaction term	With interaction term	Without interaction term	With interaction term
Constant	0.171***	0.161***	0.167***	0.136***
	(0.022)	(0.024)	(0.027)	(0.038)
Dummy variable for 1974–83	–0.015***	–0.015***	–0.015***	–0.014***
	(0.003)	(0.003)	(0.004)	(0.004)
Dummy variable for 1984–93	–0.017***	–0.016***	–0.017***	–0.016***
	(0.004)	(0.004)	(0.004)	(0.004)
Initial GDP per capita	–0.019***	–0.019***	–0.021***	–0.021***
	(0.003)	(0.003)	(0.003)	(0.003)
Initial schooling	0.003	0.003	0.003	0.003
	(0.003)	(0.003)	(0.003)	(0.003)
Population growth	–0.184	–0.209	–0.260	–0.304
	(0.192)	(0.192)	(0.204)	(0.203)
Investment-GDP ratio	0.009***	0.009***	0.008**	0.007**
	(0.003)	(0.003)	(0.003)	(0.003)
Government size	–0.016***	–0.022***	–0.023***	–0.038***
	(0.004)	(0.008)	(0.008)	(0.015)
Institutional capability	0.017*	0.041	0.027***	0.085*
(0 worst, 1 best)	(0.009)	(0.027)	(0.010)	(0.044)
Government size × Institutional capability		0.014		0.033
		(0.014)		(0.024)
Policy distortion	–0.006***	–0.006***	–0.005***	–0.005***
	(0.002)	(0.002)	(0.002)	(0.002)
Terms-of-trade changes	0.034	0.034	0.042	0.044
	(0.040)	(0.040)	(0.042)	(0.042)
Latin America dummy variable	–0.017***	–0.017***	–0.015***	–0.015***
	(0.004)	(0.004)	(0.004)	(0.004)
Sub-Saharan Africa dummy variable	–0.030***	–0.030***	–0.028***	–0.028***
	(0.006)	(0.006)	(0.006)	(0.006)
Socialist dummy variable	–0.008	–0.008	–0.013**	–0.013**
	(0.006)	(0.006)	(0.005)	(0.005)
No. of observations	271	271	258	258
R^2	0.5196	0.5213	a	a

*** Significant at the 1 percent level.
 ** Significant at the 5 percent level.
  * Significant at the 10 percent level.
Note: Growth in GDP per capita is at 1985 international prices. Standard errors, corrected for heteroskedasticity, are in parentheses.
a. The R^2 is not an appropriate measure of goodness of fit with instrumental variable regressions.

indicating better bureaucracies. The policy distortion index is obtained by principal component analysis of three key indicators: the degree to which an economy is open (as measured by the share of trade in GDP), the degree to which a country's currency has been overvalued (as measured by the black market premium on the exchange rate), and the degree to which local prices have departed from international prices. Higher values of the index indicate greater policy distortion.

The data for Figure 5 were pooled so as to exploit the information in ten-year averages covering the periods 1964–73, 1974–83, and 1984–93. Both OLS and IV regressions are reported in Table TN3. The OLS and the

IV estimates are very close; the discussion concentrates on the latter. The instruments for the policy distortion index and the investment share of GDP are their own lagged values from five years previously. The instrument for the government size variable is the prediction from the IV regression for government size reported in the Commander, Davoodi, and Lee background paper. All other variables in the regression were treated as exogenous.

The state variables all have the predicted signs. The coefficient on the initial income term indicates a conditional convergence rate of 2.1 percent per year, which is close to the 2.6 percent reported by Barro and Sala-i-Martin 1995. Human capital formation, as given by years of schooling, affects growth positively, but the effect is not statistically significant. The investment rate, on the other hand, affects growth quite significantly. Population growth exerts a negative effect on GDP growth per capita, whereas the terms-of-trade variable has a positive effect. Both, however, are insignificant. There is an unambiguously negative, and statistically significant, effect from government consumption spending. A one-standard-deviation increase in government consumption is associated with a decline of 0.65 percentage point per year, which is close to the 0.7 percentage point reported by Barro and Sala-i-Martin 1995. There is also an unambiguously negative growth effect of policy distortion, which is significant at the 1 percent level. This indicates that policy distortions, as measured by the index used here, will have a predictably negative effect on growth. However, the size of that effect, as given by the coefficient on the policy term (and controlling for other variables) is not that large, at least relative to the government size variable (0.5 percentage point per year). By contrast, the institutional capability variable exerts a sizeable, positive, and significant effect on growth. Similarly, interacting the government consumption term with the institutional capability variable—an attempt to coax out the implications of high values of the two variables occurring simultaneously—yields a positive coefficient. When evaluating the consequences of government for growth, it is not simply size that is relevant. Bad policies, as represented by overvalued currencies and pervasive trade restrictions, hold down a country's growth, while the quality of government can exert a positive effect on performance. And it is clear that countries and regions that have fared least well tend to do worst on all three indicators. It is the combination of government size and the quality of policy and institutions that seems to matter.

Chapter 2

In *Figure 2.2* the IV estimates from the growth regression reported in the Commander, Davoodi, and Lee background paper are used to decompose the sources of growth in Sub-Saharan Africa and East Asia over the period 1964–93. These sources (explained and unexplained) are added sequentially to GDP per capita in Sub-Saharan Africa in 1964.

See the technical note to Box 2 for details regarding the top two panels in *Figure 2.4*. The bottom panel in Figure 2.4 is derived from the regression reported in Table TN4. The dependent variable is the country-average rates of return for a sample of 312 development projects financed by the World Bank. Project evaluation has been completed for the projects chosen. The data are from the World Bank's Operation and Evaluation (OED) data base. The independent variables are the change in the terms of trade over the period 1984–93, the policy distortion index for 1984–93, and an index of the level of gov-

ernment credibility. The terms-of-trade and policy distortion variables (see the note to Figure 5 above) are from the Commander, Davoodi, and Lee background paper. Data on level of credibility are from the private sector survey conducted for this Report (see "The private sector survey" below). The regression also included a constant term.

Chapter 3

The data in *Figure 3.8* are simple averages of pensions, unemployment benefits, and family assistance expenditure shares in GDP across twenty-two OECD countries. The series for the years 1965–79 is constructed from data in ILO, various years. The 1980–93 data are from OECD 1996.

Chapter 5

In *Figure 5.5* the dependent variable, an index of bureaucratic capability, is the bureaucratic quality rating variable reported in the *International Country Risk Guide,* various issues, rescaled so that higher values signify higher bureaucratic quality. The independent variables are initial GDP per capita and an index of meritocracy. The regression also includes a constant term.

The correlation coefficient for the data in *Figure 5.7* is –0.37 with a *t*-statistic of –10.14. The countries represented are Botswana, Burkina Faso, Cameroon, Chad, Egypt, Gabon, the Gambia, Ghana, Kenya, Madagascar, Malawi, Mauritania, Mauritius, Morocco, Nigeria, Rwanda, Senegal, Somalia, Sudan, and Togo. The sample covers variation over time and across countries in pay and employment. The wage variable is the central government real average wage relative to real GDP per capita, both measured in local currency; the employment variable is central government employment relative to the total

Table TN4 Regression of rates of return on World Bank-financed projects on level of credibility and other variables

Independent variable	Regression coefficient
Constant	–7.080
	(12.87)
Level of credibility	35.55**
(0 worst, 1 best)	(16.18)
Change in terms of trade, 1984–93	8.078
	(31.07)
Policy distortion, 1984–93	2.481
	(2.76)
Adjusted R^2	0.088
No. of observations	30

** Statistically significant at the 5 percent level.
Note: Numbers in parentheses are standard errors. Estimation is by the OLS method.

population. Employment and nominal wages are taken from Kraay and Van Rijckeghem 1995. The real average wage is constructed by deflating total nominal wages by the product of the consumer price index and employment. Population, the consumer price index, and real GDP per capita are taken from the World Bank data base.

Chapter 6

Figure 6.1 is based on cross-country regression results presented in Table TN5. For the countries included and definitions of the corruption variables see "The private sector survey" below. The dependent variable, the investment-GDP ratio, is a simple average of the share of gross investment in GDP over the period 1990–94. The predictability of corruption is a combination of predictability of outcomes and of the size of the additional payment to be made. The regression controls for initial level of education (measured as the logarithm of secondary school enrollment in 1990), initial income (logarithm of 1990 GDP per capita, measured in PPP terms), and existing policy distortion. The policy distortion variable is taken from the Commander, Davoodi, and Lee background paper (see the technical note to Figure 5). Data on investment, education, and initial income were obtained from World Bank sources. The statistical methodology for constructing the figure is the same as for Figure 5. The level and predictability of corruption are important factors in determining the share of investment and are significant at the 5 percent level.

Chapter 7

The index of democracy in *Figure 7.1* is based on Polity III data developed by Jaggers and Gurr 1996; regional groupings follow standard World Bank classifications. The index is derived from "institutionalized democracy" and "institutionalized autocracy" indicators for each year from 1800 to 1994, for all independent countries with populations greater than 500,000 in the early 1990s (177 countries in all). The index is calculated by subtracting the latter indicator from the former. Each indicator consists of five components: competitiveness of political participation, regulation of political participation, competitiveness of executive recruitment, openness of executive recruitment, and constraints on the chief executive. Each of the components is scored according to Jaggers and Gurr 1995 (p. 472). Both indicators are additive on an eleven-point scale from 0 to 10. The advantage of using the difference between the two indicators is that it shows a regime type along a political continuum of which democracy (+10) and autocracy (–10) represent the two ends. The index of democracy is highly correlated with the Freedom House index of political rights and civil rights (Freedom House, various issues), with correlation

Table TN5 Regression of share of gross investment in GDP on level and predictability of corruption and other variables

Independent variable	Regression coefficient
Constant	19.523
	(13.49)
Level of corruption	–5.814**
	(2.23)
Predictability of corruption	6.309**
	(2.62)
Log of secondary school enrollment in 1990	1.987
	(2.18)
Log of initial GDP per capita in 1990	–1.149
	(1.87)
Policy distortion	–1.959
	(1.46)
Adjusted R^2	0.24
No. of observations	39

** Significant at the 5 percent level.
Note: Numbers in parentheses are standard errors. Estimation is by the OLS method.

coefficients of 0.92 and 0.87, respectively, for the period 1973–94.

The figures in *Box 7.3* are based on simple correlations and do not control for other characteristics of the villages. However, the relationships still hold when these characteristics are controlled for. The data on social capital are from the Social Capital and Poverty Survey (SCPS), which was carried out in rural Tanzania in April and May 1995 as part of a larger World Bank participatory poverty assessment exercise. Expenditure data are from the same source, although that part of the survey covered households in only fifty-three of the eighty-seven clusters. The village-level social capital index is the average number of groups (for example, churches, women's groups, farmers' groups) to which respondents belonged, multiplied by an index of the average characteristics of those groups along three dimensions: kin heterogeneity, income heterogeneity, and group functioning. The data on school quality are from the Human Resource Development Survey (HRDS), carried out in Tanzania in 1993, which can be matched at the cluster level with the eighty-seven clusters from the SCPS. The school quality index is a cluster-level average derived from respondents' answers to questions on the relative importance of five attributes of schools, and their assessment of the quality of their local school along those same five dimensions. The HRDS was a nationally representative survey of 5,000 households in Tanzania. The survey was a joint effort undertaken by the Department of Economics of the University of Dar es Salaam, the Government of Tanzania, and the World

Bank, and was funded by the World Bank, the Government of Japan, and the British Overseas Development Agency. See Ferreira and Griffen 1995.

Chapter 9

Figure 9.2 is based on the generalized least squares (GLS) regression reported in Table TN6. The regression captures the effects of initial conditions and institutional, demographic, and economic variables on welfare spending.

The dependent variable is government spending on pensions, unemployment, and family assistance as a share of GDP (see the technical note to Figure 3.8). Initial conditions are captured by the initial Gini index for income distribution (Deininger and Squire 1996) and the time elapsed since the start of the social security program in each country (U.S. Department of Health and Human Services 1994). The institutional variables include an indicator of bureaucratic efficiency (institutional capability, from the Commander, Davoodi, and Lee background paper) and three indicators of the political environment. Higher scores imply greater efficiency. Although efficient bureaucracies are more likely to curb fraud and abuse, they are also more likely to grant benefits to all eligible beneficiaries. Thus, the sign of the coefficient on the bureaucratic efficiency variable depends on the relative importance of these two effects. A positive coefficient implies that more efficient governments provide greater welfare coverage. Political environment indicators consist of constitutional structure, type of government, and ideological orientation of the legislature (data for the last two are from Alesina and Perotti 1995). Constitutional structure is measured as the veto power given under the constitution to minorities and interest groups to block social legislation. Higher values of the index imply less obstructive capacity. A positive coefficient implies that countries with low veto power are more likely to indulge in welfare expansion. Government is classified into six types ranging from single-party to multiparty minority. Ideological orientation is classified as right-wing, right-center, balanced, left-center, or left-wing. A positive coefficient for government type implies that single-party governments are less prone toward expansionary policies; for ideological orientation it implies that left-wing governments are more prone to such policies. The percentage of population above 65 years of age (aging), number of children 14 years and under, unemployment rate, real GDP per capita, and inflation are taken from the World Bank's Social Indicators data base; OECD, various years; ILO 1986 and 1994; IMF, various years (b); and the World Bank Economic and Social Data Base. A positive coefficient is expected for the aging and unemployment rate variables. Finally, the more affluent the country, the bigger its welfare bill. This effect is picked up by a positive coefficient for real GDP per capita.

A new variable, "residual average welfare spending," is defined by subtracting, from the sample average of welfare spending, the constant term of the regression and the following term: (coefficient × sample average of independent variables not significant at the 10 percent level or less). The contribution of each variable to welfare spending is obtained by multiplying the estimated coefficient on each variable by the sample average of that variable and dividing the result by residual average welfare spending. The reported decomposition of welfare spending is robust to retaining only those variables in the regression that were significant at the 10 percent level or better.

The back-of-the-envelope calculation for the reduction in distortions resulting from tax reform in Pakistan is based on the so-called Harberger triangle. The deadweight loss (DWL) equation is given by:

$$DWL = (0.5) \times (t^2) \times (1 - t)^{-1} \times \varepsilon_T \times TI$$

where:

t = tax rate
ε_T = compensated demand elasticity
TI = taxable income.

The prereform tax rate used is 60 percent, and the postreform rate 30 percent. The compensated demand elasticity used is 0.5, the same as in Feldstein 1995. The relevant

Table TN6 Regression of welfare spending on constitutional structure and other variables

Independent variable	Regression coefficient	Standard error
Constant	−6.37	4.229
Constitutional structure	4.40	2.189**
Aging	0.583	0.082***
Unemployment rate	0.361	0.029***
Type of government	0.227	0.063***
Efficiency of bureaucracy	1.76	0.521***
GDP per capita × 10^4	0.94	0.495*
Ideology of government	−0.04	0.045
Inflation rate	0.01	0.017
No. of children × 10^8	2.37	4.09
Starting year of program	−0.006	0.039
Gini index	−0.004	0.109
R^2	0.63	
No. of observations	365	

*** Significant at the 1 percent level.
** Significant at the 5 percent level.
* Significant at the 10 percent level.
Note: Estimation is by the generalized least-squares method. The R^2 does not have all the properties of the OLS R^2.

ratio of taxable income to GDP is 7.22 percent. Based on these figures, the deadweight loss reduction (prereform minus postreform) associated with a revenue-neutral reform is estimated at 1.4 percent of GDP.

The private sector survey

Why this survey?

A vast number of anecdotal reports document the harm done to private sector development by uncertainty about laws, policies, and regulations. Examples are De Soto 1989 on the problems of informal firms in Peru, the description by Klitgaard 1990 of the uncertainties of doing business in Equatorial Guinea, and the analysis of institutional uncertainty in Nicaragua by Borner, Brunetti, and Weder 1995.

Adequate data for such an analysis have been hard to come by, however. The private sector survey conducted for this Report sought to fill that gap by creating an internationally comparable data set, for a broad cross section of countries, on different aspects of institutional uncertainty as perceived by private entrepreneurs.

The survey questionnaire

The questionnaire first asks about some general characteristics of the responding firm. Five different dimensions are considered: size (fewer than 50 employees, between 50 and 200 employees, or more than 200 employees); the firm's line of business (manufacturing, services, or agriculture); its headquarters location (capital city, other large city, or small city or countryside); the presence or absence of foreign capital participation; and whether the firm exports its products.

The main part of the questionnaire consists of twenty-five multiple-choice questions, which are grouped in five sections, each with its own focus. The questionnaire is divided into the following five sections:

- *Predictability of laws and policies.* These questions seek to assess the uncertainties created by the lawmaking process.
- *Political instability and security of property.* These questions ask about the uncertainties that arise from both regular and irregular transfers of government power.
- *Government-business interface.* The questionnaire lists fifteen areas where the firm is confronted with government action and asks it to evaluate the degree to which each of these areas creates obstacles to doing business.
- *Law enforcement and bureaucratic red tape.* These questions focus on the degree of corruption and whether it is a predictable transactions cost or a source of uncertainty. A problem in analyzing the responses is, of course, firms' reluctance to openly admit that they pay bribes. In addition, the questionnaire asks directly whether uncertainties in dealing with the state have stifled planned investment projects, and what percentage

of senior management's time is spent dealing with legal requirements.
- *Uncertainty created by lack of government efficiency in providing services.* These questions concentrate on whether and how efficiently the government delivers certain basic services such as mail, health care, telephone service, and roads.

Implementation and results

The questionnaire was originally written in English. However, worldwide distribution required its translation into several major languages: French, German, Portuguese, Russian, and Spanish. Wherever possible the questionnaires were administered in one of these languages or in English. At times, however, it was vital to provide translations for a single country. This was done in the cases of Albania, Bulgaria, the Czech Republic, Hungary, Italy, Poland, the Slovak Republic, and Turkey.

The survey was implemented between August 1996 and January 1997. At its conclusion sixty-nine countries had participated. These include the following: *industrial countries,* Austria, Canada, France, Germany, Ireland, Italy, Portugal, Spain, Switzerland, the United Kingdom, and the United States; *South and Southeast Asia,* Fiji, India, and Malaysia; *Middle East and North Africa,* Jordan, Morocco, and the West Bank and Gaza; *Central and Eastern Europe,* Albania, Bulgaria, the Czech Republic, Estonia, Hungary, Latvia, Lithuania, Macedonia, Poland, the Slovak Republic, and Turkey; *Latin America and the Caribbean,* Bolivia, Colombia, Costa Rica, Ecuador, Jamaica, Mexico, Paraguay, Peru, and Venezuela; *Sub-Saharan Africa,* Benin, Cameroon, Chad, the Congo, Côte d'Ivoire, Ghana, Guinea, Guinea-Bissau, Kenya, Madagascar, Malawi, Mali, Mauritius, Mozambique, Nigeria, Senegal, South Africa, Tanzania, Togo, Uganda, Zambia, and Zimbabwe; *Commonwealth of Independent States,* Armenia, Azerbaijan, Belarus, Georgia, Kazakstan, the Kyrgyz Republic, Moldova, Russia, Ukraine, and Uzbekistan.

The companies selected ran the gamut of firm size, geographic location within the country, and type of business, and companies both with and without foreign capital participation were well represented. Questionnaires were sent by mail where possible, but were delivered by hand in some countries where mail delivery was unreliable. Table TN7 provides details on response rates. Considering other experience with mailed surveys, the high overall response rate for the mailed survey in developing countries (30 percent) is remarkable. The high rate can be attributed to two factors: the fact that the survey raised questions of great concern for local businesspeople, and the fact that the survey was sponsored by an international organization with considerable name recognition in developing countries.

Table TN7 Responses to the private sector survey by region

Region or group	No. of countries surveyed	No. of firms surveyed	No. of questionnaires returned			
			Average	Median	Minimum	Maximum
Industrial countries	11	254	23	20	14	56
South and Southeast Asia	3	139	46	45	41	53
Middle East and North Africa	3	109	36	42	15	52
CEE	11	771	70	70	46	114
Latin America and Caribbean	9	474	53	47	17	87
Sub-Saharan Africa	22	1,288	59	48	13	124
CIS	10	650	65	62	31	91
All developing countries	58	3,431	59	51	13	124
All countries	69	3,685	53	50	13	124

Because of budget and time constraints, in some countries the responding firms did not represent a random sample of those to which questionnaires had been distributed. In other countries, political and economic conditions allowed only limited geographical coverage. On average, however, the survey achieved its goal of fifty responses per country.

Almost half of the firms were small (fewer than fifty employees); the rest were divided more or less equally between the two larger firm sizes. The survey intended that the companies in the sample represent a variety of geographic locations within each country. Firms located in the capital city constituted about half of those responding. It is encouraging, however, that management of almost one-quarter of the firms was located in a small city or in the countryside.

The aggregate results, however, hide considerable variation within countries. The share of firms located in the capital city varies between 100 percent and 0 percent. Such variation can be explained by the distribution of private businesses over country territory. In some former republics of the Soviet Union more than half of registered businesses are in the capital. In other countries the socioeconomic and political situation limited distribution of the questionnaire to the more remote parts. In some countries the unreliability of the mails made it infeasible to distribute questionnaires to remote places and have them returned in a timely fashion.

Services and manufacturing were represented about equally among respondents, but responses from agricultural enterprises were relatively few. This bias can be explained by geography: more than three-quarters of the surveyed firms were headquartered in the capital city or another large city, where few agricultural firms are located.

Firms were evenly distributed with respect to foreign capital participation and access to foreign markets. Two-thirds of the surveyed companies reported no foreign participation. The results therefore contrast with those of other earlier attempts at subjective measurement of countries' investment climate, which concentrated entirely on the perceptions of multinational firms.

Construction of the credibility indicator

The credibility indicator was designed as a broad measure of the reliability of the institutional framework as perceived by private entrepreneurs. It encompasses several different sources of uncertainty in the interaction of government and the private sector and summarizes these into one global indicator. The credibility index is constructed as the simple mean of the average answers to five subindicators, which is then normalized such that the index for the high-income OECD countries equals one:

■ *Predictability of rulemaking,* or the extent to which entrepreneurs have to cope with unexpected changes in rules and policies, whether they expect the government to stick to announced major policies, the degree to which entrepreneurs are usually informed about important rule changes, and whether they have an opportunity to voice concerns when planned changes affect their business

■ *Subjective perception of political instability,* or whether changes in government (constitutional or unconstitutional) are perceived to be accompanied by far-reaching policy surprises that could have serious effects on the private sector

■ *Security of persons and property,* or whether entrepreneurs feel confident that the authorities will protect them and their property from criminal actions, and whether theft and other forms of crime represent serious problems for business

■ *Predictability of judicial enforcement,* or the degree of uncertainty arising from arbitrary enforcement of rules by the judiciary, and whether such unpredictability presents a problem for doing business

■ *Corruption,* or whether it is common for private entrepreneurs to have to make some irregular additional payments to get things done.

BIBLIOGRAPHICAL NOTE

THIS REPORT HAS DRAWN ON A WIDE RANGE OF World Bank documents and on numerous outside sources. World Bank sources include ongoing research as well as country economic, sector, and project work. These and other sources are listed alphabetically by author or organization in two groups: background papers commissioned for this Report and a selected bibliography. The background papers, some of which will be made available through the Policy Research Working Paper series, and the rest through the *World Development Report* office, synthesize relevant literature and Bank work. The views they express are not necessarily those of the World Bank or of this Report.

In addition to the principal sources listed, many persons, both inside and outside the World Bank, provided valuable advice and guidance. Special thanks is owed to Gregory Ingram, Arturo Israel, Ravi Kanbur, and Michael Walton. Caroline Anstey and Hans Jurgen Gruss helped facilitate inputs and consultations from many sources. Valuable comments and contributions were also provided by Sri-Ram Aiyer, Mark Baird, Shahid Javed Burki, Uri Dadush, Partha Dasgupta, Gloria Davis, Shanta Devarajan, Mamadou Dia, Jessica Einhorn, Gunnar Eskeland, Francisco Ferreira, Cesar Gaviria, Roger Grawe, Jeffrey Hammer, Ricardo Hausmann, Enrique Iglesias, Edmundo Jarquin, Robert Klitgaard, Geoff Lamb, Moises Naím, Gobind Nankani, John Nellis, Richard Newfarmer, Guillermo Perry, Guy Pfeffermann, Robert Picciotto, Boris Pleskovic, Stephen Pursey, Sarath Rajapatirana, Malcolm Rowat, Salvatore Schiavo-Campo, Nemat Shafik, Ibrahim Shihata, Mary Shirley, I. J. Singh, Andrew Steer, Nicholas Stern, Maurice Strong, Roger Sullivan, Vinod Thomas, Jacques van der Gaag, Paulo Vieira da Cunha, Steve Webb, Alan Winters, and John Williamson. Bruce Ross-Larson, Meta de Coquereaumont, Paul Holtz, and Alison Strong provided valuable editorial advice and assis-

tance at various stages. Helpful contributions on individual chapters are listed under the chapter acknowledgments.

The survey of private sector firms conducted specially for this Report was made possible through the assistance and cooperation of staff in the operational complex of the World Bank. Particular thanks go to the coordinators of the survey in the regional vice presidencies as well as the resident representatives and the staff of the resident missions in the participating countries.

A wide range of consultations was undertaken for the Report. We particularly wish to thank the following organizations for arranging consultation meetings: the Research Institute for Development Assistance, Overseas Economic Cooperation Fund, Tokyo; the German Ministry of Cooperation; the Norwegian Ministry of Foreign Affairs; the North-South Institute, Ottawa; the National Council for Applied Economic Research, New Delhi; the African Economic Research Consortium, Nairobi; the Overseas Development Agency, London; the Global Coalition for Africa, Addis Ababa; and InterAction, Washington.

We wish to thank *in Tokyo*: Yuan Gangming, Kaoru Hayashi, Mr. Hisatake, Naoko Ishii, Shigeru Ishikawa, Shinichi Jin, Yutaka Kosai, Isao Kubota, Toru Nakanishi, Nobutake Odano, Tetsuji Okazaki, Yoshio Okubo, Toru Shinotsuka, Masaki Shiratori, Akira Suehiro, Shigeki Tejima, Prof. Juro Teranishi, and Yoshio Wada; *in Brussels*: Dominique Bé, Brunet Bernard, Noel Coghlan, P. Defraigne, M. de Lange, L. de Richemont, Daniel Guyader, Maurice Guyader, Ditte Juul Jorgensen, Maral LeRoy, Françoise Moreau, L. R. Pench, Regine Roy, G. Tebbe, A. Tincani, J. Vignon, and Rutger Wissels; *in the United Kingdom*: Mandeep Bains, Bill Baker, Richard Batley, Kate Bayliss, Sarah Bernard, Graham P. Chapman, Anne Coles, Paul Collier, Sean Collins, Rosalind Eyben, Mick Foster, Peter Grant, Mr. Greif, P. Holden, Tony Killick, Robert

Lasiett, Andrew Leslie, Deborah McGurk, Dino Merotto, Mick Moore, Peter Mountfield, Rachel Phillipson, Trevor Robinson, Sally Taylor, Sandra Wallman, Jon Wilmsburst, and Geoffrey Wood; *in Stockholm*: Stefan Fölster, Jörgen Holmqvist, Erik Johnsson, Assar Lindbeck, Eva Lindström, Per Molander, and Joakim Palme; *in Ferney-Voltaire, France*: Hans Engelberts, Elie Jouen, and Mike Waghorne; *in Bonn*: Friedrich W. Bolay, Hans-Gert Braun, Hartmut Elsenhans, Ingrid Hoven, Ernst-J. Kerbusch, Elmar Kleiner, Gudrun Kochendörfer-Lucius, Rolf J. Langhammer, Hildegard Lingnau, Peter Molt, Mr. Preuss, Dirk Reinermann, Hans-Bernd Schäfer, Mr. Schröder, Christian Sigrist, Klaus Simon, Albrecht Stockmayer, Franz Thediek, Josef Thesing, Dr. Tittel-Gronefeld, Klemens van de Sand, and Peter Wolf; *in Paris*: Sophie Bismut, Catherine Bourtembourg, Christian Chavagneux, Jean Coussy, Maximin Emagna, Bénédicte Etien, Ulrich Hiemenz, Etienne Le Roy, Turkia Ould-Daddah, Michel Pipelier, and Jean Pisani Ferry; *at a meeting of NGO representatives in London*: Graham Bray, Joji Carino, Marcus Colchester, Harriet Goodman, Andrew Gray, Caroline Harper, Rob Lake, Christine Lippai, Brendon Martin, Arthur Neame, Henry Northover, Helen O'Connell, Robin Poulton, Mohammed Sulliman, Sabjit Tohal, Kitty Warnock, Alex Wilks, Christian Wisskirchen, and Jessica Woodroffe; *at the European Commission*: Roderick Abbott, Christoph Bail, Chris Boyd, Gunther Burghardt, Carlos Camino, Jim Cloos, Robert Coleman, Carlos Costa, Pierre Defraigne, Xavier de Larnaudie-Eiffel, Joly Dixon, Michael Green, Alexander Italianer, Horst Krenzler, Ed Kronenburg, François Lamoureux, Rene Leray, Jean-François Marchipont, Stefano Micossi, Agne Pantelouri, Bernard Petit, Juan Prat, Giovanni Ravasio, Alexander Schaub, Steffen Smidt, Michel van den Abeele, Robert Verrue, Jerome Vignon, Heinrich von Moltke, and Jorg Wenzel; *at Georgetown University, Washington*: Daniel Brumberg, Marsha Darling, Bruce Douglas, Steven King, Carol Lancaster, Marilyn McMorrow, Dennis McNamara, Gwendolyn Mikell, Howard Schaeffer, and Dan Unger; *at the Washington College of Law, American University*: Claudia Martin and Rochas Pronk; *at a World Bank meeting with NGO representatives*: Peter Bachrach, Deborah Brautigam, Jim Cox, George Devendorf, Jack Downey, Justin Forsyth, Jo Marie Griesgraber, Wendy Grzywacz, Kari Hamerschlag, Carola Kaps, Meg Kinghorn, Michael Kronthal, Carolyn Long, Claudia Martin, Carmen Monico, Joe Muwonge, Gabriel Negatu, Michal Nehrbass, Carolyn Reynolds, Mildred Robbins Leet, Bruce Robinson, Berta Romero, James Rosen, Frances Seymour, Gmakahn Sherman, Carla Simon, Andrea Soccobo, Julia Taft, Nicolas van de Walle, Nick Vanedwaild, and Chuck Woolery; *in Cairo*: Ismail Sabry Abdallah, Mamdouh El Beltagy, Ahmed Galal, Abdel Fattah El Gebalyl, Moha-

med El Sayed Selim, Mohamed Aboul Enein, Samiha Fawzy, Ahmed Gweily, Heba Handoussa, Taher Helmy, Mohamed Mahmoud El Imam, Mohamed Lofty Mansour, Omar Mohanna, Mohamed Ozalp, Ghada Ragab, Yasser Sobhi, Arvind Subramanian, Fouad Sultan, and El Sayed Yasseen; *in Oslo*: Ole Winkler Andersen, Christian Friis Bach, Ingrid Braenden, Adne Cappelen, Arne Disch, Thorvald Grung Moe, Tor Halvorsen, Trond Folke Lindberg, Desmond McNeill, Lars Mjoset, Frode Neergaard, Poul Engberg Pedersen, Erik Reinert, Reiulf Steen, Astri Suhrke, and Lars Udsholt; *in the Netherlands*: M. Bienefelt, K. Blekxtoon, J. de Groot, L. de Maat, K. Doornhof, J. Enneking, J. Faber, H. Gobes, A. C. M. Hamer, J. P. Ramaker, F. Roos, G. Storm, R. J. Tjeerdsma, A. van't Veer, F. Ph. M. van der Kraaji, G. van Dijk, G. J. J. M. van Empel, F. D. van Loon, L. van Maare, A. van Raverstein, and M. van Wier; *from Belgium*: Guido Dumon, Dany Ghekiere, Luc Hubloue, Thomas Lievens, and Guy Schorochoff; *at the World Health Organization*: D. Bettcher, A. Moncayo, S. Sapirie, J. Tulloch, J. Visschedijk, and Derek Yach; *at the Office of the United Nations High Commissioner for Refugees*: Jamal Benomar and Eric Morris; *in Addis Ababa*: Members of the Economic Committee of the Global Coalition for Africa; *in the West Bank and Gaza*: Samir Abdallah, Hatem Halawani, Nabil Kassis, Ali Mahmoud Khadr, Mohammad Zuhdi Nashashibi, Yousif Nasser, and Mohammad Shtayyeh; *at a meeting in Cancún, Mexico*: José Afonso, Pedro Aguayo, Kenny Anthony, Nicolás Ardito-Barletta, Edgardo Boeninger, Juan Bour, Hernán Buchi, Rubén Carles, Alejandro Carrillo, Tarsicio Castañeda, Pelegrin Castillo, José Dagnino Pastore, Andrés Dauhajre, Diego de Figueiredo Moreira Neto, Alberto Díaz Cayeros, Haydee García, Rudolf Hommes, Tasso Jereissati, Arnoldo Jiménez, Eduardo Lizano, Thereza Lobo, Rolf Lüders, Gabriel Martínez, Néstor Martínez, Helen McBain, Ambler Moss, Marthe Muse, Arturo Núñez del Prado, Tomás Pastoriza, Ramón Piñango, Fernando Romero, Luis Rubio, Ricardo Samaniego, Cezley Sampson, Antonio Sancho, Enrique Vescovi, and Eduardo Wiesner Durán; *in India*: Swaminathan Aiyar, Yoginder Alagh, Surjit Bhalla, Onkar Goswani, R. N. Malhotra, Rakesh Mohan, and Pai Panandikar; *in Bern*: Franz Blankart, Thomas Greminger, Beat Kappeler, Luzius Mader, and Mathias Meyer; *at the African Economic Research Consortium*: Ibrahim Elbadawi and Benno Ndulu; *in Berlin*: Heinz Buhler, Alexander Friedrich, Götz Link, Theo Sommer, and Carl-Dieter Spranger; *at the International Labour Organisation*: Katherine Hagen and Stanley Taylor; *at the International Confederation of Free Trade Unions*: Gemma Adaba; *in Canada*: Isabella Bakker, Manfred Bienefeld, Jim Carruthers, G. Shabbir Cheema, Roy Culpeper, Nasir Islam, Devesh Kapur, Bahman Kia, Peter Larson, Caroline Pestieau, and Alison Van Rooy; *in Addis*

Ababa: Addis Anteneh, Tedenekialesh Assfaw, Asrat Bekele, Befekadu Degefe, Getachew Demeke, Tekalign Gedamu, Murtaza Jaffer, Rehenia Jingo-Kakonge, Teshome G. Mariam, Berhane Mewa, Gabriel Negatu, Florence Nekyon, Tom L. Torome, and Kiffle Wodajo.

For this consultation process we wish to thank in particular Patricia Dufour, Tomoko Hirai, Mika Iwasaki, Ali Khadr, Geoff Lamb, S. Miyamura, Fayez Omar, Sudarshan Gooptu, Claudia Von Monbart, and Spiros Voyadzis and several Executive Directors of the World Bank and their staff based in Washington.

Chapter 1
A bold and panoramic look at the evolution of the state over the past thousand years is provided in Tilly 1990. Classic texts that deal with the state and its management include Machiavelli's *The Prince* and Kautiliya's *Arthashastra* (see Kangle 1965). Helm 1989 analyzes the shifting boundaries of the state after 1945. Díaz Alejandro 1988 considers shifting fashions in development in the Latin American context. Tanzi and Schuknecht 1995 provide a recent evaluation of the effectiveness of states. World Bank 1991b provides an overview of competing paradigms of development and the differing roles accorded to the state. Teranishi and Kosai 1993 provide a comprehensive review of Japanese economic policies. IMF 1996 provides a review of the fiscal policy issues facing developing countries. A comprehensive review of the arguments for state intervention is contained in Stiglitz 1994. See Mueller 1989 for an alternative approach. Box 1.1 is adapted from Sills 1968, Gould and Kolb 1964, and Kuper and Kuper 1996. Box 1.2 is summarized from Stiglitz 1996. Box 1.3 draws from a background note by Swaminathan Aiyar. The historical section benefited from contributions by Emma Rothschild and draws as well on the background paper by Aron, Elbadawi, and Ndulu. Box 1.4 is summarized from Stiglitz 1986. Table 1.1 benefited from valuable inputs from Jeffrey Hammer.

Chapter 2
Peter Knight contributed material for Box 2.1. Figure 2.1 draws on Alston 1996. On measurement of the state see Gemmell 1993 and Lindauer 1988. The standard reference on purchasing power parity prices is Summers and Heston 1991. The empirical work in this chapter is based on the Commander, Davoodi, and Lee background paper. There is an extensive literature on the factors determining government size: see, among others, Borcherding 1985, Buchanan 1977, Courakis, Moura-Roque, and Tridimas 1993, Lybeck 1986, Meltzer and Richard 1981, Oxley 1994, Peacock and Wiseman 1961, Ram 1987, and Rodrik 1996. On the effects of government size on growth and other indicators of well-being see Alesina and Perotti 1995, Anand and Ravallion 1993, Barro and Sala-

i-Martin 1995, Bosworth, Collins, and Chen 1995, Devarajan, Swaroop, and Zou 1996, Kormendi and Meguire 1985, Landau 1986, Ram 1986, and Slemrod 1995. Knack and Keefer 1995 look explicitly at the role of institutions. Mauro 1995 looks at the consequences of corruption for growth. The discussion of credibility draws on Borner, Brunetti, and Weder 1995, and the results reported are derived from the credibility survey conducted for this Report, which is described in detail in the Brunetti, Kisunko, and Weder background papers. The general discussion on institutions draws on North 1990, Olson 1996, and Dia 1996. The discussion of evolution in economists' thinking about growth draws on Barro and Sala-i-Martin 1995, Solow 1956, Dasgupta 1995, and Drèze and Sen 1989.

Chapter 3
This chapter benefited from valuable contributions and suggestions from Richard Ball, Jeanine Braithwaite, Lionel Demery, Jeffrey Hammer, Estelle James, Emmanuel Jimenez, Maureen Lewis, Geoffrey Shepherd, Carlos Silva, Kalanidhi Subbarao, and Dominique van de Walle.

The discussion on shared growth is based on Aoki, Murdoch, and Okuno-Fujiwara 1995 and Ishikawa 1990. Box 3.2 is drawn from Guerrero 1996. The discussion of mining in Nevada is from Libecap 1996. The material on land titling was provided by Klaus Deininger, with additional information from Feder and Nishio 1996. Berry and Levy 1994 describe patterns of export marketing by Indonesian firms. Box 3.3 builds on Stone, Levy, and Paredes 1996.

The section on the policy environment draws on World Bank 1994a for its discussion of price distortions in African agriculture. The discussion of changes in the way developing countries raise tax revenue is based on information provided by Vinaya Swaroop. The discussion of mechanisms for establishing fiscal and monetary credibility draws on the background papers by Alesina and Ball.

The discussion on patterns of public expenditure draws on Hammer 1997, Pradhan 1996, and World Bank 1994c. The discussion of benefit incidence of public spending draws on contributions by Lionel Demery and on van de Walle and Nead 1995. The discussion of the historical role of the private sector draws on Psacharopoulos and Nguyen 1997 and van der Gaag 1995. Box 3.6 is based on van der Gaag 1995.

Box 3.7 is based on Coloma 1996. Box 3.8 was provided by Nisha Agrawal.

Chapter 4
Jean Aden, Gerard Caprio, Cheryl Gray, Luis Guasch, Robert Hahn, Gordon Hughes, Pablo Spiller, and Andrew Stone made valuable contributions to this chapter. Box 4.1 was prepared by Andrew Stone.

The discussion of privatization and liberalization draws heavily on Galal and others 1994, World Bank 1995c, and the Guasch and Hahn background paper. Lau and Song 1992 delineate the evolution of public-private ownership in the Republic of Korea and Taiwan (China).

The frameworks for the discussion of financial, utilities, and environmental regulation draw heavily from, respectively, Caprio 1996, Levy and Spiller 1994, and Afsah, Laplante, and Wheeler 1996. The discussion of banking supervision draws heavily on Polizatto 1992. Box 4.3 is drawn from Sheng 1992. The World Bank study on episodes of bank insolvency is Caprio and Klingebiel 1996. The description of price-cap regulation in the United Kingdom is based on Spiller and Vogelsang 1996. The information on environmental regulation in industrial countries is from Lovei and Weiss 1996 and Rose-Ackerman 1995. The shortcomings of top-down environmental regulation are examined in Margulis 1996.

Stiglitz and Uy 1996 probe some East Asian approaches to maintaining bank solvency, and Saunders and Wilson 1995 synthesize some historical experiences with contingent liability in banking in the Western world. The discussions of telecommunications regulation in Jamaica and the Philippines are from Spiller and Sampson 1996 and Esfahani 1996. The discussion of Indonesia's experience with environmental regulation is adapted from Afsah, Laplante, and Makarim 1996. Box 4.5 is from Metropolitan Environment Improvement Program 1996.

The section on industrial policy builds on Aoki, Murdoch, and Okuno-Fujiwara 1995, Ohno 1996, World Bank 1993, Levy and others 1994, and Humphrey and Schmitz 1995. Box 4.6 is adapted from Okazaki 1997. The Philippine experience with capital-intensive projects is summarized in World Bank 1987. Lee's background paper lays out the experience with infrastructure in the Cholla region of the Republic of Korea. Tendler 1997 examines public procurement in Ceará State, Brazil.

Chapter 5

This chapter has benefited from valuable contributions, suggestions, and comments from Ladipo Adamolekun, Ed Campos, Migara da Silva, Giulio de Tommaso, Roger Grawe, Jeffrey Hammer, Malcolm Holmes, Arturo Israel, Klaus König, Alexander Kotchegura, Patricia Langan, Nicholas Manning, Ernesto May, Julie McLaughlin, Amitabha Mukherjee, Vikram Nehru, Chetana Neerchal, Barbara Nunberg, Gary Reid, Susan Rose-Ackerman, George Russell, Claude Salem, Salvatore Schiavo-Campo, Mary Shirley, Mike Stevens, Roger Sullivan, Jim Wesberry, and David Wood.

The chapter draws on the Campos and Pradhan background paper, the Schiavo-Campo, de Tommaso, and Mukherjee background paper, and background notes by Nicholas Manning and Gary Reid. Mike Stevens con-

tributed Box 5.1. Box 5.2 is from Campos and Pradhan 1996. The discussion on policymaking as the brains of government draws on Israel 1990. The discussion of policymaking in Poland and Hungary draws on Nunberg forthcoming.

The section on service delivery draws on information provided by Nicholas Manning and on Israel 1997. Box 5.3 is from World Bank 1996b. Box 5.4 draws from van der Gaag 1995 and Heyneman forthcoming. Box 5.5 is from van der Gaag 1995. The study on performance contracts with public enterprises is World Bank 1995c. The comparison of the Indian and Korean irrigation systems draws upon Wade 1994. The section on financial and management controls draws on information from Gary Reid, Chetana Neerchal, George Russell, and Jim Wesberry.

The section on building capable, motivated staff benefited from extensive contributions by Barbara Nunberg. The section on meritocratic recruitment and promotion draws from Evans 1995 and Campos and Root 1996. Box 5.6 is from Nunberg 1995. The discussion on pay and employment, including the study on wage decompression in Africa, draws on Lindauer and Nunberg 1994; the analysis of the decline of public sector wages is derived from Haque and Sahay 1996. The study of civil service reform efforts over 1981–91 is reported in World Bank 1991a. Box 5.7 is from Tendler 1997.

Chapter 6

This chapter has benefited from valuable inputs, suggestions, and comments by Ladipo Adamolekun, Robert Bates, Ed Campos, Maria Dakolias, Matthew McCubbins, Elena Panaritis, Andres Rigo Sureda, Susan Rose-Ackerman, Kenneth Shepsle, Mike Stevens, Andrew Stone, and Douglas Webb.

The section on the judiciary is based on the Webb background paper. The study on property rights and the stability of the regime is Clague and others 1996. Box 6.1 was provided by Elena Panaritis. The section on corruption draws on the Rose-Ackerman background paper. The analysis of the predictability of corruption has benefited from discussions with Ed Campos. Boxes 6.2, 6.3, and 6.4 were provided by Susan Rose-Ackerman, drawing on Brett 1993 and Ruzindana 1995 (Box 6.3) and Manion 1996 and Quah 1993 (Box 6.4). There is a vast literature on corruption, which includes Klitgaard 1988, Mauro 1995, Rose-Ackerman 1978, and Shleifer and Vishny 1993.

Chapter 7

This chapter has benefited from valuable contributions and comments from Junaid K. Ahmad, Dan Aronson, Katherine Bain, Ela Bhatt, Richard Bird, Tim Campbell, John Clark, Peter Evans, Marianne Fay, Deon Filmer, Ashraf Ghani, Jim Hicks, Michael Laver, Deepa Narayan, Vikram Nehru, Samuel Paul, Lant Pritchett, Lester Salamon, David Sewell, Anwar Shah, Jerry Silverman, Albrecht Stockmayer, and David Wildasin.

The section on voice and participation draws heavily on ideas developed in Evans 1996a and 1996b, Hirschman 1970, and Montgomery 1988. Box 7.1 is based on Linz, Lipset, and Pool n.d., Weaver and Dickens 1995, and polls conducted by Europinion, Brussels, and *India Today* 1996. The reference to electoral arrangements under parliamentary systems and women's political representation comes from Lijphart 1995. The section on diversity and representation is based on the Brautigam background paper and a background note by Jalali. The distinction among service delivery NGOs, intermediary organizations, and primary associations draws on Fisher 1993 and Carroll, Schmidt, and Bebbington 1996. The reference to Umu-Itodo, Nigeria, comes from Francis and others 1996. Box 7.3 is based on Putnam, Leonardi, and Nanetti 1993 and Narayan and Pritchett 1997. The discussion of the role of social capital in enhancing the quality of public action draws on Evans 1996a and 1996b.

The discussion of participatory mechanisms is inspired by Campos and Root 1996, Paul 1994, Picciotto 1995, and Holmes and Krishna 1996. The reference to the user assessment of water supply in Baku, Azerbaijan, comes from World Bank 1995a. Box 7.4 is based on material supplied by Patricia Langan. The evidence in Box 7.5 is based on Narayan 1995 and subsequent empirical work by Isham, Narayan, and Pritchett 1995. The example from Recife, Brazil, comes from Orstrom 1996, and the discussion of the implications for public agencies and the enabling environment draws on World Bank 1996c and 1996e.

The section on decentralization draws on the work of Bennett 1990, Campbell and Fuhr forthcoming, Oates 1972, Scharpf 1994, Shah 1994, Stiglitz 1977 and 1996, Tanzi 1995a, Wallich 1994, and World Bank research led by Hans Binswanger and Anwar Shah. Table 7.2 is based on contributions by Jeffrey Hammer. Box 7.6 was prepared by Bill Dillinger and Vikram Nehru, and Box 7.7 by Anwar Shah. Table 7.4 was prepared by Anwar Shah. Examples of decentralization initiatives in various countries are based on Barzelay 1991, Kanter 1995, Villadsen and Lubanga 1996, and information provided by Tim Campbell, Florence Eid, Armin Fidler, Vikram Nehru, Alcyone Saliba, Klaus Simon, and Markus Steinich.

Chapter 8

This chapter draws extensively on the framework set out by Stiglitz 1995. The principles of voluntary cooperation are drawn from Lawrence, Bressant, and Ito 1996. The section on ensuring more effective cooperation draws on Shihata 1996. Hoekman 1995 provides useful background materials on opening world markets. Box 8.1 is based on Hoekman 1995 and *Financial Times* 1996. The

section on basic research makes use of findings reported in Ad Hoc Committee on Health Research Relating to Future Intervention Options 1996. Box 8.2 is based on Pardey and others 1996. The discussion of international environmental agreements is based on material supplied by Laurence Boisson des Chassournes; examples of global environmental issues are drawn from Flavin 1996. Box 8.3 was prepared by Carter Brandon and Charles Feinstein. Box 8.5 draws on work by Landau 1993 and Knight, Loayza, and Villanueva 1995. The discussion of refugees and the role of the state is based on the background paper by Suhrke and Newland. Evidence on the effectiveness of aid is drawn from Burnside and Dollar 1996.

Chapter 9

This chapter benefited from written contributions by Dani Rodrik and Gary Reid and suggestions and comments from Barry Ames, Juan Cariaga, Antonio Estache, Sue Goldmark, Jorge Gorrio, Ravi Kanbur, Octavio Amorim Neto, Graham Scott, Mary Shirley, and Zafiris Tzannatos.

The information on the decentralization program in Peru is from Graham and Kane 1996. The study on inefficiency in Uruguay's water utilities is Estache, Rodriguez-Pardina, and Smith 1996. The study on political coalitions in Brazil is Alesina and Rosenthal 1995. On pension expenditure in Uruguay see Kane 1995. Box 9.2 is based on Lundahl 1992. Box 9.3 is based on Lewis 1961. The discussion of telecommunications in Sri Lanka is based on World Bank 1996g. Box 9.4 is based on Bermeo and García-Durán 1994. Box 9.5 is based on Navarro 1996.

Chapter 10

The discussion on state collapse is based on the Suhrke and Newland background paper. It also draws on discussions with Mamadou Dia and Steven Holtzman and on Tallroth 1997. Box 10.1 is based on Mubarak 1996. Box 10.2 is based on Tallroth 1997. The discussion on the regional agenda was prepared with the help of Malcolm Rowat, Salvatore Schiavo-Campo, and Michael Walton. Shahrokh Fardoust, Alan Gelb, Costas Michalopoulos, Marcelo Selowsky, Shekhar Shah, Roger Sullivan, and John Williamson also provided valuable comments.

Background papers

Aiyar, Swaminathan. "Evolution of the Role of the State in India."

Alesina, Alberto. "Politics, Procedures, and Budget Deficits."

Aron, Janine, Ibrahim Elbadawi, and Benno Ndulu. "The State and Development in Sub-Saharan Africa."

Ball, Richard. "The Institutional Foundations of Monetary Commitment: A Comparative Analysis."

Braathen, Einar, and Harald Ekker. "The State and National Reconstruction: Interdependency Between Central and Local Level."

Brautigam, Deborah. "The State and Ethnic Pluralism: Managing Conflict in Multiethnic Societies."

Brunetti, Aymo, Gregory Kisunko, and Beatrice Weder. "Credibility of Rules and Economic Growth: Evidence from a Worldwide Survey of the Private Sector." (a)

_____. "Institutional Obstacles for Doing Business: Region-by-Region Results from a Worldwide Survey of the Private Sector." (b)

Campos, Ed, and Sanjay Pradhan. "Building Institutions for a More Effective Public Sector."

Commander, Simon, Hamid Davoodi, and Une J. Lee. "The Causes and Consequences of Government for Growth and Well-Being."

De Silva, Migara. "War, Tax Revenue and the Rise of the Modern Public Administration in Western Europe."

Disch, Arne. "The Scandinavian 'Model': Successes and Limitations of the Activist State."

Guasch, J. Luis, and Robert W. Hahn. "The Costs and Benefits of Regulation: Some Implications for Developing Countries."

Jalali, Rita. "State and Ethnicity."

Lee, Kyu Sik. "Cholla Region Catches Up with Korea: The Role of Local Governments."

Molander, Per. "Public Sector Spending Control: Swedish Experiences."

Ohno, Kenichi. "Creating the Market Economy: The Japanese View on Economic Development and Systemic Transition."

Rose-Ackerman, Susan. "When Is Corruption Harmful?"

Schiavo-Campo, Rino. "Civil Service and Economic Development—A Selective Synthesis of International Facts and Experience."

Schiavo-Campo, Salvatore, Giulio de Tommaso, and Amitabha Mukherjee. "An International Statistical Survey of Government Employment and Wages."

Suhrke, Astri, and Kathleen Newland. "States and Refugees: International Cooperation on Issues of Displacement."

Van Rijckeghem, Caroline, and Beatrice Weder. "Corruption and Rate of Temptation: Do Low Wages in the Civil Service Cause Corruption?"

Webb, Douglas. "The Judiciary: The Arbiter of Rules and Resolver of Disputes."

WHO (World Health Organization). "Essential Public Health Functions: A New Initiative in Support of Health for All."

_____. "Redefining the Scope of Public Health Beyond the Year 2000."

_____. "The Role of Government in Public Health Through the Ages."

_____. "The Role of State Action in Disease Eradication and Control."

Selected bibliography

Abdallah, A. E. A. 1990. "Ethnic Conflict in Sudan." In M. L. Michael Wyzan, ed., The Political Economy of Ethnic Discrimination and Affirmative Action. New York, N.Y.: Praeger.

Adamolekun, Ladipo. 1991. "Promoting African Decentralization." Public Administration and Development 11(3): 285–91.

Aden, Jean. 1996. "Industrial Pollution Abatement in the Newly Industrializing Countries: Korea." Asia Technical Department, World Bank, Washington, D.C.

Ad Hoc Committee on Health Research Relating to Future Intervention Options. 1996. Investing in Health Research and Development: Report of the Ad Hoc Committee on Health Research Relating to Future Intervention Options. Geneva: World Health Organization.

Afsah, Shakeb, Benoit Laplante, and Nabiel Makarim. 1996. "Program-based Pollution Control Management: The Indonesian PROKASIH Program." World Bank Policy Research Working Paper No. 1602. Policy Research Department, Environment, Infrastructure and Agriculture Division, World Bank, Washington, D.C.

Afsah, Shakeb, Benoit Laplante, and David Wheeler. 1996. "Controlling Industrial Pollution: A New Paradigm." World Bank Policy Research Working Paper No. 1672. Policy Research Department, Environment, Infrastructure and Agriculture Division, World Bank, Washington, D.C.

Alesina, Alberto, R. Hausmann, R. Hommes, and E. Stein. 1996. "Budget Institutions and Fiscal Performance in Latin America." NBER Working Paper No. 5556. National Bureau of Economic Research, Cambridge, Mass.

Alesina, Alberto, and Roberto Perotti. 1995. "Fiscal Expansions and Adjustments in OECD Countries." Economic Policy: A European Forum 21 (October): 205–48.

_____. 1996. "Income Distribution, Political Instability, and Investment." European Economic Review 40: 1203–28.

Alesina, Alberto, and Howard Rosenthal. 1995. Partisan Politics, Divided Government, and the Economy. Cambridge, England: Cambridge University Press.

Alston, Lee. 1996. "Empirical Work in Institutional Economics: An Overview." In Lee Alston, T. Eggertsson, and Douglass North, eds., Empirical Studies in Institutional Change. Cambridge, England: Cambridge University Press.

Amsden, Alice. 1989. Asia's Next Giant: South Korea and Late Industrialization. New York, N.Y.: Oxford University Press.

Anand, Sudhir, and Martin Ravallion. 1993. "Human Development in Poor Countries: On the Role of Private Incomes and Public Services." Journal of Economic Perspectives 7(1): 133–50.

Andic, Fuat, and Suphan Andic. 1996. The Last of the Ottoman Grandees: The Life and Political Testament of Ali Pasha. Istanbul: Istanbul's Press.

Aoki, Masahiko, and Ronald Dore, eds. 1994. The Japanese Firm: Sources of Competitive Strength. Oxford, England: Clarendon Press.

Aoki, Masahiko, Hyung-Ki Kim, and Masahiro Okuno-Fujiwara. 1997. The Role of the Government in East Asian Economic Development: Comparative Institutional Analysis. Oxford, England: Oxford University Press.

Aoki, Masahiko, Kevin Murdoch, and Masahiro Okuno-Fujiwara. 1995. "Beyond the East Asian Miracle: Introducing the Market-Enhancing View." Stanford University Center for Economic Policy Research Discussion Paper No. 442. Stanford, Calif.

Arisawa, Hiromi, and Takahide Nakamura, eds. 1990. *Data: Design of Postwar Economic Policies,* Vol. 1. Tokyo: Tokyo University Press (in Japanese).

Bahl, Roy. 1994. "Revenues and Revenue Assignment: Intergovernmental Fiscal Relations in the Russian Federation." In Christine I. Wallich, ed., *Russia and the Challenge of Fiscal Federalism.* World Bank Regional and Sectoral Studies. Washington, D.C.: World Bank.

Bardhan, Pranab. 1996. "Efficiency, Equity and Poverty Alleviation: Policy Issues in Less Developed Countries." *Economic Journal* 106 (September): 1344–56.

Barro, Robert J. 1996. "Determinants of Democracy." Department of Economics, Harvard University, Cambridge, Mass.

Barro, Robert J., and Xavier Sala-i-Martin. 1995. *Economic Growth.* New York, N.Y.: McGraw-Hill.

Barzelay, Michael. 1991. "Managing Local Development: Lessons from Spain." *Policy Sciences* 24: 271–90.

Batley, Richard. 1996. "Public-Private Relationships and Performance in Service Provision." *Urban Studies* 33(4–5): 723–51.

Bennett, Robert J., ed. 1990. *Decentralization, Local Governments, and Markets: Toward a Post-Welfare Agenda.* Oxford, England: Oxford University Press.

Bermeo, Nancy, and José García-Durán. 1994. "Spain: Dual Transition Implemented by Two Parties." In Stephan Haggard and Steven B. Webb, *Voting for Reform: Democracy, Political Liberalization, and Economic Adjustment.* New York, N.Y.: Oxford University Press.

Berry, Albert, and Brian Levy. 1994. "Indonesia's Small and Medium-Size Exporters and Their Support Systems." Policy Research Working Paper No. 1402. Policy Research Department, Finance and Private Sector Development Division, World Bank, Washington, D.C.

Bhatt, Ela. n.d. "Moving Towards a People-Centered Economy." The Self-Employed Women's Association, Ahmedabad, India.

Bird, Richard M. 1995. "Decentralizing Infrastructure: For Good or for Ill?" In Antonio Estache, ed., *Decentralizing Infrastructure: Advantages and Limitations,* pp. 22–51. World Bank Discussion Paper No. 290. Washington, D.C.: World Bank.

Bird, Richard M., Robert D. Ebel, and Christine I. Wallich, eds. 1995. *Decentralization of the Socialist State: Intergovernmental Finance in Transition Economies.* World Bank Regional and Sectoral Studies. Washington, D.C.: World Bank.

Boadway, Robin W., Sandra Roberts, and Anwar Shah. 1994. "The Reform of Fiscal Systems in Developing and Emerging Market Economies: A Federalism Perspective." Policy Research Working Paper No. 1259. Policy Research Department, Public Economics Division, World Bank, Washington, D.C.

Borcherding, T. E. 1985. "The Causes of Government Expenditure Growth: A Survey of the U.S. Evidence." *Journal of Public Economics* 28 (December): 359–82.

Borner, Silvio, Aymo Brunetti, and Beatrice Weder. 1995. *Political Credibility and Economic Development.* New York, N.Y.: St. Martin's Press.

Boston, Jonathan, John Martin, June Pallot, and Pat Walsh. 1996. *Public Management: The New Zealand Model.* New York, N.Y.: Oxford University Press.

Bosworth, Barry, Susan Collins, and Yu-chin Chen. 1995. "Accounting for Differences in Economic Growth." Economic Studies Program, Brookings Institution, Washington, D.C.

Brautigam, Deborah. 1996. "State Capacity and Effective Governance." In Benno Ndulu and Nicholas van de Walle, eds., *Agenda for Africa's Economic Renewal,* pp. 81–108. Washington, D.C.: Overseas Development Council.

Brass, P. R. 1985. *Ethnic Groups and the State.* Totowa, N.J.: Barnes and Noble.

Bread for the World Institute. 1997. *What Governments Can Do: Seventh Annual Report on the State of World Hunger.* Silver Spring, Md.: Bread for the World Institute.

Brett, E. A. 1993. "Theorizing Crisis and Reform: Institutional Theories and Social Change in Uganda." Institute for Development Studies, Sussex University, Brighton, England.

Buchanan, J. M. 1977. "Why Does Government Grow?" In Thomas Borcherding, ed., *Budgets and Bureaucrats: The Sources of Government Growth.* Durham, N.C.: Duke University Press.

Burki, Shahid J., and Sebastian Edwards. 1996. *Dismantling the Populist State. The Unfinished Revolution in Latin America and the Caribbean.* World Bank Latin American and Caribbean Studies: Viewpoints. Washington, D.C.: World Bank.

Burnside, Craig, and David Dollar. 1996. "Aid, Policies and Growth." Policy Research Department, Macroeconomics and Growth Division, World Bank, Washington, D.C.

Buscaglia, Edgardo, and Maria Dakolias. 1996. *Judicial Reform in Latin American Courts: The Experience in Argentina and Ecuador.* World Bank Technical Paper No. 350. World Bank, Washington, D.C.

Campbell, Tim, and Harald Fuhr, eds. Forthcoming. *Does Decentralization Work? Case Studies on Innovative Local Government in Latin America.* Washington, D.C.: World Bank.

Campbell, Tim, George Peterson, and José Brakarz. 1991. "Decentralization to Local Government in LAC: National Strategies and Local Response in Planning, Spending and Management." Report No. 5. Latin America and the Caribbean Technical Department, Regional Studies Program, World Bank, Washington, D.C.

Campos, Ed, and Sanjay Pradhan. 1996. "Budgetary Institutions and Expenditure Outcomes: Binding Governments to Fiscal Performance." Policy Research Working Paper No. 1646. Policy Research Department, World Bank, Washington, D.C.

Campos, Ed, and Hilton L. Root. 1996. *The Key to the Asian Miracle: Making Shared Growth Credible.* Washington, D.C.: Brookings Institution.

Caprio, Gerard, Jr. 1996. "Bank Regulation: The Case of the Missing Model." World Bank Policy Research Working Paper No. 1574. Policy Research Department, Finance and

Private Sector Development Division, World Bank, Washington, D.C.

Caprio, Gerard, Jr., and Daniela Klingebiel. 1996. "Bank Insolvency: Bad Luck, Bad Policy, or Bad Banking?" Paper presented at the Annual World Bank Conference on Development Economics, World Bank, Washington, D.C., April 25.

Carroll, Tom, Mary Schmidt, and Tony Bebbington. 1996. "Participation Through Intermediary NGOs." Environment Department Papers No. 031. Environment Department, World Bank, Washington, D.C.

CEPAL/GTZ (Comisión Económica para América Latina/Gesellschaft für Technische Zusammenarbeit). 1996. *Descentralización Fiscal en América Latina: Balance y Principales Desafíos.* Santiago, Chile: CEPAL/GTZ.

Chellaraj, Gnanaraj, Olusoji Adeyi, Alexander S. Preker, and Ellen Goldstein. 1996. *Trends in Health Status, Services, and Finance: The Transition in Central and Eastern Europe. Volume II: Statistical Annex.* Washington, D.C.: World Bank.

Chhibber, Ajay, Mansoor Dailami, and Nemat Shafik, eds. 1992. *Reviving Private Investment in Developing Countries: Empirical Studies and Policy Lessons.* Elsevier Science Publishers, North Holland.

Chisari, Omar, Antonio Estache, and Carlos Romero. 1996. "Winners and Losers from Utilities Privatizations: Lessons from a General Equilibrium Model of Argentina." Universidad Argentina de la Empresa, Buenos Aires, and World Bank, Washington, D.C.

Clague, Christopher, Philip Keefer, Stephen Knack, and Mancur Olson. 1996. "Property and Contract Rights under Democracy and Dictatorship." *Journal of Economic Growth* 1(2): 243–76.

Clark, John. 1995. "The State, Popular Participation and the Voluntary Sector." *World Development* 23(4): 593–601.

Coase, R. H. 1960. "The Problem of Social Cost." *Journal of Law and Economics* 3 (October): 1–44.

———. 1988. *The Firm, the Market, and the Law.* Chicago, Ill.: University of Chicago Press.

Coloma, Fernando C. 1996. "Seguro de Desempleo: Teoria, Evidencia, y una Propuesta." *Cuadernos de Economía* 33(99): 295–320.

Conyers, Diana. 1985. "Decentralization: A Framework for Discussion." In Hasnat Abdul Hye, ed., *Decentralization, Local Government Institutions and Resource Mobilization,* pp. 22–42. Comilla, Bangladesh: Bangladesh Academy for Rural Development.

Courakis, Anthony, Fatima Moura-Roque, and George Tridimas. 1993. "Public Expenditure Growth in Greece and Portugal: Wagner's Law and Beyond." *Applied Economics* 25: 125–34.

Cox, Gary W., and Mathew D. McCubbins. 1996. "Structure and Policy: The Institutional Determinants of Policy Outcomes." Department of Political Science, University of California, San Diego, Calif.

Dasgupta, Partha. 1995. *An Inquiry into Well-Being and Destitution.* New York, N.Y.: Oxford University Press.

———. 1997. "Social Capital and Economic Performance." University of Cambridge, Cambridge, England.

Deininger, Klaus, and Lyn Squire. 1996. "A New Data Set on Measuring Income Inequality." *World Bank Economic Review* 10(3): 565–92.

De Soto, Hernando. 1989. *The Other Path.* New York, N.Y.: Harper & Row.

Deutsche Gesellschaft für Technische Zusammenarbeit (GTZ). n.d. "Indo-German Watershed Development Programme, Maharashtra, India." GTZ, Eschborn, Germany.

Deutsche Stiftung für internationale Entwicklung. 1996. *Zweites Deutsches Weltbank-Forum: Verantwortungsbewuße öffentlich-private Partnerschaft.* Berlin: Deutsche Stiftung für internationale Entwicklung.

Devarajan, Shantayanan, Vinaya Swaroop, and Heng-fu Zou. 1996. "The Composition of Public Expenditure and Economic Growth." *Journal of Monetary Economics* 37: 313–44.

Dia, Mamadou. 1996. *Africa's Management in the 1990s and Beyond: Reconciling Indigenous and Transplanted Institutions.* Directions in Development Series. Washington, D.C.: World Bank.

Díaz Alejandro, Carlos. 1988. *Trade, Development and the World Economy: Selected Essays.* Oxford, England: Basil Blackwell.

DiIulio, John J., Jr., ed. 1994. *Deregulating the Public Service: Can Government Be Improved?* Washington, D.C.: The Brookings Institution.

Dillinger, Bill. 1995. "Decentralization, Politics and Public Service." In Antonio Estache, ed., *Decentralizing Infrastructure: Advantages and Limitations,* pp. 5–21. World Bank Discussion Papers No. 290. Washington, D.C.: World Bank.

Dixon, Geoffrey. 1993. "Managing Budget Outlays 1983–84 to 1992–93." In Brian Galligan, ed., *Federalism and the Economy: International, National and State Issues.* Canberra: Federalism Research Centre, Australian National University.

Drèze, Jean, and A. K. Sen. 1989. *Hunger and Public Action.* Oxford, England: Oxford University Press.

Easterly, William, and Ross Levine. 1996. "Africa's Growth Tragedy: A Retrospective, 1960–89." World Bank Policy Research Paper No. 1503. Macroeconomics and Growth Division, Policy Research Department, World Bank, Washington, D.C.

Easterly, William, and Sergio Rebelo. 1993. "Fiscal Policy and Economic Growth." *Journal of Monetary Economics* (Netherlands) 32(3): 417–58.

Economic and Social Research Council. n.d. *ESRC Whitehall Programme: The Changing Nature of Central Government in Britain.* London: Economic and Social Research Council.

Edwards, Michael, and David Hulme, eds. 1992. *Making a Difference: NGOs and Development in a Changing World.* London: Earthscan Publications.

Elsenhans, Hartmut. 1996. *State, Class and Development.* New Delhi: Radiant Publishers.

Epsing-Andersen, Gøsta. 1994. "After the Golden Age: The Future of the Welfare State in the New Global Order." Occasional Paper No. 7. World Summit for Social Development, Geneva.

Esfahani, Hadi Salehi. 1996. "The Political Economy of the Telecommunications Sector in the Philippines." In Brian Levy and Pablo T. Spiller, eds., *Regulations, Institutions and*

Commitment: Comparative Studies of Telecommunications, pp. 145–201. Cambridge, England: Cambridge University Press.

Esman, Milton. 1994. *Ethnic Politics.* Ithaca, N.Y.: Cornell University Press.

Estache, Antonio, ed. 1995. *Decentralizing Infrastructure: Advantages and Limitations.* World Bank Discussion Paper No. 290. Washington, D.C.: World Bank.

Estache, Antonio, M. Rodriguez-Pardina, and W. Smith. 1996. "Towards a New Role for the State in Uruguay's Utilities." Latin America and the Caribbean Country Department I, Infrastructure and Urban Development Division, World Bank, Washington, D.C.

European Commission. 1996. "Towards a More Coherent Global Economic Order." Discussion Paper. Forward Studies Unit and Directorate-General for Economic and Financial Affairs, European Commission, Brussels.

Evans, Peter B. 1995. *Embedded Autonomy: States and Industrial Transformation.* Princeton, N.J.: Princeton University Press.

———. 1996a. "Government Action, Social Capital and Development: Reviewing the Evidence on Synergy." *World Development* 24(6): 1119–32.

———. 1996b. "Social Capital and the Functioning of Bureaucracies in Developing Countries." Paper presented at the International Conference on Governance Innovations: Building a Government-Citizen-Business Partnership, Manila, October 20–23.

Evans, Peter B., and James Rauch. 1996. "Bureaucratic Structure and Economic Growth: Some Preliminary Analysis of Data on 35 Developing Countries." University of California, Berkeley, Calif.

Fageberg, Jan, Bart Verspagen, and Nick von Tunzelmann. 1994. *The Dynamics of Technology, Trade and Growth.* Aldershot, Hants, England, and Brookfield, Vt.: Edward Elgar.

Farrington, John, and David Lewis, eds., with S. Satish and Avrea Miclat-Teves. 1993. *Nongovernmental Organizations and the State in Asia: Rethinking Roles in Sustainable Agricultural Development.* London and New York, N.Y.: Routledge.

Feder, Gershon, and Akihiko Nishio. 1996. "The Benefits of Land Registration and Titling: Economic and Social Perspectives." Paper presented at the International Conference of Land Tenure and Administration, Orlando, Fla., November 12.

Federalist Papers. 1987. Edited by Isaac Kramnick. Harmondsworth, Middlesex, England: Penguin.

Feldstein, Martin. 1995. "Tax Avoidance and the Deadweight Loss of the Income Tax." NBER Working Paper No. 5055. National Bureau of Economic Research, Cambridge, Mass.

Feldstein, Martin, and Andrew Samwick. 1996. "The Transition Path in Privatizing Social Security." Paper presented at a National Bureau of Economic Research conference on Privatizing Social Security, Cambridge, Mass., August 2.

Fernandez, Raquel, and Dani Rodrik. 1991. "Resistance to Reform: Status Quo Bias in the Presence of Individual-Specific Uncertainty." *American Economic Review* 81(5): 1146–55.

Ferreira, M. Luisa, and Charles C. Griffen. 1995. "Tanzania Human Development Survey: Final Report." Population and Human Resources, Eastern Africa Department, World Bank, Washington, D.C.

Financial Times. 1996. "Antagonists Queue for WTO Judgment." (August 8).

Fischer, Stanley. 1995. "Central-Bank Independence Revisited." *AEA Papers and Proceedings* (May): 201–06.

Fisher, Julie. 1993. *The Road from Rio: Sustainable Development and the Nongovernmental Movement in the Third World.* New York, N.Y.: Praeger.

Fiske, Edward B. 1996. *Decentralization of Education: Politics and Consensus.* Directions in Development Series. Washington, D.C.: World Bank.

Flavin, Christopher. 1996. "Facing Up to the Risks of Climate Change." In Lester R. Brown, Christopher Flavin, and Linda Starke, eds., *State of the World 1996. A Worldwatch Institute Report on Progress Toward a Sustainable Society.* New York, N.Y.: Norton.

Fölster, Stephan. 1996. "Social Insurance Based on Personal Savings Accounts: A Possible Reform Strategy for Overburdened Welfare States." Industrial Institute for Economic and Social Research, Stockholm.

Forster, Michael. 1994. *The Effects of Net Transfers on Low Income Among Non-Elderly Families.* OECD Economic Studies No. 22. Paris: OECD.

Francis, Paul, J. A. Akinwumi, P. Ngwu, S. A. Nkom, J. Odihi, J. A. Olomajeye, F. Okunmadewa, and D. J. Shehu. 1996. *State, Community and Local Development in Nigeria.* World Bank Technical Paper No. 336. Africa Region Series. Washington, D.C.: World Bank.

Francks, Penelope. 1992. *Japanese Economic Development: Theory and Practice.* London and New York, N.Y.: Routledge.

Freedom House. Various issues. *Freedom in the World: The Annual Survey of Political Rights and Civil Liberties.* New York, N.Y.: Freedom House.

Freeman, Richard B., Birgitta Swedenborg, and Robert Topel. 1995. "Economic Troubles in Sweden's Welfare State: Introduction, Summary, and Conclusions." NBER/SNS Project Reforming the Welfare State Occasional Paper No. 69. National Bureau of Economic Research, Cambridge, Mass.

Frey, Bruno S., and Reiner Eichenberger. 1994. "The Political Economy of Stabilization Programmes in Developing Countries." *European Journal of Political Economy* 10: 169–90.

Fuhr, Harald, Klaus Simon, and Albrecht Stockmayer, eds. 1993. *Subsidiarität in der Entwicklungszusammenarbeit: Dezentralisierung und Verwaltungsreformen zwischen Strukturanpassung und Selbsthilfe.* Baden-Baden, Germany: Nomos Verlagsgesellschaft.

Fukuyama, Francis. 1995. *Trust: The Social Virtues and the Creation of Prosperity.* New York, N.Y.: Simon & Schuster.

Galal, Ahmed. 1996. "Chile: Regulatory Specificity, Credibility of Commitment, and Distributional Demands." In Brian Levy and Pablo Spiller, eds., *Regulations, Institutions and Commitment: Comparative Studies of Telecommunications.* Cambridge, England: Cambridge University Press.

Galal, Ahmed, Leroy Jones, Pankaj Tandon, and Ingo Vogelsang. 1994. *Welfare Consequences of Selling Public Enterprises: An Empirical Analysis.* New York, N.Y.: Oxford University Press.

Gemmell, Norman, ed. 1993. *The Growth of the Public Sector.* London: Edward Elgar.

Gould, Julius, and William L. Kolb. 1964. *A Dictionary of the Social Sciences.* New York, N.Y.: Free Press of Glencoe.

Graham, Carol, and Cheikh Kane. 1996. "Opportunistic Government or Sustaining Reform? Electoral Trends and Public Expenditure Patterns in Peru, 1990–1995." Poverty and Social Policy Department Discussion Paper Series 89. Human Capital Development and Operations Policy Department, World Bank, Washington D.C.

Graham, Carol, and Moises Naím. 1997. "The Political Economy of Institutional Reform in Latin America." Paper presented to the MacArthur Foundation/IDB Conference on Inequality Reducing Growth in Latin America's Market Economies, January 28–29.

Gray, Cheryl. 1996. "In Search of Owners: Privatization and Corporate Governance in Transition Economies." *World Bank Research Observer* 11(2): 179–97.

Greenwood, Roystone, C. R. Hinnings, and Stewart Ranson. 1975. "Contingency Theory and the Organization of Local Authorities. Part 1: Differentiation and Integration." *Public Administration* 53: 1–23.

Gruber, Jonathan. 1994. "The Consumption Smoothing Benefits of Unemployment Insurance." NBER Working Paper Series No. 4750. National Bureau of Economic Research, Cambridge, Mass.

Guasch, J. Luis, and Pablo T. Spiller. 1997. *Managing the Regulatory Process: Concepts, Issues and the Latin America and Caribbean Story Book.* Directions in Development Series. Washington, D.C.: World Bank and Johns Hopkins University Press.

Guerrero, Rodrigo. 1996. "Epidemiology of Violence: The Case of Cali, Colombia." Paper presented at the Second Annual World Bank Conference on Development in Latin America and the Caribbean, Bogotá, Colombia, July.

Guhan, S., and Samuel Paul, eds. 1997. *Corruption in India: Agenda for Action.* New Delhi: Vision Books.

Gupta, Sanjeev, Jerald Schiff, and Benedict Clements. 1996. "Drop in World Military Spending Yields Large Dividend." *IMF Survey* (June 3).

Gurr, Ted Robert, Keith Jaggers, and Will H. Moore. 1990. "The Transformation of the Western State: The Growth of Democracy, Autocracy, and State Power Since 1800." *Studies in Comparative International Development* 25(1): 73–108.

Gustafsson, Bo. 1995. "Foundations of the Swedish Model." *Nordic Journal of Political Economy* 22: 5–26.

Gwartney, James D., Robert Lawson, and Walter Block. 1996. *Economic Freedom of the World, 1975–1995.* Vancouver: Fraser Institute.

Haggard, Stephan, and Steven B. Webb, eds. 1994. *Voting for Reform: Democracy, Political Liberalization, and Economic Adjustment.* New York, N.Y.: Oxford University Press.

Hahn, Robert W., ed. 1996. *Risks, Costs and Lives Saved: Getting Better Results from Regulation.* New York, N.Y.: Oxford University Press.

Hammer, Jeffrey S. 1997. "Economic Analysis for Health Projects." *World Bank Research Observer* 12(1): 47–71.

Haque, Nadeem Ul, and Ratna Sahay. 1996. "Do Government Wage Cuts Close Budget Deficits? Costs of Corruption." *IMF Staff Papers* 43(4): 754–78.

Helm, Dieter, ed. 1989. *The Economic Borders of the State.* Oxford, England: Oxford University Press.

Hesse, Jems-Joachim. 1993. "From Transformation to Modernization: Administrative Change in Central and Eastern Europe." *Public Administration* 71 (Spring-Summer): 219–57.

Heyneman, Stephen P. Forthcoming. "Education Choice in Eastern Europe and the Former Soviet Union: A Review Essay." *Education Economics.*

Hirsch, Joachim. 1995. *Der nationale Wettbewerbstaat: Staat, Demokratie, und Politik, in globalen Kapitalismus.* Berlin: Edition ID-Archiv.

Hirschman, Albert O. 1970. *Exit, Voice, and Loyalty: Responses to Decline in Firms, Organizations and States.* Cambridge, Mass.: Harvard University Press.

Ho, Luu Bich. 1997. "The Government's Role in Market-oriented Economic Renovation Process in Viet Nam." Paper presented at the International Symposium on Government's Role in the Market Economy, China Institute for Reform and Development, Haikou, China, January 7–8.

Hoekman, Bernard M. 1995. *Trade Laws and Institutions: Good Practices and the World Trade Organization.* World Bank Discussion Paper No. 282. Washington, D.C.: World Bank.

Holmes, Malcolm, and Anirudh Krishna. 1996. "Public Sector Management and Participation: Institutional Support for Sustainable Development." In Jennifer Rietbergen-McCracken, ed., *Participation in Practice: The Experience of the World Bank and Other Stakeholders,* pp. 29–35. World Bank Discussion Paper No. 333. Washington, D.C.: World Bank

Holsti, K. J. 1995. "War, Peace, and the State of the State." *International Political Science Review* 16(4): 319–39.

Holtzman, Steven. 1995. "Post Conflict Reconstruction." Environment Department, Social Policy and Resettlement Division, World Bank, Washington, D.C.

Hommes, Rudolf. 1995. "Conflicts and Dilemmas of Decentralization." In Michael Bruno and Boris Pleskovic, eds., *Annual World Bank Conference on Development Economics,* pp. 331–50. Washington, D.C.: World Bank.

Huber, Evelyne, Charles Ragin, and John D. Stephens. 1993. "Social Democracy, Christian Democracy, Constitutional Structure, and the Welfare State." *American Journal of Sociology* 99(3): 711–49.

Hulten, Charles R. 1996. "Infrastructure and Economic Development: Once More into the Breach." Department of Economics, University of Maryland, College Park, Md.

Humphrey, John, and Hubert Schmitz. 1995. "Principles for Promoting Clusters and Networks of Small and Medium Enterprises." Discussion Paper No. 1. Small and Medium Enterprise Branch, United Nations Industrial Development Organization, New York, N.Y.

Huntington, Samuel P. 1991. *The Third Wave: Democratization in the Late Twentieth Century.* Norman: University of Oklahoma Press.

ILO (International Labour Office). Various years. *The Cost of Social Security.* Geneva: ILO.

ILO (International Labour Organisation). 1986. *Yearbook of Labor Statistics.* Geneva: ILO.

_____. 1994. *Yearbook of Labor Statistics.* Geneva: ILO.

IMF (International Monetary Fund). 1986. *Manual on Government Finance Statistics.* Washington, D.C.: IMF.

_____. 1996. *World Economic Outlook.* Washington, D.C.: IMF.

_____. Various years—a. *Government Statistics Yearbook.* Washington, D.C.: IMF.

_____. Various years—b. *International Financial Statistics.* Washington, D.C.: IMF.

India Today. 1996. "The Maturity of Democracy." (August 31).

International Country Risk Guide. Various issues. New York, N.Y.: International Reports.

International Political Science Review. 1996. *New Trends in Federalism.* Special edition of *International Political Science Review* 17(4).

Inter-Parliamentary Union. 1996. "Women in Parliament as at 30 June 1995." Inter-Parliamentary Union, Geneva.

Isham, Jonathan, Daniel Kaufmann, and Lant Pritchett. 1995. "Governance and the Returns to Investment: An Empirical Investigation." World Bank Policy Research Working Paper No. 1550. Policy Research Department, Poverty and Human Resources Division, World Bank, Washington, D.C.

Isham, Jonathan, Deepa Narayan, and Lant Pritchett. 1995. "Does Participation Improve Performance? Establishing Causality with Subjective Data." *World Bank Economic Review* 9(2): 175–200.

Ishikawa, Shigeru. 1990. *Basic Issues of Development Economics.* Tokyo: Iwanami Shoten (in Japanese).

_____. 1996. "From Development Economics to Development Aid Policy." In S. Ishikawa, ed., *Theoretical Studies on Development Aid Policy.* Tokyo: Institute of Development Economics (in Japanese).

Israel, Arturo. 1990. "The Changing Role of the State: Institutional Dimensions." PRE Working Paper WPS 495. Country Economics Department, World Bank, Washington, D.C.

_____. 1997. "A Guide for the Perplexed: Institutional Aspects of Social Programs." SOC 96–105. Inter-American Development Bank, Washington, D.C.

Itoh, Motoshige, Kazuharu Kiyono, Masahiro Okuno, and Kotaro Suzumura. 1988. *Economic Analysis of Industrial Policy.* Tokyo: Tokyo University Press (in Japanese).

Jaggers, Keith, and Ted Robert Gurr. 1995. "Tracking Democracy's Third Wave with the Polity III Data." *Journal of Peace Research* 32(4): 469–82.

_____. 1996. "Polity III: Regime Type and Political Authority, 1800–1994." Inter-University Consortium for Political and Social Research, Ann Arbor, Mich.

Jalali, Rita, and Seymour M. Lipset. 1992–93. "Racial and Ethnic Conflicts: A Global Perspective." *Political Science Quarterly* 107(4).

Jalan, Bimal. 1992. *The Indian Economy: Problems and Prospects.* New Delhi: Penguin Books India.

Jhabvala, Renana, and Ela Bhatt. n.d. "The World of Work in the People's Sector: And Its Inherent Strength. The SEWA Experience." The Self-Employed Women's Association, Ahmedabad, India.

Jun, Jong S., and Deil S. Wright, eds. 1996. *Globalization and Decentralization: Institutional Contexts, Policy Issues and Intergovernmental Relations in Japan and the United States.* Washington, D.C.: Georgetown University Press.

Ka, Samba, and Nicolas van de Walle. 1994. "Senegal: Stalled Reform in a Dominant Party System." In Stephan Haggard and Stephen B. Webb, *Voting for Reform: Democracy, Political Liberalization, and Economic Adjustment,* pp. 290–359. New York, N.Y.: Oxford University Press.

Kabeer, Naila. 1994. *Reversed Realities: Gender Hierarchies in Development Thought.* London: Verso.

Kane, Cheikh T. 1995. "Uruguay: Options for Pension Reform." Education and Social Policy Paper Series No. 68. Human Resources Development and Operations Policy Department, World Bank, Washington, D.C.

Kane, Cheikh, and Robert Palacios. 1996. "The Implicit Pension Debt." *Finance and Development* 33 (June): 36–38.

Kangle, K. P. 1965. *The Kautiliya Arthashastra: An English Translation with Critical and Explanatory Notes.* Delhi: Motilal Banarsidass Publishers.

Kanter, Rosabeth Moss. 1995. "Thriving Locally in the Global Economy." *Harvard Business Review* (September-October): 151–60.

Kaufmann, Daniel. 1996. "Listening to Stakeholders on Development Challenges and World Bank Instruments in their Countries: Myths Meet Some Evidence on Corruption, Economic Reforms, and Bank Programs." Harvard Institute for International Development, Harvard University, Cambridge, Mass., and World Bank, Washington, D.C.

Keefer, Philip, and Stephen Knack. 1995. "The Effects of Institutions on Public Investment." Policy Research Department, World Bank, Washington, D.C.; IRIS/University of Maryland, College Park, Md.; and School of Public Affairs, American University, Washington, D.C.

Khaldaun, Ibn. n.d. *The Muqaddimah.* Translated with an Introduction by Franz Rosenthal. Princeton, N.J.: Princeton University Press.

Kim, Hyung-Ki, Michio Muramatsu, T. J. Pempel, and Kozo Yamamura, eds. 1995. *The Japanese Civil Service and Economic Development: Catalysts of Change.* Oxford, England: Clarendon Press.

Klingemann, Hans-Dieter, and Dieter Fuchs, eds. 1995. *Beliefs in Government. Volume 1: Citizens and the State.* New York, N.Y.: Oxford University Press.

Klitgaard, Robert. 1988. *Controlling Corruption.* Berkeley, Calif.: University of California Press.

_____. *Tropical Gangsters.* New York, N.Y.: Basic Books.

Knack, Stephen, and Philip Keefer. 1995. "Institutions and Economic Performance: Cross-Country Tests Using Alternative Institutional Measures." *Economics and Politics* 7(3): 207–27.

Knight, Malcolm, Norman Loayza, and Delano Villanueva. 1995. "The Peace Dividend: Military Spending Cuts and Economic Growth." IMF Working Paper No. WP/95/53.

Middle Eastern Department, International Monetary Fund, Washington, D.C.

Kohli, Atul. 1994. "Where Do High Growth Political Economies Come From? The Japanese Lineage of Korea's 'Development State.'" *World Development* 22: 1269–93.

König, Klaus. 1996. "Policy Planning and Management Dialogue with Countries in Transition." *Public Administration and Development* 16: 417–29.

_____. 1997. "Drei Welten der Verwaltungsmodernisierung." In Klaus Lüder, ed., *Staat und Verwaltung: Funfzig Jahre Hochschule für Verwaltungswissenschaften,* pp. 399–424. Berlin: Duncker & Humblot.

Kormendi, Roger, and Philip Meguire. 1985. "Macroeconomic Determinants of Growth: Cross-Country Evidence." *Journal of Monetary Economics* 16(2): 141–63.

Kraay, Aart, and Caroline Van Rijckeghem. 1995. "Employment and Wages in the Public Sector: A Cross-Country Study." IMF Working Paper WP/95/70. Fiscal Affairs Department, International Monetary Fund, Washington, D.C.

Kubota, Isao. 1996. "Roles That Governments Play in Developing, Developed States." *Japan Times,* June 17, p. 15.

Kuper, Adam, and Jessica Kuper, eds. 1996. *The Social Science Encyclopedia,* 2nd ed. London and New York, N.Y.: Routledge.

Laking, R. G. 1996. "Good Practice in Public Sector Management: Issues for the World Bank." Poverty and Social Policy Department, World Bank, Washington, D.C.

Lalor, R. Peter, and Hernan Garcia. 1996. "Reshaping Power Markets in South America." *Electricity Journal* 9(2): 63–71.

Landau, D. 1986. "Government and Economic Growth in Less Developed Countries: An Empirical Study for 1960–1980." *Economic Development and Cultural Change* 35(1): 35–75.

_____. 1993. "The Economic Impact of Military Expenditures." World Bank Policy Research Working Paper No. WPS 1138. Policy Research Department, World Bank, Washington, D.C.

Latinobarometro. 1996. "Press Release: Latinobarometro Survey 1996." Latinobarometro, Santiago, Chile.

Lau, Lawrence, and D. H. Song. 1992. "Growth versus Privatization—An Alternative Strategy to Reduce the Public Enterprise Sector: The Experiences of Taiwan and South Korea." Working Paper, Department of Economics, Stanford University, Stanford, Calif.

Lawrence, Robert Z., Albert Bressand, and Takatoshi Ito. 1996. *A Vision for the World Economy.* Washington, D.C.: Brookings Institution.

Leftwich, Adrian, ed. 1996. *Democracy and Development: Theory and Practice.* Cambridge, England, and Cambridge, Mass: Polity Press in association with Blackwell Publishers.

Leonard, David K., and Dale Rogers Marshall. 1982. "Institutions of the Rural Development for the Poor: Decentralization and Organizational Linkages." Institute of International Studies, University of California, Berkeley, Calif.

Letowski, Janusz. 1993. "Polish Public Administration Between Crisis and Renewal." *Public Administration* 71 (Spring-Summer): 1–11.

Levine, Ross, and David Renelt. 1992. "A Sensitivity Analysis of Cross-Country Growth Regressions." *American Economic Review* 82(4): 942–63.

Levy, Brian, and Pablo Spiller. 1994. "The Institutional Foundations of Regulatory Commitment: A Comparative Analysis of Telecommunications and Regulation." *Journal of Law, Economics and Organization* 10(2): 201–46.

Levy, Brian, and Pablo Spiller, eds. 1996. *Regulations, Institutions and Commitment: Comparative Studies of Telecommunications.* Cambridge, England: Cambridge University Press.

Levy, Brian, Albert Berry, Motoshige Itoh, Linsu Kim, Jeffrey Nugent, and Shujiro Urata. 1994. "Technical and Marketing Support Systems for Successful Small and Medium-Size Enterprises in Four Countries." World Bank Policy Research Working Paper No. 1400. Policy Research Department, Finance and Private Sector Division, World Bank, Washington, D.C.

Lewis, Bernard. 1961. *The Emergence of Modern Turkey.* London and New York, N.Y.: Oxford University Press.

Libecap, Gary D. 1996. "Economic Variables and the Development of Law: The Case of Western Mineral Rights." In Lee J. Alston, Thrainn Eggertsson, and Douglass C. North, eds., *Empirical Studies in Institutional Change.* New York, N.Y.: Cambridge University Press.

Lijphart, Arendt. 1969. "Consociational Democracy." *World Politics* 21.

_____. 1995. "The Virtues of Parliamentarism: But Which Kind of Parliamentarism?" In H. E. Chenabi and Alfred Stepan, eds., *Politics, Society, and Democracy: Comparative Studies.* Boulder, Colo.: Westview Press.

Lijphart, Arendt, and Carlos H. Waisman, eds. 1996. *Institutional Design in New Democracies: Eastern Europe and Latin America.* Boulder, Colo.: Westview Press.

Lim, Linda Y., and Peter Gosling, eds. 1983. *The Chinese in Southeast Asia,* vol. 1. Singapore: Naruyen Asia.

Lin, Justin Yifu. 1996. "Comparative Advantage, Development Policy, and the East Asian Miracles." Peking University, Hong Kong University of Science and Technology, and Australian National University.

Lin, Justin Yifu, Fang Cai, and Zhou Li. 1996. *The China Miracle: Development Strategy and Economic Reform.* A Friedman Lecture Fund Monograph. Hong Kong: The Chinese University Press.

Lindauer, David. 1988. "The Size and Growth of Government Spending." Policy Working Paper WPS 44. World Bank, Washington, D.C.

Lindauer, David, and Barbara Nunberg, eds. 1994. *Rehabilitating Government: Pay and Employment Reform in Africa.* Washington, D.C.: World Bank.

Lindbeck, Assar. 1995. "Hazardous Welfare State Dynamics." Reprint Series No. 538. Institute for International Economic Studies, Stockholm University, Stockholm.

Lindbeck, Assar, Per Molander, Torsten Persson, Olof Petersson, Agnar Sandmo, Birgitta Swedenborg, and Niels Thygesen. 1994. *Turning Sweden Around.* Cambridge, Mass.: MIT Press.

Linz, Juan J., Seymour Martin Lipset, and Amy Bunger Pool. n.d. "Social Conditions for Democracy in Latin America: Latin American Barometer Survey Analysis." Yale University, New Haven, Conn.

Linz, Juan J., and Alfred Stepan, eds. 1996. *Problems of Democratic Transition and Consolidation: Southern Europe, South America, and Post Communist Europe.* Baltimore, Md.: Johns Hopkins University Press.

Lipset, Seymour Martin. 1979. *The First New Nation: The United States in Historical & Comparative Perspective.* New York, N.Y.: W. W. Norton & Company.

_____. 1996. *American Exceptionalism: A Double Edged Sword.* New York, N.Y.: W. W. Norton.

Lovei, Magda, and Charles Weiss, Jr. 1996. "Environmental Management and Institutions in OECD Countries: Experience and Lessons Learned." Environment Department, World Bank, Washington, D.C.

Lundahl, Mats. 1992. *Politics or Markets?: Essays on Haitian Underdevelopment.* London and New York, N.Y.: Routledge.

Lybeck, J. A. 1986. *The Growth of Government in Developed Economies.* Aldershot, Hants, England, and Brookfield, Vt.: Gower.

Ma, Jun. 1996. *Intergovernmental Relations and Economic Management in China.* Houndsmill, Basingstoke, and London: Macmillan.

Machiavelli, Niccolò. 1513. *The Prince.* Translated with an Introduction by George Bull. London: Penguin Books, 1981.

Mainwaring, Scott. 1991. "Politicians, Parties, and Electoral Systems: Brazil in Comparative Perspective." *Comparative Politics* (October): 21–43.

Manion, Melanie. 1996. "Policy Instruments and Political Context: Transforming a Culture of Corruption in Hong Kong." Paper presented at the Annual Meeting of the Association for Asian Studies, Honolulu, Ha., April 11–14.

Manor, James. 1996. "The Political Economy of Decentralization." Agriculture and Natural Resources Department, World Bank, Washington, D.C.

Margulis, Sergio. 1996. "Environmental Regulation: Instruments and Actual Implementation." Environment Department, World Bank, Washington, D.C.

Margulis, Sergio, and Paulo Pereira de Gusmao. 1996. "Problems of Environmental Management in the Real World: The Rio de Janeiro Experience." Environment Department, World Bank, Washington, D.C.

Martin, Brendan. 1993. *In The Public Interest?: Privatization and Public Sector Reform* London: Zed Books.

Mauro, Paolo. 1995. "Corruption and Growth." *Quarterly Journal of Economics* 110: 681–712.

McLure, Charles E., Jr. 1994. "The Sharing of Taxes on Natural Resources and the Future of the Russian Federation." In Christine I. Wallich, ed., *Russia and the Challenge of Fiscal Federalism,* pp. 181–217. World Bank Regional and Sectoral Studies. Washington, D.C.: World Bank.

_____. 1995. "Comment on Prud'homme." *World Bank Research Observer* 10(2): 221–26.

Meltzer, Alan, and S. F. Richard. 1981. "A Rational Theory of the Size of Government." *Journal of Political Economy* 89: 914–27.

Metropolitan Environment Improvement Program. 1996. "Japan's Experience in Urban Environmental Management—Yokohama: A Case Study." United Nations Development Programme, New York, N.Y., and World Bank, Washington, D.C.

Milgrom, Paul R., Douglass C. North, and Barry R. Weingast. 1990. "The Role of Institutions in the Revival of Trade: The Law Merchant, Private Judges, and the Champagne Fairs." *Economics and Politics* 2(1): 1–23.

Montgomery, John D. 1988. *Bureaucrats and People: Grassroots Participation in Third World Development.* Baltimore, Md: Johns Hopkins University Press.

Montinola, Gabriella, Yingyi Qian, and Barry R. Weingast. 1995. "Federalism, Chinese Style: The Political Basis for Economic Success in China." *World Politics* 48: 50–81.

Mosley, Paul, Jane Harrigan, and John Toye. 1995. *Aid and Power: The World Bank and Policy-Based Lending. Vol. 1, Analysis and Policy Proposals,* 2nd ed. London and New York, N.Y.: Routledge.

Moser, Caroline. 1996. *Confronting Crisis: A Comparative Study of Household Responses to Poverty and Vulnerability in Four Urban Communities.* Environmentally Sustainable Development Studies and Monographs Series No. 8. Washington, D.C.: World Bank.

Mubarak, Jamil Abdalla. 1996. *From Bad Policy to Chaos in Somalia: How an Economy Fell Apart.* London: Praeger.

Mueller, D. C. 1989. *Public Choice II.* Cambridge, England: Cambridge University Press.

Mugoya, Ndungu. 1996. "Tribalism and the Politics of Patronage in Kenya." *Finance* 31 (May): 14–18.

Murphy, Ricardo López, ed. 1995. *Fiscal Decentralization in Latin America.* Washington, D.C.: Inter-American Development Bank.

Musgrave, R. A. 1976. "Adam Smith on Public Finance and Distribution." In Thomas Wilson and Andrew Skinner, eds., *The Market and the State: Essays in Honour of Adam Smith.* Oxford, England: Oxford University Press.

Naím, Moises. 1995. "Latin America's Journey to the Market: From Macroeconomic Shocks to Institutional Therapy." International Center for Economic Growth Occasional Paper No. 62. San Francisco, Calif.: Institute for Contemporary Studies Press.

Narayan, Deepa. 1995. "The Contribution of People's Participation: Evidence from 121 Rural Water Supply Projects." Environmentally Sustainable Development Occasional Paper Series No. 1. World Bank, Washington, D.C.

Narayan, Deepa, and Lant Pritchett. 1997. "Cents and Sociability: Household Income and Social Capital in Rural Tanzania." Environment Department and Policy Research Department, World Bank, Washington, D.C.

National Bureau of Economic Research. 1997. *Penn World Tables, Mark 5.6.* http://nber.harvard.edu/pwt56.html.

Navarro, Juan Carlos. 1996. "Reversal of Fortune: The Ephemeral Success of Adjustment in Venezuela, 1989–93." In Leila Frischtak and Izak Atiyas, eds., *Governance, Leadership, Communication: Building Constituencies for Economic Reform. Essays on Venezuela, Malaysia, Tanzania, Bolivia, Egypt, Ghana, Pakistan, Turkey, Brazil.* Washington, D.C.: World Bank Private Sector Development Department.

Ndulu, Benno, and Nicholas van de Walle, eds. 1996. *Agenda for Africa's Economic Renewal.* New Brunswick, N.J., and Oxford, England: Transaction Publishers.

Nellis, John R., and Dennis A. Rondinelli. 1986. "Assessing Decentralization Policies in Developing Countries: The Case for Cautious Optimism." *Development Policy Review* 4(1): 3–23.

Noonan, John T., Jr. 1994. *Bribes*. Berkeley, Calif.: University of California Press.

North, Douglass. 1990. *Institutions, Institutional Change and Economic Performance*. Cambridge, England: Cambridge University Press.

_____. 1993. Paper prepared for the Nobel Prize Lecture in Economic Science, Stockholm.

Nunberg, Barbara. 1995. *Managing the Civil Service: Reform Lessons from Advanced Industrialized Countries*. World Bank Discussion Paper No. 204. Washington, D.C.: World Bank.

_____. Forthcoming. *The State After Communism: Administrative Transitions in Central and Eastern Europe*. Public Management Division, ECA-MENA Technical Department, World Bank, Washington, D.C.

Oates, Wallace E. 1972. *Fiscal Federalism*. New York, N.Y.: Harcourt Brace Jovanovich.

_____. 1985. "Searching for the Leviathan: An Empirical Study." *American Economic Review* 74(4): 748–57.

OECD (Organization for Economic Cooperation and Development). 1993. *Managing with Market-Type Mechanisms*. Paris: OECD/PUMA.

_____. 1994. *DAC Orientations on Participatory Development and Good Governance*, Vol. 2, No. 2. OECD Working Papers. Paris: OECD.

_____. 1996. "Social Expenditure Statistics of OECD Member Countries (Provisional Version)." Labor Market and Social Policy Occasional Papers No. 17. Paris: OECD.

_____. Various years. *OECD Economic Outlook*. Paris: OECD.

Office of the United Nations High Commissioner for Refugees. 1995. *The State of the World's Refugees: In Search of Solutions*. New York, N.Y.: Office of the United Nations High Commissioner for Refugees.

Ohno, Kenichi. 1996. "Replicability of Selective Industrial Policy: The Case of Five Capital-Intensive Industries in Vietnam." Saitama University and Tsukuba University, Japan.

Okazaki, Tetsuji. 1997. "The Government-Firm Relationship in Postwar Japanese Economic Recovery: Co-ordinating the Co-ordination Failure in Industrial Rationalization." In Masahiko Aoki, Hyung-Ki Kim, and Masahiro Okuno-Fujiwara, eds., *The Role of Government in East Asian Economic Development: Comparative Institutional Analysis*. Oxford, England: Oxford University Press.

Olson, Mancur, Jr. 1971. *The Logic of Collective Action*. Cambridge, Mass.: Harvard University Press.

_____. 1996. "Big Bills Left on the Sidewalks: Why Some Nations are Rich, and Others Poor." *Journal of Economic Perspectives* 10(2): 3–24.

Orstrom, Elinor. 1996. "Crossing the Divide: Co-production, Synergy and Development." *World Development* 24(6): 1073–87.

Orstrom, Elinor, Larry Schroeder, and Susan Wynne. 1993. *Institutional Incentives and Sustainable Development: Infrastructure Policies in Perspective*. Boulder, Colo., San Francisco, Calif., and Oxford, England: Westview Press.

Osborne, David, and Ted Gaebler. 1993. *Reinventing Government: How the Entrepreneurial Spirit Is Transforming the Public Sector*. New York, N.Y.: Penguin.

Ottaway, Marina. 1994. *Democratization and Ethnic Nationalism: African and Eastern European Experiences*. Policy Essay No. 14. Washington, D.C.: Overseas Development Council.

Oxley, Les. 1994. "Cointegration, Causality and Wagner's Law: A Test for Britain, 1870–1913." *Scottish Journal of Political Economy* 41(3): 286–98.

Pardey, Philip G., and others. 1996. *Hidden Harvest: U.S. Benefits from International Research Aid*. Washington, D.C. International Food Policy Research Institute.

Pasha, Hafiz. 1996. "Governance and Fiscal Reform: A Study of Pakistan." In Leila Frischtak and Izak Atiyas, eds., *Governance, Leadership, Communication: Building Constituencies for Economic Reform. Essays on Venezuela, Malaysia, Tanzania, Bolivia, Egypt, Ghana, Pakistan, Turkey, Brazil*. Washington, D.C.: World Bank Private Sector Development Department.

Paul, Samuel. 1994. "Does Voice Matter? For Public Accountability, Yes." Policy Research Working Paper No. 1388. Policy Research Department, Finance and Private Sector Development Division, World Bank, Washington, D.C.

Peacock, A. T., and J. Wiseman. 1961. *The Growth of Public Expenditure in the United Kingdom*. NBER General Series No. 72. Princeton, N.J.: Princeton University Press.

Peters, B. Guy. 1996. *The Future of Governing: Four Emerging Models*. Lawrence, Kan.: University Press of Kansas.

Peterson, George E. 1997. *Decentralization in Latin America: Learning Through Experience*. World Bank Latin American and Caribbean Studies. Washington, D.C.: World Bank.

Peterson, Paul E. 1995. *The Price of Federalism*. A Twentieth Century Fund Book. Washington, D.C.: Brookings Institution.

Picciotto, Robert. 1995. *Putting International Economics to Work: From Participation to Governance*. World Bank Discussion Paper No. 304. Washington, D.C.: World Bank.

_____. 1996. "What Is Education Worth? From Production Function to Institutional Capital." Human Capital Development Working Papers No. 75. World Bank, Washington, D.C.

Picks Currency Yearbook. Various years. New York, N.Y.: Pick Publishing.

Pierson, Paul. 1994. *Dismantling the Welfare State*. New York, N.Y.: Cambridge University Press.

Pitschas, Rainer, and Rolf Sülzer, eds. 1995. *New Institutionalism in Development Policy: Perspectives and General Conditions of Public Administration Development in the South and East*. Berlin: Duncker and Humblot.

Platteau, Jean Philippe. 1991. "Traditional Systems of Social Security." In E. Ahmad and others, eds., *Social Security in Developing Countries*. Oxford, England: Oxford University Press.

Polizatto, Vincent P. 1992. "Prudential Regulation and Banking Supervision." In Dimitri Vittas, ed., *Financial Regulation: Changing the Rules of the Game*. EDI Development Studies. Washington, D.C.: World Bank.

Poterba, James M. 1994. "State Responses to Fiscal Crises: The Effect of Budgetary Institutions and Politics." *Journal of Political Economy* 102(4): 799.

Pradhan, Sanjay. 1996. *Evaluating Public Spending: A Framework for Public Expenditure Review.* World Bank Discussion Paper No. 323. Washington, D.C.: World Bank.

Pritchett, Lant, and L. H. Summers. 1996. "Wealthier Is Healthier." *Journal of Human Resources* 1(4): 841–68.

Prud'homme, Rémy. 1995. "The Dangers of Decentralization." *World Bank Research Observer* 10(2): 201–20.

Psacharopoulos, George. 1995. *Building Human Capital for Better Lives.* Washington, D.C.: World Bank.

Psacharopoulos, George, and Nguyen Xuan Nguyen. 1997. *The Role of Government and the Private Sector in Fighting Poverty.* World Bank Technical Paper No. 346. Washington, D.C.: World Bank.

Psacharopoulos, George, and P. Zafiris Tzannatos. 1992. *Women's Employment and Pay in Latin America: Overview and Methodology.* World Bank Regional and Sectoral Studies. Washington, D.C.: World Bank.

Putnam, Robert, with Robert Leonardi and Rafaella Y. Nanetti. 1993. *Making Democracy Work: Civic Traditions in Modern Italy.* Princeton, N.J.: Princeton University Press.

Quah, Jon. 1993. "Controlling Corruption in City-States: A Comparative Study of Hong Kong and Singapore." Paper presented at a conference on "The East Asian Miracle: Economic Growth and Public Policy," Stanford University, Palo Alto, Calif., October 25–26.

Ram, Rati. 1986. "Government Size and Economic Growth: A New Framework and Some Evidence from Cross-Section and Time-Series Data." *American Economic Review* 76(1): 191–203.

_____. 1987. "Wagner's Hypothesis in Time Series and Cross-Section Perspectives: Evidence from 'Real' Data for 115 Countries." *Review of Economics and Statistics* 69: 194–204.

Ramey, Garey, and Valerie Ramey. 1995. "Cross-Country Evidence on the Link Between Volatility and Growth." *American Economic Review* 85(5): 1138–51.

Reinert, Erik S. 1996. "The Role of the State in Economic Growth." Paper prepared for a conference on The Rise and Fall of Public Enterprises in Western Countries in Milan, October 10–12.

Rietbergen-McCracken, Jennifer, ed. 1996. *Participation in Practice: The Experience of the World Bank and Other Stakeholders.* World Bank Discussion Paper No. 333. Washington, D.C.: World Bank.

Rodrik, Dani. 1996. "Why Do More Open Economies Have Larger Governments?" John F. Kennedy School of Government, Harvard University, Cambridge, Mass.

Romer, Paul M. 1994. "The Origins of Endogenous Growth." *Journal of Economic Perspectives* 8(1): 3–22.

Rose, Richard, and Christian Haerpfer. 1990. "New Democracies Barometer III: Learning from What is Happening," *Studies in Public Policy.*

Rose-Ackerman, Susan. 1978. *Corruption: A Study in Political Economy.* New York, N.Y.: Academic Press.

_____. 1992. *Rethinking the Progressive Agenda: The Reform of the American Regulatory State.* New York, N.Y.: Free Press.

_____. 1995. *Controlling Environmental Policy: The Limits of Public Law in Germany and the United States.* New Haven, Conn.: Yale University Press.

_____. Forthcoming. "The Political Economy of Corruption." In Kimberly Ann Elliott, ed., *Corruption in the World Economy.* Washington, D.C.: Institute for International Economics.

Roy, Jayanta, ed. 1995. *Macroeconomic Management and Fiscal Decentralization.* EDI Seminar Series. Washington, D.C.: World Bank.

Ruzindana, Augustine. 1995. "Combating Corruption in Uganda." In Petter Langseth, J. Katorobo, E. Brett, and J. Munene, eds., *Uganda: Landmarks in Rebuilding a Nation.* Kampala: Fountain Publishers.

Salamon, Lester M., and Helmut K. Anheier. 1994. *The Emerging Sector—An Overview.* Baltimore, Md.: The Johns Hopkins University Institute for Policy Studies.

_____. 1996. "The Nonprofit Sector: A New Global Force." Working Paper No. 21. The Johns Hopkins Comparative Nonprofit Sector Project, The Johns Hopkins University Institute for Policy Studies, Baltimore, Md.

Saunders, Anthony, and Berry Wilson. 1995. "Contingent Liability in Banking: Useful Policy for Developing Countries?" World Bank Policy Research Working Paper No. 1538. Policy Research Department, Finance and Private Sector Development Division, World Bank, Washington, D.C.

Scharpf, Fritz W. 1994. *Optionen des Föderalismus in Deutschland und Europa.* Frankfurt, Germany, and New York, N.Y.: Campus Verlag.

Schwart, Joseph. 1994. "Democratic Solidarity and the Crisis of the Welfare State." In Lyman Legters, John Burke, and Arthur Diquatro, eds., *Critical Perspectives on Democracy.* Lanham, Md.: Rowman & Littlefield.

Scott, Graham. 1995. "Improving Fiscal Responsibility." Extract from *Agenda: A Journal of Policy Analysis and Reform* 2(1): 3–16. Heidelberg, Victoria, Australia.

_____. 1996. "The Use of Contracting in the Public Sector." *Australian Journal of Public Administration* 55(3).

Sen, Amartya. 1987. *The Standard of Living.* Cambridge, England: Cambridge University Press.

Senghaas, Dieter. 1985. *The European Experience: A Historical Critique of Development Theories.* Oxford, England: Berg Publishers.

Serven, Luis, and Andres Solimano, eds. 1994. *Striving for Growth after Adjustment: The Role of Capital Formation.* Washington, D.C.: World Bank.

Shah, Anwar. 1994. *The Reform of Intergovernmental Fiscal Relations in Developing and Emerging Market Economies.* Washington, D.C.: World Bank.

_____. 1997. "Fostering Responsible and Accountable Performance: Lessons from Decentralization Experience." Paper presented at the OED Annual Conference, World Bank, Washington, D.C., April 1–2.

Sheng, Andrew. 1992. "Bank Restructuring in Malaysia." In Dimitri Vittas, ed. *Financial Regulation: Changing the Rules of the Game.* EDI Development Studies. Washington, D.C.: World Bank.

Shihata, Ibrahim F. I. 1996. "Implementation, Enforcement and Compliance With International Environmental Agreements—Views from the World Bank." Legal Department, World Bank, Washington, D.C.

Shiratori, Masaki, and Yoshio Wada. 1996. "World Bank-OECF Periodic Conference: General Meeting on 'Role of Government.'" World Bank, Washington, D.C.

Shleifer, Andrei. 1996. "Government in Transition." Discussion Paper No. 1783. Harvard Institute of Economic Research, Harvard University, Cambridge, Mass.

Shleifer, Andrei, and Robert W. Vishny. 1993. "Corruption." *Quarterly Journal of Economics* 108: 599–617.

Shui Yan Tang. 1992. *Institutions and Collective Action: Self Governance in Irrigation.* San Francisco, Calif.: Institute for Contemporary Studies.

Sills, David L., ed. 1968. *International Encyclopedia of the Social Sciences.* New York, N.Y.: Macmillan and the Free Press, and London: Collier-Macmillan.

Silverman, Jerry M. 1992. *Public Sector Decentralization: Economic Policy and Sector Investment Programs.* World Bank Technical Paper Number 188, Africa Technical Department Series. Washington, D.C.: World Bank.

Slemrod, Joel. 1995. "What Do Cross-Country Studies Teach about Government Involvement, Prosperity and Economic Growth?" *Brookings Papers on Economic Activity* 2: 373–431.

Snider, Lewis. 1996. *Growth, Debt and Politics: Economic Adjustment and the Political Performance of Developing Countries.* Boulder, Colo.: Westview Press.

Solow, Robert. 1956. "A Contribution to the Theory of Economic Growth." *Quarterly Journal of Economics* 70: 65–94.

Soyinka, Wole. 1996. *The Open Sore of a Continent: A Personal Narrative of the Nigerian Crisis.* New York, N.Y., and Oxford, England: Oxford University Press.

Spiller, Pablo T., and Cezley Sampson. 1996. "Telecommunications Regulation in Jamaica." In Brian Levy and Pablo Spiller, eds., *Regulations, Institutions and Commitment: Comparative Studies of Telecommunications.* Cambridge, England: Cambridge University Press.

Spiller, Pablo, and Ingo Vogelsang. 1996. "The United Kingdom: A Pacesetter in Regulatory Incentives. In Brian Levy and Pablo Spiller, eds., *Regulations, Institutions and Commitment: Comparative Studies of Telecommunications.* Cambridge, England: Cambridge University Press.

Stein, Freiherr vom. 1807. "Über die zweckmäßige Bildung der obersten und der Provinzial-, Finanz- und Polizeibehörden in der preußischen Monarchie (Nassauer Denkschrift)." (Reprinted in Walther Hubatsch, ed., 1959. *Freiherr vom Stein. Briefe und amtliche Schriften,* pp. 380–98. Stuttgart, Germany: Kohlhammer.)

Stiglitz, Joseph E. 1977. "The Theory of Local Public Goods." In Martin S. Feldstein and Robert P. Inman, eds., *The Economics of Public Services,* pp. 274–333. London: Macmillan.

_____. 1986. *Economics of the Public Sector.* New York, N.Y., and London: W. W. Norton.

_____. 1994. *Whither Socialism?* Cambridge, Mass.: MIT Press.

_____. 1995. "The Theory of International Public Goods and the Architecture of International Organizations." Paper presented at the United Nations Third Meeting of the High Level Group on Development Strategy and Management of the Market Economy, Helsinki, July 8–9.

_____. 1996. "Keynote Address: The Role of Government in Economic Development." In Michael Bruno and Boris Pleskovic, eds., *Annual World Bank Conference on Development Economics,* pp. 11–23. Washington, D.C.: World Bank.

Stiglitz, Joseph, and Marilou Uy. 1996. "Financial Markets, Public Policy and the East Asian Miracle." *World Bank Research Observer* 11(2): 249–76.

Stone, Andrew, Brian Levy, and Ricardo Paredes. 1996. "Public Institutions and Private Transactions: A Comparative Analysis of the Legal and Regulatory Environment for Business Transactions in Brazil and Chile." In Lee J. Alston, Thrainn Eggertsson, and Douglass C. North, eds., *Empirical Studies in Institutional Change.* New York, N.Y.: Cambridge University Press.

Strong, Maurice F. 1996. "The CGIAR at Twenty-Five: Looking Back and Looking Forward." Sir John Crawford Memorial Lecture, International Centers Week, Washington, D.C., October 28.

Stuart, Charles E. 1981. "Swedish Tax Rates, Labor Supply, and Tax Revenues." *Journal of Political Economy* 89(51): 1020–51.

Subbarao, Kalanidhi, Aniruddha Bonnerjee, Jeanine Braithwaite, Soniya Carvalho, Kene Ezemenari, Carol Graham, and Alan Thompson. 1997. *Safety Net Programs and Poverty Reduction: Lessons from Cross Country Experience.* Directions in Development Series. Washington, D.C.: World Bank.

Summers, Robert, and Alan Heston. 1991. "The Penn World Table (Mark 5): An Expanded Set of International Comparisons, 1950–1988." *Quarterly Journal of Economics* 106 (May): 327–68.

Sweden. Ministry of Health and Social Affairs. 1994. "Pension Reform in Sweden: A Short Summary." Stockholm: Ministry of Health and Social Affairs.

Sweden. Styrelsen för Internationell Utveckling. 1994. *State, Market and Aid: Redefined Roles.* Stockholm: Swedish International Development Authority.

Tallroth, Nils Borje, III. 1997. "The Political Economy of Modern Wars in Africa." Paper presented at the Carter Center Conference on the Transition from War to Peace, Atlanta, February 19–21.

Tanzi, Vito. 1995a. "Fiscal Federalism and Decentralization: A Review of Some Efficiency and Macroeconomic Aspects." In Michael Bruno and Boris Pleskovic, eds., *Annual World Bank Conference on Development Economics,* pp. 295–316. Washington, D.C.: World Bank.

_____. 1995b. *Taxation in an Integrating World.* Washington, D.C.: Brookings Institution.

Tanzi, Vito, and Ludger Schuknecht. 1995. "The Growth of Government and the Reform of the State in Industrial Countries." IMF Working Papers WP/95/130. International Monetary Fund, Washington, D.C.

Tavares, Jose, and Romain Wacziarg. 1996. "How Democracy Fosters Growth?" Department of Economics, Harvard University, Cambridge, Mass.

Tendler, Judith. 1997. *Good Government in the Tropics.* Baltimore, Md.: Johns Hopkins University Press.

Tengs, Tammy O., and John D. Graham. 1996. "The Opportunity Costs of Haphazard Social Investments in Life-Saving." In Robert W. Hahn, ed., *Risks, Costs and Lives Saved: Getting Better Results from Regulation.* New York, N.Y.: Oxford University Press.

Teranishi, Juro, and Yukata Kosai, eds. 1993. *The Japanese Experience of Economic Reforms.* New York, N.Y.: St. Martin's Press.

Thomas, Vinod, and Jisoon Lee. 1997. "The Payoffs from Economic Reforms." In Nancy Birdsall and Frederick Jaspersen, eds., *Pathways to Growth.* Washington, D.C.: Inter-American Development Bank.

Tilly, Charles. 1990. *Coercion, Capital, and European States, AD 990–1990.* Cambridge, Mass.: Basil Blackwell.

Tlaiye, Laura, and Dan Biller. 1994. "Successful Environmental Institutions: Lessons from Colombia and Curitiba, Brazil." LATEN Dissemination Note No. 12. Latin America Technical Department, Environment Unit, World Bank, Washington, D.C.

Toye, J. 1992. "Interest Group Politics and the Implementation of Adjustment Policies in Sub-Saharan Africa." *Journal of International Development Policy, Economic and International Relations* 4(2), March–April: 183–98 (special issue on The Economic Analysis of Aid Policy).

Trebilcock, Michael J. 1996. "What Makes Poor Countries Poor? The Role of Institutional Capital in Economic Development." Faculty of Law, University of Toronto, Toronto.

Twain, Mark, Charles Warner, and Ward Just. 1877. *The Gilded Age: A Tale of Today.* Reprinted by New York, N.Y.: Oxford University Press, 1996.

United Nations Development Programme. 1997. *Reconceptualising Governance.* Discussion Paper 2. New York, N.Y.: Management Development and Governance Division, Bureau for Policy and Programme Support, United Nations Development Programme.

U.S. Department of Health and Human Services. 1994. *Social Security Programs Throughout the World.* SSA Publication No. 13-11805, Research Report No. 63. Office of Research and Statistics, Social Security Administration, Washington, D.C.

Valdeavilla, Ermelita V. 1995. "Breakthroughs and Challenges of Making Philippine Government Work for Gender Equality." *IDS Bulletin* 26(3): 94–101. Brighton, England: Institute for Development Studies, University of Sussex.

van der Gaag, Jacques. 1995. *Private and Public Initiatives: Working Together for Health and Education.* Washington, D.C.: World Bank.

van de Walle, Dominique, and Kimberley Nead, eds. 1995. *Public Spending and the Poor: Theory and Evidence.* Baltimore, Md.: Johns Hopkins University Press.

Villadsen, Søren, and Francis Lubanga, eds. 1996. *Democratic Decentralisation in Uganda: A New Approach to Local Governance.* Kampala, Uganda: Fountain.

Vittas, Dimitri, ed. 1992. *Financial Regulation: Changing the Rules of the Game.* EDI Development Studies. Washington, D.C.: World Bank.

von Hagen, J., and I. Harden. 1994. "National Budget Processes and Fiscal Performance." *European Economy, Reports and Studies* 3: 311–418.

Wade, Robert. 1994. "The Governance of Infrastructure: Organizational Issues in the Operation and Maintenance of Irrigation Canals." World Bank, Washington, D.C.

Wallich, Christine I. 1994. "Intergovernmental Fiscal Relations: Setting the Stage." In Christine I. Wallich, ed., *Russia and the Challenge of Fiscal Federalism,* pp. 19–63. World Bank Regional and Sectoral Studies. Washington, D.C.: World Bank.

Weal, Albert. 1990. "Equality, Social Welfare and the Welfare State." *Ethics* 100(3): 475.

Weaver, R. Kent, and William T. Dickens, eds. 1995. *Looking Before We Leap: Social Science and Welfare Reform.* Washington, D.C.: Brookings Institution.

Wiesner Durán, Eduardo. 1992. "Colombia: Descentralización y Federalismo Fiscal: Informe Final de la Misión para la Descentralización." Departamento Nacional de Planeación, Presidencia de la República, Bogotá, Colombia.

Wildasin, David E. 1996. "Introduction: Fiscal Aspects of Evolving Federations." *International Tax and Public Finance* (Netherlands) 3: 21–131.

Williamson, John, ed. 1994. *The Political Economy of Policy Reform.* Washington, D.C.: Institute for International Economics.

Willman, John, Stephen Pollard, Bernard Jenkin, Madsen Pirie, Eamonn Butler, and José Piñera. 1996. "The Need for Welfare Reform." In *Over to You: The Transition to Funded Fortune Accounts.* London: Adam Smith Institute.

Williamson, Oliver E. 1996. *The Mechanisms of Governance.* New York, N.Y.: Oxford University Press.

Winston, Clifford. 1993. "Economic Deregulation: Days of Reckoning for Microeconomists." *Journal of Economic Literature* 31(3): 1263–89.

Wolf, Edward. 1985. "Social Security, Pensions and the Wealth Holdings of the Poor." Institute for Research on Poverty Discussion Paper No. 799–85. University of Wisconsin-Madison, Madison, Wisc.

Wong, John. 1997. "Government Participation in Economic Development: Singapore Experiences." Paper presented at the International Symposium on Government's Role in the Market Economy, China Institute for Reform and Development, Haikou, China, January 7–8.

World Bank. 1983. *World Development Report 1983.* New York, N.Y.: Oxford University Press.

_____. 1987. "The Philippines: Issues and Policies in the Industrial Sector." Report No. 6706-PH. Asia Region, Country Department II, World Bank, Washington, D.C.

_____. 1991a. *The Reform of Public Sector Management: Lessons of Experience.* Policy Research Series 18. World Bank, Washington, D.C.

_____. 1991b. *World Development Report 1991: The Challenge of Development.* New York, N.Y.: Oxford University Press.

_____. 1993. *The East Asian Miracle: Economic Growth and Public Policy.* A World Bank Policy Research Report. New York, N.Y.: Oxford University Press.

_____. 1994a. *Adjustment in Africa: Reforms, Results and the Road Ahead.* A World Bank Policy Research Report. New York, N.Y.: Oxford University Press.

_____. 1994b. *Averting the Old Age Crisis: Policies to Protect the Old and Promote Growth.* A World Bank Policy Research Report. New York, N.Y.: Oxford University Press.

_____. 1994c. *World Development Report 1994: Infrastructure for Development.* New York, N.Y.: Oxford University Press.

_____. 1995a. "Azerbaijan: Baku Water Supply Rehabilitation Project." Environment Department Papers Series. Assessment Series Paper No. 017. World Bank, Washington, D.C.

_____. 1995b. *Better Urban Services: Finding the Right Incentives.* Washington, D.C.: World Bank.

_____. 1995c. *Bureaucrats in Business: The Economics and Politics of Government Ownership.* A World Bank Policy Research Report. New York, N.Y.: Oxford University Press.

_____. 1995d. *Development in Practice: Priorities and Strategies for Education—A World Bank Review.* Washington, D.C.: World Bank.

_____. 1995e. *Global Economic Prospects and the Developing Countries.* Washington, D.C.: World Bank.

_____. 1995f. "Vietnam Poverty Assessment and Strategy." Report No. 13442-VN. Country Department I, East Asia and Pacific Region, World Bank, Washington, D.C.

_____. 1995g. *World Development Report 1995: Workers in an Integrating World.* New York, N.Y.: Oxford University Press.

_____. 1996a. "Argentina: Reforming Provincial Utilities: Issues, Challenges and Best Practice." Report No. 15063-AR. Infrastructure Division, Country Department I, Latin America and the Caribbean Region, World Bank, Washington, D.C.

_____. 1996b. "Bangladesh: Government That Works: Reforming the Public Sector." Private Sector Development and Finance Division, Country Department I, South Asia Region, World Bank, Washington, D.C.

_____. 1996c. *Handbook on Good Practices for Laws Relating to Nongovernmental Organizations.* Prepared for the World Bank by the International Center for Non-Profit Law.

_____. 1996d. "Republic of Guinea: Public Expenditure Review." Western Africa Department, World Bank, Washington, D.C.

_____. 1996e. *Social Assistance and Poverty-Targeted Programs: A Sourcebook Prepared by the Social Assistance Program Team.* Washington, D.C.: Poverty and Social Policy Department, World Bank.

_____. 1996f. *Social Indicators of Development 1996.* Washington, D.C.: World Bank.

_____. 1996g. "Technical Annex: Democratic Republic of Sri Lanka: Telecommunications Regulation and Public Enterprise Reform Technical Assistance Project." Report No. T-6730 CE. Country Department I, Energy and Project Finance Division, South Asia Region, World Bank, Washington, D.C.

_____. 1996h. *The World Bank Participation Sourcebook.* Washington, D.C.: World Bank.

_____. 1996i. *World Development Report 1996: From Plan To Market.* New York, N.Y.: Oxford University Press.

_____. 1997. "Ukraine Public Sector Reform Loan, Preparation Mission Report, Public Administration." World Bank, Washington, D.C.

_____. Forthcoming. *The Road to Financial Integration: Private Capital Flows to Developing Countries.* Washington, D.C.: World Bank.

Wyzan, M. L. Michael, ed. 1990. *The Political Economy of Ethnic Discrimination and Affirmative Action: A Comparative Perspective.* New York, N.Y.: Praeger.

Zartman, William I., ed. 1995. *Collapsed States: The Disintegration and Restoration of Legitimate Authority.* Boulder, Colo., and London: Lynne Rienner.

APPENDIX

SELECTED INDICATORS ON PUBLIC FINANCE

DATA ON CENTRAL GOVERNMENT REVENUE AND EXpenditure are from IMF, various years (a) and (b), and IMF data files. The accounts of each country are reported using the system of common definitions and classifications in IMF 1986. See these sources for complete and authoritative explanations of concepts, definitions, and data sources.

Table A.1 Central government revenue

Current revenue includes tax receipts and nonrepayable receipts (other than grants) from the sale of land, intangible assets, government stocks, or fixed capital assets, or from capital transfers from nongovernmental sources.

Income, profit, and capital gains taxes are levied on the actual or presumptive net income of individuals, on enterprise profits, and on capital gains. *Social security contributions* includes employers' and employees' contributions and those of self-employed and unemployed people. *Domestic goods and services* taxes include general sales and turnover or value added taxes, selective excises on goods, selective taxes on services, taxes on the use of goods or property, and profits of fiscal monopolies. *International trade* taxes include import and export duties, profits of export or import monopolies, exchange profits, and exchange taxes. *Other taxes* includes employers' payroll or labor taxes, taxes on property, and taxes not allocable elsewhere. *Nontax revenue* includes requited nonrepayable receipts for public purposes, such as fines, administrative fees, or entrepreneurial income from government ownership of property, and voluntary, unrequited nonrepayable receipts other than from government sources.

Table A.2 Central government expenditure by economic type

Government expenditure includes all nonrepayable payments, whether current or capital, requited or unrequited. Expenditure can be measured either by economic type as shown here or by function as in Table A.3.

Goods and services expenditure includes all government payments in exchange for goods and services, whether in the form of wages and salaries to employees or other purchases. *Wages and salaries* consists of all cash payments to employees in return for services rendered, before taxes and pension contributions. *Interest payments* are payments for the use of borrowed money to domestic sectors and nonresidents. *Subsidies and other current transfers* includes all unrequited, nonrepayable transfers on current account to private and public enterprises, and the cost of covering the cash operating deficits of departmental enterprise sales to the public. *Capital expenditure* is expenditure to acquire fixed capital assets, land, intangible assets, government stocks, and nonmilitary, nonfinancial assets. Also included are capital grants.

Table A.3 Central government expenditure by function

Central government expenditure data by function are often incomplete, and coverage varies from country to country because functional responsibilities stretch across levels of government for which no data are available. Consequently, the data presented, especially those for education and health, may not always be comparable across countries.

Health covers public expenditure on hospitals, maternity and dental centers, and some clinics; on national health insurance schemes; and on family planning and preventive care. *Education* comprises expenditure on preprimary, primary, and secondary schools; universities and colleges; and vocational, technical, and other training institutions. *Social security and welfare* covers compensation for loss of income to the sick and temporarily disabled; payments to the elderly, the permanently disabled, and the unemployed; family, maternity, and child allowances; and the cost of welfare services, such as care of the aged, the disabled, and children. *Defense* comprises all expenditures, whether by defense or other departments, to maintain military forces. *Other* expenditures include general public services, interest payments, and items not included elsewhere.

Table A.1 Central government revenue

		Percentage of total current revenue											
		Tax revenue										Nontax revenue	
		Income, profit, and capital gains		Social security contributions		Domestic goods and services		International trade		Other taxes			
		1981–90	1991–95	1981–90	1991–95	1981–90	1991–95	1981–90	1991–95	1981–90	1991–95	1981–90	1991–95
Low-income economies													
1	Mozambique	..	..	..	..	..	..	..	..	..	..	..	..
2	Ethiopia	27.5	26.5	..	..	22.2	25.7	20.2	18.5	0.7	1.7	27.5	23.4
3	Tanzania	28.7	..	..	..	55.0	..	9.6	..	1.3	..	4.6	..
4	Burundi	22.4	..	2.9	..	28.7	..	24.0	..	2.3	..	10.8	..
5	Malawi	35.0	..	..	..	32.2	..	19.0	..	0.5	..	13.3	..
6	Chad	19.0	22.6	..	..	35.3	33.7	27.5	15.3	6.6	5.2	9.5	21.8
7	Rwanda	17.1	14.7	6.4	3.5	33.6	35.2	26.1	31.4	3.3	3.8	13.0	11.2
8	Sierra Leone	26.0	22.8	..	..	22.7	35.4	41.2	37.7	1.2	0.3	8.8	3.8
9	Nepal	8.6	8.8	..	..	38.7	39.1	29.2	28.0	0.2	..	17.2	19.3
10	Niger	..	..	..	..	..	..	..	..	..	..	..	..
11	Burkina Faso	17.8	21.5	8.2	..	17.6	..	35.8	..	5.1	2.0	13.7	25.0
12	Madagascar	11.4	16.0	..	..	21.0	24.6	45.9	46.7	0.7	0.4	19.6	11.1
13	Bangladesh	9.6	..	..	..	25.3	..	32.2	..	1.5	..	29.5	..
14	Uganda	8.2	..	..	..	31.1	..	58.6	..	0.1	..	3.1	..
15	Vietnam	..	..	..	..	..	..	..	..	..	..	..	..
16	Guinea-Bissau	9.9	..	2.1	..	15.8	..	33.5	..	8.8	..	36.6	..
17	Haiti	14.9	..	0.3	..	30.7	..	23.8	..	6.2	..	11.5	..
18	Mali	12.3	..	4.7	..	31.8	..	21.5	..	11.0	..	11.2	..
19	Nigeria	50.5	..	..	..	6.9	..	12.1	..	0.2	..	50.6	..
20	Yemen, Rep.	25.8	22.8	..	..	10.2	10.8	16.8	19.1	4.5	2.7	42.6	42.9
21	Cambodia	..	..	..	..	..	..	..	..	..	..	..	..
22	Kenya	28.6	28.5	..	..	39.9	47.5	20.1	12.4	0.9	1.0	10.6	10.6
23	Mongolia	..	34.8	..	11.6	..	24.3	..	13.1	..	0.4	..	16.0
24	Togo	33.5	..	6.4	..	11.6	..	31.2	..	0.2	..	13.2	..
25	Gambia, The	15.8	13.3	..	..	10.5	38.0	65.4	42.4	0.8	0.4	7.4	5.9
26	Central African Republic	16.1	..	6.4	..	20.8	..	39.8	..	7.4	..	9.1	..
27	India	16.0	19.7	..	..	37.8	32.9	26.2	23.3	0.1	0.2	19.5	23.8
28	Lao PDR	..	..	..	..	..	..	..	..	..	..	..	..
29	Benin	..	..	..	..	..	..	..	..	..	..	..	..
30	Nicaragua	13.5	11.2	9.7	11.8	43.8	45.1	13.2	19.4	2.1	5.3	9.5	6.6
31	Ghana	22.5	17.7	..	..	28.2	37.1	37.2	31.2	0.1	..	12.1	14.0
32	Zambia	33.2	33.5	..	..	41.2	42.5	17.8	18.5	1.2	0.1	6.4	5.1
33	Angola	..	..	..	..	..	..	..	..	..	..	..	..
34	Georgia	..	..	..	..	..	..	..	..	..	..	..	..
35	Pakistan	12.3	14.2	..	..	33.0	32.0	31.7	26.5	0.0	..	22.8	26.8
36	Mauritania	..	..	..	..	..	..	..	..	..	..	..	..
37	Azerbaijan	..	..	..	..	..	..	..	..	..	..	..	..
38	Zimbabwe	44.8	44.4	..	..	29.0	26.3	14.7	19.0	0.8	0.8	10.4	9.3
39	Guinea	8.6	10.4	..	..	16.6	25.1	47.0	46.1	0.4	0.8	27.4	17.6
40	Honduras	24.2	..	..	..	25.9	..	42.4	..	1.0	..	5.7	..
41	Senegal	20.7	..	3.5	..	26.0	..	35.6	..	2.1	..	7.1	..
42	China	31.2	33.5	..	..	17.6	29.2	13.8	17.7	..	0.8	37.4	19.4
43	Cameroon	39.0	18.1	5.7	5.6	15.1	18.4	19.7	16.9	2.9	3.6	15.0	33.4
44	Côte d'Ivoire	..	..	..	..	..	..	..	..	..	..	..	..
45	Albania	..	8.4	..	15.2	..	39.6	..	14.0	..	0.4	..	21.5
46	Congo	..	..	..	..	..	..	..	..	..	..	..	..
47	Kyrgyz Republic	..	..	..	..	..	..	..	..	..	..	..	..
48	Sri Lanka	13.4	13.2	..	..	38.5	49.6	32.6	22.1	..	..	12.7	11.1
49	Armenia	..	..	..	..	..	..	..	..	..	..	..	..
Middle-income economies													
Lower-middle-income													
50	Lesotho	11.3	15.4	..	..	16.8	15.9	59.7	55.1	0.4	0.1	11.9	13.4
51	Egypt, Arab Rep.	16.5	20.6	13.1	10.5	11.4	12.8	15.7	10.4	6.4	9.0	35.9	36.0
52	Bolivia	3.7	4.3	8.7	7.5	37.5	38.5	12.5	6.6	3.8	0.5	29.2	33.9
53	Macedonia, FYR	..	..	..	..	..	..	..	..	..	..	..	..
54	Moldova	..	..	..	..	..	..	..	..	..	..	..	..
55	Uzbekistan	..	..	..	..	..	..	..	..	..	..	..	..
56	Indonesia	61.9	52.2	..	2.0	16.9	28.0	5.2	5.4	0.5	0.5	14.1	11.5
57	Philippines	23.6	29.2	..	..	36.3	26.7	24.1	28.1	2.1	3.6	13.1	12.2
58	Morocco	19.0	22.6	4.7	3.8	39.4	39.9	17.2	18.0	3.9	1.4	13.5	12.0
59	Syrian Arab Republic	26.6	27.4	..	..	20.6	34.0	7.9	11.5	6.1	6.0	36.7	19.9
60	Papua New Guinea	46.0	45.0	..	..	12.8	10.8	23.9	23.8	1.8	1.9	15.5	18.4
61	Bulgaria	32.4	20.7	20.9	25.4	20.0	21.1	1.8	6.9	1.2	4.3	23.7	21.6
62	Kazakstan	..	..	..	..	..	..	..	..	..	..	..	..
63	Guatemala	15.7	19.4	..	..	39.4	42.4	21.2	20.1	7.5	3.5	14.8	13.7
64	Ecuador	53.9	56.0	..	..	20.8	24.9	20.2	11.6	1.1	1.0	2.5	5.5
65	Dominican Republic	19.4	17.1	4.1	4.1	28.4	25.1	33.7	44.2	1.4	0.3	12.3	8.6
66	Romania	18.9	32.4	15.4	29.6	32.6	22.7	0.5	4.0	11.1	2.5	68.3	8.8
67	Jamaica	34.5	..	4.6	..	38.0	..	7.7	..	8.7	..	4.8	..
68	Jordan	12.0	11.1	..	..	13.8	20.6	34.0	31.6	5.6	5.3	30.0	26.9
69	Algeria	..	..	..	..	..	..	..	..	..	..	..	..
70	El Salvador	20.2	22.2	..	..	39.9	49.8	25.8	17.0	0.8	0.2	8.3	7.1
71	Ukraine	..	..	..	..	..	..	..	..	..	..	..	..
72	Paraguay	12.7	9.8	13.1	..	22.6	27.7	14.6	14.8	12.7	11.9	16.7	30.0

Note: Components may not add to 100 percent because of adjustments to current revenue totals by the reporting countries. Figures in italics are for years other than those specified.

		Percentage of total current revenue										
		Tax revenue									Nontax revenue	
		Income, profit, and capital gains		Social security contributions		Domestic goods and services		International trade		Other taxes		Nontax revenue	
		1981–90	1991–95	1981–90	1991–95	1981–90	1991–95	1981–90	1991–95	1981–90	1991–95	1981–90	1991–95
73	Tunisia	13.7	13.6	9.0	12.3	21.0	23.2	27.4	28.4	2.6	2.9	24.4	17.8
74	Lithuania	..	20.7	..	29.8	..	38.2	..	3.7	..	0.3	..	6.5
75	Colombia	24.6	39.3	10.3	..	28.2	37.2	17.0	9.7	6.2	0.7	14.4	13.2
76	Namibia	34.9	26.2	..	..	21.9	26.6	29.3	33.6	0.3	0.4	12.9	12.7
77	Belarus	..	11.9	..	32.2	..	39.9	..	4.5	..	8.7	..	2.0
78	Russian Federation	..	14.2	..	33.6	..	32.7	..	12.1	..	1.4	..	6.4
79	Latvia	..	11.5	..	34.9	..	40.0	..	3.6	..	0.4	..	9.8
80	Peru	14.6	12.5	7.4	12.3	49.8	49.3	20.8	9.8	8.0	7.3	9.1	8.6
81	Costa Rica	12.3	9.8	26.2	27.7	26.0	32.2	25.5	16.1	1.2	0.7	10.6	13.1
82	Lebanon	..	10.3	..	..	..	6.8	..	35.5	..	6.7	..	30.5
83	Thailand	20.3	28.4	0.2	1.1	46.5	40.7	21.3	17.6	0.7	0.8	9.3	9.1
84	Panama	20.7	18.0	22.4	20.5	15.5	16.8	9.9	10.5	1.7	1.7	25.6	31.1
85	Turkey	44.4	37.0	..	..	28.0	35.4	6.9	4.1	3.7	2.3	15.6	20.1
86	Poland	25.8	27.6	24.0	24.7	30.0	28.0	6.6	8.1	6.4	1.1	5.3	10.4
87	Estonia	..	20.5	..	33.6	..	38.8	..	1.8	..	0.5	..	4.6
88	Slovak Republic	..	..	..	..	..	..	..	..	..	..	..	..
89	Botswana	35.6	29.7	..	..	1.3	3.0	20.4	18.6	..	..	42.5	48.6
90	Venezuela	60.0	50.6	3.9	5.5	5.5	10.4	12.6	9.1	1.1	1.3	18.3	22.3
Upper-middle-income													
91	South Africa	51.4	50.9	1.5	1.8	31.0	34.9	4.4	2.9	1.4	1.3	8.7	6.5
92	Croatia	..	10.7	..	36.9	..	38.1	..	8.3	..	0.5	..	5.1
93	Mexico	27.9	34.2	12.9	17.9	55.3	50.2	10.1	7.1	1.0	2.4	10.7	9.0
94	Mauritius	12.8	12.5	4.4	5.1	19.2	23.9	49.2	41.0	0.4	0.7	10.9	11.1
95	Gabon	40.2	27.6	0.9	0.8	10.8	23.7	17.4	17.4	1.8	0.9	29.2	29.3
96	Brazil	17.4	16.3	24.8	30.1	21.0	19.2	2.7	1.9	4.5	5.2	29.5	27.2
97	Trinidad and Tobago	62.3	..	..	..	11.0	..	8.0	..	0.6	..	17.7	..
98	Czech Republic	..	16.6	..	38.0	..	31.9	..	3.9	..	1.7	..	7.5
99	Malaysia	34.8	34.3	0.6	1.0	17.8	22.0	20.5	14.1	1.8	3.5	24.1	24.6
100	Hungary	16.9	..	22.8	..	34.7	..	6.2	..	3.5	..	13.2	..
101	Chile	13.3	18.1	8.4	6.7	41.8	45.2	8.7	9.6	6.3	3.7	21.1	16.7
102	Oman	24.3	19.9	..	..	0.7	1.0	2.5	3.2	0.5	0.7	71.9	74.9
103	Uruguay	7.4	7.3	26.1	30.1	42.2	32.4	11.4	5.6	4.9	8.4	6.4	5.9
104	Saudi Arabia	..	..	..	..	..	..	..	..	..	..	..	..
105	Argentina	4.9	2.6	26.4	45.9	33.1	26.6	13.8	7.9	6.0	4.6	11.9	9.1
106	Slovenia	..	..	..	..	..	..	..	..	..	..	..	..
107	Greece	18.5	29.6	31.7	1.1	37.8	66.5	0.9	0.1	4.7	3.9	9.7	6.4
High-income economies													
108	Korea, Rep.	27.1	31.6	2.2	6.9	40.9	33.6	14.2	6.9	2.7	6.0	11.4	12.1
109	Portugal	21.6	24.7	25.0	25.0	35.1	35.2	3.4	0.2	5.5	2.8	8.3	11.8
110	Spain	25.6	31.2	41.5	38.2	19.9	21.5	3.3	0.6	0.3	..	7.9	8.1
111	New Zealand	59.7	58.2	..	..	21.5	27.4	3.4	2.1	1.1	1.4	13.4	10.1
112	Ireland	33.9	38.6	13.6	14.7	31.2	30.9	8.2	5.9	1.4	1.5	10.0	6.4
113	†Israel	38.2	37.4	8.4	7.7	28.8	35.9	3.9	1.2	3.5	3.1	16.7	13.7
114	†Kuwait	1.7	..	..	..	0.6	..	1.6	..	..	..	96.0	..
115	†United Arab Emirates	..	..	2.5	2.1	24.1	26.0	..	..	..	..	77.3	71.9
116	United Kingdom	39.2	35.2	16.9	16.9	29.7	32.3	0.1	0.1	1.0	0.1	10.7	8.3
117	Australia	61.5	63.9	..	..	22.8	20.4	4.8	3.3	0.5	1.5	10.1	10.9
118	Italy	36.3	36.6	33.7	29.2	25.6	28.8	0.0	0.0	1.4	1.2	4.0	2.9
119	Canada	50.3	49.3	13.6	18.4	19.2	18.2	4.4	2.6	0.0	..	12.5	11.4
120	Finland	30.5	29.0	9.5	11.4	46.7	44.2	1.1	0.9	0.3	0.3	8.4	11.6
121	†Hong Kong	..	..	..	..	..	..	..	..	..	..	..	..
122	Sweden	16.9	8.9	31.5	36.0	28.6	31.6	0.6	0.8	5.1	3.0	14.5	15.8
123	Netherlands	26.0	28.7	39.0	38.5	20.6	21.6	..	..	0.4	0.9	12.0	8.0
124	Belgium	37.2	33.6	33.4	35.4	23.5	24.7	0.0	0.0	0.1	..	3.7	3.8
125	France	17.6	17.7	42.1	44.1	29.4	27.5	0.0	0.0	1.2	2.0	7.7	6.8
126	†Singapore	27.2	28.0	..	..	15.3	18.3	3.7	1.7	5.4	8.9	40.1	36.5
127	Austria	19.6	19.9	36.3	37.5	26.2	24.6	1.4	1.4	6.5	6.5	8.3	8.6
128	United States	51.4	50.9	32.4	34.5	4.4	3.9	1.5	1.5	0.0	0.0	9.2	8.1
129	Germany	17.3	15.5	53.9	47.7	22.5	25.2	0.0	..	..	..	6.2	6.2
130	Denmark	36.7	38.3	3.9	3.9	42.6	39.6	0.1	0.1	0.7	1.4	13.2	14.8
131	Norway	21.4	16.0	22.7	24.0	37.9	36.7	0.5	0.6	0.1	0.0	16.4	21.9
132	Japan	67.8	38.7	..	25.6	17.4	13.9	1.7	1.2	3.6	1.6	5.2	15.4
133	Switzerland	14.9	14.7	48.7	52.6	19.2	16.9	8.4	6.4	..	..	6.0	6.6

† Economies classified by the United Nations or otherwise regarded by their authorities as developing. As of July 1, 1997, Hong Kong is a part of China.

Table A.2 Central government expenditure by economic type

		Percentage of total expenditure									
		Goods and services		Wages and salaries[a]		Interest payments		Subsidies and other current transfers		Capital expenditure	
		1981–90	1991–95	1981–90	1991–95	1981–90	1991–95	1981–90	1991–95	1981–90	1991–95
Low-income economies											
1	Mozambique	..	..	..	..	..	..	..	..	..	..
2	Ethiopia	78.0	*74.6*	35.0	*43.9*	4.9	*7.2*	7.2	*14.9*	20.5	*13.1*
3	Tanzania	*52.4*	..	*19.0*	..	*8.9*	..	*13.1*	..	*28.6*	..
4	Burundi	*39.4*	..	*25.5*	..	*1.9*	..	*6.8*	..	*45.5*	..
5	Malawi	47.9	..	18.2	..	17.0	..	6.5	..	28.6	..
6	Chad	*34.1*	*40.9*	*24.3*	*23.9*	*1.2*	*2.8*	*2.5*	*2.7*	*61.7*	*60.3*
7	Rwanda	47.9	*60.2*	29.3	*27.3*	5.3	*8.9*	14.7	*7.1*	32.9	*31.6*
8	Sierra Leone	54.1	36.4	27.0	18.8	15.6	23.7	6.8	19.4	24.3	30.0
9	Nepal	..	..	..	..	..	..	..	..	..	..
10	Niger	..	..	..	..	..	..	..	..	..	..
11	Burkina Faso	63.8	*46.0*	53.0	*37.8*	5.8	*8.3*	12.8	*11.6*	15.3	*34.0*
12	Madagascar	*37.5*	32.1	*26.0*	20.9	*10.8*	21.9	*8.1*	7.1	*39.9*	35.4
13	Bangladesh	..	..	..	..	..	..	..	..	..	..
14	Uganda	..	..	..	..	..	..	..	..	16.9	..
15	Vietnam	..	..	..	..	..	..	..	..	..	..
16	Guinea-Bissau	*22.9*	..	*13.9*	..	*6.1*	..	*4.0*	..	*62.1*	..
17	Haiti	*70.5*	..	..	..	*3.4*	..	*15.2*	..	*10.8*	..
18	Mali	37.1	..	25.8	..	2.4	..	6.5	..	3.3	..
19	Nigeria	*16.2*	..	*9.5*	..	*31.8*	..	*12.3*	..	*38.5*	..
20	Yemen, Rep.	*64.2*	68.1	*55.0*	58.4	*8.4*	10.0	*6.5*	8.2	*33.4*	13.6
21	Cambodia	..	..	..	..	..	..	..	..	..	..
22	Kenya	53.2	49.8	31.4	31.1	15.7	26.3	14.8	8.4	16.3	15.4
23	Mongolia	..	32.1	..	8.2	..	2.5	..	47.7	..	17.7
24	Togo	48.1	..	26.2	..	*12.7*	..	*13.0*	..	28.5	..
25	Gambia, The	*49.9*	..	*25.3*	..	*8.0*	..	*10.4*	..	*30.9*	30.7
26	Central African Republic	*67.0*	..	*53.6*	..	*1.2*	..	*16.0*	..	*6.0*	..
27	India	27.2	22.8	12.3	10.0	17.1	25.6	42.6	40.1	13.1	11.5
28	Lao PDR	..	..	..	..	..	..	..	..	..	..
29	Benin	..	..	..	..	..	..	..	..	..	..
30	Nicaragua	59.9	47.9	14.6	27.9	4.0	10.7	14.6	19.2	17.2	22.1
31	Ghana	55.5	47.4	32.1	31.1	12.7	13.8	14.8	20.7	16.2	18.1
32	Zambia	*47.3*	37.6	*26.2*	19.6	*9.9*	18.4	*19.0*	16.9	*19.7*	26.0
33	Angola	..	..	..	..	..	..	..	..	..	..
34	Georgia	..	..	..	..	..	..	..	..	..	..
35	Pakistan	50.0	45.7	..	..	16.9	23.7	18.9	13.7	14.2	16.8
36	Mauritania	..	..	..	..	..	..	..	..	..	..
37	Azerbaijan	..	..	..	..	..	..	..	..	..	..
38	Zimbabwe	48.6	55.1	30.4	38.0	12.5	*15.5*	30.6	*18.2*	8.2	*11.1*
39	Guinea	*36.3*	39.4	*17.2*	22.0	*5.8*	7.2	*5.8*	4.4	*52.1*	48.9
40	Honduras	..	..	..	..	..	..	..	..	..	..
41	Senegal	*52.4*	..	*36.3*	..	*7.5*	..	*16.9*	..	*16.9*	..
42	China	..	..	..	..	..	..	..	..	..	..
43	Cameroon	*47.3*	59.0	*30.0*	47.8	*3.0*	8.1	*11.9*	14.4	*37.9*	16.0
44	Côte d'Ivoire	..	..	..	..	..	..	..	..	..	..
45	Albania	..	26.3	..	11.8	..	7.6	..	48.4	..	17.8
46	Congo	..	..	..	..	..	..	..	..	45.6	..
47	Kyrgyz Republic	..	..	..	..	..	..	..	..	..	..
48	Sri Lanka	26.3	34.4	14.2	18.4	16.7	21.8	19.6	21.6	37.4	22.2
49	Armenia	..	..	..	..	..	..	..	..	..	..
Middle-income economies											
Lower-middle-income											
50	Lesotho	*43.8*	*51.8*	*23.5*	*29.3*	*9.0*	*7.1*	*4.9*	*6.0*	*42.3*	33.2
51	Egypt, Arab Rep.	42.4	33.6	20.3	17.8	9.2	18.9	33.0	25.2	16.1	22.3
52	Bolivia	*62.6*	58.0	*41.6*	32.8	*6.6*	8.3	*18.9*	13.5	*11.8*	20.2
53	Macedonia, FYR	..	..	..	..	..	..	..	..	..	..
54	Moldova	..	..	..	..	..	..	..	..	..	..
55	Uzbekistan	..	..	..	..	..	..	..	..	..	..
56	Indonesia	23.5	25.4	14.3	16.0	9.9	11.3	19.6	14.1	47.0	48.6
57	Philippines	52.0	42.5	29.0	28.0	23.1	29.8	6.8	9.9	18.1	17.8
58	Morocco	47.3	*50.6*	34.1	*37.3*	14.6	*17.9*	12.5	*9.1*	25.7	*22.5*
59	Syrian Arab Republic	..	..	..	..	..	..	..	..	30.1	31.9
60	Papua New Guinea	61.9	57.0	35.2	28.7	9.5	9.2	19.1	22.5	9.6	11.3
61	Bulgaria	*34.0*	26.6	*2.8*	5.7	*6.9*	24.6	*54.2*	46.0	*4.9*	2.9
62	Kazakstan	..	..	..	..	..	..	..	..	..	..
63	Guatemala	52.8	50.2	37.3	34.4	9.7	11.4	14.0	15.5	25.6	25.6
64	Ecuador	*32.0*	46.1	*28.9*	42.2	*17.8*	22.7	*26.5*	11.2	*19.2*	16.7
65	Dominican Republic	47.1	33.9	34.8	22.9	4.1	6.1	13.3	10.2	34.2	48.7
66	Romania	25.9	33.4	5.9	15.8	*1.8*	1.8	34.2	53.9	39.0	10.8
67	Jamaica	*44.1*	..	*18.4*	..	*30.7*	..	*10.5*	..	*14.7*	..
68	Jordan	53.9	57.9	*48.9*	43.4	9.0	12.4	12.4	10.5	26.0	19.6
69	Algeria	..	..	..	..	..	..	..	..	..	..
70	El Salvador	61.2	51.3	51.0	41.9	8.3	13.2	14.0	17.4	10.6	16.8
71	Ukraine	..	..	..	..	..	..	..	..	..	..
72	Paraguay	55.9	53.7	35.3	42.4	6.2	7.0	20.9	22.5	16.9	16.8

Note: Components may not add to 100 percent because of adjustments to total expenditure by the reporting countries. Figures in italics are for years other than those specified.

		Percentage of total expenditure									
		Goods and services		**Wages and salaries**[a]		**Interest payments**		**Subsidies and other current transfers**		**Capital expenditure**	
		1981–90	1991–95	1981–90	1991–95	1981–90	1991–95	1981–90	1991–95	1981–90	1991–95
73	Tunisia	35.3	35.9	26.9	29.2	7.5	10.3	30.9	32.9	27.0	20.9
74	Lithuania	..	31.5	..	11.8	..	0.7	..	55.8	..	12.2
75	Colombia	28.1	25.2	19.3	16.2	7.3	10.0	45.7	42.7	20.7	22.1
76	Namibia	51.5	72.5	21.8	..	5.8	1.1	25.7	10.9	16.9	15.5
77	Belarus	..	36.4	..	2.1	..	1.8	..	46.3	..	15.5
78	Russian Federation	..	39.6	..	13.7	..	9.7	..	49.4	..	4.6
79	Latvia	..	36.8	..	18.6	..	2.4	..	56.6	..	4.2
80	Peru	46.0	29.7	18.5	15.6	21.6	19.3	15.8	35.7	16.6	15.3
81	Costa Rica	49.4	50.5	38.9	38.0	9.2	15.2	29.2	23.9	15.3	10.5
82	Lebanon	..	52.9	..	37.0	..	26.6	..	..	..	20.5
83	Thailand	59.9	58.4	30.8	32.1	13.8	5.5	8.0	7.5	18.4	28.6
84	Panama	57.3	53.0	37.6	40.1	15.8	9.7	18.9	28.9	7.9	8.3
85	Turkey	39.9	46.3	25.3	34.5	11.8	14.4	28.1	27.9	20.2	11.4
86	Poland	18.2	26.1	..	14.1	0.5	10.3	74.5	60.1	6.9	3.5
87	Estonia	..	25.1	..	7.8	..	0.2	..	72.8	..	7.5
88	Slovak Republic	..	..	..	..	..	..	..	..	..	..
89	Botswana	48.8	53.0	25.7	27.9	3.3	2.1	26.0	27.0	21.8	17.9
90	Venezuela	37.4	30.9	29.5	24.4	12.4	17.4	29.8	34.7	19.2	15.4
	Upper-middle-income										
91	South Africa	49.6	47.4	21.5	31.9	11.8	15.2	27.8	29.0	10.7	8.4
92	Croatia	..	57.5	..	21.3	..	3.1	..	33.2	..	6.2
93	Mexico	23.7	32.6	17.9	23.4	40.6	22.7	19.2	29.9	16.7	15.1
94	Mauritius	43.1	46.1	34.1	35.1	17.7	11.6	24.6	23.5	14.6	18.7
95	Gabon	35.8	..	23.0	27.1	5.5	..	6.2	3.8	45.3	45.6
96	Brazil	16.5	15.1	9.4	8.7	39.7	44.5	46.7	47.3	5.5	3.2
97	Trinidad and Tobago	40.6	..	34.8	..	6.2	..	30.2	..	23.0	..
98	Czech Republic	..	19.6	..	8.6	..	3.7	..	66.1	..	10.6
99	Malaysia	45.1	47.9	31.1	30.7	19.8	16.5	14.6	16.6	20.9	19.6
100	Hungary	19.6	..	7.0	..	3.6	..	67.9	..	8.9	..
101	Chile	30.0	28.4	19.3	18.6	5.9	6.3	54.0	50.9	10.1	14.4
102	Oman	71.4	72.1	16.5	22.4	3.9	5.2	4.7	6.5	20.0	16.2
103	Uruguay	39.9	30.3	24.9	15.8	6.5	5.9	46.4	57.5	7.2	6.3
104	Saudi Arabia	..	..	..	..	..	..	..	..	..	..
105	Argentina	28.4	29.3	19.8	22.2	11.6	10.2	50.6	57.7	9.5	2.8
106	Slovenia	..	..	..	..	..	..	..	..	..	..
107	Greece	39.2	31.4	24.8	22.1	11.1	25.8	38.6	32.3	11.6	10.4
	High-income economies										
108	Korea, Rep.	39.9	31.7	14.2	13.1	6.3	3.4	39.0	49.5	14.8	15.5
109	Portugal	31.7	38.2	22.0	28.5	16.6	15.8	40.0	33.4	10.5	12.6
110	Spain	29.0	20.5	21.6	14.9	6.6	10.2	53.5	61.7	10.7	7.7
111	New Zealand	25.2	43.6	16.1	10.5	15.2	13.6	54.5	39.4	5.1	3.4
112	Ireland	18.1	18.5	12.8	13.2	17.9	16.0	56.9	58.1	7.1	7.4
113	†Israel	38.4	34.3	11.6	13.5	22.6	15.2	35.0	39.6	3.9	11.1
114	†Kuwait	46.9	41.9	24.8	19.7	..	..	24.1	47.8	29.0	10.3
115	†United Arab Emirates	88.6	88.1	30.6	34.0	..	..	8.8	8.2	4.4	3.8
116	United Kingdom	30.6	29.8	12.8	10.4	10.0	7.2	54.1	56.4	5.3	6.6
117	Australia	22.2	23.5	11.1	10.0	8.3	5.5	63.1	65.7	6.4	5.2
118	Italy	16.0	15.3	11.7	11.7	17.1	21.8	56.0	56.5	9.5	6.0
119	Canada	20.6	18.9	9.8	9.2	17.2	17.3	60.4	60.9	1.8	1.4
120	Finland	20.3	17.9	10.4	7.8	3.6	6.3	67.0	71.1	9.0	4.7
121	†Hong Kong	..	..	..	..	..	..	..	..	..	..
122	Sweden	14.4	14.7	6.3	5.8	13.7	11.7	68.6	72.9	3.2	2.5
123	Netherlands	14.9	14.5	9.1	8.7	7.5	9.1	69.9	71.9	7.8	4.5
124	Belgium	19.9	18.0	14.2	14.2	17.1	20.1	56.6	57.4	6.4	4.6
125	France	27.4	24.9	17.8	16.3	4.2	6.0	63.8	64.3	4.6	4.9
126	†Singapore	49.2	54.1	26.3	28.2	14.7	10.2	7.4	13.0	28.6	22.7
127	Austria	25.9	24.9	10.2	9.7	7.3	9.5	58.0	57.7	8.8	7.9
128	United States	30.1	25.3	10.5	9.3	14.3	14.6	50.6	55.7	5.1	4.4
129	Germany	33.7	30.1	8.6	7.6	4.9	6.3	56.0	58.4	5.3	5.2
130	Denmark	20.4	19.8	12.6	11.4	15.1	13.6	60.3	63.0	4.2	3.5
131	Norway	18.8	19.7	9.0	8.0	7.0	5.6	70.8	69.4	3.4	5.2
132	Japan	13.4	..	..	..	18.7	..	53.0	..	14.9	..
133	Switzerland	29.3	30.4	6.5	5.0	2.5	2.8	62.1	62.0	6.2	4.8

a. Included in goods and services.   †Economies classified by the United Nations or otherwise regarded by their authorities as developing. As of July 1, 1997, Hong Kong is a part of China.

Table A.3 Central government expenditure by function

		Percentage of total expenditure									
		Health		Education		Social security and welfare		Defense		Other	
		1981–90	1991–95	1981–90	1991–95	1981–90	1991–95	1981–90	1991–95	1981–90	1991–95
Low-income economies											
1	Mozambique	..	..	..	..	..	..	..	..	..	..
2	Ethiopia	3.5	4.2	10.7	12.4	5.2	5.8	32.8	30.2	47.7	47.5
3	Tanzania	5.5	..	11.8	..	0.5	..	13.3	..	68.8	..
4	Burundi	..	..	..	..	..	..	..	..	..	..
5	Malawi	6.5	..	11.9	..	0.8	..	6.4	..	74.3	..
6	Chad	..	..	..	..	..	..	..	..	..	..
7	Rwanda	..	..	..	..	..	..	..	..	..	..
8	Sierra Leone	7.8	..	14.8	..	1.9	..	6.1	..	69.4	..
9	Nepal	4.6	3.8	10.8	12.5	0.6	..	5.9	5.7	78.4	78.0
10	Niger	..	..	..	..	..	..	..	..	..	..
11	Burkina Faso	6.1	6.9	17.3	17.3	5.5	..	19.1	14.0	53.2	61.8
12	Madagascar	5.6	5.3	14.3	13.5	2.3	1.6	7.2	5.9	73.0	73.7
13	Bangladesh	5.1	..	9.1	..	3.4	..	10.8	..	71.6	..
14	Uganda	3.7	..	12.6	..	1.5	..	20.1	..	62.0	..
15	Vietnam	..	..	..	..	..	..	..	..	..	..
16	Guinea-Bissau	6.1	..	8.0	..	4.0	..	7.2	..	75.4	..
17	Haiti	..	..	..	..	..	..	..	..	..	..
18	Mali	2.6	..	10.0	..	4.2	..	8.3	..	74.8	..
19	Nigeria	1.7	..	6.1	..	0.3	..	7.5	..	84.5	..
20	Yemen, Rep.	4.1	4.4	17.4	19.7	..	..	29.5	30.3	49.0	45.6
21	Cambodia	..	..	..	..	..	..	..	..	..	..
22	Kenya	6.4	5.6	20.6	20.3	0.1	0.1	10.7	7.6	62.1	66.4
23	Mongolia	..	2.4	..	3.6	..	22.2	..	11.3	..	60.5
24	Togo	5.1	..	18.5	..	7.8	..	8.0	..	60.6	..
25	Gambia, The	7.4	..	14.8	..	2.5	..	4.3	..	74.0	..
26	Central African Republic	5.1	..	17.6	..	6.2	..	9.7	..	61.4	..
27	India	2.0	1.7	2.2	2.0	..	..	19.2	15.1	76.7	81.3
28	Lao PDR	..	..	..	..	..	..	..	..	..	..
29	Benin	..	..	..	..	..	..	..	..	..	..
30	Nicaragua	13.3	13.4	13.7	15.4	8.3	16.3	28.5	7.6	36.2	47.3
31	Ghana	8.5	7.8	21.9	23.0	6.0	7.0	5.4	4.7	58.2	57.6
32	Zambia	6.5	9.9	11.6	12.8	1.8	2.9	..	..	80.1	74.4
33	Angola	..	..	..	..	..	..	..	..	..	..
34	Georgia	..	..	..	..	..	..	..	..	..	..
35	Pakistan	..	..	..	..	..	..	..	..	..	..
36	Mauritania	..	..	..	..	..	..	..	..	..	..
37	Azerbaijan	..	..	..	..	..	..	..	..	..	..
38	Zimbabwe	6.8	..	21.5	..	4.5	..	17.1	..	50.1	..
39	Guinea	..	..	..	..	..	..	..	..	..	..
40	Honduras	..	..	..	..	..	..	..	..	..	..
41	Senegal	4.3	..	18.0	..	5.5	..	10.0	..	62.3	..
42	China	0.4	0.4	2.1	2.4	0.1	0.1	15.4	16.3	82.0	80.8
43	Cameroon	3.8	4.8	11.8	18.0	4.6	1.0	7.5	9.4	72.3	66.8
44	Côte d'Ivoire	..	..	..	..	..	..	..	..	..	..
45	Albania	..	5.6	..	2.3	..	21.7	..	7.1	..	63.3
46	Congo	..	..	10.3	..	4.2	..	..	..	88.9	..
47	Kyrgyz Republic	..	..	..	..	..	..	..	..	..	..
48	Sri Lanka	4.7	5.5	8.6	10.2	10.8	16.9	5.4	11.8	70.5	55.6
49	Armenia	..	..	..	..	..	..	..	..	..	..
Middle-income economies											
Lower-middle-income											
50	Lesotho	8.9	12.1	15.7	21.3	1.7	1.3	7.4	6.1	66.3	59.2
51	Egypt, Arab Rep.	2.6	2.4	11.2	12.0	11.9	10.4	15.4	9.4	58.9	65.8
52	Bolivia	5.5	6.3	20.4	18.0	17.4	15.3	13.6	9.5	43.2	50.8
53	Macedonia, FYR	..	..	..	..	..	..	..	..	..	..
54	Moldova	..	..	..	..	..	..	..	..	..	..
55	Uzbekistan	..	..	..	..	..	..	..	..	..	..
56	Indonesia	2.2	2.8	9.2	9.8	..	5.3	9.7	6.6	78.9	79.5
57	Philippines	5.0	3.8	17.6	15.7	1.6	2.7	12.7	10.5	63.0	67.3
58	Morocco	2.9	3.0	17.4	17.8	5.8	6.1	14.6	14.3	59.3	58.8
59	Syrian Arab Republic	1.4	2.3	8.8	9.0	4.2	2.0	36.3	35.2	49.3	51.5
60	Papua New Guinea	9.3	8.3	17.4	16.2	0.5	0.8	4.6	3.9	68.1	70.8
61	Bulgaria	1.7	3.2	2.8	3.7	21.8	30.7	8.8	7.0	65.0	55.4
62	Kazakstan	..	..	..	..	..	..	..	..	..	..
63	Guatemala	7.7	10.1	14.1	16.8	3.5	4.4	14.1	13.9	60.9	58.2
64	Ecuador	9.0	..	24.9	..	1.4	..	12.2	..	52.6	..
65	Dominican Republic	10.1	11.0	12.4	10.1	6.4	3.7	7.2	4.9	63.8	70.4
66	Romania	3.1	8.1	3.4	9.7	21.4	27.0	7.1	8.1	65.0	47.1
67	Jamaica	..	..	..	..	..	..	..	..	..	..
68	Jordan	4.4	6.5	12.4	14.8	11.4	14.6	25.8	22.6	46.1	41.5
69	Algeria	..	..	..	..	..	..	..	..	..	..
70	El Salvador	7.5	8.0	16.7	13.4	3.3	4.5	21.7	14.0	50.8	60.1
71	Ukraine	..	..	..	..	..	..	..	..	..	..
72	Paraguay	4.3	6.3	11.9	17.6	24.6	15.6	11.9	12.1	47.3	48.5

Note: Components may not add to 100 percent because of rounding. Figures in italics are for years other than those specified.

		Percentage of total expenditure									
		Health		Education		Social security and welfare		Defense		Other	
		1981–90	1991–95	1981–90	1991–95	1981–90	1991–95	1981–90	1991–95	1981–90	1991–95
73	Tunisia	6.3	6.5	15.1	17.5	10.7	14.1	7.7	5.5	60.2	56.4
74	Lithuania	..	6.0	..	6.9	..	35.8	..	2.4	..	48.9
75	Colombia	4.6	5.4	21.1	18.3	16.7	8.3	8.0	8.0	49.5	60.1
76	Namibia	..	..	..	..	..	..	..	..	..	..
77	Belarus	..	2.5	..	17.6	..	36.5	..	4.1	..	39.3
78	Russian Federation	..	1.6	..	2.7	..	28.1	..	14.3	..	53.3
79	Latvia	..	6.4	..	13.8	..	39.0	..	3.0	..	37.9
80	Peru	5.7	..	16.9	..	..	..	20.1	..	57.2	..
81	Costa Rica	25.0	26.7	19.6	21.0	13.2	14.4	2.5	..	39.9	38.0
82	Lebanon	..	..	..	..	..	..	..	..	..	..
83	Thailand	5.7	7.6	19.7	21.3	3.2	3.6	19.1	15.6	52.4	51.8
84	Panama	17.1	20.5	16.0	18.4	14.5	22.4	7.2	5.2	49.4	33.5
85	Turkey	2.3	3.0	13.6	16.1	1.2	3.1	12.2	10.0	70.8	67.8
86	Poland	..	..	..	..	..	..	..	..	..	..
87	Estonia	..	13.1	..	8.2	..	34.9	..	2.6	..	41.9
88	Slovak Republic	..	..	..	..	..	..	..	..	..	..
89	Botswana	5.5	5.1	19.1	21.3	2.3	2.1	9.3	12.1	63.9	59.4
90	Venezuela	8.6	..	18.3	..	6.7	..	6.3	..	60.2	..
Upper-middle-income											
91	South Africa	..	..	..	..	..	..	..	..	..	..
92	Croatia	..	15.3	..	6.2	..	32.2	..	18.7	..	27.6
93	Mexico	1.4	3.0	11.9	23.7	10.0	21.0	2.2	3.8	74.5	48.6
94	Mauritius	7.9	8.8	14.5	15.5	15.8	15.9	1.1	1.5	60.7	58.3
95	Gabon	..	..	..	..	..	..	..	..	..	..
96	Brazil	7.1	5.9	3.9	3.5	26.8	30.6	3.9	2.8	58.3	57.3
97	Trinidad and Tobago	..	..	..	..	..	..	..	..	..	..
98	Czech Republic	..	17.2	..	11.2	..	27.8	..	6.1	..	37.7
99	Malaysia	4.9	5.6	18.7	20.4	4.0	5.9	10.7	11.7	61.8	56.3
100	Hungary	3.4	..	2.0	..	24.3	..	4.5	..	65.8	..
101	Chile	7.5	11.4	13.2	13.5	37.7	33.5	11.4	9.2	30.3	32.3
102	Oman	4.2	6.0	8.9	12.1	3.0	3.6	44.4	35.4	41.6	42.9
103	Uruguay	4.1	5.4	7.2	6.7	50.6	58.4	10.8	6.5	27.4	23.0
104	Saudi Arabia	..	..	..	..	..	..	..	..	..	..
105	Argentina	2.0	2.2	7.9	7.0	35.7	47.5	7.9	6.8	46.8	36.4
106	Slovenia	..	..	..	..	..	..	..	..	..	..
107	Greece	10.5	7.7	9.6	8.2	30.6	14.2	10.8	8.6	38.4	61.3
High-income economies											
108	Korea, Rep.	1.7	1.1	18.9	18.8	6.9	10.0	29.0	20.0	43.5	50.1
109	Portugal	8.7	..	9.9	..	24.2	..	6.0	..	51.3	..
110	Spain	8.2	6.2	5.9	4.4	47.0	39.0	4.9	3.7	34.0	46.7
111	New Zealand	12.8	13.5	11.8	14.4	29.4	37.7	4.9	3.8	41.1	30.7
112	Ireland	13.0	14.1	11.7	12.8	25.4	27.5	3.1	3.1	46.9	42.6
113	†Israel	3.7	5.4	8.5	12.0	17.1	23.5	27.8	20.3	43.0	38.8
114	†Kuwait	6.7	4.5	11.9	8.8	10.6	13.7	14.5	36.8	56.3	36.1
115	†United Arab Emirates	6.8	7.1	11.4	16.2	3.1	3.4	43.3	37.5	35.5	35.8
116	United Kingdom	13.6	14.0	2.7	4.2	30.0	30.5	13.0	9.2	40.7	42.2
117	Australia	9.8	12.9	7.4	7.4	27.7	32.5	9.1	7.7	46.0	39.5
118	Italy	11.0	..	8.2	..	32.8	..	3.4	..	44.6	..
119	Canada	5.8	4.9	3.3	2.8	34.7	40.6	7.8	6.5	48.5	45.1
120	Finland	10.7	2.9	14.1	12.2	32.2	45.3	5.1	4.2	37.9	35.4
121	†Hong Kong	..	..	..	..	..	..	..	..	..	..
122	Sweden	1.3	0.5	9.2	7.3	46.1	50.1	6.8	5.6	36.6	36.4
123	Netherlands	11.2	13.9	11.0	10.5	36.6	37.4	5.2	4.3	35.9	33.9
124	Belgium	1.9	..	12.9	..	40.3	..	5.0	..	39.9	..
125	France	16.1	17.8	7.5	7.0	43.0	42.9	6.6	5.7	26.8	26.6
126	†Singapore	5.5	6.8	19.1	21.0	1.5	3.3	20.6	26.5	53.2	42.3
127	Austria	12.4	13.3	9.6	9.5	45.5	45.4	2.9	2.3	29.6	29.6
128	United States	11.7	16.9	1.9	1.8	29.9	28.5	24.2	19.3	32.3	33.6
129	Germany	18.6	16.8	0.7	0.8	48.9	45.3	8.8	6.4	23.1	30.7
130	Denmark	1.2	1.0	9.4	9.8	38.7	41.1	5.4	4.5	45.2	43.6
131	Norway	9.0	3.5	7.9	6.3	35.2	36.7	8.2	7.0	39.7	46.5
132	Japan	..	1.5	..	6.2	..	37.5	..	4.4	..	50.3
133	Switzerland	13.0	20.7	3.2	2.7	49.1	46.0	10.4	7.1	24.3	23.4

† Economies classified by the United Nations or otherwise regarded by their authorities as developing. As of July 1, 1997, Hong Kong is a part of China.

SELECTED WORLD DEVELOPMENT INDICATORS

CONTENTS

INTRODUCTION TO SELECTED WORLD DEVELOPMENT INDICATORS

THESE SELECTED WORLD DEVELOPMENT INDICATORS provide a core set of data covering three development themes: people, the environment, and the economy. The layout of the seventeen tables retains the tradition of past editions of *World Development Report* of presenting comparative socioeconomic data covering more than 130 economies for the most recent year or period for which data are available and one earlier year or period. An additional table presents basic indicators for seventy-six economies with sparse data or with populations less than 1 million.

Most of the indicators presented here have been selected from more than 500 indicators covered in the new, freestanding *World Development Indicators 1997.* Published annually, *World Development Indicators* is the World Bank's flagship statistical publication. It features a broader, more integrated approach to the presentation of development statistics. In its five main sections it recognizes the interplay of a wide range of issues: human capital development, environmental sustainability, macroeconomic performance, private sector development, and the global links that influence the external environment for development. It also features, for the first time, extensive documentation of the data to highlight potential pitfalls in intercountry and intertemporal comparisons. *World Development Indicators* is complemented by a new CD-ROM data base of over 1,000 data tables and 500 time-series indicators for 209 economies.

More about the Selected World Development Indicators

Tables 1 to 3, *Summary of socioeconomic development indicators,* offer an overview of key development issues: How rich or poor are the people? What is the life expectancy of newborns? What percentage of adults are illiterate? How has the economy performed in terms of growth and infla-

tion? What kind of external economic environment do countries face?

Tables 4 to 7, *Human resources,* show the rate of progress in social development during the past decade. Data on population growth, labor force participation, and income distribution are included. Measures of well-being such as malnutrition and access to health care, school enrollment ratios, and gender differences with respect to adult illiteracy are also presented.

Tables 8 to 10, *Environmental sustainability,* include measures of human impacts on the environment—deforestation, changing land use patterns, freshwater withdrawals, and emissions of carbon dioxide—and of some of the activities that cause these impacts—energy use and urbanization. Also included is information on the extent of protected areas that preserve natural habitat and, hence, biodiversity.

Tables 11 to 17, *Economic performance,* present information on economic structure and growth, as well as on foreign investment, external debt, and degree of integration into the global economy.

Because the World Bank's primary business is providing lending and policy advice to low- and middle-income member countries, the issues covered focus mainly on these economies. Where available, information on the high-income economies is also provided for comparison. Readers may wish to refer to national statistical publications or publications of the Organization for Economic Cooperation and Development and the European Union for more information on the high-income economies.

Classification of economies

As in the Report itself, the main criterion used to classify economies and broadly distinguish stages of economic development is GNP per capita. Countries are classified into three categories according to income. The GNP per capita cutoff levels in this edition of Selected World Development Indicators are as follows: low-income, $765 or less in 1995 (forty-nine economies); middle-income, $766 to $9,385 (fifty-eight economies); and high-income, $9,386 or more (twenty-six economies). A further division, at GNP per capita $3,035, is made between lower-middle-income and upper-middle-income. Economies are further classified by region. For a list of all economies in each income group and region, including those with populations of fewer than 1 million, see the Classification of Economies table at the end of the Selected World Development Indicators.

Data sources and methodology

Socioeconomic data presented here are drawn from several sources: primary collection by the World Bank, member-country statistical publications, nongovernmental organizations such as the World Resources Institute, and other international organizations such as the United Nations and its specialized agencies, the International Monetary Fund, and the Organization for Economic Cooperation and Development. (See Data Sources at the end of the Technical Notes for a complete listing of sources.) Although international standards of coverage, definition, and classification apply to most statistics reported by countries and international agencies, there are inevitably differences in coverage, currentness, and the capabilities and resources devoted to basic data collection and compilation. In some cases, competing sources of data require review by World Bank staff to ensure that the most reliable data available are presented. Where available data are deemed too weak to provide reliable measures of levels and trends, or do not adequately adhere to international standards, the data are not shown.

Data presented in these tables are consistent with those in *World Development Indicators 1997*. Differences between data in each annual edition reflect not only newly received information, but also revisions to historical series and changes in methodology. Thus data of different vintages may be published in different editions. *Readers are advised not to compare data series between publications.* Consistent time-series data are available on the *World Development Indicators 1997 CD-ROM*.

Considerable effort has been made to standardize the data, but *full comparability cannot be ensured, and care must be taken in interpreting the indicators.* For example, the indicators in Table 5, Distribution of income or consumption, are not strictly comparable across countries, because the underlying household surveys differ in method and in the type of data collected.

All dollar figures are in current U.S. dollars unless otherwise stated. The methods used for converting from national currency figures are described in the Technical Notes.

Summary measures

Summary measures, presented in the colored bands on each table, are either totals (indicated by t), weighted averages (w), or median values (m) calculated for groups of economies. Countries for which data are not shown in the main tables have been implicitly included in the summary measures on the assumption that they followed the trend of reporting economies during the period. The countries excluded from the main tables (those presented in Table 1a, Basic indicators for other economies) have been included in the summary measures when data are available or, when not, by assuming that they follow the trend of reporting countries. This gives a more consistent aggregate measure by standardizing country coverage for each period shown. Where missing information accounts for a third or more of the overall estimate, however, the group measure is reported as not available. The method used for computing the summary measures in each table is stated in the technical note for the table.

Terminology and country coverage

The term "country" is not meant to imply political independence but may refer to any territory for which authorities report separate social or economic statistics.

Data are shown for countries or economies as they were constituted in 1995, and historical data are revised to reflect current political arrangements. Throughout the tables, exceptions are noted.

Data for China do not include data for Taiwan, China, unless otherwise noted. As of July 1, 1997, Hong Kong is a part of China.

Data are shown separately whenever possible for the Czech Republic and the Slovak Republic, the countries formed from the former Czechoslovakia.

Data are shown separately for Eritrea whenever possible; in most cases prior to 1992, however, they are included in the data for Ethiopia.

Data for Germany refer to the unified Germany unless otherwise noted.

Data for Jordan refer to the East Bank only unless otherwise noted.

In 1991 the Union of Soviet Socialist Republics was formally dissolved into fifteen countries: Armenia, Azerbaijan, Belarus, Estonia, Georgia, Kazakstan, Kyrgyz Republic, Latvia, Lithuania, Moldova, Russian Federation, Tajikistan, Turkmenistan, Ukraine, and Uzbekistan. Whenever possible, data are shown for the individual countries.

Data for the Republic of Yemen refer to that country from 1990 onward; data for previous years refer to the former People's Democratic Republic of Yemen and the former Yemen Arab Republic, unless otherwise noted.

Whenever possible, data are shown for the individual countries formed from the former Yugoslavia: Bosnia and Herzegovina, Croatia, the former Yugoslav Republic of Macedonia, Slovenia, and the Federal Republic of Yugoslavia (Serbia and Montenegro).

Table layout

The table format of this edition generally follows that of previous editions of *World Development Report*. Economies are listed in ascending order of GNP per capita in all tables except Table 1a. High-income economies marked by the symbol † are those classified by the United Nations, or otherwise regarded by their authorities, as developing. Economies with populations of fewer than 1 million and those with sparse data are not shown separately in the main tables but are included in the aggregates. Basic indicators for these economies may be found in Table 1a. The alphabetical list in the Key and Primary Data Documentation table shows the reference number for each economy.

Technical Notes

Because data quality and intercountry comparisons are often problematic, readers are encouraged to consult the Technical Notes, the Key and Primary Data Documentation table, the Classification of Economies table, and the footnotes to the tables. These describe the methods, concepts, definitions, and data sources used in compiling the tables. For more extensive documentation see *World Development Indicators 1997*. The Data Sources section at the end of the Technical Notes lists sources that contain more comprehensive definitions and descriptions of the concepts used.

For more information about the Selected World Development Indicators and the World Bank's other statistical publications, please contact:

Information Center, Development Data Group
The World Bank, 1818 H Street, N.W.
Washington, D.C. 20433
Hotline: (800) 590-1906 or (202) 473-7824
Fax: (202) 522-1498
E-mail: info@worldbank.org
World Wide Web: http:// www.worldbank.org or
    http://www.worldbank.org/wdi.

To order World Bank publications, e-mail your request to books@worldbank.org, or write to World Bank Publications at the address above, or call (703) 661-1580.

Groups of economies

For this map, economies are classified by income group, as they are for the tables that follow.
Low-income economies are those with a GNP per capita of $765 or less in 1995; middle-income,
$766–$9,385; high-income, $9,386 or more. Five middle-income economies—American Samoa (US),
Fiji, Kiribati, Tonga, and Western Samoa, one high-income economy—French Polynesia (Fr), and Tuvalu,
for which income data are not available, are not shown on the map because of space constraints.

- Low-income economies
- Middle-income economies
- High-income economies
- Data not available

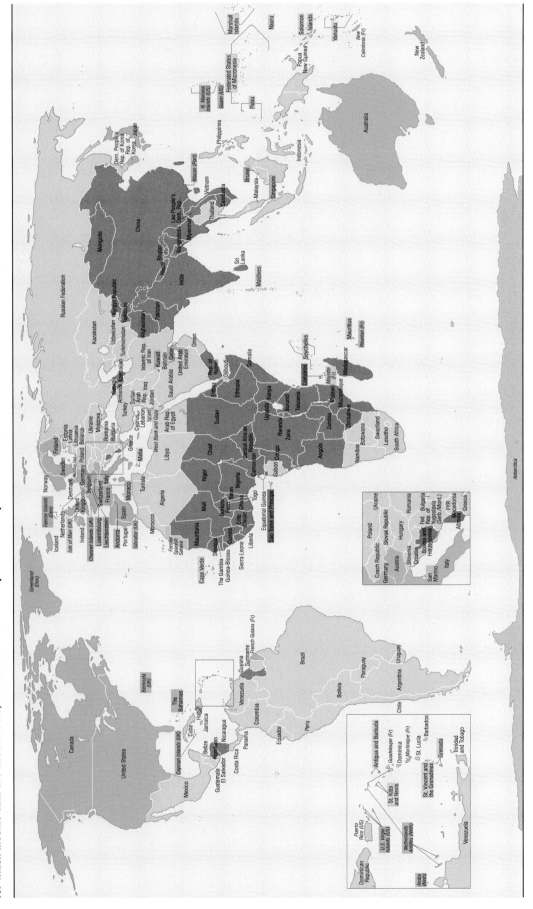

KEY AND PRIMARY DATA DOCUMENTATION

T HE KEY AND PRIMARY DATA DOCUMENTATION TABLE below provides an index to the countries included in the Selected World Development Indicators and additional information on the sources, treatment, and currentness of the principal demographic, economic, and environmental indicators for the 133 countries included in the main statistical tables.

The World Bank is not a primary data collection agency for most areas other than living standards surveys and debt. As a major user of socioeconomic data, however, the World Bank places particular emphasis on data documentation to inform users of data in economic analysis and policymaking. Differences in the methods and conventions used by the primary data collectors—usually national statistical agencies, central banks, and customs services—may give rise to significant discrepancies over time both among and within countries. See the 1997 *World Development Indicators* for a more complete treatment of primary data documentation.

In each statistical table of the Selected World Development Indicators, economies are listed in ascending order of GNP per capita. The ranking below by GNP per capita therefore indicates a country's place in the statistical tables.

Figures in the colored bands in the tables are summary measures for groups of economies. The letter *w* means weighted average; *m*, median; and *t*, total.

Except where noted in the Technical Notes, growth rates for economic data are in real terms.

The data cutoff date was February 1, 1997.

The symbol . . means not available.

A blank space means not applicable.

The figures 0 and 0.0 mean zero or less than half the unit shown.

Figures in italics indicate data that are for years or periods other than those specified.

The symbol † indicates high-income economies classified by the United Nations, or regarded by their own authorities, as developing.

Economy	GNP per capita ranking in tables	Latest population census	Latest household or demographic survey	Vital regis- tration complete	Latest water withdrawal data	Fiscal year end	National accounts base year	National accounts price valuation	Govern- ment finance accounting concept
Albania	45	1989		√	1970	Dec. 31	1993	VAP	
Algeria	69	1987	PAPCHILD, 1992		1990	Dec. 31	1980	VAB	
Angola	33	1970			1987	Dec. 31	1970	VAP	
Argentina	105	1991			1976	Dec. 31	1986	VAP	C
Armenia	49	1989		√	1989	Dec. 31	1993	VAB	
Australia	117	1991		√	1985	Jun. 30	1989	VAP	C
Austria	127	1991		√	1991	Dec. 31	1990	VAP	C
Azerbaijan	37	1989		√	1989	Dec. 31	1987	VAP	
Bangladesh	13	1991	DHS, 1994		1987	Jun. 30	1985	VAP	
Belarus	77	1989		√	1989	Dec. 31	1990	VAB	C

Economy	GNP per capita ranking in tables	Latest population census	Latest household or demographic survey	Vital regis-tration complete	Latest water withdrawal data	Fiscal year end	National accounts		Govern-ment finance accounting concept
							base year	price valuation	
Belgium	124	1991		√	1980	Dec. 31	1985	VAP	C
Benin	29	1992	WFS, 1981		1994	Dec. 31	1985	VAP	
Bolivia	52	1992	DHS, 1994		1987	Dec. 31	1980	VAP	C
Botswana	89	1991	DHS, 1988		1992	Mar. 31	1986	VAP	B
Brazil	96	1991	DHS, 1991		1990	Dec. 31	1980	VAB	C
Bulgaria	61	1992		√	1988	Dec. 31	1990	VAP	C
Burkina Faso	11	1985	SDA, 1995		1992	Dec. 31	1985	VAB	C
Burundi	4	1990			1987	Dec. 31	1980	VAB	
Cambodia	21	1962			1987	Dec. 31	1960	VAP	
Cameroon	43	1987	DHS, 1991		1987	Jun. 30	1980	VAP	C
Canada	119	1991		√	1991	Mar. 31	1986	VAB	C
Central African Rep.	26	1988	DHS, 1994–95		1987	Dec. 31	1987	VAB	
Chad	6	1993			1987	Dec. 31	1977	VAB	C
Chile	101	1992			1975	Dec. 31	1986	VAP	C
China	42	1990	Population, 1995		1980	Dec. 31	1990	VAP	B
Colombia	75	1993	DHS, 1995		1987	Dec. 31	1975	VAP	C
Congo	46	1984			1987	Dec. 31	1978	VAP	
Costa Rica	81	1984	CDC, 1993	√	1970	Dec. 31	1987	VAP	C
Côte d'Ivoire	44	1988	DHS, 1994		1986	Dec. 31	1986	VAB	C
Croatia	92	1991		√		Dec. 31	1994	VAB	
Czech Republic	98	1991	CDC, 1993	√	1991	Dec. 31	1984	VAP	C
Denmark	130	1991			1990	Dec. 31	1980	VAB	C
Dominican Republic	65	1993	DHS, 1991		1987	Dec. 31	1970	VAP	C
Ecuador	64	1990	DHS, 1994		1987	Dec. 31	1975	VAP	B
Egypt, Arab Rep.	51	1986	DHS, 1995	√	1992	Jun. 30	1987	VAB	C
El Salvador	70	1992	CDC, 1994		1975	Dec. 31	1962	VAP	B
Estonia	87	1989		√	1989	Dec. 31	1993	VAB	C
Ethiopia	2	1994	Fam. & fert., 1990		1987	Jul. 7	1981	VAB	B
Finland	120	1990		√	1991	Dec. 31	1990	VAB	C
France	125	1990	Income, 1989	√	1990	Dec. 31	1980	VAP	C
Gabon	95	1993				Dec. 31	1989	VAP	B
Gambia, The	25	1993			1982	Jun. 30	1976	VAB	B
Georgia	34	1989		√	1989	Dec. 31	1987	VAB	
Germany	129			√	1991	Dec. 31	1990	VAP	C
Ghana	31	1984	DHS, 1993		1970	Dec. 31	1975	VAP	C
Greece	107	1991		√	1980	Dec. 31	1970	VAB	C
Guatemala	63	1994	DHS, 1995		1970	Dec. 31	1958	VAP	B
Guinea	39	1991	SDA, 1991		1991	Dec. 31	1986	VAP	
Guinea-Bissau	16	1983	SDA, 1994–95		1987	Dec. 31	1989	VAP	C
Haiti	17	1982	DHS, 1994–95		1987	Sep. 30	1976	VAP	
Honduras	40	1988	DHS, 1994		1992	Dec. 31	1978	VAB	
† Hong Kong	121	1991		√		Dec. 31	1990	VAB	
Hungary	100	1990	Income, 1995	√	1991	Dec. 31	1991	VAB	C
India	27	1991	Nat. fam. hlth., 1992–93		1975	Mar. 31	1980	VAB	C
Indonesia	56	1990	DHS, 1994		1987	Mar. 31	1993	VAP	C
Ireland	112	1996		√	1980	Dec. 31	1985	VAB	C
† Israel	113	1983		√	1989	Dec. 31	1990	VAB	C
Italy	118	1991		√	1990	Dec. 31	1985	VAP	C
Jamaica	67	1991	LSMS, 1994	√	1975	Dec. 31	1986	VAP	
Japan	132	1990		√	1990	Mar. 31	1985	VAP	C
Jordan	68	1994	DHS, 1990		1975	Dec. 31	1990	VAB	B

Economy	GNP per capita ranking in tables	Latest population census	Latest household or demographic survey	Vital registration complete	Latest water withdrawal data	Fiscal year end	National accounts base year	National accounts price valuation	Government finance accounting concept
Kazakstan	62	1989		√	1989	Dec. 31	1994	VAB	
Kenya	22	1989	DHS, 1993		1990	Jun. 30	1982	VAB	B
Korea, Rep.	108	1995			1992	Dec. 31	1990	VAP	C
† Kuwait	114	1995		√	1974	Jun. 30	1984	VAP	C
Kyrgyz Republic	47	1989	LSMS, 1994	√	1989	Dec. 31	1993	VAB	
Lao PDR	28	1985			1987	Dec. 31	1990	VAP	
Latvia	79	1989		√	1989	Dec. 31	1993	VAB	C
Lebanon	82	1970			1975	Dec. 31	1990	VAB	
Lesotho	50	1986	DHS, 1991		1987	Mar. 31	1980	VAB	C
Lithuania	74	1989		√	1989	Dec. 31	1993	VAB	C
Macedonia, FYR	53	1994		√		Dec. 31	1990	VAP	
Madagascar	12	1993	SDA, 1993		1984	Dec. 31	1984	VAB	C
Malawi	5	1987	DHS, 1992		1994	Mar. 31	1978	VAB	B
Malaysia	99	1991		√	1975	Dec. 31	1978	VAP	C
Mali	18	1987	DHS, 1987		1987	Dec. 31	1987	VAB	
Mauritania	36	1988	PAPCHILD, 1990		1985	Dec. 31	1985	VAB	
Mauritius	94	1990	CDC, 1991	√	1974	Jun. 30	1992	VAB	C
Mexico	93	1990	DHS, 1987		1991	Dec. 31	1980	VAP	C
Moldova	54	1989		√	1989	Dec. 31	1993	VAB	
Mongolia	23	1989			1987	Dec. 31	1986	VAB	C
Morocco	58	1994	DHS, 1995		1992	Dec. 31	1980	VAP	C
Mozambique	1	1980			1992	Dec. 31	1987	VAB	
Namibia	76	1991	DHS, 1992		1991	Mar. 31	1990	VAB	C
Nepal	9	1991			1987	Jul. 14	1985	VAB	C
Netherlands	123	1971		√	1991	Dec. 31	1990	VAP	C
New Zealand	111	1991		√	1991	Jun. 30	1982	VAP	B
Nicaragua	30	1995	LSMS, 1993		1975	Dec. 31	1980	VAP	C
Niger	10	1988	Hsld. bgt. & cons., 1993			Dec. 31	1987	VAP	
Nigeria	19	1991	Cons. expenditure, 1992		1987	Dec. 31	1987	VAB	
Norway	131	1990		√	1985	Dec. 31	1990	VAP	C
Oman	102	1993	Child health, 1989		1975	Dec. 31	1978	VAP	B
Pakistan	35	1981	LSMS, 1991		1975	Jun. 30	1981	VAB	C
Panama	84	1990			1975	Dec. 31	1992	VAB	C
Papua New Guinea	60	1990			1987	Dec. 31	1983	VAP	B
Paraguay	72	1992	CDC, 1992		1987	Dec. 31	1982	VAP	C
Peru	80	1993	LSMS, 1994		1987	Dec. 31	1979	VAP	C
Philippines	57	1990	DHS, 1993		1975	Dec. 31	1985	VAP	B
Poland	86	1988		√	1991	Dec. 31	1990	VAP	C
Portugal	109	1991		√	1990	Dec. 31	1985	VAP	C
Romania	66	1992	LSMS, 1995	√	1994	Dec. 31	1993	VAB	C
Russian Federation	78	1989	LSMS, 1994	√	1991	Dec. 31	1993	VAB	C
Rwanda	7	1991	DHS, 1992		1993	Dec. 31	1985	VAB	C
Saudi Arabia	104	1992	Mat'l. & child hlth., 1993	√	1975	Hijri year	1970	VAP	
Senegal	41	1988	DHS, 1992–93		1987	Dec. 31	1987	VAP	
Sierra Leone	8	1985	SHEHEA, 1989–90		1987	Jun. 30	1985	VAB	B
† Singapore	126	1990		√	1975	Mar. 31	1985	VAP	C
Slovak Republic	88	1991		√	1991	Dec. 31	1993	VAP	
Slovenia	106	1991		√		Dec. 31	1992	VAB	
South Africa	91	1991	LSMS, 1993		1990	Mar. 31	1990	VAB	C

Economy	GNP per capita ranking in tables	Latest population census	Latest household or demographic survey	Vital registration complete	Latest water withdrawal data	Fiscal year end	National accounts base year	National accounts price valuation	Government finance accounting concept
Spain	110	1991		√	1991	Dec. 31	1996	VAP	C
Sri Lanka	48	1981	DHS, 1993	√	1970	Dec. 31	1982	VAB	C
Sweden	122	1990		√	1991	Jun. 30	1990	VAB	C
Switzerland	133	1990		√	1991	Dec. 31	1990	VAP	C
Syrian Arab Republic	59	1994			1976	Dec. 31	1985	VAP	C
Tanzania	3	1988	LSMS, 1993		1994	Jun. 30	1992	VAB	
Thailand	83	1990	DHS, 1987		1987	Sep. 30	1988	VAP	C
Togo	24	1981	DHS, 1988		1987	Dec. 31	1978	VAP	
Trinidad and Tobago	97	1990	DHS, 1987	√	1975	Dec. 31	1985	VAB	
Tunisia	73	1994			1990	Dec. 31	1990	VAP	C
Turkey	85	1990	Pop. & health, 1983		1991	Dec. 31	1994	VAB	C
Uganda	14	1991	DHS, 1995		1970	Jun. 30	1991	VAB	
Ukraine	71	1989		√	1989	Dec. 31	1990	VAB	
† United Arab Emirates	115	1980			1980	Dec. 31	1985	VAB	B
United Kingdom	116	1991		√	1991	Dec. 31	1990	VAB	C
United States	128	1990	Current pop., 1994	√	1990	Sep. 30	1985	VAP	C
Uruguay	103	1985			1965	Dec. 31	1983	VAP	C
Uzbekistan	55	1989		√	1989	Dec. 31	1987	VAB	
Venezuela	90	1990	LSMS, 1993		1970	Dec. 31	1984	VAP	C
Vietnam	15	1989	Intercensal demo., 1995		1992	Dec. 31	1989	VAP	
Yemen, Rep.	20	1994	DHS, 1991–92		1987	Dec. 31	1990	VAB	C
Zambia	32	1990	SDA, 1993		1994	Dec. 31	1977	VAP	C
Zimbabwe	38	1992	DHS, 1994		1987	Jun. 30	1980	VAB	C

Notes:

- *Latest population census* shows the most recent year in which a census was conducted.

- *Latest household or demographic survey* gives information on the surveys used in compiling household and demographic data. PAPCHILD is the Pan Arab Project for Child Development; DHS is Demographic and Health Survey; WFS is World Fertility Study; LSMS is Living Standards Measurement Study; SDA is Social Dimensions of Adjustment; CDC is Centers for Disease Control and Prevention; and SHEHEA is Survey of Household Expenditure and Household Economic Activities.

- *Vital registration complete* identifies countries judged to have complete registries of vital statistics (√) by the United Nations Department of Economic and Social Information and Policy Analysis, Statistical Division, and reported in Population and Vital Statistics Reports. Countries with complete vital statistics registries may have more accurate and more timely demographic indicators.

- *Latest water withdrawal survey* refers to the most recent year for which data have been compiled from a variety of sources.

- *Fiscal year end* is the date of the end of the fiscal year for the central government. Fiscal years for other levels of government and the reporting years for statistical surveys may differ, but if a country is designated as a fiscal year reporter in the following column, the date shown is the end of its national accounts reporting period.

- *National accounts base year* is the year used as the base period for constant price calculations in the country's national accounts. Price indexes derived from national accounts aggregates, such as the GDP deflator, express the price level relative to prices in the base year. Constant price data reported in the World Bank are partially rebased to a common 1987 base year.

- *National accounts price valuation* shows whether value added in the national accounts is reported at basic or producers' prices (VAB) or at purchasers' prices (VAP). Purchasers' prices include the value of taxes levied on value added and collected from consumers and thus tend to overstate the actual value added in production.

- *Government finance accounting concept* describes the accounting basis for reporting central government financial data. For most countries government finance data have been consolidated (C) into one set of accounts capturing all fiscal activities of the central government. Budgetary central government accounts (B) exclude central government units.

Table 1. Basic indicators

	Population (millions) mid-1995	Surface area (thousands of sq. km)	GNP per capita[a] Dollars 1995	GNP per capita[a] Avg. ann. growth (%) 1985–95	PPP estimates of GNP per capita[b] US=100 1987	PPP estimates of GNP per capita[b] US=100 1995	PPP estimates of GNP per capita[b] Current int'l $ 1995	Poverty % of people living on less than $1 a day (PPP) 1981–95	Life expectancy at birth (years) 1995	Adult illiteracy (%) 1995
Low-income economies	3,179.9 t	40,606 t	430 w	3.8 w					63 w	34 w
Excluding China and India	1,050.3 t	27,758 t	290 w	–1.4 w					56 w	46 w
1 Mozambique	16.2	802	80	3.6	2.5	3.0	810c	..	47	60
2 Ethiopia	56.4	1,097	100	–0.3	2.0	1.7	450	33.8	49	65
3 Tanzania[d]	29.6	945	120	1.0	2.6	2.4	640	16.4	51	32
4 Burundi	6.3	28	160	–1.3	3.2	2.3	630c	..	49	65
5 Malawi	9.8	118	170	–0.7	3.1	2.8	750	..	43	44
6 Chad	6.4	1,284	180	0.6	2.5	2.6	700c	..	48	52
7 Rwanda	6.4	26	180	–5.4	3.8	2.0	540	45.7	46	40
8 Sierra Leone	4.2	72	180	–3.6	3.2	2.2	580	..	40	..
9 Nepal	21.5	141	200	2.4	4.0	4.3	1,170c	53.1	55	73
10 Niger	9.0	1,267	220	..	3.6	2.8	750c	61.5	47	86
11 Burkina Faso	10.4	274	230	–0.2	3.3	2.9	780c	..	49	81
12 Madagascar	13.7	587	230	–2.2	3.1	2.4	640	72.3	52	..
13 Bangladesh	119.8	144	240	2.1	4.8	5.1	1,380	..	58	62
14 Uganda	19.2	236	240	2.7	4.7	5.5	1,470c	50.0	42	38
15 Vietnam	73.5	332	240	..	..	..	..	..	68	6
16 Guinea-Bissau	1.1	36	250	2.0	2.8	2.9	790c	87.0	38	45
17 Haiti	7.2	28	250	–5.2	5.8	3.4	910c	..	57	55
18 Mali	9.8	1,240	250	0.8	2.3	2.0	550	..	50	69
19 Nigeria	111.3	924	260	1.2	4.4	4.5	1,220	28.9	53	43
20 Yemen, Rep.	15.3	528	260	..	..	..	..	..	53	..
21 Cambodia	10.0	181	270	..	..	..	..	..	53	35
22 Kenya	26.7	580	280	0.1	5.7	5.1	1,380	50.2	58	22
23 Mongolia	2.5	1,567	310	–3.8	10.6	7.2	1,950	..	65	..
24 Togo	4.1	57	310	–2.7	5.5	4.2	1,130c	..	56	48
25 Gambia, The	1.1	11	320	..	4.5	3.5	930c	..	46	61
26 Central African Republic	3.3	623	340	–2.4	5.0	4.0	1,070c	..	48	40
27 India	929.4	3,288	340	3.2c	4.4	5.2	1,400	52.5	62	48
28 Lao PDR	4.9	237	350	2.7	..	..	..	..	52	43
29 Benin	5.5	113	370	–0.3	6.9	6.5	1,760	..	50	63
30 Nicaragua	4.4	130	380	–5.4	11.8	7.4	2,000c	43.8	68	34
31 Ghana	17.1	239	390	1.4	7.4	7.4	1,990c	..	59	..
32 Zambia	9.0	753	400	–0.8	4.2	3.5	930	84.6	46	22
33 Angola	10.8	1,247	410	–6.1	8.9	4.9	1,310	..	47	..
34 Georgia[f]	5.4	70	440	–17.0	28.1	5.5	1,470	..	73	..
35 Pakistan	129.9	796	460	1.2	8.4	8.3	2,230	11.6	60	62
36 Mauritania	2.3	1,026	460	0.5	6.0	5.7	1,540c	31.4	51	..
37 Azerbaijan[f]	7.5	87	480	–16.3	21.8	5.4	1,460	..	70	..
38 Zimbabwe	11.0	391	540	–0.6	8.6	7.5	2,030	41.0	57	15
39 Guinea	6.6	246	550	1.4	..	..	..	26.3	44	..
40 Honduras	5.9	112	600	0.1	7.9	7.0	1,900	46.5	67	27
41 Senegal	8.5	197	600	..	7.3	6.6	1,780	54.0	50	67
42 China	1,200.2	9,561	620	8.3	6.3	10.8	2,920	29.4	69	19
43 Cameroon	13.3	475	650	–6.6	15.1	7.8	2,110	..	57	37
44 Côte d'Ivoire	14.0	322	660	..	8.2	5.9	1,580	17.7	55	60
45 Albania	3.3	29	670	..	..	..	..	..	73	..
46 Congo	2.6	342	680	–3.2	11.5	7.6	2,050	..	51	25
47 Kyrgyz Republic[f]	4.5	199	700	–6.9	13.6	6.7	1,800	18.9	68	..
48 Sri Lanka	18.1	66	700	2.6	10.6	12.1	3,250	4.0	72	10
49 Armenia[f]	3.8	30	730	–15.1	25.4	8.4	2,260	..	71	..
Middle-income economies	1,590.9 t	60,838 t	2,390 w	–0.7 w				..	68 w	18 w
Lower-middle-income	1,152.6 t	40,323 t	1,670 w	–1.3 w				..	67 w	..
50 Lesotho	2.0	30	770	1.2	6.1	6.6	1,780c	50.4	61	29
51 Egypt, Arab Rep.	57.8	1,001	790	1.1	14.3	14.2	3,820	7.6	63	49
52 Bolivia	7.4	1,099	800	1.8	9.1	9.4	2,540	7.1	60	17
53 Macedonia, FYR	2.1	26	860	..	..	..	..	..	73	..
54 Moldova[f]	4.3	34	920	..	..	..	..	6.8	69	..
55 Uzbekistan[f]	22.8	447	970	–3.9	12.6	8.8	2,370	..	70	..
56 Indonesia	193.3	1,905	980	6.0	9.8	14.1	3,800	14.5	64	16
57 Philippines	68.6	300	1,050	1.5	10.3	10.6	2,850	27.5	66	5
58 Morocco	26.6	447	1,110	0.9	13.2	12.4	3,340	1.1	65	56
59 Syrian Arab Republic	14.1	185	1,120	0.9	18.5	19.7	5,320	..	68	..
60 Papua New Guinea	4.3	463	1,160	2.3	8.5	9.0	2,420c	..	57	28
61 Bulgaria	8.4	111	1,330	–2.6	23.4	16.6	4,480	2.6	71	..
62 Kazakstan[f]	16.6	2,717	1,330	–8.6	24.2	11.2	3,010	..	69	..
63 Guatemala	10.6	109	1,340	0.3	13.2	12.4	3,340	53.3	66	44
64 Ecuador	11.5	284	1,390	0.8	15.8	15.6	4,220	30.4	69	10
65 Dominican Republic	7.8	49	1,460	2.1	13.7	14.3	3,870	19.9	71	18
66 Romania	22.7	238	1,480	–3.8	22.2	16.2	4,360	17.7	70	..
67 Jamaica	2.5	11	1,510	3.6	11.3	13.1	3,540	4.7	74	15
68 Jordan	4.2	89	1,510	–4.5	23.8	15.1	4,060c	2.5	70	13
69 Algeria	28.0	2,382	1,600	–2.4	26.5	19.6	5,300	1.6	70	38
70 El Salvador	5.6	21	1,610	2.8	8.2	9.7	2,610	..	67	29
71 Ukraine[f]	51.6	604	1,630	–9.2	20.7	8.9	2,400	..	69	..
72 Paraguay	4.8	407	1,690	1.2	13.3	13.5	3,650	..	68	8

Note: For other economies, see Table 1a. For data comparability and coverage, see the technical notes. Figures in italics are for years other than those specified.

		Population (millions) mid-1995	Surface area (thousands of sq. km)	GNP per capita[a] Dollars 1995	GNP per capita[a] Avg. ann. growth (%) 1985–95	PPP estimates of GNP per capita[b] US=100 1987	PPP estimates of GNP per capita[b] US=100 1995	PPP estimates of GNP per capita[b] Current int'l $ 1995	Poverty % of people living on less than $1 a day (PPP) 1981–95	Life expectancy at birth (years) 1995	Adult illiteracy (%) 1995
73	Tunisia	9.0	164	1,820	1.9	18.3	18.5	5,000	3.9	69	33
74	Lithuania[f]	3.7	65	1,900	–11.7	25.2	15.3	4,120	2.1	69	..
75	Colombia	36.8	1,139	1,910	2.6	20.7	22.7	6,130	7.4	70	9
76	Namibia	1.5	824	2,000	2.9	15.8	15.4	4,150[c]	..	59	..
77	Belarus[f]	10.3	208	2,070	–5.2	26.3	15.6	4,220	..	70	..
78	Russian Federation[f]	148.2	17,075	2,240	–5.1	30.9	16.6	4,480	1.1	65	..
79	Latvia[f]	2.5	65	2,270	–6.6	24.5	12.5	3,370	..	69	..
80	Peru	23.8	1,285	2,310	–1.6	17.9	14.0	3,770	49.4	66	11
81	Costa Rica	3.4	51	2,610	2.8	19.8	21.7	5,850	18.9	77	5
82	Lebanon	4.0	10	2,660	..	..	..	..	..	68	8
83	Thailand	58.2	513	2,740	8.4	16.2	28.0	7,540	0.1	69	6
84	Panama	2.6	76	2,750	–0.4	26.1	22.2	5,980	25.6	73	9
85	Turkey	61.1	779	2,780	2.2	20.4	20.7	5,580	..	67	18
86	Poland	38.6	313	2,790	1.2	21.5	20.0	5,400	6.8	70	..
87	Estonia[f]	1.5	45	2,860	–4.3	25.5	15.6	4,220	6.0	70	..
88	Slovak Republic	5.4	49	2,950	–2.8	17.6	13.4	3,610	12.8	72	..
89	Botswana	1.5	582	3,020	6.1	15.3	20.7	5,580	34.7	68	30
90	Venezuela	21.7	912	3,020	0.5	33.0	29.3	7,900	11.8	71	9
	Upper-middle-income	438.3 t	20,514 t	4,260 w	0.2 w					69 w	14 w
91	South Africa	41.5	1,221	3,160	–1.1	22.4	18.6	5,030[c]	23.7	64	18
92	Croatia	4.8	57	3,250	..	..	..	..	..	74	..
93	Mexico	91.8	1,958	3,320	0.1	27.8	23.7	6,400	14.9	72	10
94	Mauritius	1.1	2	3,380	5.4	39.0	49.0	13,210	..	71	17
95	Gabon	1.1	268	3,490	–8.2	..	..	..	..	55	37
96	Brazil	159.2	8,512	3,640	–0.8	24.2	20.0	5,400	28.7	67	17
97	Trinidad and Tobago	1.3	5	3,770	–1.7	38.1	31.9	8,610[c]	..	72	2
98	Czech Republic	10.3	79	3,870	–1.8	44.9	36.2	9,770	3.1	73	..
99	Malaysia	20.1	330	3,890	5.7	22.9	33.4	9,020	5.6	71	17
100	Hungary	10.2	93	4,120	–1.0	28.9	23.8	6,410	0.7	70	..
101	Chile	14.2	757	4,160	6.1	24.6	35.3	9,520	15.0	72	5
102	Oman	2.2	212	4,820	0.3	33.2	30.2	8,140[c]	..	70	..
103	Uruguay	3.2	177	5,170	3.1	23.6	24.6	6,630	..	73	3
104	Saudi Arabia	19.0	2,150	7,040	–1.9	43.0	..	..	..	70	37
105	Argentina	34.7	2,767	8,030	1.8	31.6	30.8	8,310	..	73	4
106	Slovenia	2.0	20	8,200	..	..	..	..	..	74	..
107	Greece	10.5	132	8,210	1.3	44.2	43.4	11,710	..	78	..
	Low- and middle-income	4,770.8 t	101,444 t	1,090 w	0.4 w					65 w	30 w
	Sub-Saharan Africa	583.3 t	24,271 t	490 w	–1.1 w					52 w	43 w
	East Asia and Pacific	1,706.4 t	16,249 t	800 w	7.2 w					68 w	17 w
	South Asia	1,243.0 t	5,133 t	350 w	2.9 w					61 w	51 w
	Europe and Central Asia	487.6 t	24,355 t	2,220 w	–3.5 w					68 w	..
	Middle East and N. Africa	272.4 t	11,021 t	1,780 w	–0.3 w					66 w	39 w
	Latin America and Caribbean	477.9 t	20,414 t	3,320 w	0.3 w					69 w	13 w
	High-income economies	902.2 t	32,039 t	24,930 w	1.9 w					77 w	..
108	Korea, Rep.	44.9	99	9,700	7.7	27.3	42.4	11,450	..	72	h
109	Portugal	9.9	92	9,740	3.6	41.6	47.0	12,670	..	75	..
110	Spain	39.2	505	13,580	2.6	50.5	53.8	14,520	..	77	..
111	New Zealand	3.6	271	14,340	0.8	63.3	60.6	16,360	..	76	h
112	Ireland	3.6	70	14,710	5.2	44.2	58.1	15,680	..	77	h
113	†Israel	5.5	21	15,920	2.5	56.3	61.1	16,490	..	77	..
114	†Kuwait	1.7	18	17,390	1.1	86.3	88.2	23,790[c]	..	76	21
115	†United Arab Emirates	2.5	84	17,400	–2.8	84.4	61.1	16,470	..	75	21
116	United Kingdom	58.5	245	18,700	1.4	72.0	71.4	19,260	..	77	h
117	Australia	18.1	7,713	18,720	1.4	70.1	70.2	18,940	..	77	h
118	Italy	57.2	301	19,020	1.8	72.5	73.7	19,870	..	78	h
119	Canada	29.6	9,976	19,380	0.4	84.6	78.3	21,130	..	78	h
120	Finland	5.1	338	20,580	–0.2	72.9	65.8	17,760	..	76	h
121	†Hong Kong	6.2	1	22,990[g]	4.8	70.7	85.1	22,950[g]	..	79	8
122	Sweden	8.8	450	23,750	–0.1	77.7	68.7	18,540	..	79	h
123	Netherlands	15.5	37	24,000	1.9	70.5	73.9	19,950	..	78	h
124	Belgium	10.1	31	24,710	2.2	76.3	80.3	21,660	..	77	h
125	France	58.1	552	24,990	1.5	77.6	78.0	21,030	..	78	h
126	†Singapore	3.0	1	26,730	6.2	56.1	84.4	22,770[c]	..	76	9
127	Austria	8.1	84	26,890	1.9	75.0	78.8	21,250	..	77	h
128	United States	263.1	9,364	26,980	1.3	100.0	100.0	26,980	..	77	h
129	Germany	81.9	357	27,510	..	..	74.4	20,070	..	76	h
130	Denmark	5.2	43	29,890	1.5	78.7	78.7	21,230	..	75	h
131	Norway	4.4	324	31,250	1.7	78.6	81.3	21,940	..	78	h
132	Japan	125.2	378	39,640	2.9	75.3	82.0	22,110	..	80	h
133	Switzerland	7.0	41	40,630	0.2	105.4	95.9	25,860	..	78	h
	World	5,673.0 t	133,483 t	4,880 w	0.8 w					67 w	..

†Economies classified by the United Nations or otherwise regarded by their authorities as developing. a. Atlas method; see the technical notes. b. Purchasing power parity; see the technical notes. c. The estimate is based on regression; others are extrapolated from the latest International Comparison Programme benchmark estimates. d. In all tables, GDP and GNP cover mainland Tanzania. e. GDP growth rates were revised after the statistics for this publication were finalized. f. Estimates for economies of the former Soviet Union are preliminary; their classification will be kept under review. g. Data refer to GDP. h. According to UNESCO, illiteracy is less than 5 percent.

Table 2. Macroeconomic indicators

| | | Central gov't. curr. deficit/surplus[a] (% of GDP) | | Money and quasi money | | | Nominal interest rates of banks (average annual %) | | | | Average annual inflation (%) (GDP deflator) | Current account balance (% of GDP) | | Gross international reserves (months of import cov.) | | Net present value of external debt (% of GNP) |
| | | | | Avg. ann. nominal growth (%) | Average outstanding as % of GDP | | Deposit rate | | Lending rate | | | | | | | |
		1980	1995	1985–95	1980	1995	1980	1995	1980	1995	1985–95	1980	1995	1980	1995	1995
Low-income economies																
Excluding China and India																
1	Mozambique	..	..	..	21.6[b]	42.1	..	..	..	..	52.2	–18.1	..	..	..	333
2	Ethiopia	–1.7[b]	..	..	..	11.5	..	15.1	..		..	–4.1[b]	–1.9	4.0[b]	7.0	61
3	Tanzania	–1.3	..	..	40.7	30.7	4.0	24.6	11.5	42.8	32.3	–7.1	–17.5	0.2	1.5	148
4	Burundi	1.9	..	..	13.5	19.9	2.5	..	12.0	15.3	6.1	..	–0.6	..	8.7	50
5	Malawi	1.1	..	23.6	18.0	15.2	7.9	37.3	16.7	47.3	22.1	–21.0	–35.0	1.4	1.5	65
6	Chad	..	..	–0.6	20.0	13.7	5.5	5.5	11.0	16.0	3.1	1.2	–4.1	1.7	4.2	38
7	Rwanda	3.5	..	7.3	13.6	6.3	5.0	5.0	13.5	15.0	10.8	–4.2	–6.5	6.7	4.7	40
8	Sierra Leone	–4.4	–3.3	51.4	19.4	9.8	9.2	7.0	11.0	28.8	61.6	–14.2	–10.1	0.7	2.7	137
9	Nepal	..	..	..	21.9	33.7	4.0	..	14.0	..	11.6	–4.8	–8.9	8.9	4.9	26
10	Niger	5.0	..	1.1	13.3	14.2	6.2	..	14.5	..	1.3	–10.9	–8.2	1.6	2.6	53
11	Burkina Faso	2.0	..	9.3	13.8	24.3	6.2	..	14.5	..	2.6	–2.9	0.8	1.5	7.1	27
12	Madagascar	..	–2.8	24.2	18.2	17.9	..	..	..	..	18.4	–13.8	–8.6	0.1	1.1	98
13	Bangladesh	..	..	14.1	18.4	35.6	8.3	6.0	11.3	14.0	6.4	–6.5	–3.5	1.5	4.2	32
14	Uganda	–2.2	..	69.0	12.7	10.1	6.8	7.6	10.8	20.2	65.7	–6.6	–7.6	0.1	3.8	43
15	Vietnam	..	..	..	..	..	..	..	..	..	88.3	..	–9.9	..	0.0	138
16	Guinea-Bissau	..	..	..	..	13.8	..	26.5	..	32.9	62.5	–48.0	–16.1	..	2.5	235
17	Haiti	–3.2	..	16.9	24.0	42.9	10.0	..	..	..	14.7	–6.9	–3.3	0.6	1.6	25
18	Mali	–1.4	..	6.5	17.9	20.2	6.2	..	14.5	..	4.6	–8.0	–8.9	0.6	4.0	73
19	Nigeria	..	..	23.8	25.1	..	5.3	13.5	8.4	20.2	33.0	5.6	–1.9	5.8	1.5	132
20	Yemen, Rep.	..	–13.4	..	..	47.0	..	..	..	..	..	..	3.0	..	2.5	128
21	Cambodia	..	..	..	..	7.7	..	8.7	..	18.7	..	..	–6.7	..	0.8	52
22	Kenya	2.5	–0.3	21.3	29.8	37.6	5.8	13.6	10.6	28.8	13.0	–12.1	–4.4	2.1	1.2	72
23	Mongolia	..	8.6	..	..	25.7	..	60.1	..	114.9	51.6	–34.7	4.5	..	3.4	39
24	Togo	1.8	..	0.5	29.0	28.9	6.2	..	14.5	..	..	–8.4	–5.8	1.4	3.6	75
25	Gambia, The	6.7	7.4	14.4	21.1	23.1	5.0	12.5	15.0	25.0	9.0	–37.2	–2.1	0.4	5.3	59
26	Central African Republic	–2.1	..	6.1	18.9	20.9	5.5	5.5	10.5	16.0	3.8	–5.4	–2.8	2.2	9.0	52
27	India	0.0	–1.6	16.8	34.7	46.0	..	..	16.5	16.3	9.8	–1.7	–1.8	8.0	5.2	23
28	Lao PDR	..	..	..	..	12.7	..	14.0	..	25.7	22.6	..	–12.7	..	1.8	43
29	Benin	..	..	10.1	17.1	25.1	6.2	..	14.5	..	..	–2.5	2.4	0.4	3.2	46
30	Nicaragua	–1.5	3.1	836.2	24.0	30.0	..	11.1	..	19.9	961.6	–19.2	–36.9	0.9	1.2	520
31	Ghana	–2.9	–0.9	38.4	16.2	15.4	11.5	28.7	19.0	..	28.6	0.7	–6.5	3.1	4.3	61
32	Zambia	–8.1	3.4	75.1	28.4	12.6	7.0	..	9.5	113.3	91.5	–13.3	..	1.2	..	139
33	Angola	..	..	..	..	..	..	..	..	..	169.5	..	–18.1	..	..	260
34	Georgia	..	..	..	..	..	..	..	..	..	310.0	..	..	..	..	44
35	Pakistan	1.8	0.3	15.6	38.7	40.9	..	..	..	..	9.2	–4.8	–3.8	3.1	2.1	38
36	Mauritania	..	..	7.5	20.5	19.3	5.5	..	12.0	..	6.9	–18.8	–2.6	3.6	1.7	166
37	Azerbaijan	..	..	..	..	9.5	..	..	..	162.5	..	..	–10.9	..	..	8
38	Zimbabwe	–9.0	..	22.1	29.5	26.0	3.5	25.9	17.5	34.7	20.9	–2.8	–7.3	2.7	..	65
39	Guinea	..	..	..	..	8.8	..	17.5	..	21.5	..	..	–5.3	..	1.0	59
40	Honduras	..	..	18.6	21.1	25.2	10.6	12.0	16.5	27.0	14.3	–12.3	–5.1	1.5	1.5	101
41	Senegal	1.8	..	3.9	26.6	20.0	6.2	..	14.5	..	3.7	–12.8	0.1	0.2	1.9	54
42	China	..	..	28.3	33.2	92.4	5.4	11.0	5.0	12.1	9.3	2.8	0.2	10.5	6.3	16
43	Cameroon	5.8	0.2	–2.9	20.6	16.2	7.5	5.5	13.0	16.0	2.0	–10.1	–2.2	1.1	0.1	97
44	Côte d'Ivoire	3.8	..	2.2	26.7	26.2	6.2	..	14.5	..	4.0	–18.0	–2.7	0.1	1.5	185
45	Albania	..	–4.7	..	..	47.5	..	15.3	..	19.7	27.3	..	–0.5	..	3.7	32
46	Congo	..	..	1.1	14.8	14.7	6.5	5.5	11.0	16.0	2.2	–9.8	–26.4	0.9	0.4	325
47	Kyrgyz Republic	..	..	..	..	..	..	..	..	..	..	..	–9.5	..	..	15
48	Sri Lanka	–4.5	–1.5	17.0	28.4	31.8	14.5	16.1	19.0	14.7	11.8	–16.3	–4.7	1.5	4.2	44
49	Armenia	..	..	..	..	..	..	..	..	..	183.1	..	–13.6	..	..	14
Middle-income economies																
Lower-middle-income																
50	Lesotho	1.3	18.0	13.9	39.7	28.9	9.6	13.3	11.0	16.4	13.4	15.3	12.2	1.3	5.4	26
51	Egypt, Arab Rep.	9.0	6.5	19.0	52.2	96.8	8.3	10.9	13.3	16.5	15.7	–1.9	–2.0	3.1	11.8	56
52	Bolivia	..	–1.2	43.1	16.2	44.9	18.0	18.9	28.0	51.0	18.4	–0.2	–4.0	6.0	6.7	67
53	Macedonia, FYR	..	..	..	..	..	..	..	..	..	..	..	..	..	1.7	57
54	Moldova	..	..	..	..	11.5	..	..	..	..	..	..	–2.7	..	2.9	16
55	Uzbekistan	..	..	..	..	..	..	..	..	..	..	..	0.0	..	..	7
56	Indonesia	9.6	9.9	..	13.2	..	6.0	..	..	17.1	8.8	–0.6	–3.5	2.9	3.0	54
57	Philippines	4.1	2.0	20.7	22.0	45.4	12.3	8.4	14.0	14.7	9.8	–5.9	–2.7	4.6	2.6	49
58	Morocco	0.5	..	13.1	38.5	65.2	4.9	..	7.0	10.0	4.8	–7.5	–4.7	1.7	3.6	62
59	Syrian Arab Republic	–3.5	7.1	..	40.9	63.2	5.0	..	..	..	16.0	1.9	2.6	2.2	..	118
60	Papua New Guinea	–6.2	–4.1	..	32.9	30.2	6.9	5.1	11.2	9.2	4.5	–11.3	13.8	3.5	1.3	45
61	Bulgaria	..	–4.1	..	..	..	..	..	..	..	45.9	4.8	2.7	..	..	87
62	Kazakstan	..	..	..	..	..	..	..	..	..	..	..	–2.4	..	2.8	22
63	Guatemala	2.1	0.8	22.7	20.5	23.5	9.0	7.9	11.0	21.2	18.6	–2.1	–3.9	4.3	2.4	19
64	Ecuador	0.9	3.3	55.3	21.2	26.6	..	43.3	9.0	55.7	45.5	–5.5	–4.6	4.1	3.4	76
65	Dominican Republic	2.9	8.3	31.9	17.8	24.4	..	..	..	..	26.4	–10.9	–1.1	1.5	0.7	33
66	Romania	15.5	2.2	51.3	33.4	19.9	..	..	..	..	68.7	..	–3.8	2.1	2.9	18
67	Jamaica	..	..	33.4	32.8	44.0	9.5	23.2	15.6	43.6	28.3	–5.1	–5.6	0.8	2.0	123
68	Jordan	..	2.5	10.2	..	104.5	..	3.3	..	9.0	..	..	–9.0	6.3	5.3	108
69	Algeria	..	..	14.8	53.3	38.8	..	..	..	..	22.9	0.6	–5.6	5.8	5.0	64
70	El Salvador	–0.4	0.8	21.2	28.0	36.1	..	14.4	..	19.1	14.9	0.9	–0.7	3.6	3.2	22
71	Ukraine	..	..	..	..	0.0	..	70.3	..	122.7	..	..	–1.4	..	0.7	10
72	Paraguay	3.3	3.0	36.5	19.8	26.4	..	21.2	..	31.0	24.9	–13.5	–19.0	6.7	..	27

Note: For data comparability and coverage, see the technical notes. Figures in italics are for years other than those specified.

| | | Central gov't. curr. deficit/surplus[a] (% of GDP) | | Money and quasi money | | | Nominal interest rates of banks (average annual %) | | | | Average annual inflation (%) (GDP deflator) | Current account balance (% of GDP) | | Gross international reserves (months of import cov.) | | Net present value of external debt (% of GNP) |
| | | | | Avg. ann. nominal growth (%) | Average outstanding as a % of GDP | | Deposit rate | | Lending rate | | | | | | | |
		1980	1995	1985–95	1980	1995	1980	1995	1980	1995	1985–95	1980	1995	1980	1995	1995
73	Tunisia	9.2	..	9.8	37.6	44.3	2.5	..	7.3	..	6.0	–4.0	–4.1	2.0	2.1	52
74	Lithuania	..	0.7	..	..	22.6	..	8.4	..	27.1	..	..	–8.7	..	2.5	9
75	Colombia	1.5	2.8	31.6	17.1	19.5	..	32.3	..	42.7	25.2	–0.6	–5.4	12.5	5.0	27
76	Namibia	..	0.7	..	..	38.7	..	10.8	..	18.5	10.4	..	1.6	..	1.3	..
77	Belarus	..	..	..	..	10.5	..	100.8	..	175.0	..	..	–1.2	..	0.9	6
78	Russian Federation	..	–5.6	..	..	11.6	..	102.0	..	319.5	148.9	..	2.8	..	2.5	35
79	Latvia	..	–2.5	..	..	25.0	..	14.8	..	34.6	72.5	..	–0.4	..	3.2	7
80	Peru	2.0	0.5	388.5	16.5	17.2	..	16.0	..	36.6	398.5	–0.5	–7.4	6.6	8.6	52
81	Costa Rica	–3.5	–0.4	23.6	38.8	32.2	18.3	23.9	25.0	36.7	18.4	–13.7	–1.5	1.2	3.0	40
82	Lebanon	..	–11.2	63.4	..	117.6	12.9	16.3	16.8	24.7	..	..	–45.7	..	14.6	25
83	Thailand	–0.1	8.1	19.7	34.5	73.8	12.0	11.6	18.0	14.4	5.0	–6.4	–8.1	3.3	5.0	35
84	Panama	0.4	2.8	11.3	32.8	67.9	..	7.2	..	11.1	1.7	–9.2	–2.2	0.2	0.9	98
85	Turkey	2.6	–2.4	73.9	14.2	24.8	8.0	76.1	..	..	64.6	–5.0	–1.4	4.3	3.7	43
86	Poland	..	–0.8	87.2	57.0	31.8	..	26.8	8.0	33.5	91.8	–6.0	–3.6	0.3	4.9	31
87	Estonia	..	..	..	..	22.5	..	8.7	..	16.0	77.2	..	–4.6	..	2.2	6
88	Slovak Republic	..	..	..	..	62.9	..	9.0	..	15.6	10.6	..	3.7	..	4.4	31
89	Botswana	10.8	21.1	19.2	28.2	25.9	5.0	10.0	8.5	14.2	11.5	–15.6	7.9	4.3	22.5	13
90	Venezuela	7.4	2.6	36.3	28.9	23.1	..	24.7	..	32.2	37.6	6.8	3.0	9.4	6.3	47
Upper-middle-income																
91	South Africa	4.4	–4.2	14.5	50.1	51.7	5.5	13.5	9.5	17.9	13.9	4.5	–2.6	3.6	1.4	..
92	Croatia	..	2.1	..	..	22.1	..	5.5	..	20.2	..	..	–9.5	..	2.5	18
93	Mexico	3.8	2.4	46.1	25.2	30.7	20.6	39.2	28.1	..	36.7	–5.3	–0.3	1.4	2.1	67
94	Mauritius	–1.9	1.9	20.3	40.0	73.2	9.3	12.2	12.2	20.8	8.8	–10.3	–0.6	1.9	4.2	..
95	Gabon	..	..	1.2	15.3	14.6	7.5	5.5	12.5	16.0	5.0	9.0	8.1	0.7	0.8	89
96	Brazil	4.1	–13.3	995.5	11.1	26.1	115.0	52.2	..	..	875.3	–5.5	–2.6	2.3	7.9	23
97	Trinidad and Tobago	24.1	..	4.3	27.1	40.1	6.6	6.9	10.0	15.2	6.8	5.7	5.5	11.4	1.8	52
98	Czech Republic	..	4.0	..	..	81.0	..	7.0	..	12.8	12.2	..	–3.1	..	6.5	36
99	Malaysia	7.1	7.3	15.5	46.1	85.0	6.2	5.9	7.8	7.6	3.3	–1.1	–5.9	4.6	3.2	39
100	Hungary	4.7	..	..	..	43.0	3.0	26.1	..	32.6	19.9	–2.3	–5.8	..	6.7	72
101	Chile	6.7	5.3	25.5	21.0	33.9	37.7	13.7	47.1	18.2	17.9	–7.1	0.2	5.9	8.8	41
102	Oman	7.9	–4.3	5.7	13.8	31.3	..	6.5	..	9.4	–0.2	15.8	–8.1	3.2	2.6	28
103	Uruguay	2.1	0.6	71.3	31.2	33.4	50.3	38.2	66.6	99.1	70.7	–7.0	–2.0	12.5	5.3	31
104	Saudi Arabia	..	..	5.1	13.8	50.4	..	..	..	..	2.8	26.5	–6.5	5.0	2.7	..
105	Argentina	–2.6	..	257.9	19.0	18.8	79.6	11.9	..	17.8	255.6	–6.3	–1.4	7.0	6.2	31
106	Slovenia	..	..	..	..	32.5	..	15.3	..	24.8	..	..	–0.2	..	2.1	18
107	Greece	–0.4	–14.4	..	50.5	53.0	14.5	15.8	21.3	23.1	15.4	–5.5	–3.2	3.7	7.0	..
Low- and middle-income																
Sub-Saharan Africa																
East Asia and Pacific																
South Asia																
Europe and Central Asia																
Middle East and N. Africa																
Latin America and Caribbean																
High-income economies																
108	Korea, Rep.	2.8	6.0	18.5	29.0	40.9	19.5	8.8	18.0	9.0	6.7	–8.3	–1.8	1.3	2.5	..
109	Portugal	–2.7	–3.4	15.5	70.1	78.1	19.0	8.4	18.8	13.8	11.2	–3.7	–0.2	15.2	6.2	..
110	Spain	0.4	–4.9	11.2	75.4	78.6	13.1	7.7	16.9	10.0	6.3	–2.6	0.2	6.0	3.2	..
111	New Zealand	–1.6	3.8	19.2	26.4	77.6	11.0	8.5	12.6	12.2	3.9	–4.3	–6.6	0.6	2.4	..
112	Ireland	–5.7	–1.8	11.4	43.8	50.1	12.0	0.4	16.0	6.6	2.5	–10.6	2.3	2.7	2.0	..
113	† Israel	–16.9	–2.4	22.1	14.8	67.3	..	14.1	176.9	20.2	17.1	–3.9	–6.0	3.6	2.5	..
114	† Kuwait	70.5	..	3.2	33.1	77.7	9.2	6.5	9.2	8.4	–0.5	53.4	15.8	6.2	4.1	..
115	† United Arab Emirates	–11.0	–8.8	4.6	19.0	54.0	9.5	..	12.1	..	..	..	..	..	..	..
116	United Kingdom	–1.2	–3.4	..	..	..	14.1	4.1	16.2	6.7	5.1	1.3	–0.4	2.0	1.3	..
117	Australia	0.6	–1.9	11.9	36.4	61.3	8.6	..	10.6	..	3.7	–2.8	–5.5	2.5	1.9	..
118	Italy	–6.4	–8.4	..	70.9	62.5	12.7	6.4	19.0	12.5	6.0	–2.3	2.4	6.4	2.4	..
119	Canada	–2.4	..	8.9	45.1	59.3	12.9	7.1	14.3	8.6	2.9	–0.6	–1.5	2.3	0.8	..
120	Finland	2.0	–9.0	6.6	39.8	56.7	9.0	3.2	9.8	7.7	3.8	–2.7	4.5	1.6	2.9	..
121	† Hong Kong	..	..	..	60.7	..	..	..	..	..	8.7	–4.4	..	..	..	..
122	Sweden	–2.5	–5.9	..	..	..	11.3	6.2	15.2	11.1	5.5	–3.4	2.0	2.0	3.1	..
123	Netherlands	1.2	–2.3	5.6	67.3	82.0	6.0	4.4	13.5	7.2	1.7	–0.5	4.1	4.4	2.5	..
124	Belgium	–2.9	–2.6	13.0	45.0	80.2	7.7	4.0	18.0	8.4	3.2	..	..	..	..	..
125	France	2.2	–3.8	3.7	71.6	64.4	7.3	4.5	12.5	8.1	2.8	–0.6	1.1	5.2	1.5	..
126	† Singapore	9.8	15.0	14.3	57.7	82.6	9.4	3.5	11.7	6.4	3.9	–13.3	18.0	3.0	5.7	..
127	Austria	0.6	–1.5	7.0	72.6	89.5	5.0	2.2	..	..	3.2	–5.0	–2.2	6.4	2.5	..
128	United States	–0.5	–1.4	3.9	60.4	59.4	13.1[c]	5.9[c]	15.3	8.8	3.2	0.1	–2.1	6.2	2.0	..
129	Germany	..	–0.2	8.1	..	62.0	7.9	3.9	12.0	10.9	..	..	–0.9	5.3	2.1	..
130	Denmark	–1.2	–1.2	4.4	42.6	57.8	10.8	3.9	17.2	10.3	2.8	–3.3	0.8	1.5	1.5	..
131	Norway	4.0	1.0	5.9	47.1	55.6	5.0	5.0	12.6	7.8	3.0	1.7	3.0	3.0	5.5	..
132	Japan	–3.2	..	5.9	83.4	112.7	5.5	0.7	8.3	3.4	1.4	–1.0	2.2	2.8	4.1	..
133	Switzerland	0.8	–3.4	4.6	107.4	126.3	8.8	1.3	5.6	5.5	3.4	–0.2	7.2	13.3	7.7	..
World																

a. Refers to current budget balance excluding grants. b. Includes Eritrea. c. Certificate of deposit rate.

Table 3. External economic indicators

		Net barter terms of trade (1987=100)		Trade (% of GDP)		Aggregate net resource flows (% of GNP)		Net private capital flows (millions $)		Aid (% of GNP)	
		1985	1995	1980	1995	1980	1995	1980	1995	1980	1994
	Low-income economies	111 m	91 m			3.4 w	5.9 w	7,368 t	53,446 t	1.9 w	4.3 w
	Excluding China and India	112 m	91 m			6.3 w	7.3 w	4,769 t	5,517 t	4.1 w	12.6 w
1	Mozambique	113	124	61	102	3.9	76.8	0	67	8.4	101.0
2	Ethiopia	119[a]	74	27[a]	39	8.3[a]	12.0	26[a]	−42	4.7[a]	22.7
3	Tanzania	126	83	37	96	16.4	18.1	100	137	12.4	29.9
4	Burundi	133	52	32	43	8.1	24.5	−3	1	12.8	31.6
5	Malawi	99	87	64	69	15.7	22.4	30	−14	12.6	38.0
6	Chad	99	103	65	46	3.3	16.2	0	7	4.9	23.9
7	Rwanda	136	75	41	32	9.3	53.8	14	1	13.4	95.9
8	Sierra Leone	109	89	62	40	5.2	22.7	−7	−28	8.0	36.0
9	Nepal	98	85	30	60	6.5	6.4	0	−2	8.3	10.9
10	Niger	91	101	63	30	12.9	8.6	199	−23	6.8	25.0
11	Burkina Faso	103	103	43	45	8.4	13.9	4	0	12.5	23.7
12	Madagascar	124	82	43	54	8.7	8.4	131	4	5.8	10.2
13	Bangladesh	126	94	24	37	13.0	3.5	11	10	9.9	6.8
14	Uganda	149	58	45	33	8.9	10.1	44	112	9.0	19.2
15	Vietnam	..	..	..	83	..	4.4	0	1,487	..	5.9
16	Guinea-Bissau	91	92	52	48	108.0	26.4	18	1	56.6	74.3
17	Haiti	89	52	52	17	5.2	28.0	20	2	7.3	37.3
18	Mali	100	103	51	38	12.1	13.9	10	1	16.6	24.5
19	Nigeria	167	86	48	81	0.9	0.8	694	453	0.0	0.6
20	Yemen, Rep.	131	84	..	88	..	3.6	97	−2	..	4.6
21	Cambodia	..	..	..	36	..	15.1	0	164	..	14.3
22	Kenya	124	98	67	72	8.8	5.6	301	−42	5.6	9.7
23	Mongolia	..	..	58	..	0.0	16.0	0	−4	0.0	27.6
24	Togo	139	90	107	65	12.7	11.3	83	0	8.3	13.8
25	Gambia, The	137	111	119	103	35.0	9.0	21	10	24.4	19.8
26	Central African Republic	109	91	69	46	10.7	12.5	4	3	13.9	19.4
27	India	92	150	17	27	1.4	1.0	868	3,592	1.3	0.8
28	Lao PDR	..	..	..	53	..	16.1	0	88	..	14.2
29	Benin	111	110	66	64	7.2	10.7	4	1	6.4	17.4
30	Nicaragua	111	95	68	76	13.8	33.3	−26	−7	10.9	46.1
31	Ghana	93	64	18	59	4.1	17.4	−26	525	4.3	8.5
32	Zambia	89	85	87	71	14.6	12.5	175	30	8.9	20.7
33	Angola	153	86	..	132	..	21.3	38	523	..	11.0
34	Georgia	..	..	..	46	..	66.2	0	0	..	7.5
35	Pakistan	112	114	37	36	5.4	4.1	230	1,443	5.1	3.1
36	Mauritania	110	106	104	104	29.4	17.8	27	3	26.2	27.7
37	Azerbaijan	..	..	..	66	..	7.9	0	110	..	3.8
38	Zimbabwe	100	84	64	74	4.2	7.2	23	99	3.1	10.2
39	Guinea	120	91	..	46	..	9.1	80	20	..	11.0
40	Honduras	118	77	80	80	11.7	6.5	137	65	4.2	9.5
41	Senegal	107	107	72	69	9.0	8.4	18	−24	9.0	17.2
42	China	109	105	13	40	1.0	7.9	1,732	44,339	0.0	0.6
43	Cameroon	113	79	54	46	10.9	2.8	409	49	4.4	10.0
44	Côte d'Ivoire	109	81	76	76	11.8	7.9	936	36	2.2	24.8
45	Albania	..	..	..	52	..	9.2	0	70	..	9.1
46	Congo	150	93	120	128	35.5	1.1	440	−49	6.0	24.9
47	Kyrgyz Republic	..	..	..	58	..	6.1	0	15	..	5.5
48	Sri Lanka	106	88	87	83	10.6	6.0	129	140	9.8	5.1
49	Armenia	..	..	..	85	..	7.2	0	8	..	9.8
	Middle-income economies	..	94 m			2.8 w	4.1 w	44,334 t	130,742 t	0.6 w	1.0 w
	Lower-middle-income	..	..			..	..	..	..	1.3 w	1.4 w
50	Lesotho	..	..	143	138	10.5	8.4	7	32	14.9	8.9
51	Egypt, Arab Rep.	147	95	73	54	14.2	1.9	1,133	294	6.5	6.4
52	Bolivia	130	67	38	47	14.1	12.9	203	191	5.9	10.9
53	Macedonia, FYR	..	..	..	86	..	3.0	0	0	..	..
54	Moldova	..	..	..	78	..	4.9	0	79	..	1.5
55	Uzbekistan	..	..	..	125	..	2.3	0	235	..	0.1
56	Indonesia	145	79	53	53	2.5	6.8	987	11,648	1.3	1.0
57	Philippines	99	114	52	80	3.9	5.2	840	4,605	0.9	1.6
58	Morocco	99	90	45	62	8.6	2.9	731	572	4.9	2.2
59	Syrian Arab Republic	138	78	54	..	19.7	1.9	42	43	13.0	5.3
60	Papua New Guinea	94	90	97	106	16.8	10.8	106	578	13.1	6.4
61	Bulgaria	95	106	66	94	1.7	3.7	339	489	0.0	1.6
62	Kazakstan	..	..	..	69	..	4.7	0	500	..	0.2
63	Guatemala	114	93	47	47	2.8	1.7	91	85	0.9	1.7
64	Ecuador	143	71	51	56	7.4	4.8	594	561	0.4	1.4
65	Dominican Republic	115	123	48	55	7.1	1.5	150	237	1.9	0.7
66	Romania	66	111	75	60	..	4.4	1,360	687	..	0.5
67	Jamaica	89	105	102	145	12.3	5.5	9	188	5.1	2.9
68	Jordan	127	128	..	121	35.0	8.4	28	−143	..	6.5
69	Algeria	173	83	65	57	3.1	2.6	897	129	0.4	1.0
70	El Salvador	122	89	67	55	3.2	1.6	−17	8	2.8	3.9
71	Ukraine	..	..	..	..	..	0.9	0	247	..	0.3
72	Paraguay	110	101	44	82	3.6	4.3	121	174	0.7	1.3

Note: For data comparability and coverage, see the technical notes. Figures in italics are for years other than those specified.

		Net barter terms of trade (1987=100)		Trade (% of GDP)		Aggregate net resource flows (% of GNP)		Net private capital flows (millions $)		Aid (% of GNP)	
		1985	1995	1980	1995	1980	1995	1980	1995	1980	1994
73	Tunisia	123	91	86	93	7.2	5.7	337	751	2.7	0.7
74	Lithuania	..	..	..	108	..	3.6	0	194	..	1.1
75	Colombia	124	80	32	35	2.9	2.7	688	3,741	0.3	0.2
76	Namibia	..	..	142	110	..	..	..	..	0.0	4.7
77	Belarus	..	..	..	..	..	1.4	0	103	..	0.5
78	Russian Federation	..	..	..	44	..	0.5	2,817	1,116	..	0.6
79	Latvia	..	..	..	91	..	2.2	0	224	..	0.9
80	Peru	111	83	42	30	1.8	6.4	−67	3,532	1.0	0.8
81	Costa Rica	111	92	63	81	9.2	1.6	248	384	1.4	0.9
82	Lebanon	105	95	..	70	..	11.3	70	1,153	..	2.5
83	Thailand	103	100	54	90	6.5	6.1	1,465	9,143	1.3	0.4
84	Panama	104	86	..	79	4.1	10.1	65	228	1.3	0.6
85	Turkey	82	109	17	45	3.0	0.8	660	2,000	1.4	0.1
86	Poland	95	109	59	53	5.5	5.6	2,265	5,058	0.0	2.0
87	Estonia	..	..	..	160	..	6.5	0	207	..	1.1
88	Slovak Republic	98	86	..	124	..	4.3	0	653	..	0.6
89	Botswana	97	152	116	101	20.3	2.3	115	64	11.8	2.2
90	Venezuela	166	82	51	49	2.6	0.0	1,825	848	0.0	0.1
	Upper-middle-income	**110 m**	**95 m**			..	..	..	..	**0.1 w**	**0.1 w**
91	South Africa	101	111	64	44	..	..	..	346	..	0.2
92	Croatia	..	..	..	93	..	1.9	0	346	..	..
93	Mexico	145	92	24	48	4.8	8.7	8,181	13,068	0.0	0.1
94	Mauritius	77	103	113	120	8.4	7.9	48	304	3.0	0.4
95	Gabon	154	90	96	101	−1.9	9.6	−93	−125	1.4	5.6
96	Brazil	101	101	20	15	2.9	2.6	5,656	19,097	0.0	0.1
97	Trinidad and Tobago	138	86	89	68	6.3	6.4	258	271	0.1	0.5
98	Czech Republic	98	86	..	108	0.0	9.2	0	5,596	0.0	0.4
99	Malaysia	114	92	113	194	8.7	14.7	1,913	11,924	0.6	0.1
100	Hungary	103	97	80	67	3.3	17.4	596	7,841	0.0	0.5
101	Chile	91	94	50	54	8.7	4.7	2,447	4,230	0.0	0.3
102	Oman	182	77	100	89	3.3	1.3	33	126	3.1	1.0
103	Uruguay	91	112	36	41	5.3	1.8	479	217	0.1	0.5
104	Saudi Arabia	175	92	101	70	..	..	..	..	0.0	0.0
105	Argentina	123	120	12	16	4.6	4.1	3,475	7,204	0.0	0.1
106	Slovenia	..	..	..	113	..	4.0	0	838	..	..
107	Greece	96	111	47	57	..	..	..	..	0.1	0.0
	Low- and middle-income	**111 m**	**93 m**			**2.9 w**	**4.5 w**	**51,702 t**	**184,188 t**	**1.0 w**	**3.3 w**
	Sub-Saharan Africa	110 m	91 m			5.5 w	8.3 w	7,906 t	9,128 t	3.4 w	16.3 w
	East Asia and Pacific	..	..			2.9 w	7.8 w	7,135 t	84,137 t	0.7 w	1.1 w
	South Asia	109 m	94 m			3.0 w	1.6 w	1,238 t	5,191 t	2.4 w	1.9 w
	Europe and Central Asia	..	..			1.7 w	3.8 w	26,164 t	30,059 t	0.4 w	0.9 w
	Middle East and N. Africa	147 m	92 m			1.9 w	0.4 w	−1,040 t	1,414 t	1.1 w	..
	Latin America and Caribbean	111 m	94 m			4.2 w	4.3 w	24,590 t	54,261 t	0.3 w	1.7 w
	High-income economies	**96 m**	**97 m**			..	..	..	..	..	..
108	Korea, Rep.	94	102	74	67					0.2	0.0
109	Portugal	117	92	61	66					..	..
110	Spain	82	114	34	47					..	..
111	New Zealand	90	108	62	62					..	..
112	Ireland	96	90	108	136					..	..
113	† Israel	99	109	91	69					4.1	1.6
114	† Kuwait	165	88	113	104					0.0	0.0
115	† United Arab Emirates	181	93	112	139					0.0	0.0
116	United Kingdom	104	102	52	57					..	..
117	Australia	110	101	34	40					..	..
118	Italy	84	107	47	49					..	..
119	Canada	99	100	55	71					..	..
120	Finland	88	95	67	68					..	..
121	† Hong Kong	118	87	181	297					0.0	0.0
122	Sweden	92	102	61	77					..	..
123	Netherlands	101	103	103	99					..	..
124	Belgium	96[b]	101[b]	128	143					..	..
125	France	89	106	44	43					..	..
126	† Singapore	108	89	423	..					0.1	0.0
127	Austria	92	87	76	77					..	..
128	United States	101	102	21	24					..	..
129	Germany	84[c]	96	..	46					..	..
130	Denmark	91	100	66	64					..	..
131	Norway	142	95	81	71					..	..
132	Japan	73	127	28	17					..	..
133	Switzerland	85	60	77	68					..	..
	World	..	..							..	..

a. Includes Eritrea. b. Includes Luxembourg. c. Data refer to the Federal Republic of Germany before unification.

Table 4. Population and labor force

		Population						Labor force								
		Total (millions)		Avg. annual growth rate (%)		Aged 15–64 (millions)		Total[a] (millions)		Avg. annual growth rate (%)		Female (%)		Agriculture (%)		Industry (%)
		1980	1995	1980–90	1990–95	1980	1995	1980	1995	1980–90	1990–95	1980	1995	1980	1990	1980	1990
Low-income economies		2,378 t	3,180 t	2.0 w	1.7 w	1,351 t	1,934 t	1,156 t	1,575 t	2.2 w	1.7 w	40 w	41 w	73 w	69 w	13 w	15 w
Excluding China and India		709 t	1,050 t	2.7 w	2.4 w	371 t	563 t	317 t	467 t	2.6 w	2.5 w	40 w	41 w	72 w	67 w	10 w	12 w
1	Mozambique	12	16	1.6	2.6	6	9	7	8	1.2	2.4	49	48	84	83	7	8
2	Ethiopia	38	56	3.1	1.9	19	28	17	25	2.9	2.3	42	41	86	80	2	2
3	Tanzania	19	30	3.2	3.0	9	15	10	15	3.2	2.9	50	49	86	84	4	5
4	Burundi	4	6	2.8	2.6	2	3	2	3	2.6	2.7	50	49	93	92	2	3
5	Malawi	6	10	3.3	2.7	3	5	3	5	3.0	2.5	51	49	88	95	5	5
6	Chad	4	6	2.4	2.5	2	3	2	3	2.1	2.5	43	44	88	81	3	4
7	Rwanda	5	6	3.0	–1.7	3	4	3	4	3.2	2.0	49	49	93	92	3	3
8	Sierra Leone	3	4	2.1	1.0	2	2	1	2	1.8	2.0	36	36	70	67	14	15
9	Nepal	15	21	2.6	2.5	8	12	7	10	2.4	2.4	39	40	95	95	1	0
10	Niger	6	9	3.3	3.3	3	4	3	4	3.0	2.9	45	44	93	91	3	4
11	Burkina Faso	7	10	2.6	2.8	4	5	4	5	2.0	2.1	48	47	92	92	3	2
12	Madagascar	9	14	2.9	3.1	5	7	4	6	2.5	3.1	45	45	85	84	6	7
13	Bangladesh	87	120	2.4	1.6	44	64	41	60	2.8	2.1	42	42	74	64	9	16
14	Uganda	13	19	2.4	3.2	6	9	7	9	2.2	2.7	48	48	89	93	4	5
15	Vietnam	54	73	2.1	2.1	28	43	26	37	2.7	1.9	48	49	73	72	13	14
16	Guinea-Bissau	1	1	1.8	2.1	0	1	0	1	1.3	1.8	40	40	86	85	2	2
17	Haiti	5	7	1.9	2.0	3	4	3	3	1.3	1.7	45	43	71	68	8	9
18	Mali	7	10	2.5	2.9	3	5	3	5	2.3	2.7	47	46	93	93	2	2
19	Nigeria	71	111	3.0	2.9	38	58	30	44	2.6	2.8	36	36	55	43	8	7
20	Yemen, Rep.	9	15	3.3	5.0	4	8	2	5	3.7	4.9	33	29	70	58	13	16
21	Cambodia	6	10	2.9	2.8	3	5	3	5	2.8	2.5	56	53	76	74	7	8
22	Kenya	17	27	3.4	2.7	8	14	8	13	3.6	2.7	46	46	83	80	6	7
23	Mongolia	2	2	2.9	2.1	1	1	1	1	3.1	2.9	46	46	40	32	21	22
24	Togo	3	4	3.0	3.0	1	2	1	2	2.6	2.8	39	40	69	66	10	10
25	Gambia, The	1	1	3.6	3.7	0	1	0	1	3.4	3.2	45	45	84	82	7	8
26	Central African Republic	2	3	2.4	2.2	..	2	1	2	1.7	1.8	48	47	85	80	3	3
27	India	687	929	2.1	1.8	394	562	300	398	1.9	2.0	34	32	70	64	13	16
28	Lao PDR	3	5	2.7	3.0	2	3	2	2	2.3	2.7	45	47	80	78	6	6
29	Benin	3	5	3.1	2.9	2	3	2	2	2.7	2.5	47	48	67	62	7	8
30	Nicaragua	3	4	2.9	3.1	1	2	1	2	2.9	4.0	28	36	39	28	24	26
31	Ghana	11	17	3.3	2.8	6	9	5	8	3.1	2.7	51	51	61	60	13	13
32	Zambia	6	9	3.0	2.9	3	5	2	4	3.1	2.8	45	45	76	75	8	9
33	Angola	7	11	2.7	3.1	4	5	3	5	2.1	2.8	47	46	76	75	8	8
34	Georgia	5	5	0.7	–0.2	3	4	3	3	0.4	–0.1	49	46	32	26	27	31
35	Pakistan	83	130	3.1	2.9	44	70	29	46	2.9	3.3	23	26	62	56	15	20
36	Mauritania	2	2	2.6	2.5	1	1	1	1	2.0	2.7	45	44	72	55	7	10
37	Azerbaijan	6	8	1.5	1.0	4	5	3	3	1.0	1.7	47	44	35	31	28	29
38	Zimbabwe	7	11	3.3	2.4	3	6	3	5	3.6	2.2	44	44	74	69	12	8
39	Guinea	4	7	2.5	2.7	2	3	2	3	2.1	2.4	47	47	91	87	1	2
40	Honduras	4	6	3.3	3.0	2	3	1	2	3.6	3.8	25	30	56	40	14	19
41	Senegal	6	8	2.9	2.7	3	4	3	4	2.6	2.7	42	42	81	76	6	7
42	China	981	1,200	1.5	1.1	586	811	539	709	2.2	1.1	43	45	76	74	14	15
43	Cameroon	9	13	2.8	2.9	5	7	4	5	2.4	3.1	37	38	73	70	8	9
44	Côte d'Ivoire	8	14	3.8	3.1	4	7	3	5	3.1	2.3	32	33	65	60	8	10
45	Albania	3	3	2.1	–0.1	2	2	1	2	2.6	0.8	39	41	57	55	23	23
46	Congo	2	3	3.1	2.9	1	1	1	1	3.1	2.6	43	43	58	48	13	14
47	Kyrgyz Republic	4	5	1.9	0.5	2	3	2	2	1.6	1.2	48	47	34	32	29	26
48	Sri Lanka	15	18	1.4	1.3	9	12	5	8	2.3	2.0	27	35	52	49	18	21
49	Armenia	3	4	1.4	1.2	2	2	1	2	1.1	1.4	48	48	21	17	43	41
Middle-income economies		1,236 t	1,591 t	1.8 w	1.4 w	717 t	981 t	513 t	688 t	2.1 w	1.8 w	36 w	38 w	38 w	32 w	28 w	27 w
Lower-middle-income		905 t	1,153 t	1.7 w	1.4 w	527 t	712 t	387 t	507 t	1.8 w	1.7 w	38 w	40 w	41 w	36 w	27 w	27 w
50	Lesotho	1	2	2.7	2.1	1	1	1	1	2.3	2.3	38	37	41	41	33	28
51	Egypt, Arab Rep.	41	58	2.5	2.0	23	34	14	21	2.5	2.7	26	29	61	43	17	23
52	Bolivia	5	7	2.0	2.4	3	4	2	3	2.6	2.6	33	37	53	47	18	18
53	Macedonia, FYR	2	2	0.7	0.9	1	1	1	1	1.2	1.3	36	41	34	22	31	41
54	Moldova	4	4	0.9	–0.1	3	3	2	2	0.2	0.2	50	49	43	33	26	30
55	Uzbekistan	16	23	2.5	2.1	9	13	6	9	2.2	2.8	48	46	38	34	25	25
56	Indonesia	148	193	1.8	1.6	83	120	59	89	2.9	2.5	35	40	59	57	12	14
57	Philippines	48	69	2.4	2.2	27	40	19	28	2.7	2.7	35	37	52	45	15	15
58	Morocco	19	27	2.2	2.0	10	16	7	10	2.6	2.6	34	35	56	45	20	25
59	Syrian Arab Republic	9	14	3.3	3.0	4	7	2	4	3.0	3.5	23	26	39	34	28	24
60	Papua New Guinea	3	4	2.2	2.3	2	2	2	2	2.1	2.3	42	42	83	79	6	7
61	Bulgaria	9	8	–0.2	–0.7	6	6	5	4	–0.4	–0.6	45	48	20	14	45	50
2	Kazakstan	15	17	1.2	–0.2	9	10	7	8	1.1	0.5	48	47	24	22	32	31
63	Guatemala	7	11	2.8	2.9	4	6	2	4	2.9	3.5	22	26	54	52	19	17
64	Ecuador	8	11	2.5	2.2	4	7	3	4	3.5	3.2	20	26	40	33	20	19
65	Dominican Republic	6	8	2.2	1.9	3	5	2	3	3.1	2.6	25	29	32	25	24	29
66	Romania	22	23	0.4	–0.4	14	15	11	11	–0.2	0.1	46	44	35	24	41	47
67	Jamaica	2	3	1.2	1.0	1	2	1	1	2.1	1.8	46	46	31	24	16	23
68	Jordan	2	4	3.7	5.7	1	2	1	1	4.9	5.3	15	21	24	21	32	32
69	Algeria	19	28	2.9	2.2	9	16	5	9	3.7	4.1	21	24	36	26	27	31
70	El Salvador	5	6	1.0	2.2	2	3	2	2	1.7	3.4	27	34	43	36	19	21
71	Ukraine	50	52	0.4	–0.1	33	34	26	26	–0.1	–0.2	50	49	25	20	39	40
72	Paraguay	3	5	3.0	2.7	2	3	1	2	2.9	2.9	27	29	45	39	20	23

Note: For data comparability and coverage, see the technical notes. Figures in italics are for years other than those specified.

		Population						Labor force									
		Total (millions)		Avg. annual growth rate (%)		Aged 15–64 (millions)		Total[a] (millions)		Avg. annual growth rate (%)		Female (%)		Agriculture (%)		Industry (%)	
		1980	1995	1980–90	1990–95	1980	1995	1980	1995	1980–90	1990–95	1980	1995	1980	1990	1980	1990
73	Tunisia	6	9	2.5	1.9	3	5	2	3	2.7	3.0	29	30	39	28	30	32
74	Lithuania	3	4	0.9	0.0	2	2	2	2	0.7	–0.2	50	48	28	18	38	40
75	Colombia	28	37	1.9	1.8	16	23	9	16	3.9	2.7	26	37	39	25	20	22
76	Namibia	1	2	2.7	2.7	1	1	0	1	2.3	2.5	40	41	56	49	15	15
77	Belarus	10	10	0.6	0.2	6	7	5	5	0.5	0.2	50	49	26	20	38	40
78	Russian Federation	139	148	0.6	0.0	95	99	76	77	0.2	0.0	49	49	16	14	44	42
79	Latvia	3	3	0.5	–1.2	2	2	1	1	0.2	–1.1	51	50	16	16	42	40
80	Peru	17	24	2.2	2.0	9	14	5	9	3.1	3.1	24	29	40	36	18	18
81	Costa Rica	2	3	2.8	2.3	1	2	1	1	3.8	2.5	21	30	35	26	23	27
82	Lebanon	3	4	2.5	1.9	2	2	1	1	3.5	2.9	23	28	13	5	26	22
83	Thailand	47	58	1.7	0.9	26	39	24	34	2.6	1.3	47	46	71	64	10	14
84	Panama	2	3	2.1	1.7	1	2	1	1	3.1	2.4	30	34	29	26	19	16
85	Turkey	44	61	2.3	1.7	25	38	19	28	2.9	2.1	35	35	60	53	16	18
86	Poland	36	39	0.7	0.3	19	26	19	19	0.1	0.6	45	46	30	27	38	36
87	Estonia	1	1	0.6	–1.1	1	1	1	1	0.4	–0.8	51	49	15	14	43	41
88	Slovak Republic	5	5	0.6	0.3	3	4	2	3	0.9	0.7	45	48	14	12	36	32
89	Botswana	1	1	3.5	2.5	0	1	0	1	3.4	2.5	50	46	64	46	10	20
90	Venezuela	15	22	2.6	2.3	8	13	5	8	3.5	3.0	27	33	15	12	28	28
	Upper-middle-income	331 t	438 t	2.0 w	1.7 w	191 t	269 t	126 t	182 t	2.7 w	2.0 w	29 w	34 w	31 w	21 w	29 w	27 w
91	South Africa	29	41	2.4	2.2	16	24	11	16	2.7	2.4	35	37	17	14	35	32
92	Croatia	5	5	0.4	0.0	3	3	2	2	0.3	0.1	40	43	24	15	32	32
93	Mexico	67	92	2.3	1.9	35	54	22	36	3.5	2.8	27	31	37	28	29	24
94	Mauritius	1	1	0.9	1.3	1	1	0	0	2.3	1.8	26	32	27	17	28	43
95	Gabon	1	1	3.0	2.8	0	1	0	1	2.1	1.9	45	44	76	61	14	19
96	Brazil	121	159	2.0	1.5	71	101	48	71	3.2	1.6	28	35	37	23	24	23
97	Trinidad and Tobago	1	1	1.3	0.8	1	1	0	1	1.2	1.8	32	36	11	11	39	31
98	Czech Republic	10	10	0.1	–0.1	6	7	5	6	0.2	0.4	47	47	13	11	56	45
99	Malaysia	14	20	2.6	2.4	8	12	5	8	2.8	2.7	34	37	41	27	19	23
100	Hungary	11	10	–0.3	–0.3	7	7	5	5	–0.8	0.1	43	44	18	15	43	38
101	Chile	11	14	1.7	1.5	7	9	4	6	2.7	2.1	26	32	21	19	25	25
102	Oman	1	2	3.9	6.0	1	1	0	1	3.4	5.1	7	14	50	48	22	26
103	Uruguay	3	3	0.6	0.6	2	2	1	1	1.6	1.0	31	40	17	14	28	27
104	Saudi Arabia	9	19	5.2	3.7	5	10	3	6	6.5	3.2	8	13	45	20	16	20
105	Argentina	28	35	1.5	1.3	17	21	11	14	1.3	2.0	28	31	13	12	34	32
106	Slovenia	2	2	0.5	–0.1	1	1	1	1	0.3	0.1	46	46	15	5	42	44
107	Greece	10	10	0.5	0.6	6	7	4	4	1.2	0.9	28	36	31	23	29	28
	Low- and middle-income	3,614 t	4,771 t	2.0 w	1.6 w	2,069 t	2,916 t	1,669 t	2,263 t	2.2 w	1.7 w	38 w	40 w	63 w	58 w	17 w	18 w
	Sub-Saharan Africa	381 t	583 t	3.0 w	2.6 w	196 t	305 t	173 t	257 t	2.7 w	2.6 w	42 w	42 w	72 w	68 w	9 w	9 w
	East Asia and Pacific	1,360 t	1,706 t	1.6 w	1.3 w	796 t	1,119 t	704 t	951 t	2.3 w	1.3 w	43 w	45 w	73 w	70 w	14 w	15 w
	South Asia	903 t	1,243 t	2.2 w	1.9 w	508 t	732 t	389 t	532 t	2.1 w	2.1 w	34 w	33 w	70 w	64 w	13 w	16 w
	Europe and Central Asia	437 t	488 t	0.9 w	0.3 w	277 t	317 t	219 t	238 t	0.6 w	0.5 w	46 w	46 w	27 w	23 w	37 w	36 w
	Middle East and N. Africa	175 t	272 t	3.1 w	2.7 w	91 t	151 t	54 t	88 t	3.2 w	3.3 w	24 w	26 w	48 w	36 w	21 w	24 w
	Latin America and Caribbean	358 t	478 t	2.0 w	1.7 w	201 t	293 t	130 t	197 t	3.0 w	2.3 w	27 w	33 w	34 w	25 w	25 w	24 w
	High-income economies	816 t	902 t	0.7 w	0.7 w	522 t	605 t	368 t	432 t	1.2 w	0.9 w	39 w	42 w	9 w	5 w	35 w	31 w
108	Korea, Rep.	38	45	1.2	0.9	24	32	16	22	2.3	1.9	39	40	37	18	27	35
109	Portugal	10	10	0.1	0.1	6	7	5	5	0.4	0.5	39	43	26	18	36	34
110	Spain	37	39	0.4	0.2	23	27	14	17	1.3	1.0	28	36	19	12	37	33
111	New Zealand	3	4	0.8	1.4	2	2	1	2	2.0	1.5	34	44	11	10	33	25
112	Ireland	3	4	0.3	0.5	2	2	1	1	0.4	1.7	28	33	19	14	34	29
113	† Israel	4	6	1.8	3.5	2	3	1	2	2.3	3.5	34	40	6	4	32	29
114	† Kuwait	1	2	4.4	–4.9	1	1	0	1	5.8	–1.6	13	27	2	1	32	25
115	† United Arab Emirates	1	2	5.7	5.8	1	1	1	1	5.1	3.9	5	13	4	7	37	24
116	United Kingdom	56	59	0.2	0.3	36	38	27	29	0.6	0.3	39	43	3	2	38	29
117	Australia	15	18	1.5	1.1	10	12	7	9	2.3	1.4	37	43	6	5	32	26
118	Italy	56	57	0.1	0.2	36	39	23	25	0.8	0.4	33	38	13	9	38	32
119	Canada	25	30	1.2	1.3	17	20	12	15	1.9	1.0	40	45	7	3	33	25
120	Finland	5	5	0.4	0.5	3	3	2	3	0.6	0.1	46	48	12	8	35	31
121	† Hong Kong	5	6	1.2	1.6	3	4	2	3	1.6	1.3	34	37	1	1	50	37
122	Sweden	8	9	0.3	0.6	5	6	4	5	1.0	0.3	44	48	..	..	..	..
123	Netherlands	14	15	0.6	0.7	9	11	6	7	2.0	0.6	31	40	6	5	31	26
124	Belgium	10	10	0.1	0.4	6	7	4	4	0.2	0.5	34	40	3	3	35	28
125	France	54	58	0.5	0.5	34	38	24	26	0.4	0.8	40	44	8	5	35	29
126	† Singapore	2	3	1.7	2.0	2	2	1	1	2.3	1.7	35	38	2	0	44	36
127	Austria	8	8	0.2	0.8	5	5	3	4	0.5	0.5	40	41	10	8	41	37
128	United States	228	263	0.9	1.0	151	172	110	133	1.4	1.1	42	46	3	3	31	28
129	Germany	78	82	0.1	0.6	52	56	37	40	0.6	0.3	40	42	7	4	45	38
130	Denmark	5	5	0.0	0.3	3	4	3	3	0.7	0.1	44	46	7	6	31	28
131	Norway	4	4	0.4	0.5	3	3	2	2	0.9	0.7	40	46	8	6	29	25
132	Japan	117	125	0.6	0.3	79	87	57	66	1.1	0.6	38	41	11	7	35	34
133	Switzerland	6	7	0.6	1.0	4	5	3	4	1.5	0.8	37	40	6	6	39	35
	World	4,429 t	5,673 t	1.7 w	1.5 w	2,590 t	3,521 t	2,037 t	2,695 t	2.0 w	1.6 w	38 w	40 w	53 w	49 w	20 w	20 w

a. Participation rates from ILO are applied to population estimates to derive labor force estimates.

Table 5. Distribution of income or consumption

		Survey year	Gini index	Percentage share of income or consumption						
				Lowest 10%	Lowest 20%	Second quintile	Third quintile	Fourth quintile	Highest 20%	Highest 10%
Low-income economies										
Excluding China and India										
1	Mozambique		..	..	..	..	..	..	..	..
2	Ethiopia		..	..	..	..	..	..	..	..
3	Tanzania	1993[a,b]	38.1	2.9	6.9	10.9	15.3	21.5	45.4	30.2
4	Burundi		..	..	..	..	..	..	..	..
5	Malawi		..	..	..	..	..	..	..	..
6	Sierra Leone		..	..	..	..	..	..	..	..
7	Rwanda	1983–85[a,b]	28.9	4.2	9.7	13.2	16.5	21.6	39.1	24.2
8	Chad		..	..	..	..	..	..	..	..
9	Nepal	1995–96[a,b]	36.7	3.2	7.6	11.5	15.1	21.0	44.8	29.8
10	Niger	1992[a,b]	36.1	3.0	7.5	11.8	15.5	21.1	44.1	29.3
11	Madagascar	1993[a,b]	43.4	2.3	5.8	9.9	14.0	20.3	50.0	34.9
12	Burkina Faso		..	..	..	..	..	..	..	..
13	Vietnam	1993[a,b]	35.7	3.5	7.8	11.4	15.4	21.4	44.0	29.0
14	Bangladesh	1992[a,b]	28.3	4.1	9.4	13.5	17.2	22.0	37.9	23.7
15	Uganda	1992–93[a,b]	40.8	3.0	6.8	10.3	14.4	20.4	48.1	33.4
16	Mali		..	..	..	..	..	..	..	..
17	Guinea-Bissau	1991[a,b]	56.2	0.5	2.1	6.5	12.0	20.6	58.9	42.4
18	Haiti		..	..	..	..	..	..	..	..
19	Nigeria	1992–93[a,b]	45.0	1.3	4.0	8.9	14.4	23.4	49.3	31.3
20	Yemen, Rep.		..	..	..	..	..	..	..	..
21	Cambodia		..	..	..	..	..	..	..	..
22	Kenya	1992[a,b]	57.5	1.2	3.4	6.7	10.7	17.0	62.1	47.7
23	Togo		..	..	..	..	..	..	..	..
24	Mongolia		..	..	..	..	..	..	..	..
25	Gambia, The		..	..	..	..	..	..	..	..
26	India	1992[a,b]	33.8	3.7	8.5	12.1	15.8	21.1	42.6	28.4
27	Central African Republic		..	..	..	..	..	..	..	..
28	Lao PDR	1992[a,b]	30.4	4.2	9.6	12.9	16.3	21.0	40.2	26.4
29	Benin		..	..	..	..	..	..	..	..
30	Nicaragua	1993[a,b]	50.3	1.6	4.2	8.0	12.6	20.0	55.2	39.8
31	Ghana	1992[a,b]	33.9	3.4	7.9	12.0	16.1	21.8	42.2	27.3
32	Zambia	1993[a,b]	46.2	1.5	3.9	8.0	13.8	23.8	50.4	31.3
33	Angola		..	..	..	..	..	..	..	..
34	Georgia		..	..	..	..	..	..	..	..
35	Pakistan	1991[a,b]	31.2	3.4	8.4	12.9	16.9	22.2	39.7	25.2
36	Mauritania	1988[a,b]	42.4	0.7	3.6	10.6	16.2	23.0	46.5	30.4
37	Azerbaijan		..	..	..	..	..	..	..	..
38	Zimbabwe	1990[a,b]	56.8	1.8	4.0	6.3	10.0	17.4	62.3	46.9
39	Guinea	1991[a,b]	46.8	0.9	3.0	8.3	14.6	23.9	50.2	31.7
40	Honduras	1992[c,d]	52.7	1.5	3.8	7.4	12.0	19.4	57.4	41.9
41	Senegal	1991[a,b]	54.1	1.4	3.5	7.0	11.6	19.3	58.6	42.8
42	China	1995[c,d]	41.5	2.2	5.5	9.8	14.9	22.3	47.5	30.9
43	Cameroon		..	..	..	..	..	..	..	..
44	Côte d'Ivoire	1988[a,b]	36.9	2.8	6.8	11.2	15.8	22.2	44.1	28.5
45	Albania		..	..	..	..	..	..	..	..
46	Congo		..	..	..	..	..	..	..	..
47	Sri Lanka	1990[a,b]	30.1	3.8	8.9	13.1	16.9	21.7	39.3	25.2
48	Kyrgyz Republic		..	..	..	..	..	..	..	..
49	Armenia		..	..	..	..	..	..	..	..
Middle-income economies										
Lower-middle-income										
50	Lesotho	1986–87[a,b]	56.0	0.9	2.8	6.5	11.2	19.4	60.1	43.4
51	Egypt, Arab Rep.	1991[a,b]	32.0	3.9	8.7	12.5	16.3	21.4	41.1	26.7
52	Bolivia	1990[c,d]	42.0	2.3	5.6	9.7	14.5	22.0	48.2	31.7
53	Macedonia, FYR		..	..	..	..	..	..	..	..
54	Moldova	1992[c,d]	34.4	2.7	6.9	11.9	16.7	23.1	41.5	25.8
55	Uzbekistan		..	..	..	..	..	..	..	..
56	Indonesia	1993[a,b]	31.7	3.9	8.7	12.3	16.3	22.1	40.7	25.6
57	Philippines	1988[a,b]	40.7	2.8	6.5	10.1	14.4	21.2	47.8	32.1
58	Morocco	1990–91[a,b]	39.2	2.8	6.6	10.5	15.0	21.7	46.3	30.5
59	Syrian Arab Republic		..	..	..	..	..	..	..	..
60	Papua New Guinea		..	..	..	..	..	..	..	..
61	Bulgaria	1992[c,d]	30.8	3.3	8.3	13.0	17.0	22.3	39.3	24.7
62	Kazakstan	1993[c,d]	32.7	3.1	7.5	12.3	16.9	22.9	40.4	24.9
63	Guatemala	1989[c,d]	59.6	0.6	2.1	5.8	10.5	18.6	63.0	46.6
64	Ecuador	1994[a,b]	46.6	2.3	5.4	8.9	13.2	19.9	52.6	37.6
65	Dominican Republic	1989[c,d]	50.5	1.6	4.2	7.9	12.5	19.7	55.7	39.6
66	Romania	1992[c,d]	25.5	3.8	9.2	14.4	18.4	23.2	34.8	20.2
67	Jordan	1991[a,b]	43.4	2.4	5.9	9.8	13.9	20.3	50.1	34.7
68	Jamaica	1991[a,b]	41.1	2.4	5.8	10.2	14.9	21.6	47.5	31.9
69	Algeria	1988[a,b]	38.7	2.8	6.9	11.0	15.1	20.9	46.1	31.5
70	El Salvador		..	..	..	..	..	..	..	..
71	Ukraine	1992[c,d]	25.7	4.1	9.5	14.1	18.1	22.9	35.4	20.8
72	Paraguay		..	..	..	..	..	..	..	..

Note: For data comparability and coverage, see the technical notes.

		Survey year	Gini index	Percentage share of income or consumption						
				Lowest 10%	Lowest 20%	Second quintile	Third quintile	Fourth quintile	Highest 20%	Highest 10%
73	Tunisia	1990[a,b]	40.2	2.3	5.9	10.4	15.3	22.1	46.3	30.7
74	Lithuania	1993[c,d]	33.6	3.4	8.1	12.3	16.2	21.3	42.1	28.0
75	Colombia	1991[c,d]	51.3	1.3	3.6	7.6	12.6	20.4	55.8	39.5
76	Namibia		..	..	..	..	..	..	..	..
77	Belarus	1993[c,d]	21.6	4.9	11.1	15.3	18.5	22.2	32.9	19.4
78	Russian Federation	1993[a,b]	49.6	1.2	3.7	8.5	13.5	20.4	53.8	38.7
79	Latvia	1993[c,d]	27.0	4.3	9.6	13.6	17.5	22.6	36.7	22.1
80	Peru	1994[a,b]	44.9	1.9	4.9	9.2	14.1	21.4	50.4	34.3
81	Costa Rica	1989[c,d]	46.1	1.2	4.0	9.1	14.3	21.9	50.7	34.1
82	Lebanon		..	..	..	..	..	..	..	..
83	Thailand	1992[a,b]	46.2	2.5	5.6	8.7	13.0	20.0	52.7	37.1
84	Panama	1989[c,d]	56.6	0.5	2.0	6.3	11.6	20.3	59.8	42.2
85	Turkey		..	..	..	..	..	..	..	..
86	Poland	1992[a,b]	27.2	4.0	9.3	13.8	17.7	22.6	36.6	22.1
87	Estonia	1993[c,d]	39.5	2.4	6.6	10.7	15.1	21.4	46.3	31.3
88	Slovak Republic	1992[c,d]	19.5	5.1	11.9	15.8	18.8	22.2	31.4	18.2
89	Venezuela	1990[c,d]	53.8	1.4	3.6	7.1	11.7	19.3	58.4	42.7
90	Botswana		..	..	..	..	..	..	..	..
Upper-middle-income										
91	South Africa	1993[a,b]	58.4	1.4	3.3	5.8	9.8	17.7	63.3	47.3
92	Croatia		..	..	..	..	..	..	..	..
93	Mexico	1992[a,b]	50.3	1.6	4.1	7.8	12.5	20.2	55.3	39.2
94	Mauritius		..	..	..	..	..	..	..	..
95	Gabon		..	..	..	..	..	..	..	..
96	Brazil	1989[c,d]	63.4	0.7	2.1	4.9	8.9	16.8	67.5	51.3
97	Trinidad and Tobago		..	..	..	..	..	..	..	..
98	Czech Republic	1993[c,d]	26.6	4.6	10.5	13.9	16.9	21.3	37.4	23.5
99	Malaysia	1989[c,d]	48.4	1.9	4.6	8.3	13.0	20.4	53.7	37.9
100	Hungary	1993[a,b]	27.0	4.0	9.5	14.0	17.6	22.3	36.6	22.6
101	Chile	1994[c,d]	56.5	1.4	3.5	6.6	10.9	18.1	61.0	46.1
102	Oman		..	..	..	..	..	..	..	..
103	Uruguay		..	..	..	..	..	..	..	..
104	Saudi Arabia		..	..	..	..	..	..	..	..
105	Argentina		..	..	..	..	..	..	..	..
106	Slovenia	1993[c,d]	28.2	4.1	9.5	13.5	17.1	21.9	37.9	23.8
107	Greece		..	..	..	..	..	..	..	..
Low- and middle-income										
Sub-Saharan Africa										
East Asia and Pacific										
South Asia										
Europe and Central Asia										
Middle East and N. Africa										
Latin America and Caribbean										
High-income economies										
108	Korea, Rep.		..	..	..	..	..	..	..	..
109	Portugal		..	..	..	..	..	..	..	..
110	Spain	1988[e,f]	..	..	8.3	13.7	18.1	23.4	36.6	21.8
111	New Zealand	1981–82[e,f]	..	..	5.1	10.8	16.2	23.2	44.7	28.7
112	Ireland		..	..	..	..	..	..	..	..
113	† Israel	1979[e,f]	..	..	6.0	12.1	17.8	24.5	39.6	23.5
114	† Kuwait		..	..	..	..	..	..	..	..
115	† United Arab Emirates		..	..	..	..	..	..	..	..
116	United Kingdom	1988[e,f]	..	..	4.6	10.0	16.8	24.3	44.3	27.8
117	Australia	1985[e,f]	..	..	4.4	11.1	17.5	24.8	42.2	25.8
118	Italy	1986[e,f]	..	..	6.8	12.0	16.7	23.5	41.0	25.3
119	Canada	1987[e,f]	..	..	5.7	11.8	17.7	24.6	40.2	24.1
120	Finland	1981[e,f]	..	..	6.3	12.1	18.4	25.5	37.6	21.7
121	† Hong Kong	1980[e,f]	..	..	5.4	10.8	15.2	21.6	47.0	31.3
122	Sweden	1981[e,f]	..	..	8.0	13.2	17.4	24.5	36.9	20.8
123	Netherlands	1988[e,f]	..	..	8.2	13.1	18.1	23.7	36.9	21.9
124	Belgium	1978–79[e,f]	..	..	7.9	13.7	18.6	23.8	36.0	21.5
125	France	1989[e,f]	..	..	5.6	11.8	17.2	23.5	41.9	26.1
126	† Singapore	1982–83[e,f]	..	..	5.1	9.9	14.6	21.4	48.9	33.5
127	Austria		..	..	..	..	..	..	..	..
128	United States	1985[e,f]	..	..	4.7	11.0	17.4	25.0	41.9	25.0
129	Germany	1988[e,f]	..	..	7.0	11.8	17.1	23.9	40.3	24.4
130	Denmark	1981[e,f]	..	..	5.4	12.0	18.4	25.6	38.6	22.3
131	Norway	1979[e,f]	..	..	6.2	12.8	18.9	25.3	36.7	21.2
132	Japan	1979[e,f]	..	..	8.7	13.2	17.5	23.1	37.5	22.4
133	Switzerland	1982[e,f]	..	..	5.2	11.7	16.4	22.1	44.6	29.8
World										

a. Refers to expenditure shares by percentiles of persons. b. Ranked by per capita expenditure. c. Refers to income shares by percentiles of persons. d. Ranked by per capita income. e. Refers to income shares by percentiles of households. f. Ranked by household income.

Table 6. Health

		Percentage of total population with access to						Infant mortality rate (per 1,000 live births)		Prevalence of malnutrition (% under 5)	Contraceptive prevalence rate (%)	Total fertility rate		Maternal mortality ratio (per 100,000 live births)
		Health care		Safe water		Sanitation								
		1980	1993	1980	1994–95	1980	1994–95	1980	1995	1989–95	1989–95	1980	1995	1989–95
	Low-income economies							98 w	69 w			4.3 w	3.2 w	
	Excluding China and India							116 w	89 w			6.3 w	5.0 w	
1	Mozambique	..	..	9	28	10	23	145	113	..	..	6.5	6.2	1,512[a]
2	Ethiopia	..	55	4	27	..	10	155	112	47	4	6.6	7.0	1,528[a]
3	Tanzania	72	93	..	49	..	86	104	82	28	10	6.7	5.8	748[a]
4	Burundi	..	80	..	58	..	48	121	98	..	..	6.8	6.5	1,327[a]
5	Malawi	40	..	..	54	..	63	169	133	27	13	7.6	6.6	620[b]
6	Chad	..	26	..	29	..	32	147	117	..	..	5.9	5.9	1,594[a]
7	Rwanda	..	..	..	..	..	..	128	133	28	21	8.3	6.2	1,512[a]
8	Sierra Leone	26	..	..	..	13	..	190	179	23	..	6.5	6.5	..
9	Nepal	10	..	11	48	0	6	132	91	70	..	6.4	5.3	515[c]
10	Niger	..	30	..	57	..	15	150	119	..	4	7.4	7.4	593[b]
11	Burkina Faso	..	..	35	..	5	14	121	99	..	8	7.5	6.7	939[a]
12	Madagascar	..	..	..	32	..	17	138	89	32	17	6.5	5.8	..
13	Bangladesh	80	74	..	83	..	30	132	79	84	40	6.1	3.5	887[a]
14	Uganda	..	..	..	42	..	60	116	98	23	15	7.2	6.7	506[c]
15	Vietnam	75	..	..	38	..	21	57	41	45	..	5.0	3.1	105[d]
16	Guinea-Bissau	30	..	24	27	..	20	168	136	..	..	6.0	6.0	..
17	Haiti	..	..	..	28	..	24	123	72	27	18	5.9	4.4	600[b]
18	Mali	20	..	..	44	..	44	184	123	..	..	7.1	6.8	1,249[a]
19	Nigeria	40	67	..	43	..	63	99	80	43	6	6.9	5.5	..
20	Yemen, Rep.	16	..	..	52	..	51	141	100	30	..	7.9	7.4	1,471[a]
21	Cambodia	..	..	..	13	..	..	201	108	..	..	4.7	4.7	..
22	Kenya	..	..	..	49	..	43	72	58	23	27	7.8	4.7	..
23	Mongolia	90	..	..	..	..	..	82	55	10	..	5.4	3.4	..
24	Togo	..	..	..	67	..	20	110	88	..	..	6.6	6.4	626[a]
25	Gambia, The	90	..	42	61	..	34	159	126	..	..	6.5	5.3	..
26	Central African Republic	..	..	16	..	..	..	117	98	..	..	5.8	5.1	649
27	India	50	..	..	63	..	29	116	68	63	43	5.0	3.2	437[d]
28	Lao PDR	..	..	..	41	..	30	127	90	40	..	6.7	6.5	..
29	Benin	..	42	..	70	..	22	122	95	36	..	6.5	6.0	..
30	Nicaragua	..	..	..	57	..	..	90	46	12	44	6.2	4.1	..
31	Ghana	..	25	..	56	..	29	100	73	27	20	6.5	5.1	742[a]
32	Zambia	..	..	..	47	..	42	90	109	27	15	7.0	5.7	..
33	Angola	70	24	..	32	..	16	153	124	20	..	6.9	6.9	..
34	Georgia	..	..	..	..	..	..	25	18	..	..	2.3	2.2	55[d]
35	Pakistan	65	85	38	60	16	30	124	90	40	14	7.0	5.2	..
36	Mauritania	..	..	..	41	..	64	120	96	..	..	6.3	5.2	..
37	Azerbaijan	..	..	..	..	..	..	30	25	..	..	3.2	2.3	29[d]
38	Zimbabwe	55	..	..	74	5	58	82	55	16	..	6.8	3.8	..
39	Guinea	..	45	..	49	12	6	161	128	18	..	6.1	6.5	880[d]
40	Honduras	..	..	..	70	..	68	70	45	19	47	6.5	4.6	..
41	Senegal	..	40	..	..	..	..	91	62	20	7	6.7	5.7	..
42	China	..	..	..	83	..	..	42	34	17	83	2.5	1.9	115[e]
43	Cameroon	20	..	..	41	..	40	94	56	14	16	6.5	5.7	..
44	Côte d'Ivoire	..	..	20	82	17	54	108	86	..	11	7.4	5.3	887[a]
45	Albania	100	..	92	..	..	100	47	30	..	..	3.6	2.6	23[d]
46	Congo	..	..	..	60	..	9	89	90	..	..	6.2	6.0	822[a]
47	Kyrgyz Republic	..	..	..	75	..	53	43	30	..	..	4.1	3.3	80[d]
48	Sri Lanka	90	..	..	57	..	66	34	16	38	..	3.5	2.3	30[d]
49	Armenia	..	..	..	..	..	..	26	16	..	..	2.3	1.8	35[d]
	Middle-income economies							65 w	39 w			3.8 w	3.0 w	
	Lower-middle-income							68 w	41 w			3.7 w	3.0 w	
50	Lesotho	..	..	18	57	12	35	108	76	21	23	5.6	4.6	598[a]
51	Egypt, Arab Rep.	100	99	90	84	70	..	120	56	9	48	5.1	3.4	..
52	Bolivia	..	..	..	60	..	44	118	69	13	45	5.5	4.5	373[b]
53	Macedonia, FYR	..	..	..	..	..	..	54	23	..	..	2.5	2.2	12[d]
54	Moldova	..	..	..	..	..	50	35	22	..	..	2.4	2.0	34[d]
55	Uzbekistan	..	..	..	..	..	18	47	30	..	..	4.8	3.7	43[d]
56	Indonesia	..	..	..	63	..	55	90	51	39	55	4.3	2.7	390
57	Philippines	..	..	..	84	..	75	52	39	30	40	4.8	3.7	208[b]
58	Morocco	..	62	32	59	50	63	99	55	9	50	5.4	3.4	372[c]
59	Syrian Arab Republic	..	99	71	87	45	78	56	32	..	..	7.4	4.8	179[d]
60	Papua New Guinea	..	..	..	31	..	26	67	64	..	..	5.7	4.8	..
61	Bulgaria	..	..	96	..	..	99	20	15	..	..	2.1	1.2	20[d]
62	Kazakstan	..	..	..	..	..	..	33	27	..	..	2.9	2.3	53[d]
63	Guatemala	..	..	..	64	..	71	75	44	..	32	6.2	4.7	464[a]
64	Ecuador	..	..	..	70	..	64	67	36	45	57	5.0	3.2	..
65	Dominican Republic	..	..	..	79	..	85	76	37	10	56	4.2	2.9	..
66	Romania	..	..	77	..	50	49	29	23	..	57	2.4	1.4	48[d]
67	Jamaica	..	..	..	70	..	74	21	13	10	55	3.7	2.4	..
68	Jordan	..	90	89	89	76	30	41	31	17	..	6.8	4.8	132[a]
69	Algeria	..	77	..	..	..	..	98	34	9	51	6.7	3.5	140[d]
70	El Salvador	..	..	..	62	..	73	81	36	22	53	5.3	3.7	..
71	Ukraine	..	..	..	97	50	49	17	15	..	..	2.0	1.5	33[d]
72	Paraguay	..	..	..	..	..	30	50	41	4	48	4.8	4.0	180[d]

Note: For data comparability and coverage, see the technical notes. Figures in italics are for years other than those specified.

		Percentage of total population with access to						Infant mortality rate (per 1,000 live births)		Prevalence of malnutrition (% under 5)	Contraceptive prevalence rate (%)	Total fertility rate		Maternal mortality ratio (per 100,000 live births)
		Health care		Safe water		Sanitation								
		1980	1993	1980	1994–95	1980	1994–95	1980	1995	1989–95	1989–95	1980	1995	1989–95
73	Tunisia	95	90	72	86	46	72	71	39	..	..	5.2	2.9	138[a]
74	Lithuania	..	..	..	96	..	..	20	14	..	..	2.0	1.5	16[d]
75	Colombia	88	..	..	96	..	70	45	26	10	72	3.8	2.8	107[a]
76	Namibia	..	..	..	57	..	36	90	62	..	29	5.9	5.0	518
77	Belarus	..	..	..	..	50	100	16	13	..	..	2.0	1.4	25[d]
78	Russian Federation	..	..	..	..	..	..	22	18	..	..	1.9	1.4	52[d]
79	Latvia	..	..	..	..	..	..	20	16	..	..	2.0	1.3	..
80	Peru	..	..	..	60	..	47	81	47	16	55	4.5	3.1	..
81	Costa Rica	..	..	..	100	..	99	20	13	2	..	3.7	2.8	..
82	Lebanon	..	..	92	..	59	..	48	32	..	..	4.0	2.8	..
83	Thailand	30	59	..	81	..	87	49	35	13	..	3.5	1.8	..
84	Panama	..	..	..	82	..	87	32	23	7	..	3.7	2.7	..
85	Turkey	..	..	67	92	..	94	109	48	..	..	4.3	2.7	183[c]
86	Poland	100	..	67	..	50	100	21	14	..	..	2.3	1.6	10[d]
87	Estonia	..	..	..	..	..	..	17	14	..	..	2.0	1.3	41[d]
88	Slovak Republic	..	..	..	..	43	51	21	11	..	..	2.3	1.5	8[d]
89	Botswana	..	..	..	70	..	55	69	56	..	..	6.7	4.4	220[a]
90	Venezuela	..	..	..	88	..	55	36	23	6	..	4.1	3.1	200[a]
Upper-middle-income								57 w	35 w			3.9 w	2.9 w	
91	South Africa	..	..	..	..	..	46	67	50	..	..	4.9	3.9	404[a]
92	Croatia	..	..	..	96	..	68	21	16	..	..	1.9	1.5	10[d]
93	Mexico	51	..	..	87	..	70	51	33	..	..	4.5	3.0	..
94	Mauritius	100	99	..	100	..	100	32	16	..	75	2.7	2.2	112[d]
95	Gabon	..	..	..	67	..	76	116	89	..	..	4.5	5.2	483[a]
96	Brazil	..	..	..	92	..	73	70	44	18	..	3.9	2.4	200[d]
97	Trinidad and Tobago	..	..	..	82	..	56	35	13	..	..	3.3	2.1	..
98	Czech Republic	..	..	..	..	..	..	16	8	..	69	2.1	1.3	12[d]
99	Malaysia	..	88	..	90	75	94	30	12	23	..	4.2	3.4	34[f]
100	Hungary	..	..	..	..	..	94	23	11	..	..	1.9	1.6	10[d]
101	Chile	..	..	..	96	..	71	32	12	1	..	2.8	2.3	..
102	Oman	75	89	15	56	..	72	41	18	..	9	9.9	7.0	..
103	Uruguay	..	..	..	83	..	82	37	18	..	..	2.7	2.2	..
104	Saudi Arabia	85	98	91	93	76	86	65	21	..	..	7.3	6.2	18[d]
105	Argentina	..	..	..	64	..	89	35	22	..	..	3.3	2.7	140[d]
106	Slovenia	..	..	..	..	..	90	15	7	..	..	2.1	1.3	5[d]
107	Greece	..	..	..	..	..	96	18	8	..	..	2.2	1.4	..
Low- and middle-income								87 w	60 w			4.1 w	3.1 w	
Sub-Saharan Africa								114 w	92 w			6.7 w	5.7 w	
East Asia and Pacific								56 w	40 w			3.1 w	2.2 w	
South Asia								120 w	75 w			5.3 w	3.5 w	
Europe and Central Asia								40 w	26 w			2.5 w	2.0 w	
Middle East and N. Africa								97 w	54 w			6.1 w	4.2 w	
Latin America and Carribbean								60 w	37 w			4.1 w	2.8 w	
High-income economies								13 w	7 w			1.9 w	1.7 w	
108	Korea, Rep.	..	100	..	89	..	100	26	10	..	..	2.6	1.8	30[d]
109	Portugal	..	..	57	..	..	100	24	7	..	..	2.2	1.4	21
110	Spain	..	..	98	99	95	97	12	7	..	..	2.2	1.2	..
111	New Zealand	..	100	87	..	..	..	13	7	..	..	2.1	2.1	..
112	Ireland	..	..	..	..	..	100	11	6	..	60	3.2	1.9	..
113	†Israel	..	..	..	99	..	70	15	8	..	..	3.2	2.4	..
114	†Kuwait	100	..	100	..	100	..	27	11	..	..	5.3	3.0	18[d]
115	†United Arab Emirates	96	90	100	98	75	95	55	16	..	..	5.4	3.6	20[a]
116	United Kingdom	..	..	..	100	..	96	12	6	..	..	1.9	1.7	..
117	Australia	99	..	99	95	99	90	11	6	..	..	1.9	1.9	..
118	Italy	..	..	99	..	99	100	15	7	..	..	1.6	1.2	..
119	Canada	..	..	97	100	60	85	10	6	..	..	1.7	1.7	..
120	Finland	..	..	..	100	100	100	8	5	..	..	1.6	1.8	..
121	†Hong Kong	..	..	..	..	..	..	11	5	..	..	2.0	1.2	..
122	Sweden	..	..	..	..	85	100	7	4	..	..	1.7	1.7	..
123	Netherlands	..	..	100	100	100	100	9	6	..	..	1.6	1.6	..
124	Belgium	..	..	..	..	99	100	12	8	..	..	1.7	1.6	..
125	France	..	..	..	100	85	96	10	6	..	..	1.9	1.7	..
126	†Singapore	..	..	100	100	..	100	12	4	14	..	1.7	1.7	..
127	Austria	..	..	100	..	85	100	14	6	..	..	1.6	1.5	..
128	United States	..	..	..	90	98	85	13	8	..	..	1.8	2.1	..
129	Germany	..	..	..	..	..	100	12	6	..	..	1.6	1.2	..
130	Denmark	..	..	100	100	100	100	8	6	..	..	1.5	1.8	..
131	Norway	..	..	..	100	100	100	8	5	..	..	1.7	1.9	..
132	Japan	..	100	..	95	..	85	8	4	3	..	1.8	1.5	6[d]
133	Switzerland	..	..	..	100	85	100	9	6	..	..	1.6	1.5	..
World								80 w	55 w			3.7 w	2.9 w	

a. UNICEF/WHO estimate based on statistical modeling. b. Indirect estimate based on sample survey. c. Based on sample survey. d. Official estimate. e. Based on a survey covering thirty provinces. f. Based on civil registration.

Table 7. Education

		School enrollment as a % of age group										Percentage of cohort reaching grade 4				Adult illiteracy (%)	
		Primary				Secondary				Tertiary		Female		Male		Female	Male
		Female		Male		Female		Male									
		1980	1993	1980	1993	1980	1993	1980	1993	1980	1993	1980	1990	1980	1990	1995	1995
Low-income economies		81 w	98 w	104 w	112 w	26 w	41 w	42 w	..	3 w	..					45 w	24 w
Excluding China and India		64 w	..	85 w	..	14 w	..	25 w	..	3 w	..					55 w	37 w
1	Mozambique	84	51	114	69	3	6	8	9	0	0	..	54	..	60	77	42
2	Ethiopia[a]	23	19	44	27	6	11	11	12	0	1	48	56	42	56	75	55
3	Tanzania	86	69	99	71	2	5	4	6	..	..	89	90	90	89	43	21
4	Burundi	21	63	32	76	2	5	4	9	1	1	83	79	83	79	78	51
5	Malawi	48	77	72	84	2	3	5	6	1	1	55	68	62	73	58	28
6	Sierra Leone	43	..	61	..	8	..	20	..	1	..					82	55
7	Rwanda	60	76	66	78	3	9	4	11	0	..	74	76	73	73	48	30
8	Chad	..	30	..	62	..	..	..	..	..	1	..	65	..	74	65	38
9	Nepal	49	87	117	129	9	23	33	46	3	6	..	..	..	..	86	59
10	Niger	18	21	33	35	3	4	7	9	0	1	79	..	82	..	93	79
11	Madagascar	133	72	139	75	..	14	..	14	3	4	..	72	..	68	..	..
12	Burkina Faso	14	30	23	47	2	6	4	11	0	..	79	90	79	86	91	71
13	Vietnam	106	..	111	..	40	..	44	..	2	2	67	..	71	..	9	4
14	Bangladesh	46	105	76	128	9	12	26	26	3	..	30	46	29	44	74	51
15	Uganda	43	83	56	99	3	10	7	17	1	1	..	..	..	..	50	26
16	Mali	19	24	34	38	5	6	12	12	1	..	77	84	73	87	77	61
17	Guinea-Bissau	43	..	94	..	2	2	10	10	..	..	47	..	63	..	58	32
18	Haiti	70	..	82	..	13	..	14	..	1	..	64	60	63	60	58	52
19	Nigeria	104	82	135	105	14	27	27	32	2	..	..	76	..	74	53	33
20	Yemen, Rep.	..	..	..	..	..	..	..	..	..	..	..	..	..	..	..	..
21	Cambodia	..	46	..	48	..	..	..	..	..	..	..	..	..	..	47	20
22	Kenya	110	91	120	92	16	23	23	28	1	..	85	78	84	76	30	14
23	Togo	91	81	146	122	16	12	51	34	2	3	84	82	90	87	63	33
24	Mongolia	107	..	107	..	97	87	85	..	..	..					..	..
25	Gambia, The	35	61	67	84	7	13	16	25	..	..	..	..	..	..	75	47
26	India	67	91	98	113	20	..	39	..	5	..	52	..	57	..	62	35
27	Central African Republic	51	..	92	92	7	..	21	..	1	2	..	..	..	..	48	32
28	Lao PDR	104	92	123	123	16	19	25	31	0	2	31	..	31	..	56	31
29	Benin	41	44	87	88	9	7	24	17	2	..	73	58	77	58	74	51
30	Nicaragua	102	105	96	101	45	44	39	39	13	9	55	62	51	55	33	35
31	Ghana	71	70	89	83	31	28	51	44	2	..	82	..	87	..	47	24
32	Zambia	83	99	97	109	11	..	22	..	2	..	..	..	..	..	29	14
33	Angola	..	..	..	..	..	..	..	..	0	1	..	37	..	49	..	..
34	Georgia	..	..	..	..	..	..	..	..	30	..					..	..
35	Pakistan	27	49	51	80	8	..	20	..	..	..	41	45	53	55	76	50
36	Mauritania	26	62	47	76	4	11	17	19	..	4	86	83	96	82	74	50
37	Azerbaijan	..	87	..	91	..	88	..	89	25	26	..	..	..	..	..	..
38	Zimbabwe	..	114	..	123	..	40	..	51	1	6	..	..	..	..	20	10
39	Guinea	25	30	48	61	10	6	24	17	5	..	..	78	..	81	78	50
40	Honduras	99	112	98	111	31	37	29	29	8	9	..	..	..	..	27	27
41	Senegal	37	50	56	67	7	11	15	21	3	3	90	..	93	..	77	57
42	China	103	116	121	120	37	51	54	60	1	4	..	..	..	..	27	10
43	Cameroon	89	..	107	..	13	..	24	..	2	2	81	..	81	..	48	25
44	Côte d'Ivoire	63	58	95	80	12	17	27	33	3	..	91	82	94	85	70	50
45	Albania	111	97	116	95	63	..	70	..	8	10	96	..	97	..	..	..
46	Congo	..	..	..	..	..	..	..	..	..	..	91	..	91	..	33	17
47	Sri Lanka	100	105	105	106	57	78	52	71	3	6	..	96	..	95	13	7
48	Kyrgyz Republic	..	..	..	..	..	..	..	80	28	21	..	..	..	..	..	..
49	Armenia	..	93	..	87	..	90	..	80	30	49	..	..	..	..	..	..
Middle-income economies		99 w	101 w	106 w	105 w	48 w	62 w	53 w	64 w	21 w	20 w					23 w	14 w
Lower-middle-income		97 w	101 w	106 w	106 w	50 w	61 w	56 w	65 w	24 w	22 w					..	..
50	Lesotho	120	105	85	90	21	31	14	21	2	2	77	85	61	75	38	19
51	Egypt, Arab Rep.	61	89	84	105	39	69	61	81	16	17	83	..	75	..	61	36
52	Bolivia	81	..	92	..	32	..	42	..	16	23	50	..	52	..	24	10
53	Macedonia, FYR	..	87	..	88	..	55	..	53	28	16	..	..	..	..	..	..
54	Moldova	..	77	..	78	..	72	..	67	29	35	..	..	..	..	..	..
55	Uzbekistan	..	79	..	80	..	92	..	96	30	33	..	..	..	..	..	..
56	Indonesia	100	112	115	116	23	39	35	48	..	10	..	..	..	..	22	10
57	Philippines	112	..	113	..	69	..	61	..	24	26	..	82	..	78	6	5
58	Morocco	63	60	102	85	20	29	32	40	6	10	89	81	90	83	69	43
59	Syrian Arab Republic	88	99	111	111	35	42	57	52	17	18	91	96	94	97	44	14
60	Papua New Guinea	51	67	66	80	8	10	15	15	2	..	..	70	..	72	37	19
61	Bulgaria	98	84	98	87	84	70	85	66	16	23	95	91	98	93	..	..
62	Kazakstan	..	86	..	86	..	91	..	89	34	42	..	..	..	..	..	..
63	Guatemala	65	79	77	89	17	23	20	25	8	..	56	..	66	..	51	38
64	Ecuador	116	122	119	124	53	56	53	54	35	..	76	..	78	..	12	8
65	Dominican Republic	..	99	..	95	..	43	..	30	..	..	..	..	..	..	18	18
66	Romania	101	86	102	87	69	82	73	83	12	12	..	94	..	93	..	..
67	Jordan	102	95	105	94	73	54	79	52	27	19	95	97	95	99	21	7
68	Jamaica	104	108	103	109	71	70	63	62	7	6	..	100	..	98	11	19
69	Algeria	81	96	108	111	26	55	40	66	6	11	91	95	92	96	51	26
70	El Salvador	75	80	75	79	23	30	26	27	4	15	55	..	52	..	30	27
71	Ukraine	..	87	..	87	..	95	..	65	42	46	..	..	..	..	..	..
72	Paraguay	101	110	107	114	..	38	..	36	8	10	..	78	..	79	9	7

Note: For data comparability and coverage, see the technical notes. Figures in italics are for years other than those specified.

		School enrollment as a % of age group										Percentage of cohort reaching grade 4				Adult illiteracy (%)	
		Primary				Secondary				Tertiary		Female		Male		Female	Male
		Female		Male		Female		Male									
		1980	1993	1980	1993	1980	1993	1980	1993	1980	1993	1980	1990	1980	1990	1995	1995
73	Tunisia	88	113	118	123	20	49	34	55	5	11	90	93	94	95	45	21
74	Lithuania	..	90	..	95	..	79	..	76	49	39	..	..	..	..	..	..
75	Colombia	126	120	123	118	41	68	40	57	9	10	46	74	42	72	9	9
76	Namibia	..	138	..	134	..	61	..	49	..	3	..	64	..	65	..	..
77	Belarus	..	95	..	96	..	96	..	89	39	44	..	..	..	..	..	..
78	Russian Federation	102	107	102	107	97	91	95	84	46	45	..	..	..	..	..	..
79	Latvia	..	82	..	83	..	90	..	84	45	39	..	..	..	..	..	..
80	Peru	111	..	117	..	54	..	63	..	17	40	83	..	85	..	17	6
81	Costa Rica	104	105	106	106	51	49	44	45	21	30	84	91	80	90	5	5
82	Lebanon	..	114	..	117	..	78	..	73	30	29	..	..	..	..	10	5
83	Thailand	97	97	100	98	28	37	30	38	13	19	..	..	..	..	8	4
84	Panama	105	..	108	..	65	65	58	..	21	23	88	88	87	85	10	9
85	Turkey	90	98	102	107	24	48	44	74	5	16	..	98	..	98	28	8
86	Poland	99	97	100	98	80	87	75	82	18	26	..	..	..	..	..	..
87	Estonia	..	83	..	84	..	96	..	87	43	38	..	..	..	..	..	..
88	Slovak Republic	..	101	..	101	..	90	..	87	..	17	..	..	..	..	..	..
89	Venezuela	..	97	..	95	25	41	18	29	21	29	..	..	..	..	10	8
90	Botswana	100	120	83	113	20	55	17	49	1	3	98	94	91	92	40	20
	Upper-middle-income	103 w	..	106 w	..	43 w	..	43 w	..	13 w	16 w					14 w	12 w
91	South Africa	..	110	..	111	..	84	..	71	..	13	..	..	..	..	18	18
92	Croatia	..	..	..	..	..	86	..	80	..	27	..	..	..	..	..	..
93	Mexico	121	110	122	114	46	58	51	57	14	14	63	..	85	..	13	8
94	Mauritius	91	106	94	107	49	60	51	58	1	4	97	98	97	99	21	13
95	Gabon	..	136	..	132	..	..	..	..	..	3	79	80	82	82	47	26
96	Brazil	97	..	101	..	36	..	31	..	11	12	..	..	..	..	17	17
97	Trinidad and Tobago	100	94	98	94	..	78	..	74	4	8	89	97	83	96	3	1
98	Czech Republic	..	100	..	99	..	88	..	85	18	16	..	..	..	..	..	..
99	Malaysia	92	93	93	93	46	61	50	56	4	..	..	99	..	98	22	11
100	Hungary	97	95	96	95	67	82	72	79	14	17	96	97	96	97	..	..
101	Chile	108	98	110	99	56	67	49	65	12	27	81	95	78	95	5	5
102	Oman	36	82	69	87	6	57	19	64	..	5	..	..	..	..	..	..
103	Uruguay	107	108	107	109	62	..	61	..	17	30	99	98	93	98	2	3
104	Saudi Arabia	49	73	74	78	23	43	36	54	7	14	90	..	81	..	50	29
105	Argentina	106	107	106	108	..	75	..	70	22	41	76	..	73	..	4	4
106	Slovenia	..	97	..	97	..	90	..	88	..	28	..	..	..	..	..	..
107	Greece	103	..	103	..	77	..	85	..	17	..	98	..	98	..	..	..
	Low- and middle-income	87 w	99 w	105 w	110 w	33 w	49 w	45 w	..	8 w	..					39 w	21 w
	Sub-Saharan Africa	68 w	65 w	90 w	78 w	10 w	22 w	20 w	27 w	1 w	..					54 w	35 w
	East Asia and Pacific	102 w	116 w	118 w	120 w	36 w	51 w	51 w	60 w	3 w	5 w					24 w	9 w
	South Asia	61 w	87 w	91 w	110 w	18 w	35 w	36 w	..	5 w	..					64 w	37 w
	Europe and Central Asia	..	97 w	..	97 w	..	90 w	..	81 w	31 w	32 w					..	..
	Middle East and N. Africa	74 w	91 w	98 w	103 w	32 w	51 w	52 w	65 w	11 w	14 w					50 w	28 w
	Latin America and Caribbean	105 w	..	108 w	..	41 w	..	40 w	..	14 w	15 w					14 w	12 w
	High-income economies	103 w	103 w	103 w	103 w	..	98 w	..	97 w	35 w	56 w					..	..
108	Korea, Rep.	111	102	109	100	74	92	82	93	15	48	96	100	96	100	b	b
109	Portugal	123	118	124	122	40	..	34	..	11	23	..	..	..	..	..	..
110	Spain	109	105	110	104	89	120	85	107	23	41	94	95	92	94	..	..
111	New Zealand	111	101	111	102	84	104	82	103	27	58	..	99	..	98	b	b
112	Ireland	100	103	100	103	95	110	85	101	18	34	100	99	97	98	b	b
113	†Israel	..	96	..	95	..	91	..	84	29	35	..	97	..	98	..	..
114	†Kuwait	100	..	105	..	76	..	84	..	11	..	..	..	..	..	25	18
115	†United Arab Emirates	88	108	90	112	49	94	55	84	3	11	..	93	..	94	20	21
116	United Kingdom	103	113	103	112	85	94	82	91	19	37	..	..	..	..	b	b
117	Australia	110	107	112	108	72	86	70	83	25	42	97	100	94	98	b	b
118	Italy	100	99	100	98	70	82	73	81	27	37	..	..	..	..	b	b
119	Canada	99	104	99	106	89	103	87	104	52	103	97	98	94	95	b	b
120	Finland	96	100	97	100	105	130	94	110	32	63	99	98	99	98	b	b
121	†Hong Kong	106	..	107	..	65	..	63	..	10	21	..	..	..	..	12	4
122	Sweden	97	100	96	100	93	100	83	99	31	38	100	..	99	..	b	b
123	Netherlands	101	99	99	96	90	120	95	126	29	45	100	..	97	..	b	b
124	Belgium	103	100	104	99	92	104	90	103	26	..	81	..	78	..	b	b
125	France	110	105	112	107	92	107	77	104	25	50	..	..	..	..	b	b
126	†Singapore	106	..	109	..	59	..	56	..	8	..	100	100	99	100	14	4
127	Austria	98	103	99	103	87	104	98	109	22	43	97	99	92	97	b	b
128	United States	100	106	101	107	..	97	..	98	56	81	..	..	..	..	b	b
129	Germany[c]	..	98	..	97	..	100	..	101	..	36	98	99	96	97	b	b
130	Denmark	95	98	96	97	104	115	105	112	28	41	..	..	..	..	b	b
131	Norway	100	99	100	99	96	114	92	118	26	54	..	..	..	..	b	b
132	Japan	101	102	101	102	94	97	92	95	31	30	100	100	100	100	b	b
133	Switzerland	..	102	..	100	..	89	..	93	18	31	94	..	92	..	b	b
	World	90 w	99 w	104 w	109 w	39 w	57 w	50 w	..	13 w	..					..	..

a. Data for 1980 include Eritrea. b. According to UNESCO, illiteracy is less than 5 percent. c. Data before 1990 refer to the Federal Republic of Germany before unification.

Table 8. Commercial energy use

		Total (thous. metric tons)		Per capita (kg)		Avg. annual growth rate (%)	GDP per kg. (1987 $)		Net energy imports as % of energy consumption		Total (mill. metric tons)		Per capita (metric tons)	
		1980	1994	1980	1994	1980–94	1980	1994	1980	1994	1980	1992	1980	1992
	Low-income economies	587,124 t	1,154,712 t	248 w	369 w	4.4 w	0.9 w	1.1 w			2,063 t	3,880 t	0.9 w	1.3 w
	Excluding China and India	80,087 t	137,034 t	114 w	134 w	2.3 w		2.6 w			223 t	443 t	0.3 w	0.5 w
1	Mozambique	1,123	619	93	40	–2.5	1.4	3.3	–15	74	3	1	0.3	0.1
2	Ethiopia	624	1,193	17	22	5.2	..	6.9	91	87	2	3	0.0	0.1
3	Tanzania	1,023	975	55	34	0.7	..	4.5	92	83	2	2	0.1	0.1
4	Burundi	58	143	14	23	6.8	13.9	8.3	98	97	0	0	0.0	0.0
5	Malawi	334	370	54	39	1.5	3.2	3.4	70	59	1	1	0.1	0.1
6	Chad	93	100	21	16	0.6	6.2	10.9	100	100	0	0	0.0	0.0
7	Rwanda	190	209	37	34	–0.4	9.3	4.9	85	78	0	0	0.0	0.1
8	Sierra Leone	310	323	96	77	0.5	2.3	2.4	100	100	1	0	0.2	0.1
9	Nepal	174	582	12	28	8.7	12.5	7.3	91	88	1	1	0.0	0.1
10	Niger	210	327	38	37	2.1	12.1	7.3	93	83	1	1	0.1	0.1
11	Burkina Faso	144	160	21	16	1.1	11.2	16.0	100	100	0	1	0.1	0.1
12	Madagascar	391	479	45	36	1.7	6.7	5.6	90	83	2	1	0.2	0.1
13	Bangladesh	2,809	7,566	32	64	7.7	4.5	3.1	60	28	8	17	0.1	0.2
14	Uganda	320	425	25	23	1.3	..	22.6	52	58	1	1	0.1	0.1
15	Vietnam	4,024	7,267	75	101	3.1	..	7.5	32	–55	17	22	0.3	0.3
16	Guinea-Bissau	31	39	38	37	2.1	3.8	5.8	100	100	0	0	0.2	0.2
17	Haiti	240	200	45	29	1.2	9.5	7.9	77	93	1	1	0.1	0.1
18	Mali	164	205	25	22	1.8	11.2	11.5	87	80	0	0	0.1	0.0
19	Nigeria	9,879	17,503	139	162	3.8	3.1	2.2	–968	–484	68	97	1.0	0.9
20	Yemen, Rep.	1,364	3,044	160	206	4.1	..	..	100	–463	3	10	0.4	0.7
21	Cambodia	393	512	60	52	2.2	..	2.4	97	96	0	0	0.0	0.1
22	Kenya	1,991	2,872	120	110	3.1	3.1	3.3	95	83	6	5	0.4	0.2
23	Mongolia	1,943	2,550	1,168	1,058	2.0	1.2	1.2	38	15	7	9	4.0	4.0
24	Togo	195	183	75	46	1.8	6.3	6.9	99	100	1	1	0.2	0.2
25	Gambia, The	53	60	83	56	0.9	3.5	4.9	100	100	0	0	0.2	0.2
26	Central African Republic	59	93	26	29	2.7	16.2	12.1	71	76	0	0	0.0	0.1
27	India	93,907	226,638	137	248	6.6	1.9	1.6	21	21	350	769	0.5	0.9
28	Lao PDR	107	182	33	38	2.6	..	9.1	–121	–18	0	0	0.1	0.1
29	Benin	149	107	43	20	–3.5	8.3	18.0	93	–194	0	1	0.1	0.1
30	Nicaragua	756	1,273	270	300	3.3	5.1	2.7	83	63	2	2	0.7	0.6
31	Ghana	1,303	1,542	121	93	2.5	3.6	4.4	57	66	2	4	0.2	0.2
32	Zambia	1,685	1,296	294	149	–2.6	1.3	1.8	32	31	4	2	0.6	0.3
33	Angola	937	931	133	89	0.3	..	7.0	–722	–2,576	5	5	0.8	0.5
34	Georgia	..	3,325	..	614	..	..	0.7	..	85	..	14	..	2.5
35	Pakistan	11,698	32,133	142	254	7.4	1.8	1.5	38	40	32	72	0.4	0.6
36	Mauritania	214	229	138	103	0.5	3.8	4.8	100	100	1	3	0.4	1.4
37	Azerbaijan	15,001	16,274	2,433	2,182	–2.7	..	0.2	1	1	..	64	..	8.7
38	Zimbabwe	2,797	4,722	399	438	3.9	1.5	1.4	28	24	10	19	1.4	1.8
39	Guinea	356	418	80	65	1.3	..	6.1	89	86	1	1	0.2	0.2
40	Honduras	843	1,173	230	204	2.1	4.2	4.4	76	82	2	3	0.6	0.6
41	Senegal	875	803	158	97	–0.1	4.2	6.3	100	100	3	3	0.5	0.4
42	China	413,130	791,040	421	664	5.0	0.3	0.7	–4	–1	1,489	2,668	1.5	2.3
43	Cameroon	774	1,335	89	103	2.6	10.0	6.9	–269	–333	4	2	0.4	0.2
44	Côte d'Ivoire	1,435	1,406	175	103	1.4	6.8	6.8	87	70	5	6	0.6	0.5
45	Albania	3,058	1,093	1,145	341	–4.8	0.6	2.4	0	3	7	4	2.8	1.2
46	Congo	262	847	157	331	3.7	5.7	2.8	–1,193	–1,013	0	4	0.2	1.6
47	Kyrgyz Republic	..	2,755	..	616	..	..	0.9	..	47	..	15	..	3.4
48	Sri Lanka	1,411	1,728	96	97	1.9	3.4	5.1	91	80	3	5	0.2	0.3
49	Armenia	1,071	1,441	346	384	1.6	4.3	1.4	..	79	..	4	..	1.1
	Middle-income economies	1,873,142 t	2,313,337 t	1,537 w	1,475 w	–1.7 w	..	..			2,831 t	7,221 t	2.9 w	4.8 w
	Lower-middle-income	1,448,776 t	1,647,009 t	1,632 w	1,449 w	–3.0 w	..	..			1,664 t	5,565 t	2.6 w	5.1 w
50	Lesotho	..	..	..	..	..	..	..				0		0.0
51	Egypt, Arab Rep.	15,176	34,071	371	600	5.7	1.6	1.2	–120	–79	45	84	1.1	1.5
52	Bolivia	1,713	2,698	320	373	1.6	2.7	2.1	–107	–61	5	7	0.8	1.0
53	Macedonia, FYR	..	2,686	..	1,279	..	..	..	..	44	..	4	..	2.0
54	Moldova	..	4,763	..	1,095	..	..	..	..	99	0	14	0.0	3.3
55	Uzbekistan	..	41,825	..	1,869	..	..	0.3	..	0	..	123	..	5.7
56	Indonesia	25,028	69,740	169	366	8.3	2.1	1.8	–275	–120	95	185	0.6	1.0
57	Philippines	13,406	21,199	277	316	3.5	2.4	1.9	79	71	37	50	0.8	0.8
58	Morocco	4,927	8,509	254	327	4.1	3.1	2.9	87	95	16	27	0.8	1.1
59	Syrian Arab Republic	5,343	13,675	614	997	6.1	1.9	1.2	–78	–130	19	42	2.2	3.3
60	Papua New Guinea	705	990	228	236	2.4	3.9	4.8	89	–150	2	2	0.6	0.6
61	Bulgaria	28,476	20,568	3,213	2,438	–2.7	0.7	1.0	74	56	75	54	8.4	6.4
62	Kazakstan	76,799	56,664	5,153	3,371	–2.3	..	0.3	0	–25	..	298	..	17.6
63	Guatemala	1,443	2,165	209	210	3.2	5.0	4.3	84	74	4	6	0.6	0.6
64	Ecuador	4,209	6,345	529	565	2.7	2.3	2.2	–156	–231	13	19	1.7	1.8
65	Dominican Republic	2,083	2,591	366	337	1.4	2.0	2.5	93	94	6	10	1.1	1.4
66	Romania	63,846	39,387	2,876	1,733	–3.1	0.5	0.7	19	27	191	122	8.6	5.4
67	Jamaica	2,169	2,703	1,017	1,083	2.3	1.3	1.5	99	100	8	8	4.0	3.3
68	Jordan	1,710	4,306	784	1,067	5.2	..	1.5	100	96	5	11	2.2	3.0
69	Algeria	12,078	24,834	647	906	4.9	4.1	2.6	–452	–318	66	79	3.5	3.0
70	El Salvador	1,000	2,032	220	370	4.0	4.5	2.6	63	70	2	4	0.5	0.7
71	Ukraine	108,290	165,132	2,164	3,180	–1.4	..	0.4	–1	48	..	611	..	11.7
72	Paraguay	550	1,402	175	299	6.9	6.0	3.5	88	–123	1	3	0.5	0.6

Note: For data comparability and coverage, see the technical notes. Figures in italics are for years other than those specified.

		Energy use (oil equivalent)							Net energy imports as % of energy consumption		Carbon dioxide emissions[a]			
		Total (thous. metric tons)		Per capita (kg)		Avg. annual growth rate (%)	GDP per kg. (1987 $)				Total (mill. metric tons)		Per capita (metric tons)	
		1980	1994	1980	1994	1980–94	1980	1994	1980	1994	1980	1992	1980	1992
73	Tunisia	..	7,555	..	595	..	..	0.8	..	70	..	22	..	5.9
74	Lithuania	13,972	22,470	501	2,030	3.5	2.1	2.1	7	−99	39	61	1.4	1.8
75	Colombia	..	..	..	622	..	..	..	..	..	..	0	..	0.0
76	Namibia	2,385	24,772	247	..	13.4	..	0.8	−8	88	..	102	..	9.9
77	Belarus	750,240	595,440	5,397	2,392	−2.6	0.6	0.5	0	−53	..	2,103	..	14.1
78	Russian Federation	..	3,997	..	4,014	..	..	1.2	..	90	..	15	..	5.6
79	Latvia	8,139	8,555	471	1,569	−0.2	2.5	2.7	−36	0	24	22	1.4	1.0
80	Peru	1,292	1,843	566	367	3.5	3.1	3.4	86	67	2	4	1.1	1.2
81	Costa Rica	2,376	3,790	840	558	2.3	..	..	97	98	6	11	2.2	2.9
82	Lebanon	12,093	44,395	259	964	13.4	2.8	2.2	96	61	40	112	0.9	2.0
83	Thailand	1,376	1,597	703	769	1.2	3.2	3.9	97	87	4	4	1.9	1.7
84	Panama	31,314	57,580	705	618	4.4	1.9	1.8	45	53	76	145	1.7	2.5
85	Turkey	124,500	92,537	3,499	957	−2.0	0.5	0.7	3	−2	460	342	12.9	8.9
86	Poland	..	5,560	..	2,401	..	..	0.7	..	39	0	21	0.3	13.5
87	Estonia	..	17,343	..	3,709	..	..	0.9	..	72	..	37	..	7.0
88	Slovak Republic	35,011	46,300	2,354	3,243	2.3	1.3	1.2	−280	−269	90	116	6.0	5.7
89	Botswana	424,366	666,328	1,282	387	2.6	2.3	1.7	..	..	1,167	1,656	3.7	4.0
90	Venezuela	384	549	426	2,186	2.6	2.1	4.7	32	55	1	2	1.1	1.6
	Upper-middle-income	424,366 t	666,328 t	1,282 w	1,544 w	2.6 w	2.3 w	1.7 w			1,167 t	1,656 t	3.7 w	4.0 w
91	South Africa	60,511	86,995	2,074	2,146	2.1	1.2	1.0	−14	−35	213	290	7.3	7.5
92	Croatia	..	6,667	..	1,395	..	..	..	..	43	..	16	..	3.4
93	Mexico	97,434	140,840	1,464	1,561	2.6	1.3	1.2	−49	−48	260	333	3.9	3.8
94	Mauritius	339	431	351	387	2.8	3.7	6.3	94	92	1	1	0.6	1.3
95	Gabon	759	692	1,098	652	−0.4	5.0	5.5	−1,106	−2,212	5	6	6.9	5.5
96	Brazil	72,141	112,795	595	718	3.9	3.4	2.8	65	39	184	217	1.5	1.4
97	Trinidad and Tobago	3,863	6,935	3,570	5,436	2.9	1.5	0.7	−240	−87	17	21	15.4	16.5
98	Czech Republic	29,394	39,982	2,873	3,868	45.2	..	0.8	−29	7	..	136	..	13.1
99	Malaysia	9,522	33,410	692	1,699	10.0	2.4	1.7	−58	−71	28	70	2.0	3.8
100	Hungary	28,322	24,450	2,645	2,383	−0.9	0.8	1.0	49	47	82	60	7.7	5.8
101	Chile	7,743	14,155	695	1,012	5.0	2.3	2.3	50	68	27	35	2.4	2.6
102	Oman	1,346	5,018	1,223	2,392	9.1	2.9	2.4	−1,024	−787	6	10	5.3	5.3
103	Uruguay	2,208	1,971	758	622	3.2	3.4	4.6	89	67	6	5	2.0	1.6
104	Saudi Arabia	35,496	83,772	3,787	4,566	5.5	2.7	1.1	−1,361	−463	131	221	14.0	13.1
105	Argentina	39,669	51,405	1,411	1,504	1.6	2.8	2.7	8	−18	107	117	3.8	3.5
106	Slovenia	..	5,195	..	2,612	..	..	..	..	51	..	6	..	2.8
107	Greece	15,973	23,560	1,656	2,260	3.3	2.8	2.2	77	62	51	74	5.3	7.2
	Low- and middle-income	2,460,266 t	3,468,049 t	686 w	739 w	−0.1 w	1.4 w	1.1 w			4,893 t	11,101 t	1.5 w	2.4 w
	Sub-Saharan Africa	94,721 t	133,471 t	249 w	237 w	1.2 w	2.2 w	2.0 w			353 t	472 t	0.9 w	0.9 w
	East Asia and Pacific	514,066 t	1,000,586 t	378 w	593 w	4.8 w	0.7 w	0.9 w			1,846 t	3,378 t	1.4 w	2.1 w
	South Asia	110,906 t	271,293 t	123 w	222 w	6.4 w	2.0 w	1.7 w			395 t	866 t	0.4 w	0.7 w
	Europe and Central Asia	1,279,071 t	1,288,624 t	3,105 w	2,647 w	−4.6 w	..	0.6 w			944 t	4,506 t	..	9.3 w
	Middle East and N. Africa	143,540 t	323,064 t	825 w	1,220 w	4.8 w	3.2 w	1.7 w			500 t	849 t	2.9 w	3.4 w
	Latin America and Caribbean	317,962 t	451,011 t	888 w	960 w	2.9 w	2.3 w	2.0 w			855 t	1,029 t	2.4 w	2.3 w
	High-income economies	3,789,479 t	4,543,482 t	4,644 w	5,066 w	1.9 w	2.9 w	3.4 w			9,877 t	10,246 t	12.4 w	11.9 w
108	Korea, Rep.	41,426	132,538	1,087	2,982	9.5	1.8	1.8	77	86	126	290	3.3	6.6
109	Portugal	10,291	18,090	1,054	1,827	4.7	3.5	2.8	86	88	27	47	2.8	4.8
110	Spain	68,692	96,200	1,837	2,458	2.8	3.6	3.6	77	69	200	223	5.4	5.7
111	New Zealand	9,202	15,070	2,956	4,245	4.1	3.4	2.8	39	15	18	26	5.7	7.6
112	Ireland	8,485	11,200	2,495	3,137	2.2	3.1	3.9	78	68	25	31	7.4	8.7
113	†Israel	8,616	14,624	2,222	2,717	4.9	3.4	3.7	98	96	21	42	5.4	8.1
114	†Kuwait	9,500	13,968	6,909	8,622	0.3	2.7	2.0	−739	−693	25	16	18.0	11.2
115	†United Arab Emirates	8,558	25,137	8,205	10,531	6.3	3.6	..	−996	−454	36	71	34.8	33.9
116	United Kingdom	201,200	220,270	3,572	3,772	0.8	2.8	3.5	2	−10	588	566	10.4	9.8
117	Australia	70,399	95,280	4,792	5,341	2.3	2.4	2.6	−22	−83	203	268	13.8	15.3
118	Italy	139,190	154,600	2,466	2,707	1.4	4.8	5.5	86	81	372	408	6.6	7.2
119	Canada	193,170	229,730	7,854	7,854	1.5	1.7	2.0	−7	−47	430	410	17.5	14.4
120	Finland	24,998	30,520	5,230	5,997	1.7	2.9	3.0	72	58	55	41	11.5	8.2
121	†Hong Kong	5,628	13,243	1,117	2,185	6.4	5.3	5.3	100	100	16	29	3.3	5.0
122	Sweden	40,992	50,250	4,933	5,723	1.3	3.4	3.3	61	38	71	57	8.6	6.6
123	Netherlands	65,106	70,440	4,601	4,580	1.3	3.0	3.7	−10	7	153	139	10.8	9.2
124	Belgium	46,122	51,790	4,684	4,684	1.5	2.8	3.2	83	78	128	102	13.0	10.1
125	France	190,660	234,160	3,539	4,042	2.0	4.1	4.4	75	95	484	362	9.0	6.3
126	†Singapore	6,049	23,743	2,651	8,103	9.9	2.2	1.6	100	100	30	50	13.2	17.7
127	Austria	23,449	26,500	3,105	3,301	1.6	4.6	5.4	67	66	52	57	6.9	7.2
128	United States	1,801,000	2,037,980	7,908	7,819	1.6	2.1	2.6	14	19	4,623	4,881	20.3	19.1
129	Germany	359,170	336,490	4,587	4,128	−0.1	..	..	49	58	1,068	878	13.6	10.9
130	Denmark	19,488	20,700	3,804	3,977	0.8	4.4	5.5	97	28	63	54	12.3	10.4
131	Norway	18,865	23,060	4,611	5,318	1.6	3.9	4.6	−195	−638	40	60	9.8	14.1
132	Japan	347,120	481,850	2,972	3,856	2.8	5.5	6.2	88	81	934	1,093	8.0	8.8
133	Switzerland	20,840	25,380	3,298	3,629	1.7	7.3	7.4	66	57	41	44	6.5	6.4
	World	6,249,745 t	8,011,531 t	1,419 w	1,433 w	1.0 w	2.3 w	2.4 w			14,770 t	21,347 t	3.6 w	4.0 w

a. From industrial processes.

Table 9. Land use and urbanization

		Land use (% of total land area)						Urban population			Population in urban agglomerations of 1 million or more as % of			
		Cropland		Permanent pasture		Other		As % of total population		Avg. annual growth rate (%)	Urban		Total	
		1980	1994	1980	1994	1980	1994	1980	1995	1980–95	1980	1995	1980	1995
	Low-income economies	12 w	12 w	31 w	32 w	57 w	55 w	21 w	29 w	4.0 w	32 w	34 w	7 w	10 w
	Excluding China and India	8 w	8 w	32 w	32 w	60 w	60 w	21 w	28 w	4.6 w	28 w	31 w	6 w	9 w
1	Mozambique	4	4	56	56	40	40	13	38	8.5	48	36	6	14
2	Ethiopia	..	11	..	20	..	69	11	13	4.5	30	29	3	4
3	Tanzania	3	4	40	40	57	56	15	24	6.7	30	24	5	6
4	Burundi	46	46	39	39	15	15	4	8	6.8	0	0	0	0
5	Malawi	14	18	20	20	66	62	9	13	6.0	0	0	0	0
6	Sierra Leone	7	8	31	31	62	62	25	39	4.9	0	0	0	0
7	Rwanda	41	47	28	28	30	24	5	8	4.7	0	0	0	0
8	Chad	3	3	36	36	62	62	19	21	3.4	0	0	0	0
9	Nepal	17	17	14	15	69	68	7	14	7.8	0	0	0	0
10	Niger	3	3	8	8	90	89	13	23	7.2	0	0	0	0
11	Madagascar	5	5	41	41	54	53	18	27	5.7	0	0	0	0
12	Burkina Faso	10	13	22	22	68	65	9	27	11.3	0	0	0	0
13	Vietnam	20	21	1	1	79	78	19	21	2.7	27	31	5	7
14	Bangladesh	70	74	5	5	25	21	11	18	5.6	46	47	5	9
15	Uganda	28	34	9	9	63	57	9	12	5.2	0	0	0	0
16	Mali	2	2	25	25	74	73	19	27	5.3	0	0	0	0
17	Guinea-Bissau	10	12	38	38	51	50	17	22	3.7	0	0	0	0
18	Haiti	32	33	18	18	49	49	24	32	3.9	55	56	13	18
19	Nigeria	33	36	44	44	23	20	27	39	5.6	23	27	6	11
20	Yemen, Rep.	3	3	30	30	67	67	20	34	7.6	0	0	0	0
21	Cambodia	12	22	3	8	85	70	12	21	6.7	..	..	..	..
22	Kenya	8	8	37	37	55	55	16	28	7.0	32	28	5	8
23	Togo	43	45	4	4	53	52	23	31	5.1	0	0	0	0
24	Mongolia	1	1	79	75	20	24	52	60	3.6	0	0	0	0
25	Gambia, The	16	17	19	19	65	64	18	26	6.3	0	0	0	0
26	India	57	57	4	4	39	39	23	27	3.1	25	35	6	10
27	Central African Republic	3	3	5	5	92	92	35	39	3.1	0	0	0	0
28	Lao PDR	3	4	3	3	94	93	13	22	6.3	0	0	0	0
29	Benin	16	17	4	4	80	79	32	42	5.1	0	0	0	0
30	Nicaragua	10	10	40	45	50	44	53	62	3.9	42	44	23	27
31	Ghana	15	19	37	37	48	44	31	36	4.3	30	27	9	10
32	Zambia	7	7	40	40	53	53	40	45	4.0	23	33	9	15
33	Angola	3	3	43	43	54	54	21	32	5.9	63	64	13	20
34	Georgia	17	16	39	24	44	60	52	58	1.3	42	43	22	25
35	Pakistan	26	28	6	6	67	66	28	35	4.6	39	53	11	18
36	Mauritania	0	0	38	38	62	62	29	54	6.8	0	0	0	0
37	Azerbaijan	22	23	27	25	51	52	53	56	1.7	48	44	26	25
38	Zimbabwe	7	7	44	44	49	48	22	32	5.7	0	0	0	0
39	Guinea	3	3	44	44	54	53	19	30	5.8	65	77	12	23
40	Honduras	16	18	13	14	71	68	36	48	5.2	0	0	0	0
41	Senegal	12	12	30	30	58	58	36	42	4.0	49	55	18	23
42	China	11	10	36	43	53	47	19	30	4.2	41	35	8	11
43	Cameroon	15	15	4	4	81	81	31	45	5.3	19	22	6	10
44	Côte d'Ivoire	10	12	41	41	49	47	35	44	5.2	44	46	15	20
45	Albania	26	26	15	15	59	59	34	37	2.1	0	0	0	0
46	Congo	0	0	29	29	70	70	41	59	5.6	0	0	0	0
47	Sri Lanka	29	29	7	7	64	64	22	22	1.6	0	0	0	0
48	Kyrgyz Republic	8	7	47	44	45	48	38	39	1.6	0	0	0	0
49	Armenia	..	..	..	..	..	..	66	69	1.6	51	51	34	35
	Middle-income economies	9 w	10 w	28 w	23 w	62 w	67 w	52 w	60 w	2.8 w	31 w	33 w	16 w	20 w
	Lower-middle-income	10 w	11 w		18 w	..	71 w	48 w	56 w	2.8 w	28 w	30 w	13 w	17 w
50	Lesotho	10	11	66	66	24	24	13	23	6.5	0	0	0	0
51	Egypt, Arab Rep.	2	4	0	0	98	96	44	45	2.5	52	51	23	23
52	Bolivia	2	2	25	24	73	73	46	58	3.9	30	29	14	17
53	Macedonia, FYR	..	26	..	25	..	49	53	60	1.5	0	0	0	0
54	Moldova	67	66	11	13	23	21	40	52	2.4	0	0	0	0
55	Uzbekistan	10	11	57	50	33	39	41	42	2.5	28	24	11	10
56	Indonesia	14	17	7	7	79	77	22	34	4.8	33	39	7	13
57	Philippines	29	31	3	4	67	65	38	53	4.9	33	25	12	14
58	Morocco	18	21	47	47	35	32	41	49	3.3	26	37	11	18
59	Syrian Arab Republic	31	30	46	45	24	25	47	53	4.1	60	52	28	28
60	Papua New Guinea	1	1	0	0	99	99	13	16	3.6	0	0	0	0
61	Bulgaria	38	38	18	16	44	46	61	71	0.6	20	23	12	16
62	Kazakstan	13	13	70	70	16	17	54	60	1.6	12	13	6	8
63	Guatemala	16	18	12	24	72	58	37	42	3.6	0	0	0	0
64	Ecuador	9	11	15	18	77	71	47	58	3.9	29	44	14	26
65	Dominican Republic	29	31	43	43	27	26	51	65	3.8	49	51	25	33
66	Romania	46	43	19	21	35	36	49	55	1.0	18	17	9	9
67	Jordan	4	5	9	9	87	87	60	72	5.8	49	39	29	28
68	Jamaica	22	20	24	24	54	56	47	55	2.2	0	0	0	0
69	Algeria	3	3	15	13	82	83	43	56	4.5	25	24	11	13
70	El Salvador	35	35	29	29	36	35	42	45	2.0	0	0	0	0
71	Ukraine	61	59	12	13	27	28	62	70	1.0	22	22	14	15
72	Paraguay	4	6	40	55	56	40	42	54	4.7	0	0	0	0

Note: For data comparability and coverage, see the technical notes. Figures in italics are for years other than those specified.

		Land use (% of total land area)						Urban population			Population in urban agglomerations of 1 million or more as % of			
		Cropland		Permanent pasture		Other		As % of total population		Avg. annual growth rate (%)	Urban		Total	
		1980	1994	1980	1994	1980	1994	1980	1995	1980–95	1980	1995	1980	1995
73	Tunisia	30	32	22	20	48	48	51	57	3.0	34	40	17	23
74	Lithuania	49	47	8	7	43	46	61	72	1.8	0	0	0	0
75	Colombia	5	5	37	39	58	56	64	73	2.7	34	38	22	28
76	Namibia	1	1	46	46	53	53	23	38	6.2	0	0	0	0
77	Belarus	31	31	16	14	53	55	56	71	2.0	24	24	14	17
78	Russian Federation	8	8	..	5	..	87	70	73	0.8	23	26	16	19
79	Latvia	28	28	12	13	60	59	68	73	0.5	0	0	0	0
80	Peru	3	3	21	21	76	76	65	72	2.9	40	44	26	31
81	Costa Rica	10	10	39	46	51	44	43	50	3.7	0	0	0	0
82	Lebanon	30	30	1	1	69	69	73	87	3.7	..	..	..	..
83	Thailand	36	41	1	2	63	58	17	20	2.6	59	56	10	11
84	Panama	7	9	17	20	75	71	50	56	2.8	0	0	0	0
85	Turkey	37	36	13	16	50	48	44	70	5.4	39	35	17	24
86	Poland	49	48	13	13	38	39	58	65	1.2	31	28	18	18
87	Estonia	24	27	8	7	68	66	70	73	0.4	0	0	0	0
88	Slovak Republic	41	34	13	17	45	49	52	59	1.3	0	0	0	0
89	Venezuela	4	4	20	20	76	75	83	93	3.3	20	29	16	27
90	Botswana	1	1	45	45	54	54	15	31	8.4	0	0	0	0
	Upper-middle-income	7 w	7 w	30 w	32 w	63 w	60 w	64 w	73 w	2.8 w	38 w	38 w	24 w	28 w
91	South Africa	11	11	67	67	22	23	48	51	2.7	23	38	11	19
92	Croatia	29	22	28	20	42	59	50	64	2.0	0	0	0	0
93	Mexico	13	13	39	39	48	48	66	75	3.1	41	37	27	28
94	Mauritius	53	52	3	3	44	44	42	41	0.6	0	0	0	0
95	Gabon	2	2	18	18	80	80	36	50	5.4	0	0	0	0
96	Brazil	6	6	20	22	74	72	66	78	3.0	42	42	27	33
97	Trinidad and Tobago	23	24	2	2	75	74	63	68	1.7	0	0	0	0
98	Czech Republic	41	44	13	12	45	45	64	65	0.2	18	18	12	12
99	Malaysia	15	23	1	1	85	76	42	54	4.3	16	11	7	6
100	Hungary	58	54	14	12	28	34	57	65	0.5	34	30	19	20
101	Chile	6	6	17	18	77	76	81	86	2.0	41	41	33	36
102	Oman	0	0	5	5	95	95	8	13	8.6	0	0	0	0
103	Uruguay	8	7	78	77	14	15	85	90	1.0	49	46	42	42
104	Saudi Arabia	1	2	40	56	60	42	67	79	6.0	28	27	19	21
105	Argentina	10	10	52	52	38	38	83	88	1.8	42	44	35	39
106	Slovenia	..	14	..	25	..	61	48	64	2.2	0	0	0	0
107	Greece	30	27	41	41	29	32	58	65	1.4	54	54	31	35
	Low- and middle-income	10 w	11 w	29 w	27 w	60 w	63 w	32 w	39 w	3.3 w	32 w	33 w	10 w	13 w
	Sub-Saharan Africa	6 w	7 w	34 w	34 w	60 w	59 w	23 w	31 w	5.0 w	23 w	26 w	5 w	8 w
	East Asia and Pacific	11 w	12 w	30 w	34 w	59 w	54 w	21 w	31 w	4.2 w	37 w	34 w	8 w	11 w
	South Asia	44 w	45 w	11 w	10 w	45 w	45 w	22 w	26 w	3.4 w	27 w	38 w	6 w	10 w
	Europe and Central Asia	13 w	13 w	..	16 w	..	71 w	58 w	65 w	1.6 w	24 w	25 w	14 w	16 w
	Middle East and N. Africa	5 w	6 w	21 w	24 w	74 w	70 w	48 w	56 w	4.2 w	36 w	36 w	17 w	20 w
	Latin America and Caribbean	7 w	7 w	28 w	29 w	65 w	63 w	65 w	74 w	2.8 w	37 w	38 w	24 w	28 w
	High-income economies	12 w	12 w	25 w	24 w	62 w	63 w	75 w	75 w	0.7 w	41 w	43 w	31 w	33 w
108	Korea, Rep.	22	21	1	1	77	78	57	81	3.5	65	64	37	52
109	Portugal	34	32	9	11	57	58	29	36	1.3	46	53	13	19
110	Spain	41	40	22	21	37	38	73	77	0.6	27	23	20	18
111	New Zealand	13	14	53	50	34	35	83	84	1.0	0	0	0	0
112	Ireland	16	19	67	45	17	36	55	58	0.5	0	0	0	0
113	†Israel	20	21	6	7	74	72	89	..	..	41	..	37	35
114	†Kuwait	0	0	8	8	92	92	90	97	0.9	67	68	60	66
115	†United Arab Emirates	0	0	2	2	97	97	72	84	5.8	0	0	0	0
116	United Kingdom	29	25	47	46	24	29	89	90	0.3	28	26	25	23
117	Australia	6	6	57	54	37	40	86	85	1.3	55	68	47	58
118	Italy	42	38	17	15	40	47	67	66	0.1	39	30	26	20
119	Canada	5	5	3	3	92	92	76	77	1.4	38	47	29	36
120	Finland	8	9	1	0	91	91	60	63	0.8	0	0	0	0
121	†Hong Kong	7	7	1	1	92	92	92	95	1.5	100	95	91	90
122	Sweden	7	7	2	1	91	92	83	83	0.4	20	21	17	17
123	Netherlands	24	28	35	31	41	41	88	89	0.6	8	16	7	14
124	Belgium	..	24	..	21	..	55	95	97	0.3	13	11	12	11
125	France	34	35	23	19	42	45	73	73	0.5	29	28	21	21
126	†Singapore	13	2	0	0	87	98	100	100	1.8	106	95	106	95
127	Austria	20	18	25	24	56	57	55	56	0.5	49	46	27	26
128	United States	21	21	26	26	53	53	74	76	1.2	49	51	36	39
129	Germany	36	34	17	15	47	51	83	87	0.6	46	47	38	41
130	Denmark	63	56	6	7	31	37	84	85	0.2	32	30	27	25
131	Norway	3	3	0	0	97	97	71	73	0.7	0	0	0	0
132	Japan	13	12	2	2	85	87	76	78	0.6	44	48	34	37
133	Switzerland	10	11	40	29	49	60	57	61	1.2	0	0	0	0
	World	11 w	11 w	28 w	26 w	60 w	63 w	40 w	45 w	2.5 w	35 w	36 w	14 w	16 w

Table 10. Forest and water resources

		Forest areas			Nationally protected areas, 1994[a]			Annual freshwater withdrawal, 1995[b]			
		Total area (thousand sq. km) 1990	Ann. deforestation, 1980–90							Per capita (cu. m)	
			Thousand sq. km	% change	Thousand sq. km	Number	As % of land area	Total (cu. km)	As % of total water resources	Domestic	Other
	Low-income economies	7,916 t	65.5 t	0.8 w	2,001.1 t	1,842 t	5.2 w				
	Excluding China and India	6,152 t	53.3 t	0.8 w	1,276.9 t	795 t	4.9 w				
1	Mozambique	173	1.4	0.8	0.0	1	0.0	0.6	0.4c	13	42
2	Ethiopia	142	0.4	0.3	60.2	23	6.0	2.2	2.0	6	45
3	Tanzania	336	4.4	1.2	139.4	31	15.8	1.2	1.3c	7	28
4	Burundi	2	0.0	0.6	0.9	3	3.5	0.1	2.8	7	13
5	Malawi	35	0.5	1.4	10.6	9	11.3	0.9	5.0c	7	13
6	Chad	114	0.9	0.7	114.9	9	9.1	0.2	0.4c	6	29
7	Rwanda	2	0.0	0.2	3.3	2	13.3	0.8	12.2	6	18
8	Sierra Leone	19	0.1	0.6	0.8	2	1.1	0.4	0.2	7	92
9	Nepal	50	0.5	1.0	11.1	12	8.1	2.7	1.6	6	144
10	Niger	24	0.1	0.4	84.2	5	6.6	0.5	0.9c	9	33
11	Burkina Faso	44	0.3	0.7	26.6	12	9.7	0.4	1.4	5	13
12	Madagascar	158	1.3	0.8	11.2	36	1.9	16.3	4.8c	16	1,568
13	Bangladesh	8	0.4	4.1	1.0	8	0.7	22.5	1.0c	7	213
14	Uganda	63	0.6	1.0	19.1	31	9.6	0.2	0.3c	7	14
15	Vietnam	83	1.4	1.5	13.3	52	4.1	28.9	7.7	54	361
16	Guinea-Bissau	20	0.2	0.8	. .	. .	. .	0.0	0.0c	3	8
17	Haiti	0	0.0	5.1	0.1	3	0.4	0.0	0.4	2	5
18	Mali	121	1.1	0.8	40.1	11	3.3	1.4	1.4c	3	159
19	Nigeria	156	1.2	0.7	29.7	19	3.3	3.6	1.3	13	28
20	Yemen, Rep.	41	0.0	0.0	0.0	0	0.0	3.4	136.0	17	318
21	Cambodia	122	1.3	1.0	30.0	20	17.0	0.5	0.1	3	61
22	Kenya	12	0.1	0.6	35.0	36	6.2	2.1	7.0c	14	37
23	Mongolia	139	1.3	0.9	61.7	15	3.9	0.6	2.2	30	243
24	Togo	14	0.2	1.5	6.5	11	11.9	0.1	0.8c	17	11
25	Gambia, The	1	0.0	0.8	0.2	5	2.3	0.0	0.3c	2	27
26	Central African Republic	306	1.3	0.4	61.1	13	9.8	0.1	0.0	5	20
27	India	517	3.4	0.6	143.4	339	4.8	380.0	18.2c	18	594
28	Lao PDR	132	1.3	0.9	. .	. .	. .	1.0	0.4	21	239
29	Benin	49	0.7	1.3	7.8	2	7.0	0.1	0.4c	7	19
30	Nicaragua	60	1.2	1.9	9.0	59	7.4	0.9	0.5	92	275
31	Ghana	96	1.4	1.4	11.0	9	4.9	0.3	0.6c	12	23
32	Zambia	323	3.6	1.1	63.6	21	8.6	1.7	1.5c	54	32
33	Angola	231	1.7	0.7	26.4	5	2.1	0.5	0.3	8	49
34	Georgia	28	0.2	0.7	1.9	15	2.7	4.0	6.5	156	586
35	Pakistan	19	0.8	3.5	37.2	55	4.8	153.4	32.8c	21	2,032
36	Mauritania	6	0.0	0.0	17.5	4	1.7	1.6	14.0c	59	436
37	Azerbaijan	10	0.1	1.3	1.9	12	2.2	15.8	56.4c	90	2,158
38	Zimbabwe	89	0.6	0.7	30.7	25	7.9	1.2	6.1c	19	117
39	Guinea	67	0.9	1.2	1.6	3	0.7	0.7	0.3	14	126
40	Honduras	46	1.1	2.2	8.6	43	7.7	1.5	2.1c	12	282
41	Senegal	75	0.5	0.7	21.8	9	11.3	1.4	3.5c	10	191
42	China	1,247	8.8	0.7	580.8	463	6.2	460.0	16.4	28	433
43	Cameroon	204	1.2	0.6	20.5	14	4.4	0.4	0.1	17	20
44	Côte d'Ivoire	109	1.2	1.0	19.9	12	6.3	0.7	0.9	15	52
45	Albania	14	0.0	0.0	0.3	11	1.2	0.2	0.9c	6	88
46	Congo	199	0.3	0.2	11.8	10	3.4	0.0	0.0c	12	7
47	Kyrgyz Republic	7	0.1	1.2	2.8	5	1.5	11.7	24.0	82	2,647
48	Sri Lanka	17	0.3	1.4	8.0	56	12.3	6.3	14.6	10	493
49	Armenia	3	0.2	3.9	2.1	4	7.6	3.8	45.8c	149	996
	Middle-income economies	20,913 t	114.4 t	0.5 w	2,994.3 t	2,662 t	5.0 w				
	Lower-middle-income	13,525 t	65.6 t	0.5 w	2,199.7 t	1,664 t	5.6 w				
50	Lesotho	0	0.0	0.0	0.1	1	0.2	0.1	1.0	7	24
51	Egypt, Arab Rep.	0	0.0	0.0	7.9	12	0.8	56.4	97.1c	67	889
52	Bolivia	493	6.3	1.2	92.3	25	8.5	1.2	0.4	20	181
53	Macedonia, FYR	9	0.0	0.1	2.2	16	8.5	. .	. .	. .	. .
54	Moldova	4	−0.2	−6.7	0.1	3	0.4	3.7	29.1c	60	793
55	Uzbekistan	14	1.0	5.5	2.4	10	0.6	82.2	76.4c	165	3,956
56	Indonesia	1,095	12.1	1.1	185.6	168	10.2	16.6	0.7	12	83
57	Philippines	78	3.2	3.4	6.1	27	2.0	29.5	9.1	123	562
58	Morocco	90	−1.2	−1.4	3.7	11	0.8	10.9	36.2	23	404
59	Syrian Arab Republic	7	−0.3	−4.3	0.0	0	0.0	3.3	9.4	30	405
60	Papua New Guinea	360	1.1	0.3	0.8	5	0.2	0.1	0.0	8	20
61	Bulgaria	37	−0.1	−0.2	3.7	46	3.3	13.9	6.8c	43	1,501
62	Kazakstan	0	0.0	0.0	9.9	20	0.4	37.9	30.2	92	2,202
63	Guatemala	42	0.8	1.8	13.3	18	12.3	0.7	0.6	13	127
64	Ecuador	120	2.4	1.8	111.1	15	40.1	5.6	1.8	41	541
65	Dominican Republic	11	0.4	2.9	10.5	17	21.7	3.0	14.9	22	423
66	Romania	63	0.0	0.0	10.7	39	4.7	26.0	12.5c	91	1,044
67	Jamaica	2	0.3	7.8	0.0	1	0.2	0.3	3.9	11	148
68	Jordan	1	0.0	−1.0	2.9	10	3.3	0.5	32.1	50	123
69	Algeria	41	0.3	0.8	119.2	19	5.0	4.5	30.4c	35	125
70	El Salvador	1	0.0	2.3	0.1	2	0.2	1.0	5.3	17	228
71	Ukraine	92	−0.2	−0.3	4.9	19	0.8	34.7	40.0c	108	565
72	Paraguay	129	4.0	2.8	15.0	20	3.8	0.4	0.1c	16	93

Note: For data comparability and coverage, see the technical notes. Figures in italics are for years other than those specified.

		Forest areas			Nationally protected areas, 1994[a]			Annual freshwater withdrawal, 1995[b]			
		Total area (thousand sq. km) 1990	Ann. deforestation, 1980–90						As % of total water resources	Per capita (cu. m)	
			Thousand sq. km	% change	Thousand sq. km	Number	As % of land area	Total (cu. km)		Domestic	Other
73	Tunisia	7	−0.1	−1.9	0.4	6	0.3	3.1	79.5[c]	41	276
74	Lithuania	20	0.0	0.0	6.3	76	9.6	4.4	19.0[c]	83	1,107
75	Colombia	541	3.7	0.7	93.8	80	9.0	5.3	0.5	71	103
76	Namibia	126	0.4	0.3	102.2	12	12.4	0.2	0.3[c]	7	103
77	Belarus	63	−0.3	−0.4	2.7	11	1.3	3.0	5.4[c]	94	200
78	Russian Federation	7,681	15.5	0.2	705.4	209	4.2	117.0	2.7[c]	134	656
79	Latvia	28	−0.1	−0.2	7.8	45	12.5	0.7	2.2[c]	110	152
80	Peru	679	2.7	0.4	41.8	22	3.3	6.1	15.3	57	243
81	Costa Rica	14	0.5	3.0	6.5	28	12.7	1.4	1.4	31	749
82	Lebanon	1	0.0	0.6	0.0	1	0.4	0.8	15.6	30	241
83	Thailand	127	5.2	3.5	70.2	111	13.7	31.9	17.8[c]	24	578
84	Panama	31	0.6	1.9	13.3	14	17.8	1.3	0.9	91	664
85	Turkey	202	0.0	0.0	10.7	49	1.4	33.5	17.3[c]	140	445
86	Poland	87	−0.1	−0.1	30.7	111	10.1	12.3	21.9[c]	42	279
87	Estonia	19	−0.2	−1.2	4.1	38	9.7	3.3	21.2	105	1,992
88	Slovak Republic	18	0.0	0.1	10.2	40	21.1	1.8	5.8	. .	. .
89	Botswana	143	0.8	0.5	106.6	9	18.8	0.1	0.6[c]	5	94
90	Venezuela	457	6.0	1.2	263.2	100	29.8	4.1	0.3[c]	164	218
	Upper-middle-income	7,387 t	48.8 t	0.6 w	794.6 t	998 t	3.9 w				
91	South Africa	45	−0.4	−0.8	69.7	238	5.7	13.3	26.6[c]	47	348
92	Croatia	20	0.0	0.1	3.9	30	7.0	. .	. .	. .	. .
93	Mexico	486	6.8	1.3	98.5	68	5.2	77.6	21.7	54	845
94	Mauritius	1	0.0	0.2	0.0	1	2.0	0.4	16.4	66	344
95	Gabon	182	1.2	0.6	10.5	6	4.1	0.1	0.0	41	16
96	Brazil	5,611	36.7	0.6	321.9	272	3.8	36.5	0.5[c]	54	191
97	Trinidad and Tobago	2	0.0	−2.1	0.2	5	3.1	0.2	2.9	40	108
98	Czech Republic	26	0.0	0.0	10.7	34	13.8	2.7	4.7	109	157
99	Malaysia	176	4.0	2.1	14.8	51	4.5	9.4	2.1	177	592
100	Hungary	17	−0.1	−0.5	5.7	53	6.2	6.8	5.7[c]	59	601
101	Chile	88	−0.1	−0.1	137.3	66	18.3	16.8	3.6	98	1,528
102	Oman	41	0.0	0.0	9.9	28	4.6	0.5	24.0	17	547
103	Uruguay	7	0.0	−0.6	0.3	8	0.2	0.7	0.5[c]	14	227
104	Saudi Arabia	12	0.0	0.0	62.0	10	2.9	3.6	163.6	224	273
105	Argentina	592	0.9	0.1	43.7	84	1.6	27.6	2.8[c]	94	949
106	Slovenia	10	0.0	0.0	1.1	10	5.4	. .	. .	. .	. .
107	Greece	60	0.0	0.0	2.2	21	1.7	5.0	8.6[c]	42	481
	Low- and middle-income	28,828 t	179.8 t	0.6 w	4,995.4 t	4,504 t	5.1 w				
	Sub-Saharan Africa	5,322 t	40.7 t	0.7 w	1,362.5 t	673 t	5.8 w				
	East Asia and Pacific	3,986 t	43.5 t	1.0 w	966.3 t	1,172 t	6.2 w				
	South Asia	658 t	5.5 t	0.8 w	212.4 t	485 t	4.4 w				
	Europe and Central Asia	8,630 t	16.6 t	0.2 w	860.0 t	964 t	3.6 w				
	Middle East and N. Africa	446 t	−1.4 t	−0.3 w	290.8 t	170 t	3.0 w				
	Latin America and Caribbean	9,786 t	74.8 t	0.7 w	1,303.4 t	1,040 t	6.5 w				
	High-income economies	10,766 t	−46.4 t	−0.5 w	3,607.9 t	5,506 t	11.9 w				
108	Korea, Rep.	65	0.1	0.1	6.9	27	7.0	27.6	41.8	117	515
109	Portugal	31	−0.1	−0.5	5.8	24	6.3	7.3	10.5[c]	111	628
110	Spain	256	0.0	0.0	42.5	214	8.5	30.8	27.6[c]	94	687
111	New Zealand	75	0.0	0.0	60.7	182	22.6	2.0	0.6	271	318
112	Ireland	4	0.0	−1.2	0.5	11	0.7	0.8	1.6[c]	37	196
113	† Israel	1	0.0	−0.3	3.1	15	14.9	1.9	84.1[c]	65	343
114	† Kuwait	0	0.0	0.0	0.3	2	1.5	0.5	. .	336	189
115	† United Arab Emirates	0	0.0	0.0	0.0	0	0.0	0.9	300.0	97	787
116	United Kingdom	24	−0.2	−1.1	51.1	168	21.1	11.8	16.6	41	164
117	Australia	1,456	0.0	0.0	940.8	889	12.3	14.6	4.3	607	327
118	Italy	86	0.0	0.0	22.8	171	7.7	56.2	33.7[c]	138	848
119	Canada	4,533	−47.1	−1.1	823.6	627	8.9	45.1	1.6	288	1,314
120	Finland	234	−0.1	0.0	27.4	81	9.0	2.2	1.9[c]	53	387
121	† Hong Kong	0	0.0	−0.5	. .	. .	. .	. .	. .	. .	. .
122	Sweden	280	−0.1	0.0	29.8	197	7.2	2.9	1.6[c]	123	218
123	Netherlands	3	0.0	−0.3	4.3	85	12.6	7.8	8.7[c]	26	492
124	Belgium	6	0.0	−0.3	0.8	3	2.3	9.0	72.2[c]	101	816
125	France	135	−0.1	−0.1	56.0	102	10.2	37.7	19.1[c]	106	559
126	† Singapore	0	0.0	2.3	0.0	1	4.9	0.2	31.7	38	46
127	Austria	39	−0.1	−0.4	20.8	170	25.2	2.4	2.6[c]	101	203
128	United States	2,960	3.2	0.1	1,302.1	1,585	14.2	467.3	18.9[c]	244	1,626
129	Germany	107	−0.5	−0.4	91.9	497	26.3	46.3	27.1[c]	64	518
130	Denmark	5	0.0	0.0	13.9	114	32.8	1.2	9.2[c]	70	163
131	Norway	96	−1.2	−1.4	55.4	113	18.0	2.0	0.5[c]	98	390
132	Japan	238	0.0	0.0	27.6	80	7.3	90.8	16.6	125	610
133	Switzerland	12	−0.1	−0.6	7.3	109	18.5	1.2	2.4[c]	40	133
	World	39,595 t	133.4 t	0.3 w	8,603.2 t	10,010 t	6.7 w				

a. Data may refer to earlier years and are the most recent reported by the World Conservation Monitoring Centre b. Refers to any year from 1970 to 1995. c. Total water resources include river flows from other countries.

Table 11. Growth of the economy

		GDP		GDP deflator		Agriculture		Industry		Services[a]		Exports of goods and services		Gross domestic investment	
		1980–90	1990–95	1980–90	1990–95	1980–90	1990–95	1980–90	1990–95	1980–90	1990–95	1980–90	1990–95	1980–90	1990–95
Low-income economies		6.0 w	6.8 w	13.4 w	62.0 w	3.6 w	3.1 w	7.7 w	11.6 w	6.9 w	6.4 w	6.1 w	11.0 w	6.2 w	10.5 w
Excluding China and India		2.7 w	1.8 w	28.4 w	170.8 w	2.6 w	1.9 w	2.9 w	..	2.8 w	..	2.5 w	4.4 w	–1.3 w	3.6 w
1	Mozambique	–0.2	7.1	38.4	48.6	1.6	2.4	–9.8	–2.4	–0.1	15.0	–5.0	7.2	–2.5	8.6
2	Ethiopia[b]	2.3	..	3.4	..	1.4	..	1.8	..	3.1	..	0.3	..	3.5	..
3	Tanzania	3.8	3.2	35.7	22.4	4.9	4.1	3.4	8.4	1.6	1.7	..	..	..	..
4	Burundi	4.4	–2.3	4.4	8.5	3.1	–4.1	4.5	–5.0	5.4	–1.5	4.5	–2.6	4.5	–5.0
5	Malawi	2.3	0.7	15.0	30.4	2.0	1.7	2.9	0.4	3.4	–1.0	2.5	2.3	–2.8	–11.2
6	Chad	6.3	1.9	1.1	8.9	2.7	6.9	8.0	–9.9	9.9	1.2	7.7	–15.8	19.0	–2.9
7	Rwanda	2.3	–12.8	3.9	18.2	0.7	–10.8	1.8	–17.0	5.4	–12.3	3.5	17.8	3.7	–6.3
8	Sierra Leone	1.6	–4.2	62.2	39.6	4.4	–2.8	5.7	–2.8	–1.1	–5.9	2.8	–15.2	–6.5	–20.0
9	Nepal	4.6	5.1	11.1	11.0	4.0	1.5	6.0	9.3	4.8	7.2	1.1	25.8	1.8	6.3
10	Niger	–1.1	0.5	2.9	6.5	1.8	..	–3.3	..	–5.2	..	–4.6	–5.2	–5.9	0.3
11	Burkina Faso	3.7	2.6	3.1	6.2	3.1	4.6	3.7	1.4	4.7	1.7	–0.6	–1.2	8.6	–5.8
12	Madagascar	1.3	0.1	16.9	23.5	2.5	1.6	0.9	0.5	0.8	–0.6	–2.0	4.9	4.9	–4.5
13	Bangladesh	4.3	4.1	9.5	4.6	2.7	1.1	4.9	7.3	5.7	5.4	7.7	14.2	1.4	8.2
14	Uganda	3.1	6.6	125.6	23.7	2.3	3.8	6.0	11.0	3.0	8.2	2.3	11.7	9.6	7.9
15	Vietnam	..	8.3	210.7	26.3	..	5.2	..	..	..	..	..	..	..	..
16	Guinea-Bissau	4.5	3.5	56.1	49.5	6.7	4.8	0.4	1.9	3.3	2.2	–1.7	11.3	5.8	1.2
17	Haiti	–0.2	–6.5	7.5	22.4	..	..	..	..	..	..	1.2	–19.0	–0.6	–45.7
18	Mali	1.8	2.5	5.3	10.1	4.3	3.1	2.7	5.3	–1.7	1.2	5.2	5.3	5.4	6.1
19	Nigeria	1.6	1.6	16.6	47.1	3.3	2.3	–1.0	–1.2	3.2	4.5	–0.3	1.1	–8.6	1.2
20	Yemen, Rep.	..	..	..	..	..	..	..	..	..	..	..	..	..	..
21	Cambodia	..	6.4	..	56.2	..	2.1	..	11.3	..	8.3	..	..	..	..
22	Kenya	4.2	1.4	9.0	18.5	3.3	–0.4	3.9	1.5	4.9	3.1	4.3	3.0	0.8	0.0
23	Mongolia	5.5	–3.3	–1.2	126.7	2.9	..	4.6	..	..	..	3.1	12.8	1.7	..
24	Togo	1.8	–3.4	4.7	4.9	5.6	3.3	1.1	–6.0	–0.3	–8.6	0.6	–10.6	2.9	–16.4
25	Gambia, The	3.4	1.6	18.7	5.0	0.4	2.6	6.0	0.4	3.9	2.5	0.6	–0.8	0.8	3.0
26	Central African Republic	1.7	1.0	5.6	8.5	2.7	1.5	3.1	–4.6	–0.1	–1.6	–3.7	4.4	4.8	–8.7
27	India[c]	5.8	4.6	8.0	10.1	3.1	3.1	7.1	5.1	6.7	6.1	5.9	12.5	6.5	5.3
28	Lao PDR	..	6.5	37.8	10.1	..	..	..	..	..	..	..	5.9	..	..
29	Benin	2.6	4.1	1.6	7.9	5.1	4.9	2.1	3.5	1.2	3.5	–2.7	6.3	–6.2	12.1
30	Nicaragua	–2.0	1.1	422.6	98.3	–2.2	0.3	–1.7	–4.4	–2.0	2.2	–3.8	7.2	–4.7	4.1
31	Ghana	3.0	4.3	42.4	23.8	1.0	2.4	3.3	4.4	6.4	6.5	2.5	6.7	4.5	0.9
32	Zambia	0.8	–0.2	42.4	107.8	3.6	–0.5	1.0	–1.2	0.1	0.7	–3.3	10.8	–2.7	–10.2
33	Angola	3.7	–4.1	5.9	774.5	0.5	–1.8	6.4	0.9	2.2	–10.8	13.3	2.9	–6.8	0.1
34	Georgia	0.5	–26.9	1.9	2,280.2	0.7	–31.4	1.8	–34.1	–1.4	–22.3	..	..	0.3	–21.2
35	Pakistan	6.3	4.6	6.7	11.2	4.3	3.4	7.3	5.7	6.8	5.0	8.1	7.7	5.9	4.0
36	Mauritania	1.7	4.0	8.6	6.8	1.7	4.9	4.9	3.9	0.4	3.2	3.4	–1.0	–4.1	–1.3
37	Azerbaijan	..	–20.2	..	747.6	..	..	..	..	..	..	..	..	..	..
38	Zimbabwe	3.5	1.0	11.5	27.6	2.4	1.6	3.6	–3.6	2.9	1.7	5.4	5.5	1.3	1.5
39	Guinea	..	3.8	..	10.1	..	4.5	..	2.3	..	4.5	..	1.3	..	0.6
40	Honduras	2.7	3.5	5.7	19.2	2.7	2.9	3.3	4.9	2.5	1.3	1.1	0.2	2.9	10.0
41	Senegal	3.1	1.9	6.5	7.6	2.8	1.3	3.7	2.0	3.0	2.0	3.9	–0.9	3.9	4.7
42	China	10.2	12.8	5.8	12.4	5.9	4.3	11.1	18.1	13.6	10.0	11.5	15.6	11.0	15.5
43	Cameroon	3.1	–1.8	5.9	5.1	2.2	2.2	5.9	–6.8	2.1	–1.4	5.9	2.2	–2.7	–4.1
44	Côte d'Ivoire	0.1	0.7	3.4	10.4	–0.5	0.3	4.4	1.7	–1.3	0.2	1.9	–0.9	–28.8	138.3
45	Albania	3.0	1.4	–1.9	76.4	2.4	7.6	3.2	–15.6	3.2	5.9	..	..	–0.3	38.4
46	Congo	3.6	–0.6	0.3	7.8	3.4	–0.9	5.2	1.2	2.5	–2.1	4.8	4.0	–11.9	–7.9
47	Kyrgyz Republic	..	–14.7	..	337.3	..	–7.6	..	..	..	..	..	..	..	..
48	Sri Lanka	4.2	4.8	10.8	10.4	2.2	2.4	4.6	6.5	4.7	6.3	6.8	11.0	0.6	6.8
49	Armenia	3.3	–21.2	0.3	896.6	–3.9	–0.6	5.1	–28.7	4.6	–19.7	..	..	6.2	–17.7
Middle-income economies		1.9 w	0.1 w	64.8 w	298.8 w	..	0.9 w	..	..	2.6 w	3.9 w	..	..	..	..
Lower-middle-income		2.3 w	–1.5 w	17.5 w	286.7 w	..	0.5 w	..	..	..	..	..	..	..	..
50	Lesotho	4.3	7.5	13.6	11.0	2.6	–3.4	7.2	12.3	5.2	6.1	4.1	11.4	6.9	12.1
51	Egypt, Arab Rep.	5.0	1.3	11.7	13.3	1.5	2.1	2.6	0.4	8.4	1.5	5.2	4.2	2.7	–1.5
52	Bolivia	0.0	3.8	316.7	10.5	2.0	..	–2.9	..	–0.1	..	3.5	6.7	–9.9	4.2
53	Macedonia, FYR	..	..	..	..	..	..	..	..	..	..	..	..	..	..
54	Moldova	..	..	..	..	..	..	..	..	..	..	..	..	..	..
55	Uzbekistan	..	–4.4	..	628.4	..	–0.9	..	–6.7	..	–6.6	..	..	..	–9.2
56	Indonesia	6.1	7.6	8.5	7.6	3.4	2.9	6.9	10.1	7.0	7.4	2.9	10.8	7.0	16.3
57	Philippines	1.0	2.3	14.9	9.2	1.0	1.6	–0.9	2.2	2.8	2.7	3.5	9.4	–2.1	3.2
58	Morocco	4.2	1.2	7.2	3.9	6.7	–5.9	3.0	1.7	4.2	2.8	6.8	3.1	2.5	–2.5
59	Syrian Arab Republic	1.5	7.4	15.3	8.5	–0.6	..	6.6	..	..	..	3.6	..	–7.0	..
60	Papua New Guinea	1.9	9.3	5.3	5.7	1.8	4.7	1.9	17.8	2.0	4.8	3.3	13.3	–0.9	0.4
61	Bulgaria	4.0	–4.3	1.2	81.2	–2.1	–1.9	5.2	–7.5	7.2	–20.7	–3.5	–0.7	2.4	–7.1
62	Kazakstan	..	–11.9	..	805.5	..	–18.0	..	19.2	..	6.1	..	..	..	–16.7
63	Guatemala	0.8	4.0	14.6	14.2	2.3	2.5	2.1	4.2	2.1	4.9	–2.1	4.8	–1.8	10.7
64	Ecuador	2.0	3.4	36.4	37.2	4.4	2.5	1.2	4.9	1.8	2.7	5.4	7.4	–3.8	5.3
65	Dominican Republic	2.7	3.9	21.5	11.7	0.4	2.5	2.2	3.3	3.7	4.5	2.8	4.6	3.7	4.9
66	Romania	0.5	–1.4	2.5	158.4	..	–0.4	..	–2.1	..	–2.8	..	..	..	–10.0
67	Jamaica	2.0	2.9	18.6	38.5	0.6	8.3	2.4	–0.5	1.9	6.0	5.4	–1.0	–0.1	5.8
68	Jordan	–1.5	8.2	7.0	4.7	13.2	10.2	–1.3	7.9	–8.2	6.2	5.9	8.2	7.3	6.5
69	Algeria	2.8	0.1	8.0	25.8	4.6	1.3	2.3	–1.1	3.8	1.3	4.1	0.2	–2.3	–4.7
70	El Salvador	0.2	6.3	16.4	11.2	–1.1	1.2	0.1	2.9	0.7	9.3	–3.4	13.6	2.2	14.7
71	Ukraine	..	–14.3	..	1,040.5	..	–9.7	..	–21.6	..	..	..	..	..	..
72	Paraguay	2.5	3.1	24.4	18.0	3.6	1.4	–0.3	1.9	3.4	4.1	11.5	13.8	–0.8	2.6

Note: For data comparability and coverage, see the technical notes. Figures in italics are for years other than those specified.

		Average annual growth rate (%)												
		GDP		GDP deflator		Agriculture		Industry		Services[a]		Exports of goods and services		Gross domestic investment	
		1980–90	1990–95	1980–90	1990–95	1980–90	1990–95	1980–90	1990–95	1980–90	1990–95	1980–90	1990–95	1980–90	1990–95
73	Tunisia	3.3	3.9	7.4	5.4	2.8	−2.1	3.1	4.0	3.6	5.6	5.6	5.6	−1.8	1.4
74	Lithuania	..	−9.7	..	241.4	..	..	..	..	..	..	..	..	..	..
75	Colombia	3.7	4.6	24.6	23.3	2.9	1.4	5.0	3.0	3.1	6.4	7.5	7.2	0.5	19.0
76	Namibia	1.1	3.8	13.6	9.3	1.8	6.8	−1.1	2.9	2.7	4.6	1.5	6.9	11.9	−2.8
77	Belarus	..	−9.3	..	878.8	..	−11.2	..	−10.9	..	−6.9	..	..	..	−17.0
78	Russian Federation	1.9	−9.8	3.2	517.0	..	..	..	..	..	..	..	..	..	..
79	Latvia	3.4	−13.7	..	149.1	2.3	−16.4	4.3	−25.1	3.1	−2.1	..	..	3.4	−37.1
80	Peru	−0.2	5.3	229.6	62.4	..	..	..	..	..	..	−1.7	8.3	−4.2	7.4
81	Costa Rica	3.0	5.1	23.5	19.1	3.1	3.6	2.8	5.2	3.1	5.6	6.1	9.5	5.3	6.6
82	Lebanon	..	..	..	..	..	..	..	..	..	..	..	..	..	..
83	Thailand	7.6	8.4	3.9	4.6	4.0	3.1	9.9	10.8	7.3	7.8	14.0	14.2	9.4	10.2
84	Panama	0.3	6.3	2.4	1.8	..	4.4	..	14.9	..	5.5	..	4.3	..	15.3
85	Turkey	5.3	3.2	45.3	75.6	1.3	0.9	7.8	4.2	4.4	3.3	16.9	9.4	5.3	2.0
86	Poland	1.9	2.4	53.7	34.9	−0.1	−2.0	−0.9	3.7	5.1	2.4	4.5	9.4	0.9	1.1
87	Estonia	2.1	−9.2	2.4	151.4	..	−8.9	..	−14.9	..	−3.8	..	..	..	−13.4
88	Slovak Republic	2.0	−2.8	1.8	16.0	1.6	1.0	2.0	−10.4	0.8	6.2	..	17.8	1.1	−7.7
89	Botswana	10.3	4.2	13.1	9.2	2.2	0.7	11.4	1.4	11.0	7.7	2.8	4.9	−5.3	..
90	Venezuela	1.1	2.4	19.3	38.4	3.0	1.9	1.6	3.4	0.5	1.7	2.8	4.9	−5.3	3.8
	Upper-middle-income	1.3 w	2.6 w	138.0 w	320.5 w	2.4 w	1.8 w	0.7 w	2.6 w	2.0 w	3.4 w	5.9 w	7.4 w	−1.4 w	5.6 w
91	South Africa	1.3	0.6	14.8	11.5	3.0	−0.3	−1.1	−0.1	3.1	0.9	1.9	2.4	−4.8	4.7
92	Croatia	..	..	..	..	..	..	..	..	..	..	..	..	..	..
93	Mexico	1.0	1.1	70.4	15.5	0.6	0.4	1.0	0.5	1.1	1.5	6.6	6.8	−3.1	−1.2
94	Mauritius	6.2	4.9	9.4	6.7	2.9	−1.4	10.3	5.6	5.4	6.4	10.4	4.8	10.2	1.7
95	Gabon	0.5	−2.5	1.9	13.0	1.7	−0.2	1.0	2.7	−0.3	−10.0	2.8	4.1	−4.6	−0.5
96	Brazil	2.7	2.7	284.5	965.3	2.8	3.7	2.0	1.7	3.5	3.6	7.5	7.4	0.2	3.5
97	Trinidad and Tobago	−2.5	1.0	4.1	7.2	−5.8	1.3	−5.5	0.2	−3.3	−0.1	8.9	12.5	−10.1	1.0
98	Czech Republic	1.7	−2.6	1.5	18.3	..	..	..	..	..	..	..	..	2.3	0.9
99	Malaysia	5.2	8.7	1.7	3.9	3.8	2.6	7.2	11.0	4.2	8.6	10.9	14.4	2.6	16.0
100	Hungary	1.6	−1.0	8.6	22.3	0.6	−7.0	−2.6	0.5	3.6	−4.6	4.0	−1.5	−0.4	6.6
101	Chile	4.1	7.3	20.9	14.7	5.6	5.2	3.7	6.1	4.2	8.4	7.0	9.2	9.6	11.9
102	Oman	8.3	6.0	−3.6	−2.9	7.9	..	10.3	..	6.0	..	..	..	..	..
103	Uruguay	0.4	4.0	61.3	55.6	0.0	4.5	−0.2	0.1	0.9	6.2	4.3	4.4	−7.8	12.9
104	Saudi Arabia	−1.2	1.7	−3.7	1.0	13.4	..	−2.3	..	−1.2	..	..	..	..	..
105	Argentina	−0.3	5.7	389.0	20.5	0.9	0.5	−0.9	5.9	0.0	6.4	3.7	6.9	−4.7	16.0
106	Slovenia	..	..	..	..	..	..	..	..	..	..	..	..	..	..
107	Greece	1.4	1.1	18.3	13.1	−0.1	3.1	1.3	−0.8	4.9	0.6	7.1	4.5	−0.9	1.9
	Low- and middle-income	2.8 w	2.1 w	50.6 w	235.8 w	3.1 w	2.0 w	3.9 w	4.9 w	3.6 w	4.5 w	..	..	1.8 w	6.5 w
	Sub-Saharan Africa	1.7 w	1.4 w	19.0 w	47.4 w	1.9 w	1.5 w	0.6 w	0.2 w	2.5 w	1.5 w	1.9 w	2.5 w	−4.0 w	3.4 w
	East Asia and Pacific	7.6 w	10.3 w	10.1 w	11.5 w	4.8 w	3.9 w	8.9 w	15.0 w	9.0 w	8.4 w	8.8 w	13.9 w	8.5 w	14.4 w
	South Asia	5.7 w	4.6 w	8.0 w	9.9 w	3.2 w	3.0 w	6.9 w	5.3 w	6.6 w	6.0 w	6.4 w	11.9 w	6.1 w	5.3 w
	Europe and Central Asia	2.3 w	−6.5 w	12.2 w	461.5 w	..	..	..	..	..	..	..	..	..	..
	Middle East and N. Africa	0.2 w	2.3 w	8.2 w	19.4 w	4.5 w	3.3 w	1.1 w	..	1.2 w	..	..	..	..	..
	Latin America and Caribbean	1.7 w	3.2 w	179.4 w	380.9 w	2.0 w	2.3 w	1.4 w	2.5 w	1.9 w	3.8 w	5.4 w	7.0 w	−1.5 w	5.7 w
	High-income economies	3.2 w	2.0 w	4.8 w	2.4 w	2.3 w	0.6 w	3.2 w	0.7 w	3.4 w	2.3 w	5.2 w	6.4 w	4.1 w	−0.2 w
108	Korea, Rep.	9.4	7.2	5.9	6.2	2.8	1.3	13.1	7.3	8.2	7.9	12.0	13.4	11.9	7.2
109	Portugal	2.9	0.8	18.1	8.7	..	..	..	..	..	..	8.7	3.3	..	..
110	Spain	3.2	1.1	9.3	5.2	..	−1.7	..	..	..	..	5.7	10.1	5.7	−2.6
111	New Zealand	1.8	3.6	10.8	0.6	4.4	0.9	1.3	3.8	1.7	3.5	4.1	5.2	1.7	12.4
112	Ireland	3.1	4.7	6.6	2.2	..	..	..	..	..	..	8.9	10.7	..	−3.8
113	† Israel	3.5	6.4	101.5	12.2	..	..	..	..	..	..	5.5	9.5	2.2	11.5
114	† Kuwait	0.9	12.2	−2.4	−2.0	14.7	..	1.0	..	0.9	..	−2.3	..	−4.5	..
115	† United Arab Emirates	−2.0	..	0.7	..	9.6	9.3	−4.2	−1.8	3.4	4.9	0.0	..	−8.7	..
116	United Kingdom	3.2	1.4	5.7	3.6	..	..	..	..	..	..	3.9	4.3	6.4	..
117	Australia	3.4	3.5	7.3	1.3	3.3	−2.4	2.8	3.3	3.7	3.7	7.0	6.8	2.7	5.8
118	Italy	2.4	1.0	9.9	4.7	0.6	1.6	..	..	..	..	4.1	8.1	2.1	−3.2
119	Canada	3.4	1.8	4.4	1.5	1.5	0.3	2.9	1.2	3.7	1.8	6.0	9.5	5.2	2.3
120	Finland	3.3	−0.5	6.8	1.8	−0.2	0.0	3.3	−1.2	5.3	−2.7	2.2	9.8	3.0	−8.3
121	† Hong Kong	6.9	5.6	7.7	8.1	..	..	..	..	..	..	14.4	13.5	4.0	11.7
122	Sweden	2.3	−0.1	7.4	3.2	1.5	−1.9	2.8	−0.7	2.5	−0.1	4.3	6.7	4.3	−7.2
123	Netherlands	2.3	1.8	1.6	2.2	3.4	3.0	1.6	0.4	2.6	2.1	4.5	3.7	3.1	−0.3
124	Belgium	1.9	1.1	4.4	3.1	1.8	4.0	2.2	..	1.8	..	4.6	4.6	3.2	−0.9
125	France	2.4	1.0	6.0	2.1	2.0	−1.1	1.1	−1.0	3.0	1.5	3.7	4.0	2.8	−2.8
126	† Singapore	6.4	8.7	2.0	3.7	−6.2	0.5	5.4	9.2	7.2	8.4	10.0	..	3.7	6.0
127	Austria	2.1	1.9	3.7	3.5	1.1	−1.8	1.9	1.7	2.3	2.2	4.6	2.5	2.5	3.6
128	United States	3.0	2.6	4.1	2.4	4.0	3.6	2.8	1.2	3.1	2.1	5.2	7.3	3.4	4.1
129	Germany[d]	2.2	..	2.6	..	1.7	..	1.2	..	2.9	..	4.4	..	2.0	..
130	Denmark	2.4	2.0	5.5	1.8	3.1	0.3	2.9	1.6	2.3	1.3	4.4	2.8	4.0	−1.1
131	Norway	2.9	3.5	5.5	1.3	0.9	..	3.5	..	2.6	..	5.0	5.1	0.6	..
132	Japan	4.0	1.0	1.7	0.9	1.3	−2.2	4.2	0.0	3.9	2.3	4.5	3.4	5.3	−0.8
133	Switzerland	2.2	0.1	3.7	2.3	..	..	..	..	..	..	3.4	1.5	4.9	0.0
	World	3.1 w	2.0 w	15.0 w	56.6 w	2.8 w	1.3 w	3.3 w	1.4 w	3.4 w	2.6 w	5.3 w	6.8 w	3.7 w	0.8 w

a. Services include unallocated items. b. Data prior to 1992 include Eritrea. c. GDP growth rates were revised after the statistics for this publication were finalized. d. Data prior to 1990 refer to the Federal Republic of Germany before unification.

Table 12. Structure of the economy: production

		GDP (million $)		Distribution of gross domestic product (%)							
				Agriculture value added		Industry value added		(Manufacturing[a]) value added		Services[b] value added	
		1980	1995	1980	1995	1980	1995	1980	1995	1980	1995
	Low-income economies	739,236 t	1,352,256 t	34 w	25 w	32 w	38 w	21 w	27 w	32 w	35 w
	Excluding China and India	390,472 t	316,889 t	..	33 w	..	25 w	..	13 w	..	41 w
1	Mozambique	2,028	1,469	37	33	31	12	..	..	32	55
2	Ethiopia[c]	5,179	5,287	56	57	12	10	6	3	31	33
3	Tanzania	5,702	3,602	46	58	18	17	11	8	37	24
4	Burundi	920	1,062	62	56	13	18	7	12	25	26
5	Malawi	1,238	1,465	37	42	19	27	12	18	44	31
6	Chad	727	1,138	54	44	12	22	..	16	34	35
7	Rwanda	1,163	1,128	50	37	23	17	16	3	27	46
8	Sierra Leone	1,166	824	33	42	21	27	5	6	47	31
9	Nepal	1,946	4,232	62	42	12	22	4	10	26	36
10	Niger	2,538	1,860	43	39	23	18	4	..	35	44
11	Burkina Faso	1,709	2,325	33	34	22	27	16	21	45	39
12	Madagascar	4,042	3,198	30	34	16	13	..	13	54	53
13	Bangladesh	12,950	29,110	50	31	16	18	11	10	34	52
14	Uganda	1,267	5,655	72	50	4	14	4	6	23	36
15	Vietnam	..	20,351	..	28	..	30	..	22	..	42
16	Guinea-Bissau	105	257	44	46	20	24	..	7	36	30
17	Haiti	1,462	2,043	..	44	..	12	..	9	..	44
18	Mali	1,629	2,431	61	46	10	17	4	6	29	37
19	Nigeria	93,082	26,817	27	28	40	53	8	5	32	18
20	Yemen, Rep.	..	4,790	..	22	..	27	..	14	..	51
21	Cambodia	..	2,771	..	51	..	14	..	6	..	34
22	Kenya	7,265	9,095	33	29	21	17	13	11	47	54
23	Mongolia	2,328	861	..	..	..	..	..	..	..	..
24	Togo	1,136	981	27	38	25	21	8	9	48	41
25	Gambia, The	233	384	30	28	16	15	7	7	53	58
26	Central African Republic	797	1,128	40	44	20	13	7	..	40	43
27	India	172,321	324,082	38	29	26	29	18	19	36	41
28	Lao PDR	..	1,760	..	52	..	18	..	14	..	30
29	Benin	1,405	1,522	35	34	12	12	8	7	52	53
30	Nicaragua	2,144	1,911	23	33	31	20	26	16	45	46
31	Ghana	4,445	6,315	58	46	12	16	8	6	30	38
32	Zambia	3,884	4,073	14	22	41	40	18	30	44	37
33	Angola	..	3,722	..	12	..	59	..	3	..	28
34	Georgia	..	2,325	..	67	..	22	..	18	..	11
35	Pakistan	23,690	60,649	30	26	25	24	16	17	46	50
36	Mauritania	709	1,068	30	27	26	30	..	13	44	43
37	Azerbaijan	..	3,475	..	27	..	32	..	..	..	41
38	Zimbabwe	5,355	6,522	14	15	34	36	25	30	52	48
39	Guinea	..	3,686	..	24	..	31	..	5	..	45
40	Honduras	2,566	3,937	24	21	24	33	15	18	52	46
41	Senegal	3,016	4,867	19	20	25	18	15	12	57	62
42	China	201,688	697,647	30	21	49	48	41	38	21	31
43	Cameroon	6,741	7,931	29	39	23	23	9	10	48	38
44	Côte d'Ivoire	10,175	10,069	27	31	20	20	13	18	53	50
45	Albania	..	2,192	..	56	..	21	..	..	..	23
46	Congo	1,706	2,163	12	10	47	38	7	6	42	51
47	Kyrgyz Republic	..	3,028	..	44	..	24	..	..	..	32
48	Sri Lanka	4,024	12,915	28	23	30	25	18	16	43	52
49	Armenia	..	2,058	..	44	..	35	..	..	25	20
	Middle-income economies	2,461,307 t	4,033,376 t	..	11 w	..	35 w	..	18 w	..	52 w
	Lower-middle-income	..	2,025,853 t	..	13 w	..	36 w	..	..	..	49 w
50	Lesotho	368	1,029	24	10	29	56	7	18	47	34
51	Egypt, Arab Rep.	22,913	47,349	18	20	37	21	12	15	45	59
52	Bolivia	3,074	6,131	18	..	35	..	15	..	47	..
53	Macedonia, FYR	..	1,975	..	..	..	..	..	..	..	..
54	Moldova	..	3,518	..	50	..	28	..	26	..	22
55	Uzbekistan	..	21,590	..	33	..	34	..	18	..	34
56	Indonesia	78,013	198,079	24	17	42	42	13	24	34	41
57	Philippines	32,500	74,180	25	22	39	32	26	23	36	46
58	Morocco	18,821	32,412	18	14	31	33	17	19	51	53
59	Syrian Arab Republic	13,062	16,783	20	..	23	..	..	..	56	..
60	Papua New Guinea	2,548	4,901	33	26	27	38	10	8	40	34
61	Bulgaria	20,040	12,366	14	13	54	34	..	..	32	53
62	Kazakstan	..	21,413	..	12	..	30	..	6	..	57
63	Guatemala	7,879	14,489	..	25	..	19	..	..	..	56
64	Ecuador	11,733	17,939	12	12	38	36	18	21	50	52
65	Dominican Republic	6,631	11,277	20	15	28	22	15	15	52	64
66	Romania	..	35,533	..	21	..	40	..	..	..	39
67	Jamaica	2,679	4,406	8	9	38	38	17	18	54	53
68	Jordan	..	6,105	..	8	..	27	..	14	..	65
69	Algeria	42,345	41,435	10	13	54	47	9	9	36	41
70	El Salvador	3,574	9,471	38	14	22	22	16	..	40	65
71	Ukraine	..	80,127	..	18	..	42	..	37	..	41
72	Paraguay	4,579	7,743	29	24	27	22	16	16	44	54

Note: For data comparability and coverage, see the technical notes. Figures in italics are for years other than those specified.

		GDP (million $)		Distribution of gross domestic product (%)								
				Agriculture value added		Industry value added		(Manufacturing[a]) value added		Services[b] value added		
		1980	1995	1980	1995	1980	1995	1980	1995	1980	1995	
73	Tunisia	8,743	18,035	14	12	31	29	12	19	55	59	
74	Lithuania	..	7,089	..	11	..	36	..	30	..	53	
75	Colombia	33,399	76,112	19	14	32	32	23	18	49	54	
76	Namibia	2,190	3,033	12	14	53	29	5	9	35	56	
77	Belarus	..	20,561	..	13	..	35	..	22	..	52	
78	Russian Federation	..	344,711	..	7	..	38	..	31	..	55	
79	Latvia	..	6,034	..	9	..	31	..	18	..	60	
80	Peru	20,661	57,424	10	7	42	38	20	24	48	55	
81	Costa Rica	4,831	9,233	18	17	27	24	19	19	55	58	
82	Lebanon	..	11,143	..	7	..	24	..	10	..	69	
83	Thailand	32,354	167,056	23	11	29	40	22	29	48	49	
84	Panama	3,592	7,413	..	11	..	15	..	..	..	74	
85	Turkey	68,790	164,789	26	16	22	31	14	21	51	53	
86	Poland	57,068	117,663	..	6	..	39	..	26	..	54	
87	Estonia	..	4,007	..	8	..	28	..	17	..	64	
88	Slovak Republic	..	17,414	..	6	..	33	..	..	..	61	
89	Botswana	971	4,318	13	5	44	46	4	4	43	48	
90	Venezuela	69,377	75,016	5	5	46	38	16	17	49	56	
Upper-middle-income		**989,317 t**	**1,981,511 t**	**8 w**	**9 w**	**47 w**	**37 w**	**20 w**	**18 w**	**43 w**	**53 w**	
91	South Africa	78,744	136,035	7	5	50	31	23	24	43	64	
92	Croatia	..	18,081	..	12	..	25	..	20	..	62	
93	Mexico	194,914	250,038	8	8	33	26	22	19	59	67	
94	Mauritius	1,132	3,919	12	9	26	33	15	23	62	58	
95	Gabon	4,285	4,691	7	..	60	..	5	..	33	..	
96	Brazil	235,025	688,085	11	14	44	37	33	24	45	49	
97	Trinidad and Tobago	6,236	5,327	2	3	60	42	9	9	38	54	
98	Czech Republic	29,123	44,772	7	6	63	39	..	..	30	55	
99	Malaysia	24,488	85,311	22	13	38	43	21	33	40	44	
100	Hungary	22,163	43,712	..	8	..	33	..	24	..	59	
101	Chile	27,572	67,297	7	..	37	..	21	..	55	..	
102	Oman	5,982	12,102	3	..	69	..	1	..	28	..	
103	Uruguay	10,132	17,847	14	9	34	26	26	18	53	65	
104	Saudi Arabia	156,487	125,501	1	..	81	..	5	..	18	..	
105	Argentina	76,962	281,060	6	6	41	31	29	20	52	63	
106	Slovenia	..	18,550	..	5	..	39	..	1	..	57	
107	Greece	40,147	90,550	27	21	48	36	30	21	24	43	
Low- and middle-income		**3,192,729 t**	**5,393,142 t**	**..**	**14 w**	**..**	**36 w**	**..**	**20 w**	**..**	**48 w**	
Sub-Saharan Africa		292,557 t	296,748 t	24 w	20 w	36 w	30 w	12 w	15 w	38 w	48 w	
East Asia and Pacific		464,719 t	1,341,265 t	27 w	18 w	39 w	44 w	27 w	32 w	32 w	38 w	
South Asia		219,283 t	439,203 t	39 w	30 w	24 w	27 w	15 w	17 w	35 w	41 w	
Europe and Central Asia		..	1,103,330 t	..	..	..	..	..	..	..	..	
Middle East and N. Africa		463,031 t	..	9 w	..	57 w	..	7 w	..	32 w	..	
Latin America and Caribbean		758,569 t	1,688,195 t	10 w	10 w	37 w	33 w	25 w	21 w	51 w	55 w	
High-income economies		**7,758,074 t**	**22,485,548 t**	**3 w**	**2 w**	**37 w**	**32 w**	**24 w**	**21 w**	**58 w**	**66 w**	
108	Korea, Rep.	63,661	455,476	15	7	40	43	29	27	45	50	
109	Portugal	28,526	102,337	..	..	..	..	..	..	..	..	
110	Spain	211,543	558,617	..	3	..	..	..	..	..	..	
111	New Zealand	22,469	57,070	11	..	31	..	22	..	58	..	
112	Ireland	20,080	60,780	..	..	..	..	..	..	..	..	
113	† Israel	22,579	91,965	..	..	..	..	..	..	..	..	
114	† Kuwait	28,639	26,650	0	0	75	53	6	11	25	46	
115	† United Arab Emirates	29,625	39,107	1	2	77	57	4	8	22	40	
116	United Kingdom	537,382	1,105,822	2	2	43	32	27	21	54	66	
117	Australia	160,109	348,782	5	3	36	28	19	15	58	70	
118	Italy	452,648	1,086,932	6	3	39	31	28	21	55	66	
119	Canada	263,193	568,928	5	..	40	..	22	..	55	..	
120	Finland	51,306	125,432	12	6	49	37	35	28	39	57	
121	† Hong Kong	28,495	143,669	1	0	32	17	24	9	67	83	
122	Sweden	125,557	228,679	4	2	37	32	25	23	59	66	
123	Netherlands	171,861	395,900	3	3	32	27	18	18	64	70	
124	Belgium	118,022	269,081	2	2	34	..	24	..	64	..	
125	France	664,597	1,536,089	4	2	34	27	24	19	62	71	
126	† Singapore	11,718	83,695	1	0	38	36	29	27	61	64	
127	Austria	76,882	233,427	4	2	40	34	28	24	56	63	
128	United States	2,708,150	6,952,020	3	2	34	26	22	18	64	72	
129	Germany	..	2,415,764	..	..	..	..	..	..	..	..	
130	Denmark	66,322	172,220	6	4	33	29	22	21	61	67	
131	Norway	63,283	145,954	4	..	36	..	15	..	60	..	
132	Japan	1,059,253	5,108,540	4	2	42	38	29	24	54	60	
133	Switzerland	101,646	300,508	..	..	..	..	..	..	..	..	
World		**10,768,090 t**	**27,846,241 t**	**7 w**	**5 w**	**38 w**	**33 w**	**23 w**	**21 w**	**53 w**	**63 w**	

a. Because manufacturing is generally the most dynamic part of the industrial sector, its share is shown separately. b. Services include unallocated items. c. Data prior to 1992 include Eritrea.

Table 13. Structure of the economy: demand

		Distribution of gross domestic product (%)												
		General govt. consumption		Private consumption		Gross domestic investment		Gross domestic saving		Exports of goods and services		Resource balance	
		1980	1995	1980	1995	1980	1995	1980	1995	1980	1995	1980	1995
	Low-income economies	12 w	12 w	66 w	59 w	24	32 w	22 w	30 w	13 w	19 w	−2 w	−1 w
	Excluding China and India	..	13 w	..	80 w	..	20 w	..	10 w	..	24 w	−8 w	−6 w
1	Mozambique	21	20	78	75	22	60	1	5	20	23	−22	−55
2	Ethiopia	14[a]	12	83[a]	81	9[a]	17	3[a]	7	11[a]	15	−6[a]	−11
3	Tanzania	12	10	69	97	29	31	19	−7	14	30	−10	−38
4	Burundi	9	12	92	95	14	11	−1	−7	9	12	−15	−18
5	Malawi	19	20	70	76	25	15	11	4	25	29	−14	−11
6	Chad	8	17	99	93	4	9	−6	−10	24	13	−17	−19
7	Rwanda	12	14	83	93	16	13	5	−7	15	6	−11	−20
8	Sierra Leone	8	11	91	98	18	6	2	−9	23	13	−16	−15
9	Nepal	7	8	82	79	18	23	11	12	12	24	−7	−12
10	Niger	10	17	67	82	37	6	23	1	24	13	−14	−4
11	Burkina Faso	10	16	95	78	17	22	−6	6	10	14	−23	−16
12	Madagascar	12	7	89	91	15	11	−1	3	13	23	−16	−8
13	Bangladesh	6	14	92	78	15	17	2	8	6	14	−13	−8
14	Uganda	11	10	89	83	6	16	0	7	19	12	−6	−9
15	Vietnam	..	7	..	77	..	27	..	16	..	36	..	−11
16	Guinea-Bissau	29	8	77	98	30	16	−6	−5	8	13	−36	−22
17	Haiti	10	6	82	101	17	2	8	−7	22	4	−9	−9
18	Mali	10	11	91	79	17	26	−2	10	16	22	−19	−16
19	Nigeria	12	10	56	69	22	18	32	20	29	25	10	4
20	Yemen, Rep.	..	29	..	61	..	12	..	10	..	43	..	−2
21	Cambodia	..	11	..	82	..	19	..	6	..	11	..	−13
22	Kenya	20	15	62	72	29	19	18	13	28	33	−11	−6
24	Togo	22	11	53	80	30	14	25	9	51	31	−5	−4
23	Mongolia	b	..	74	..	46	..	27	..	19	..	−36	2
25	Gambia, The	20	19	79	76	26	21	1	5	47	53	−26	−15
26	Central African Republic	15	13	94	80	7	15	−10	6	26	18	−17	−9
27	India	10	10	73	68	21	25	17	22	7	12	−4	−2
28	Lao PDR	..	..	..	..	..	..	..	..	..	..	..	..
29	Benin	9	9	96	82	15	20	−5	9	23	27	−20	−6
30	Nicaragua	20	14	83	95	17	18	−2	−9	24	24	−19	−27
31	Ghana	11	12	84	77	6	19	5	10	8	25	−1	−8
32	Zambia	26	9	55	88	23	12	19	3	41	31	−4	−7
33	Angola	..	47	..	9	..	27	..	43	..	74	..	33
34	Georgia	13	7	56	103	29	3	..	−9	..	17	..	−1
35	Pakistan	10	12	83	73	18	19	7	16	12	16	−12	−3
36	Mauritania	25	9	68	80	36	15	7	11	37	50	−29	−3
37	Azerbaijan	..	b	..	96	..	16	..	4	..	27	..	−16
38	Zimbabwe	20	19	64	64	19	22	16	17	30	34	−3	−6
39	Guinea	..	8	..	81	..	15	..	11	..	21	..	−4
40	Honduras	13	14	70	73	25	23	17	14	36	36	−8	−10
41	Senegal	22	11	78	79	15	16	0	10	28	32	−16	−5
42	China	15	12	51	46	35	40	35	42	6	21	0	2
43	Cameroon	10	9	70	71	21	15	20	21	27	26	−1	6
44	Côte d'Ivoire	17	12	63	67	27	13	20	20	35	41	−6	7
45	Albania	9	15	56	93	35	16	..	−8	..	14	..	−24
46	Congo	18	12	47	64	36	27	36	23	60	62	0	−4
47	Kyrgyz Republic	..	23	..	67	..	16	..	10	..	26	..	−18
48	Sri Lanka	9	12	80	74	34	25	11	14	32	36	−23	−11
49	Armenia	16	13	47	116	29	9	..	−29	..	24	..	−53
	Middle-income economies	..	14 w	..	59 w	..	25 w	..	25 w	..	24 w	..	−1 w
	Lower-middle-income	..	..	..	..	..	..	..	..	..	..	..	..
50	Lesotho	36	23	124	85	42	87	−60	−9	20	21	−102	−96
51	Egypt, Arab Rep.	16	13	69	81	28	17	15	6	31	21	−12	−3
52	Bolivia	14	13	67	79	15	15	19	8	21	20	4	−7
53	Macedonia, FYR	..	14	..	82	..	15	..	4	..	37	..	−11
54	Moldova	..	20	..	81	..	7	..	−1	..	35	..	−7
55	Uzbekistan	..	25	..	59	..	23	..	24	..	63	..	0
56	Indonesia	11	8	52	56	24	38	37	36	33	25	13	1
57	Philippines	9	11	67	74	29	23	24	15	24	36	−5	−8
58	Morocco	18	15	68	71	24	21	14	13	17	27	−10	−8
59	Syrian Arab Republic	23	..	67	..	28	..	10	..	18	..	−17	..
60	Papua New Guinea	24	12	61	48	25	24	15	39	43	61	−10	15
61	Bulgaria	6	15	55	61	34	21	39	25	36	49	5	2
62	Kazakstan	..	15	..	65	..	22	..	19	..	34	..	−3
63	Guatemala	8	6	79	86	16	17	13	8	22	19	−3	−6
64	Ecuador	15	13	60	67	26	19	26	21	25	29	0	2
65	Dominican Republic	8	4	77	80	25	20	15	16	19	26	−10	0
66	Romania	5	12	60	66	40	26	35	21	35	28	..	−5
67	Jamaica	20	9	64	80	16	17	16	10	51	69	0	−7
68	Jordan	..	22	..	75	..	26	..	3	..	49	..	−24
69	Algeria	14	16	43	56	39	32	43	29	34	27	4	−3
70	El Salvador	14	8	72	86	13	19	14	6	34	21	1	−16
71	Ukraine	..	..	..	..	..	..	..	..	..	..	..	−3
72	Paraguay	6	7	76	79	32	23	18	14	15	36	−13	−19

Note: For data comparability and coverage, see the technical notes. Figures in italics are for years other than those specified.

		Distribution of gross domestic product (%)											
		General govt. consumption		Private consumption		Gross domestic investment		Gross domestic saving		Exports of goods and services		Resource balance	
		1980	1995	1980	1995	1980	1995	1980	1995	1980	1995	1980	1995
73	Tunisia	14	16	62	63	29	24	24	20	40	45	−5	−4
74	Lithuania	..	20	..	63	..	19	..	16	..	58	..	−3
75	Colombia	10	9	70	75	19	20	20	16	16	15	1	−3
76	Namibia	17	31	44	52	29	20	39	17	76	53	10	−7
77	Belarus	..	22	..	58	..	25	..	20	..	43	..	−5
78	Russian Federation	15	16	62	58	22	25	..	26	..	22	..	3
79	Latvia	8	20	60	65	26	21	..	16	..	43	..	−5
80	Peru	11	6	57	83	29	17	32	11	22	12	3	−5
81	Costa Rica	18	17	66	60	27	25	16	24	26	41	−10	−1
82	Lebanon	..	12	..	110	..	29	..	−22	..	10	..	−62
83	Thailand	12	10	65	54	29	43	23	36	24	42	−6	−7
84	Panama	..	15	..	64	..	24	..	22	..	39	..	−2
85	Turkey	10	10	78	70	18	25	11	20	5	20	−7	−5
86	Poland	9	18	67	63	26	17	23	19	28	28	−3	2
87	Estonia	..	23	..	58	..	27	..	18	..	75	..	−9
88	Slovak Republic	..	20	..	50	..	28	..	30	..	63	..	2
89	Botswana	19	32	53	45	38	25	28	23	53	49	−10	−2
90	Venezuela	12	6	55	73	26	16	33	21	29	27	7	5
Upper-middle-income		**12 w**	**15 w**	**56 w**	**61 w**	**25**	**21 w**	**32 w**	**23 w**	**27 w**	**22 w**	**7 w**	**−1 w**
91	South Africa	13	21	50	61	28	18	36	18	36	22	8	0
92	Croatia	..	33	..	66	..	14	..	1	..	40	..	−13
93	Mexico	10	10	65	71	27	15	25	19	11	25	−2	3
94	Mauritius	14	12	75	65	21	25	10	22	51	58	−10	−3
95	Gabon	13	10	26	42	28	26	61	48	65	61	33	22
96	Brazil	9	17	70	62	23	22	21	21	9	7	−2	−1
97	Trinidad and Tobago	12	13	46	62	31	14	42	25	50	39	11	11
98	Czech Republic	..	20	..	60	..	25	..	20	..	52	..	−5
99	Malaysia	17	12	51	51	30	41	33	37	58	96	3	−3
100	Hungary	10	11	61	68	31	23	29	21	39	35	−2	−2
101	Chile	12	9	67	62	25	27	20	29	23	29	−4	2
102	Oman	25	31	28	42	22	17	47	27	63	49	25	10
103	Uruguay	12	13	76	74	17	14	12	13	15	19	−6	−1
104	Saudi Arabia	16	27	22	43	22	20	62	30	71	40	41	10
105	Argentina	b	b	76	82	25	18	24	18	5	9	−1	0
106	Slovenia	..	21	..	58	..	22	..	21	..	56	..	−1
107	Greece	16	19	60	74	29	19	23	7	21	22	−5	−12
Low- and middle-income		**14 w**	**14 w**	**57 w**	**63 w**	**26**	**27 w**	**30 w**	**22 w**	**23 w**	**22 w**	**2 w**	**−1 w**
Sub-Saharan Africa		**14 w**	**17 w**	**60 w**	**67 w**	**23**	**19 w**	**27 w**	**16 w**	**31 w**	**28 w**	**3 w**	**−3 w**
East Asia and Pacific		**12 w**	**11 w**	**58 w**	**51 w**	**28**	**39 w**	**28 w**	**38 w**	**16 w**	**29 w**	**1 w**	**−1 w**
South Asia		**9 w**	**11 w**	**75 w**	**69 w**	**20**	**23 w**	**15 w**	**20 w**	**8 w**	**14 w**	**−6 w**	**−3 w**
Europe and Central Asia		..	..	..	..	..	..	..	..	..	..	..	..
Middle East and N. Africa		**16 w**	..	**39 w**	..	**26**	..	**45 w**	..	**47 w**	..	**16 w**	..
Latin America and Caribbean		**11 w**	**12 w**	**67 w**	**67 w**	**25**	**20 w**	**23 w**	**19 w**	**16 w**	**17 w**	**−2 w**	**−2 w**
High-income economies		**17 w**	**15 w**	**60 w**	**63 w**	**23**	**21 w**	**23 w**	**21 w**	**22 w**	**22 w**	**0 w**	**2 w**
108	Korea, Rep.	12	10	64	54	32	37	25	36	34	33	−7	−1
109	Portugal	14	17	65	65	34	28c	21	18	24	28	−13	−9
110	Spain	13	16	66	62	23	21	21	22	16	24	−2	0
111	New Zealand	18	15	62	60	21	24	20	26	30	32	−1	2
112	Ireland	19	15	67	57	27	13	14	27	48	75	−13	15
113	†Israel	39	29	50	58	22	24	11	13	40	29	−11	−10
114	†Kuwait	11	33	31	49	14	12	58	18	78	55	44	6
115	†United Arab Emirates	11	18	17	54	28	27	72	27	78	70	43	1
116	United Kingdom	22	21	59	64	17	16c	19	15	27	28	2	−1
117	Australia	18	17	59	60	25	23	24	22	16	20	−2	−1
118	Italy	15	16	61	62	27	18	24	22	22	26	−3	3
119	Canada	19	19	55	60	24	19	25	21	28	37	2	2
120	Finland	18	21	54	54	29	16	28	24	33	38	−1	8
121	†Hong Kong	6	9	60	59	35	35	34	33	90	147	−1	−2
122	Sweden	29	26	51	55	21	14	19	19	29	41	−2	4
123	Netherlands	17	14	61	57	22	22	22	29	51	53	0	7
124	Belgium	18	15	63	62	22	18	19	24	63	74	−3	6
125	France	18	20	59	60	24	18	23	20	22	23	−1	2
126	†Singapore	10	9	53	40	46	33	38	..	207	..	−9	..
127	Austria	18	19	56	55	28	27	26	26	37	38	−2	−1
128	United States	18	16	63	68	20	16	19	15	10	11	−1	−2
129	Germany	..	20	..	58	..	21	..	23	..	23	..	1
130	Denmark	27	25	56	54	19	16	17	21	33	35	−1	6
131	Norway	18	21	51	50	25	23c	31	29	43	38	6	6
132	Japan	10	10	59	60	32	29	31	31	14	9	−1	2
133	Switzerland	13	14	67	59	24	23	20	27	37	36	−4	4
World		**16 w**	**15 w**	**59 w**	**63 w**	**24**	**23 w**	**25 w**	**21 w**	**22 w**	**22 w**	**1 w**	**1 w**

a. Includes Eritrea. b. General government consumption figures are not available separately; they are included in private consumption. c. Includes statistical discrepancy.

Table 14. Central government budget

		Percentage of GDP							Percentage of total expenditure[b]				Overall deficit/surplus[c] (% of GDP)	
		Total revenue[a]				Total expenditure				Defense		Social services[d]			
		Tax		Nontax		Current		Capital							
		1980	1995	1980	1995	1980	1995	1980	1995	1980	1995	1980	1995	1980	1995
Low-income economies															
Excluding China and India															
1	Mozambique	..	..	..	..	..	..	..	..	..	..	..	..	..	..
2	Ethiopia	12.8e	11.9	3.7e	..	18.0e	..	3.3e	..	35.5e	..	19.6e	..	−3.1e	−8.5
3	Tanzania	17.1	..	9.4	..	19.2	..	10.4	..	9.2	..	35.0	..	−7.0	..
4	Burundi	13.2	..	3.5	..	11.5	..	11.0	..	..	..	..	..	−3.9	..
5	Malawi	16.6	..	5.9	..	18.0	..	16.6	..	12.8	..	30.7	..	−15.9	..
6	Chad	..	..	..	..	..	..	..	..	..	..	..	..	..	..
7	Rwanda	11.0	..	2.5	..	9.3	..	5.0	..	..	..	..	..	−1.7	−6.9
8	Sierra Leone	14.0	12.5	2.5	4.5	19.6	13.3	5.0	6.5	..	..	..	..	−12.1	−5.0
9	Nepal	6.6	9.1	2.9	4.3	..	..	..	..	6.7	..	..	..	−3.0	..
10	Niger	12.2	..	2.6	..	9.4	..	9.0	..	3.8	..	50.5	..	−4.7	..
11	Burkina Faso	10.4	..	1.9	..	9.8	..	2.3	..	17.0	..	36.0	..	0.2	..
12	Madagascar	12.9	8.2	5.2	2.2	..	11.3	..	7.5	..	..	..	34.6	..	−4.8
13	Bangladesh	7.7	..	2.9	..	..	..	..	..	9.4	..	..	..	2.5	..
14	Uganda	3.0	..	1.3	..	5.3	..	0.8	..	25.2	..	24.1	..	−3.1	..
15	Vietnam	..	..	..	..	..	..	..	..	..	..	..	..	..	..
16	Guinea-Bissau	..	..	..	..	..	..	..	..	..	..	..	..	..	..
17	Haiti	9.3	..	1.6	..	13.9	..	3.5	..	..	..	..	..	−4.7	..
18	Mali	9.5	..	4.0	..	12.3	..	1.9	..	11.0	..	37.8	..	−4.6	..
19	Nigeria	..	..	..	..	..	..	..	..	..	..	..	..	..	..
20	Yemen, Rep.	..	13.0	..	2.6	..	34.7	..	3.8	..	30.3	..	30.8	..	−17.3
21	Cambodia	..	..	..	..	..	..	..	..	..	..	..	..	..	..
22	Kenya	19.1	19.6	8.5	10.0	19.4	22.1	5.9	5.3	16.4	6.2	36.0	27.1	−4.5	−3.2
23	Mongolia	..	20.3	..	5.0	..	18.1	..	3.3	..	11.5	..	38.8	..	−1.9
24	Togo	27.0	..	4.6	..	23.7	..	8.9	..	7.1	..	56.2	..	−2.0	..
25	Gambia, The	20.0	21.8	0.8	7.5	16.7	15.8	15.5	4.6	..	..	38.2	..	−4.5	3.5
26	Central African Republic	15.0	..	3.4	..	18.5	..	1.3	..	9.7	..	34.5	..	−3.5	..
27	India	9.8	9.6	5.0	4.1	11.7	14.2	1.6	1.8	19.8	14.5	8.8	11.9	−6.5	−5.4
28	Lao PDR	..	..	..	..	..	..	..	..	..	..	..	..	..	..
29	Benin	..	..	..	..	..	..	..	..	..	..	..	..	..	..
30	Nicaragua	20.3	23.6	8.7	10.7	24.8	22.0	4.7	8.4	7.7	0.0	41.3	63.5	−7.2	−4.3
31	Ghana	6.4	12.9	1.9	5.6	9.8	17.6	1.1	3.0	3.7	4.9	38.3	42.3	−4.2	−2.5
32	Zambia	23.1	13.4	10.8	7.0	33.0	10.7	4.0	6.1	0.0	..	23.4	59.0	−18.5	−2.9
33	Angola	..	..	..	..	..	..	..	..	..	..	..	..	..	..
34	Georgia	..	..	..	..	..	..	..	..	..	..	..	..	..	..
35	Pakistan	13.3	15.3	5.5	7.2	14.5	19.1	3.1	4.1	..	..	..	..	−5.7	−4.8
36	Mauritania	..	..	..	..	..	..	..	..	..	..	..	..	..	..
37	Azerbaijan	..	..	..	..	..	..	..	..	..	..	..	..	..	..
38	Zimbabwe	19.2	..	6.7	..	33.0	..	1.8	..	25.0	..	30.2	..	−10.9	..
39	Guinea	..	..	..	..	..	..	..	..	..	..	..	..	..	..
40	Honduras	13.6	..	3.5	..	..	..	..	..	..	..	..	..	..	−0.2
41	Senegal	20.7	..	6.3	..	22.3	..	1.9	..	16.8	..	38.5	..	0.9	0.0
42	China	..	5.7	..	4.6	..	..	..	..	..	12.4	..	..	..	−1.9
43	Cameroon	15.0	9.5	2.9	2.8	10.5	14.0	5.2	1.5	9.1	9.4	38.2	29.0	0.5	−1.7
44	Côte d'Ivoire	21.1	..	5.7	..	19.1	..	9.0	..	..	..	..	..	−10.8	..
45	Albania	..	18.3	..	9.2	..	28.0	..	6.1	..	7.1	..	40.2	..	−9.9
46	Congo	27.0	..	2.7	..	21.8	..	17.7	..	..	16.1	12.6	..	−5.2	−0.1
47	Kyrgyz Republic	..	..	..	..	..	..	..	..	..	..	..	..	..	..
48	Sri Lanka	19.1	18.0	5.4	10.8	24.7	22.1	16.6	6.5	1.7	2.6	40.5	46.2	−18.3	−0.1
49	Armenia	..	..	..	..	..	..	..	..	..	..	..	..	..	..
Middle-income economies															
Lower-middle-income															
50	Lesotho	29.5	44.4	3.5	7.5	32.9	33.3	..	..	..	..	31.4	..	..	..
51	Egypt, Arab Rep.	28.9	26.3	4.0	5.6	36.6	34.8	9.0	8.0	13.5	8.7	32.1	39.1	−6.3	2.0
52	Bolivia	..	11.8	..	7.1	..	18.7	..	5.4	..	8.2	..	52.3	..	−3.6
53	Macedonia, FYR	..	..	..	..	..	..	..	..	..	..	..	..	..	..
54	Moldova	..	..	..	..	..	..	..	..	..	..	..	..	..	..
55	Uzbekistan	..	..	..	..	..	..	..	..	..	..	..	..	..	..
56	Indonesia	20.2	16.4	1.8	6.2	11.7	8.4	10.4	7.8	13.5	6.2	23.7	70.4	−2.3	0.6
57	Philippines	12.5	16.0	5.9	4.9	9.9	15.4	3.5	3.0	15.7	10.6	25.4	26.3	−1.4	−1.5
58	Morocco	20.4	..	8.1	..	22.8	..	10.3	..	17.9	..	39.5	..	−9.7	..
59	Syrian Arab Republic	10.5	17.8	1.4	8.2	30.3	15.5	17.9	11.1	35.8	28.2	28.0	26.8	−9.7	−3.8
60	Papua New Guinea	20.5	18.9	2.8	2.3	29.2	26.1	5.2	3.3	4.4	3.3	29.8	30.5	−1.9	−4.1
61	Bulgaria	..	29.0	..	10.4	..	41.4	..	1.6	..	6.3	..	35.0	..	−5.5
62	Kazakstan	..	..	..	..	..	..	..	..	..	..	..	..	..	..
63	Guatemala	8.7	6.8	2.9	3.7	7.3	6.9	5.1	2.3	10.6	15.2	47.5	38.4	−3.4	−1.2
64	Ecuador	12.2	13.9	2.2	4.1	11.9	12.4	2.3	3.3	12.5	..	52.5	..	−1.4	0.0
65	Dominican Republic	11.1	14.9	3.1	5.5	11.4	8.2	5.2	8.7	7.8	4.7	53.0	87.1	−2.6	0.0
66	Romania	10.1	26.3	0.0	6.9	29.8	27.7	15.0	4.3	3.8	6.2	28.3	54.8	0.5	0.0
67	Jamaica	27.9	..	14.3	..	..	..	..	..	..	..	..	..	−15.5	..
68	Jordan	..	20.4	..	6.5	..	24.7	..	6.1	25.3	20.7	38.5	46.8	..	1.1
69	Algeria	..	..	..	..	..	..	..	..	..	..	..	..	..	..
70	El Salvador	11.1	12.1	3.4	6.4	11.7	11.2	2.8	3.7	8.8	5.2	47.0	37.2	−5.7	0.0
71	Ukraine	..	..	..	..	..	..	..	..	..	..	..	..	..	..
72	Paraguay	9.8	9.1	1.9	5.0	7.5	11.1	2.4	1.9	12.4	10.7	47.0	54.1	0.3	1.2

Note: For data comparability and coverage, see the technical notes. Figures in italics are for years other than those specified.

		Percentage of GDP								Percentage of total expenditure[b]				Overall deficit/surplus[c] (% of GDP)	
		Total revenue[a]				Total expenditure				Defense		Social services[d]			
		Tax		Nontax		Current		Capital							
		1980	1995	1980	1995	1980	1995	1980	1995	1980	1995	1980	1995	1980	1995
73	Tunisia	23.9	..	7.5	..	22.1	..	9.4	..	12.2	..	53.7	..	−2.8	..
74	Lithuania	..	24.4	..	12.6	..	24.7	..	2.7	..	1.9	..	53.2	..	..
75	Colombia	10.3	14.0	2.7	6.8	10.4	11.9	4.1	2.5	6.7	8.7	58.5	40.8	−1.8	−0.5
76	Namibia	..	31.4	..	10.1	..	34.6	..	6.1	..	..	..	..	..	−4.8
77	Belarus	..	..	..	..	..	..	..	..	..	..	..	..	..	..
78	Russian Federation	..	16.1	..	6.3	..	25.8	..	1.3	..	16.4	..	34.6	..	−10.5
79	Latvia	..	23.1	..	10.9	..	29.2	..	1.2	..	2.6	..	63.7	..	−4.2
80	Peru	15.8	14.4	6.4	7.7	15.0	15.8	4.4	3.1	21.0	..	27.4	0.0	−2.4	0.0
81	Costa Rica	16.8	22.0	5.4	8.4	21.3	26.0	5.2	2.4	2.6	0.0	73.9	63.0	−7.4	−2.9
82	Lebanon	..	10.8	..	1.1	..	25.8	..	..	..	..	..	..	..	..
83	Thailand	13.2	17.1	6.6	7.4	14.4	10.5	4.4	..	21.7	..	37.8	57.7	−4.9	1.8
84	Panama	19.7	20.1	4.5	4.8	26.5	25.4	5.9	2.9	..	5.4	48.5	69.6	−5.5	4.3
85	Turkey	14.3	14.3	3.6	7.3	15.5	20.9	5.9	6.1	15.2	15.8	33.0	21.6	−3.1	0.0
86	Poland	..	36.7	..	11.6	..	41.9	..	1.5	..	..	..	..	..	−2.3
87	Estonia	..	33.2	..	13.6	..	..	..	..	..	3.1	..	..	..	1.4
88	Slovak Republic	..	..	..	..	..	..	..	..	..	..	..	..	..	..
89	Botswana	24.9	28.1	0.3	1.7	23.1	38.3	10.8	..	9.8	..	41.5	35.6	−0.2	..
90	Venezuela	18.9	14.8	0.9	4.0	14.9	16.3	4.0	2.5	5.8	..	48.0	..	0.0	−4.1
Upper-middle-income															
91	South Africa	20.5	25.2	5.6	10.0	19.1	31.0	3.0	2.2	..	..	..	..	−2.3	−6.2
92	Croatia	..	43.0	..	18.7	..	42.8	..	3.7	..	21.1	..	60.9	..	−0.9
93	Mexico	14.3	14.8	4.4	8.0	11.3	14.3	5.5	..	2.3	..	57.6	65.7	−3.0	..
94	Mauritius	18.4	18.2	3.6	5.5	22.7	19.1	4.6	4.2	0.8	1.5	55.9	60.0	−10.3	−1.4
95	Gabon	23.6	..	1.7	..	..	..	..	..	..	..	..	..	6.1	..
96	Brazil	17.8	18.6	7.3	4.9	18.6	39.0	2.2	..	..	..	43.5	34.5	−2.2	..
97	Trinidad and Tobago	35.7	..	1.6	..	18.4	..	12.0	..	..	..	..	..	7.2	..
98	Czech Republic	..	37.5	..	13.0	..	36.9	..	5.1	..	5.7	..	65.7	..	0.5
99	Malaysia	23.4	20.6	4.4	6.6	19.2	18.1	9.9	5.1	14.8	12.7	45.3	48.0	−6.0	0.8
100	Hungary	44.9	..	20.5	..	48.7	..	7.5	..	4.4	..	31.0	..	−2.8	..
101	Chile	25.6	17.8	11.4	9.7	25.3	16.2	2.7	3.3	12.4	8.8	65.3	77.9	5.4	1.6
102	Oman	10.7	8.5	0.2	0.4	30.3	36.0	8.2	6.9	51.2	36.5	9.7	26.3	0.4	−11.2
103	Uruguay	21.0	27.6	9.6	9.6	20.1	29.2	1.7	2.6	13.4	7.3	67.6	79.8	0.0	−2.8
104	Saudi Arabia	..	..	..	..	..	..	..	..	..	..	..	..	..	..
105	Argentina	10.4	..	2.6	..	18.2	..	2.7	..	14.3	..	28.6	..	−2.6	0.0
106	Slovenia	..	..	..	..	..	..	..	..	..	..	..	..	..	..
107	Greece	27.4	26.0	9.7	17.8	31.1	38.8	5.5	4.4	12.6	8.9	58.8	34.1	−5.0	−15.7
Low- and middle-income															
Sub-Saharan Africa															
East Asia and Pacific															
South Asia															
Europe and Central Asia															
Middle East and N. Africa															
Latin America and Caribbean															
High-income economies															
108	Korea, Rep.	15.3	17.7	8.0	6.5	14.6	14.2	2.4	3.6	34.3	18.1	30.0	42.1	−2.2	−0.2
109	Portugal	24.3	30.9	8.8	12.8	28.9	37.7	4.4	..	7.4	..	55.9	..	−8.5	..
110	Spain	22.2	28.7	3.1	6.5	23.8	36.8	3.0	2.6	4.3	6.8	77.4	54.0	−4.2	0.0
111	New Zealand	30.6	34.4	6.1	10.8	35.7	35.0	2.4	1.2	5.1	3.6	63.8	70.1	−6.7	0.1
112	Ireland	30.9	35.1	10.4	11.4	40.4	39.3	4.6	3.2	3.4	3.0	57.7	61.6	−12.5	−0.2
113	† Israel	43.3	33.4	12.4	13.0	67.2	40.9	2.8	4.3	39.8	19.4	29.0	57.5	−15.6	−2.9
114	† Kuwait	2.7	1.2	0.2	0.0	18.9	44.1	8.9	7.3	12.2	25.5	39.1	44.2	58.7	..
115	† United Arab Emirates	0.0	0.6	0.0	0.6	11.2	11.3	0.9	0.5	47.5	37.1	24.0	29.2	2.1	0.2
116	United Kingdom	30.6	33.5	9.8	11.8	36.4	39.6	1.8	4.4	13.8	..	48.2	54.5	−4.6	−0.1
117	Australia	19.6	22.3	5.1	5.2	21.1	26.6	1.5	2.5	9.4	16.8	50.1	58.0	−1.5	−0.1
118	Italy	29.1	38.4	7.7	11.2	37.6	48.0	2.2	1.9	3.4	..	55.3	..	−10.7	−10.5
119	Canada	16.2	..	3.1	..	21.0	..	0.3	..	7.7	10.8	46.1	..	−3.5	..
120	Finland	25.1	29.3	13.3	14.2	25.2	42.0	3.0	1.7	5.6	3.9	59.7	63.5	−2.2	−13.4
121	† Hong Kong	..	..	..	..	..	..	..	..	..	..	..	..	..	..
122	Sweden	30.1	32.8	10.2	11.2	37.5	43.6	1.8	1.4	7.7	5.6	67.0	64.6	−8.1	−6.9
123	Netherlands	44.2	42.9	10.3	10.5	48.2	48.3	4.6	2.5	5.6	3.9	70.5	68.7	−4.6	−4.9
124	Belgium	41.7	43.7	10.5	11.4	46.6	47.9	4.3	5.5	5.7	7.0	67.0	7.2	−8.2	−0.5
125	France	36.7	38.1	12.2	11.5	37.4	44.4	2.1	2.4	7.4	..	74.1	72.5	−0.1	−5.5
126	† Singapore	17.5	17.2	4.0	4.6	15.6	10.7	4.5	4.2	25.2	37.4	37.5	48.5	2.1	0.0
127	Austria	32.0	32.9	8.8	9.1	34.0	37.5	3.4	2.9	3.0	3.7	78.8	77.8	−3.4	−0.1
128	United States	18.5	19.0	0.9	0.8	20.7	22.1	1.4	0.8	21.2	18.1	54.2	55.0	−2.8	−2.3
129	Germany	..	30.0	..	7.3	..	32.2	..	1.7	9.1	..	74.9	..	..	−2.5
130	Denmark	31.3	35.4	16.7	16.5	36.7	42.0	2.7	1.5	6.5	4.0	61.2	56.9	−2.7	−2.0
131	Norway	33.9	31.6	14.8	15.4	33.4	39.1	1.2	..	7.7	..	55.9	51.1	−1.7	..
132	Japan	11.0	17.6	2.4	3.0	14.8	..	3.6	..	..	4.1	..	..	−7.0	0.0
133	Switzerland	18.3	21.5	3.8	3.4	18.9	25.9	1.4	1.2	10.2	15.2	69.0	75.2	−0.2	0.1
World															

a. Refers to current revenue. b. Includes lending minus repayments. c. Includes grants. d. Refers to education, health, social security, welfare, housing, and community amenities. e. Includes Eritrea.

Table 15. Exports and imports of merchandise

		Exports Total (million $)		Manufactures (% of total)		Imports Total (million $)		Food (% of total)		Fuel (% of total)		Export volume		Import volume	
		1980	1995	1980	1993	1980	1995	1980	1993	1980	1993	1980–90	1990–95	1980–90	1990–95
	Low-income economies	84,204 t	245,456 t			97,748 t	251,806 t					5.3 w	8.3 w	1.6 w	13.0 w
	Excluding China and India	58,817 t	64,769 t			65,465 t	86,058 t					1.4 w	2.7 w	–4.2 w	5.0 w
1	Mozambique	281	169	2	20	800	784	..	..	..	..	–10.5	–0.3	–1.0	2.9
2	Ethiopia[a]	425	423	0	4	717	1,033	8	6	25	11	1.2	–9.4	3.3	–3.3
3	Tanzania	511	639	14	..	1,250	1,619	13	..	21	..	–1.8	10.0	–3.3	12.7
4	Burundi	65	106	3	30	168	234	..	..	..	..	7.4	–4.8	1.4	–14.6
5	Malawi	295	325	7	6	439	491	8	..	15	..	0.1	–1.8	1.3	–1.6
6	Chad	71	156	8	..	74	220	..	..	..	..	5.4	–10.0	10.5	–12.1
7	Rwanda	72	45	0	..	243	235	12	..	13	..	5.6	–19.6	1.3	–1.9
8	Sierra Leone	224	42	40	27	427	135	24	..	2	..	–2.1	–4.3	–9.9	–1.1
9	Nepal	80	348	31	84	342	1,374	4	..	18	..	7.8	22.1	4.9	6.8
10	Niger	566	225	2	..	594	309	14	..	26	..	–6.4	–2.0	–4.5	2.5
11	Burkina Faso	161	274	..	..	359	549	..	..	..	..	5.4	1.3	2.1	8.3
12	Madagascar	401	364	6	20	600	499	9	11	15	12	–0.1	–6.8	–4.6	–5.6
13	Bangladesh	793	3,173	69	81	2,600	6,496	24	15	10	14	7.5	12.7	1.8	5.3
14	Uganda	345	461	3	1	293	1,058	8	..	30	..	–1.4	3.9	–0.6	28.7
15	Vietnam	339	5,026	..	..	1,310	7,272	..	..	..	..	..	..	..	..
16	Guinea-Bissau	11	23	..	..	55	70	20	..	6	..	–5.1	–18.3	1.3	–5.4
17	Haiti	226	110	..	..	375	653	24	..	13	..	–2.9	–11.2	–4.4	–6.8
18	Mali	205	326	9	..	439	529	19	..	35	..	2.6	–3.7	1.2	–3.4
19	Nigeria	26,000	11,670	0	3	16,700	7,900	17	..	2	..	–2.4	–1.9	–17.5	7.6
20	Yemen, Rep.	..	1,937	51	..	..	1,962	28	..	7	..	1.5	7.2	–5.9	11.1
21	Cambodia	..	855	..	..	..	1,213	..	..	..	..	..	..	..	..
22	Kenya	1,250	1,878	12	18	2,120	2,949	8	8	34	33	2.6	16.6	1.1	–5.6
23	Mongolia	..	324	..	..	..	223	..	..	..	..	..	..	..	..
24	Togo	338	209	11	6	551	386	17	23	23	10	4.9	9.0	1.1	–11.2
25	Gambia, The	31	16	9	37	165	140	23	..	11	..	2.3	26.9	1.0	9.0
26	Central African Republic	116	187	29	..	81	174	21	..	2	..	2.5	3.5	6.0	–3.3
27	India	8,590	30,764	59	75	14,900	34,522	9	4	45	30	6.3	7.0	4.5	2.7
28	Lao PDR	31	348	8	..	29	587	..	..	..	..	..	..	..	..
29	Benin	63	163	8	..	331	493	26	..	8	..	7.7	–0.3	–6.3	29.4
30	Nicaragua	451	520	14	7	887	962	15	23	20	15	–4.4	–8.7	–4.1	7.3
31	Ghana	1,260	1,227	1	23	1,130	1,580	10	..	27	..	3.9	9.1	1.6	12.8
32	Zambia	1,300	781	..	..	1,340	1,258	5	..	22	..	–3.5	26.9	–5.0	–6.2
33	Angola	1,880	3,508	13	..	1,330	1,748	24	..	1	..	11.3	4.2	–3.4	–4.1
34	Georgia	..	347	..	..	..	687	..	..	..	..	..	..	..	..
35	Pakistan	2,620	7,992	49	85	5,350	11,461	13	14	27	17	9.5	8.8	2.1	10.3
36	Mauritania	194	404	2	1	286	700	30	..	14	..	7.8	3.5	1.1	4.4
37	Azerbaijan	..	612	..	..	..	955	..	..	..	..	..	..	..	..
38	Zimbabwe	1,415	1,885	38	37	1,448	2,241	3	18	1	12	2.2	–6.6	–2.2	–5.1
39	Guinea	401	583	..	..	270	690	..	..	..	..	–3.6	–8.6	–2.9	–2.8
40	Honduras	830	1,061	13	13	1,010	1,219	10	11	16	13	1.3	10.7	–1.0	7.0
41	Senegal	477	340	15	21	1,050	704	25	29	25	11	2.6	3.6	1.0	6.1
42	China*	18,100	148,797	48	81	19,900	129,113	..	3	..	6	11.4	14.3	10.0	24.8
43	Cameroon	1,380	2,331	4	13	1,600	1,241	9	16	12	3	4.5	–1.7	–1.4	–11.2
44	Côte d'Ivoire	3,130	3,939	..	17	2,970	2,808	13	..	16	..	3.3	–7.5	–4.0	5.4
45	Albania	367	205	..	..	..	354	..	..	..	..	..	..	..	..
46	Congo	911	952	7	..	580	670	19	..	14	..	5.5	9.7	–2.0	2.5
47	Kyrgyz Republic	..	409	..	..	..	610	..	..	..	..	..	..	..	..
48	Sri Lanka	1,070	3,798	16	73	2,040	5,185	20	16	24	9	6.3	17.0	2.0	15.0
49	Armenia	..	271	..	..	..	674	..	..	..	..	..	..	..	..
	Middle-income economies	586,567 t	893,331 t			455,925 t	987,309 t					2.6 w	6.9 w	–0.2 w	11.0 w
	Lower-middle-income	..	..			..	..					..	..	..	..
50	Lesotho	58	143	..	..	464	821	..	..	..	..	..	..	..	..
51	Egypt, Arab Rep.	3,050	3,435	11	33	4,860	11,739	32	24	1	2	–0.2	–0.1	–0.7	–2.9
52	Bolivia	942	1,101	3	19	665	1,424	19	9	1	5	1.7	–5.4	–2.8	18.9
53	Macedonia, FYR	..	1,244	..	..	..	1,420	..	..	..	..	..	..	..	..
54	Moldova	..	746	..	..	..	841	..	..	..	..	..	..	..	..
55	Uzbekistan	..	3,805	..	..	..	3,598	..	..	..	..	..	..	..	..
56	Indonesia	21,900	45,417	2	53	10,800	40,918	13	7	16	8	5.3	21.3	1.2	9.1
57	Philippines	5,740	17,502	37	76	8,300	28,337	8	8	28	12	2.9	10.2	2.4	15.2
58	Morocco	2,490	4,802	24	57	4,160	8,563	20	17	24	14	4.2	0.8	2.9	1.7
59	Syrian Arab Republic	2,110	3,970	6	9	4,120	4,616	14	19	26	4	6.4	–3.2	–9.3	22.3
60	Papua New Guinea	1,030	2,644	3	12	1,180	1,451	21	..	15	..	4.5	19.3	–0.2	2.1
61	Bulgaria	10,400	5,100	..	..	9,650	5,015	..	8	..	36	..	..	..	..
62	Kazakstan	..	5,197	..	..	..	5,692	..	..	..	..	..	..	..	..
63	Guatemala	1,520	2,156	24	30	1,600	3,293	8	11	24	14	–1.3	8.2	–0.6	19.3
64	Ecuador	2,480	4,307	3	7	2,250	4,193	8	5	1	2	3.0	8.9	–3.9	10.0
65	Dominican Republic	962	765	24	52	1,640	2,976	17	..	25	..	–1.0	–10.2	2.6	8.9
66	Romania	11,200	7,548	..	77	12,800	9,424	..	14	..	26	–6.8	–4.7	–0.9	–5.3
67	Jamaica	963	1,414	63	65	1,100	2,757	20	14	38	19	1.2	1.3	3.1	7.0
68	Jordan	574	1,769	34	51	2,400	3,698	18	20	17	13	7.4	7.1	–3.1	13.0
69	Algeria	13,900	8,594	0	3	10,600	9,570	21	29	3	1	2.5	–0.8	–5.1	–5.7
70	El Salvador	967	998	35	48	966	2,853	18	15	18	14	–2.8	13.0	1.3	16.2
71	Ukraine	..	13,647	..	..	..	15,945	..	..	..	..	..	..	..	..
72	Paraguay	310	817	12	17	615	2,370	..	11	..	12	9.9	–1.9	3.2	7.3
*	Data for Taiwan, China	19,800	111,585	88	93	19,700	103,698	8	6	25	8	11.6	5.9	12.8	14.1

Note: For data comparability and coverage, see the technical notes. Figures in italics are for years other than those specified.

		Exports Total (million $)		Manufactures (% of total)		Imports Total (million $)		Food (% of total)		Fuel (% of total)		Average annual growth rate (%) Export volume		Import volume	
		1980	1995	1980	1993	1980	1995	1980	1993	1980	1993	1980–90	1990–95	1980–90	1990–95
73	Tunisia	2,200	5,475	36	75	3,540	7,903	14	8	21	8	6.2	7.7	1.3	6.4
74	Lithuania	..	2,707	..	64	..	3,083	..	11	..	45	..	..	..	..
75	Colombia	3,920	9,764	20	40	4,740	13,853	12	8	12	4	9.7	4.8	−1.9	22.3
76	Namibia	..	1,353	..	..	..	1,196	..	..	..	..	..	..	..	..
77	Belarus	..	4,621	..	..	..	5,149	..	..	..	..	..	..	..	..
78	Russian Federation	..	81,500	..	..	..	58,900	..	..	..	..	..	..	..	..
79	Latvia	..	1,305	..	..	..	1,818	..	..	..	..	..	..	..	..
80	Peru	3,900	5,575	18	17	2,500	9,224	20	20	2	8	−1.9	11.0	−1.0	12.1
81	Costa Rica	1,000	2,611	34	33	1,540	3,253	9	8	15	9	4.9	10.1	2.8	15.1
82	Lebanon	868	982	65	..	3,650	6,721	16	..	15	..	−1.2	−7.8	−7.4	23.5
83	Thailand	6,510	56,459	28	73	9,210	70,776	5	5	30	8	14.3	21.6	12.1	12.7
84	Panama	358	625	9	16	1,450	2,511	10	10	31	13	2.6	23.3	−4.1	14.3
85	Turkey	2,910	21,600	27	72	7,910	35,710	4	6	48	14	12.0	8.8	11.3	11.2
86	Poland	14,200	22,892	71	60	16,700	29,050	14	12	18	17	4.8	3.9	1.5	26.4
87	Estonia	..	1,847	..	..	..	2,539	..	..	..	..	..	..	..	..
88	Slovak Republic	..	8,585	..	..	..	9,070	..	..	..	..	..	..	..	..
89	Botswana	502	2,130	..	..	692	1,907	..	..	..	..	11.4	−0.8	7.7	−5.6
90	Venezuela	19,221	18,457	2	14	11,827	11,968	15	11	2	1	1.6	−0.1	−6.1	19.3
Upper-middle-income		**246,329 t**	**372,898 t**			**161,848 t**	**379,450 t**					**1.7 w**	**7.3 w**	**−0.6 w**	**12.6 w**
91	South Africa	25,500	27,860	39	74	19,600	30,555	3	6	0	1	0.9	2.8	−0.8	5.3
92	Croatia	..	4,633	..	71	..	7,582	..	9	..	10	..	..	..	..
93	Mexico	15,600	79,543	12	75	19,500	72,500	16	8	2	2	12.2	14.7	5.7	18.7
94	Mauritius	431	1,537	27	67	609	1,959	26	13	14	9	8.6	2.0	11.0	2.5
95	Gabon	2,170	2,713	..	4	674	882	19	..	1	..	0.6	5.7	−2.0	2.0
96	Brazil	20,100	46,506	39	60	25,000	53,783	10	10	43	16	6.1	6.6	−1.5	8.5
97	Trinidad and Tobago	3,960	2,455	4	34	3,160	1,714	11	15	38	16	−4.3	4.9	−12.1	8.1
98	Czech Republic	..	21,654	..	..	..	26,523	..	..	..	..	..	..	..	..
99	Malaysia	13,000	74,037	19	65	10,800	77,751	12	7	15	4	11.5	17.8	6.0	15.7
100	Hungary	8,670	12,540	66	68	9,220	15,073	8	6	16	13	3.0	−1.8	0.7	7.9
101	Chile	4,710	16,039	10	18	5,800	15,914	15	6	18	10	5.7	10.5	1.4	14.5
102	Oman	2,390	6,065	3	70	1,730	4,248	15	19	11	3	13.1	9.8	−1.6	18.5
103	Uruguay	1,060	2,106	38	43	1,680	2,867	8	8	29	9	2.9	−3.1	−2.0	21.7
104	Saudi Arabia	109,000	46,624	1	9	30,200	27,458	14	..	1	..	−8.2	4.0	−8.4	5.9
105	Argentina	8,020	20,967	23	32	10,500	20,122	6	5	10	2	3.1	−1.0	−8.6	45.8
106	Slovenia	..	8,286	..	86	..	9,452	..	8	..	11	..	..	..	..
107	Greece	5,150	9,384	47	48	10,500	21,466	9	6	23	25	5.1	11.9	5.8	12.8
Low- and middle-income		**660,833 t**	**1,152,249 t**			**547,417 t**	**1,233,749 t**					**3.0 w**	**7.2 w**	**0.2 w**	**11.4 w**
Sub-Saharan Africa		77,237 t	72,847 t			66,593 t	77,574 t					0.9 w	0.9 w	−3.8 w	1.9 w
East Asia and Pacific		69,623 t	359,102 t			65,139 t	368,683 t					9.3 w	17.8 w	7.1 w	17.0 w
South Asia		13,848 t	46,455 t			25,863 t	60,512 t					6.6 w	8.6 w	3.5 w	5.3 w
Europe and Central Asia		..	..			..	..					..	..	..	..
Middle East and N. Africa		203,379 t	106,441 t			103,850 t	110,841 t					−2.0 w	1.1 w	−5.8 w	5.9 w
Latin America and Caribbean		98,589 t	221,210 t			107,971 t	237,576 t					5.2 w	6.6 w	−0.5 w	15.1 w
High-income economies		**1,393,926 t**	**3,997,288 t**			**1,503,743 t**	**4,037,671 t**					**5.2 w**	**5.4 w**	**6.2 w**	**4.6 w**
108	Korea, Rep.	17,500	125,058	90	93	22,300	135,119	10	6	30	18	13.7	7.4	11.2	7.7
109	Portugal	4,640	22,621	72	78	9,310	32,339	14	19	24	24	12.2	0.5	9.8	2.4
110	Spain	20,700	91,716	72	78	34,100	115,019	13	14	39	11	6.9	11.2	10.1	5.3
111	New Zealand	5,420	13,738	20	27	5,470	13,958	6	8	23	7	3.6	5.4	4.9	5.5
112	Ireland	8,400	44,191	58	75	11,200	32,568	12	10	15	5	9.3	11.4	4.7	5.6
113	†Israel	5,540	19,046	82	91	9,780	29,579	11	7	27	7	5.9	10.0	4.6	12.3
114	†Kuwait	19,700	12,977	10	88	6,530	7,784	15	13	1	1	−2.0	42.3	−6.3	23.0
115	†United Arab Emirates	20,700	25,650	3	..	8,750	21,024	11	..	11	..	6.1	6.3	−1.3	21.0
116	United Kingdom	110,000	242,042	74	82	116,000	263,719	13	11	14	5	4.4	1.8	0.5	0.9
117	Australia	21,900	52,692	20	35	22,400	61,280	5	5	14	6	5.8	8.1	4.9	5.1
118	Italy	78,100	231,336	85	89	101,000	204,062	13	13	28	10	4.3	6.0	5.3	−1.7
119	Canada	67,700	192,198	49	66	62,500	168,426	8	6	12	4	5.7	8.4	6.2	6.3
120	Finland	14,200	39,573	70	83	15,600	28,114	7	7	29	13	2.3	8.7	4.4	−1.9
121	†Hong Kong	19,800	173,754	92	95	22,400	192,774	12	6	6	2	15.4	15.3	11.0	15.8
122	Sweden	30,900	79,908	79	85	33,400	64,438	7	8	24	9	4.6	7.4	4.9	5.0
123	Netherlands	74,000	195,912	51	63	76,600	176,420	15	15	24	9	4.5	5.8	4.6	4.3
124	Belgium[b]	64,500	136,864	..	..	71,900	125,297	..	..	..	..	4.4	4.2	4.0	0.3
125	France	116,000	286,738	74	78	135,000	275,275	10	11	27	9	4.1	2.3	5.0	0.8
126	†Singapore	19,400	118,268	50	80	24,000	124,507	9	6	29	11	12.2	16.2	8.6	12.1
127	Austria	17,500	45,200	83	89	24,400	55,300	6	5	16	5	6.4	3.9	5.8	1.9
128	United States	226,000	584,743	68	82	257,000	770,852	8	5	33	10	3.6	5.6	7.2	7.4
129	Germany[c]	193,000	523,743	86	90	188,000	464,220	12	10	23	8	4.6	2.2	4.9	2.9
130	Denmark	16,700	49,036	56	66	19,300	43,223	12	13	22	6	4.4	5.4	3.6	3.4
131	Norway	18,600	41,746	32	31	16,900	32,702	8	7	17	3	6.8	6.5	4.2	0.7
132	Japan	130,000	443,116	96	97	141,000	335,882	12	18	50	21	5.0	0.4	6.5	4.0
133	Switzerland	29,600	77,649	91	94	36,300	76,985	8	7	11	4	6.0	3.3	4.9	−6.7
World		**2,003,797 t**	**5,144,770 t**			**2,027,078 t**	**5,246,326 t**					**4.7 w**	**6.0 w**	**4.9 w**	**5.8 w**

a. Data prior to 1992 include Eritrea. b. Includes Luxembourg. c. Data prior to 1990 refer to the Federal Republic of Germany before unification.

Table 16. Balance of payments

		Exports of goods, services, and income (million $)		Imports of goods, services, and income (million $)		Current transfers				Current account balance (million $)		Gross international reserves (million $)	
						Net workers' remittances (million $)		Other net transfers (million $)					
		1980	1995	1980	1995	1980	1995	1980	1995	1980	1995	1980	1995
Low-income economies													
Excluding China and India													
1	Mozambique	452	490	875	1,368	0	..	56	..	−367	..	..	..
2	Ethiopia[a]	590	828	797	1,400	..	..	80	532	−126	−93	262	815
3	Tanzania	762	1,253	1,412	2,236	0	0	128	354	−522	−629	20	270
4	Burundi	..	139	..	297	..	0	..	151	..	−6	105	216
5	Malawi	315	419	638	937	0	0	63	124	−260	−450	76	115
6	Chad	71	274	83	540	−4	−15	25	206	9	−38	12	147
7	Rwanda	182	91	335	338	−14	−7	118	196	−48	−129	187	126
8	Sierra Leone	276	137	494	374	−2	0	54	47	−165	−89	31	52
9	Nepal	239	1,110	368	1,592	..	..	36	108	−93	−375	272	646
10	Niger	644	291	1,016	496	−47	−41	143	108	−277	−126	132	99
11	Burkina Faso	225	356	596	652	100	29	223	226	−49	15	75	352
12	Madagascar	518	756	1,121	1,161	−30	−2	77	131	−556	−276	9	109
13	Bangladesh	976	4,292	2,622	6,747	..	..	802	1,426	−844	−1,029	331	2,376
14	Uganda	331	642	450	1,440	..	0	36	370	−83	−428	3	459
15	Vietnam	..	7,368	..	9,865	..	..	..	477	−792	−2,021	0	3
16	Guinea-Bissau	17	24	83	95	−14	−1	..	31	−80	−41	..	20
17	Haiti	309	209	498	780	52	0	36	505	−101	−67	27	106
18	Mali	263	533	537	967	40	69	104	162	−130	−164	26	330
19	Nigeria	27,759	9,879	22,005	50,427	−410	2,567	−166	−1,894	5,178	−510	10,640	1,709
20	Yemen, Rep.	..	2,154	..	3,075	..	..	..	1,067	..	146	..	638
21	Cambodia	..	979	..	1,442	..	10	..	267	..	−186	..	192
22	Kenya	2,061	2,974	3,095	3,874	0	−4	156	503	−878	−400	539	384
23	Mongolia	476	511	1,283	550	0	0	0	77	−808	39	..	158
24	Togo	570	520	752	655	1	5	85	25	−95	−57	85	135
25	Gambia, The	66	181	181	241	0	0	28	52	−87	−8	6	106
26	Central African Republic	205	234	329	319	−19	−27	100	91	−43	−25	62	238
27	India	12,348	40,995	18,130	54,303	..	..	2,860	7,478	−2,922	−5,830	12,010	22,865
28	Lao PDR	..	453	..	673	..	0	..	−3	..	−224	..	99
29	Benin	241	489	428	769	75	65	76	84	−36	36	15	202
30	Nicaragua	514	655	1,049	1,436	0	75	124	0	−411	−706	75	142
31	Ghana	1,213	1,586	1,264	2,264	−4	12	84	264	30	−414	330	804
32	Zambia	1,625	1,500	1,987	1,691	−61	..	−93	..	−516	..	206	192
33	Angola	..	3,655	..	4,701	..	−83	..	249	..	−769	..	..
34	Georgia	..	..	..	..	..	..	..	..	..	..	..	..
35	Pakistan	3,011	8,403	6,042	12,758	..	..	1,895	2,390	−1,137	−1,965	1,568	2,528
36	Mauritania	270	533	493	636	−27	−20	117	76	−134	−27	146	90
37	Azerbaijan	..	..	..	1,273	..	..	..	110	..	−379	..	84
38	Zimbabwe	1,714	2,372	1,895	2,836	8	−2	23	41	−149	−425	419	888
39	Guinea	..	714	..	1,090	..	−10	..	189	..	−197	..	87
40	Honduras	967	1,667	1,306	2,110	0	120	22	123	−317	−201	159	270
41	Senegal	830	1,501	1,337	1,898	−15	13	135	375	−387	3	25	283
42	China *	24,729	152,431	19,541	152,248	538	350	−52	1,085	5,674	1,618	10,091	80,288
43	Cameroon	1,813	2,070	2,478	2,250	..	..	−17	9	−682	−171	206	15
44	Côte d'Ivoire	3,640	4,527	4,761	4,502	−716	−449	10	155	−1,826	−269	46	546
45	Albania	386	376	375	865	0	385	6	93	16	−12	..	265
46	Congo	1,029	1,252	1,195	1,825	−38	−27	37	29	−167	−570	93	64
47	Kyrgyz Republic	..	340	..	490	..	..	..	43	..	−288	..	..
48	Sri Lanka	1,340	4,843	2,269	6,041	152	715	121	75	−657	−546	283	2,088
49	Armenia	..	301	..	741	..	12	..	148	..	−279	..	..
Middle-income economies													
Lower-middle-income													
50	Lesotho	363	663	482	1,021	0	0	175	471	56	108	50	457
51	Egypt, Arab Rep.	6,516	11,337	9,745	17,353	2,696	3,417	95	5,060	−438	−956	2,480	17,122
52	Bolivia	1,046	1,283	1,112	1,794	0	−1	60	226	−6	−218	553	1,005
53	Macedonia, FYR	..	1,321	..	2,184	..	..	..	..	..	..	..	275
54	Moldova	..	865	..	999	..	..	..	40	..	−95	..	240
55	Uzbekistan	..	3,746	..	3,253	..	..	..	..	..	−8	..	..
56	Indonesia	24,878	52,505	25,694	60,367	0	629	250	210	−566	−7,023	6,803	14,908
57	Philippines	7,997	32,862	10,348	35,722	202	296	232	584	−1,917	−1,980	3,978	7,757
58	Morocco	3,270	9,118	5,807	12,900	989	1,890	141	371	−1,407	−1,521	814	3,874
59	Syrian Arab Republic	2,568	5,929	4,610	6,406	774	385	1,520	532	251	440	828	..
60	Papua New Guinea	1,089	3,014	1,561	2,415	0	0	184	75	−289	674	458	267
61	Bulgaria	9,443	6,680	8,547	6,478	0	0	58	132	954	334	..	..
62	Kazakstan	..	5,296	..	5,874	..	..	..	59	..	−519	..	1,660
63	Guatemala	1,834	2,868	2,107	3,933	0	350	110	144	−163	−572	753	783
64	Ecuador	2,975	5,298	3,647	6,351	0	0	30	231	−642	−822	1,257	1,788
65	Dominican Republic	1,313	5,106	2,237	6,100	183	795	21	−266	−720	−125	279	373
66	Romania	12,160	9,094	14,580	10,799	0	3	0	360	−2,420	−1,342	2,511	2,624
67	Jamaica	1,422	3,327	1,678	4,107	51	414	70	121	−136	−245	105	681
68	Jordan	1,782	3,606	3,318	5,200	..	..	594	1,118	−942	−476	1,745	2,279
69	Algeria	14,500	10,954	14,552	12,512	241	..	60	168	249	−2,310	7,064	4,164
70	El Salvador	1,271	2,103	1,289	3,562	11	1,061	41	328	34	−70	382	940
71	Ukraine	..	17,337	..	18,961	..	..	..	472	..	−1,152	..	1,069
72	Paraguay	781	..	1,399	4,173	2	..	−2	42	−618	−1,473	783	1,040
*	Data for Taiwan, China	22,627	134,484	23,445	126,626	..	..	−95	−2,202	−913	5,656	4,055	95,559

Note: For data comparability and coverage, see the technical notes. Figures in italics are for years other than those specified.

		Exports of goods, services, and income (million $)		Imports of goods, services, and income (million $)		Current transfers				Current account balance (million $)		Gross international reserves (million $)	
						Net workers' remittances (million $)		Other net transfers (million $)					
		1980	1995	1980	1995	1980	1995	1980	1995	1980	1995	1980	1995
73	Tunisia	3,356	8,098	4,119	9,646	304	659	106	152	−353	−737	700	1,689
74	Lithuania	..	3,242	..	3,966	..	1	..	109		−614	..	829
75	Colombia	5,860	14,794	6,231	19,588	68	172	97	506	−206	−4,116	6,474	8,205
76	Namibia	..	1,899	..	2,082	..	4	..	230		50	..	225
77	Belarus	..	2,773	..	3,209	..	..	..	182		−254	..	377
78	Russian Federation	..	95,100	..	85,800	..	..	..	304		9,604	..	18,024
79	Latvia	..	2,151	..	2,246	..	..	..	68		−27	..	602
80	Peru	4,832	7,382	5,080	12,097	0	334	147	157	−101	−4,223	2,804	8,653
81	Costa Rica	1,219	3,945	1,897	4,241	0	0	15	154	−664	−143	197	1,060
82	Lebanon	..	1,512	..	6,953	..	..	..	350		−5,092	7,025	8,100
83	Thailand	8,575	74,093	10,861	88,134	0	0	210	487	−2,076	−13,554	3,026	36,939
84	Panama	7,853	9,542	8,225	9,584	−36	−7	76	210	−331	−141	117	782
85	Turkey	3,672	38,069	9,251	44,904	2,071	3,327	100	1,169	−3,408	−2,339	3,298	13,891
86	Poland	16,200	33,169	20,338	36,929	0	35	721	−520	−3,417	−4,245	574	14,957
87	Estonia	..	2,801	..	3,112	..	−1	..	127		−184	..	583
88	Slovak Republic	..	11,185	..	10,629	..	0	..	93		648	..	3,863
89	Botswana	748	2,908	954	2,539	−17	−157	72	129	−151	342	344	4,764
90	Venezuela	22,232	22,406	17,065	20,262	−418	−173	−21	284	4,728	2,255	13,360	10,715
Upper-middle-income													
91	South Africa	29,258	33,471	25,989	36,994	0	0	239	23	3,508	−3,500	7,888	4,464
92	Croatia	..	7,375	..	9,733	..	..	..	646		−1,712	..	2,036
93	Mexico	23,987	93,529	35,243	98,145	687	3,672	147	290	−10,422	−654	4,175	17,046
94	Mauritius	579	2,402	718	2,525	0	0	22	101	−117	−22	113	887
95	Gabon	2,434	2,793	1,926	2,415	−143	−152	19	0	384	378	115	153
96	Brazil	23,275	56,098	36,250	77,855	−80	2,773	224	848	−12,831	−18,136	6,875	51,477
97	Trinidad and Tobago	3,371	2,875	2,972	2,577	1	30	−43	−35	357	294	2,813	379
98	Czech Republic	..	29,399	..	31,345	..	0	..	572		−1,374	..	14,613
99	Malaysia	14,836	84,212	15,100	92,440	0	0	−2	163	−266	−4,147	5,755	24,699
100	Hungary	9,780	17,933	10,374	21,528	0	−14	63	1,073	−531	−2,535	..	12,095
101	Chile	6,276	20,014	8,360	20,214	0	0	113	357	−1,971	157	4,128	14,860
102	Oman	3,852	6,403	2,650	5,671	−362	−1,740	102	29	942	−979	704	1,251
103	Uruguay	1,594	3,679	2,312	4,069	0	0	9	32	−709	−358	2,401	1,813
104	Saudi Arabia	114,208	55,091	62,710	45,583	−4,094	−16,616	−5,901	−1,000	41,503	−8,108	26,129	10,399
105	Argentina	11,202	28,052	15,999	30,874	0	0	23	432	−4,774	−2,390	9,297	15,979
106	Slovenia	..	10,731	..	10,812	..	53	..	−8		−37	..	1,821
107	Greece	8,374	16,835	11,670	27,707	1,066	2,982	21	5,026	−2,209	−2,864	3,607	16,119
Low- and middle-income													
Sub-Saharan Africa													
East Asia and Pacific													
South Asia													
Europe and Central Asia													
Middle East and N. Africa													
Latin America and Caribbean													
High-income economies													
108	Korea, Rep.	22,477	151,826	28,342	160,490	96	486	496	−73	−5,273	−8,251	3,101	32,804
109	Portugal	6,846	35,666	10,916	43,026	2,928	3,348	78	3,783	−1,064	−229	13,863	22,063
110	Spain	33,863	146,042	41,089	149,863	1,647	2,119	−1	2,983	−5,580	1,280	20,474	40,531
111	New Zealand	6,561	18,572	7,630	22,428	143	174	−47	−96	−973	−3,778	365	4,410
112	Ireland	10,418	53,126	13,754	53,530	0	..	1,204	1,782	−2,132	1,379	3,071	8,770
113	† Israel	9,858	28,659	13,458	39,750	0	0	2,729	5,600	−871	−5,491	4,055	8,123
114	† Kuwait	27,344	19,276	10,463	13,232	−692	−1,347	−888	−499	15,302	4,198	5,425	4,543
115	† United Arab Emirates	..	..	..	..	..	..	..	..	..	..	2,355	7,778
116	United Kingdom	201,137	458,728	189,683	452,359	0	..	−4,592	−11,001	6,862	−4,632	31,755	49,144
117	Australia	26,668	74,417	30,702	93,535	..	..	−416	−67	−4,774	−19,184	6,366	14,952
118	Italy	104,979	330,286	116,668	299,954	1,609	98	−507	−4,724	−10,587	25,706	62,428	60,690
119	Canada	77,980	224,135	79,845	232,458	..	..	173	−370	−1,691	−8,693	15,462	16,369
120	Finland	17,332	50,798	18,620	44,813	0	..	−114	−343	−1,403	5,642	2,451	10,657
121	† Hong Kong	24,190	219,346	25,448	219,500	..	..	..	..	−1,258	..	..	..
122	Sweden	39,388	109,063	42,495	101,439	0	106	−1,224	−3,098	−4,331	4,633	6,996	25,909
123	Netherlands	103,143	250,990	102,850	228,460	−320	−423	−828	−5,916	−855	16,191	37,549	47,162
124	Belgium[b]	88,925	305,010	92,625	286,809	−270	−393	−961	−2,848	−4,931	14,960	27,974	24,120
125	France	174,118	498,203	174,156	475,234	−2,591	−1,364	−1,578	−5,162	−4,208	16,443	75,592	58,510
126	† Singapore	25,239	159,437	26,695	143,456	0	0	−106	−888	−1,563	15,093	6,567	68,695
127	Austria	29,152	106,474	32,951	110,085	−67	28	1	−1,531	−3,865	−5,113	17,725	23,369
128	United States	344,470	969,220	333,820	1,082,260	−810	−12,230	−7,690	−22,960	2,150	−148,230	171,413	175,996
129	Germany[c]	238,177	706,502	238,524	686,512	−4,437	−5,305	−8,422	−35,661	−13,205	−20,976	104,702	121,816
130	Denmark	23,176	92,772	24,891	90,398	0	0	−161	−961	−1,875	1,413	4,347	11,652
131	Norway	28,252	50,837	26,658	45,573	−23	−236	−493	−1,384	1,079	3,645	6,746	22,976
132	Japan	158,230	687,136	167,450	568,143	0	..	−1,530	−7,747	−10,750	111,246	38,919	192,620
133	Switzerland	59,462	154,840	58,524	129,113	−603	−2,519	−537	−1,586	−201	21,622	64,748	68,620
World													

a. Data prior to 1992 include Eritrea. b. Includes Luxembourg. c. Data prior to 1990 refer to the Federal Republic of Germany before unification.

Table 17. External debt

| | | Total external debt (million $) | | External debt as percentage of | | | | Debt service as % of exports of goods and services | | Ratio of present value to nominal value of debt (%) | Multilateral debt as % of total external debt | |
| | | | | GNP | | Exports of goods and services | | | | | | |
		1980	1995	1980	1995	1980	1995	1980	1995	1995	1980	1995
	Low-income economies	106,209 t	534,794 t	16.3 w	38.7 w	96.8 w	183.9 w	9.6 w	15.4 w		17.2 w	25.5 w
	Excluding China and India	..	..	..	..		..	..	..		..	..
1	Mozambique	..	5,781	..	443.6	..	1,192.5	..	35.3	76.6	..	22.7
2	Ethiopia[a]	824	5,221	..	99.9	134.5	458.2	7.3	13.6	65.8	41.2	45.3
3	Tanzania	2,460	7,333	..	207.4	323.0	585.2	21.1	17.4	73.5	23.0	39.1
4	Burundi	166	1,157	18.2	110.1	..	829.3	..	27.7	45.2	35.7	80.1
5	Malawi	821	2,140	72.1	166.8	260.8	499.6	27.7	25.9	47.6	26.7	78.8
6	Chad	285	908	39.5	81.4	399.6	339.0	8.4	5.9	48.7	26.1	73.0
7	Rwanda	190	1,008	16.3	89.1	103.5	657.3	4.1	..	47.6	47.8	80.4
8	Sierra Leone	435	1,226	38.3	159.7	157.7	1,163.5	23.2	60.3	62.6	14.2	34.3
9	Nepal	205	2,398	10.4	53.3	85.4	198.0	3.3	7.8	49.2	62.0	81.3
10	Niger	863	1,633	34.5	91.2	132.8	571.7	21.7	19.8	62.2	16.5	53.2
11	Burkina Faso	330	1,267	19.5	55.0	88.0	346.1	5.9	11.1	51.0	42.8	77.6
12	Madagascar	1,241	4,302	31.1	141.7	239.3	562.2	20.3	9.2	74.1	14.7	39.2
13	Bangladesh	4,230	16,370	32.6	56.3	360.4	298.2	23.7	13.3	55.9	30.2	59.7
14	Uganda	689	3,564	54.6	63.7	208.1	555.1	17.3	21.3	52.4	11.5	61.8
15	Vietnam	..	26,495	..	130.2	..	396.0	..	5.2	88.0	..	1.2
16	Guinea-Bissau	145	894	137.8	353.7	..	1,874.3	..	66.9	65.1	20.1	56.1
17	Haiti	302	807	20.9	39.8	72.8	386.8	6.2	45.2	49.1	43.8	75.7
18	Mali	732	3,066	45.4	131.9	227.3	467.1	5.1	12.6	58.9	23.7	45.2
19	Nigeria	8,921	35,005	10.1	140.5	32.1	274.5	4.1	12.3	94.1	6.4	14.1
20	Yemen, Rep.	1,684	6,212	..	155.2	..	192.1	..	3.2	82.2	14.9	20.6
21	Cambodia	..	2,031	..	73.5	..	205.4	..	0.6	70.7	..	5.8
22	Kenya	3,383	7,381	48.1	97.7	164.1	248.2	21.0	25.7	74.1	18.6	39.5
23	Mongolia	..	512	..	61.5	..	100.2	..	9.1	64.2	..	33.2
24	Togo	1,052	1,486	95.9	121.2	181.3	464.5	9.0	5.7	61.7	11.3	48.4
25	Gambia, The	137	426	61.5	..	..	206.6	6.2	14.0	50.3	29.9	76.0
26	India	20,581	93,766	11.9	28.2	136.0	201.2	9.3	27.9	80.0	29.5	32.0
27	Central African Republic	195	944	24.4	..	94.8	403.9	4.9	6.8	53.4	27.4	67.2
28	Lao PDR	350	2,165	..	124.9	..	478.3	..	5.8	34.3	5.9	28.7
29	Benin	424	1,646	30.2	81.8	133.1	285.6	6.3	8.4	55.9	24.5	52.3
30	Nicaragua	2,192	9,287	108.5	589.7	426.5	1,272.7	22.3	38.7	88.2	19.2	16.0
31	Ghana	1,398	5,874	31.6	95.1	115.2	366.5	13.1	23.1	64.3	19.9	50.8
32	Zambia	3,261	6,853	90.7	191.3	200.7	528.7	25.3	174.4	72.4	12.2	31.9
33	Angola	..	11,482	..	274.9	..	314.3	..	12.5	94.6	..	1.7
34	Georgia	..	1,189	..	51.6	..	..	..	..	85.9	..	19.7
35	Pakistan	9,930	30,152	42.4	49.5	208.7	257.9	18.3	*35.3*	77.6	15.4	40.5
36	Mauritania	843	2,467	125.5	243.3	306.1	458.5	17.3	21.5	68.3	14.8	36.8
37	Azerbaijan	..	321	..	9.2	..	..	..	..	86.3	..	30.8
38	Zimbabwe	786	4,885	14.9	78.9	45.6	..	3.8	*25.6*	82.2	0.4	33.1
39	Guinea	1,134	3,242	..	91.2	..	453.4	..	25.3	64.9	11.5	45.2
40	Honduras	1,473	4,567	60.6	124.6	152.2	255.5	21.4	31.0	81.2	31.1	47.3
41	Senegal	1,473	3,845	50.5	82.3	162.7	224.3	28.7	18.7	65.3	17.8	48.4
42	China	4,504	118,090	2.2	17.2	..	77.3	..	9.9	91.4	0.0	13.8
43	Cameroon	2,588	9,350	37.9	124.4	140.7	338.3	15.2	20.1	80.0	16.7	17.9
44	Côte d'Ivoire	7,462	18,952	77.1	251.7	205.0	418.6	38.7	23.1	87.6	7.0	20.6
45	Albania	..	709	..	31.6	..	93.2	..	1.0	101.6	..	15.6
46	Congo	1,526	6,032	99.0	365.8	148.2	481.8	10.6	14.4	88.8	7.7	11.7
47	Kyrgyz Republic	..	610	..	20.2	..	..	..	4.8	73.9	..	29.9
48	Sri Lanka	1,841	8,230	46.1	64.4	123.4	140.3	12.0	7.3	67.7	11.7	34.7
49	Armenia	..	374	..	17.6	..	119.1	..	2.9	77.9	..	55.7
	Middle-income economies	509,503 t	1,530,883 t	22.4 w	39.9 w	84.6 w	142.6 w	13.6 w	17.4 w		5.6 w	10.4 w
	Lower-middle-income	..	..	..	..	..	..	..	..		..	..
50	Lesotho	72	659	11.4	44.6	19.8	108.8	1.5	6.0	58.4	56.0	69.6
51	Egypt, Arab Rep.	19,131	34,116	89.2	73.3	207.7	208.1	13.4	14.6	75.8	13.7	12.4
52	Bolivia	2,702	5,266	93.4	90.6	258.4	410.1	35.0	28.9	74.0	16.5	48.9
53	Macedonia, FYR	..	1,213	..	65.8	..	79.9	..	11.8	86.1	..	24.0
54	Moldova	..	691	..	17.8	..	79.9	..	8.0	90.0	..	31.3
55	Uzbekistan	..	1,630	..	7.5	..	35.3	..	6.0	91.7	..	15.1
56	Indonesia	20,938	107,831	28.0	56.9	..	202.9	..	30.9	95.7	8.8	18.6
57	Philippines	17,417	39,445	53.7	51.5	212.4	121.7	26.6	16.0	95.8	7.5	21.5
58	Morocco	9,247	22,147	50.7	71.0	213.9	200.9	33.4	32.1	90.0	7.8	30.8
59	Syrian Arab Republic	3,552	21,318	27.2	134.8	106.3	336.8	11.4	4.6	87.7	8.8	4.8
60	Papua New Guinea	719	2,431	28.9	53.3	66.0	80.6	13.8	20.8	84.6	21.2	38.3
61	Bulgaria	..	10,887	..	92.3	..	163.0	..	18.8	94.6	..	16.8
62	Kazakstan	..	3,712	..	23.5	..	60.8	..	4.6	92.6	..	10.6
63	Guatemala	1,166	3,275	14.9	22.3	63.6	101.5	7.9	10.6	85.4	30.0	28.8
64	Ecuador	5,997	13,957	53.8	84.1	201.6	263.4	33.9	26.7	90.1	5.4	21.4
65	Dominican Republic	2,002	4,259	31.2	36.5	133.8	128.5	25.3	7.8	90.5	10.2	24.0
66	Romania	9,762	6,653	..	19.5	80.3	73.1	12.6	10.6	94.0	8.3	25.5
67	Jamaica	1,913	4,270	78.0	134.9	129.9	113.2	19.0	17.9	91.2	14.9	28.5
68	Jordan	1,971	7,944	..	126.2	79.0	163.8	8.4	12.6	85.9	8.0	14.9
69	Algeria	19,365	32,610	47.1	83.1	129.9	264.2	27.4	38.7	76.9	1.5	11.6
70	El Salvador	911	2,583	26.1	27.0	71.1	81.6	7.5	8.9	81.4	28.3	52.4
71	Ukraine	..	8,434	..	10.7	..	48.6	..	5.3	93.4	..	7.3
72	Paraguay	955	2,288	20.7	29.4	122.2	53.8	18.6	..	92.7	20.2	34.0

Note: For data comparability and coverage, see the technical notes. Figures in italics are for years other than those specified.

		Total external debt (million $)		External debt as percentage of GNP		External debt as percentage of Exports of goods and services		Debt service as % of exports of goods and services		Ratio of present value to nominal value of debt (%)	Multilateral debt as % of total external debt	
		1980	1995	1980	1995	1980	1995	1980	1995	1995	1980	1995
73	Tunisia	3,527	9,938	41.6	57.3	96.0	113.2	14.8	17.0	89.8	12.3	37.2
74	Lithuania	..	802	..	10.1	..	24.7	..	1.4	87.9	..	20.7
75	Colombia	6,941	20,760	20.9	28.2	117.1	138.7	16.0	25.2	95.8	19.5	25.6
76	Namibia	..	..	..	..	..	..	..	..	..	..	..
77	Belarus	..	1,648	..	7.9	..	33.3	..	..	80.7	..	11.4
78	Russian Federation	..	120,461	..	37.6	..	126.7	..	6.6	92.7	..	1.7
79	Latvia	..	462	..	7.6	..	21.5	..	1.6	93.1	..	30.3
80	Peru	9,386	30,831	47.6	54.1	194.2	399.5	44.5	15.3	96.5	5.5	12.1
81	Costa Rica	2,744	3,800	59.7	42.5	225.2	96.3	29.1	16.4	93.0	16.4	35.5
82	Lebanon	510	2,966	..	25.5	..	152.7	..	13.1	97.2	15.2	6.7
83	Thailand	8,297	56,789	25.9	34.9	96.8	76.6	18.9	10.2	101.2	12.0	5.6
84	Panama	2,975	7,180	81.8	101.4	37.5	74.7	6.2	3.9	97.2	11.0	8.5
85	Turkey	19,131	73,592	27.4	44.1	333.1	177.8	28.0	27.7	91.3	11.2	12.2
86	Poland	..	42,291	..	36.1	..	127.3	..	12.2	84.5	..	4.9
87	Estonia	..	309	..	6.7	..	11.0	..	0.8	92.6	..	42.2
88	Slovak Republic	..	5,827	..	33.5	..	52.1	..	9.7	93.2	..	16.3
89	Botswana	147	699	16.3	16.3	19.6	24.0	2.1	3.2	80.0	57.4	68.0
90	Venezuela	29,344	35,842	42.1	49.0	132.0	160.0	27.2	21.7	95.5	0.7	9.2
Upper-middle-income		..	..	..	..	..	..	..	..		..	..
91	South Africa	..	..	..	..	..	..	..	..	..	..	..
92	Croatia	..	3,662	..	20.3	..	49.7	..	5.7	88.9	..	14.4
93	Mexico	57,378	165,743	30.5	69.9	232.4	170.5	44.4	24.2	96.1	5.6	11.2
94	Mauritius	467	1,801	41.6	45.9	80.8	75.0	9.0	9.0	90.6	16.6	15.0
95	Gabon	1,514	4,492	39.2	121.6	62.2	160.3	17.7	15.8	79.8	2.7	14.8
96	Brazil	71,520	159,130	31.2	24.0	306.5	269.8	63.3	37.9	95.4	4.3	5.9
97	Trinidad and Tobago	829	2,556	14.0	53.6	24.6	87.9	6.8	14.8	97.4	8.6	20.7
98	Czech Republic	..	16,576	..	37.0	..	67.4	..	8.7	97.2	..	6.1
99	Malaysia	6,611	34,352	28.0	42.6	44.6	40.8	6.3	7.8	90.5	11.3	4.8
100	Hungary	9,764	31,248	44.8	72.8	..	174.2	..	39.1	99.4	0.0	10.5
101	Chile	12,081	25,562	45.5	43.3	192.5	127.7	43.1	25.7	95.5	2.9	11.2
102	Oman	599	3,107	11.2	29.5	15.4	48.2	6.4	7.5	94.9	5.8	5.7
103	Uruguay	1,660	5,307	17.0	32.4	104.1	144.3	18.8	23.5	96.4	11.0	23.7
104	Saudi Arabia	..	..	..	..	..	..	..	..	..	..	..
105	Argentina	27,157	89,747	35.6	33.1	242.4	320.2	37.3	34.7	92.5	4.0	10.5
106	Slovenia	..	3,489	..	18.7	..	33.3	..	6.7	96.5	..	15.4
107	Greece	..	..	..	..	..	..	..	..	..	..	..
Low- and middle-income		615,711 t	2,065,676 t	21.0 w	39.6 w	86.5 w	151.4 w	13.0 w	17.0 w		7.6 w	14.3 w
Sub-Saharan Africa		84,119 t	226,483 t	30.6 w	81.3 w	91.7 w	241.7 w	9.8 w	14.5 w		9.0 w	24.3 w
East Asia and Pacific		64,600 t	404,458 t	17.3 w	32.9 w	81.8 w	98.3 w	11.5 w	12.8 w		8.4 w	13.3 w
South Asia		38,014 t	156,778 t	17.4 w	30.5 w	160.5 w	218.7 w	11.7 w	24.6 w		24.6 w	36.4 w
Europe and Central Asia		87,919 t	425,319 t	9.9 w	39.9 w	47.1 w	130.7 w	7.4 w	13.8 w		5.4 w	7.9 w
Middle East and N. Africa		83,793 t	216,046 t	18.3 w	37.3 w	41.1 w	133.4 w	5.7 w	14.9 w		6.7 w	10.6 w
Latin America and Caribbean		257,266 t	636,594 t	36.0 w	41.0 w	201.8 w	212.0 w	36.3 w	26.1 w		5.5 w	11.4 w
High-income economies												
108	Korea, Rep.											
109	Portugal											
110	Spain											
111	New Zealand											
112	Ireland											
113	† Israel											
114	† Kuwait											
115	† United Arab Emirates											
116	United Kingdom											
117	Australia											
118	Italy											
119	Canada											
120	Finland											
121	† Hong Kong											
122	Sweden											
123	Netherlands											
124	Belgium											
125	France											
126	† Singapore											
127	Austria											
128	United States											
129	Germany											
130	Denmark											
131	Norway											
132	Japan											
133	Switzerland											
World		..	..	..	..	..	..	..	..		..	..

a. Includes Eritrea.

Table 1a. Basic indicators for other economies

		Population (thousands) mid-1995	Surface area (thousands of sq. km)	GNP per capita[a] Dollars 1995	GNP per capita[a] Avg. ann. growth (%) 1985–95	PPP estimates of GNP per capita[b] US=100 1987	PPP estimates of GNP per capita[b] US=100 1995	PPP estimates of GNP per capita[b] Current int'l $ 1995	Poverty % of people living on less than $1 a day (PPP) 1981–95	Life expectancy at birth (years) 1995	Adult illiteracy (%) 1995
1	Afghanistan	23,481	652.09	c	..	..	..	..	..	44	69
2	American Samoa	57	0.20	d	..	..	..	..	..	..	..
3	Andorra	..	0.45	e	..	..	..	..	..	..	..
4	Antigua and Barbuda	65	0.44	d	..	..	..	..	..	75	..
5	Aruba	..	0.19	e	..	..	..	..	..	..	..
6	Bahamas, The	276	13.88	11,940	−0.8	68.8	54.5	14,710[f]	..	73	2
7	Bahrain	577	0.68	7,840	0.2	54.2	49.7	13,400[f]	..	72	15
8	Barbados	266	0.43	6,560	0.8	45.1	39.4	10,620[f]	..	..	3
9	Belize	216	22.96	2,630	3.9	17.0	20.0	5,400[f]	..	70	..
10	Bermuda	63	0.50	e	..	..	..	..	..	..	..
11	Bhutan	695	47.00	420	4.9	4.5	4.7	1,260[f]	..	..	58
12	Bosnia and Herzegovina	4,383	51.13	c	..	..	..	..	..	..	..
13	Brunei	285	5.77	e	..	..	..	..	..	75	12
14	Cape Verde	380	4.03	960	..	6.6	6.9	1,870[f]	..	65	28
15	Cayman Islands	..	0.26	e	..	..	..	..	..	..	..
16	Channel Islands	142	0.20	e	..	..	..	..	..	78	..
17	Comoros	499	2.23	470	−1.4	6.5	4.9	1,320[f]	..	56	43
18	Cuba	11,011	110.86	g	..	..	..	..	..	76	4
19	Cyprus	734	9.25	e	..	44.5	..	..	..	78	..
20	Djibouti	634	23.20	g	..	..	..	..	..	50	54
21	Dominica	73	0.75	2,990	4.1	..	..	..	..	73	..
22	Equatorial Guinea	400	28.05	380	..	..	..	..	..	49	..
23	Eritrea	3,574	124.80	c	..	..	..	..	..	48	..
24	Faeroe Islands	..	1.40	e	..	..	..	..	..	..	..
25	Fiji	775	18.27	2,440	2.0	19.1	21.4	5,780[f]	..	72	8
26	French Guiana	..	90.00	e	..	..	..	..	..	..	..
27	French Polynesia	225	4.00	e	..	..	..	..	..	70	..
28	Greenland	..	341.70	e	..	..	..	..	..	68	..
29	Grenada	91	0.34	2,980	..	..	..	..	..	..	..
30	Guadeloupe	424	1.71	d	..	..	..	..	..	75	..
31	Guam	149	0.55	e	..	..	..	..	..	73	..
32	Guyana	835	214.97	590	0.6	8.2	9.0	2,420[f]	..	66	2
33	Iceland	268	103.00	24,950	1.0	88.1	75.8	20,460	..	79	..
34	Iran, Islamic Rep.	64,120	1,648.00	g	−1.5	21.6	20.3	..	..	68	28
35	Iraq	20,097	438.32	g	..	..	..	..	..	66	42
36	Isle of Man	..	0.59	d	..	..	..	..	..	..	..
37	Kiribati	79	0.73	920	−0.6	..	..	..	..	..	..
38	Korea, Dem. Rep.	23,867	120.54	g	..	..	..	..	..	70	..
39	Liberia	2,733	97.75	c	..	7.0	..	..	..	54	..
40	Libya	5,407	1,759.54	d	..	43.9	..	..	..	65	..
41	Liechtenstein	..	0.16	e	..	..	..	..	..	..	..
42	Luxembourg	410	2.59	41,210	0.9	154.1	140.6	37,930	..	76	h
43	Macao	450	0.02	e	..	..	..	..	..	..	..
44	Maldives	253	0.30	990	5.9	7.5	11.4	3,080[f]	..	63	7
45	Malta	372	0.32	d	..	38.2	..	..	..	77	..
46	Marshall Islands	..	0.18	g	..	..	..	..	..	..	..
47	Martinique	380	1.10	e	..	..	..	..	..	77	..
48	Mayotte	..	0.37	d	..	..	..	..	..	..	..
49	Micronesia, Fed. Sts.	107	0.70	g	..	..	..	..	..	..	..
50	Monaco	..	0.20	e	..	..	..	..	..	..	..
51	Myanmar	45,106	676.58	c	..	..	..	..	..	59	17
52	Netherlands Antilles	200	0.80	e	..	..	..	..	..	77	..
53	New Caledonia	185	18.58	e	..	..	..	..	..	..	..
54	Northern Mariana Islands	..	0.48	e	..	..	..	..	..	..	..
55	Puerto Rico	3,717	8.90	d	..	41.8	..	..	..	75	..
56	Qatar	642	11.00	11,600	−4.2	85.4	65.6	17,690[f]	..	72	21
57	Reunion	653	2.51	e	..	..	..	..	..	74	..
58	São Tomé and Principe	129	0.96	350	−2.1	..	..	..	..	69	..
59	Seychelles	74	0.45	6,620	..	..	..	..	..	72	21
60	Solomon Islands	375	28.90	910	3.2	7.9	8.1	2,190[f]	..	63	..
61	Somalia	9,491	637.66	c	..	2.3	..	..	..	49	..
62	St. Kitts and Nevis	41	0.36	5,170	4.8	28.2	34.9	9,410[f]	..	69	..
63	St. Lucia	158	0.62	3,370	3.9	..	..	..	..	71	..
64	St. Vincent and the Grenadines	111	0.39	2,280	3.8	..	..	..	..	72	..
65	Sudan	26,707	2,505.81	c	..	8.1	..	..	..	54	54
66	Suriname	410	163.27	880	3.5	11.9	8.3	2,250[f]	..	70	7
67	Swaziland	900	17.36	1,170	−1.4	12.5	10.7	2,880	..	58	23
68	Tajikistan[i]	5,836	143.10	340	..	12.1	3.4	920	..	67	..
69	Tonga	104	0.75	1,630	0.5	..	..	..	..	69	..
70	Turkmenistan[i]	4,508	488.10	920	..	..	..	..	4.9	..	..
71	Vanuatu	169	12.19	1,200	−1.1	9.4	8.5	2,290[f]	..	..	..
72	Virgin Islands (U.S.)	99	0.34	e	..	0.0	..	..	..	76	..
73	West Bank and Gaza	..	6.10	g	..	..	..	..	..	..	..
74	Western Samoa	165	2.84	1,120	0.2	8.9	7.5	2,030[f]	..	68	..
75	Yugoslavia, Fed. Rep. (Serb./Mont.)	10,518	102.17	g	..	..	..	..	..	..	..
76	Zaire	..	..	120	..	..	..	490[f]	..	..	..

a. Atlas method; see the technical notes. b. Purchasing power parity; see the technical notes. c. Estimated to be low income ($765 or less). d. Upper middle income ($3,036 to $9,385). e. Estimated to be high income ($9,386 or more). f. The estimate is based on regression; others are extrapolated from the latest International Comparison Programme benchmark estimates. g. Estimated to be lower middle income ($766 to $3,035). h. According to UNESCO, illiteracy is less than 5 percent. i. Estimates for economies of the former Soviet Union are preliminary; their classification will be kept under review.

TECHNICAL
NOTES

These technical notes discuss the sources and methods used to compile the 124 indicators included in the 1997 Selected World Development Indicators. The notes are organized by table and, within each table, by indicator in order of appearance in the table.

The 133 economies covered in the main tables are listed in ascending order of gross national product (GNP) per capita. A separate table (Table 1a) shows basic indicators for an additional 76 economies that have sparse data or populations of fewer than 1 million.

Sources

The data in the Selected World Development Indicators are taken from *World Development Indicators 1997*. Except for a few corrections made to the data base after that volume went to press, they are identical in source and vintage to the data published there. Although some countries have produced revised statistical series since the publication of *World Development Indicators 1997*, those revisions are not included here. They will appear in the next edition of the *World Development Indicators*.

The World Bank draws on a variety of sources for the indicators published in the *World Development Indicators*. Data on external debt are reported directly to the World Bank by developing member countries, through the Debtor Reporting System. Other data are drawn mainly from the United Nations, its specialized agencies, the International Monetary Fund (IMF), and country reports to the World Bank. Bank staff estimates are also used to improve currentness or consistency. For most countries, national accounts estimates are obtained from member governments through World Bank economic missions. In some instances these are adjusted by Bank staff to ensure conformity with international definitions and concepts. Most social data from national sources are drawn from regular administrative files, special surveys, or periodic census inquiries. Citations of specific sources are included in the Key and Primary Data Documentation table and in the notes below.

Data consistency and reliability

Considerable effort has been made to standardize the data, but full comparability cannot be assured, and care must be taken in interpreting the indicators. Many factors affect availability, comparability, and reliability: statistical systems in many developing economies are still weak; statistical methods, coverage, practices, and definitions differ widely; and cross-country and intertemporal comparisons involve complex technical and conceptual problems that cannot be unequivocally resolved. For these reasons, although the data are drawn from the sources thought to be most authoritative, they should be construed only as indicating trends and characterizing major differences among economies rather than offering precise quantitative measures of those differences. Also, national statistical agencies tend to revise their historical data, particularly for recent years. Thus, data of different vintages may be published in different editions of World Bank publications. Readers are advised not to compare such data from different editions. Consistent time series are available on the *World Development Indicators 1997 CD-ROM*. In addition, data issues have yet to be resolved for the fifteen economies of the former Soviet Union: coverage is sparse, and the data are subject to more than the normal range of uncertainty.

Data in italics are for years or periods other than those specified: up to two years before or after the date shown for economic indicators, and up to three years for social indicators, because the latter tend to be collected less regularly and change less dramatically over short periods.

Ratios and growth rates

For ease of reference, data are often presented as ratios or rates of growth. The underlying absolute data are available on the *World Development Indicators 1997 CD-ROM*.

Unless otherwise noted, period-average growth rates are computed using the least-squares regression method (see Statistical methods below). Because this method takes into account all available observations in a period, the resulting growth rates reflect general trends and are not unduly influenced by exceptional values. To exclude the effects of inflation, constant-price economic indicators are used in calculating growth rates.

Constant-price series

To facilitate international comparisons and capture the effects of changes in intersectoral relative prices for the national accounts aggregates, constant-price data for most economies are first partially rebased to three sequential base years and then "chain-linked" together and expressed in prices of a common base year, 1987. The year 1970 is the base year for the period from 1960 to 1975, 1980 for 1976 to 1982, and 1987 for 1983 and beyond.

During the chain-linking procedure, components of GDP by industrial origin are individually rescaled and summed to provide the rescaled GDP. In this process a rescaling deviation may occur between constant-price GDP as measured by industrial origin and constant-price GDP as measured by expenditure. Such rescaling deviations are absorbed in private consumption expenditures, on the assumption that GDP by industrial origin is the more reliable estimate. Independent of the rescaling, value added in the services sector also includes a statistical discrepancy as reported by the original source.

Summary measures

The summary measures across countries for regions and income groups, presented in the blue bands in the tables, are calculated by simple addition when they are expressed as levels. Growth rates and ratios are usually combined by a base-year value-weighting scheme. The summary measures for social indicators are weighted by population or subgroups of population, except for infant mortality, which is weighted by the number of births. See the notes on specific indicators for more information.

For summary measures that cover many years, calculations are based on a uniform group of economies so that changes in the composition of the aggregate do not produce spurious changes in the indicator. Group measures are compiled only if data are available for a given year for at least two-thirds of the full group, as defined by the 1987 benchmarks. As long as that criterion is met, countries with missing data are assumed to behave like those that provided estimates. Readers should keep in mind that the summary measures are estimates of representative aggregates for each topic, and that nothing meaningful can be deduced about behavior at the country level by working back from group indicators. In addition, the

weighting process may result in discrepancies between subgroup and overall totals.

Table 1. Basic indicators

Basic indicators for economies with sparse data or with populations of fewer than 1 million are shown in Table 1a.

Population estimates for mid-1995 are based on the de facto definition of population, which counts all residents regardless of legal status or citizenship. Refugees not permanently settled in the country of asylum are generally considered to be part of the population of their country of origin.

Population estimates are derived from national censuses. Precensus and postcensus estimates are often based on interpolations or projections. The international comparability of population indicators is limited by differences in the concepts, definitions, data collection procedures, and estimation methods used by national statistical agencies and other organizations that collect the data. In addition, the frequency and quality of coverage of population censuses vary by country and region. For more information on the compilation of population data, see the notes to Table 4.

Surface area is measured in square kilometers and comprises land area and inland waters. Data on surface area come from the Food and Agriculture Organization (FAO) and are published in the FAO *Production Yearbook.*

Gross national product (GNP) per capita is the sum of gross value added by all resident producers, plus any taxes (less subsidies) that are not included in the valuation of output, plus net receipts of primary income (employee compensation and property income) from nonresident sources, divided by the midyear population and converted to U.S. dollars using the World Bank's Atlas method. This involves using a three-year average of exchange rates to smooth the effects of transitory exchange rate fluctuations. For further discussion of the Atlas method see Statistical methods below. The growth rate of GNP per capita is computed from GNP measured in constant 1987 prices using the least-squares growth rate method.

GNP per capita is estimated by World Bank staff based on national accounts data collected by World Bank staff during economic missions or reported by national statistical offices to other international organizations such as the Organization for Economic Cooperation and Development (OECD). For high-income OECD economies the data come from the OECD. GNP per capita in U.S. dollars is used by the World Bank to classify countries for analytical purposes and to determine eligibility for borrowing. For definitions of the income groups used in this book, see the table on Classification of Economies by Income and Region.

PPP estimates of GNP per capita are calculated by converting GNP to U.S. dollars using purchasing power parities (PPP) instead of exchange rates as conversion factors. The resulting estimates are expressed in international dollars, a unit of account that has the same purchasing power over total GNP as the U.S. dollar in a given year. The denominator is the midyear population estimate for the year shown.

Relative prices of goods and services not traded on international markets tend to vary substantially from one country to another, leading to large differences in the relative purchasing power of currencies and thus in welfare as measured by GNP per capita. The use of PPP conversion factors corrects for these differences and may therefore provide a better comparison of average income or consumption between economies. However, caution should be used in interpreting PPP-based indicators. PPP estimates employ price comparisons of comparable items, but not all items can be matched perfectly in quality across countries and over time. Services are particularly difficult to compare, in part because of differences in productivity. Many services—for example, government services—are not sold in markets in all countries, so they are compared using input prices (mostly wages). Because this approach ignores productivity differences, it may inflate estimates of real quantities in lower-income countries.

The source of PPP data is the International Comparison Programme (ICP), coordinated by the U.N. Statistical Division. The World Bank collects detailed ICP benchmark data from regional sources, establishes global consistency across the regional data sets, and computes regression-based estimates for nonbenchmark countries. For detailed information on the regional sources and compilation of benchmark data see World Bank 1993. For information on how regression-based PPP estimates are derived see Ahmad 1992.

The percentage of people living on less than $1 a day (PPP) at 1985 international (purchasing power parity) prices is a widely used measure of poverty. A person is said to be poor if he or she lives in a household whose total income or consumption per person is less than the poverty line. Although it is impossible to create an indicator of poverty that is strictly comparable across countries, the use of a standard, international poverty line helps to reduce comparability problems in several ways. In estimating living standards, nationally representative surveys have been used, conducted either by national statistical offices or by private agencies under government or international agency supervision. Whenever possible, consumption has been used as the welfare indicator for deciding who is poor. The measure of consumption is generally comprehensive, including that from own production as well as all food and nonfood goods purchased. When only household incomes

are available, the average level of income has been adjusted to accord with either a survey-based estimate of mean consumption (when available) or an estimate based on consumption data from national accounts.

Poverty measures are prepared by the Poverty and Human Resources Division of the World Bank's Policy Research Department. International poverty lines are based on primary household survey data obtained from government statistical agencies and World Bank country departments. The poverty measures are based on the most recent PPP estimates, from the latest version of the Penn World Tables (Mark 5.6a).

Life expectancy at birth is the number of years a newborn infant would live if prevailing patterns of mortality at the time of its birth were to stay the same throughout its life. Estimates of life expectancy are derived from vital registration systems or, in their absence, from demographic and household surveys using models to obtain age-specific mortality rates.

Adult illiteracy is the proportion of adults age 15 and above who cannot, with understanding, read and write a short, simple statement on their everyday life. Literacy and illiteracy are difficult both to define and to measure. The definition here is based on the concept of "functional" literacy. To measure literacy using such a definition requires census or sample survey measurements under controlled conditions. In practice, many countries estimate the number of illiterate adults from self-reported data or from estimates of school completion. Because of these problems, comparisons across countries—and even over time for one country—should be made with caution. Data on illiteracy rates are supplied by UNESCO (United Nations Educational, Scientific, and Cultural Organization) and published in its *Statistical Yearbook.*

Table 2. Macroeconomic indicators

Central government current deficit/surplus is defined as current revenue of the central government less current expenditure. Grants are not included in revenue. This is a useful measure of the government's own fiscal capacity. The overall deficit or surplus, including grants and the capital account, is shown in Table 14. The data come from the IMF's *Government Finance Statistics Yearbook.*

Money and quasi money comprise most liabilities of a country's monetary institutions to residents other than the central government. This definition of the money supply is sometimes referred to as M2. Money comprises currency held outside banks and demand deposits other than those of the central government. Quasi money comprises time and savings deposits and similar bank accounts that the issuer can exchange for money with little, if any, delay or penalty, and foreign currency deposits of residents other than those of the central government. Where nonmonetary financial institutions are important issuers of quasi-monetary liabilities, their liabilities may be included in quasi money.

The source of data on the money supply is the IMF's *International Financial Statistics*. Money and quasi money are the sum of IFS lines 34 and 35.

The *average annual nominal growth rate* of the money supply is calculated from year-end figures using the least-squares method. The average of the year-end figures for the specified year and the previous year is used to calculate the *average outstanding as a percentage of GDP*.

Nominal interest rates of banks show the deposit rate paid by commercial or similar banks for demand, time, or savings deposits and the lending rate charged by these banks on loans to prime customers. The data are of limited international comparability, partly because coverage and definitions vary. Interest rates are expressed in nominal terms; therefore much of the variation among countries stems from differences in inflation. The data come from *International Financial Statistics*, lines 60l and 60p.

Average annual inflation is measured by the rate of change in the GDP implicit deflator. The implicit deflator is calculated by dividing annual GDP at current prices by the corresponding value of GDP at constant prices, both in national currency. The least-squares method is used to calculate the growth rate of the GDP deflator for the period.

The GDP implicit deflator is the broadest-based measure of inflation, showing price movements for all goods and services produced in the economy, but like all price indexes it is subject to conceptual and practical limitations. Deflators for developing economies are estimated from national accounts data collected by the World Bank. Data for high-income economies are derived from data provided by the OECD.

Current account balance is the sum of net exports of goods, services, and income and net current transfers. Capital transfers are excluded. (See also Table 16.) The data come from the IMF's *International Financial Statistics* and from estimates provided by World Bank country teams.

Gross international reserves comprises holdings of monetary gold, special drawing rights (SDRs), the reserve position of members with the IMF, and holdings of foreign exchange under the control of monetary authorities. Gross international reserves in U.S. dollars are shown in Table 16. Reserve holdings as months of import coverage are calculated as the ratio of gross international reserves to the current U.S. dollar value of imports of goods and services, multiplied by 12.

The summary measures in this table are computed as the ratio of group aggregates for gross international reserves and total imports of goods and services in current dollars.

Net present value of external debt is the value of short-term debt plus the discounted sum of all debt service payments due over the life of existing loans, at current prices. The debt figures are converted into U.S. dollars from currencies of repayment at end-of-year official exchange rates. To calculate the ratio of debt to GNP, GNP is converted at official exchange rates or, in exceptional cases, by an alternative, single-year conversion factor determined by World Bank staff. (See also the notes to Tables 12 and 17.)

Table 3. External economic indicators

Net barter terms of trade measures the relative movement of export prices against that of import prices. Calculated as the ratio of a country's average export price index to its average import price index, this indicator shows changes relative to a base year (1987). The data come from the U.N. Conference on Trade and Development (UNCTAD) data base, the IMF's *International Financial Statistics,* and World Bank staff estimates. (See also Table 15.)

Trade is measured as the ratio of the sum of exports and imports of goods and services to the current value of GDP. The trade-GDP ratio is a commonly used measure of the openness of an economy or its integration with the global economy. The data come from the World Bank's national accounts data files.

Aggregate net resource flows is the sum of net flows of long-term debt (excluding use of IMF credits), official grants (excluding technical assistance), net foreign direct investment, and net portfolio equity flows. Total net flows of long-term debt are disbursements less repayments of principal on public, publicly guaranteed, and private nonguaranteed long-term debt. Official grants are transfers made by an official agency in cash or in kind, in respect of which no legal debt is incurred by the recipient. The data are taken from the World Bank's Debtor Reporting System and from the IMF's *International Financial Statistics.*

Net private capital flows consists of private debt and nondebt flows and bank and trade-related lending. Private debt flows include commercial bank lending, bonds, and other private credits. Nondebt private flows are made up of net foreign direct investment and portfolio investment. Foreign direct investment is investment made to acquire a lasting management interest in an enterprise operating in an economy other than that of the investor. It is the sum of net flows of equity capital, reinvested earnings, other long-term capital, and short-term capital as shown in the balance of payments. Portfolio investment flows include net non-debt-creating portfolio equity flows (the sum of country funds, depository receipts, and direct purchases of shares by foreign investors) and net portfolio debt flows (bond issues purchased by foreign investors).

The principal source of data on private capital flows is the World Bank's Debtor Reporting System. Additional data come from *International Financial Statistics* and World Bank data files.

Aid comprises financial assistance classified as official development assistance (ODA) or official aid (OA) by the Development Assistance Committee (DAC) of the OECD. ODA comprises loans and grants made on concessional financial terms by all bilateral official agencies and multilateral sources to promote economic development and welfare. Net disbursements equal gross disbursements less payments to the originators of aid for amortization of past aid receipts. To qualify as ODA, a transaction must meet the following tests: it is administered with the promotion of the economic development and welfare of developing countries as its main objective, and it is concessional in character and conveys a grant element of at least 25 percent. OA comprises assistance provided on ODA-like terms to the countries of Eastern Europe, the former Soviet Union, and other economies on the DAC's "part II" list. The data on aid are provided by the DAC and published in its annual report, *Development Co-operation*. Data for GNP are World Bank estimates.

Summary measures for aid as a percentage of GNP are computed from the ratio of group totals for aid and for GNP in current U.S. dollars.

Table 4. Population and labor force

Population estimates for mid-1995 come from a variety of sources, including the U.N. Population Division, national statistical offices, and World Bank country departments. The World Bank uses the de facto definition of a country's population, which counts all residents regardless of legal status or citizenship. However, refugees not permanently settled in the country of asylum are generally considered to be part of the population of their country of origin.

The notes to Table 1 provide additional information about population estimates. The Key and Primary Data Documentation table lists the date of the most recent census or demographic survey.

Average annual growth rate of population is computed using the exponential end-point method. See the section on Statistical methods for more information.

Population aged 15–64 is the age group generally considered to be the most economically active. In many developing economies, however, many children under 15 work full or part time. And in some high-income economies many workers postpone retirement past age 65.

Total labor force comprises those people who meet the International Labour Organization's definition of the economically active population: all people who supply labor for the production of goods and services during a specified period. It includes both the employed and the unemployed. Although national practices vary in the treatment of such groups as the armed forces and seasonal or part-time workers, in general the labor force includes the armed forces, the unemployed, and first-time job-seekers, but excludes homemakers and other unpaid caregivers and workers in the informal sector.

Average annual growth rate of the labor force is computed using the exponential end-point method. See the section on Statistical methods for more information.

Females as a percentage of the labor force shows the extent to which women are active in the labor force. Labor force estimates are derived by applying participation rates from the International Labour Organization to World Bank population estimates.

Agricultural labor force includes people engaged in farming, forestry, hunting, and fishing.

Industrial labor force includes people working in the mining, manufacturing, construction, and electricity, water, and gas industries.

Activity rates or labor force participation rates of the economically active population are compiled by the International Labour Organization from the latest national censuses or surveys and are published in its *Yearbook of Labour Statistics*. Labor force numbers in some developing countries reflect a significant underestimation of female participation rates. Estimates of the rural labor force may also fail to capture the extent of family and seasonal labor.

All summary measures are country data weighted by population or population subgroup.

Table 5. Distribution of income or consumption

Survey year is the year in which the underlying data were collected.

The *Gini index* measures the extent to which the distribution of income (or, in some cases, consumption expenditures) among individuals or households within an economy deviates from a perfectly equal distribution. A Lorenz curve plots the cumulative percentages of total income received against the cumulative number of recipients, starting with the poorest individual or household. The Gini index measures the area between the Lorenz curve and a hypothetical line of absolute equality, and is expressed as a percentage of the maximum area under the line. Thus a Gini index of zero represents perfect equality, and an index of 100 percent perfect inequality.

Percentage share of income or consumption is the share that accrues to subgroups of population indicated by deciles or quintiles. Percentage shares by quintiles may not sum to 100 because of rounding.

Inequality in the distribution of income is reflected in the percentage share of income or consumption accruing to segments of the population ranked by income or consumption levels. The segments ranked lowest by personal or family income typically receive the smallest share of total income. The Gini index provides a convenient summary measure of the degree of inequality.

Data on personal or household income or consumption come from nationally representative household surveys. The data sets refer to different years between 1985 and 1994. Footnotes to the survey year indicate whether the rankings are based on income or consumption per capita or, in the case of high-income economies, household income. Where the original data from the household survey were available, they have been used to directly calculate the income (or consumption) shares by quintile. Otherwise, shares have been estimated from the best available grouped data.

The distribution indicators for low- and middle-income economies have been adjusted for household size, providing a more consistent measure of income or consumption per capita. No adjustment has been made for geographic differences in the cost of living within countries, because the data needed for such calculations are generally unavailable. For further details on the estimation method for low- and middle-income economies, see Ravallion and Chen 1996.

Because the underlying household surveys differ in method and in the type of data collected, the distribution indicators are not strictly comparable across countries. These problems are diminishing as survey methods improve and become more standardized, but strict comparability is still impossible.

The following sources of noncomparability should be noted. First, the surveys differ as to whether they use income or consumption expenditure as the living standard indicator. For thirty-seven of the sixty-six low- and middle-income economies for which data are available, the data refer to consumption expenditure. Income is typically more unequally distributed than consumption. In addition, the definitions of income used in the surveys are usually very different from the economic definition of income (the maximum level of consumption consistent with keeping productive capacity unchanged). For these reasons, consumption is usually a much better measure. Second, the surveys differ as to whether they use the household or the individual as their unit of observation. Furthermore, household units differ in size and in the extent to which income is shared among members. Individuals differ in age and consumption needs. Where households are used as the observation unit, the deciles or quintiles refer to the percentage of households rather than of population. Third, the surveys differ according to whether they rank the units of observation by household or per capita income (or consumption).

World Bank staff have made an effort to ensure that the data for low- and middle-income economies are as comparable as possible. Whenever possible, consumption has been used rather than income. Households have been ranked by consumption or income per capita in forming the percentiles, and the percentiles are based on population, not households. The comparability of the data for high-income economies is more limited, because the unit of observation is usually a household unadjusted for size, and households are ranked according to total household income rather than income per household member. These data are presented pending the publication of improved data from the Luxembourg Income Study, which ranks households by the average disposable income per adult equivalent. The estimates in the table should therefore be treated with considerable caution.

Data on distribution for low- and middle-income economies are compiled by the Poverty and Human Resources Division of the World Bank's Policy Research Department, using primary household survey data obtained from government statistical agencies and World Bank country departments. Data for high-income economies are from national sources, supplemented by the Luxembourg Income Study 1990 data base, the Eurostat *Statistical Yearbook,* and the United Nations' *National Accounts Statistics: Compendium of Income Distribution Statistics* (1985).

Table 6. Health

Access to health care is measured by the share of the population for whom treatment of common diseases and injuries, including essential drugs on the national list, is available within one hour's walk or travel. Facilities tend to be concentrated in urban areas.

Access to safe water shows the percentage of the population with reasonable access to adequate amounts of safe water (including treated surface waters or untreated but uncontaminated water from sources such as springs, sanitary wells, and protected boreholes). In an urban area such a source may be a public fountain or standpost located not more than 200 meters away. In rural areas access implies that members of the household do not have to spend a disproportionate part of the day fetching water. The definition of safe water has changed over time.

Access to sanitation refers to the percentage of the population with at least adequate excreta disposal facilities that can effectively prevent human, animal, and insect contact with excreta.

The *infant mortality rate* is the number of deaths of infants under 1 year of age per thousand live births in a given year. The data are a combination of observed values and interpolated and projected estimates.

Prevalence of malnutrition is the percentage of children under age 5 whose weight for age is more than 2 standard deviations below the mean of the reference population. Weight for age is a composite indicator of weight for height (wasting) and height for age (stunting). Although this indicator does not distinguish wasting from stunting, it is useful for comparisons with earlier surveys, as weight for age was the first anthropometric measure in general use. The reference population, adopted by the World Health Organization (WHO) in 1983, consists of children in the United States who are assumed to be well nourished. For some countries, if weight for age cannot be estimated, the prevalence assessment for the country was estimated from survey data by the WHO. This approach has minor effects on the estimated rates, which the WHO considers generally comparable across countries.

Contraceptive prevalence rate is the proportion of women who are practicing, or whose husbands are practicing, any form of contraception. Contraceptive usage is generally measured for married women age 15 to 49. A few countries use measures relating to other age groups, especially 15 to 44. Data are mainly derived from demographic, health, and contraceptive prevalence surveys.

The *total fertility rate* represents the number of children that would be born to a woman were she to live to the end of her childbearing years and bear children at each age in accordance with prevailing age-specific fertility rates. The data are a combination of observed, interpolated, and projected estimates.

The *maternal mortality ratio* is the number of female deaths that occur during pregnancy and childbirth per 100,000 live births. Because deaths during childbirth are defined more widely in some countries, to include complications of pregnancy or the period after childbirth or of abortion, and because many pregnant women die from lack of suitable health care, maternal mortality is difficult to measure consistently and reliably across countries. Clearly, many maternal deaths go unrecorded, particularly in countries with remote rural populations. This may account for some of the low estimates shown in the table, especially for several African countries. The data are drawn from diverse national sources. Where national administrative systems are weak, estimates are derived from demographic and health surveys using indirect estimation techniques or from other national sample surveys. For a number of developing countries, maternal mortality estimates are derived by the WHO and the United Nations Children's Fund (UNICEF) using statistical modeling techniques.

All summary measures, except for infant mortality, are weighted by population or by subgroups of the population. Infant mortality is weighted by the number of births.

Table 7. Education

Primary school enrollment data are estimates of the ratio of children of all ages enrolled in primary school to the country's population of primary school-age children. Although many countries consider primary school age to be 6 to 11 years, others use different age groups. Gross enrollment ratios may exceed 100 percent because some pupils are younger or older than the country's standard primary school age.

Secondary school enrollment data are calculated in the same manner, and again the definition of secondary school age differs among countries. It is most commonly considered to be 12 to 17 years. Late entry of students as well as repetition and the phenomenon of "bunching" in final grades can influence these ratios.

Tertiary enrollment data are calculated by dividing the number of pupils enrolled in all postsecondary schools and universities by the population age 20 to 24, although people above and below this age group may be registered in tertiary institutions.

Percentage of cohort reaching grade 4 is the proportion of children starting primary school in 1980 and 1988 who continued to the fourth grade by 1983 and 1991, respectively. Figures in italics represent earlier or later cohorts.

Data on enrollment flows are compiled by UNESCO from reports by national authorities.

Adult illiteracy is defined as the proportion of the population age 15 years and older who cannot, with understanding, read and write a short, simple statement on their everyday life. This is only one of three widely accepted definitions, and its application is subject to qualifiers in a number of countries. The data are from the illiteracy estimates and projections prepared by UNESCO.

The summary enrollment measures in this table are weighted by population.

Table 8. Commercial energy use

Total energy use refers to domestic primary energy use before transformation to other end-use fuels (such as electricity and refined petroleum products) and is calculated as indigenous production plus imports and stock changes, minus exports and international marine bunkers. Energy consumption also includes products for nonenergy uses, mainly derived from petroleum. The use of firewood, dried animal excrement, and other traditional fuels, although substantial in some developing countries, is not taken into account, because reliable and comprehensive data are not available.

Energy use per capita is based on total population estimates in the years shown.

GDP per kilogram of commercial energy use is the U.S. dollar estimate of GDP produced (at constant 1987 prices) per kilogram of oil equivalent.

To calculate *net energy imports as a percentage of energy consumption,* both imports and consumption are measured in oil equivalents. A negative sign indicates that the country is a net exporter.

Data on commercial energy use come primarily from the International Energy Agency and the U.N. *Energy Statistics Yearbook.* They refer to commercial forms of primary energy—petroleum (crude oil, natural gas liquids, and oil from unconventional sources), natural gas, solid fuels (coal, lignite, and other derived fuels), and primary electricity (nuclear, hydroelectric, geothermal, and other)—all converted into oil equivalents. For converting nuclear electricity into oil equivalents, a notional thermal efficiency of 33 percent is assumed; hydroelectric power is represented at 100 percent efficiency.

Carbon dioxide emissions measures industrial contributions to the carbon dioxide flux from solid fuels, liquid fuels, gas fuels, gas flaring, and cement manufacture. The data are based on several sources as reported by the World Resources Institute. The main source is the Carbon Dioxide Information Analysis Center (CDIAC), Environmental Science Division, Oak Ridge National Laboratory.

CDIAC annually calculates emissions of carbon dioxide from the burning of fossil fuels and the manufacture of cement for most countries of the world. These calculations are based on data on the net apparent consumption of fossil fuels from the World Energy Data Set maintained by the U.N. Statistical Division, and from data on world cement manufacture based on the Cement Manufacturing Data Set maintained by the U.S. Bureau of Mines. Emissions are calculated using global average fuel chemistry and usage. Estimates do not include bunker fuels used in international transport because of the difficulty of apportioning these fuels among the countries benefiting from that transport. Although the estimates of world emissions are probably within 10 percent of actual emissions, estimates for individual countries may have larger error bounds.

Summary measures for total energy use and carbon dioxide emissions are simple totals. The summary growth rates are computed from the group totals using the least-squares method. For energy consumption per capita and carbon dioxide emissions per capita, population weights are used to compute group averages.

Table 9. Land use and urbanization

Cropland includes land used to cultivate temporary and permanent crops, temporary meadows, market and kitchen gardens, and land that is temporarily fallow. Permanent crops are those that do not need to be replanted after each harvest, excluding land used to grow trees for wood or timber.

Permanent pasture is land used for five or more years for forage, including natural crops and cultivated crops. Only a few countries regularly report data on permanent pasture, as this category is difficult to assess because it includes wild land used for pasture.

Other land includes forest and woodland and the land under natural or planted stands of trees, as well as logged-over areas that will be forested in the near future. It also includes uncultivated land, grassland not used for pasture, wetlands, wastelands, and built-up areas. Built-up areas are residential, recreational, and industrial lands and areas covered by roads and other fabricated infrastructure.

Data on land use are from the Food and Agriculture Organization (FAO), which gathers these data from national agencies through annual questionnaires and national agricultural censuses. However, countries sometimes use different definitions of land use. The FAO often adjusts the definitions of land use categories and sometimes substantially revises earlier data. Because data on land use reflect changes in data reporting procedures as well as actual land use changes, apparent trends should be interpreted with caution. Most land use data are from 1994.

Urban population is the midyear population of areas defined as urban in each country. The definition varies slightly from country to country.

Population in urban agglomerations of 1 million or more is expressed as the percentage of a country's population living in metropolitan areas that in 1990 had a population of 1 million or more people.

Estimates of the urban population come from the United Nations' *World Urbanization Prospects: The 1994 Revision.* To compute the growth rate of the urban population, the United Nations' ratio of urban to total population is first applied to the World Bank's estimates of total population (Table 4). The resulting series of urban population estimates are also used to compute the population in urban agglomerations as a percentage of the urban population. Because the estimates in this table are based on different national definitions of what is urban, cross-country comparisons should be made with caution.

The summary measures for urban population as a percentage of total population are calculated from country percentages weighted by each country's share in the aggregate population. The other summary measures are weighted in the same fashion, using the urban population.

Table 10. Forest and water resources

Forest areas refers to natural stands of woody vegetation in which trees predominate.

Annual deforestation refers to the permanent conversion of forestland to other uses, including shifting cultivation, permanent agriculture, ranching, settlements, or infrastructure development. Deforested areas do not include areas logged but intended for regeneration or areas degraded by fuelwood gathering, acid precipitation, or forest fires. The extent and percentage of total area shown refer to the average annual deforestation of natural forest area.

Estimates of forest area are derived from country statistics assembled by the FAO and the United Nations Economic Commission for Europe (UNECE). In 1993 new assessments were published for tropical countries by the FAO and for temperate zones jointly by the UNECE and the FAO—but with different definitions. The FAO defines natural forest in tropical countries either as closed forest, where trees cover a large portion of the ground with no continuous grass cover, or as open forest, a mix of forest and grassland with at least 10 percent tree cover and a continuous grass layer on the forest floor. The UNECE-FAO assessment defines a forest as land where tree crowns cover more than 20 percent of the area. Also included are open forest formations; forest roads and firebreaks; small, temporarily cleared areas; young stands expected to achieve at least 20 percent crown cover on maturity; and windbreaks and shelter belts.

Nationally protected areas refers to areas of at least 1,000 hectares that fall into one of five management categories: scientific reserves and strict nature reserves; national parks of national or international significance (not materially affected by human activity); natural monuments and natural landscapes with some unique aspects; managed nature reserves and wildlife sanctuaries; and protected landscapes and seascapes (which may include cultural landscapes). This table does not include sites protected under local or provincial law or areas where consumptive uses of wildlife are allowed. The data are subject to variations in definition and in reporting to the organizations, such as the World Conservation Monitoring Centre, that compile and disseminate them.

Annual freshwater withdrawal refers to total water withdrawal, not counting evaporation losses from storage basins. Withdrawals also include water from desalination plants in countries where that source is a significant part of all water withdrawal. Withdrawal data are for single years between 1970 and 1995. Withdrawals can exceed 100 percent of renewable supplies when extractions from nonrenewable aquifers or desalination plants are considerable or if there is significant water reuse. Data are expressed as totals and as a percentage of total freshwater resources, which include both internal renewable resources and, where noted in the table, river flows from other countries. Internal renewable water resources include flows of rivers and groundwater from rainfall in the country.

Freshwater withdrawal per capita is calculated by dividing a country's total withdrawal by its population in the year for which withdrawal estimates are available. For most countries, data on sectoral withdrawal per capita are calculated using sectoral withdrawal percentages estimated for 1987 to 1995. *Domestic use* includes drinking water, municipal use or supply, and use for public services, commercial establishments, and homes. *Other* withdrawals are those for direct industrial use, including withdrawals for cooling thermoelectric plants and for agriculture (irrigation and livestock production).

Data on annual freshwater withdrawal are subject to variation in collection and estimation methods but are indicative of the magnitude of water use in both total and per capita terms. These data, however, also hide what can be significant variations in total renewable water resources from one year to another. They also fail to distinguish the seasonal and geographic variations in water availability within a country. Because freshwater resources are based on long-term averages, their estimation explicitly excludes decade-long cycles of wet and dry. The data for water indicators were compiled by the World Resources Institute from various sources and published in *World Resources 1996–97*. The Département Hydrogéologie in Orléans, France, compiles water resource and withdrawal data from published documents, including national, U.N., and professional literature. The Institute of Geography at the National Academy of Sciences in Moscow also compiles global water data on the basis of published work and, where necessary, estimates water resources and consumption from models that use other data, such as area under irrigation, livestock populations, and precipitation. Data for small countries and countries in arid and semiarid zones are less reliable than those for larger countries and countries with more rainfall.

Table 11. Growth of the economy

Gross domestic product at purchasers' prices is the sum of the gross value added by all resident and nonresident producers in the economy plus any taxes and minus any subsidies not included in the value of the products. It is calculated without making deductions for depreciation of fabricated assets or for depletion and degradation of natural resources.

The *GDP deflator* is calculated implicitly as the ratio of current-price GDP to constant-price GDP. The GDP deflator is the most broadly based measure of changes in the overall price level. (See also the note to Table 2.)

Agriculture comprises value added from forestry, hunting, and fishing as well as cultivation of crops and livestock production. In developing countries with high levels of subsistence farming, much agricultural production is either not exchanged or not exchanged for money. This increases the difficulty of measuring the contribution of agriculture to GDP and reduces the reliability and comparability of such numbers.

Industry comprises value added in mining, manufacturing (also reported as a separate subgroup), construction, electricity, water, and gas.

Manufacturing refers to industries belonging to divisions 15–37 in the International Standard Industrial Classification, Revision 2.

Services includes value added in all other branches of economic activity, such as wholesale and retail trade (including hotels and restaurants), transport, and government, financial, professional, and personal services such as education, health care, and real estate services. Also included are imputed bank service charges, import duties, and any statistical discrepancies noted by national compilers as well as discrepancies arising from rescaling.

Exports of goods and services represents the value of all goods and other market services provided to the world. Included is the value of merchandise, freight, insurance, travel, and other nonfactor services. Factor and property income (formerly called factor services), such as investment income, interest, and labor income, is excluded. Transfer payments are excluded from the calculation of GDP.

Growth rates of GDP and its components are calculated using constant-price data in the local currency. Regional and income group growth rates are calculated after converting local currencies to U.S. dollars using the World Bank's International Economics Department (IEC) conversion factor. Growth rates are estimated by fitting a linear trend line to the logarithmic annual values of the given variable using the least-squares growth rate method. This produces an average growth rate that corresponds to a model of periodic compound growth. The least-squares growth rate method and the IEC conversion factor are described in the section on Statistical methods.

In calculating the summary measures, constant 1987 U.S. dollar values for each indicator are calculated for each year of the periods covered, and the values are aggregated across countries for each year. The least-squares procedure is used to compute the aggregate growth rates.

Table 12. Structure of the economy: production

The definitions of GDP and its components are those of the U.N. System of National Accounts (SNA), Series F, No. 2, Version 3. Version 4 of the SNA was completed only in 1993, and it is likely that many countries will continue to use the recommendations of Version 3 for the next few years. Estimates are obtained from national sources, sometimes reaching the World Bank through other international agencies but more often collected by World Bank staff. For definitions of specific components, see the technical note to Table 11.

National accounts data for developing countries are collected from national statistical organizations and central banks by visiting and resident World Bank missions. Data for industrial countries come from OECD data files.

For information on the OECD national accounts series see OECD, *National Accounts, 1960–1994,* volumes 1 and 2. The complete set of national accounts time series is available on the *World Development Indicators CD-ROM.*

World Bank staff review the quality of national accounts data and, in some instances, adjust national series. Because of the sometimes limited capabilities of statistical offices and basic data problems, strict international comparability cannot be achieved, especially in economic activities that are difficult to measure, such as parallel market transactions, the informal sector, and subsistence agriculture.

The figures for GDP are U.S. dollar values converted from domestic currencies using single-year official exchange rates. For a few countries where the official exchange rate does not reflect the rate effectively applied to actual foreign exchange transactions, an alternative conversion factor is used. Note that the table does not use the three-year averaging ("Atlas") technique applied to GNP per capita in Table 1.

Summary measures are computed from group aggregates of sectoral GDP in current U.S. dollars.

Table 13. Structure of the economy: demand

General government consumption includes all current expenditures for purchases of goods and services by all levels of government, but excluding most government enterprises. Most capital expenditures on national defense and security are regarded as a general government consumption expenditure.

Private consumption is the market value of all goods and services, including durable products (such as cars, washing machines, and home computers), purchased or received as income in kind by households and nonprofit institutions. It excludes purchases of dwellings but includes imputed rent for owner-occupied dwellings. In practice, it may include any statistical discrepancy in the use of resources.

Gross domestic investment consists of outlays on additions to the fixed assets of the economy plus net changes in the level of inventories.

Gross domestic saving is calculated by deducting total consumption from GDP.

Exports of goods and services represents the value of all goods and other market services provided to the world. Included is the value of merchandise, freight, insurance, travel, and other nonfactor services. Factor and property income (formerly called factor services), such as investment income, interest, and labor income, is excluded. Transfer payments are excluded from the calculation of GDP.

Resource balance is the difference between exports of goods and services and imports of goods and services.

Summary measures in this table are computed from group aggregates of sectoral GDP in current U.S. dollars.

Table 14. Central government budget

Total revenue is derived from tax and nontax sources. *Tax revenue* comprises compulsory, unrequited, nonrepayable receipts for public purposes. It includes interest collected on tax arrears and penalties collected on nonpayment or late payment of taxes, and is shown net of refunds and other corrective transactions. *Nontax revenue* comprises receipts that are not compulsory, nonrepayable payments for public purposes, such as fines, administrative fees, or entrepreneurial income from government ownership of property. Proceeds of grants and borrowing, funds arising from the repayment of previous lending by governments, incurrence of liabilities, and proceeds from the sale of capital assets are not included.

Total expenditure comprises expenditures by all government offices, departments, establishments, and other bodies that are agencies or instruments of the central authority of a country. It includes both *current* and *capital* (development) expenditures.

Defense comprises all expenditures, whether by defense or other departments, on the maintenance of military forces, including the purchase of military supplies and equipment, construction, recruiting, and training. Also in this category are closely related items such as military aid programs. Defense does not include expenditure on public order and safety, which is classified separately.

Social services comprises expenditures on health, education, housing, welfare, social security, and community amenities. It also covers compensation for loss of income to the sick and temporarily disabled; payments to the elderly, the permanently disabled, and the unemployed; family, maternity, and child allowances; and the cost of welfare services, such as care of the aged, the disabled, and children. Many expenditures relevant to environmental defense, such as pollution abatement, water supply, sanitary affairs, and refuse collection, are included indistinguishably in this category.

Overall deficit/surplus is defined as current and capital revenue and official grants received, less total expenditure and lending minus repayments. This is a broader concept than the current government deficit or surplus shown in Table 2.

Because of differences in coverage of available data, the individual components of central government expenditure and revenue shown may not be strictly comparable across all economies.

Inadequate statistical coverage of state, provincial, and local governments requires the use of central government data; this may seriously understate or distort the statistical portrayal of the allocation of resources for various purposes, especially in countries where lower levels of government have considerable autonomy and are responsible for many economic and social services. In addition, "central government" can mean either of two accounting concepts: consolidated or budgetary. For most countries, central government finance data have been consolidated into one overall account, but for others only the budgetary central government accounts are available. Because budgetary accounts do not always include all central government units, the overall picture of central government activities is usually incomplete. The concept employed by the reporting country is noted in the Key and Primary Data Documentation table.

In general, the data presented, especially those for social services, are not comparable across countries. In many economies, private health and education services are substantial; in others, public services represent the major component of total expenditure but may be financed by lower levels of government. Caution should therefore be exercised in using the data for cross-country comparisons.

Data on central government revenues and expenditures are from the IMF's *Government Finance Statistics Yearbook* (1995) and IMF data files. The accounts of each country are reported using the system of common definitions and classifications found in the IMF's *A Manual on Government Finance Statistics* (1986). For complete and authoritative explanations of concepts, definitions, and data sources, see these IMF sources.

Table 15. Exports and imports of merchandise

Merchandise *exports* and *imports,* with some exceptions, covers international movements of goods across customs' borders; trade in services is not included. Exports are valued f.o.b. (free on board) and imports c.i.f. (cost plus insurance and freight) unless otherwise specified in the foregoing sources. These values are in current U.S. dollars.

The categorization of exports and imports follows the Standard International Trade Classification (SITC), Series M, No. 34, Revision 1. *Manufactures* are commodities classified in Sections 5 through 9, excluding Division 68 (nonferrous metals). *Food* commodities are those in SITC Sections 0, 1, and 4 and Division 22 (food and live animals, beverages and tobacco, animal and vegetable oils and fats, oilseeds, oil nuts, and oil kernels). *Fuels* are the commodities in SITC Section 3 (mineral fuels, lubricants, and related materials). For some countries, data for certain commodity categories are unavailable.

Average annual growth rates of exports and imports are calculated from values at constant prices, which are derived from current values deflated by the relevant price index. The World Bank uses the price indexes produced by UNCTAD for low- and middle-income economies, and those presented in the IMF's *International Financial Statistics* for high-income economies. These growth rates can differ from those derived from national sources because national price indexes may use different base years and weighting procedures from those used by UNCTAD or the IMF.

The main source of current trade values is the UNCTAD trade data base, supplemented by the data from the IMF's *International Financial Statistics,* the U.N.'s Commodity Trade (COMTRADE) data base, and World Bank estimates. The shares in these tables are derived from trade values in current dollars reported in the UNCTAD trade data system, supplemented by data from the U.N. COMTRADE system.

The summary measures for the growth rates are calculated by aggregating the 1987 constant U.S. dollar price series for each year and then applying the least-squares growth rate procedure for the periods shown.

Table 16. Balance of payments

Exports and *imports of goods, services, and income* comprise all transactions involving a change of ownership of goods and services between residents of a country and the rest of the world, including merchandise, services, and income. Receipts of compensation to employees by, and investment income from, nonresident entities are treated as exports; payments to residents by nonresidents are treated as imports.

Net workers' remittances covers payments and receipts of income by migrants who are employed or expect to be employed for more than a year in their new economy, where they are considered residents. These remittances are classified as private unrequited transfers, whereas those derived from shorter-term stays are included in services as labor income. The distinction accords with internationally agreed guidelines, but some developing countries classify workers' remittances as a factor income receipt (hence a component of GNP). The World Bank adheres to international guidelines in defining GNP, and therefore its definitions may differ from national practices.

Other net transfers comprises net unrequited transfers other than workers' remittances.

The *current account balance* is the sum of net exports of goods and services and net transfers.

Gross international reserves comprises holdings of monetary gold, special drawing rights (SDRs), the reserve position of members in the IMF, and holdings of foreign exchange under the control of monetary authorities. The gold component of these reserves is valued at year-end (December 31) London prices ($589.50 an ounce in 1980 and $386.75 an ounce in 1995). Because of differences in

the definition of international reserves, in the valuation of gold, and in reserve management practices, the levels of reserve holdings published in national sources may not be strictly comparable. The reserve levels for 1980 and 1995 refer to the end of the year indicated and are in current U.S. dollars at prevailing exchange rates. See Table 2 for reserve holdings expressed as months of import coverage.

The data for this table are based upon IMF data files. World Bank staff also make estimates and, in rare instances, adjust coverage or classification to enhance comparability between the national accounts and the balance of payments. Definitions and concepts are based on the IMF's *Balance of Payments Manual, Fifth Edition* (1993). Values are in U.S. dollars converted at official exchange rates.

The summary measures are computed from group aggregates for gross international reserves.

Table 17. External debt

Total external debt is the sum of public, publicly guaranteed, and private nonguaranteed long-term debt, use of IMF credit, and short-term debt. Long-term debt has three components: public, publicly guaranteed, and private nonguaranteed loans. Public loans are external obligations of public debtors, including the national government, its agencies, and autonomous public bodies. Publicly guaranteed loans are external obligations of private debtors that are guaranteed for repayment by a public entity. Private nonguaranteed loans are external obligations of private debtors that are not guaranteed for repayment by a public entity. Use of IMF credit denotes repurchase obligations to the IMF for all uses of IMF resources, excluding those resulting from drawings in the reserve tranche. It comprises purchases outstanding under the credit tranches, including enlarged access resources, and all special facilities (the buffer stock, compensatory financing, extended fund, and oil facilities), trust fund loans, and operations under the enhanced structural adjustment facilities. Use of IMF credit outstanding at year-end (a stock) is converted to U.S. dollars at the dollar-SDR exchange rate then in effect. Short-term debt is debt with an original maturity of one year or less. It includes interest arrears on long-term debt outstanding and disbursed that are due but not paid on a cumulative basis. Available data permit no distinction between public and private nonguaranteed short-term debt.

External debt as a percentage of GNP and of *exports of goods and services* are calculated in U.S. dollars. Workers' remittances are included in exports of goods and services.

Debt service as a percentage of exports of goods and services is the sum of principal repayments and interest payments on total external debt. It is one of several conventional measures used to assess a country's ability to service debt. Workers' remittances are included in exports of goods and services.

The *ratio of present value to nominal value of debt* is the discounted value of future debt service payments divided by the face value of total external debt. The present value of external debt is the discounted sum of all debt service payments due over the life of existing loans. The present value can be higher or lower than the nominal value of debt. The determining factors for the present value being above or below par are the interest rates on loans and the discount rate used in the present value calculation. A loan with an interest rate higher than the discount rate yields a present value that is larger than the nominal value of debt; the opposite holds for loans with an interest rate lower than the discount rate.

The discount rates used to calculate the present value are interest rates charged by OECD countries for officially supported export credits. The rates are specified for the Group of Seven (G-7) currencies: British pounds, Canadian dollars, French francs, German marks, Italian lire, Japanese yen, and U.S. dollars. International Bank for Reconstruction and Development (IBRD) loans and International Development Association (IDA) credits are discounted at the most recent IBRD lending rate, and IMF loans are discounted at the SDR lending rate. For debt denominated in other currencies, discount rates are the average of interest rates on export credits charged by other OECD countries. For variable rate loans, for which future debt service payments cannot be precisely determined, debt service is calculated using the end-1994 rates for the base period specified for the loan.

Multilateral debt as a percentage of total external debt conveys information about the borrower's receipt of aid from the World Bank, regional development banks, and other multilateral and intergovernmental agencies. Excluded are loans from funds administered by an international organization on behalf of a single donor government.

The data on debt in this table come from the World Bank Debtor Reporting System, supplemented by World Bank estimates. The system is concerned solely with developing economies and does not collect data on external debt for other groups of borrowers or for economies that are not members of the World Bank. Debt is stated in U.S. dollars converted at official exchange rates. The data on debt include private nonguaranteed debt reported by thirty developing countries and complete or partial estimates for an additional twenty that do not report but for which this type of debt is known to be significant.

The summary measures are taken from the World Bank's *Global Development Finance 1997*.

Statistical methods

This section describes the calculation of the least-squares growth rate, the exponential (end-point) growth rate, the Gini index, and the World Bank's Atlas methodology for estimating the conversion factor used to estimate GNP and GNP per capita in U.S. dollars.

Least-squares growth rate
The least-squares growth rate, r, is estimated by fitting a least-squares linear regression trend line to the logarithmic annual values of the variable in the relevant period. The regression equation takes the form:

$$\log X_t = a + bt,$$

which is equivalent to the logarithmic transformation of the geometric growth rate equation:

$$X_t = X_o (1 + r)^t.$$

In these equations, X is the variable, t is time, and $a = \log X_o$ and $b = \log(1 + r)$ are the parameters to be estimated. If b^* is the least-squares estimate of b, then the average annual growth rate, r, is obtained as [antilog $(b^*) - 1$] and is multiplied by 100 to express it as a percentage.

The calculated growth rate is an average rate that is representative of the available observations over the period. It does not necessarily match the actual growth rate between any two periods. Assuming that geometric growth is the appropriate way of modeling the data, the least-squares estimate of the growth rate is consistent and efficient.

Exponential end-point growth rate
The growth rate between two points in time for certain demographic data, notably labor force and population, is calculated from the equation:

$$r = \ln(p_n / p_1) / n$$

where p_n and p_1 are the last and first observations in the period, respectively, n is the number of years in the period, and ln is the natural logarithm operator.

This growth rate is based on a model of continuous, exponential growth. To obtain a growth rate for discrete periods comparable to the least-squares growth rate, one takes the antilog of the calculated growth rate and subtracts 1.

The Gini index
The Gini index measures the extent to which the distribution of income (or, in some cases, consumption expenditure) among individuals or households within an econ-

omy deviates from a perfectly equal distribution. A Lorenz curve plots the cumulative percentages of total income received against the cumulative percentage of recipients, starting with the poorest individual or household. The Gini index measures the area between the Lorenz curve and a hypothetical line of absolute equality, expressed as a percentage of the maximum area under the line. Thus a Gini index of zero presents perfect equality, whereas an index of 100 percent implies maximum inequality.

The World Bank employs a numerical analysis program, POVCAL, to estimate values of the Gini index; see Chen, Datt, and Ravallion 1992.

World Bank Atlas method

The Atlas conversion factor for any year is the average of a country's exchange rate (or alternative conversion factor) for that year and its exchange rates for the two preceding years, after adjustment for differences in rates of inflation between the country in question and the G-5 countries (France, Germany, Japan, the United Kingdom, and the United States). The inflation rate for the G-5 countries is represented by changes in the SDR deflators. This three-year averaging smoothes annual fluctuations in prices and exchange rates for each country. The Atlas conversion factor is applied to the country's GNP. The resulting GNP in U.S. dollars is divided by the midyear population for the latest of the three years to derive GNP per capita.

The following formulas describe the procedures for computing the conversion factor for year t:

$$e_t^* = \frac{1}{3}\left[e_{t-2}\left(\frac{p_t}{p_{t-2}} \Big/ \frac{p_t^{S\$}}{p_{t-2}^{S\$}} \right) + e_{t-1}\left(\frac{p_t}{p_{t-1}} \Big/ \frac{p_t^{S\$}}{p_{t-1}^{S\$}} \right) + e_t \right]$$

and for calculating GNP per capita in U.S. dollars for year t:

$$Y_t^\$ = (Y_t / N_t) / e_t^*$$

where:

Y_t = current GNP (in local currency) for year t;

p_t = GNP deflator for year t;

e_t = average annual exchange rate (units of national currency per U.S. dollar) for year t;

N_t = midyear population for year t;

$p_t^{S\$}$ = SDR deflator in U.S. dollar terms for year t.

Alternative conversion factors

The World Bank systematically assesses the appropriateness of official exchange rates as conversion factors. An alternative conversion factor is used when the official exchange rate is judged to diverge by an exceptionally large margin from the rate effectively applied to domestic transactions of foreign currencies and traded products; this is the case for only a small number of countries (see the Key and Primary Data Documentation table). Alternative conversion factors are used in the Atlas method and elsewhere in the World Development Indicators as single-year conversion factors.

DATA SOURCES

Ahmad, Sultan. 1992. "Regression Estimates of Per Capita GDP Based on Purchasing Power Parities." Policy Research Working Paper 956. World Bank, International Economics Department, Washington, D.C.

Bos, Eduard, My T. Vu, Ernest Massiah, and Rodolfo A. Bulatao. 1994. *World Population Projections, 1994–95 Edition.* Baltimore, Md.: Johns Hopkins University Press.

Council of Europe. 1995. *Recent Demographic Developments in Europe and North America.* Council of Europe Press.

Eurostat (Statistical Office of the European Communities). Various years. *Statistical Yearbook.* Luxembourg.

FAO (Food and Agriculture Organization). Various years. *Production Yearbook.* FAO Statistics Series. Rome.

IEA (International Energy Agency). 1996. *Energy Statistics and Balances of Non-OECD Countries 1993–94.* Paris.

———. 1996. *Energy Statistics of OECD Countries 1993–94.* Paris.

ILO. (International Labour Organisation). 1995. *Year Book of Labour Statistics.* Geneva.

———. 1995. *Labour Force Estimates and Projections, 1950–2010.* Geneva.

———. 1995. *Estimates of the Economically Active Population by Sex and Age Group and by Main Sectors of Economic Activity.* Geneva.

IMF. (International Monetary Fund). 1986. *A Manual on Government Finance Statistics.* Washington, D.C.

———. 1993. *Balance of Payments Manual. 5th ed.* Washington, D.C.

———. Various years. *Government Finance Statistics Yearbook.* Washington, D.C.

———. Various years. *International Financial Statistics.* Washington, D.C.

OECD. (Organization for Economic Cooperation and Development). 1988. *Geographical Distribution of Financial Flows to Developing Countries.* Paris.

———. 1996. *Development Co-operation: 1995 Report.* Paris.

———. 1996. *National Accounts 1960–1994.* Vol. 1, *Main Aggregates.* Paris.

———. 1996. *National Accounts 1960–1994.* Vol. 2, *Detailed Tables.* Paris.

———. Various years. *Development Co-operation.* Paris.

Ravallion, Martin, and Shaohua, Chen. 1996. "What Can New Survey Data Tell Us About Recent Changes in Living Standards in Developing and Transitional Economies?" World Bank, Policy Research Department, Washington, D.C.

U. S. Bureau of the Census. 1996. *World Population Profile.* Washington, D.C.: U.S. Government Printing Office.

UNCTAD (United Nations Conference on Trade and Development). Various years. *Handbook of International Trade and Development Statistics.* Geneva.

UNESCO (United Nations Educational, Scientific, and Cultural Organization). Various years. *Statistical Yearbook.* Paris.

UNICEF (United Nations Children's Fund). 1997. *The State of the World's Children 1997.* Oxford: Oxford University Press.

UNIDO (United Nations Industrial Development Organization). 1996. *International Yearbook of Industrial Statistics 1996.* Vienna.

United Nations. 1968. *A System of National Accounts: Studies and Methods.* Series F. No. 2. Rev. 3. New York.

———. 1985. *National Accounts Statistics: Compendium of Income Distribution Statistics.* New York.

———. 1994. *World Urbanization Prospects, 1994 Revision.* New York.

———. 1996. *World Population Prospects: The 1996 Edition.* New York.

———. Various years. *Energy Statistics Yearbook.* New York.

———. Various years. *Levels and Trends of Contraceptive Use.* New York.

———. Various issues. *Monthly Bulletin of Statistics.* New York.

———. Various years. *Population and Vital Statistics Report.* New York.

———. Various years. *Statistical Yearbook.* New York.

———. Various years. *Update on the Nutrition Situation.* Administrative Committee on Co-ordination, Subcommittee on Nutrition. Geneva.

———. Various years. *Yearbook of International Trade Statistics.* New York.

WHO. (World Health Organization). 1991. *Maternal Mortality: A Global Factbook.* Geneva.

———. Various years. *World Health Statistics.* Geneva.

———. Various years. *World Health Statistics Report.* Geneva.

World Bank. 1993. *Purchasing Power of Currencies: Comparing National Incomes Using ICP Data.* Washington, D.C.

———. 1997. *Global Development Finance 1997.* Washington, D.C.

World Resources Institute in collaboration with UNEP (United Nations Environment Programme) and UNDP (United Nations Development Programme). 1994. *World Resources 1994–95: A Guide to the Global Environment.* New York: Oxford University Press.

World Resources Institute, UNEP (United Nations Environment Programme), UNDP (United Nations Development Programme), and World Bank. 1996. *World Resources 1996–97: A Guide to the Global Environment.* New York: Oxford University Press.

Table 1. Classification of economies by income and region, 1997

| Income group | Subgroup | Sub-Saharan Africa | | Asia | | Europe and Central Asia | | Middle East and North Africa | | Americas |
		East and Southern Africa	West Africa	East Asia and Pacific	South Asia	Eastern Europe and Central Asia	Rest of Europe	Middle East	North Africa	
Low-income		Angola Burundi Comoros Eritrea Ethiopia Kenya Madagascar Malawi Mozambique Rwanda Somalia Sudan Tanzania Uganda Zaire Zambia Zimbabwe	Benin Burkina Faso Cameroon Central African Republic Chad Congo Côte d'Ivoire Equatorial Guinea Gambia, The Ghana Guinea Guinea-Bissau Liberia Mali Mauritania Niger Nigeria São Tomé and Principe Senegal Sierra Leone Togo	Cambodia China Lao PDR Mongolia Myanmar Vietnam	Afghanistan Bangladesh Bhutan India Nepal Pakistan Sri Lanka	Albania Armenia Azerbaijan Bosnia and Herzegovina Georgia Kyrgyz Republic Tajikistan		Yemen, Rep.		Guyana Haiti Honduras Nicaragua
Middle-income	Lower	Botswana Djibouti Lesotho Namibia Swaziland	Cape Verde	Fiji Indonesia Kiribati Korea, Dem. Rep. Marshall Islands Micronesia, Fed. Sts. Papua New Guinea Philippines Solomon Islands Thailand Tonga Vanuatu Western Samoa	Maldives	Belarus Bulgaria Estonia Kazakstan Latvia Lithuania Macedonia, FYR[a] Moldova Poland Romania Russian Federation Slovak Republic Turkmenistan Ukraine Uzbekistan Yugoslavia, Fed. Rep.[b]	Turkey	Iran, Islamic Rep. Iraq Jordan Lebanon Syrian Arab Republic West Bank and Gaza	Algeria Egypt, Arab Rep. Morocco Tunisia	Belize Bolivia Colombia Costa Rica Cuba Dominica Dominican Republic Ecuador El Salvador Grenada Guatemala Jamaica Panama Paraguay Peru St. Vincent and the Grenadines Suriname Venezuela
	Upper	Mauritius Mayotte Seychelles South Africa	Gabon	American Samoa Malaysia		Croatia Czech Republic Hungary Slovenia	Greece Isle of Man Malta	Bahrain Oman Saudi Arabia	Libya	Antigua and Barbuda Argentina Barbados Brazil Chile Guadeloupe Mexico Puerto Rico St. Kitts and Nevis St. Lucia Trinidad and Tobago Uruguay
Subtotal:	158	26	23	21	8	27	4	10	5	34

Table 1. *(continued)*

| Income group | Subgroup | Sub-Saharan Africa | | Asia | | Europe and Central Asia | | Middle East and North Africa | | Americas |
		East and Southern Africa	West Africa	East Asia and Pacific	South Asia	Eastern Europe and Central Asia	Rest of Europe	Middle East	North Africa	
High-income	OECD countries			Australia Japan New Zealand Korea, Rep.			Austria Belgium Denmark Finland France Germany Iceland Ireland Italy Luxembourg Netherlands Norway Portugal Spain Sweden Switzerland United Kingdom			Canada United States
	Non-OECD countries	Reunion		Brunei French Polynesia Guam Hong Kong Macao New Caledonia N. Mariana Islands Singapore OAE[c]			Andorra Channel Islands Cyprus Faeroe Islands Greenland Liechtenstein Monaco	Israel Kuwait Qatar United Arab Emirates		Aruba Bahamas, The Bermuda Cayman Islands French Guiana Martinique Netherlands Antilles Virgin Islands (U.S.)
Total:		210	27	23	34	8	27	28	14	5	44

a. Former Yugoslav Republic of Macedonia.
b. Federal Republic of Yugoslavia (Serbia/Montenegro).
c. Other Asian economies—Taiwan, China.

For operational and analytical purposes, the World Bank's main criterion for classifying economies is gross national product (GNP) per capita. Every economy is classified as low-income, middle-income (subdivided into lower-middle and upper-middle), or high-income. Other analytical groups, based on geographic regions, exports, and levels of external debt, are also used.

Low-income and middle-income economies are sometimes referred to as developing economies. The use of the term is convenient; it is not intended to imply that all economies in the group are experiencing similar development or that other economies have reached a preferred or final stage of development. Classification by income does not necessarily reflect development status.

Definitions of groups

These tables classify all World Bank member countries and all other economies with populations of more than 30,000.

Income group: Economies are divided according to 1995 GNP per capita, calculated using the *World Bank Atlas* method. The groups are: low-income, $765 or less; lower-middle-income, $766–$3,035; upper-middle-income, $3,036–$9,385; and high-income, $9,386 or more.

The estimates for the republics of the former Soviet Union are preliminary and their classification will be kept under review.

Distributors of World Bank Publications

Prices and credit terms vary from country to country. Consult your local distributor before placing an order.

ARGENTINA
Oficina del Libro Internacional
Av. Cordoba 1877
1120 Buenos Aires
Tel: (54 1) 815-8354
Fax: (54 1) 815-8156

AUSTRALIA, FIJI, PAPUA NEW GUINEA, SOLOMON ISLANDS, VANUATU, AND WESTERN SAMOA
D.A. Information Services
648 Whitehorse Road
Mitcham 3132
Victoria
Tel: (61) 3 9210 7777
Fax: (61) 3 9210 7788
E-mail: service@dadirect.com.au
URL: http://www .dadirect.com.au

AUSTRIA
Gerold and Co.
Weihburggasse 26
A-1011 Wien
Tel: (43 1) 512-47-31-0
Fax: (43 1) 512-47-31-29
URL: http://www .gerold.co/at.online

BANGLADESH
Micro Industries Development
  Assistance Society (MIDAS)
House 5, Road 16
Dhanmondi R/Area
Dhaka 1209
Tel: (880 2) 326427
Fax: (880 2) 811188

BELGIUM
Jean De Lannoy
Av. du Roi 202
1060 Brussels
Tel: (32 2) 538-5169
Fax: (32 2) 538-0841

BRAZIL
Publicacões Tecnicas Internacionais
  Ltda.
Rua Peixoto Gomide, 209
01409 Sao Paulo, SP.
Tel: (55 11) 259-6644
Fax: (55 11) 258-6990
E-mail: postmaster@pti.uol.br
URL: http://www .uol.br

CANADA
Renouf Publishing Co. Ltd.
5369 Canotek Road
Ottawa, Ontario K1J 9J3
Tel: (613) 745-2665
Fax: (613) 745-7660
E-mail: order .dept@renoufbooks.com
URL: http:// www .renoufbooks.com

CHINA
China Financial & Economic
  Publishing House
8, Da Fo Si Dong Jie
Beijing
Tel: (86 10) 6333-8257
Fax: (86 10) 6401-7365

COLOMBIA
Infoenlace Ltda.
Carrera 6 No. 51-21
Apartado Aereo 34270
Santafé de Bogotá, D.C.
Tel: (57 1) 285-2798
Fax: (57 1) 285-2798

COTE D'IVOIRE
Center d'Edition et de Diffusion
Africaines (CEDA)
04 B.P. 541
Abidjan 04
Tel: (225) 24 6510;24 6511
Fax: (225) 25 0567

CYPRUS
Center for Applied Research
Cyprus College
6, Diogenes Street, Engomi
P.O. Box 2006
Nicosia
Tel: (357 2) 44-1730
Fax: (357 2) 46-2051

CZECH REPUBLIC
National Information Center
prodejna, Konviktska 5
CS – 113 57 Prague 1
Tel: (42 2) 2422-9433
Fax: (42 2) 2422-1484
URL: http://www .nis.cz/

DENMARK
SamfundsLitteratur
Rosenoerns Allé 11
DK-1970 Frederiksberg C
Tel: (45 31) 351942
Fax: (45 31) 357822

EGYPT, ARAB REPUBLIC OF
Al Ahram Distribution Agency
Al Galaa Street
Cairo
Tel: (20 2) 578-6083
Fax: (20 2) 578-6833

The Middle East Observer
41, Sherif Street
Cairo
Tel: (20 2) 393-9732
Fax: (20 2) 393-9732

FINLAND
Akateeminen Kirjakauppa
P.O. Box 128
FIN-00101 Helsinki
Tel: (358 0) 121-4418
Fax: (358 0) 121-4435
E-mail: akatilaus@stockmann.fi
URL: http://www .akateeminen.com/

FRANCE
World Bank Publications
66, avenue d'Iéna
75116 Paris
Tel: (33 1) 40-69-30-56/57
Fax: (33 1) 40-69-30-68

GERMANY
UNO-Verlag
Poppelsdorfer Allee 55
53115 Bonn
Tel: (49 228) 212940
Fax: (49 228) 217492

GREECE
Papasotiriou S.A.
35, Stournara Str.
106 82 Athens
Tel: (30 1) 364-1826
Fax: (30 1) 364-8254

HAITI
Culture Diffusion
5, Rue Capois
C.P. 257
Port-au-Prince
Tel: (509 1) 3 9260

HONG KONG, MACAO
Asia 2000 Ltd.
Sales & Circulation Department
Seabird House, unit 1101-02
22-28 Wyndham Street, Central
Hong Kong
Tel: (852) 2530-1409
Fax: (852) 2526-1107
E-mail: sales@asia2000.com.hk
URL: http://www .asia2000.com.hk

INDIA
Allied Publishers Ltd.
751 Mount Road
Madras - 600 002
Tel: (91 44) 852-3938
Fax: (91 44) 852-0649

INDONESIA
Pt. Indira Limited
Jalan Borobudur 20
P.O. Box 181
Jakarta 10320
Tel: (62 21) 390-4290
Fax: (62 21) 421-4289

IRAN
Ketab Sara Co. Publishers
Khaled Eslamboli Ave.,
6th Street
Kusheh Delafrooz No. 8
P.O. Box 15745-733
Tehran
Tel: (98 21) 8717819; 8716104
Fax: (98 21) 8712479
E-mail: ketab-sara@neda.net.ir

Kowkab Publishers
P.O. Box 19575-511
Tehran
Tel: (98 21) 258-3723
Fax: (98 21) 258-3723

IRELAND
Government Supplies Agency
Oifig an tSoláthair
4-5 Harcourt Road
Dublin 2
Tel: (353 1) 661-3111
Fax: (353 1) 475-2670

ISRAEL
Yozmot Literature Ltd.
P.O. Box 56055
3 Yohanan Hasandlar Street
Tel Aviv 61560
Tel: (972 3) 5285-397
Fax: (972 3) 5285-397

R.O.Y. International
PO Box 13056
Tel Aviv 61130
Tel: (972 3) 5461423
Fax: (972 3) 5461442
E-mail: royil@netvision.net.il

Palestinian Authority/Middle East
Index Information Services
P.O.B. 19502 Jerusalem
Tel: (972 2) 6271219
Fax: (972 2) 6271634

ITALY
Licosa Commissionaria Sansoni
SPA
Via Duca Di Calabria, 1/1
Casella Postale 552
50125 Firenze
Tel: (55) 645-415
Fax: (55) 641-257
E-mail: licosa@ftbcc.it
Url: http://www .ftbcc.it/licosa

JAMAICA
Ian Randle Publishers Ltd.
206 Old Hope Road
Kingston 6
Tel: 809-927-2085
Fax: 809-977-0243
E-mail: irpl@colis.com

JAPAN
Eastern Book Service
3-13 Hongo 3-chome, Bunkyo-ku
Tokyo 113
Tel: (81 3) 3818-0861
Fax: (81 3) 3818-0864
E-mail: orders@svt-ebs.co.jp
URL: http://www .bekkoame.or.jp/
~svt-ebs

KENYA
Africa Book Service (E.A.) Ltd.
Quaran House, Mfangano Street
P.O. Box 45245
Nairobi
Tel: (254 2) 223 641
Fax: (254 2) 330 272

KOREA, REPUBLIC OF
Daejon Trading Co. Ltd.
P.O. Box 34, Youida
706 Seoun Bldg
44-6 Youido-Dong, Yeongchengpo-
Ku
Seoul
Tel: (82 2) 785-1631/4
Fax: (82 2) 784-0315

MALAYSIA
University of Malaya Cooperative
  Bookshop, Limited
P.O. Box 1127
Jalan Pantai Baru
59700 Kuala Lumpur
Tel: (60 3) 756-5000
Fax: (60 3) 755-4424

MEXICO
INFOTEC
Av. San Fernando No. 37
Col. Toriello Guerra
14050 Mexico, D.F.
Tel: (52 5) 624-2800
Fax: (52 5) 624-2822
E-mail: infotec@rtn.net.mx
URL: http://rtn.net.mx

NEPAL
Everest Media International
    Services (P.) Ltd.
GPO Box 5443
Kathmandu
Tel: (977 1) 472 152
Fax: (977 1) 224 431

NETHERLANDS
De Lindeboom/InOr-Publikaties
P.O. Box 202
7480 AE Haaksbergen
Tel: (31 53) 574-0004
Fax: (31 53) 572-9296
E-mail: lindeboo@worldonline.nl
URL: http://
    www.worldonline.nl/~lindeboo

NEW ZEALAND
EBSCO NZ Ltd.
Private Mail Bag 99914
New Market
Auckland
Tel: (64 9) 524-8119
Fax: (64 9) 524-8067

NIGERIA
University Press Limited
Three Crowns Building Jericho
Private Mail Bag 5095
Ibadan
Tel: (234 22) 41-1356
Fax: (234 22) 41-2056

NORWAY
NIC Info A/S
Book Department
Postboks 6512 Etterstad
N-0606 Oslo
Tel: (47 22) 97-4500
Fax: (47 22) 97-4545

PAKISTAN
Mirza Book Agency
65, Shahrah-e-Quaid-e-Azam
Lahore 54000
Tel: (92 42) 735 3601
Fax: (92 42) 758 5283

Oxford University Press
5 Bangalore Town
Sharae Faisal
PO Box 13033
Karachi-75350
Tel: (92 21) 446307
Fax: (92 21) 4547640
E-mail: oup@oup.khi.erum.com.pk

Pak Book Corporation
Aziz Chambers 21
Queen's Road
Lahore
Tel: (92 42) 636 3222; 636 0885
Fax: (92 42) 636 2328
E-mail: pbc@brain.net.pk

PERU
Editorial Desarrollo SA
Apartado 3824
Lima 1
Tel: (51 14) 285380
Fax: (51 14) 286628

PHILIPPINES
International Booksource Center
Inc.
1127-A Antipolo St.
Barangay, Venezuela
Makati City
Tel: (63 2) 896 6501; 6505; 6507
Fax: (63 2) 896 1741

POLAND
International Publishing Service
Ul. Piekna 31/37
00-677 Warzawa
Tel: (48 2) 628-6089
Fax: (48 2) 621-7255
E-mail: books%ips@ikp.atm.com.pl
URL: http://
    www.ipscg.waw.pl/ips/export/

PORTUGAL
Livraria Portugal
Apartado 2681
Rua Do Carmo 70-74
1200 Lisbon
Tel: (1) 347-4982
Fax: (1) 347-0264

ROMANIA
Compani De Librarii Bucuresti S.A.
Str. Lipscani no. 26, sector 3
Bucharest
Tel: (40 1) 613 9645
Fax: (40 1) 312 4000

RUSSIAN FEDERATION
Isdatelstvo <Ves Mir>
9a, Lolpachniy Pereulok
Moscow 101831
Tel: (7 095) 917 87 49
Fax: (7 095) 917 92 59

**SINGAPORE, TAIWAN,
MYANMAR, BRUNEI**
Asahgate Publishing Asia
    Pacific Pte. Ltd.
41 Kallang Pudding Road #04-03
Golden Wheel Building
Singapore 349316
Tel: (65) 741-5166
Fax: (65) 742-9356
E-mail: ashgate@asianconnect.com

SLOVENIA
Gospodarski Vestnik Publishing
Group
Dunajska cesta 5
1000 Ljubljana
Tel: (386 61) 133 83 47; 132 12 30
Fax: (386 61) 133 80 30
E-mail: belicd@gvestnik.si

SOUTH AFRICA, BOTSWANA
For single titles:
Oxford University Press
    Southern Africa
P.O. Box 1141
Cape Town 8000
Tel: (27 21) 45-7266
Fax: (27 21) 45-7265

For subscription orders:
International Subscription Service
P.O. Box 41095
Craighall
Johannesburg 2024
Tel: (27 11) 880-1448
Fax: (27 11) 880-6248
E-mail: iss@is.co.za

SPAIN
Mundi-Prensa Libros, S.A.
Castello 37
28001 Madrid
Tel: (34 1) 431-3399
Fax: (34 1) 575-3998
E-mail: libreria@mundiprensa.es
URL: http://www .mundiprensa.es/

Mundi-Prensa Barcelona
Consell de Cent, 391
08009 Barcelona
Tel: (34 3) 488-3492
Fax: (34 3) 487-7659
E-mail: barcelona@mundiprensa.es

SRI LANKA, THE MALDIVES
Lake House Bookshop
100, Sir Chittampalam Gardiner
Mawatha
Colombo 2
Tel: (94 1) 32105
Fax: (94 1) 432104
E-mail: LHL@sri.lanka.net

SWEDEN
Wennergren-Williams AB
P. O. Box 1305
S-171 25 Solna
Tel: (46 8) 705-97-50
Fax: (46 8) 27-00-71
E-mail: mail@wwi.se

SWITZERLAND
Librairie Payot
Service Institutionnel
Côtes-de-Montbenon 30
1002 Lausanne
Tel: (41 21) 341-3229
Fax: (41 21) 341-3235

ADECO Van Diermen Editions
    Techniques
Ch. de Lacuez 41
CH1807 Blonay
Tel: (41 21) 943 2673
Fax: (41 21) 943 3605

TANZANIA
Oxford University Press
Maktaba Street
PO Box 5299
Dar es Salaam
Tel: (255 51) 29209
Fax: (255 51) 46822

THAILAND
Central Books Distribution
306 Silom Road
Bangkok 10500
Tel: (66 2) 235-5400
Fax: (66 2) 237-8321

**TRINIDAD & TOBAGO,
AND THE CARRIBBEAN**
Systematics Studies Unit
9 Watts Street
Curepe
Trinidad, West Indies
Tel: (809) 662-5654
Fax: (809) 662-5654
E-mail: tobe@trinidad.net

UGANDA
Gustro Ltd.
PO Box 9997
Madhvani Building
Plot 16/4 Jinja Rd.
Kampala
Tel: (256 41) 254 763
Fax: (256 41) 251 468

UNITED KINGDOM
Microinfo Ltd.
P.O. Box 3
Alton, Hampshire GU34 2PG
England
Tel: (44 1420) 86848
Fax: (44 1420) 89889
E-mail: wbank@ukminfo.demon.co.uk
URL: http://www .microinfo.co.uk

VENEZUELA
Tecni-Ciencia Libros, S.A.
Centro Cuidad Comercial Tamanco
Nivel C2
Caracas
Tel: (58 2) 959 5547; 5035; 0016
Fax: (58 2) 959 5636

ZAMBIA
University Bookshop
University of Zambia
Great East Road Campus
P.O. Box 32379
Lusaka
Tel: (260 1) 252 576
Fax: (260 1) 253 952

ZIMBABWE
Longman Zimbabwe (Pvt.)Ltd.
Tourle Road, Ardbennie
P.O. Box ST125
Southerton
Harare
Tel: (263 4) 6216617
Fax: (263 4) 621670

04/28/97